# A Gathering

*of*

# Spiritual Riches

# A Gathering

## *of*

# Spiritual Riches

by Saint Tikhon of Zadonsk

Translated from the Russian
by Seraphim F. Englehardt

HOLY TRINITY PUBLICATIONS
Printshop of Saint Job of Pochaev
Holy Trinity Monastery
Jordanville, New York
2023

Printed with the blessing of His Grace,
Bishop Luke of Syracuse and Abbot of Holy Trinity Monastery

---

A Gathering of Spiritual Riches
© 2023 Holy Trinity Monastery

PRINTSHOP OF
SAINT JOB OF POCHAEV

An imprint of

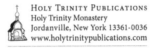

HOLY TRINITY PUBLICATIONS
Holy Trinity Monastery
Jordanville, New York 13361-0036
www.holytrinitypublications.com

ISBN: 978-0-88465-482-7 (paperback)
ISBN: 978-0-88465-494-0 (ePub)

Library of Congress Control Number: 2022946156

Cover Art: Vector background of floral pattern with traditional Russian by
Antuanetto. Source: stock.adobe.com. 63108250.

New Testament Scripture passages taken from the New King James Version.
Copyright © 1982 by Thomas Nelson, Inc. Used by permission.
Psalms taken from A Psalter for Prayer, trans. David James
(Jordanville, N.Y.: Holy Trinity Publications, 2011).
Old Testament and Apocryphal passages taken
from the Orthodox Study Bible.
Copyright © 2008 by Thomas Nelson, Inc. Used by permission.

# Contents

x   *Contents*

# *Foreword*

St Tikhon of Zadonsk (1724–1793) was a Bishop of the Orthodox Church in Russia who has bequeathed to us an array of spiritual wisdom and counsel. The world of eighteenth-century Russia in which he engaged in his own spiritual struggle is vastly different to our own: it was a predominantly agrarian society in which many lived in serfdom. The various situations that St Tikhon chooses to draw out are from this society and so at first we may need to adjust ourselves to them.

Nonetheless they remain apt: As the writer of Ecclesiastes reminds us "there is nothing new under the sun" (Eccl 1:9). So it is with the spiritual life and the struggle to overcome sin and to acquire virtue as is befitting a Christian. The circumstances of our lives may be very different from those of St Tikhon's time, but the fundamental battles that we must wage against the passions have not changed, and so we may appropriate his examples to our own circumstances without much difficulty.

The modern American salesman and motivational speaker Zig Ziglar (1926–2012) is particularly known for saying: "Repetition is the mother of learning, the father of action, which makes it the architect of accomplishment." St Tikhon would agree with him and evinced this understanding some two hundred years earlier. He repeats again and again the same themes and frequently employs the repetition of a word or phrase to drive his point home. For our distracted generation with increasingly short attention spans this style becomes particularly effective.

We are grateful to the servant of God Seraphim for his labors in making this work available for an English-language readership and ask for the prayers of St Tikhon of Zadonsk in helping all of us who read this to acquire the wealth of spiritual riches that have been gathered here for us.

Holy Trinity Monastery

*As a merchant gathers various goods from
different countries and carries them home
and stores them up, so the Christian may
gather edifying thoughts and lay them up
in the storeroom of his heart, and enrich
his soul with them.*

# 1. The World

Nothing exists independently. No city is built by itself but by someone; no house is built by itself but by someone. No letter exists by itself but is written for others. No book is composed by itself but by others. In a word, no thing is made by itself but by another. In the same way, this world does not exist on its own but was made by its Creator. "He spake, and they came to be; He commanded, and they were created" (Ps 148:5). This Creator is our God in one nature but believed in, confessed, and worshipped in three persons— the Father, the Son and the Holy Spirit. The Creator did not create the world in the same way that people create things. People create one thing out of another; that is, they make the thing out of some kind of material, and that with difficulty. But God created this world, that is, heaven and earth with the fullness thereof, from nothing and without any difficulty, only by His desire and word. "He spake, and they came to be; He commanded, and they were created"—this work is attributed to God's almighty power. Our reason, which tells us that comes out of nothing, cannot understand how this vast world can be made from nothing. But faith augments the shortcomings of reason and persuades it to acknowledge that for God, being almighty, all things are possible. "For with God nothing will be impossible" (Luke 1:37).

"By faith we understand that the worlds were framed by the word of God, so that things which are seen were not made of things which are visible" (Heb 11:3). It hears the witness of the Holy Spirit: "In the beginning God made heaven and earth" (Gen 1:1), and does not question this. One could say that the author of a book makes something out of nothing when he draws the words out of his mind and writes them on paper and in this way composes a book. In a like manner the wise and almighty Creator created everything that He thought of and that He desired and as it were composed a book of two sheets, consisting of heaven and earth. In this book, we see God's omnipotence, wisdom, and goodness: omnipotence—because He created everything out of nothing by His desire and word; wisdom—because He created everything wisely: "In wisdom hast Thou made them all" (Ps 103:24); goodness—because He created everything not for His own sake, but for ours. Good is done for its own sake. Because God does not require anything, and as before time began, so now, and unto the ages of ages He abides in all-perfect blessedness.

## 2. The Sun

Before the sun rises, darkness and night prevail, but as day breaks, the darkness recedes and the light begins to shine. In like manner, before the coming of Christ, Who is the Sun of Righteousness, darkness covered the whole world, and the night was deep. But as soon as this radiant Sun shone forth and emitted its warming rays onto the whole world, a most propitious and sweet day dawned on our souls. Then the saying of the prophet was fulfilled, "A people who walk in darkness, behold a great light; and to you who dwell in the country of the shadow of death, upon you a light will shine" (Isa 9:1 (also Matt 4:16)). "The night is far spent, the day is at hand. Therefore let us cast off the works of darkness, and let us put on the armor of light. Let us walk properly, as in the day, not in revelry and drunkenness, not in lewdness and lust, not in strife and envy. But put on the Lord Jesus Christ, and make no provision for the flesh, to fulfill its lusts," says the Apostle (Rom 13:12–14). Let us behave according to the Apostle's exhortation, and we will be sons of Light and day.

Everyone lives under the sun that shines in the heavens, and it looks down on each and every one. In like manner, people live in the presence of God, Who is everywhere present and looks down on all. Whatever anyone does, thinks, undertakes, or plans, the eyes of the Lord see them all. "The Lord looked down from heaven, and beheld all the children of men; From His prepared habitation, He considered all them that dwell on the earth, Having made the hearts of every one of them, and understanding all their works"

(Ps 32:13–15). And also: "Your eyes are upon the ways of the sons of men, to give everyone according to his way" (Jer 39:19 LXX (32:19)). And again: "the eyes of the Lord are ten thousand times brighter than the sun, and look upon all the ways of men, and observe even the secret places. Before all things were created, everything was known to Him, and the end of all things is also known to Him" (Sir 23:19–20 LXX). We should walk before God as before One Who is all-seeing and Who renders to each what is proper. With apprehension, fear, and reverence, we should do what is pleasing to His holy will, so as not to anger His majesty. "See then that you walk circumspectly, not as fools, but as wise," the Apostle tells us (Eph 5:15). O man! God watches you and sees whatever you do, or think, or undertake, or plan; everything that you love or hate; whatever consoles you; whatever offends you; whatever you seek; whatever you flee from; how you relate to Him, your Creator; and how you act toward your neighbor. He hears how and what you say, how and what you ask and answer, and will render to you properly and according to the fruit of your endeavors. See, beloved, "that you walk circumspectly, not as fools, but as wise!"

When the sun shines in the sky, everything is clear. Each person sees the path on which he needs to go, and where his destination is, what to do, and what not to. He sees and distinguishes one thing from another, the beneficial from the harmful, and so on. "Man shall go forth to his work, and to his labor, until the evening" (Ps 103:23). This is how it is in the soul, which Christ, the Sun of Righteousness, enlightens. Such a soul sees everything clearly and recognizes the delight or delusion and vanity of this world. It perceives good and evil, vice and virtue, harm and benefit, distinguishing the trail leading to perdition and the path to eternal life. Such a soul acts in a way pleasing to God and beneficial to himself. For it the word of God is as sweet as God Himself. Such a soul considers everything pleasant and dear in this world as nothing, remembering the word of the Saviour—"For what profit is it to a man if he gains the whole world, and loses his own soul?" (Matt 16:26)—and always strives for a blessed eternity. It has in its mind only one thing: how to please God and to be in the number of the saved. Blessed is the soul, which the Divine Light shines upon!

When the sun sets, night and darkness fall. Then people can see nothing, cannot distinguish one thing from another, and walk as blind men. They fall into ditches and do not know how to avoid harm. Such is the condition of those souls on which the light of Christ has not shone! They feel like blind men, cannot differentiate good from evil, do not distinguish benefit and harm, and sink from one sin to another. They snatch at trivialities and set aside that which is sublime. They think that they are going by the straight path but do not know that it leads to the pit of perdition. Such in essence are those who have been joined with the vanity of this world and only learn how to amass great wealth, to earn high honors, to become famous in this world, and so on, but who think little about the eternal treasure of salvation and have it as their last concern. This is worthy of astonishment or rather sorrow! They see that those who die and leave this world leave everything behind and depart just as naked as when they entered. But they try to grow rich as if they will live in the world forever. And it is astonishing that not only pagans who have no hope and have become tangled up in such vanity, but that Christians, called to everlasting life and eternal good things, of which they always hear in the Gospel, also do this. O poor, wretched man! How you do not see the deception of this world: you chase after what is of little value and quickly disappears like smoke. How can you abandon what is true and abides forever? Everything that we have in this world, excepting virtue alone, will leave us, but what we will receive in eternity will never be separated from us. But in order to be freed from such blindness and darkness and to be enlightened by the light of Christ, we need to approach Him who is the true Light, and with tears to beg Him, "Have mercy on us, O Lord, Son of David" (Matt 20:30). We must always regard the example of His holy life and follow in His sanctified footsteps. Then the true Light, Christ, will enlighten such a man because when we have before us a light and we look at it, we are enlightened. In the same way, the soul, when it draws near to Christ, and looks at the manner of His most holy life, and follows Him, is enlightened by His light. The closer we are to the light, the more we are enlightened. The Light is Christ. As we come closer to Him we will no longer be walking in the darkness. "I am the light of the world: he that follows me shall not walk in darkness, but have the light of life" (John 8:12). For he who walks in Christ will not stride in darkness, but he who moves away from this Light will unfailingly tread in darkness.

The sun warms everything under heaven and in a sense gives it life. Likewise, God, the eternal Sun, by the warmth of His love warms and gives life to all creation and, most of all, the human race. "For in him we live, and move, and have our being" (Acts 17:28). And most of all, He poured out the warmth of His love on us by sending His only-begotten Son to us, who had forsaken Him and were perishing. "For God so loved the world, that he gave his only begotten Son, that whoever believes in him should not perish, but have everlasting life. For God did not send his Son into the world to condemn the world; but that the world through him might be saved" (John 3:16–17). "O praise the Lord, all ye nations; praise Him, all ye peoples, For His merciful kindness is ever more and more towards us, and the truth of the Lord endureth for ever" (Ps 116:1–2). You, too, should praise the Lord, O my soul! May the name of the Lord be blessed from henceforth and forevermore! Think, O Christian, about this great work and give thanks to the Lord!

Everyone looks at the sun and, wishing to be warmed by it, is drawn toward it. So also all the faithful look to God and are warmed by His mercy. "The eyes of all look unto Thee, O Lord, and Thou givest them their food in due season. Thou openest Thine hand and fillest every living thing with benevolence" (Ps 144:15–16). "Hear us, O God of our salvation, the hope of all the ends of the earth and of them that be afar off at sea" (Ps 64:6). Lift up your eyes to God, O Christian, that you may be warmed by His mercy and may often say with the Prophet from the depth of your heart: "Unto Thee have I lifted up mine eyes, O Thou that dwellest in heaven. Behold even as the eyes of servants are upon the hands of their masters, and as the eyes of a maid are upon the hand of her mistress, even so are our eyes upon the Lord our God, until He have pity on us" (Ps 122:1–2).

Without the sun, no fruit grows and ripens. So also, without God, the eternal Sun, no good work is begun, done, or finished. Our highest desire, our good beginning, middle, and end are His work. He begins in us, works in us, and finishes in us. Without Him we cannot do anything: "for without me you can do nothing" (John 15:5). Therefore, O Christian, learn: (1) To get to know your weakness, sinfulness, and nothingness, to learn that you in and of yourself are nothing more than a dried-up tree that can bear no fruit. (2) Learn humility from this. (3) Attribute to God alone every good work that you have done or are doing, that you may not ascribe His work for yourself, and misappropriate His glory, and thereby sin grievously. (4) At all times, send up your sighs to God, that He may not take away His almighty hand from you, since without God's help you will fall from sin to sin. Repeat the prayer of the Psalmist often: "Forsake me not, O Lord my God, be not far from me. Attend unto my help, O Lord of my salvation" (Ps 37:22–23). (5) When God sends you misfortune, grief, and sorrow, He wants to correct you and make you into a fruitful tree. Be patient with your Lord, as you are patient with the physician who treats you with bitter medicine. Bitter medicine is grief and sorrow for the flesh, but the ailing soul is cured by it. "Wait thou on the Lord, be of good courage, and let thine heart stand firm, and wait thou on the Lord" (Ps 26:14).

The sun never stops its movement but always goes from east to west and pours its light and warmth onto the earth. In the same way God never ceases His beneficence and always does good to us—such is His nature. God is good in essence, hence "no one is good save One, that is, God" (Matt 19:17), as the Saviour attests, and therefore cannot not do good.

The sun shines and pours its warmth both on the evil and the good. Likewise the eternal Sun, God, does good to the just and unjust, the pious and impious. "Bless the Lord, O my soul" (Ps 102:1). Let us too imitate the Creator in this and do good to the just and unjust, to those who love us and those who hate us, after the exhortation of the Apostle: "Therefore be imitators of God as dear children" (Eph 5:1). "For He makes His sun rise on the evil and on the good, and sends rain on the just and on the unjust" (Matt 5:45).

The sun pours its warmth equally on all things. But some things melt from its warmth, like wax, while others harden, like clay. In the same way God does good to all and sends down the warmth of His goodness equally. But some people are softened by His goodness and repent, while others become hardened and perish, as, for example, pharaoh became hardened and perished. This even now happens in the world. "O man ... do you despise the riches of His goodness, forbearance, and longsuffering, not knowing that the goodness of God leads you to repentance" (Rom 2:3–4)? Beware, O man, of becoming hardened by the goodness of God; for your salvation, it is better to be moved to repentance and to contemplate God's long-suffering.

The sun is seen clearly in clean, still water, and its likeness is reflected there. So also, God, the eternal Sun, shows Himself in a quiet, pure, unsullied soul, and His image is reflected in it. "Therefore, having these promises, beloved, let us cleanse ourselves from all filthiness of the flesh and spirit, perfecting holiness in the fear of God" (2 Cor 7:1). Let God, the eternal Sun, take up His abode in us and let His holy image be reflected in us.

Thick and dense things—earth, stone, wooden walls, etc.—do not allow sunlight to pass through. But glass, clean water, crystal, etc., on the other hand, do. In like manner, the mind, darkened by the sins and lusts of this world, cannot admit God's enlightenment. Like admits like. "Therefore he says, 'Awake you who sleep, Arise from the dead, And Christ wall give you light'" (Eph 5:14). Repent, and cleanse your soul by repentance and tears, and drive off the cloud of your vain thoughts, and then Christ will enlighten you.

The higher the sun is, the smaller the shadow is; the lower it is, the longer the shadow is. And as the sun sets, the shadow disappears. So the closer God draws to a person, the smaller the person becomes within himself, and the more he feels humiliated and humbled. He sees his unworthiness and nothingness and the majesty of God and therefore is humbled. On the other hand, the further God distances Himself from a person, the more a person rises in self-importance, exalts himself, and becomes proud. And when God completely distances Himself from a person, they perish, as the shadow disappears when the sun sets. Beware, O man, of haughtiness, lest you perish as did the devil. Do not be haughty, but be afraid. "For everyone who exalts himself will be humbled, and he who humbles himself will be exalted" (Luke 18:14).

Whoever wants to be enlightened and warmed by the sun must emerge from a dark place and place themselves under its rays. Likewise he, who wants to be enlightened by God, the Eternal Sun, and be warmed by His sweetest love, must leave the darkness of sin, to hate his iniquitous and impure life, and to turn to Him, take up repentance and brokenness of heart, and pray. And then he will be enlightened by His Divine light and his heart will be warmed by His Divine love. "Come unto Him and be enlightened, and your faces shall not be ashamed" (Ps 33:6). So then, let us turn, O Christian, to God with our whole hearts, be enlightened by His light, and be warmed by His love.

Diseased eyes cannot look at the sun and see it. Likewise the soul, afflicted by cunningness, vainglory, pride, self-importance, self-esteem, and the love of this world, cannot see the eternal Divinity. God is seen by an unpretentious and healthy spiritual eye. It is impossible to know and see God without God Himself, and He reveals Himself to simple and gentle babies. "You have hidden these things from the wise and prudent and have revealed them to babes" (Matt 11:25). Christians, let us be simple and pure in heart, and then we shall see God.

If anyone often looks at the sun with diligence and attention, his eyes will be darkened and injured. So, if anyone scrutinizes God, the eternal Sun, with curiosity, and attempts to learn His incomprehensible mysteries, his mind is darkened and he will fall into serious error. Beware, O man, to investigate what you do not need to know. We should theorize about God only as His Holy Word has revealed.

Whoever walks toward the sun is followed by his shadow. Whoever walks away from the sun sees his shadow retreat from him. Likewise, for the very reason that someone draws near to Christ, the Sun of Righteousness, and follows Him with faith and love, he will be followed constantly by hatred, malice, and the persecution of this world. The world, blinded by the falsehood of the devil, does not love God's truth. And therefore, as it hated and persecuted Christ, the Truth itself, in like manner it hates and persecutes the Christian who holds to the truth. The Apostle wrote of this: "And all that desire to live godly in Christ Jesus will suffer persecution" (2 Tim 3:12). Do not grieve, beloved Christian, that the world hates you. Christ is incomparably greater and better than the whole world, and His love is sweeter than it. Whoever Christ loves and has mercy on will in no way be harmed by the hatred and malice of this world. Only mind that you are Christ's. Christ does not abandon His own. He endured and suffered so much for you, so will He abandon you in your need? Hear His comforting promise to His servants: "I am with him in trouble, and I will deliver him" (Ps 90:15). And the Apostle indicates how to learn who Christ is: "Those who are Christ's have crucified the flesh with its passions and desires" (Gal 5:24). And further: "Let everyone who names the name of Christ depart from iniquity" (2 Tim 2:19). Be Christ's, and the whole world, and all the devils will not harm you, since He is incomparably stronger than all of them, and all on earth and the nether regions tremble before His Divine power.

When the sky is covered with thick and dark clouds, and a great storm is gathering, it seems that the sun is abandoning us. Even at such a time, however, it always pours its diaphanous rays upon us. Thus, when the dark cloud and storm of temptations come upon us and cover us, it seems that God has abandoned us. But even in such darkness God does not abandon his faithful one, but with His hidden power keeps him safe. "But God is faithful, who will not allow you to be tempted beyond what you are able, but with the temptation will also make the way of escape, that you may be able to bear it" (1 Cor 10:13). Do not despair, beloved Christian, when some temptation befalls you, but pray and call upon Him. Then wait for help from Him, according to His truthful promise: "And call upon Me in the day of thy trouble, and I will deliver thee, and thou shalt glorify Me" (Ps 49:15). God waits your patience and struggle, not despondency and indignation. "Wait thou on the Lord; be of good courage, and let thine heart stand firm, and wait thou on the Lord" (Ps 26:14), without Whose counsel and will nothing takes place.

When bad weather and storm pass, the sun shines on us most pleasantly. Likewise, when the storm of temptations passes by, the pleasantness and kindness of the Lord's goodness can be felt in a person's heart. Then the sweetest calm shines in the soul. Then the soul is comforted and is sated with peace and rest as at the most tasty supper. Then, "mercy and truth are met together, justice and peace have kissed each other" (Ps 84:11) in such a soul. Then the soul tastes and sees "that the Lord is good" (Ps 33:9). Such a sweetness follows in the human heart after enduring temptation. Endure the onslaught of temptations, O Christian, and you will feel then a pleasant and sweet calm in your soul.

Also, when we look at the sun, O Christian, we remember how Christ the Lord said, "Then the righteous will shine forth as the sun in the kingdom of their Father" (Matt 13:43). The chosen ones of God will be clothed in such great and wondrous glory that they will shine like the sun. We will look with the eyes of our soul at this glory and will scorn the fraudulent glory and honor of this world.

# 3. Father and Children

Children are begotten of a father. Likewise Christians, people—renewed and the sons of God by grace—are begotten of God. "But as many as received Him, to them He gave the right to become children of God, to those who believe in His name: who were born, not of blood, nor of the will of the flesh, nor of the will of man, but of God" (John 1:12–13).

Children are begotten of the seed of the father. Christians are begotten of water and the Spirit, the Word of God and faith. "Of his own will He brought us forth by the word of truth" (Jas 1:18). "Having been born again, not of corruptible seed but incorruptible, through the word of God which lives and abides forever" (1 Pet 1:23).

Children are begotten of a father in the flesh. Christians are begotten of the Father in the Spirit. "That which is born of the flesh is flesh, and that which is born of the Spirit is spirit" (John 3:6).

The characteristics and likeness of the father are perceived in children, just as the characteristics and likeness of the Heavenly Father should be in Christians. They too should be holy, good, merciful, meek, patient, etc. This is what they are told: "But as He who called you is holy, you also be holy in all your conduct, because it is written, 'Be holy, for I am holy'" (1 Pet 1:15–16). "Therefore be merciful, just as your Father also is merciful" (Luke 6:36).

Whatever children see their father doing, they try to do likewise. In the same way Christians should imitate their Heavenly Father as much as possible. "Therefore be imitators of God as dear children" (Eph 5:1). God offends no one; in the same way they should not offend anyone. God does good to all; likewise, they should do good to all. God remits the sins of all who repent; likewise, as God forgives us our trespasses, so should Christians forgive those who trespass against them. God hates sin; in like manner, Christians should hate sin and avoid it. God "desires all men to be saved and to come to the knowledge of the truth" (1 Tim 2:4); likewise, Christians should desire salvation for all with their whole hearts.

A father loves his children, and children love their father. Likewise God loves Christians, and Christians should love God, as their Father, with their whole hearts.

Children try to please their father. Likewise Christians should try to please God, their Father. Children shun everything that offends their father. Likewise Christians should always move away from whatever offends their Heavenly Father—and every sin and disdain for virtue offends Him.

A father and his children converse with each other with love. Likewise God speaks with faithful souls with love in the Sacred Scriptures, and faithful souls speak with God lovingly in prayer and glorification. Oh, the loving and sweet talk that takes place between the majesty of God and an ignoble human, who is earth and ashes. "Lord, what is man, that Thou hast had such respect unto him? Or the son of man, that Thou so regardest him" (Ps 143:3)?

A father rejoices in his children, and his children reciprocate by taking comfort in their father. Likewise the Heavenly Father rejoices in faithful souls, and they rejoice in Him. "My heart and my flesh have rejoiced in the living God" (Ps 83:3).

Out of love, children call their father "Father" or "Papa." Likewise, out of love Christians call God "Father" and cry to Him "Abba, Father" (Rom 8:15). "And because you are sons, God has sent forth the Spirit of his Son into your hearts, crying out, 'Abba, Father'" (Gal 4:6).

"Our Father in heaven ..." (Matt 6:9). Children ask their father for everything, but he does not give them everything, only that which is necessary and beneficial. Likewise the Christians ask for everything from their Heavenly Father, but He does not grant them everything, only what is necessary and beneficial. "Or what man is there among you who, if his son asks for bread, will give him a stone? Or if he asks for a fish, will he give him a serpent?

If you then, being evil, know how to give good gifts to your children, how much more will your Father who is in heaven give good things to those who ask Him!" (Matt 7:9–11).

Children act reverently before their father, doing and saying nothing improper, and rendering him every respect. Likewise, Christians should walk with fear and reverence before the omnipresent and all-seeing God, not doing, saying, or thinking anything indecent.

A father cares for his children, looks after them, and trains them. Likewise, God cares for Christians, looks after them, and educates them with His Word and the life-giving Mysteries. Children run to the protection of their father from the calumnies of malicious people. Likewise, Christians run under the protection and defense of their Heavenly Father from the calumnies of the devil and his minions. "Father ... deliver us from the evil one" (Matt 6:13). They dare to sing: "God is our refuge and strength, a very present helper in the troubles which greatly afflict us" (Ps 45:2).

A father punishes his children for their transgressions but with love. Likewise, God, our Heavenly Father, punishes Christians for their sins not out of anger, but out of love. "'For whom the Lord loves he chastens, and scourges every son whom he receives.' If you endure chastening, God deals with you as with sons; for what son is there whom a father does not chasten" (Heb 12:6–7)?

Good children humble themselves and confess their transgressions and acknowledge themselves guilty before their father. Likewise, Christians should humble themselves, confess their sins, and acknowledge their falsehoods and confess: "It is good for me that Thou didst humble me" (Ps 118:71). A father punishes his children so they may be honorable. God "chastens" us so that we may be partakers of His holiness (Heb 12:10). A father prepares an inheritance for his children. Likewise God is preparing eternal life and the kingdom of heaven as an inheritance for Christians. A father gives an inheritance to his children in due time. Likewise God, when the time comes, will give an inheritance to Christians and will comfortingly tell them: "Come, you blessed of my Father, inherit the kingdom prepared for you from the foundation of the world" (Matt 25:34).

Good children try everywhere to behave honorably in order not to defame the name of their father. Likewise Christians should live so that the name of God is not deprecated. A father is honored and praised when his children continually live good lives. Likewise, the name of the Heavenly Father is glorified when Christians live piously and worthy of their calling. The Lord calls us to this: "Let your light so shine before men, that they may see your good works and glorify your Father in heaven" (Matt 5:16). Likewise, children, no matter how much they honor and try to please their father, are only rendering what is due to him, as a parent, educator, and breadwinner; otherwise they would be ungrateful. In the same way, Christians, no matter how they try to please their Heavenly Father, are rendering Him His due and cannot merit anything by this. What they receive from God, they accept as a gift. We cannot repay God in any way for the blessings He has given and is giving to us, but we always remain in His debt. Children, when someone dishonors or offends them in their father's presence, do not take revenge on him who has offended them but look to their father and entrust their grievance to him. Likewise, when someone wounds them, Christians should not take revenge for themselves but lift up their mental eyes to their Heavenly Father, and to entrust vengeance to Him, the righteous Judge, Who says, "Vengeance is Mine; I will repay" (Rom 12:19).

A father disowns a son who is inconstant and careless even after considerable punishment, disinherits him, and turns him out to live as he wills. Likewise, the Heavenly Father disowns careless Christians who do not want to listen to Him, excludes them from inheriting eternal life, and lets them go to live as they like. "But My people would not hear My voice, and Israel would not heed Me. So I gave them up unto their hearts' lusts; they shall walk in their own imaginations" (Ps 80:12–13).

A father does not punish someone else's children, although he may see them behaving badly. Likewise, our Heavenly Father leaves without punishment those people who are not members of His household and not His family, as not His own: "But if you are without chastening, of which all have become partakers, then you are illegitimate and not sons" (Heb 12:8).

A father not only punishes his children but also comforts them. Likewise the Heavenly Father not only punishes His children, the true Christians, but also comforts them. "For He who humbles will have compassion according to the abundance of his mercy" (Lam 3:28 LXX). "According to the multitude of my sorrows in my heart have Thy comforts refreshed my soul" (Ps 93:19).

Ponder, O Christian, and see how God acts toward Christians and how they should act toward God.

Christians derive comfort and joy from this: (1) How close a union and fellowship true Christians have with God, like that of children with their father: "and truly our fellowship is with the Father, and with his Son Jesus Christ, says the Apostle" (1 John 1:3). It is impossible for the mind to grasp how great and glorious this is. (2) How great and lofty is the dignity of Christians. It is great to be a child of a certain master, more so of a lord, and even much more so to be the child of a king. How incomparably greater it is to be a child of God! The holy Apostle is amazed at this and says, "Behold what manner of love the Father has bestowed on us, that we should be called the children of God! Therefore the world does not know us, because it did not know Him" (1 John 3:1). (3) If Christians are the children of God, then in glory they will be clothed when they are revealed! An earthly king clothes his children in beautiful and radiant clothing. In what glorious and radiant clothing will the children of God be clothed! "[He] will transform our lowly body that it may be conformed to His glorious body" (Phil 3:21). "Beloved, now we are children of God; and it has not yet been revealed what we shall be, but we know that when He is revealed, we shall be like Him, for we shall see Him as He is" (1 John 3:2). "Remember us, O Lord, according to the favor that Thou bearest unto Thy people; O visit us with Thy salvation, That we may see the goodness of Thy nation, and be glad in the gladness of Thy nation, and glory with Thine inheritance" (Ps 105:4–5).

# 4. Master and Servant

A servant is called by the name of his master. Likewise, a Christian is called a Christian, because he is the servant of Christ. A servant is called the servant of a certain master because he works for him, carries out his will, and tries to please him. Likewise, the Christian is called the servant of Christ because he works for Him, carries out His will, and tries to please Him. A master deems a servant of his who does not carry out his will to be unfaithful. Likewise, Christ deems the Christian who does not fulfill His commandments to be an unfaithful servant. "Why do you call me, 'Lord, Lord,' and do not do the things which I say" (Luke 6:46)?

A servant behaves before his master with fear and reverence in order not to anger him. Likewise, Christians before Christ, their Lord, should walk with fear and reverence in order not to anger Him. Although He is not visible to them, He sees and watches everyone.

A servant does not know when his master will summon him, and therefore a good servant is ready at all times and waits for him. Likewise, a Christian does not know when Christ the Lord will call him to Himself. Christ calls everyone to Himself through death, and therefore a good Christian is always ready for his end. When a master leaves for somewhere, a good servant always awaits his return. Likewise, the Christian should always await the coming of Christ from the heavens and prepares to meet Him. "Let your waist be girded and your lamps burning; and you yourselves be like men who wait for their master, when he will return from the wedding, that when he comes and knocks they may open to him immediately" (Luke 12:35–36).

A servant, when he shows his master that he is careless, is punished. Likewise, the Christian, when he shows Christ the Lord that he is careless, will be punished.

The servant, no matter how faithfully he works for his master, does what he must do. Likewise, the Christian, although he faithfully works for Christ the Lord, must, however, acknowledge himself unworthy. "When you have done all those things which you are commanded, say, 'We are unprofitable servants. We have done what was our duty to do'" (Luke 17:10). A servant receives a reward and payment for faithful service from his good master only because of the latter's mercy. Likewise, Christians, servants of Christ, will receive a reward from Christ the Lord in the age to come, but only because of His mercy, and not for their merits.

Behind their master's back, inconstant and malicious servants live as they wish and are self-willed. They do what they want, thinking that their master does not see them. Likewise, many shameless Christians act against their conscience and the law of God, as if Christ does not see them, and all but say, "Christ is in heaven, far from us; He does not see us and what we do." And perhaps, many do think and speak this way. But the Psalmist sings to all, "The Lord looked down from heaven, and beheld all the children of men. From His prepared habitation, He considereth all them that dwell on the earth, having made the hearts of every one of them, and understanding all their works" (Ps 32:13–15). And the Prophet Jeremiah says to the Lord, "Your eyes are upon the ways of the sons of men, to give to everyone according to his way" (Jer 39:19 LXX (32:19)). And the holy David denounces them, "Take heed, ye thoughtless among the people, and ye fools, when will you be wise? He that planted the ear, shall He not hear? Or He that made the eye, shall He not see? He that chasteneth the heathen, shall He not rebuke, He that teacheth man knowledge" (Ps 93:8–10)? And the Lord Himself says to the sinner, "I will reprove thee, and set thy sins before thy face" (Ps 49:21).

If a servant came into such madness and frenzy that he dared to yell, make a fuss, laugh excessively, jump, dance, and engage in other sorts of rowdiness, he would be displaying extreme disrespect and scorning toward his master and would call forth his wrath. Christians who transgress and are self-willed before Christ the Lord, the All-Seeing, show such madness and frenzy. This includes unseemly shouting, fistfights, dances, foul and unseemly songs, horse races, quarrels and swearing, oaths, slander and judgment of neighbors, scandalous gatherings, banquets, drunkenness, fornication, adultery, swindling, theft, and so on. All this is madness and frenzy, which is done by blind Christians before the Almighty Lord Jesus Christ. All of them display extreme disrespect and scorning toward Christ the Lord and thus move Him to righteous anger. Therefore, such terrible punishments happen as terrible fires, plagues, invasions of foreigners, earthquakes, and so on. Great indeed is human blindness and madness! A servant is afraid to commit excesses in front of his—human—master. But Christians do not fear to do in front of Christ—God—what a man does not dare to do before another man, although he hears from the Holy Scripture that God sees everything. This is how Satan blinds the minds of people so that they will not see their perdition. Beware, O man, of doing before God what you fear doing before earthly authority and what you are ashamed of doing before an upright person. God has been patient with you until now, but whether He will be patient henceforth is unknown. "Our God *is* a consuming fire" (Heb 12:29). "It is a fearful thing to fall into the hands of the living God" (Heb 10:31; 12:29). Think about this.

# 5. A King and His Honored Subject—a Criminal

It happens that a king favors a subject of his, gives him high rank, enriches him, and shows him his sublime favor in other ways. But he, having become proud at the king's sublime mercy, displays ingratitude even to the king instead of gratitude, violates his laws and becomes a foe to the homeland. Desiring to repudiate such an ungrateful and shameless person, the king airs his grievances against him to the whole homeland and says of his villainy and ingratitude, "I showed such and such favors to that person, that subject of mine. But he nevertheless both scorned me and rendered evil to his homeland." And such a criminal is deprived of all royal favor and is given over to execution. Likewise, God, the Heavenly King, airs his grievances before the whole world against the people, His subjects, who know His name but do not honor Him. They are enriched by various benefactions from Him, but they forget all of this, and are ungrateful to Him; they violate His holy and righteous law; and they grieve and exasperate Him, as we read in the Books of the Prophets and in the Psalms about the ungrateful Jews: "They forgat His good deeds, and the wonderful works that He had showed for them" (Ps 77:11).

What is there that the Lord who loves mankind has not done for them? What favors has He not bestowed? What benefactions has He not shown? He chose them as His people and revealed His name to them. He heard the groans of those who had come into Egypt and became embittered at the tormentor, stood up for them, and delivered them. He smote Egypt with its first-born and led Israel out of it by His mighty hand and upstretched arm. He divided the Red Sea and led Israel through it. He plunged pharaoh and his army into the Red Sea. He led them through the desert and satisfied them there with all sorts of good things. He struck down great kings before them and killed powerful kings. And He gave land as an inheritance to Israel, His servant. And so "He brought them to the mountain of His holiness, even to the mountain which His right hand had purchased. He cast out the heathen also before them, and gave them the land by lot, and settled the tribes of Israel in their tents" (Ps 77:54–55). "But how often did they provoke Him in the wilderness, and anger Him in the desert?" (Ps 77:40), as is written of this in the books of Moses. Just as entering the Promised Land, "they tempted and displeased the most high God, and kept not His testimonies; But turned backward, and fell away like their fathers, becoming like a sprung bow. And they angered Him in their hill places, and vexed Him with their idols. God heard and turned away, and greatly disparaged Israel" (Ps 77:56–59).

And He bears witness to their ingratitude before heaven and earth: "Hear, O heavens, and listen, O earth. For the Lord has spoken: 'I have begotten and brought up sons, but they rejected Me. The ox knows its owner and the donkey its master's crib; but Israel does not know me, and the people do not understand me'" (Isa 1:2–3). He sent to them his servants, the Prophets, to lead them to repentance and to turn them to Himself. But Israel not only did not receive them but even killed them. Then He Himself came to them in human form. But the holy Evangelist with pity bears witness to the world that "He came to his own, and his own did not receive Him" (John 1:11). And not only did they not receive Him, but they cursed Him, provoked Him, swore at Him, and killed Him Who came to save them. No matter what Christ the Lord did for them, no matter how much He tried to turn them to repentance, they remained unhealed and hard-hearted. "O Jerusalem, Jerusalem, the one who kills the prophets and stones those who are sent to her! How often I wanted to gather your children together, as a hen gathers her chicks under her wings, but you were not willing!" Finally, they heard the terrifying words of God: "See, your house is left to you desolate" (Matt 23:37–38). "Wrath is come upon them to the uttermost" (1 Thess 2:16). And so the whole world sees God's righteous Judgments and acknowledges that they have been justly cast away from God.

And the word that Christ spoke was fulfilled: "The kingdom of God will be taken from you, and given to a nation bearing the fruits of it" (Matt 21:43). God turned and called to Himself the gentiles instead of the Jews. The Gentiles, having turned from idols to the Living God, were made the people of God. But those who hypocritically honor God, and confess God's name with their lips, but by their actions reject Him are following the hypocritical and obstinate Jews. Such Christians promised at Baptism to serve God but serve the devil (The one whose will he fulfills, is the one he serves). And the denunciation by the prophets and the Lord Himself of the Jews for their unjust and ungrateful hearts also applies to false Christians as well. Christians have taken the place of the Jews. They have taken the books of the Word of God into their hands but do not want to live by it. They have received Christ but oppose Him by their works. They always listen to preachers as if they were prophets sent from God but do not want to obey their teaching. What is worse, they swear at them, say spiteful things about them, and revile them. Therefore, as the Jews are now denounced before the whole world in the holy books, so also ungrateful and false Christians will be denounced at Christ's Second Coming on the last day before the holy angels and God's chosen. And they will be deprived of the kingdom of God, and then all the saints will see and acknowledge God's righteous Judgment. For whatever a person has done, said, planned, undertaken, desired, and sought now in this world will follow him into the next age and will appear with him at Christ's Judgment. People's good, evil, secret deeds, words, and thoughts will be revealed to all the angels and the people, says St. Basil the Great in his letter to a fallen virgin.

"Let us fear, O Christians, and bear fruits worthy of repentance. Let us expiate our sins now by repentance and tears, lest they, as our accusers, appear with us at Christ's judgment, denouncing us. Let it not be said to us then, 'Look at that person and his works!' Woe to that person whose sins appear with him at that universal, shameful spectacle. For it will be rendered to him according to his deeds."

# 6. Captives and Their Liberator

It happens that people fall into captivity in a foreign country and there suffer every kind of evil from the tormentor who has taken them prisoner. A good king, having mercy on and pitying his people who have fallen into such suffering, will send to them a liberator, who will either ransom them with silver or free them in some other way. Likewise, the Eternal King, the Heavenly Father, pitying us prisoners, sent His only-begotten Son to us to deliver us from bitter captivity and bears witness to us from the heavens, "This is My beloved Son, in whom I am well pleased. Hear him!" (Matt 17:5). And the Son of God Himself says, "The Spirit of the Lord is upon me, Because he hath anointed me To preach the gospel to the poor; He has sent Me to heal the brokenhearted, To proclaim liberty to the captives And recovery of sight to the blind, to set at liberty those who are oppressed; To proclaim the acceptable year of the Lord" (Luke 4:18–19). When our forebears in paradise obeyed the counsel of the serpent and transgressed God's commandment, they became captives of the devil with all of their posterity, that is, the whole human race. And he, being the evil Leviathan and tormentor, exulted over them and mocked them, and did with them whatever he wished. It was not enough for people to worship the sun and other heavenly bodies instead of God; they worshiped beasts, cattle, plants; there was hardly any creature that they did not make idols of. It is shameful even to speak of the other acts by which they carried out the will of their enemy. In what bitter captivity the poor human found himself! "In Judea is God known; His Name is great in Israel" (Ps 75:2). But the always-scheming enemy tried so hard to destroy the true worship of God even in this tiny corner of the world! How many times did he lead Israel into idol worship! How many other serious sins did he cause them to fall into, so that "They sacrificed their sons and their daughters unto demons, And shed innocent blood, even the blood of their sons and of their daughters, whom they sacrificed to the graven images of Canaan, and the land was putrid with their blood" (Ps 105:37–38).

No one could be found who would free us from his tormenting hands. He Who was stronger and more powerful than anyone had to come and save us. "How can one enter a strong man's house and plunder his goods, unless he first binds the strong man? And then he will plunder his house" (Matt 12:29). Christ, the Son of God, seeing that we had no helper, stood up for us through the good will of His Heavenly Father, as He Himself says through His prophet, "I looked, but there was no helper; and I observed, and there was no one to help; therefore, my arm delivered them, and My anger was suddenly present" (Isa 63:5). This Most Merciful Protector is the Lord, "strong and mighty, even the Lord mighty in battle" (Ps 23:8), joined in struggle for us and defeated the enemy, our tormentor. And as David defeated Goliath not with a weapon, but with a sling, so also Christ defeated the devil, our enemy, not with armaments, but by the power of His Cross. By suffering and patience, Christ smashed Satan's inimical head and cast him to the ground like a corpse. And the one who had mocked us and trampled on us, He gave to us, His servants, to trample on, and led us into freedom. About this Protector of ours, the Conqueror of Death and Hades, Jesus, we dare to say: if He is for us, who is against us? Strengthened by His might, we tread on the serpent, the scorpion, and on all the enemy's power, and we triumph, exclaiming, "'O Death, where is your sting? O Hades, where is your victory?' But thanks be to God, Who gives us the victory through our Lord Jesus Christ" (1 Cor 15:55, 57).

What should we, who have been delivered from such a tormentor, do, O Christians? The answers are these: (1) From a pure heart to thank our Great Benefactor, Who freed us from the bitter captivity of the enemy, from whom we could in no way liberate ourselves by our own power. We would have eternally been in the power of darkness, if merciful Jesus, the Son of God, had not offered a helping hand. For this, may He be glorified with His Father and the Holy Spirit! (2) To always remember His great deed and to sing a song of victory to Him, as the Conqueror of our enemy. "The Lord became my helper and the shield of my salvation; He is my God and I will glorify Him" (Exod 15:2). Our enemy has fallen, and we have risen up and reformed our ways. He was disgraced, and we were glorified. He, who had held us captive, was himself imprisoned, and we were set free. He, having been exalted, was humbled, and we, who had been humbled, were exalted, "for in our humbleness the Lord remembered us" (Ps 135:23). (3) From a pure heart to love such a Great and Lofty Benefactor, Who cannot and will not be surpassed. If we love a human benefactor who has done us some minor good deed, then even more so should we love Christ, Who has given us so much that we can never repay Him. (4) To render Him fervent obedience and to keep His holy commandments, lest we insult Him. This will show our love for Him, as He Himself says: "He who has my commandments and keeps them, it is he who loves Me" (John 14:21). (5) Take care not to fall again into the captivity of the devious enemy, lest we become his eternal prisoners. Christ led us out to freedom; let us try to keep it.

# 7. A Master and the Servant Whom He Purchased

We see that a servant toils for the master who bought him from another. Christ, the Son of God, ransomed us for Himself from the devil and his dark rule. He ransomed us not with silver and gold or any other perishable asset, but with His own Blood. He did not spare His Own Blood for our sake and did not refuse to suffer and die in order to redeem us and take possession of us. And although Satan would have taken possession of us with flattery and made us his servants, Christ our Lord took our part and delivered us from bitter slavery, and took possession of us for Himself, and made us His servants. And when we entered Christianity in Holy Baptism, we renounced this enemy, his pride, and all his evil works, and promised to serve Jesus our Redeemer. "And you are not your own. For you were bought at a price" (1 Cor 6:19–20). What price was given for us? Silver or gold? No! Then what? Precious blood was shed! Whose was it? An ordinary man's? No! Who is He, Who so mercifully dealt with us that He did not spare His own Blood for us, who were enslaved by the enemy and tormentor? It is our Lord and God! "He purchased [us] with His own blood" (Acts 20:28).

Oh, truly, a great price, an inestimable amount, was paid for us! We are truly not our own, but servants bought by Christ! We should serve Christ as our Lord who bought us and should do His will and fulfill His commandments. "And He died for all, that those who live should live no longer for themselves, but for Him who died for them and rose again" (2 Cor 5:15). The master orders the servant, and the servant obeys him. He tells him, "Do this," and he does it. "Go there," and he goes. "Lay the table," and he lays it. Christ our Lord orders us, "Christian, love your neighbor, as yourself; be merciful, humble, meek, and kind; avoid every sin," and so on. We should, as servants whom He has purchased, do what He orders us, especially since we of our own will promised to serve Him, and this service is beneficial to us, and not Him. He held us so dear that He did not spare even Himself for our sake. O Lord! "What is man, that Thou art mindful of him? Or the son of man, that Thou visitest him" (Ps 8:5)? Let us honor Him as He honored us. Let us serve Him with all humility, as our Lord. Then He will recognize and acknowledge us as His servants in the day of His Second Coming and will say to each of us, "'Good and faithful servant ... enter into the joy of your lord'" (Matt 25:21).

## 8. A Captive and His Liberator

Imagine if someone were in captivity and was suffering every torture from the tormentor that had taken him captive. He could expect nothing from his tormentor than a bitter death, until some good and powerful person came to him and said to him, "Look, I am freeing you from this bitter servitude and all of your misery and will bring you into your homeland, only come, follow me," Oh, with what great joy that poor captive would want to go and follow that merciful liberator! Christ, the Almighty and all-good Son of God, came down from heaven to us captives, sent from His Heavenly Father, and tells us: "I have been sent from My Heavenly Father to free you and to lead you to Him into His heavenly kingdom." "'I am the way, the truth, and the life. No man comes to the Father except through me'" (John 14:6). "If you want to come into eternal blessedness and to inherit the kingdom of heaven, come follow Me and I shall lead you there." "'If anyone desires to come after me, let him deny himself, and take up his cross, and follow me'" (Matt 16:24). Christians, let us then follow Christ, our Deliverer, Who came to us and mercifully visited us, and calls us into His heavenly kingdom, and will lead us into that most blessed rest and eternal joy, the abode of all who are joyful! Jesus is the true and faithful Leader, and without him, no one will enter the Kingdom of God. Let us entrust ourselves to His leadership and follow Him inseparably, and He will lead us into a place of eternal repose. His elect follow Christ not on foot but with the heart and faith, love, humility, patience, and meekness. Let us love this path of Christ and follow Him. This path is lowly, humble, and scorned by many, but only it leads into the homeland on high: heaven (see Matt 7:14).

There is no other path to eternal life except the path of the Cross: "'And he who does not take his cross and follow after me is not worthy of me' the Lord says" (Matt 10:38). If someone is unworthy of Christ, then who else will he be deserving of, other than His enemy? Whatever you think, O man, and wherever you turn your thoughts, you must carry your cross and follow Christ: Follow His humility, love, patience, meekness, so as to endure without grumbling whatever happens to you that is sorrowful, because Christ, your Saviour, endured things in this way. Endure without grumbling everything that God's holy right hand may send you, drain whatever cup the Heavenly Father may send you, and you will be a true member of the spiritual Body of Christ, and so you will follow your Head, Christ. And as you suffer with Him, so you will be glorified with Him, as the member with its head. As is said in the Scriptures, "if indeed we suffer with Him, that we may also be glorified together" (Rom 8:17). And "if anyone serves Me, let him follow Me; and where I am, there My servant will be also" (John 12:26). "Wait thou on the Lord; be of good courage, and let thine heart stand firm, and wait thou on the Lord" (Ps 26:14).

# 9. Joyous News for Criminals

Imagine if some people seriously transgressed before the King and were sent by him into incarceration or exile. A messenger then came from him and announced to them his pardon and forgiveness of their crime. They were to be returned again to their native land and their home, and were granted to live in peace and quiet there. What joyous news that would be to those poor convicts! We with our forefather Adam have all sinned before God, the Heavenly King, and were sent from Paradise to this world, as into confinement and exile. Christ, the Son of God, the Angel of Great Counsel, came to us, exiled and condemned, and brought the sweet news from His Heavenly Father and announced to us His forgiveness, and restoration to His favor. "And He came and preached peace to you who were afar off and to those that were near" (Eph 2:17), the Apostle says. And Christ proclaims to us about Himself. "He (the Father) has anointed me to preach the gospel to the poor; He has sent me to heal the brokenhearted, to proclaim liberty to the captives and recovery of sight to the blind, to set at liberty those who are oppressed; to proclaim the acceptable year of the Lord" (Luke 4:18–19). He as it were said, "Do not be afraid, do not be terrified, poor and outcast people! I have brought you good news from My Heavenly Father. You have sinned—He forgives you your sins.

You have turned away from Him—He is turning you again to Himself. You distanced yourself and were banished from Him—He again returns you to Himself. You were perishing—He saves you through me. You were driven out of paradise for your sin–He by His grace gives you heaven instead of paradise. Receive Me as His Messenger. "Let not your heart be troubled; you believe in God, believe also in Me. In My Father's house are many mansions" (John 14:1–2). I am calling and returning you, who were exiled into those mansions."

O what tidings, the dearest, sweetest, and most propitious for the whole world! Truly there could be nothing more pleasant than these tidings for us poor sinners! Food for the hungry, cool water for the thirsty, freedom for the imprisoned, light for those sitting in darkness, rest for the weary, health for the ill, are not so pleasant as this news is to us poor, cast-out, condemned, and perishing sinners, who are far from God. Do not fear, do not despair, poor sinner! Christ, the Son of the Living God, the King and beloved and Only-Begotten Son of the Heavenly King, sent from His Heavenly Father, came to save you and to lead you into His heavenly kingdom. "For the Son of man has come to seek and to save that which was lost" (Luke 19:10). "This is a faithful saying and worthy of all acceptance, that Christ Jesus came into the world to save sinners; of whom I am chief" (1 Tim 1:15). "For God so loved the world that He gave His only-begotten Son, that whoever believes in Him should not perish but have everlasting life. For God did not send His Son into the world to condemn the world, but that the world through Him might be saved" (John 3:16–17).

We thank You, O Lover of Mankind, Only-Begotten Son and Word of God, that You have brought us such sweet and comforting tidings from Your Heavenly Father, and by this have delighted our hearts, pained by the poison of the ancient serpent! We believe in You, the Son of the Living God, and in Your Heavenly Father Who sent You, and we hope to come to Him through You, Who are the Way, the Truth, and the Life. And we will glorify You forever with Your Father and the Holy Spirit! "Let Thy mercy, O Lord, be upon us, according as we have put our trust in Thee" (Ps 32:22). We have put our hope in Thee, O Lord, let us never be put to shame. Amen! O sorrowing soul, who has sinned and is repenting, be comforted by these most sweet tidings, the Gospel of our Lord Jesus Christ! During your life, they will be a refreshment during spiritual drought, and, in the hour of your death struggle, a real comfort. The Son of God came to save sinners, not just certain ones, but all of them, no matter who they may be. As long as they repent, believe in Jesus

Christ, Who came to save sinners, paradise will be opened by the hand of Christ crucified on the Cross. You, too, should repent, O sinner, and believe in this holy and most sweet Gospel and, without a doubt, you will enter into paradise with the thief. "Blessed is the Lord God of Israel, For he has visited and redeemed his people, And has raised up a horn of salvation for us in the house of His servant David, As He spoke by the mouth of his holy prophets, Who have been since the world began" (Luke 1:68–70).

# 10. The King Who out of Compassion Visits People Living in Poverty

If the King came and visited people who were in captivity, undergoing every suffering and looking forward to nothing but a bitter death, and he wished to talk with them and to suffer for them in order to deliver them out of that bitter slavery and to return them to their home, so great and marvelous would be that event that all ages would celebrate him with great wonder. And indeed there cannot be more love and mercy, more condescension to a subject from his King. But the King, although an exalted personage, is, however, a mortal man just like his subject, the same earth and ashes, and subject to the same corruption as other people. It is marvelous and surpasses every wonder that our Great and Incomprehensible God, the Creator of heaven and earth, drew near to us poor ones and visited us and came to us in our image. An Immaterial Spirit, to be clothed in human flesh like ours, One Who had shone forth incorruptibly from the Father, God from God, Light from Light, to be born of the Most Holy Virgin Who knew not wedlock, and to call her Mother, and to be called Her Son—O marvel of marvels! God deigned to call His handmaiden His Mother, and the Son of God to be called the Son of the Virgin, and thus He Who was without beginning received a beginning, the Invisible One became visible, the Intangible One became tangible, He who was inaccessible to the Cherubim and Seraphim became accessible to sinners. The King of heaven came down to earth. God became like us humans, lived with us on earth, and humbled Himself with us and for our sake. The Almighty became feeble; the All-powerful became powerless. And what is even more wonderful: The Lord meekly and voluntarily endured abuse—disgrace, reviling, tying up, insult, mockery, reproach, trials, condemnation, being spit upon, being slapped in the face, being slandered, calumniated, beaten, and wounded—from His wicked servants even though it led to His death: to being nailed on the Cross and numbered with the lawless. For whose sake? For you and me, who were His enemies! This is such a great and wondrous thing, that foreseeing it from afar, the prophet cried out in terror, "Lord, I have heard Your report and was afraid" (Hab 3:2).

You should also be astonished, O Christian, at this great work of your Lord, which is not and could not be a greater. Sing and glorify His love for mankind, which it is impossible to describe with the pen or comprehend with the mind. With the Prophet we may truly exclaim, "Lord, what is man, that Thou hast had such respect unto him? Or the son of man, that Thou so regardest him" (Ps 143:3)? You came down from heaven for my sake, to raise me up to heaven. You were humbled in order to lift me up. You Who are God became man for my sake, so that You may make me "a partaker of Your Divine nature" (2 Pet 1:4). For my sake You were born in the flesh, so that I might be born in the spirit. For my sake You endured persecution, so that You would lead me who had been banished back into paradise. For my sake You deigned to wander, and You will return me, a captive, to my homeland. For my sake You were cursed at, so that You would close the mouth of my enemy, the slanderer, the devil. For my sake, You were bound, so that You would release me from the bonds of sin. For my sake, You grieved, mourned, were sad, and wept to deliver me from eternal morning, sorrow, and tears. For my sake, You were dishonored and cursed at, so that You might glorify me. For my sake, You were numbered among the transgressors, so that You might justify me. For my sake, my life, You tasted of death, so that You might grant me life. I am amazed at Your love for mankind. I sing Your mercy! I bow down to Your extreme humility and condescension! What shall I render unto the Lord for what He has given me, Your poor and wretched servant? Picture, O Christian, this great work before the eyes of your mind often, and You will always see a wonder that is greater than all wonders.

If at any time you wish to see a miracle, contemplate the incarnation and passion of Christ. And from this soul-saving contemplation will follow: (1) A living faith. If Christ suffered and died for all, then that included you and me. If He is the Saviour of all who truly believe in Him, then He is your Saviour and mine. The lamp of faith is lit by this contemplation. (2) Hope will follow. If He suffered so much for you, will He abandon you in your need? If He died for you, will He refuse to help you in your misfortune? He is able and willing to help you. He is able, since He is most wise and all-powerful; He is willing, since He is good and loves you. From His goodness and love, he suffered for you. If He tarries, it is because He is awaiting your patience. So be patient and wait for Him. He will come without fail and will not delay, since He is faithful in His words. (3) Love for Him will follow. He so loved you and me, His enemies, that He died for us. There is nothing greater than this love. Therefore, how can we not love such a One Who loves and not repay love for love? We love the person who has done us some small favor. Would we not love Christ, the Son of God, such an exalted and great Benefactor? (4) Obedience will follow, for in order for the one who is loved not to offend the beloved, we must constantly render him obedience. And through obedience, love is shown, as He Himself teaches, "He who has My commandments and keeps them, it is he who loves Me" (John 14:21). (5) Gratitude follows. He redeemed you from eternal death not with gold and silver and not with any other price, but with His Own Blood. Reasoning thus, you will certainly be persuaded to thank Him from a pure heart and out of gratitude to try to please Him, as our great Benefactor. There is not and there cannot be anything greater than this benefaction. This benefaction of Christ, rendered to us, the unworthy, is so great that it is impossible ever to repay in any way or with anything. Even if you lived a hundred or two hundred years and every day suffered the cruelest torture for the name and honor of Christ, this would be nothing compared to His benefaction, since you, and I, and everyone are nothing compared to such a lofty and great figure as Christ. For we are human, earth and ashes, and He is our Lord and God, Who showed such condescension to us. This requires the most earnest thanksgiving from us. For the greater the benefaction the greater should be the gratitude for it. (6) Fear will follow. For if Christ's sufferings will not be of benefit for someone and for his eternal salvation, that person will have a greater condemnation. This especially applies to Christians who have known Christ, but do not obey Him. Fear to sin, lest you be deprived of God's grace and lest the very Blood of Christ, which was shed for you, but which you have disdained, cry out against you to God. (7) Consolation for one who has sinned and is repenting follows. If Christ suffered and died for you, how will He not receive one who has sinned and repents? Is it difficult for Him to remit sin for you, who come to Him with compunction and a contrite heart and ask forgiveness—to Him, for Whom it was not difficult to suffer and die for you? He Who died for your sins will joyfully remit your sins for you who repent. (8) From this know, O Christian, the nobility, honor, dignity, and preeminence of the human soul. For its deliverance and redemption, not an angel, not any other kind of mediator sent from God, but the Lord God Himself came. He Himself honored and visited it by His coming. And He redeemed it from the devil, death, Hades, and the other enemies, not with silver or gold, or by any other corruptible material, but by His own Precious Blood. He honored us in our creation, when he created us in His image and likeness. But He honored us even more when He Himself came to us, fallen and perishing, in our image, and suffered and died for us. The Lord put such a high price on the human soul that He Himself came to recover it and shed His Blood to acquire it. The more valuable the item, the higher the price is given for it. And since there is not and cannot be anything more valuable than Christ and His Blood, we can understand the preciousness of the human soul from the fact that Christ, the Son of God, did not spare Himself and His Blood for it.

Understand, Christian, the preciousness of your soul and do not be tempted by the seductive ranks and titles of this world, by which the sons of this age are tempted and fall into folly. The honor, glory, and dignity of your soul are greater than the glory of the whole world. Your soul is the bride, betrothed forever to Christ, the Son of God, and redeemed by His holy Blood. Understand its nobility. The Bridegroom is noble and the bride joined to Him is noble. You do not see this nobility and dignity now, but you will see it when the children of God are revealed. "It has not yet been revealed what we shall be, but we know that when He is revealed, we shall be like Him, for we shall see Him as. He is" (1 John 3:2). All the nobility, dignity, and preeminence of this world, gathered together, are dung compared to the honor and nobility of the human soul. (9) From here follows humility. How? This is how. If an earthly king were to come to you, a lowly person, and visit you, and came, not invited by you, but of his own accord, would you not be terrified and, falling down before him, would you not say, "Who am I, that my Great Lord has visited me, who am lowly and unworthy?" Not an earthly king, but the Heavenly King, King of Kings and Lord of Lords, came to us, His poor and lowly servants, and visited us not in answer to our supplication but in accordance with His merciful promise, and not only visited but endured suffering and death for us. Humble yourself, O Christian, when you see such condescension of your King, your God and Lord; bow and fall down before Him and say to Him with fear and humility, "Who am I, earth and ashes, a sinner and worthless servant, that my Lord and my God has come to me? But so He willed in His unparalleled goodness! Glory to His goodness, glory to His love for mankind and unbounded munificence!" (10) We see how our Lord humbled Himself for us. Let us also humble ourselves, O Christians, for His sake and for ours: for His sake because there is nothing so pleasant and dear to Him as our humility; for our sake because there is nothing so beneficial for us as humility, since "God resists the proud, But gives grace to the humble" (1 Pet 5:5). He did not feel aversion to us, ignoble and sinful servants. And, looking to that living example of humility, let us not feel aversion to our brothers who, although lower than us, are still of like nature with us. That is, let all men treat one another as brothers: lords–their servants, the high-ranking–the low-ranking, the rich–the poor, the honored–the base, the wise–the foolish, the learned–the unlearned, and let no one hold another in contempt. Our kindred nature demands this. He did not despise us, base and degraded; let us, the base and degraded, not despise the base and degraded. All of us, to the very last person, are by our essence and nature destitute, wretched, poor and cursed, from the prince and the lord even to the simplest peasant. Why should the poor disdain the poor, when the Lord and King of Glory did not disdain us, the ignoble and poor? (11) Since we cannot give worthy thanks to Christ for His exalted beneficence to us, and He does not want anything so much as our salvation (for this, He came into the world, suffered, and died), so let us try to be saved by His grace and by this to please Him, that in the future life, through all of never-ending eternity, we may sing a song of thanksgiving, praise, and glorification to Him with His Father and the Holy Spirit. Amen.

# 11. The Death Penalty for a Condemned Man

It happens that, as his just deserts and in accordance with the law, a man is sentenced to death. They lead him out of the city, and a multitude of people follows him, and at the appointed place, he is put to death. From this shameful spectacle, O Christian, turn your mind and thought to the dreadful and terrible spectacle of the saving passion of Christ. Christ, the Son of God, was judged and condemned to death. But He was led to death unjustly and without blame, as a lamb to sacrifice, "And a great multitude of the people followed Him" (Luke 23:27). And outside the city He was led to the place of death, and there between two criminals, He suffered death on the Cross. A terrible and touching spectacle! The Son of God and Lord of Glory, like a criminal, was condemned and led to death and was executed! By whom? By His evil servants! For whom? For His useless servants! The servants sinned, and the Master suffered the punishment! "He was wounded because of our lawlessness, and became sick because of our sins" (Isa 53:5). Where? Outside the gates of Jerusalem! Before whom? Before the eyes of God, of the angels, and of men. You see, O Christian, the dreadful and terrible spectacle. Look and contemplate its cause! Its cause was our sins. This is how my sins, and yours, and the sins of the whole world were cleansed. This is how God's righteousness, which had been vexed by the sins of the world, was satisfied. This is how God was reconciled with the world and the world with God! This is how justification was earned for us sinners, and eternal salvation was effected! This is how we were delivered from the captivity and power of the devil, the torments of hell, and eternal death! This is how ascent to heaven has been prepared for us, and the heavenly kingdom, closed by our sins, has been opened, and everything that we lost in Adam was returned! In Adam, we were subjected to the devil and his dark power, and through Christ's passion, we were delivered from it. In Adam, we sinned and became cursed, but through Christ's passion, God's justification and blessing were returned to us. In Adam, we died and perished, but by Christ's passion, we came to life again and were saved. In Adam, we were distanced from God, but by Christ's passion we were led to God. In Adam, we were exiled from paradise, but by Christ's passion we were returned to not an earthly paradise, but a heavenly one. In Adam we were dishonored and disgraced, but through Christ's passion we were honored and glorified. In Adam we were deprived of everything good and fell into every affliction and wretchedness, but by Christ's passion, we received every good thing and were delivered from every misfortune.

And so our entire well-being flows from Christ's passion as the fountain of salvation. His suffering is the cause of our consolation. His death is the cause of our life. By His trial and condemnation, we were delivered from trial and eternal condemnation. We were healed by His wounds. The fetters with which He was bound have loosed us from the chains of sin, for which we hymn Him with the Prophet, "Thou hast broken my bonds in sunder. I will offer unto Thee a sacrifice of thanksgiving" (Ps 115:7–8). Peace and eternal joy have flowed out to us from His sorrow and grief. His merciful tears have wiped dry the tears of our eyes and are effectual before the Heavenly Father. The stripping of His Divine Body became for us a robe of salvation and garment of gladness. His humility and degradation raised us up. His humiliation and disgrace resulted in eternal honor and glory for us. In a word, all spiritual and eternal blessedness flowed from this saving Fountain. For this, we send up eternal thanksgiving to Him, the Author of our life, with the Father and the Holy Spirit. Always remember, O Christian, the time in which this, our blessedness, was secured. Remember that time in which God in human and servile form appeared and lived on earth for our sake, moved about among sinners, ate, drank, and talked with sinners; the time in which He suffered abuse and persecution from His evil servants; in which for the sake of our sins He sorrowed, grieved, was terrified, and sweat blood; in which He was sold and betrayed by a smooth-tongued and ungrateful disciple and abandoned by the other disciples; in which He was bound, led to trial, judged and condemned to death, sworn at, spit on, and slapped in the face; in which they cried at Him: "Crucify Him, Crucify Him" (John 19:6); in which He was numbered with the transgressors and died on the Cross for our salvation. And try to follow and be pleasing to your Redeemer by faith, love, humility, and patience, and you will eternally reign with Him.

# 12. A King, Awaited by Citizens, His Arrival in the City, and His Reception by the Citizens

A king, wishing to come to a city, first sends a herald there to announce his arrival to the citizens. Therefore the citizens wait for the king and prepare to meet and receive him with appropriate honor. In like manner the Heavenly King, getting ready to come into the world as to a splendid city built with His hands, sent heralds ahead of Him, His servants, the prophets, to announce to all His approaching advent into the world, which they repeatedly foretold in diverse ways. All the Old-Testament faithful and saints awaited Him with great desire. "Many prophets and righteous men desired to see ... and to hear" (Matt 13:17) Christ, the Son of God, in the flesh. When the time came, Jesus Christ, the King of Heaven, came into the world, and all those who loved His Divine appearing met and received Him. The Heavenly King lived on earth, and accomplished salvation there, for the sake of which He had come, and then ascended into heaven, and sat on the Throne of His Glory. His servants, the Apostles, preached His saving providence in all the ends of the earth, and all who receive their saving preaching will be saved. Thus, the prophets and Apostles of the only Saviour of the World, the Son of God, preached to us. The prophets preached of the One preparing to come, and the Apostles preached of the One Who had already come into the world and had accomplished salvation. The Old-Testament faithful believed in the coming Christ and were saved. The new grace-filled believers in the Christ Who came are being saved.

So one Christ, in the Old and New Testaments, is the Saviour of the faithful. We Christians now need to do nothing more than to try to please our Lord and Saviour Jesus, the Heavenly King, and look after receiving the eternal salvation accomplished by His labors and afflictions, and await His second coming from heaven. His first coming took place; His second will, too. The prophets preached His first coming, saying, "The Christ is coming into the world, the Christ is coming into the world." And Christ came into the world quietly and unexpectedly: "He shall come down like the rain upon a fleece of wool, even as the drops that water the earth" (Ps 71:6). Church pastors and teachers say about the Second Coming, "Christ is coming into the world, Christ is coming into the world, again He will appear unexpectedly, but this time, in glory and causing dread." As citizens await the coming of their King and prepare to meet him, likewise we Christians should await the coming of our Heavenly King and prepare to meet Him properly, especially since we do not know the day and hour in which He will come. He will come not to live, teach, and suffer—that already took place—but to judge and to render to each according to his deeds. Let us try, O Christians, to keep vigil and be ready to meet our King, remembering His word of exhortation, "Watch therefore, for you know neither the day nor the hour in which the Son of Man is coming" (Matt 25:13). May we have the honor of standing on His right hand at His coming!

# 13. A Low-ranking Person Adopted by a High-ranking Person

It happens that a high-ranking person adopts a low-ranking person as his son, takes off his rags, washes him, dresses him in clothing fitting for his own station, and thus makes him his son and his heir. This is how God, the Heavenly King, acts with a poor and ignoble person. This is achieved in Holy

Baptism. A person does not see this with bodily eyes, but this Mystery is comprehended by faith. Then God in His sublime mercy receives the poor person, does not recollect his former sins and transgressions, and remits every wrongdoing. He sets aside the righteous anger that He had against him, as against a child of anger. He removes his stinking sinful rags, washes him with pure water, and puts on him the beautiful purple robe of Christ's justification, and makes him His son and heir of the eternal heavenly kingdom. The priest says from the Word of God to the person being baptized, "But you were washed, but you were sanctified, but you were justified in the name of the Lord Jesus and by the Spirit of our God" (1 Cor 6:11). O, God's ineffable Love for mankind for us, poor and outcast people! Oh, the incomprehensible kindness! God receives man—a criminal and apostate from Him, His enemy—into such great favor and the highest—supremely high—dignity! The holy Apostle is rightly amazed at this great and incomprehensible love: "Behold what manner of love the Father has bestowed on us, that we should be called children of God! Therefore the world does not know us, because it did not know Him. Beloved, now we are children of God; and it has not yet been revealed what we shall be, but we know that when He is revealed, we shall be like Him, for we shall see Him as He is" (1 John 3:1–2). Christians, it remains for us to do nothing other than the following: (1) To always thank Him from a pure heart for this sublime Divine favor and love for mankind. (2) To love Him, as children do their father. (3) To sincerely show Him filial obedience and desire to please. (4) To avoid every sin, which insults Him, lest we offend Him. (5) To imitate Him, as children imitate their father in accordance with the exhortation of the Apostle, "Be imitators of God as dear children" (Eph 5:1). He took us into His sublime favor—let us remember this mercy of His. He created us as His children, let us be His true, and not pretended, children, that is, let us do deeds fitting for children of God. He is holy; let us imitate His holiness, doing holy deeds in the fear of God. He is good and merciful—let us "be kind to one another, tenderhearted, forgiving one another, even as God in Christ forgave you" (Eph 4:32). "He makes His sun rise on the evil and on the good, and sends rain on the just and on the unjust" (Matt 5:45)—let us do good to all, acquaintances and strangers, our own people and outsiders, people of our own faith and of another, friends and enemies, those who do us good and those who do us evil. He has long endured the transgressions of the whole world, awaiting all to come to repentance; let us be patient with those who transgress against us. Let us do all this and more, not for our own sake, but for the sake of His glory, after the exhortation of the Saviour: "Let your light so shine before men, that they may see your good works and glorify your Father in heaven" (Matt 5:16).

If this ignoble person honored by his benefactor devoted himself to disgraceful deeds, and threw off the honor and presentable attire and clothed himself again in shabby and shameless rags, this matter would be worthy of amazement, pity, and laughter from everyone. And indeed, this would be a serious insult to the benefactor who had honored him. And some people would pity, others would be astonished at, and others would laugh at the foolishness of this stupid person. Such a thing happens to the Christian who has been taken into such sublime favor of God's and has been honored by God in Holy Baptism. Such a Christian, I say, who devotes himself to iniquitous deeds, and violates God's law without fear, befits the proverb, "A dog returns to his own vomit,' and, 'a sow, having washed, to her wallowing in the mire" (2 Pet 2:22). The beautiful and sacred clothing in which his soul was attired is taken off. He is deprived of the sublime honor of Divine adoption and an eternal inheritance. He is clothed in the dishonorable and shameless rags of sin and becomes the basest servant. There is sorrow and weeping by the holy angels and all God's chosen inhabitants of heaven, who had previously all rejoiced at his blessedness. Laughter, and mockery, and joy begin among the evil spirits, who previously had envied him. Every Christian who transgresses falls into such a miserable condition. Such a soul will fall again into the same affliction and dreadful condition in which it was before Baptism, but even more wretched. Of such people, the Apostle wrote that "the latter end is worse for them than the beginning. For it would have been better for them not to have known the way of righteousness, than having known it, to turn from the holy commandment delivered to them" (2 Pet 2:20–21). To his misfortune, such a poor person sees neither the blessedness he is deprived of nor the affliction into which he is falling because neither one nor the other is of the body, but within, in the soul. For both true Christian blessedness and affliction have in common that they are in the soul. Oh, if only a person would see what blessedness he loses after Baptism through sin and in what affliction he falls, he would be sobbing and weeping continuously and inconsolably! The poor sinners will see this when the glory of the sons of God and their own disgrace are revealed. They will see this, but to their great sorrow. Then they will begin to weep and sob, but then it will be to no avail.

The causes of such a miserable condition after baptism are as follows: (1) weakness and corruption that is hidden within, in the person's heart, and is born with him. (2) A bad upbringing. The cause of this is parents who do not take trouble either for themselves or for their children, and so are headed for perdition and are leading their offspring there. (3) Pastoral negligence by those who do not take care of Christ's flock entrusted to them. (4) Temptations from bad parents and other evil people; upon observing them, the young people are tempted and become corrupted. (5) The machinations of the common enemy of Christians, the devil, who walks about "like a roaring lion, seeking whom he may devour" (1 Pet 5:8). (6) Carelessness and negligence concerning himself, as is a person who listens to the Word of God read in church, but instead of heeding it walks like a blind man into a ditch—eternal perdition. And from this, it follows: (7) How necessary a good upbringing and instruction is for young children. The law of God obliges Christians to teach their children, not what present-day people care about most of all, but to live a Christian life. Even if children do not know any language, but live a Christian life, they will not be deprived of true blessedness. (8) How carefully the young must be protected from temptations that rouse the evil that hides in their hearts. (9) One hope remains for the Christian who has gone astray from the true path after baptism: true repentance. For this, sinful soul, turn to the Heavenly Father, as the Prodigal Son did and fall before His merciful eyes, and with contrition and groaning of heart, cry out to Him: "'Father, I have sinned against heaven and before you, and I am no longer worthy to be called your son. Make me like one of your hired servants'" (Luke 15:18–19). And believe without doubting that He will receive you and will clothe you in the finest clothing, and so there will be joy for you before the angels of God.

# 14. A Benefactor and the Ungrateful Man Who Receives a Benefaction from Him

If someone lived in the house of a good and merciful master and was receiving food, drink, clothing, protection, and other benefits from him, but were not to show him fitting gratitude as his benefactor, displaying every kind of rudeness, disrespect, and scorn, and abused and cursed at him, it would be deplorable, and everyone would be indignant at such a senseless person. And, indeed, such a person would be worthy of every indignation and vilification! Ingratitude is a great evil, folly, and blindness and is loathsome to everyone. In this vice abide children who do not honor their parents; people who abuse and malign their pastor; pupils who annoy their teachers; subordinates who do not show fitting honor and love to authorities, who look after the general welfare; beggars who do not love those who give them alms and do not remember their benefaction, and so on. Wayward Christians show God this kind of ingratitude and even incomparably worse. For whatever good one man does to another, it is not his, but God's good that he does, since He is the Source and Cause of any good in the world. God will give us His true good. What good and benefaction has God not shown us, O Christians! He created us, not as beasts, but humans endowed with reason. He created by His extraordinary counsel: "Let Us make man" (Gen 1:26). He created man in His image and likeness. What greater honor can there be for a person than to be created in the image of God! For this alone we shall never be able to show our gratitude to God in any way. But when we sinned, fell, and were lost, even then our all-good Creator did not leave us to our ruin. And how many means did He not devise to restore us and bring us to Himself? He sent us His prophets, who returned us who had departed from Him. He gave us His holy word like a letter in which He revealed and proclaimed His holy will. And since we were so struck and wounded by that fierce robber, our enemy, the devil, that nothing could heal us, our Merciful Creator had mercy on us poor ones, to the point that He did not spare His only-begotten Son for our sake, but sent Him to us, to seek out and save us the lost ones, to heal the wounded and grief-stricken. Regarding this the only-begotten Son of God Himself proclaims to us, "For God so loved the world that He gave His only begotten Son, that whoever believes in Him should not perish but have everlasting life. For God did not send His Son into the world to condemn the world, but that the world through Him might be saved" (John 3:16–17). What did He, living, or rather, wandering on earth, not do? What benefactions did He not grant? What did He not suffer for our sake? What name-calling, bad-mouthing, what insults from His own ungrateful people He suffered? Finally, He died the death on the Cross for our salvation! And all of this our all-good Master did by the good will of His Heavenly Father and His own free will.

Having thus shown His wondrous Providence for us, our God, Plenteous in Mercy, called us to His holy faith and washed us, sanctified, and justified us in the name of our Lord Jesus Christ and His Holy Spirit, as the Apostle says to Christians, "But you were washed, but you were sanctified, but you were justified in the name of the Lord Jesus and by the Spirit of our God" (1 Cor 6:11). This and other benefactions of God appertain to our soul and eternal life. The entire world bears witness to what good He renders to our body and temporal life. O man, turn your mind and eyes to all His creation and consider: Whom does it serve? Is it not us? Whom do the sun, moon, and stars serve? Is it not us? Whom do the air and the clouds serve? Is it not us? Whom does the earth with its fruits serve? Is it not us? Whom the cattle, beasts, and birds serve? Is it not us? Whom the water with its fish and the other things living in it serve? Is it not for us, O Christians? All creation serves us by God's command, since we cannot live the shortest time without it. Who can live without bread and water or without clothing? Air is so necessary to us that we cannot live even minutes without it. What would our life be like if God took light away from us? Wouldn't we all wander about like blind men? Who would be able to remain unharmed by the invisible enemy, the devil, were it not for God saving us by His almighty hand from the enemy, who rages with seething malice against our race, and "walks about like a roaring lion, seeking whom he may devour" (1 Pet 5:8). But why enumerate so many? We need to acknowledge that God's benefactions that every one of us has been favored with are without number. Everyone is embraced in God's love and benefactions. Wherever you look, wherever you turn your mind, everything shows God's love for us and His benefaction. Gehenna itself, of which He testified, is a benefactor to us, since it inspires fear in us. Let us repent and weep before the Lord, who made us, that He would have mercy on us and deliver us from it. Our Creator tolerates the devil himself for our benefit. And as much as He tolerates him, so much does it benefit us, and as much as this enemy tempts us, so much does it benefit us. How does it benefit us? It rouses us up from laziness and prompts us to prayer. Feeling the presence of this enemy, we flee to God and ask help and protection from Him. And as the more a soldier is in battle, the more skillful he becomes, so the more temptations the Christian bravely endures from this enemy, the better and more skillful he becomes in the Christian calling, and the more victories he will gain over this enemy, the more beautiful the crown he will be honored with from the Source and Judge of struggles, Jesus Christ. "Having care," says St. John Chrysostom, "for our salvation, God let loose the devil so that he would rouse us from laziness, and prepared an opportunity for us to receive a crown" (Homily 23 on Genesis, 2) And St. Paul says: "A thorn in the flesh was given to me, a messenger of Satan to buffet me, lest I be exalted above measure" (2 Cor 12:7). Do you see how beneficial for us is the hostile spirit? Do you see how it leads the proud to humility? He plays dirty tricks on us lest we become puffed up. And thus the evil and malicious spirit promotes our welfare through his bad intention.

But when the Christian transgresses, he forgets all these benefactions of God and he does not honor God, his Benefactor, and is very ungrateful to Him—he becomes like one who reviles his human benefactor and curses Him, and regards the benefaction rendered him as nothing. The Christian does not honor and disdains God because he does not want to obey Him. This is a strange saying, O Christian, but a true one! How is that? Listen and pay attention. God orders: Do not swear by My Name in vain. But the lawless Christian swears. God orders: Honor your parents and the authorities. But the lawless Christian does not honor them. God orders: Do not get angry, do not nurse a grudge against your neighbor, and do not hate him. But the lawless Christian holds on to anger, remembers wrongs, and hates his neighbor, who is created in the image of God. God orders: Do not fornicate and do not commit adultery. But the lawless Christian commits either adultery or fornication and thus defiles his own and another's soul and body, defiles, I say, a soul created in the image of God. God commands: Do not steal, and do not purloin what belongs to another. But the lawless Christian steals and purloins. God commands: Do not bear false witness, do not say spiteful things, do not curse at your neighbor, do not lie, do not cheat, do not judge, and do not slander. But the lawless Christian disregards this commandment of God, he bears false witness, he lies, he cheats, he reviles, he curses, he judges, and he condemns a man like him, and sometimes a better one. Do you see how the lawless one disobeys and disdains his Creator? What kind of honoring of the father by the son and the master by the servant is it, when the son does not obey the father and the servant does not obey the master? Is it not manifest scorn and disrespect? Oh, how many on earth are those who scorn and despise God? How many enemies of God are there even among those who think that they honor Him?

Oh, into what a sad state Christianity has arrived! The Christian, who has received and is receiving so many favors and benefactions from God, becomes an enemy of God, his Most High Benefactor; he who knows that the Son of God came into the world, suffered and died both for the sake of all, and for his sake; he who was called by the Word of God to eternal life; he who is washed, sanctified, justified by God through the bath of Baptism. Oh, how the devil, the murderer, has infected unfortunate mankind! He has made man the enemy of God, just as he is. See, Christian, where your sin leads you! Through sin, you, who should be a lover of God and one who honors God, have become an enemy of God. It seems sweet to you, but its fruits are bitter. You do not see this now, but you will see it, when all the deeds and thoughts of men will be revealed. It is painful for you, a man, to endure it when a man like you, who has received some small benefaction from you, does not express gratitude to you. How much more painful is ingratitude to God, the Source of all good things! From here we see that God everywhere complains of ingratitude: "they forgat His good deeds ... and the wonderful works that He had showed for them" (Ps 77:11). "And again: Hear, O heavens, and listen, O earth. For the Lord has spoken: 'I have begotten and brought up sons, but they rejected Me'" (Isa 1:2). And again: "They sinned; the blameworthy children are not His, A generation twisted and perverse. Is this how you repay the Lord?" (Deut 32:5–6), and in other places in Scripture.

So come to yourself, O Christian, and, acknowledging your ingratitude and sins, fall down with humility before God's merciful eyes and from the depths of your heart cry out to Him: "I have sinned, O Lord, have mercy on me! Receive me, the lost sheep, and number me among Thy chosen flock. Give me a heart, O God, the Knower of Hearts, that honors Thee, that fears Thee, that loves Thee, that follows Thy will. Guide me on Thy way, and I will walk in Thy truth. Look down upon me, and have mercy on me, according to the judgment of them that love Thy name." And when, having turned around, you will begin to repent and embark on a new Christian life, your former lawless life will not hurt you, and then you will learn what kind of person you were in God's eyes. "When you return and groan, then you will be saved and know where you were" (Isa 30:15). You will understand in what a calamitous state you were and how far you had strayed from the way of truth. You will understand that you were unworthy of the name of Christian, although you called yourself a Christian; and that in reality you were dead, although you dreamed that you were alive. Everyone who lives in sin is dead to God, just as one who lives in God is dead to sin. Then will come true for you what is said: "'For this my son was dead and is alive again; he was lost and is found'" (Luke 15:24). And then there will be joy for you in heaven before God's angels. Oh, may this come to pass! "O Lord God of hosts, convert us; show the light of Thy countenance, and we shall be saved" (Ps 79:20).

When a person who is ungrateful to his benefactor comes to his senses and repents for his ingratitude, he begins to think and say to himself, "What am I, the wretched one, doing? Is that how I should repay my benefactor? Hatred for love, and evil for good? I have indeed lost my senses!" And he thus regrets and grieves over his iniquitous behavior. And he is ashamed to look at his benefactor; he falls down before him with humility and asks his forgiveness, fearing nothing from him, but only regretting that he has vilified, cursed at, and insulted the one whom, being one who loved him, he should have loved and honored. This is true repentance. You see, Christian, what a person does to his human benefactor when he displays ingratitude to him and then comes to repentance. Likewise, a Christian, when he comes to his senses and thinks about God's benefactions rendered both to others and to him, and about God, his Benefactor, Whom he has forgotten and disdained, he becomes extremely distressed and downcast with sorrow in God, he is wounded as by an arrow, and he becomes angry at himself as at an enemy; he judges himself as one unworthy of neither heaven nor earth, nor a piece of bread, nor of rags. In a word, he does not consider himself worthy of anything except punishment. He sees that he should have honored Him as his Creator and God, but he did not honor Him. He should have obeyed Him but did not. He should have loved Him but did not. He should have humbled himself before Him but did not. He should have submitted himself to Him but did not. And thus offended Him in whose love and benefactions he is enclosed; Him, Who is only love and goodness; Him, Who has all the ends of the earth; and he himself, in his hand, Him, Whom the angels worship, honor, and hymn with fear and love. This is sorrow in God, which effects deep-rooted repentance for salvation! A heart broken by such sadness cannot but shed tears. Along with the prophet, he will wish for a fountain of tears. For such a one, it is hard to sin in the future. He would rather die than sin. This is true Christian repentance, which proceeds from reflection on our disdain for God our Benefactor and His benefactions! Oh, if only every Christian would reason what good God does for him, and how badly he offends Him by sin, Him from Whom he receives every benefaction, and would consider God's majesty and his own unworthiness, he would never want to sin! But the trouble is that he has closed spiritual eyes and therefore does not see what he is doing. "Awake, you who sleep, Arise from the dead, And Christ will give you light" (Eph 5:14). Wake up, O unfortunate soul! Satan wants to deprive you forever of the eternal treasure.

# 15. A King and His Subject
## Who Asks a Favor of Him

When a person stands before his King and asks a favor of him, he looks on him with humility and reverence, he kneels and falls down before him, and he has his whole mind and thoughts concentrated on disposing the king to mercy and to receive what he desires. You see, O Christian, how a man asks mercy from a man! What attention, humility, and reverence he shows, wishing to receive what he is asking for! From this example, we learn how we should stand before the Lord God and our King in prayer, to look with humility on His all-holy face, to bend our knees with humility and fall down before His majesty, and to ask for what we wish. O man! Remember in your prayer that you are standing before God, are conversing with God, and are speaking with God: "Lord, have mercy! Lord, be generous, Lord, hear me! Lord, save!" and so forth. And if you read psalms, or sing church songs, you are singing to God; you are raising up your voice to God: "Thou, O Lord!" "To Thee, O Lord!" and so on. Who are you? Earth, ashes, and a sinner. Before Whom do you stand and talk? Before a God Who is Holy and frightening, before Whom all creation, visible and invisible, is as nothing. You, a small and poor little worm, and besides that a sinner, stand praying before the Eternal, Incomprehensible, and Almighty God. Consider what humility and reverence this requires of you. We stand with humility before an earthly King and ask him, and the more so before the King of Heaven! From this it follows: (1) The reading of prayers with haste, as fast as the tongue can manage, does not yield any benefit. (2) Hurriedly read verses or sung songs only make noise and are not only not beneficial for those who read and sing but are turned into sin. (3) From this it happens that priests, clerics, and other people who read and sing like this not only do not improve but even become worse, for they never pray, even though they often go to church frequently and pray. Prayer is our intercession for all good things for us. This is why, without prayer, it is impossible to improve ourselves, to live in a Christian way, and do good. We must ask God for every good. Being always inclined to evil, we cannot be good without God. (4) Inasmuch as prayer is the cause of all good for us, Satan, our enemy, knowing this great benefit that we receive from prayer, hinders us in every way, first offering thoughts about worldly matters, then pestering us with evil thoughts, and then instilling despondency. That is why the pious need to be careful in prayer, to resist the enemy, not to allow thoughts to be distracted, and to pay attention only to God, so that we may stand before God both in body and spirit and that we may fall down before Him both in the body and in the spirit, so that the mind and heart will not be silent concerning what the tongue speaks of—in a word, that the interior of the one praying be in harmony with the exterior.

Everyone approaches a good and merciful person, although he be of high rank, with ease, for his goodness and mercy attracts everyone to him, and the hope of his mercy makes access to him comfortable. Everyone thinks of him, "Although he is mighty and high-ranking, he is still accessible to all the poor who come to him and ask mercy of him, and he opens the doors of mercy." Even more so should we think so about our Lord God, O Christian! Although He is both Mighty and terrifying, and His majesty is incomprehensible, His greatness is equaled by His Goodness and mercy, and His majesty is equaled by his mercy. "The Lord is merciful and gracious, longsuffering, and of great kindness. The Lord is good unto all, and His mercies are upon all His works" (Ps 144:8–9). And every holy word of His preaches to us nothing so much as His goodness and mercy for our hope and comfort, that we may approach him without doubting and will knock on the door of His mercy. And He Himself commands us to approach Him with prayer and supplication in our needs. "Ask, and it will be given to you; seek, and you will find; knock, and it will be opened to you. For everyone who asks receives, and he who seeks finds, and to him who knocks it will be opened" (Matt 7:7–8). What can be more comforting than these words to us poor sinners? To what person, so good, merciful, generous, and meek, is access so easy as it is to God, Who has planted goodness, mercy, munificence, and meekness in the human heart? From what father do children so easily and quickly ask what they desire, as human sons do from God? Our God not only looks on a petition and grants it but listens even to the desire of His poor people. "Thou hast heard the desire of the poor, O Lord; Thine ear hearkeneth unto the disposition of their hearts" (Ps 9:38). Our Sweetest Saviour Jesus opened to us the doors of mercy and access to God by His inestimable merits. And do not let His majesty deter us from approaching Him with prayer, but let His goodness and love for mankind encourage us. "Let us therefore come boldly to the throne of grace, that we may obtain mercy and find grace to help in time of need" (Heb 4:16).

We see that one cannot approach a King or some other high personage with a petition at any time or in any place. But to our God, Christian, it is not so: it is always and everywhere easy to come to God. He is always and everywhere ready to listen to our prayer. Night and day, evening and morning, and any time and hour are suitable for prayer. Also, it is expedient to approach Him in any place, for He is with all of us always and everywhere. We can approach Him with our petition in church, at home, in a meeting, on the way, at work, in bed, walking and sitting, working and resting, and at any time. For we can always and everywhere raise our mind and heart to Him, and offer the petition of our hearts to Him, and fall down with prostrate hearts before His merciful eyes, and await mercy from Him. For we draw near to God not with our feet but with our hearts. Draw near, Christian, always and everywhere to your Merciful Creator; confess and acknowledge your destitution, poverty, and sinfulness, and you will receive a wealth of goodness from Him.

# 16. The Vine and the Branches

The relationship between Christ and Christians parallels that between a vine and its branches. The branches are connected to the vine. So also are Christians spiritually connected with Christ. The branches receive their sap from the vine and bear fruit, just as Christians receive the life-giving force of decency and virtues from Christ and bear the fruits of good works. Although fruit appears on the branches, it is ascribed to the vine; likewise, although Christians yield the fruit of virtues, these are ascribed to Christ, the Son of God. Branches of themselves cannot yield fruit without the vine; likewise, Christians without Christ cannot produce anything. Workers prune the branches, that they will produce better and more fruit. Likewise the Heavenly Father chastens Christians so they may yield more numerous and pleasing fruits of virtues. From the outside, branches are not attractive, but inside contain good and pleasant sap and fruit; likewise, Christians are unprepossessing and contemptible on the outside but are good on the inside; they do not speak beautifully, but they live beautifully. The more branches become heavy with fruit, the more they bend over and sink down. Likewise, the more good works Christians do, the more humble they become. Branches bear fruit by way of the labor of the worker; likewise Christians do good works in accordance with the word of the Heavenly Father, from Whom every good thing proceeds. The branch that does not bear fruit is cut from the vine; likewise, the Christian who does not bear good fruit is torn away from Christ. The branch that is cut from the vine withers; likewise, the Christian who is torn away from Christ ruins his whole spiritual life force and withers spiritually. The withered branch is not fit for anything other than to be burned; likewise, the Christian who has been torn away from Christ and has withered is giving himself up to eternal fire (see John 15:4–6).

From here you can see, O Christian: (1) How close is the union and fellowship of true Christians with Christ! He is the Vine, and they are the branches. (2) What a great and lofty dignity this is! For what is more excellent than to have fellowship with Christ, the Heavenly King? It is most excellent to have fellowship with an earthly king or prince, but it is incomparably more excellent with Christ, the King of Kings. (3) How great is their blessedness! If Christ is with Christians, who can be against them? All the world and all of hell can do anything against the Christian, since Christ is his Might and his Strength. (4) We cannot be virtuous and do good works without Christ, for the branches cannot bear fruit without the vine. (5) From this it follows that, first of all, one must be planted in Christ and so bear the fruits of good works—we must first of all become good and then do good. "A bad tree [cannot] bear good fruit" (Matt 7:18). (6) How calamitous is the state of those Christians who have torn themselves away from Christ by an iniquitous life! For they are like the withered branches. (7) Everyone who wants to be saved must turn to God with a pure heart and wash himself with repentance and tears, and so be grafted onto Christ, the True Vine. For there is no salvation apart from Christ and outside of Christ. Christ is Life and Light, and that is why he who has separated himself from these will find himself in death and in darkness. Think about this, Christian, and wash away your sins by repentance and tears, so that you may be joined again with Life—Christ.

## 17. Head and Body

What the head and body are to each other, so are Christ and Christians. The head is joined with the body just as Christians are spiritually joined with Christ. The head governs the rest of the body just as Christ governs His spiritual Body or His holy Church. The head looks after the benefit and safety of the whole body, just as Christ looks after the benefit and salvation of His Church or the faithful. Whatever the head plans and desires, the members of the body do. The hands do what the head wishes. The feet go where the head wishes. No member does anything without the head willing it. Likewise, Christians should do everything in accordance with the will of Christ, that is, what He wishes. All the members of the body obey the head, just as

Christians should obey Christ. When the head suffers, all the members of the body suffer along with it. Likewise, Christians in this world should suffer with Christ, Who has suffered; should be mocked with Christ, Who was mocked; should be sworn at with Him who was sworn at —in a word, to take up their cross with Christ, Who carried His Cross, and follow Him. When the head is glorified, the members of the body join in the same glory. Likewise, His spiritual members—Christians—are glorified with the glorified Christ in His kingdom. The members of the body are the tools of the head: the head does everything, but through its members. Likewise, Christians are the tools of the Head, Christ, Who through them performs good works. Whatever good the members do is ascribed to the head. Thus, everything good that Christians do should be ascribed to Christ. When someone strikes the head, the hands protect it in every way possible and defend it from whoever is striking it, lest it be injured. Likewise, when Christ is abused and dishonored, Christians should stand up and defend the glory of His name, even if he himself has to suffer. All the felicity of the body depends on the head. Likewise the happiness of all Christians depends on Christ. When the body or some member suffers, the head suffers as well. Likewise, when Christians suffer, Christ suffers with them. The head imputes to itself whatever happens to a bodily member. Is an offense or some evil done to a Christian? All this is done to Christ Himself. Is the Christian persecuted, sworn at, reviled, or reproached? All this concerns Christ Himself. Does the Christian do a good deed or some benefaction? Christ imputes this to Himself.

Christ speaks about this: "Inasmuch as you did it to one of the least of these My brethren, you did it to Me." And again, "Inasmuch as you did not do it to one of the least of these, you did not do it to Me" (Matt 25:40, 45). From this you see, Christian, (1) what kind of union and relationship Christians have with Christ, like the members of the body with the head. (2) Christ is the Holy Head. His members—Christians—must join in His holiness and perform acts of holiness in the fear of God. Otherwise, "what fellowship has righteousness with lawlessness? And what communion has light with darkness?" (2 Cor 6:14). We must purify ourselves with true repentance and bear fruits worthy of it, in order to be true Christians, living members of Christ, and so join in His holiness. (3) How great is the preeminence and blessedness of Christians! For what could be greater for a person than to be a member of Christ the King, the Head higher than the heavens? (4) What a serious sin those Christians commit who offend Christians, inasmuch as this offense bears on Christ Himself, which is terrible even to say, but it is so in reality.

(5) From this, Christians should be comforted that Christ—their Head—will suffer along with them in their trials, and whatever happens to them, He imputes to Himself. (6) Christians, let us try to be true Christians and to join ourselves to Christ's sanctity and to the blessedness of true Christians.

# 18. The Members of the Body among Themselves

Christians relate to one another as do members of the body. The body is composed of many members, just as Christians make up the spiritual body. The members are joined into one body, just as Christians are united into one spiritual body. The members of the body are joined and connected by sinews, just as Christians are united and bound together by faith, spirit, and love. The members of the body do not cause harm to each other, just as Christians should not offend or injure one another. Members of the body are peaceable and harmonious with each other, just as among Christians there should be tranquility and concord. Members of the body help each other and protect each other, just as Christians should assist and defend each other. When one member of the body suffers, the other members suffer along with it. Likewise Christians, when any Christian suffers, should empathize with them and should weep with those who weep. Members of the body do not disdain each other and are not haughty toward one other, just as Christians should not have contempt or be arrogant toward one another. Members of the body are all of equal dignity, as are all Christians. Bodily members guard each other against approaching harm, for example: the eyes, by sight; the ears, by hearing; the legs, by running, and so on, just as Christians should watch out for each other: some by word, some by advice, some by fear, some by prayer. The head looks after and takes care of the whole body, just as Christ, the Head, is concerned and watches over His whole spiritual Body. To Him be glory forever, amen! You see, Christian, what is the nature of Christians and what love, peace, harmony, mercy, empathy, and so on should be among them. Consider whether you belong to this holy community. It is written of the first Christians: "[T]he multitude of those who believed were of one heart and one soul" (Acts 4:32). Oh, if only it were that way now! But with sorrow and lamentation, we see the opposite (see Rom 12:4–5; 1 Cor 10:17; 12:12–13; and others).

## 19. Sheep

Christians are called sheep in Sacred Scripture because there is considerable similarity between these. Sheep do not offend any other animals. Likewise, Christians do not offend anyone. Simplicity is characteristic among sheep. When a wolf kills a sheep, they do not run off, but all of them watch. Likewise, Christians are simple-hearted: "wise in what is good, and simple concerning evil" (Rom 16:19). Sheep bring great benefit to their owners; that is, they provide them with wool, milk, leather, and meat. Likewise, Christians are good and beneficial to all and offer a sacrifice of praise and confession to God, their Lord. Peace and harmony are observed among sheep, for many of them can be accommodated even in a small pen. Likewise, Christians are peaceful and harmonious among themselves. Meekness and patience are observed among sheep: they are silent when they are shorn and when they are slaughtered. Likewise, Christians are humble, meek, and patient. Envy is not observed among sheep, for, when they eat, they do not fight with each other. Likewise, Christians are not envious. Sheep are very greedy, for they eat a lot. Likewise Christians, although they may be pious, always hunger and thirst after righteousness. Sheep are obedient to their shepherd. Likewise, Christians are obedient to their Shepherd and Lord, Jesus Christ. "'My sheep hear My voice,' Christ says" (John 10:27).

You see, Christian, the characteristics of Christ's sheep, the true Christians. Think of yourself, whether you belong to this blessed flock. If you want to be in the heavenly enclosure, you absolutely need to be one of Christ's sheep.

## 20. Goats

Evil people are likened to goats, since there is considerable similarity between them. Goats butt and hurt almost any animal with their horns. Likewise, evil people hurt any person, good and evil, either by word or deed. Pride is characteristic of goats, since they move mostly in high and steep places and often climb up onto buildings. Likewise, evil people are haughty and conceited. In a herd, goats always try to be in front. Likewise, evil people always want to be in charge or be in first place. Goats, when they are dragged somewhere or slaughtered, are not silent but cry out. Likewise, evil people, when they are punished, do not have patience, but grumble, and often even use abusive language, saying, "What fault is it of mine? What did I do wrong?" and so on. Goats give off a certain peculiar stench. Likewise, evil people stink of depravity and iniquitous/lawless life.

Take note, Christian of the similarity of goats and evil people and remember what is written about sheep and goats: "All the nations will be gathered before Him [Christ the King], and He will separate them one from another, as a shepherd divides his sheep from the goats. And He will set the sheep on His right hand, but the goats on the left" (Matt 25:32–33). Correct yourself by repentance and prayer, that you may be one of Christ's sheep and that you will not be like a goat when the good are separated from the evil, as the sheep from the goats.

# 21. Shepherd and Flock

We see in this world that people entrust livestock to shepherds to tend and protect it. Likewise, Christ's sheep, Christians, are entrusted by Christ the Lord to pastors, bishops and priests, to tend them and protect them. Shepherds are chosen who are good and sensible, lest they lose the livestock. Likewise, good and sensible pastors must be chosen, lest they lose Christ's rational sheep, lest what is written might also come true for them: "if the blind leads the blind, both will fall into a ditch" (Matt 15:14). Shepherds drive livestock into the field, to grass and good pasture, and graze them there. Pastors should feed Christ's sheep with the Word of God and the Holy Mysteries. Shepherds look after their flock and protect it from wolves and other wild animals. Likewise, pastors should look after and protect the flock of Christ's sheep from the devil, demons, heretics, and other wild beasts of the soul. Pastors search for the animal that has been separated from the flock and become lost and drive it back into the flock. Likewise pastors should search for the lost Christian and return him to Christ's flock. And every Christian is lost who does not live in a Christian way.

Shepherds drive their flock home from the field to their owners. Likewise, pastors should send the flock of Christ's sheep from this world into the heavenly enclosure, so that when they later arrive, they can say: "Here I am with your sheep that You gave me, Lord!" Shepherds receive pay from owners for their work, for tending the livestock. Likewise pastors will receive pay for their work and for tending His flock: "the crown of glory that does not fade away" (1 Pet 5:4). If shepherds do not drive one of the animals home, the owners ask: "Where is such and such an animal of mine?" Likewise, if a Christian perishes and does not appear in the heavenly enclosure, Christ the Lord will ask of pastors, "Where is such and such a sheep of mine? Where is the sheep that I acquired not by silver or gold, but by My Blood? Where is the sheep that you received in order to tend and keep it?" A shepherd cannot say to the owner, "I do not know where it is," because he had been the caretaker of the flock. Likewise, a pastor cannot say to Christ the Lord, "I do not know where the sheep is," because he was the caretaker of Christ's flock (see Ezek 34:8–31). The owner deprives the shepherd of pay for the loss of the animal. Likewise, the pastor is deprived by Christ of wages for the loss of the rational sheep and is given over for punishment. The shepherd is not culpable if the animal perishes for some reason other than his negligence. Likewise, the pastor will not be culpable when the Christian perishes because of his own carelessness and willfulness rather than because of his pastor's negligence and lack of supervision, that is, if the pastor taught him, exhorted him, admonished him, and showed him an example of good works, but he did not listen to him.

A flock of livestock obeys the shepherds and therefore goes where they drive it. Likewise, Christians ought to obey their pastors and do what they teach, after the Apostle's exhortation: "Obey those who rule over you, and be submissive, for they watch out for your souls, as those who must give account. Let them do so with joy and not with grief" (Heb 13:17). Pastor! Remember that you are the caretaker of the flock of Christ's sheep. People! Pay attention to what Christ says about pastors who teach, but do not do: "The scribes and the Pharisees sit in Moses' seat. Therefore whatever they tell you to observe, that observe and do, but do not do according to their works; for they say, and do not do" (Matt 23:2–3).

## 22. Bridegroom and Bride

As a bridegroom and bride are to each other, so is Christ and the Christian soul. The bride is betrothed to the bridegroom. Likewise the human soul is betrothed to Christ, the Son of God, and is washed in the bath of baptism. The bride leaves home and parents and cleaves to her bridegroom alone. Likewise the Christian soul, being betrothed to Christ, the Son of God, must leave the world and its fancies and cleave only to its Bridegroom, Jesus Christ, to which the Holy Spirit exhorts us through the prophet: "Hearken, O daughter, and see, and incline thine ear, and forget thy people and thy father's house, and the King shall greatly desire thy beauty" (Ps 44:11–12). The bride is dressed in a colorful dress and is adorned to be pleasing to her bridegroom. Likewise the Christian soul must dress in suitable clothing and adorn itself within to be pleasing to its Bridegroom, Jesus Christ. The Holy Spirit identifies the attire of the soul through the Apostle: "Therefore, as the elect of God, holy and beloved, put on tender mercies, kindness, humility, meekness, longsuffering" (Col 3:12).

A good bride is faithful to her bridegroom. Likewise, a Christian soul should be faithful to Jesus Christ until death, concerning which Christ Himself says to it: "Be faithful until death, and I will give you the crown of life" (Rev 2:10). The good bride loves no one as much or more than her bridegroom. Likewise, the Christian soul should not love anyone as much as or more than Christ, its Bridegroom. A bride is not pleasing to her bridegroom when she renders equal or especially more love to another. Likewise, a Christian soul does not please Christ when it loves another equally to Christ, or, what is worse, more than Him. "He who loves father or mother more than Me is not worthy of Me. And he who loves son or daughter more than Me is not worthy of Me, Christ says" (Matt 10:37). The nobility, honor, and dignity of the bride are dependent on the bridegroom. Likewise, the honor, nobility, and dignity of the Christian soul depend on Christ. The more noble the bridegroom, the more noble is the bride betrothed to him. But since there is no one more honorable, noble, and worthy than Christ, the son of God, then for the Christian soul there cannot be a greater honor and dignity than to be the betrothed bride of Christ, the Son of God. The honor, nobility, and dignity of the bride are not apparent until she is joined with her bridegroom in marriage. Likewise, the honor and glory of the Christian soul are not apparent until it is united in marriage with Jesus Christ in the age to come. "Beloved, says the apostle, it has not yet been revealed what we shall be" (1 John 3:2). The glory and dignity of the bride will be revealed when she is joined with her bridegroom in the most honorable marriage. Thus will be revealed the supreme glory of the Christian soul, when in His Second Coming, it will be joined with Him in marriage. Then it will be like its most excellent Bridegroom. "But we know that when He is revealed, we shall be like Him, for we shall see Him as He is" (1 John 3:2).

After the wedding, the bride is led with gladness to the house of the bridegroom. Likewise, the Christian soul will be led into the house and chamber of its Heavenly Bridegroom, Jesus Christ, "with joy and gladness" (Ps 44:16). "For with the Lord's help, they shall return and come to Zion with gladness and everlasting joy; for exceeding joy. Praise and gladness shall come on them, and pain, grief, and sighing shall depart from them" (Isa 51:11). After a wedding, feasting and merriment take place. Likewise, at this wedding, there will be joy, gladness, and a great supper. Then they will eat, they will drink, they will rejoice, and they will be glad in the gladness of their hearts (see Isa 65:13–14). This was revealed to the holy Apostle John: "And I heard, as it were, the voice of a great multitude, as the sound of many waters and as the sound of mighty thunderings, saying, 'Alleluia! For the Lord God Omnipotent reigns! Let us be glad and rejoice and give Him glory, for the marriage of the Lamb has come, and His wife has made herself ready.' And to her it was granted to be arrayed in fine linen, clean and bright, for the fine linen is the righteous acts of the saints" (Rev 19:6–8).

The bridegroom rejoices in his bride, and the bride in her bridegroom. Likewise, Christ, the Heavenly Bridegroom, rejoices in the souls of those who have been saved and glorified. "And as a bridegroom rejoices over his bride, so the Lord shall rejoice over you" (Isa 62:5). And souls will rejoice in their most sweet and beautiful Bridegroom unto the ages of ages. "Let my soul rejoice exceedingly in the Lord, for He clothed me with the garment of salvation and the tunic of gladness. He put a miter around me like a bridegroom and adorned me with ornaments like a bride" (Isa 61:10). The Lord speaks of this mystical betrothal and wedding through the prophet, "I will betroth you to Myself forever; Yes, I will betroth you to Myself in righteousness and justice, And in mercy and compassions. I will betroth you to Myself in faithfulness, And you shall know the Lord" (Hos 2:19–20). And the Apostle tells Christians, "I have betrothed you to one husband, that I may present you as a chaste virgin to Christ" (2 Cor 11:2). Let us try, beloved Christian, to purify ourselves by repentance and to adorn our souls with the tunic of virtues. May we find favor with our Heavenly Bridegroom, Jesus Christ, and He will receive us into His heavenly and eternal chamber.

# 23. *Warfare*

In this world, we see that when kingdom rises up against kingdom, a war takes place between them. Likewise, Christians have their enemies who rise up against them, and there is warfare between them. In a battle of this world, people rise up against people. Likewise, in the Christian battle, Satan and his evil angels rise up against Christians. People who rise up against people are visible. But Satan and his angels, our enemies, are invisible to us. In a battle of this world, each opposing side sees the other, and so they are wary of each other. But in Christian warfare, the Christians are visible to their enemies the demons but do not see them. Our visible enemies are fierce and dangerous. But more fierce and dangerous for us are our invisible enemies, that is, the demons. In visible warfare, the more evil and cunning the enemy, the more dangerous he is. But since there is no more evil and cunning an enemy than Satan and his demons, warfare with them is very dangerous for us. When people fight against people, they rest from battle for a time. But Satan and his evil angels never sleep but are always vigilant and are trying to bring us down. Warfare that is carried out among people, although it may be prolonged, does nevertheless end, and peace is concluded. But Christians have a continuous battle, even until death, against their enemies, and is only ended by death. It happens in battle that the foe retreats and seems to be discontinuing the battle, but then it is more dangerous, since he is exercising his cunningness and is planning how more skillfully to defeat the opposing side. Our enemy Satan does likewise. He often ostensibly retreats from us and discontinues the battle, but this is his cunningness and craftiness since he is planning by this to lead us into inadvertence and carelessness in order to bring us down more easily.

In battle, people engage each other with weapons and wound and kill each other. Likewise, there are weapons in the Christian battle. Both the demons and the Christians have theirs. The demons strike us with the weapons of the passions and of our members. And they have as many weapons as there are passions in our flesh. The Christian weapons are the Word of God and prayer. With these weapons, Christians fight and defend themselves against the demons and make the arrows of their enemies ineffective. What the sword and other weapons are to the warrior, prayer and the Word of God are to the Christian. The Christian without prayer and the Word of God is like the warrior without sword and gun. Warriors in battle always carry a sword and other arms. Likewise Christians always should be armed with the spiritual sword of the Word of God and the weapon of prayer. For they have constant warfare against their enemies. Therefore, they are commanded, "Pray without ceasing" (1 Thess 5:17). Warriors in battle stay vigilant and are extremely cautious because of the enemies surrounding them. Likewise, Christians in their battle should always be vigilant and act cautiously, for the enemies always surround them. Therefore it is said to them, "Be sober, be vigilant; because your adversary the devil walks about like a roaring lion, seeking whom he may devour. Resist him, steadfast in the faith" (1 Pet 5:8–9). Warriors in battle all stand as one against the enemy and fight. Likewise, Christians should all stand as one against the enemy, the devil, and fight. Warriors in battle help each other. Likewise, Christians should help each other against their enemy, either by advice, or by exhortation, or by prayer. The enemy, when he senses his weariness, calls other allies to help him. Likewise, our enemy the devil, when he is not having success against the Christian, looks for evil people and fights the Christian through them. Therefore, every Christian, when he tempts, persecutes, exasperates, and in any way leads his neighbor into sin, is taking up arms together with the devil against him. Watch out, Christian so that you do not find yourself working with the devil.

In battle, there are superior officers and commanders, who train, admonish, and encourage to a good effort against the enemy. Likewise in the Christian battle, the superior officers are the pastors and teachers, who arm the Christians with the Word of God against the enemy, the devil, and train and admonish how to stand and fight against him. The enemy in battle tries first of all to hit and kill the superior officers and commanders of the opposing side in order to throw the entire force into disorder and confusion and in this way to kill or capture them, for the entire safety and well-being of the force depends on the superior officers and commanders, especially the wise ones. Likewise, in the Christian battle, the enemy, the devil, tries most of all to bring down pastors and teachers, so that it would be easier to capture and destroy them. The entire safety and well-being of the Christian congregation depends on the pastors and teachers. Without a good and prudent pastor, Christians are like lost sheep. And when the enemy cannot bring down a pastor, he stirs up people who do his [the devil's] will against the pastor, to spread malicious rumors about him, so that people would not believe his teaching. Therefore it happens that pastors and teachers suffer much slander, vilification, backbiting, persecution, and expulsion, to which all ages bear witness. No one so vexes this enemy as pastors and good teachers. They destroy his dark kingdom and authority by the Word of God and the power of the Holy Spirit and snatch Christian souls, his favorite catch, from his hands. Therefore, the malicious spirit rages and grows savage against no one as much as at pastors and teachers. And so, Christian, avoid backbiting any person, and especially pastors and teachers, lest you be scheming in concert with the devil.

In a battle of this world, people try to protect their borders and cities or seize them from the opposing side. But in the Christian battle, it is otherwise. The enemy, the devil, is not trying to capture cities, borders, or our riches, but our souls—to capture not the body, but our souls, and ruin them forever, to take away not earthly and temporal happiness, but that which is heavenly and eternal. All of his efforts and attentions are directed to this—to draw us to perdition with himself. Behold, Christian, your enemy's malice, enmity, and ferocity against you, and shun him. The enemy is trying to take away from you not gold, not silver, or other perishable matter, but an eternal and imperishable treasure—your salvation. Guard this not only more closely than your possessions but more closely than your life. In a battle of this world, it sometimes happens that the events of the war at first develop unfavorably for one side, but in the end, the action takes a favorable turn for them, and so victory is ascribed to those who successfully finish the battle. The side that at first was being beaten is victorious at the end of the battle and thus ends the battle successfully. It is also like this in the Christian battle. From the beginning of their lives, many Christians are being vanquished by their enemy, the devil. But then, rising by the grace of God and strengthened by the power of Christ, they take up arms against the enemy and defeat him, and so finish the warfare successfully. The end determines success and failure. He who began well is not successful, but who ends well. The more a warrior takes part in battles and engagements, the more skillful and braver he becomes. Likewise, the more often a Christian falls into temptations, misfortunes, and tribulations, the more proficient he becomes in the Christian life. Therefore, the Apostle says, "My brethren, count it all joy when you fall into various trials, knowing that the testing of your faith produces patience. But let patience have its perfect work, that you may be perfect and complete, lacking nothing" (Jas 1:2–4). When the battle ends, the victors return to their homeland with celebration and rejoicing and receive honor from their king. Likewise, Christians who have successfully finished their battle and blessedly ended their temporal life go into the heavenly homeland with celebration and gladness and receive the crown of righteousness from the heavenly King, Jesus Christ. "I have fought the good fight, I have finished the race, I have kept the faith. Finally, there is laid up for me the crown of righteousness, which the Lord, the righteous Judge, will give to me on that Day, and not to me only but also to all who have loved His appearing" (2 Tim 4:7–8). The Apostle pictures this Christian battle for us and forearms us:

> Finally, my brethren, be strong in the Lord and in the power of His might. Put on the whole armor of God, that you may be able to stand against the wiles of the devil. For we do not wrestle against flesh and blood, but against principalities, against powers, against the rulers of the darkness of this age, against spiritual hosts of wickedness in the heavenly places. Therefore take up the whole armor of God, that you may be able to withstand in the evil day, and having done all, to stand. Stand therefore, having girded your waist with truth, having put on the breastplate of righteousness, and having shod your feet with the preparation of the gospel of peace; above all, taking the shield of faith with which you will be able to quench all the fiery darts of the wicked one. And take the helmet of salvation, and the sword of the Spirit, which is the word of God. (Eph 6:10–17)

From this you see, Christian: (1) The Christian life in this world is nothing other than a constant battle. (2) The battle is not against flesh and blood, that is people, but against the devil and the demons. (3) These enemies, which are invisible, very malicious, hostile, and cunning, are risen against us and fight with us. (4) They are trying to take away from us not temporary booty, but eternal salvation, and to bring us to perdition. (5) Therefore, you see what a fierce and difficult battle we have against these enemies. For this, we must not slumber, but stay awake and be careful. Here eternal salvation is either gained or lost. (6) This struggle and victory do not take place without Christ's help. Here, human strength can do nothing. For this, we must pray and sigh to Christ, the Master and Judge of Struggles, that He may help and strengthen us. We continually require His help since the enemies continually surround us. (7) Inasmuch as our enemies concentrate more on pastors and teachers, all Christians should pray for them more, so that the Lord might help them. (8) Inasmuch as the Word of God and prayer are the Christian weapons, then he who abandons the Word of God and prayer does the same as a warrior who, during combat, throws down his sword and other weapons; this is a sign that he has yielded to the enemy. (9) Having joined in the struggle, do not be dejected, do not despair on seeing such a terrible battle, but stand fast. Christians, Christ reassures us, "Be of good cheer, I have overcome the world" (John 16:33). Be daring, Christian. God stands up for us. "If God is for us, who can be against us" (Rom 8:31)? "Through God we shall do great deeds, and it is He that shall wipe out our enemies" (Ps 107:14). (10) Having fallen down and lying prostrate, get up, as usually happens with warriors in battle. They fall and get up, they are wounded, and they inflict wounds. You should do likewise, Christian! Get up on your feet and take heart and, calling on the Lord of Hosts, Jesus Christ, for help, stand and fight. And He will without fail help you, seeing your diligence and zeal. He Who was made like you for your sake, and suffered and died for you, will help you. Warfare is at first terrifying for soldiers who are not used to battle, but later it is not so, and they go into battle with daring. Likewise, at first this struggle is terrifying for you, but later it will be easy. Take courage, beloved; go and fight against your enemy. Christ is our King, Christ is our Protector, Christ is strong and mighty in battle. He calls us to battle and to struggle against our enemy, who trembles at His name alone. He calls us and promises to grant us His help: "Be of good cheer, I have overcome the world" (John 16:33) And He will overcome it in us: only let us stand up and stand aright, and He will rise to our help and will be a pillar of strength for us in the face of the enemy. "Arise, O Lord; help us, and deliver us for Thy Name's sake" (Ps 43:27). (11) Pastor, the leader in this spiritual battle, you see how prudent and wise you need to be. If skillful and wise leaders are required in visible warfare, where people fight people and flesh with flesh, how much more so are prudent and wise leaders needed in the spiritual battle, where the battle is by people against the demons, and by flesh and blood against the invisible and cunning spirits. O pastor! You, who must exhort and teach others, ought above all else to be learned in the Word of God. You above all else need to gird yourself with the sword of the Word of God, and to put on the whole armor, and be vigilant, and be cautious in this battle, in which the foe is trying above all to wound and destroy you, and so save yourself and those entrusted to you. All Christian souls will be required from your hand. Remember this, beloved, and lay it up in your heart, and be watchful as you stand on guard for the Lord! (12) Warriors in a battle take heart in the hope of victory and higher rank and so fight bravely. Beloved Christian! Your victory is not over flesh and blood, but over the spirit of malice, and therefore will be glorious, and your crown, and honor, and glory, and praise, and peace, and celebration are not temporal and earthly, but heavenly and eternal, promised not from man, but from God, Who cannot lie. "Be faithful until death, and I

will give you the crown of life" (Rev 2:10). The sons of this age labor and fight
for the sake of the temporary and corruptible. Are we not to fight for the sake
of eternal and ineffable good things? (13) The weapons of the demons, with
which they fight us and lead us to evil, are evil thoughts that they stir up in our
hearts. This is how they shoot at us. As many times as we assent to, or think,
or speak, or do evil, they defeat us. As many times as we resist them, we defeat
them, and we honor our God, Who mercifully visits and encourages us to
fight against them, Who helps us defeat them, strengthens us lest we weaken
in the warfare, promises us the incorruptible crown, that we will remain in the
struggle until the end. "Be faithful until death, and I will give you the crown
of life" (Rev 2:10).

In a battle of this world, people are victorious when they pursue the opposing side. And on the contrary, they are defeated when they yield to the enemy.
In the Christian battle, it is not so. Christians are victorious when they yield to
their enemies; when they endure evil from people but do not themselves do
evil; when people curse at them and mock them; when people beat them, but
they do not retaliate, and so on. For when they yield to people, then they do
not give ground to the devil. This is the Christian victory, which consists of
patience, and not revenge. It is a great wound to the devil and a glorious victory of Christians when they love their enemies, bless those who curse them,
do good to those who hate them, and pray for those who offend them and
persecute them (see Matt 5:4). The glorious Christian victory is to defeat the
malice of their enemies by love and goodness. Christ gave us an example of
this and showed how we should defeat our enemies; He prayed for His enemies: "Father, forgive them" (Luke 23:34). There, Christian, is the Christian
victory—not to take revenge on enemies, but to pray for our enemies. "Do not
be overcome by evil, but overcome evil with good" (Rom 12:21).

Since the Word of God and prayer are the Christian weapons, listen and
heed. The devil incites you to sin, but answer him in your heart, "I do not want
to do it, for this is offensive to God; God has forbidden it." If the devil arouses
in you a foul and filthy thought, answer him: "My God has forbidden this." If
the devil arouses in you anger and a plan for vengeance, cut off this thought

with the sword of the Word of God, saying in your heart, God did not command this." If the devil shows you someone else's property and incites you to steal it, say in your heart: God forbade this: "You shall not steal ... You shall not covet" (Exod 20:15, 17). Act likewise with other thoughts that are contrary to God's law that arise in your heart and see whether your thought is in accordance with or opposed to the law of God. Accept any that are in accordance and put them into action. Ward off any contrary to the law, lest, having become stronger, they overcome you. Christ, our Saviour, gave us an example of this when to every temptation of the devil He answered the tempter, "It is written ... It is written" (Matt 4:4, 7, 10). Satan leads you into despair and says to your heart, "There is no salvation for you, you have sinned much, you have done so much evil." Answer him, "You are the condemned, not the judge, eternal fire is prepared for you, not salvation. My hope and salvation is Christ God, Who came into the world to save sinners. He will save even me, since I am one of the sinners whom He came to save."

But everywhere another weapon is needed, that is, prayer, without which all of our effort and resistance are powerless. In any temptation, we need to raise our eyes to Christ and pray to him, "Lord, help me," or ask help of Him in some other way. Be strong, Christian, "in the Lord and in the power of His might" (Eph 6:10). And as the gardener prunes twigs and shoots that are injurious to the tree, so they will not cause harm to the tree when they grow larger, likewise, immediately cut off with the sword of the Word of God and prayer evil thoughts that spring up so that, having grown stronger, they will not harm or kill the inner person. Snuff out the spark before it grows into a flame, and kill the enemy, while it is still small. If you do not snuff out the spark, it will become a great fire, and if you do not kill the enemy while it is small, then, when it grows up, it will gain strength, overcome, and destroy you. "Blessed is he that shall seize and dash thine infants against a rock" (Ps 136:9).

## 24. A Wayfarer

A person who leaves one place and goes toward a destination is called a wayfarer. Likewise, Christians, we are wayfarers from the day of our birth to that of death; we are walking along life's path. One wayfarer has a long path, another, a short one. Likewise, for us our path of life is not an equal one—one quickly finishes his path, and another goes farther. The wayfarer on his path fears every misfortune. "See then that you walk circumspectly, not as fools but as wise, redeeming the time, because the days are evil" (Eph 5:15–16). The wayfarer is subject to every kind of bad weather and storm. So with us, walking on our path, we experience every storm of troubles, misfortunes, and disasters. The wayfarer disregards all this but, enduring everything, continues to his destination. Likewise we should disregard all troubles that happen to us, endure them, and go on to our desired Homeland. Robbers often attack a wayfarer and strip him, and often kill him, and so he is unable to get to his destination. The same thing also happens to us, as demons, like robbers, attack and injure and kill the careless, and prevent them from reaching their desired Homeland. Wayfarers defend themselves from robbers with weapons. Likewise, we should defend ourselves from the demons by prayer and the Word of God. The wayfarer always has in his mind the place where he is headed, and he tries to reach it. Likewise, we should always have the heavenly Homeland in our mind and how to reach it. "Run in such a way that you may obtain it, the holy apostle tells us" (1 Cor 9:24).

The farther the wayfarer walks on the path, the shorter his way becomes. So the more we continue the way of our life, the more we approach the end. The wayfarer, coming to the place where he was going, is in safety, and becomes calm, and rejoices on the successful conclusion of his journey. Likewise, we Christians, when we successfully finish our path and come into the heavenly Homeland, shall be safe, we shall be freed from all troubles and misfortunes, we shall become calm, and we shall rejoice in our eternal blessedness that we shall receive by the grace and the love for mankind of our Lord Jesus Christ. Amen! "Unto Thee have I lifted up mine eyes, O Thou that dwellest in heaven. Behold, even as the eyes of servants are upon the hand of their masters, and as the eyes of a maid are upon the hand of her mistress, even so are our eyes upon the Lord our God, until He have pity upon us. Have mercy upon us, O Lord, have mercy upon us! For we have had our fill of humiliation. Our soul is fed up with the scornful reproof of the wealthy, and the disparaging of the proud" (Ps 122:1–4).

## 25. A Wayfarer and a Guide

We see in this world that a wayfarer, for whom the path to his destination is unfamiliar and unknown, requires and looks for a guide, and without a guide goes astray and does not get to his destination. Beloved Christians! We are wayfarers in this world and wish to get to our desired heavenly Homeland, as said earlier, a Homeland of which we were deprived through sin; a Homeland longed-for, beloved, most sweet, beautiful, quiet, peaceful, filled with all good things, of which "[e]ye has not seen, nor ear heard, Nor have entered into the heart of man the things which God has prepared for those who love Him" (1 Cor 2:9); a Homeland to which we look with tearful eyes from this vale of tears. This Homeland is most precious, I say, but the path to it is unknown and frightening to us—unknown, since we do not know how to get there; frightening, since the innumerable demons, like robbers, surround it, and impede those on the path, and try to preclude entrance to it. We absolutely require a skillful and wise guide in such an important matter. But where can we find him? Among the wise and prudent of this age? No! For all, not only the simple, but also the wise, having gone astray, have left this path: "All we like sheep have gone astray. Man has gone astray in his way" (Isa 53:6).

Therefore, even the most wise of this age require a guide to this Homeland. But where should we seek him? The prophets, apostles, and teachers all point to Jesus Christ, the Son of God. He alone is the reliable and wise Guide to the heavenly Homeland. No one will come there, if He does not lead them there, as He Himself testifies concerning this, saying, "No one comes to the Father except through Me" (John 14:6). God, wishing to lead Israel out of Egyptian bondage and lead it into the Promised Land, sent on this great undertaking Moses, His faithful servant, who led Israel out of bitter bondage and led it through the desert into the Promised Land. After the death of Moses, the Lord raised up as their guide Joshua the son of Nun, who led God's people into the land flowing with milk and honey. Christian! Moses and Joshua the son of Nun served as types of Jesus Christ, the Son of God; the old Israel—of the new Israel, of Christians; Egyptian bondage—of the oppressive bondage to the devil; the passage through the sea—of holy Baptism; Israel's going through the desert—of the life of Christian in this world. The Promised Land signifies the heavenly Homeland. God sent to us His only-begotten Son, Jesus Christ, so that He, leading us out of the bondage to the devil, would bring us to His Heavenly Father. His Heavenly Father bore witness of Him from heaven: "This is My beloved Son, in whom I am well pleased. Hear Him!" (Matt 17:5). All the prophets, Apostles, and teachers of the Church bear witness of Him and teach us to follow Him. "Christ also suffered for us, leaving us an example, that you should follow His steps" (1 Pet 2:21). And He Himself says, "For I have given you an example, that you should do as I have done to you" (John 13:15). And again, "If anyone serves Me, let him follow Me; and where I am, there My servant will be also" (John 12:26). All the saints followed Him, and He led them into a land flowing with milk and honey of heavenly sweetness. His faithful servants follow Him now as well. They follow with faith, love, humility, patience, and meekness. And He will lead them into this Homeland, and, as the Good Shepherd, taking them on His shoulders, brings them to His Heavenly Father. O Christians! Let us also join this blessed and holy fellowship, and let us follow Jesus with faith, love, humility, and He will lead us not into the land of Canaan, but into the eternal Kingdom of God, and will grant each his portion. O Jesus, Strength of our salvation! Guide me on Your way; draw me after You; we will run after You.

## 26. A Stranger or Wanderer

A person who absents himself from his home and homeland and lives in a foreign land is a stranger or wanderer there, as a Russian, located in Italy or in another such land, would be. Likewise, a Christian, expelled from his heavenly Homeland and living in this dismal world, is a stranger or wanderer. The holy Apostle speaks with the faithful about this: "For here we have no continuing city, but we seek the one to come" (Heb 13:14). And the Holy David confesses this: "For I am a sojourner with Thee, and a pilgrim, as all my fathers were" (Ps 38:13). And he prays again: "I am a pilgrim upon earth, O hide not Thy commandments from me" (Ps 118:19). A pilgrim, living in a foreign land, applies every effort to complete what he came to the foreign land for. Likewise, the Christian, called by the Word of God and renewed for eternal life by holy Baptism, tries not to be deprived of eternal life, which is either gained or lost here in this world. The pilgrim lives in a foreign land with no small apprehension because he is living among unfamiliar people. Likewise, the Christian, living in this world, as in a foreign land, fears and is wary of everything, that is, of the spirits of malice, demons, sin, the delights of the world, and evil and godless people. All shun the wanderer as not their own and a foreigner. Likewise, all lovers of this world and sons of this age shun, retreat from, and hate the true Christian, as not their own and repugnant to them. The Lord says concerning this, "If you were of the world, the world would love its own. Yet because you are not of the world, but I chose you out of the world, therefore the world hates you" (John 15:19). The sea does not keep a dead body within itself but disgorges it, as they say. Likewise, the inconstant world, like the sea, drives out the pious soul, as one having died to the world. The lover of the world is the favorite child of the world, while the despiser of the world and its seductive lusts is its enemy.

The wanderer does not acquire any real property, that is, neither houses nor gardens, nor anything of the like in a foreign land, except for what is necessary, without which it is impossible to live. Likewise, for the true Christian, everything in this world is real property; he will leave everything in this world, even his very body. About this, the holy Apostle says, "For we brought nothing into this world, and it is certain we can carry nothing out" (1 Tim 6:7). Therefore, the true Christian looks for nothing in this world, except what is necessary, saying with the Apostle, "Having food and clothing, with these we shall be content" (1 Tim 6:8). The wanderer sends or carries personal property, for example, money and goods, into his homeland. Likewise, for the true Christian the personal property in this world, which he can take with himself and carry into the next age, is good works. He tries to gather them here, while living in the world, like a spiritual merchant gathering spiritual goods, and carry them into his heavenly Homeland, and to appear with them before the Heavenly Father. The Lord exhorts us about this, Christians: "Lay up for yourselves treasures in heaven, where neither moth nor rust destroys and where thieves do not break in and steal" (Matt 6:20).

The sons of this age care for the mortal body, but pious souls care for the immortal soul. The sons of this age seek their temporal and earthly treasures, while pious souls strive toward eternal and heavenly ones and desire such good things that "[e]ye has not seen, nor ear heard, Nor have entered into the heart of man" (1 Cor 2:9). They look with faith at this invisible and incomprehensible treasure and scorn all earthly things. The sons of this age try to be glorified on earth, but true Christians seek glory in heaven, where their Homeland is. The sons of this age adorn the body with all manner of attire, but the sons of the Kingdom of God adorn their immortal souls and put on, as the Apostle exhorts, "tender mercies, kindness, humility, meekness, longsuffering" (Col 3:12). And that is why the sons of this age are foolish and senseless, for they seek that which is in and of itself nothing. The Sons of the Kingdom of God are sensible and wise, since they care for what eternal blessedness comprises.

The wanderer finds life in a foreign country tiresome. Likewise, the true Christian finds life in this world tiresome and doleful. Everywhere in this world he finds exile, prison, and a place of banishment, being one expelled from the heavenly Homeland. "Woe is me, says the holy David, for my wandering hath been prolonged" (Ps 119:5). Other saints also lament and sigh about this. Although it is tiresome for the wanderer to live in a foreign land, he lives there because of the need for which he left his homeland. Likewise, although it is doleful the true Christian to live in this world, he lives and endures this wandering for as long as God commands. The wanderer always has his home and homeland in his mind and memory and wishes to return to his homeland. The Jews, while in Babylon, always had in their mind and memory their home, Jerusalem, and eagerly wished to return there. Likewise, true Christians in this world, as at the waters of Babylon, sit and weep, remembering the Jerusalem on high—the heavenly Homeland, and lift up our eyes to it with lamentation and tears, wishing to go there. "For in this we groan, earnestly desiring to be clothed with our habitation which is from heaven, sighs Saint Paul with the faithful" (2 Cor 5:2). For the sons of this age, who have become addicted to the world, the world is like a homeland and paradise, and they therefore do not want to be separated from it. But the sons of the Kingdom of God, separated in their hearts from the world, and enduring every sorrow in the world, wish to come to that Homeland. To the true Christian in this world, life is nothing other than constant suffering and a cross. When a wanderer returns to his homeland and to his own home, his family, neighbors, and friends rejoice for him and welcome his safe arrival. So, when a Christian, having finished his wandering in the world, goes to the heavenly Homeland, all the angels and all the holy heavenly inhabitants rejoice for him. The wanderer who arrives in his homeland and his home lives in safety and rests content. Likewise, the Christian, entering the heavenly Homeland, rests content, lives in safety and fears nothing, rejoices, and is glad in his blessedness.

From this, you see, Christian: (1) Our life in this world is nothing other than wandering and migration, as the Lord says, "In My sight you are resident aliens and sojourners" (Lev 25:23). (2) Our true homeland is not here but in the heavens, and we were created for it, renewed by Baptism, and called by the Word of God. (3) We should not, as ones called to heavenly blessings, seek earthly things and cleave to them, except what is necessary, that is, food, clothing, a house, and so on. (4) For the Christian living in the world, there is nothing more to desire than eternal life, "For where your treasure is, there your heart will be also" (Matt 6:21). (5) Whoever wants to be saved needs to tear his heart away from the world before his soul departs from the world. (6) Whoever in this world seeks to become rich and famous shows by this that he has the world and not heaven as his homeland, and thus deludes himself, which he will comprehend on the day of his death.

# 27. A Citizen

We see that in this world, a person wherever he may live and wherever he is located is called an inhabitant or citizen of the city in which he has his home; for example, an inhabitant of Moscow is a Muscovite, an inhabitant of Novgorod is a Novgorodian, and so on. Likewise, true Christians, although they live in this world, have a city in the heavenly Homeland, "whose builder and maker is God" (Heb 11:10). And he is called a citizen of this city. This city is the heavenly Jerusalem that the holy Apostle John saw in his revelation: "The construction of its wall was of jasper; and the city was pure gold, like clear glass ... And the street of the city was pure gold, like transparent glass ... The city had no need of the sun or of the moon to shine in it, for the glory of God illuminated it. The Lamb is its light" (Rev 21:18, 21, 23). "In its streets is continuously sung the sweet hymn, 'Alleluia!'" (see Rev 19:1, 3, 4, 6). In this city, "there shall by no means enter it anything that defiles, or causes an abomination or a lie, but only those who are written in the Lamb's Book of Life" (Rev 21:27). "But outside are dogs and sorcerers and sexually immoral and murderers and idolaters, and whoever loves and practices a lie" (Rev 22:15).

True Christians are called citizens of this beautiful and shining city, although they wander on the earth. They have habitations there, prepared for them by Jesus Christ, their Redeemer. They direct the eyes of their souls and their sighs there from their wandering. Inasmuch as nothing foul will enter this city, as we saw earlier, "let us cleanse ourselves, beloved Christian, from all filthiness of the flesh and spirit, perfecting holiness in the fear of God" (2 Cor 7:1). And may we be citizens of this shining city, and when we depart this world, may we be found worthy to enter it by the grace of our Saviour, Jesus Christ, to Whom be glory with the Father and the Holy Spirit forever, Amen.

# 28. A Dinner or Supper

As we see, it happens in this world that a distinguished and rich person arranges a rich and splendid supper or dinner and invites to that dinner many people. Likewise God, the Heavenly King, created a great supper of eternal blessedness, full of every ineffable consolation, delight, joy, and festivity and, in his love for mankind, invites everyone. Everyone, I say: famous and infamous; high-born and low-born; rich and poor; wise and foolish; and people of every sex, calling, and rank. He invited through the prophets, he invited through His only-begotten Son, and He invited through the holy Apostles. And He is inviting now through preachers of His Word, pastors and teachers: "Come, for all things are now ready" (Luke 14:17). Beloved Christian! Thanks be to God, we, too, the unworthy, have been called by the man-loving God to this magnificent supper. Let us accept this mercy of the Heavenly King to us and hasten with joy to this holy and most sweet supper. There, we will see the Heavenly King "face to face" (1 Cor 13:12). We shall see His flaming servants, the angels and archangels. We shall see the assembly of the patriarchs, the assembly of the prophets, the assembly of the apostles and hierarchs, the assembly of martyrs, the assembly of monastic saints, and all who have been pleasing to God, and we shall have gracious friendship with all of them.

We see that many, as they once rejected, now also refuse to go to this splendid supper. And instead of eternal and heavenly good things, they choose temporary and earthly ones and thereby prefer a phantom to the truth. And so, they make themselves unworthy of eternal blessedness and show themselves to be ungrateful to the Heavenly King, their Great Benefactor, and they are therefore provoking his righteous anger. "For I say to you," says the Lord, "that none of those men who were invited shall taste my supper, for many are called, but few are chosen" (Luke 14:24). Christians! Let us lay up in our ears and fasten in our memories this word of God, "none of those men who were invited shall taste my supper." We see here that the Lord is angry at those ungrateful people, who have been called by His word to eternal blessedness, to the splendid and most sweet supper but, disdaining this great grace of His, have turned to acquiring temporary honor, glory, riches, various forms of gratification, and other treasures of this world. "None of those men who were invited shall taste my supper."

We read in Moses's book of Numbers that when the sons of Israel, leaving Egypt, grumbled, "Who will give us meat to eat? We remember the fish we ate freely in Egypt, and the cucumbers, the melons, the leeks, the onions, and the garlic." The Lord heard their grumbling and His anger was greatly aroused, and a fire from the Lord burned among them (Num 11:4, 5, 10). Christians! The grumbling Israelites signify those Christians who prefer transient good things to eternal and heavenly ones, just as the Israelites preferred Egyptian meat and other food to the heavenly manna, and for this reason raised up God's anger against themselves, and fire, not temporary, but eternal, is kindled for them. "I say to you that none of those men who were invited shall taste my supper." This saying is fearsome, Christians, but true. It will be this way with those who disdain God's call. Let us be fearful, Christian, and having obeyed the Lord Who calls us, "Set your mind on things above, not on things on the earth" (Col 3:2). When an earthly king calls, as you yourself know, it is shameful and deplorable not to go to his supper. The more so not to go to the supper that God, the Heavenly King, has prepared and to which He constantly calls through his servants. We shall hear His saving voice and shall go with thanksgiving and haste to this most sweet feast. The supper is prepared, splendid, eternal, and most sweet. The servants of God, whom God sends to us, call us, "Come, for all things are now ready." The doors are open; the Heavenly King, Who loves mankind and is all-good, calls everyone and waits. Those who hear His voice enter with thanksgiving and partake of that heavenly sweetness. Christians! Let us too join this holy fellowship and follow it, and the King will lead us into His palace. Amen!

In this world, it happens that the renowned and rich invite to their suppers mostly the renowned and rich like themselves. It is not so with the Heavenly King, the man-loving God. He, in His love for mankind, disdains no one but calls everyone equally to His heavenly supper without respect of persons: rich and poor, renowned and low-born—in a word, every person, male and female—He opens the doors to all. But for the most part, the paupers, the destitute, the poor, and the low-born hear this saving call and go to His splendid supper, but the rich and renowned for the most part decline, for they do not want to leave their pride, magnificence, and luxury. They want to enjoy themselves and to rule here in this world and therefore disdain that great supper; they see the good things of this world but do not see the eternal good things. It is written of the Israelites, "They thought scorn of that longed-for land; they gave no credence unto His word" (Ps 105:24). Thus, the rich and renowned, having joined themselves to the good things of this world, disparage that great supper and do not believe the Lord Who calls them to it. This is why the Apostle writes, "For you see your calling, brethren, that not many wise according to the flesh, not many mighty, not many noble, are called. But God has chosen the foolish things of the world to put to shame the wise, and God has chosen the weak things of the world to put to shame the things which are mighty; and the base things of the world and the things which are despised God has chosen, and the things which are not, to bring to nothing the things that are, that no flesh should glory in His presence" (1 Cor 1:26–29). The paupers and the poor, those of humble birth and the despised of this world, listen more eagerly to the voice of the Lord calling them and go to that supper, for they have few of the good things of this world. Love of honor, glory, riches, pleasures, and luxuries of this world blind the eyes of the soul and hinder them from seeing the eternal good things. And what a person does not see he does not want.

Oh, if only a person saw the future good things, then he would rush to them just as "the hart panteth after the waterbrooks" (Ps 41:2). But in all lovers of this world, a darkness, like a kind of veil, lies over the eyes of the soul, and for this reason they do not see those good things. But for whoever with a pure heart "turns to the Lord, the veil is taken away" (2 Cor 3:16), and he sees those good things with the eye of faith and eagerly seeks them. Christian, rich or poor, renowned or wretched! Let us turn away from the world to the Lord, and our eyes will be opened, and we shall speedily go to that supper and shall believe the Word of God, by which He calls us. We are called by God to great, heavenly, eternal and ineffable good things, so why do we join our heart to that which is nothing in itself and which we will soon leave? Not in vain does the Apostle exhort us, "Do not love the world or the things in the world" (1 John 2:15), and so on. And again, "If then you were raised with Christ, seek those things which are above, where Christ is, sitting at the right hand of God. Set your mind on things above, not on things on the earth" (Col 3:1–2), since love of this world hobbles our legs and prevents us from going to that splendid supper. Christian! Leave the good things of this world, and we shall receive all blessings and incomparably better ones there, which "[e]ye has not seen, nor ear heard, Nor have entered into the heart of man" (1 Cor 2:9). Be confident of those good things and, I assure you, having held the world in contempt, you will without fail seek them with all zeal.

It happens in this world that when all those invited to the supper gather, then the host who invited them will lead them into the decorated hall prepared for the supper, and all will be seated at their places. This is how it will be for those who have been invited to the heavenly supper and have come to it. Then the Heavenly King will say to those who have heard His call and have come to His supper, "Come, you blessed of My Father, inherit the kingdom prepared for you from the foundation of the world" (Matt 25:34). And they will go with exultation and rejoicing into His splendid, heavenly, eternal, and royal palace, not made with hands, "and sit down with Abraham, Isaac, and Jacob in the kingdom of heaven" (Matt 8:11). Then the word of the prophet will be fulfilled, "And those gathered by the Lord shall return and come to Zion with gladness, and with everlasting gladness over their head. For praise and exceeding joy will be on their head, and gladness shall possess them. Pain sorrow, and sighing fled away" (Isa 35:10). Christians! Let us hear now the Lord's voice and turn to the Lord with our whole heart and repent, so that we may then hear His most sweet voice, "Come, you blessed of My Father," and so on.

Those sitting and feasting at a distinguished supper of this world are dressed in bright and beautiful clothing. So it will be also at that splendid and magnificent heavenly supper. Those attending will be dressed in the robe of salvation and the clothing of gladness, and clothed "in garments of gold" (Ps 44:10, 14), clothed in clean and bright linen. "And to her, that is, the Church, it was granted to be arrayed in fine linen, clean and bright, for the fine linen is the righteous acts of the saints, says St. John in his Revelation" (Rev 19:8). Christ, our Saviour, also showed this by the glorification of His holy Body on Mount Tabor, where "His face shone like the sun, and His clothes became as white as the light" (Matt 17:2). There the bodies of God's saints will conform to the glorified Body of Christ, of which the holy Apostle assures us, "For our citizenship is in heaven, from which we also eagerly wait for the Savior, the Lord Jesus Christ, who will transform our lowly body that it may be conformed to His glorious body, according to the working by which He is able even to subdue all things to Himself" (Phil 3:20–21). And Christ Himself says, "Then the righteous will shine forth as the sun in the kingdom of their Father" (Matt 13:43). Christian! Let us pray to the Lightgiver Christ, and may He grant us the bright robe of justification, and let us attend this supper with His elect. "I see Thy bridal chamber adorned, O my Savior, and I have no wedding garment that I may enter there. Make the robe of my soul to shine, O Giver of Light, and save me" (Hymn from the Bridegroom Matins).

At a splendid supper of this world, every good thing is provided for the comfort and enjoyment of those sitting and feasting. It will be similar at the heavenly supper. Every good thing will be provided there, but it will be incomparably better than the earthly supper. At that supper, God's holy people will be sated with all the heavenly blessings that the good and man-loving Lord has prepared for them. "They shall neither hunger anymore nor thirst anymore; the sun shall not strike them, nor any heat; for the Lamb who is in the midst of the throne will shepherd them and lead them to living fountains of waters. And God will wipe away every tear from their eyes" (Rev 7:16–17). "My servants shall eat, … shall drink, … shall be glad, … shall rejoice exceedingly in gladness" (Isa 65:13–14). "They shall be drunk from the plenteousness of Thy house, and Thou shalt give them drink of Thy pleasure, as out of a river. For with Thee is the fountain of life; in Thy light shall we see light" (Ps 35:9–10). "For thus says the Lord: 'Behold, I will turn to them like a river of peace and like a brook, to flood them with the glory of the Gentiles. Their children shall be taken up on shoulders and comforted on knees. Like someone a mother comforts, so also will I comfort you, and you shall be comforted in Jerusalem.' You shall see, and your heart will rejoice" (Isa 66:12–14). "For now we see in a mirror dimly, but then face to face" (1 Cor 13:12). "Eye has not seen, nor ear heard, Nor have entered into the heart of man The things which God has prepared for those who love Him" (1 Cor 2:9), and so on. For there will be such blessedness there: (1) We shall see God face to face, from which will flow ineffable consolation, gladness, joy, and heartfelt jubilation. We shall see the Face of God and shall shout with joy. (2) We shall see our Lord and Redeemer Jesus Christ in His divine glory and see Him Who for us suffered so terribly and died a reviled death and so delivered us from death. (3) We shall then enjoy all the gifts of the Holy Spirit, as the Life-creating Source. (4) We shall have a loving friendship with the holy angels and all the saints who have been pleasing to God from the creation of the world. (5) We shall triumph over all our enemies. "O Death, where is your sting? O Hades, where is your victory" (1 Col 15:55)? "But thanks be to God, who gives us the victory through our Lord Jesus Christ" (1 Cor 15:57). Christian! Our Merciful God is still calling everyone. Stop chasing after the temporary and earthly; rather hurry to this heavenly supper, where God is seen face to face, and from Him, as the life-creating and ever-flowing Source, springs every consolation, delight, and joyful jubilation. Hurry, hurry, while the doors are still open, lest, arriving late, you find yourself standing outside and knocking on the door to no avail, saying, "Lord, Lord, open for us" (Luke 13:25).

It happens at suppers of this world that the host says to the arriving guests, "There are the good things laid out on my table. Eat, drink, and be merry!" Likewise, our Lord, Who loves Mankind, will say to those who have heard His call and come to His heavenly supper: "Here are the good things that I have prepared for you, that I have promised you, and that in faith and hope you awaited from Me, that 'Eye has not seen, nor ear heard, Nor have entered into the heart of man The things which God has prepared for those who love Him'" (1 Cor 2:9).

> Here are My good things that I promised you. I promised you the resurrection of your dead bodies—here you see it. You have risen from the dead. I promised you a spiritual body, incorruptible and immortal—you have it now. I promised you a glorified body, pure, bright, and shining—now you are shining like the sun and like the stars of heaven (see 1 Cor 15:42–46). I promised you eternal life—now you have eternal life. Live forever! I promised you the Kingdom of Heaven—now I am giving it to you. Inherit it and reign forever! I promised you to show you My Face–behold My Face. Look at it and be glad. I promised you the garland of life, the unfading garland—here is that garland! I promised you honor and glory—here is your glory, as my children. I promised to comfort you—now I am consoling you as a mother consoles her children. I promised you to give continual peace in your hearts—I say, "My peace I give to you" (John 14:27). I promised to take away from you sorrow, sickness, and sighing—and sorrow, sickness, and sighing have been eliminated from your hearts. I promised you food and drink, sweetness and joy for eternity—here is this consolation and enjoyment: "O friends, eat and drink, and O brothers, drink abundantly."
>
> (Song 5:1)

"Ye that have trod the narrow way of sorrow; all ye that in life have taken up the Cross as a yoke, and have followed me in faith, come, enjoy the honours and heavenly crowns which I have prepared for you,"[1] the Lord says. Then will be fulfilled what has been written, "Like as we have heard, so have we seen in the city of the Lord of Hosts, in the city of Our God; God hath established her for ever. We have received Thy mercy, O God, in the midst of Thy temple" (Ps 47:9–10). Oh, Christian who has gotten drunk on the love of the world! Sober up, while there is still time, and look for the heavenly blessings that God promised to those who love him, lest you seek them later, but not receive them.

At a splendid supper of this world, music and singing are performed for the entertainment of the feasting guests. There will be singing also at that heavenly supper, but it will be incomparably better. The most sweet singing of the holy angels, praising and hymning the Lord, their Creator: "Holy, Holy, Holy, is the Lord of Hosts; the whole earth is full of His glory" (Isa 6:3) will be heard there. And the most holy of God's people who live in God's house will exalt the Lord unto the ages of ages and together with the heavenly Hosts will hymn the Holy Trinity. O the beautiful music! O the most sweet hymns! O the wondrous harmony of the angels and angel-like people, hymning the Lord, their Creator! "Blessed is the Lord God of Israel, For He has visited and redeemed His people, And has raised up a horn of salvation for us In the house of His servant David" (Luke 1:68–69). Bless the Lord, O my soul (Ps 102:1–2). "Blessed are You, O Lord God of our Fathers, For You are praiseworthy And exalted beyond measure unto the ages. Blessed is Your name and the temple of Your glory, and You are praised exceedingly And exalted beyond measure unto the ages" (Dan 3:52). Let us hasten, beloved Christian, let us hasten to that magnificent and marvelous supper, where we shall hear the most sweet heavenly music, and shall exalt the Lord, our Creator and Redeemer, not only in faith, as we do now, but face to face. "O Lord God of Hosts, hear my prayer; hearken, O God of Jacob. Behold, O God, our Defender, and look upon the face of Thy Christ. For one day in Thy courts is better than a thousand; I have preferred to be a doorkeeper in the house of my God, than to dwell in the tents of sinners" (Ps 83:9–11).

In this world, the guests who come to a supper, having eaten to satisfaction, no longer wish to eat, and so stop. It will be different at that heavenly supper. They will eat and drink but without becoming satiated; they will feast but always with hunger. They will always have a certain incessant, but very pleasant, hunger. They will be satiated with heavenly food but will always want more. They will see God face to face and will be gratified by this most sweet sight, but never filled, but will always desire this joyful and pleasant gratification. And the more they are gratified by this sight of God, the more and more they will desire it. To see God's face is a joy greater than any joy, a consolation greater than any consolation, and a sweetness greater than any sweetness. This is the food and drink of the holy angels and chosen of God. Hence, just as from an ever-flowing and life-giving spring a river is formed, a continuous desire to see the face of God forms continuous joy, gladness, consolation, enjoyment, jubilation, and a certain skipping of the heart. And as a river flows uninterruptedly and continually, so the blessedness of the heavenly supper will flow uninterruptedly and continually. This, Christian, is the great heavenly supper, to which we are called by God! This is the Divine Paradise, filled with joy and sweetness, which had in its middle the tree of life, from which those who eat will never die but will live forever! This is eternal life and blessed eternity. Christians! Let us seek out this consolation by repentance and faith. Let us seek while it can be sought and found. It can be sought and found only here.

At a banquet in this world, lighted lamps and candles are set out. At that heavenly supper, such illumination will not be needed, nor the light from the sun and the moon, for there will be no night there. The glory of the Lord will illuminate everything. "The city had no need of the sun or of the moon to shine in it, for the glory of God illuminated it. The Lamb is its light" (Rev 21:23). "There shall be no night there: They need no lamp nor light of the sun, for the Lord God gives them light" (Rev 22:5). "The sun shall no longer be your light by day, nor shall the rising of the moon shine on you at night, but the Lord shall be your everlasting light, and God, your glory. For your sun shall no longer set, nor shall your moon be eclipsed, for the Lord shall be your everlasting light" (Isa 60:19–20). "Lord, in Thy light shall we see light! Continue Thy mercy unto them that know Thee" (Ps 35:10–11). "Let Thy mercy, O Lord, be upon us, according as we have put our trust in Thee" (Ps 32:22).

In this world, a supper lasts a short while, for the guests, satisfied with all they have received from the host, disperse to their own homes. So both the supper and its pleasure come to an end. Every temporary pleasure and enjoyment, like smoke, vanishes quickly. It will not be like that at that great supper. Having once started, it will continue forever. The participants will endlessly see God's face, and will be gratified by the sweetest contemplation of Him, without satiation unto the ages. They will eat this heavenly food and drink this sweet drink without end and without becoming satiated. As there will be no end to Christ's kingdom, so also God's holy people will reign with Him, as members with the head, unto the ages of ages. "Blessed are they that dwell in Thy house, for ever and ever will they praise Thee, … my King and my God (Ps 83:4–5). Remember us, O Lord, according to the favor that Thou bearest unto Thy people; O visit us with Thy salvation, That we may see the goodness of Thy chosen, and be glad in the gladness of Thy nation, and glory with

Thine inheritance" (Ps 105:4–5). "Turn again then into thy rest, O my soul, for the Lord hath prospered thee. For He hath delivered my soul from death, mine eyes from tears, and my feet from stumbling. I will be well-pleasing before the Lord in the land of the living" (Ps 114:6–8). "Lord Jesus! Say unto my soul, I am thy salvation" (Ps 34:3). "Assuredly, I say to you, today you will be with Me in Paradise" (Luke 23:43). May it be, may it be! Amen.

## 29. A Curtain or Veil

We do not see whatever is covered by a curtain or veil. Thus, we do not see the sun when it is covered by clouds. We do not see a person who is covered by a kerchief or clothing. We do not see things located behind a curtain, and so on. Thus, a kind of curtain hangs over the eyes of every unrepentant sinner, every fornicator and adulterer, every plunderer, thief, and bribe-taker, every liar and cheat—in a word, every shameless person, and it is as though a kind of veil hangs over the eyes of the soul and hinders it from seeing what good things it is being deprived of, and how it is headed for bitter perdition. It is headed into a ditch, and does not see it, and will fall into it if it does not take heed. Satan, the enemy of mankind, arranges this curtain and veil for those people who live carelessly, do not heed the Word of God as a lamp to our feet, and abandon prayer, without which any person is blind; he arranges it so that they do not see their perdition. This curtain or veil is taken away when a person turns to God with a true heart. Then he will see his calamitous situation and his ruination. Then he will comprehend where he was and how he was going astray. Then he will begin to sigh, weep, and sob. Then, as if wakening from sleep, he will begin to walk as he previously did. "Therefore He says: 'Awake, you who sleep, Arise from the dead, And Christ will give you light'" (Eph 5:14). "Convert us, O God; show the light of Thy countenance, and we shall be saved" (Ps 79:4).

## 30. A Deaf Man

The body and the soul have their hearing. Not every body has clear hearing. Nor does every soul. God speaks to the soul: do not kill, do not steal, do not commit adultery, turn away from evil and do good, and so on, and the soul that has clear hearing apprehends and listens to what God says and does what God commands. It is impossible for the soul, truly impossible, not to listen to God and not do what he commands if he has ears that hear. A person listens to an earthly king and lower authority and does what he commands. Will the soul not listen to God as He speaks when it has clear hearing? Truly! He will hear with diligence and delight and say to Him, "My heart is ready, O God, my heart is ready" (Ps 107:2). Clear hearing of the soul was possessed by the holy Patriarch Abraham, to whom God said, "'Get out of your country, from your kindred and from your father's house, To a land I will show you' ... Then Abram departed as the Lord said to him" (Gen 12:1, 4). All those to whom Christ said, "'Follow Me' ... and ... they ... followed Him" (Matt 4:19–22) had clear hearing. Everyone who with diligence tries to fulfill God's commandments has clear hearing of the soul. Not in vain does Christ the Lord say in the Gospel, "He who has ears to hear, let him hear!" (Luke 8:8, 15).

Everyone has ears, but not everyone has ears to hear. By ears to hear means to have ears of the soul that clearly hear. Bodily ears bring us no benefit when the ears of the soul do not function. The body has its own deafness, when its ears do not hear well. Likewise, the soul has its deafness, when hearing is impeded. The bodily deaf man does not hear what a person tells him, orders him, or promises him, since he cannot hear. Likewise, the deaf in soul, that is, one who has the hearing of his soul impeded, does not hear what God tells Him, orders him, or promises him. How can one hear without clear hearing? Every fornicator and adulterer, plunderer, robber, bribe-taker, bribe-giver, lover of money, voluptuary—in a word, every iniquitous person—has impeded ears of the soul. How many such people hear the Word of God but do not listen to God and do not reform. They listen and do not hear. They hear with their bodily ears but do not hear with their souls' ears. And how can they hear with them when they do not function? How many people hear Christ's word, "Come to Me, all you who labor and are heavy laden, and I will give you rest" (Matt 11:28), but do not want to come to Christ and have rest. They hold on to the world, as to a beloved treasure of theirs, although it both worries them and ruins them. This is deafness of the soul. "Behold, I stand at the door and knock. If anyone hears My voice and opens the door, I will come in to him and dine with him, and he with Me," says Christ the Lord (Rev 3:20). This word is true and sure! The Merciful Jesus poured out His blood for all, wants to save all, and visits each and every one. He stands at the house of each one's heart and knocks at the door and wants to enter and make a most sweet supper. But the deaf soul does not hear this sweet voice. If it heard His voice, what soul would not open the doors of its house and receive such a great, such a dear, such a longed-for Guest with cheerfulness and joy? This Guest does not need our food and drink. He will lay His own table for us and will delight us with His own heavenly food and His own sweet drink. But the trouble is that the poor soul does not hear the voice of Jesus, and for that reason does not open the doors to Him, and is deprived of His visit and His most sweet feast. Bodily deafness is disastrous, as you yourself know, O man. But even more disastrous is deafness of the soul, for it allows no word of God, and so all understandings have no good end. O Merciful Jesus! Open the ears of our souls. May we hear Your holy word! Look down from your holy heaven and say to us, "Ephphatha," that is, "Be opened" (Mark 7:34).

With every deaf person, hearing is impeded to every word, bad or good. But with the person deaf in the soul, it is not so. For everything bad: for slanders, for unsuitable fables, for foul and corrupting songs, for the whisperings of the devil, for stories about carnal and worldly caprices—he has clear hearing. On the other hand, for the hearing of God's Word, His marvelous works, and His praises, he has impeded hearing. Someone will say to him, "You know, such and such a person somehow or other has acquired quite a bit of property for himself, such and such a governor or such and such a secretary collected so many thousands in money and bought so many peasants," he immediately begins to think within himself how could he also manage that. When they say that such and such cloth, such and such a coach, such and such wines, and so on, which serve human whims, are for sale, he immediately thinks of how to see them and have them in his house. And when God's Word is preached and says to him, "Repent, correct yourself, begin a new Christian life, fear God and His righteous Judgment, shun sin, love virtue and try to practice it," and so on, then he heeds that just as a deaf man does a song. Truly great is the deafness of the soul! What is more terrible than eternal perdition? And what is more desirable than eternal life? God in His Scriptures speaks, and through preachers, His servants, thunders, "Poor soul! You will perish, you will perish forever, if you do not repent."

"Upon sinners He shall rain down snares; fire and brimstone, and the stormy wind, shall be the portion of their cup. For the Lord is righteous and loveth righteousness; His countenance hath beheld just things" (Ps 10:6–7). "But the cowardly, unbelieving, abominable, murderers, sexually immoral, sorcerers, idolaters, and all liars shall have their part in the lake which burns with fire and brimstone, which is the second death" (Rev 21:8). But the poor soul does not hear God's powerful voice and remains without repentance, as before. God calls, "Turn to me soul, and you will be saved, and you will live eternally." But the soul does not hear God's call; it goes and heads toward perdition as before. It does not hear since it does not have unimpeded hearing. The voice is terrible: "You will perish forever, if you do not repent." The kind and longed-for voice: "You will be saved forever if you repent." Oh, if the soul heard that voice, it would be horror-struck, and would begin to tremble, and would choose true repentance, in order to avoid perdition and receive eternal salvation! Therefore, every Christian should endeavor to open the inner hearing of his soul and pray for this. This forms the beginning both of conversion and true repentance, and of salvation. O poor Christian, deaf Christian! Wake up, please, wake up, and force yourself, fall down before Christ, sigh and fervently pray to Him that He will open the hearing of your soul by His Divine power, and then with longing and joy you will hear the Lord's voice. O Jesus, Strength and Hope of our salvation, Who has opened the eyes of the blind and the ears of the deaf! Open the hearing of our souls, so that we may hear Your Divine word. Say to our sinful soul: "'Ephphatha,' that is, 'Be opened,'" and its ears will be opened. The signs of deafness of the soul are these: (1) when Christians hear the Word of God and do not correct themselves and (2) love for this world, that is, for honor, glory, wealth, luxury, and pleasures. Satan arranges this deafness by his whispering, so that people would not be able to hear the Word of God and so would perish.

When in a house there are various sounds, noise, shouting and bustle, then no matter what is said to a person, he does not hear, since this noise impedes his hearing. This also happens in the soul. When all kinds of noise and tumult of worldly lusts cause disturbance it cannot then hear the Word of God, since worldly lusts, which "war against the soul" (1 Pet 2:11), and surround it, do not permit God's words to reach it, and repel and drive it away. What will the voice of the Word of God be able to do in such noise? As music to the deaf man, so is the Word of God to the soul enveloped in noise. Often such a one hears the preaching of God's Word and praises it but receives no benefit from it. He goes away from preaching the same as when he came to it, if not worse, for the Word of God that is heard yields greater harm to one who

hears it but is not corrected by it. So the scribes and Pharisees often heard
the Word of God from Christ and did not correct themselves and therefore
became worse. Satan, the enemy of human souls, tries with all his strength to
tangle a person's soul in worldly lust, as a fish in a net, so that the Word of God
would not gain access to it and the soul would perish. Christian! I advise you
and beseech you for the sake of your salvation, take a rest from this pernicious
noise, if only for a short time. Then you will recognize the truth and see that
God's Word drives out the tumult of worldly lusts from the soul. Then you
will feel a certain movement to eternity, as a still small voice. Then, little by
little the thought will come to you, who are you and what end you are coming to, what awaits you after death, and so on. And it is this that is the sign of
God's Word coming into the soul, for God's Word, like a seed, bears fruit like
unto itself.

Whoever has clear bodily hearing and does not have any impediments
hears everything that is said. He hears something terrifying and is frightened.
He hears something pleasant and is comforted. He hears something funny
and laughs. He hears something that he needs, and wishes it and looks for
it. The Christian whose soul has clear hearing does the same thing. He hears
every word of God and admits it to the interior of his soul and is roused by
its power as a horse is by spurs. God's word has a Divine power that rouses
the human soul, as strong vodka or spirits affect the sense of smell. And since
God's word is spiritual, it rouses it to spiritual activity. Such a Christian hears
the word about God's righteous Judgment and fears it. He hears the word
about eternal torment, and is terrified, and tries to escape it. He hears about
eternal life and its blessedness and is delighted in his heart and takes care that
he would not be deprived of it. He hears what a great and pernicious evil sin
is, and with all his power shuns it. He hears how fine and advantageous virtue
is and tries to acquire it. He hears a sermon about repentance and immediately feels within himself a desire for and an impulse to it and contemplates
how to actually carry this out. He hears a sermon denouncing sin, and seeing
it in his conscience, he feels sorrow for this sin, Godly sorrow, and is pierced
as if by an arrow, is indignant and angry with himself, and often even sheds
tears from a contrite heart. He hears how God's wondrous goodness to the
human race was revealed in the incarnation of the Son of God and marvels at
this salvific and man-loving Providence of God. He hears that even he is one

of those for whose sake the Son of God, the great God appeared in the flesh and "has come to save that which was lost" (Matt 18:11) and gives thanks from his whole heart and bows down with humility to the man-loving God for this. He hears the consoling word of the Gospel and feels within a kind of poignant spiritual consolation. For the Gospel, as God's joyful tidings sent from the heavens to mankind, does not fail to console the soul that hears it. This is the action of God's Word, which penetrates into the very depths of the soul!

So the Word of God, which has taken up its abode in a Christian soul, renews the Christian and makes him divinely wise, God-fearing, pious, holy— in a word, "a new creation ... in Christ" (2 Cor 5:17). As balsam that is brought into a house fills the house with fragrance, likewise, when it enters a human soul, God's Word, like a spiritual and salubrious balsam, releases a fragrance in it. The fragrance of this balsam is the fear of God, love of God and neighbor, repentance, sorrow in God, a contrite soul, sighing, tender emotion, tears, consolation, and spiritual joy. The Holy Spirit creates this heavenly fragrance in the soul through His holy Word.

Christian! You too will sense this beneficent fragrance of heavenly balsam in your soul when, having separated your soul from the noise and tumult of worldly whims, you open the ears of your soul to God's Word. How can one feel the power and activity of God's Word who thinks not of salvation but of the whims of this world? Cast out this harmful and pernicious noise out of your soul, and your soul will feel that heavenly balsam acting within it. Cease thinking of how to win honor, glory, riches in this world, how to set a rich table, how to receive guests and to go visiting, how to build and decorate a palatial home, how to dress in the best clothing, how to be seen as more wise and illustrious than others, how to go for rides with splendid horses and rich carriages, how to acquire more land and peasants, how to build the most splendid gardens, how to build beautiful porticoes and dig attractive ponds in them, and so on. But think instead how to receive eternal salvation. Let this be for you the very first consideration in all your plans, undertakings, and activities. Then, I assure you, your soul will hear the Word of God and will bear fruit corresponding to it. Otherwise, even if you learn the entire Holy Bible and other Christian books by heart, you will not receive any benefit for your soul from them if you do not give up the whims that so deafen your soul and refuse admittance to the God's Word. Give them up, so that the Word of God may enter your soul.

# 31. A Seed

In this world, we see that whatever kind of seed that is sown will bear the same kind of fruit, for example, wheat from wheat, rye from rye, oats from oats, and so on. "That which is born of the flesh is flesh" (John 3:6). Likewise, God's Word, like a seed sown in the earth of human hearts, bears fruit like itself. God's Word is a spiritual seed, good, heavenly, holy, and life-giving. Sown in the human heart, it bears a person like it; that is, it makes him spiritual, good, heavenly, holy, and alive. Consider, O man, how you hear the Word of God: from listening, do you feel a power and activity like the Word of God? Do you feel in your soul spiritual, good, heavenly thoughts and desires? If you do not feel this, it is a sign that the seed of the Word of God is perishing in you. "He who has ears to hear, let him hear!" says the Lord (Luke 8:8, 15).

Seed is sown in the same way but does not fall on the same ground. Likewise, the Word of God is preached equally to all, but its power and fruit are not present in all. Some seed falls on *the wayside* and is carried away by *the birds of the air*. Likewise, the Word of God is preached to human hearts, through which, as along the wayside, various thoughts pass, perish, and are unfruitful because *evil spirits*, like birds, carry it away, *lest people should believe and be saved.* Other seed falls on *rocky* ground and therefore does not have enough soil for it to put down and establish its roots. It will quickly sprout up, but not having roots, it withers from the sun's heat. Likewise, the Word of God, having fallen into human hearts, but not having gone deep and not having put down roots, although it is received with joy, however from the onslaught of temptations, sorrow, and persecution, is deprived of nourishment and so is unfruitful. Other seeds fall among thorns and are choked by the thorns that spring up, and therefore these too are unfruitful. Like this, many people hear the Word of God but, having hearts choked by "the cares of this world and the deceitfulness of riches" as by thorns, bear no fruit. And this is why the Word of God bears no fruit in them. Another seed falls on good ground, and it alone bears fruit. Likewise, the Word of God, when good hearts hear it, bears its fruit and produces "some a hundredfold, some sixty, some thirty" (see Matt 13:3–23; Mark 4:3–20; Luke 8:5–15).

From this, you see, Christian: (1) You must listen with all assiduousness and attention to the Word of God that is preached, that is, the Gospel or epistle being read, or something from the Old Testament, or the sermon of a preacher. May the evil spirits not snatch away the Word of God that is preached to you, as the birds snatch away the seed sewn on the wayside, and may you not be unfruitful. (2) You must bury and enroot in the depths of your heart the Word of God that you hear or read, and study it day and night, as the Psalmist says of himself and presents himself as a model for us: "Thy words have I hid within my heart, that I should not sin against Thee" (Ps 118:11). And again, "Thy servant occupied himself in Thy statutes. For Thy testimonies are my consolation, and Thy statues are my counsel" (Ps 118:23–24). And again, "And my study was in Thy commandments, which I greatly loved" (Ps 118:47). And again, "And I occupied myself in Thy statutes" (Ps 118:48). And again, "O how I have loved Thy law, O Lord; It is my study all day" (Ps 118:97). And again, "Grief and want have found me, yet are Thy commandments my comfort" (Ps 118:143). Therefore, it is written of the righteous man, "The law of his God is in his heart, and his foot-steps shall not slide" (Ps 36:31) and that person is called blessed whose "delight is in the law of the Lord, and in His law will he exercise himself day and night." Therefore, he is compared to a tree planted by the streams of the waters "that will bring forth his fruit in due season; his leaf also shall not fall, and all whatsoever he doeth, it shall prosper" (Ps 1:1–3). (3) Since the fancies of this world choke the word of God sown in the soul like the seeds that "fell among thorns, which grew up and choked the plants" (Matt 13:7 [The Parable of the Sower]), it is necessary to root out these harmful thorns from the heart, and "Do not love the world or the things in the world" (1 John 2:15). Otherwise the seed of God's word will not bear fruit. (4) Whoever wishes to serve God and to bear the fruit of His word for Him encounters various temptations, as it is written, "My son, if you draw near to serve the Lord, Prepare your soul for temptation" (Sir 2:1). Therefore, it is necessary to vanquish all temptations by patience. That is why the holy Evangelist says that "having heard the word with a noble and good heart, [they] keep it and bear fruit with patience" (Luke 8:15). That is why those who desire to bear the fruit of God's Word need patience. (5) Human effort without the help of God is feeble. An earthen field—the human heart—cannot combine with heavenly seed and bear fruit. Here the power and aid of the Heavenly Husbandman are needed, as He Himself says, "Without Me you can do nothing" (John 15:5). Therefore, one who desires and is trying to bear the fruit of the Word of God must fervently pray that the Lord Himself would produce and mature the fruit of His Word in our hearts. "Ask, and it will be given to you; seek, and you will find; knock, and it will be opened to you. For everyone who asks receives, and he who seeks finds, and to him who knocks it will be opened" (Matt 7:7–8). It is for this reason that the Psalmist prays with such great zeal throughout the entire Psalm 118 that God Himself would lead him on the way of His Commandments and mature the fruit of His Word. Lord Jesus Christ, Word of Your Beginingless Father, help us!

Although the soil on which the seed is sown is good, it cannot produce fruit if it is not warmed by the sunshine and watered by the rain. So, although the seed of the Word of God falls on a good heart, it will not bear any fruit if the warmth of God's grace does not heat it and the dew from above does not water it. Therefore, as the seeds that have been sown need sunshine and rain to bear fruit, so the Word of God that is heard needs God's grace to warm and water it, lest it be fruitless. This is why the Holy David says, "I ran the way of Thy commandments, when Thou didst enlarge my heart" (Ps 118:32). Therefore, we must always sigh to the Lord that by His grace He would warm and water our hearts. We require God's grace every hour and every minute. Without it, like babies still not being able to walk, we shall fall down and lie there. "Thy mercy shall follow me all the days of my life" (Ps 22:6). O Lord, by Thy almighty hand put us on the path of Thy commandments and strengthen and lead us!

# 32. Sowing and Harvesting

Farmers have sowing and harvesting. So do Christians. Farmers have seeds; likewise, Christians have their own seeds. Farmers' seeds come into being from seeds; likewise, for Christians, spiritual seeds come into being from the seed of the Word of God. Farmers have rye, wheat, barley seeds, and so on. Christians' seeds are repentance, godly sorrow, sighing, tears, prayer, thanksgiving, singing, works of mercy, patience, and so on. These spiritual seeds come into being from the seed of the Word of God that fall into human hearts. Farmers have an appropriate time for sowing and harvesting and so do Christians. Farmers know the time when they should sow. Likewise, Christians have an appropriate time when they should sow their seeds; this is the time of the present life. "Behold, now is the accepted time; behold, now is the day of salvation" (2 Cor 6:2). Sensible and wise farmers do not let pass the time in which they should sow but work and sow at that time. So sensible and wise Christians do not let pass the time of the present life but work and sow their seeds, repent, perform works of repentance, do acts of mercy, and so on. Only the present time is the time of sowing; in the age to come this will not be done. Now is the acceptable time to repent, weep for our sins, pray, and do good to all, but in the age to come, all this ceases. Farmers labor and sow, hoping for the fruit produced from the seed. Likewise, Christians labor and sow with the hope for spiritual fruit, a merciful recompense from God. Farmers reap the ripe fruits of their labors during the harvest. Likewise, Christians will reap the fruits of their labors and seeds at the end of the age and the resurrection of the dead. Farmers, gathering the fruits of their labors, rejoice. Likewise, Christians, seeing and gathering the fruits of their labors and seeds, will rejoice. "They that sow in tears, shall reap in joy. They went on their way and wept, sowing their seed, but they shall return in joy, bearing their sheaves" (Ps 125:5–6). Lazy and careless farmers who do not sow at the proper time also do not gather fruits during harvest. Likewise, foolish, careless, negligent Christians, who now do not sow spiritual seeds will not reap any fruits at the end of the age and the resurrection of the dead but will appear before the Lord without having borne fruit. How will they gather then, when they have not scattered now? How will they reap then, when they have not sown now? Christians! Let us labor and sow our seeds now. And then we shall reap the fruits of our labors with joy.

Farmers who sow more seeds will reap a greater harvest than those who plant less. Likewise Christians who sow more spiritual seeds in the present life will, on the last day, that of Christ's Judgment, at which all the works of everyone will be revealed, will reap more fruits. But those who sow scantily will reap less, as the Apostle says, "He who sows sparingly will also reap sparingly" (2 Cor 9:6). Our Lord is just: He "will render to each one according to his deeds" (Rom 2:6). Therefore, the Apostle exhorts us, "Let us not grow weary while doing good, for in due season we shall reap if we do not lose heart. Therefore, as we have opportunity, let us do good to all, especially to those who are of the household of faith" (Gal 6:9–10). Christians! Let us write this word of the Apostle, "as we have opportunity," in our hearts. This is the time of our present life. Only now may we do good works and give alms—in the world to come all this will come to an end. Let us try to sow now, and then we shall reap and try now to labor for the sake of the good, and then we shall rest here, let us distribute our possessions, and there we shall gather much more. Let us give our gold and silver into the hands of the poor, and then we shall receive it back from Christ the Lord with interest. Do not be afraid, Christian! "For He who promised is faithful" (Heb 10:23). You give your silver into the hand of beggars, but Christ promised to repay you for them, and He will repay with great gain. Everything will perish that is spent on fancies and luxury, rich and beautiful houses, abundant cuisines, for rich clothing, splendid carriages, horses, and so on. All of these expenditures are vain and will perish. You will know this on the day of your death, when you leave everything here. But whatever is put into the hands of the poor will not perish but will bear a hundred-fold fruit, as the seed that falls in good ground does not perish but bears fruit for him who has sown it. Let us entrust our property into the hands of the poor in Christ's name and let us receive back from Christ a hundred-fold.

When a farmer sows his seeds, a foolish person who, not knowing the fruit that comes from the seed, laughs at this, thinking that the farmer is spoiling his seed to no purpose, throwing it on the ground. But the farmer, hoping that the seed that he has thrown into the earth will bring him more fruit than he is sowing, does not cease sowing. This is how foolish and senseless people act. They, seeing that the Christian is distributing his possessions and giving to paupers, laugh about this, thinking that he is undoing of his property. These people think on that which is visible, and think only possessions that are expended on do not perish—on vanity and the fancies of this world. This is why they themselves expend their possessions not on alms but on carnal lusts and laugh at those who give to paupers. Laugh, O man, laugh. But later you will weep and sob bitterly—you, who do not begrudge spending thousands or hundreds on the trousseau of your daughter, on the building and decoration of palatial houses, on expensive wines, and on abundant tables, on silk and linen, on carriages and horses, on hunts with dogs and other fancies, but for the sake of Christ, Who suffered and died for you, Who so loved you, His enemy, that He did not even spare Himself for your sake. For the sake of Christ, I say, such a Great and High Benefactor, you begrudge giving even a penny or a half a penny, even from His bounty that He has given you. For all the good things that we have are His. "The earth is the Lord's, and the fullness thereof" (Ps 23:1). Think like this, and you will constantly grieve and weep. And if you do not grieve and weep now, then at the second coming of Christ and the day of retribution, you will grieve and weep, but it will be too late and in vain. As lazy bumpkins and idlers, upon seeing farmers gathering the fruits of the seeds that they have scattered and rejoicing in them, complain and lament, seeing nothing in their own hands, since they did not labor, did not sow, and therefore are not gathering fruits, and thus remain without hope for subsistence, so at the end of the age and the resurrection from the dead—this will be the Christian harvest (see Matt 13:30)—Christians who love luxury and are idlers will be ashamed and disgraced and will weep and sob when they see the good Christians reaping the fruits of their seeds, and will see themselves empty-handed, in extreme poverty. Then they will indeed see that wealth wasted on vanity and luxury perishes and plunges wastrel into perdition. But wealth in the hands of the poor and paupers, invested there in Christ's Name, is preserved and is returned much improved and with great gain. "Blessed are the merciful, For they shall obtain mercy" (Matt 5:7). The wretched unmerciful ones will be deprived of mercy, "For judgment is without mercy to the one who has shown no mercy" (Jas 2:13). Then the merciful, who have performed works of mercy, will hear from the Righteous Judge,

> "Come, you blessed of My Father, inherit the kingdom prepared for you from the foundation of the world: for I was hungry and you gave Me food; I was thirsty and you gave Me drink; I was a stranger and you took Me in; I was naked and you clothed Me; I was sick and you visited Me; I was in prison and you came to Me." But the unmerciful, who loved luxury, and the idlers, who squandered our kind Lord's property not on the destitute, but on their own whims, as unprofitable servants and unfaithful stewards, will hear, "Depart from Me, you cursed, into the everlasting fire prepared for the devil and his angels: for I was hungry and you gave Me no food; I was thirsty and you gave Me no drink; I was a stranger and you did not take Me in, naked and you did not clothe Me, sick and in prison and you did not visit Me." (Matt 25:34–43)

Christ does not require our good things, but He Himself will give us everything. I say that Christ does not require them, but Christians, our brothers, require them. And in His love for mankind, Christ imputes to Himself whatever is given to Christians, for He says, "[I]nasmuch as you did it to one of the least of these My brethren, you did it to Me" (Matt 25:40). And whatever is not done for Christians is not done for Christ Himself, as is said, "[I]nasmuch as you did not do it to one of the least of these, you did not do it to Me" (Matt 25:45). For what is done for the members is done for the head as well. And what is not done for the members is not done for the head. If good is done for the members, the head imputes it for itself as well. If good is not done for the members, it is not done for the head itself. Think about this, O man, stingy in giving alms, generous to your own whims and luxuries! Blessed Christian! Christ-loving soul! Do not look at the sons of this age, who in every way try to please this world and not Christ, who died for us. But do not cease doing good: "for in due season we shall reap if we do not lose heart" (Gal 6:9). Beloved, do not imitate what is evil, but imitate what is good. "He who does good is of God, but he who does evil has not seen God" (3 John 1:11). Imitate the farmer who sows at the proper time with hope for fruit. Sow your seeds now, and during the harvest, you will reap with joy. "Whatever a man sows, that he will also reap. For he who sows to his flesh will of the flesh reap corruption, but he who sows to the Spirit will of the Spirit reap ever-lasting life" (Gal 6:7–8). How longed-for and sweet will be the words, "Come, you blessed!" But terrible and frightful will be: "Depart from Me, you cursed!" Christians, may these two words ever ring in your ears: "Come" and "Depart." Let us have mercy on our brothers, and we ourselves shall obtain mercy. Let us give, and it will be given to us. Amen.

Farmers do not just throw their seeds onto the ground but first imagine the harvest, look at the fruits produced from the seeds to be sown, and wish for them with eagerness. Looking at the future gain, they get to work and sow. Likewise, merchants do not simply travel through foreign countries but first consider the wealth to be gathered from trade, before beginning their trip. Likewise, wayfarers do not simply set out on journey but first consider the place to which they want to go and plan the trip and make preparations before leaving for the destination. Likewise, soldiers do not just go into a battle but beforehand with their minds' eyes imagine victory and the glory and honor that will follow it. Then they go into battle and fight against the enemy. Like-wise, everyone in this world does not just start to work but first considers the result for which he begins it, and the fruit that will ensue, before they start. For no one begins and does anything without a proposal and intention. Beloved Christian, you should imitate such toilers, who labor for the sake of temporary good things. They labor, looking toward corruptible and transient goods. You should look to eternal good things with the eye of faith, good things that "eye has not seen, nor ear heard, Nor have entered into the heart of man The things which God has prepared for those who love Him" (1 Cor 2:9). Prepare and sow with the hope of receiving these good things. Look at that harvest that will be gathered on the last day, one that is not earthly, but heavenly; not corruptible, but incorruptible; not temporary, but from which eternal fruits are gathered. And so now, on earth, while there is time, before the sowing and proper time for it has passed, sow your seeds, and during this harvest, you will reap fruits. Farmers and others who labor for earthly blessings often are disappointed in their hope. For good fruit does not always come forth, and people do not always receive what they desire and what they work for. But whoever with faith, with hope and zeal, seeks eternal blessings is not disappointed, but receives them, since "He who promised is faithful" (Heb 10:23). You, too, should prepare and sow now; sow with faith and hope. Do not be afraid: the seed will not perish. You give into the hands of the poor, but what has been given is found in the hands of Christ and will be returned to you with great increase. Lay up in your mind and set in your memory that your homeland and home is in heaven. "Do not lay up for yourselves treasures on earth, where moth and rust destroy and where thieves break in and steal; but lay up for yourselves treasures in heaven, where neither moth nor rust destroys and where thieves do not break in and steal" (Matt 6:19–20). Do not fear: your laid-up treasure will be all intact and on the last day will be announced before the whole world and will be handed over to you, and will be ever present with you unto the ages of ages. From this, it follows: (1) You will show that you have left this world in soul, mind, and heart, and you have your citizenship in heaven, although you are present in the body and in the world. And you may say with the Apostle, "For our citizenship is in heaven, from which we also eagerly wait for the Savior, the Lord Jesus Christ (Phil 3:20). For where your treasure is, there your heart will be also" (Matt 6:21). You will unfailingly be present in your spirit, heart, and thought where your treasure is laid up. (2) You will receive it in due course. You will hear from Christ on that day, "Beloved, here is your treasure that you laid up not on earth, but in heaven, according to My word. Here, it is being returned to you in its entirety. Take it and take comfort in it. And be rich not in corruptible, but in non-corruptible wealth" (see Matt 6:19–21). (3) A treasure, laid up on earth, brings fear and sorrow to the one who lays it up; he fears lest it be stolen. You, laying up your treasure in heaven, are freed from this fear and sorrow and will feel free, calm, and peaceful in your soul, which is the greatest good of the soul. Christian! No matter where you turn your thought, you will not have peace unless you send your treasure to this Homeland in advance. Even if you bury it in the earth, even if you lock it in your room and in trunks, even if you entrust it to guards, even if you squander it on whims and luxuries, you will not escape an agonizing worry about it. Always and everywhere, wherever you may be, care, sorrow, and fear will be with you, and as a worm inside a tree, this evil inside your heart and your soul will gnaw at you and torment you. And so you will suffer from a two-fold evil—you will sin and be tormented. But when you send it to heaven through the hands of the destitute and paupers, this will free you from evil. Therefore, believe the word of Christ: "[W]here your treasure is, there will your heart be also" (Matt 6:21), and transfer your treasure from earth to heaven, and there your heart will be present with it. What is more dear and sweet than to live on earth in the body and to be in heaven with the soul and heart? O Jesus, the Light of the eyes of our souls! Open the eyes of our souls that we may see these blessings that You have "prepared for those who love" You (1 Cor 2:9), and we will search for them with desire and zeal. Beloved Christian! If you had seen even a small part of these blessings, you would rush to them, despising everything in this world. But please believe the true Word of God, which is more trustworthy than anything you may see, and seek after them.

Impoverished farmers, who have few fruits that they have gathered, even though they are enduring need, save them so there will be something to sow and fruits to harvest. Wretched Christian! Do the same as these wretched but sensible laborers. You have scant possessions, but do not squander them all on household expenditures. Save, so that there will be something to sow and to gather at harvest time. Spare a portion of the little you have for Christ, Who in His own time will return to you a hundredfold. If you only sow a few seeds into the hands of the poor, may your fruit be multiplied by God's grace! Give with zeal to him who asks you, and the little given from a well-wishing giver will be counted as much, and Jesus, the Lover of Mankind, will accept it, as he accepted the two mites from the poor widow. "Assuredly, I say to you that this poor widow has put in more than all those who have given to the treasury; for they all put in out of their abundance, but she out of her poverty put in all that she had, her whole livelihood" (Mark 12:43–44). You too should put mites, if nothing more, into the hands of the poor, like seed in the earth, and in due time you will reap with joy. And a cup of cool water given in Christ's name is not forgotten by Him (see Mark 9:41).

# 33. The Right Hand

We see that the right hand does not contain anything in itself, but what it receives, it gives away again. Christian! A person has nothing of his own, except infirmity, sins, poverty, and wretchedness, but receives from his Creator intellect, health, strength, wealth, silver and gold, a house, clothing, bread, food, drink, livestock, and so on. This is the hand that receives. But there should also be a hand that gives. Many receive, but not everyone gives. Christian, be not only a receiving hand, but also a giving one. You have received good things from God; do not hold on to them, but give them away to the glory of God and the benefit of our neighbor. You received intellect from God—do not hide it, but give to the foolish and senseless, and your talent will increase. You received health and strength—do not conceal them, but use them for blessed labors. You received wealth—do not hide it in the earth, in storerooms and chests. Do not waste God's bounty on whims and luxuries, but distribute them to poor and destitute people—your brothers. You receive bread—share it with those who want it. You have clothing—do not keep it in your storeroom, but clothe your naked brethren with it. You have livestock—let it serve not only you but other people as well. You have a house—do not lock it, but open it to visitors, wanderers, etc. There, Christian, is your right hand! Be not only a receiving but also a giving right hand. You receive every good thing from God—give it away to the glory of the Bestower of good things and the edification of the one who needs your good things. Then you will be a faithful steward of God's gifts. And what you will receive from God, you will return to Him, to His Glory. For this, God will render to you, as his faithful steward, not earthly, but heavenly, not temporary, but eternal good things. If you do not do this, then, like the evil and unfaithful servant, you will be punished by the Lord and will hear: "Cast the unprofitable servant into the outer darkness. There will be weeping and gnashing of teeth" (Matt 25:30).

# 34. The Giving King
# and the Thief of His Gift

If a king gave some gift to his subject and immediately some impudent fellow stole that gift right out of the recipient's hands in his sight, what would the king then do to the thief? Without fail, a fierce anger would flare up at the thief. And rightly so, since this would be a great vexation to the king who gave the gift, and an insult to the servant who received it. God, the heavenly King, in his goodness and love for mankind, gives His blessings to all people. And He places them in their hands, so that everyone would be contented with His blessings and would know and gave thanks to Him as their Benefactor. But bold people steal God's gifts from people and as it were tear them out of their hands, and do this lawless act before God's all-seeing eyes. God gives His good things to His servants, as a gift into their hands, but they steal the good things that God has given. And whomever God honors, they as it were make dishonorable. And whomever God endows, they deprive. And whomever God enriches, they impoverish. And God sees this, their lawless action. Think, O man, how these thieves vex God and insult people. And we cannot describe how fiercely God's anger will flare up against them for this. Those who have not helped their brothers—the poor and wretched people—he sends to eternal fire (see Matt 25), but what will happen to those who not only do not help but even steal and rob. Consider this, dear thief, who gorges on other people's property. Such lawless acts are done by (1) Robbers, who attack travelers and take their belongings. (2) Powerful but bold people who take away land, groves, and other valuable property needed to sustain life from poor widows and other people not having protectors. (3) Superiors who do not give subordinates their wages, appointed for them by the Sovereign, or give it, but not in full, without any good reason retaining it for themselves, for their own delicacies of the table. (4) Judges and officials who take money from those coming to court and do not handle the case without payment. They have the customary ruse: "Come tomorrow"; but this expression means: "Bring something, and the case will be taken care of." (5) Landowners, who burden their peasants either with high quit-rents or much work. This is serious misappropriation, although the blinded master does not even see it. The poor peasant labors and sweats the whole summer, but he and his family have nothing to feed and clothe themselves with. He plows and sows, but the landowner gathers almost everything. Our homeland groans and sighs because of these "noble" souls, as well as "impartial" judges! O Lord, have mercy on Your creation! (6) Stealthy robbers and thieves, who steal from shops, houses, barns, and secretly steal other types of people's belongings. (7) Lawless merchants, who sell a bad item for a good one and a cheap item for an expensive one, and in any transaction cheats his neighbor. (8) Anyone who by whatever means purloins another's property. All such people are stealing God's good things, put by God into human hands, and it is as if they are tearing them out of their hands in the eyes of God. O Man! God gives your neighbor His good things into his possession as if into his hands, and you snatch these good things out of his hands. And God sees your lawless act, sees it and writes it down in His book, and will display it to you at His Judgment. Then you will see how badly you have acted! But repent and return what you have stolen, and scatter the good things that have been gathered through sin, so that they might not appear with you at the judgment and it not be said of you, "Behold the man that took not God for his helper, but trusted unto the multitude of his riches, and puffed up his vanity" (Ps 51:9 LXX). "Behold the man and his acts!"

The thief of a king's gift hurts himself more than the person from whom he steals the gift. Likewise, every thief, swindler, and robber hurts himself more than the one from whom he steals. The thief of a king's gift is deprived of the monarch's favor and will be subjected to his anger. Likewise, every thief and swindler who steals someone else's good things is deprived of God's favor and will be subject to His righteous anger. The thief of the king's gift, like an enemy of the king and one who vexes His Royal Majesty, is excluded from the number of good citizens and is handed over for punishment. Likewise, every plunderer is excluded from the number of good Christians and will be subject to both temporal and eternal punishment. We can see that he is subject to temporal punishment. We see how property unjustly gathered by thieves disintegrates and perishes, and they themselves suffer in this world from dishonor, remorse, and pangs of conscience. And it often happens that such people for a certain time become rich and flourish like a flower in a field, but suddenly, like the flower, wither and fall and become like one of the poor and wretched. Stolen property, like fire spreading to a house, consumes all the other belongings, for God's curse abides where there is fraud. No good thing, but every misfortune, will be wherever God's curse is. Extortioners and robbers are like a person who scoops up water with a sieve. So also everything that they steal or gather flows out from their hands in various streams. Steal and grab, O man, as you like and what you like. But everything will flow out from your hands, and your iniquitous belongings, like fire, will be destroyed. But that the swindler and the thief is subject to eternal punishment is clear from what the Apostle wrote: "Neither ... thieves, nor covetous, nor drunkards, nor revilers, nor extortioners will inherit the kingdom of God" (1 Cor 6:10).

Those who do not show mercy to their neighbors will be banished and sent into eternal fire (see Matt 25:41). How much then will those who have stolen other people's belongings suffer? So the thief and the robber hurt themselves more than their neighbor from whom they steal; harm themselves more than him. O man! You temporarily profit from another's belongings, but you will pay for this by eternal suffering. Eternal suffering is horrifying even to hear of, let alone endure. But you will not escape it, really you won't, if you do not repent and are reconciled with your brother. The Lord tells you, "Agree with your adversary quickly, while you are on the way with him, lest your adversary deliver you to the judge, the judge hand you over to the officer, and you be thrown into prison. Assuredly, I say to you, you will by no means get out of there till you have paid the last penny" (Matt 5:25–26). Be reconciled, O man, be reconciled quickly with everyone whom you have offended. Be reconciled while you are on your life's way, before the Righteous Judge calls you to His Judgment. For He calls everyone through death. And however you are when you are called, that is how you will stand before His Judgment.

# 35. Turn Back! Do Not Go That Way!

In this world, it happens that a person calls back a person who is walking and yells after him: "Do you hear? Come back! Don't go there." So also God speaks in a person's conscience and cries out to him when he wishes to do evil: "Come back, O man! Don't go there." "Shun evil" (Ps 33:15). Christian! Do you want to take revenge on, harm, or what is worse, kill your neighbor? God cries to you, "Turn back, O man." Do you want to commit fornication and defile your body? God cries to you, "Turn back, O man." Do you want to steal, swindle, and take your neighbor's property? God thunders in your conscience, "Turn back, O man." Do you want to deceive and cheat your neighbor? God cries to you, "Turn back, O man." Do you want to slander, condemn, curse, or defame your brother? God turns you away from this and says, "Turn around, O man." "Keep thy tongue from evil" (Ps 33:14). In the same way, God turns you away from other sins as well and calls to your conscience, "Turn back, O man." "Shun evil, and do good" (Ps 33:15). And He tells you in His holy Word the same thing that He tells you in your conscience. An innocent conscience and the Word of God are in harmony. Whatever the conscience says is what the Word of God says. From whatever the conscience restrains from and turns away from, likewise does the Word of God. Whatever the conscience denounces, the Word of God does as well. And whatever the conscience praises, the Word of God does as well. For example, your conscience denounces you for theft—so does the Word of God. Your conscience praises you for mercy shown to your neighbor; God's Word praises you as well. "Blessed are the merciful" (Matt 5:7). Therefore, when our conscience turns us away and restrains us from something, this is God's voice calling within us, turning us away and restraining us from evil. Christians! Let us listen to God's voice and turn away from evil, in accordance with the admonition of the Holy Spirit: Today if you will hear His voice, "Harden not your hearts" (Ps 94:7–8). And we shall cry out, and the Lord will hear us.

## 36. Don't Touch That! It's Poison!

It happens that a person, wanting to warn another person lest he be harmed, holds him back and tells him. "Don't touch that! Poison is hidden in there." We see many such instances in the world. Likewise, God's word cautions us against sin and says to each of us: "Shun sin, O man, poison is hidden in sin. When you touch it, it will kill you." "The wages of sin is death" (Rom 6:23). There is poison in hatred, rancor, and murder—shun it! There is poison in fornication and in every impurity—shun it! There is poison in drunkenness, luxury, and sensual pleasure—shun it! There is poison in enmity and quarreling—shun it! There is poison in theft, embezzlement, violence, bribery, and every unjust deed—shun it! There is poison in idleness and laziness—shun it! There is poison in slander, condemnation, backbiting, swearing, foul language, foolish talk, blasphemy, and every unwholesome and rotten word—shun this, O man! There is poison also in pride, love of fame, vainglory, and hypocrisy—shun it! There is poison in every impious action, word, thought, and undertaking—beware of it! Shun every sin, O man, lest it destroy you! Poison kills the body, but sin—the soul. You try to avoid bodily death; the more so should you try to avoid the death of the soul that sin causes. The soul is more honorable and precious than the body; this is all the more reason why we should take care of it. Whether you try to avoid bodily death or not, you will not escape it. It is necessary for everyone—and for you, too.

But if you will protect your soul from the deadly poison of sin, you will live forever, even if you die, for by God's grace you will rise up not in death but to eternal life. My soul, shun every sin, as a deadly poison, lest it kill you. "Come, ye children," the Holy Spirit tells us, "and hearken unto me; I will teach you the fear of the Lord. What man is he that lusteth to life, and would gladly see good days? Keep thy tongue from evil, and thy lips, that they speak no guile. Shun evil and do good; seek peace, and pursue it. The eyes of the Lord are over the righteous, and His ears are open unto their prayers. But the countenance of the Lord is against them that do evil, to root out the remembrance of them from the earth" (Ps 33:12–17). Blessed is the person who hears the admonitions and warnings of God's Word and shuns every sin. Wretched is he who does not heed God's soul-saving voice.

We see that when a person, through carelessness, consumes poison or some other harmful thing and feels pain in his stomach, he does not tarry but immediately hastens to a physician and seeks healing. Christian! Don't you tarry either, when, through carelessness and the action of the devil, you consume the poison of sin. Do not tarry, I say, but immediately seek healing. Hasten with faith to Christ, the Physician of souls and bodies, ask of Him healing of your soul. Tell Him of the wound with which the enemy has wounded you. Tell Him, even though He already knows of it. Fall down before Him and with contrite heart acknowledge your illness. Do not be ashamed and do not be afraid! He knows your illness even before your confession. But He requires your willing and voluntary confession, so that you accuse yourself before Him and do not conceal your sin. Tell Him and confess your transgression: "I have sinned, O Lord, have mercy on me! Heal my soul, for I have sinned against Thee" (Ps 40:5). When they came out of Egypt and went into the Promised Land, the children of Israel were bitten by serpents in the desert. God, having mercy on them, ordered Moses to raise up a copper serpent on a pole, so that the people who had been bitten would look at that serpent for their healing and, when they looked, they were healed (see Num 21:6–9). Christians! We are going to the Promised Land, the heavenly homeland promised to us, and passing through the desert of this world, we suffer much from the serpent of hell, the devil. The moment that, because of our carelessness, this fierce serpent bites us, and we feel his harmful poison in our soul, let us immediately lift up our eyes to Christ, the Son of God, Who sits at the right hand of the Father, and Who once was raised up upon the wood of the Cross, was crucified, and died for our sins. "And as Moses lifted up the serpent in the wilderness, even so must the Son of Man be lifted up, that whoever believes in Him should not perish but have eternal life" (John 3:14–15). O Jesus, Power and Hope of our salvation, Who sits at the right hand of the Father in the Father's glory! Have mercy on us, whom You redeemed by Your precious Blood.

# 37. Weeping

In the world, we see that people weep. They are born with weeping, they live with weeping, and they die with weeping. People weep because they live in the world, a place of weeping, a vale of tears. There are many reasons why people weep. And everyone who weeps has his own reason for doing so. You should weep, too, Christian! Since you live in a vale of tears, you too have many reasons for which you should weep. Weep, before the time has passed when tears are helpful. Weep, that you will not do so eternally. Weep, and you will be comforted. "Blessed are those who mourn, For they shall be comforted" (Matt 5:4). People weep because they are unhappy. You should weep, Christian, because you are sinful, because you have sinned against your Lord, for this is a great misfortune. People weep that they do not have health of body. You should weep that you do not have health of soul. People weep that they are infirm and ill. You should weep that your soul is ailing, ill, and feeble. Pride, envy, anger, impurity, sensuality, love of fame, and greed are serious ailments. And there are as many passions and lusts as there are sicknesses that torment us. "Heal me, O Lord, and I shall be healed" (Jer 17:14), for You are God, my Saviour. People weep, because they have lost riches. You too should weep, Christian, that you have lost the riches given you from your Heavenly Father in Holy Baptism. People weep that they are in poverty and want. You should weep that you are destitute and needy, poor and wretched. Sin is intolerable poverty. "Bow down Thine ear, O Lord, and hear me, for I am poor and in misery" (Ps 85:1). People weep that they do not have food and drink. You should weep that your soul grows weak from hunger and that it is deprived of the hearing of the Word of God. It is a profound and severe hunger not to hear God's Word. People weep that they are without clothing and do not have anything to cover their nakedness. You should weep that your soul is naked—sin has stripped it bare. Bodily nakedness is shameful, but that of the souls is even more shameful. People see bodily nakedness, but God and His holy angels see nakedness of soul. "Blessed is he who watches, and keeps his garments, lest he walk naked and they see his shame" (Rev 16:15). Wretched and poor is he who does not keep watch and does not keep his garments, for he walks naked and they see his shame. Grant me a vesture of light, O most merciful Christ my God, Who wraps Thyself with light as it were a garment (cf. Ps 103:2). People weep that they fall and hurt themselves. Christian, you should weep that you fall into sin and hurt yourself, and your soul grows faint. Sin is a serious and severe fall. It is better that your body falls down because of your legs than your soul because of sin. "Let him who thinks he stands take heed lest he fall" (1 Cor 10–12). People weep for deceased parents, brothers, relatives, and friends. You should weep, Christian, for your dead soul, as Martha and Mary did for Lazarus (see John 11:31–33). May the Heavenly Father say about you as well, "for this my son was dead and is alive again; he was lost and is found" (Luke 15:24). O Jesus, Raiser of the dead! Resurrect my soul deadened by sins, as you resurrected the widow's son who had died (see Luke 7:12–15). People weep that they endure insult and violence from their enemies. You should weep before God, Christian, for the enemies of your soul, who try to take away eternal salvation. These enemies are the devil and his evil angels. "Judge them, O Lord, that do me wrong; fight Thou against them that fight against me. Lay hold of shield and buckler, and come to my help. Draw forth the sword, and stop the way against them that persecute me; say unto my soul, I am thy salvation" (Ps 34:1–3). People weep when they are summoned and brought into court, fearing that they may be disgraced in court, and be found guilty, and fall under punishment. You should weep too, Christian, for you too will be summoned to court, not a human one, but God's tribunal at which the Judge will not call witnesses, for He Himself knows all our deeds, words, and thoughts. Weep now, before you are summoned. Weep, so that you may mollify the Judge by your tears. Weep that you may not be found guilty and be cast into outer darkness. "There will be weeping and gnashing of teeth" (Matt 25:30). "And enter not into judgment with Thy servant, for before Thee shall no man living be justified" (Ps 142:2). People weep because they have many debts, and not having anything to repay, they fear that they will be cast into prison. You should weep too, Christian, that you are a great debtor to the Heavenly King by your sins, and indeed you have nothing with which to pay. Weep and mollify Him by your tears, so that He may forgive you your debt, and you may not be cast into the eternal prison. "Father … forgive us our debts" (Matt 6:9–12). People confined to prison weep because they do not see light. You too should weep, Christian, that your soul is enveloped by the darkness of the passions and does not see the Divine light. "Bring my soul out of prison, that I may give thanks unto Thy name" (Ps 141:8). People in chains and fetters weep because they do not have freedom. You too should weep, Christian, that your soul is bound by sins, like chains, and does not have its freedom. "Therefore if the Son makes you free, you shall be free indeed" (John 8:36). O Jesus, Redeemer of our captive souls! Break apart our bonds, so that we may offer a sacrifice of praise to Thee. People weep because they endure beating and wounds. You too should weep, Christian, that your evil conscience hurts and torments your soul more than any tormentor. "Have mercy upon me, O God, after Thy great goodness, and according to the multitude of Thy mercies do away mine offences" (Ps 50:3). People living in a foreign land weep because they do not see their home and their beloved homeland. The Jews being in the Babylonian captivity wept thus, as they themselves confess: "By the waters of Babylon, there we sat down and we wept" (Ps 136:1). You too should weep, Christian, that you live in this world, as in a foreign land, and do not see the heavenly and beautiful Homeland, Jerusalem on high. "Woe is me, for my wandering hath been prolonged" (Ps 119:5). You too should weep, my soul, that you may be comforted both here and there. "Who will give water to my head, and a fountain of tears to my eyes, that I might weep … day and night" (Jer 8:21 LXX [Jer 9:1]). "Hear my prayer, O Lord, and give ear unto my petition; hold not Thy peace at my tears. For I am a sojourner with Thee, and a pilgrim, as all my fathers were. O spare me, that I may recover my strength, before I go hence, and be no more" (Ps 38:13–14). "O come, let us worship and fall down before Him, and weep before the Lord that made us. For He is our God, and we are the people of His pasture, and the sheep of His hand" (Ps 94:6–7). "Hear us, O God of our salvation, the hope of all the ends of the earth, and of them that be afar off at sea" (Ps 64:6). "We have sinned, we have transgressed, we have done evil in Thy sight; we have not kept or followed Thy commandments. But reject us up not utterly; O God of our Fathers."[2]

# 38. *Debt*

It happens in the world that one person will borrow some money or some other items from another; what is lent is called a debt, and the person who borrows it, a debtor. And the more he borrows the more he increases his debt and owes back to the lender. Likewise, a person, when he breaks God's commandment and sins before God, falls into debt before God and becomes

His debtor. And the more he breaks God's commandments and sins against his Creator, the greater the burden of debt he amasses and the greater a debtor he becomes to God's majesty. Hence, the sins of people are called debts to God, and sinners, debtors, as we read in the Lord's Prayer: "And forgive us our debts, As we forgive our debtors" (Matt 6:12). The law obliges the debtor to repay the debt to the lender. Likewise, every sinner is obliged by God's law to recompense God for sins. The debtor, if he does not repay the debt to the lender, is thrown into prison. Likewise, the sinner, if he does not repay his debt to His Creator, is thrown into the eternal prison. But how can the sinner, who has so many times offended God's infinite majesty, repay his debt to God? There is no way to pay for one sin, so how can many and serious sins be paid for, for even one sin, being an affront to God's infinite majesty, is worthy of death and eternal punishment, as Christian theology teaches. Christian! It is hard to become a debtor to a man, but it is incomparably worse to incur debts to God because of sins. It is grim and terrifying to be thrown into a temporal prison, but incomparably grimmer and more terrible to be committed to the eternal prison. Sin is sweet for people, but its fruits are bitter. "The wages of sin is death," says the Apostle Paul (Rom 6:23). It is easy to commit sin, but it is difficult to be freed from it. One must continually be liberated by Him Who says, "If the Son makes you free, you shall be free indeed" (John 8:36). It happens that if the debtor cannot repay his debt to the lender, the lender by his mercy alone forgives him the debt, and the debtor is freed. Christians, we are God's debtors. We could not and cannot repay our debts to God, to Whom we were and remain in debt. But He in His unparalleled mercy forgives us the debts of our sins. We are the debtor Who owed ten thousand talents to his king and did not have anything with which to repay his debt. "And the king ... was moved with compassion, released him, and forgave him the debt" (Matt 18:24–28). The Heavenly King forgives the many and serious debts of sins, as the ten thousand talents, for we do not have anything with which to repay them, but He pardons whoever comes to Him with a pure heart and repents for the sins he has committed, and falls down before Him and begs mercy from Him. He remits by grace and love for mankind of His only-begotten Son, our Lord Jesus Christ, "Who was delivered up because of our offenses, and was raised because of our justification; ... [Who] was wounded because of our lawlessness, and became sick because of our sins" (Rom 4:25; Isa 53:5). He forgives, I say, those who repent. For the sinner who does not repent and does not abandon his sins remains in a debt of sin before God, the Heavenly

King. And as often as he boldly breaks God's commandment, he incurs debt before God. And the more sins he commits, the more he increases his debt. As often as a fornicator, an adulterer, and every impure person transgresses, the more he adds to his debt. The more a swindler, a thief, or an extortioner steals, the more he is burdened by his debt of sin. The more a slanderer and user of foul language, a person who speaks foolishly, a blasphemer, and every reviler defiles his tongue by his rotten and evil speech, the greater a debtor he becomes before God. In a word, the more every wrongdoer boldly violates God's law, the more he adds to the burden of his sin and thus subjects himself to greater punishment. O man! Sin, by which you offend God's infinite majesty and arouse His righteous anger against you, is sweet to you. Sin, for which Christ, the Son of God, drained the most bitter cup of suffering and death, is sweet to you. Sin, for which you will taste the grief of eternal death unless you repent, is sweet to you. You see how bitter are the fruits of sin, although it seems sweet to you. But enough of being burdened by debt! It is time to throw off this burden from your shoulders, lest you appear with them at Christ's Judgment. Woe to the person who appears there with this heavy burden. It will without fail plunge him into the bottom of hell. Fall down, poor man, before your Creator, and with humble and broken heart cry out to Him, imitating the publican, "God, be merciful to me a sinner!" (Luke 18:13). And the Lord will look after you with a merciful eye and will remit all your debts. But in future, by all means avoid offending Him and going into His debt. And knowing God's mercy to you, show mercy to your neighbor as well and forgive his sins, lest you learn again the anger of God against yourself, and lest your forgiven debt return to you, as happened with that evil servant, mentioned in the parable (see Matt 18:28–35). Remembrance of wrongs closes the door to receiving God's mercy and forgiveness of sins. "For if you forgive men their trespasses, your heavenly Father will also forgive you. But if you do not forgive men their trespasses, neither will your Father forgive your trespasses" (Matt 6:14–15). "Father ... forgive us our debts, as we forgive our debtors" (Matt 6:9–12).

The debtor, having received mercy from the lender and seeing his debt forgiven, rejoices. Likewise, the sinner, having received the utmost mercy and forgiveness of sins from God, feels in his heart a warm consolation and rejoices in the mercy that God pours out on sinners. The repentant and contrite heart that truly turns to God is not deprived of consolation by its Merciful Creator, for God, Who is Merciful and loves mankind, lovingly and mercifully looks on a heart that turns to Him, falling before Him with contrition, and so "a contrite and humble heart God shall not despise" (Ps 50:19), and on such a heart He pours out the oil of His mercy, from which the grieved heart is healed like a wound by a recuperative bandage, and is restored. "The Lord ... healeth those that are broken in heart and bindeth up their wounds" (Ps 146:2–3). This is a true Gospel consolation that is vouchsafed to the repentant heart from its Merciful Creator! These are the same tidings of which Christ, the Redeemer of the world, speaks: "He has anointed Me to preach the gospel to the poor; He has sent Me to heal the brokenhearted, to proclaim liberty to the captives and recovery of sight to the blind, to set at liberty those who are oppressed; to proclaim the acceptable year of the Lord" (Luke 4:18–19). The debtor loves the lender as his merciful benefactor; he remains grateful to him all his life and remembers his benefaction even until death. Likewise the sinner, feeling God's great mercy, loves Him sincerely, thanks Him warmly, and remembers this grace of His even until death. For gratitude is remembrance of benefactions. Where there is remembrance of benefactions, there is gratitude as well. Where benefaction is forgotten, ingratitude rears its head. The debtor, seeing the mercy shown by the lender and remembering this mercy, himself shows mercy to his own debtor, if he has one, and remits his debt. This is the sign of a good-natured and grateful person. Likewise, a grateful and good-hearted Christian, seeing God's mercy to himself and feeling the remission of his sins, himself shows mercy to his neighbor and forgives him his sins. It happens that a wicked debtor, having received forgiveness of a debt, himself does not want to forgive a debt owed him. This justly moves his lender to anger, and the debtor sees his debt reinstated, and he becomes a debtor as before. Likewise, the ungrateful and wicked Christian, feeling God's great mercy to him on having received remission of serious sins from God, himself does not want to forgive his neighbor even minor transgressions. I say minor transgressions since, when a person sins against another person, no matter how he does this, it is far less than when we transgress against God. And it so moves God, his Creator, to great and righteous anger, that he reverts to being His debtor, but even greater one than he was before. Read, Christian, the parable of the king and his debtor, and you will see how serious and dangerous it is to be nasty and vengeful toward your neighbor (see Matt 18:23–35). There is nothing safer than to forgive, and there is nothing more dangerous than not to forgive and to take vengeance on your neighbor for an offense. "For judgment is without mercy to the one who has shown no mercy" (Jas 2:13). God in His goodness shows mercy to all of us; we feel it not just every day but every hour. But when a person, being vouchsafed God's mercy, does not wish to show mercy to a person like himself, then God takes away His mercy from him, as from an ungrateful and wicked servant. As a result, that person, instead of mercy, is subject to God's righteous Judgment and will be judged for all the sins he ever committed in his life. We see, Christians, how terrible and dangerous it is to not forgive and to take vengeance on our neighbor. "You wicked servant!" the king says to his debtor, whose debt he would have forgiven, "I forgave you all that debt because you begged me. Should you not also have had compassion on your fellow servant, just as I had pity on you?" The Heavenly King says the same thing to the Christian who does not have mercy on his neighbor. "And his master was angry, and delivered him to the torturers until he should pay all that was due to him. So," Christ the Lord concludes the parable, "My heavenly Father also will do to you if each of you, from his heart, does not forgive his brother his trespasses" (Matt 18:32–35).

# 39. A Master Who Is Calling a Servant

It happens that a master, wishing to call a certain faithful servant, says to other servants, "Send me that servant." And they call him, "Go, the master is sending for you," and he goes. Like this, Christ, the Lord of all, calls a person from this world—and he leaves it. The master calls his servant unexpectedly. So also Christ the Lord called everyone unexpectedly. Death is each person's summons. Blessed is the servant who is in a good state when called by his master. Cursed is he who is deficient when he appears. Blessed is the man who, called by Christ the Lord, appears before Him in a good state. Cursed is he who is deficient when he appears. Christians! Our good state is true repentance. Our deficiency is neglect of true repentance. Our summons to the Lord is our demise. We see our approaching end; we see in this our summons. Our demise is both known to us and unknown: known because we shall die; unknown because we do not know when we shall die, so also the Lord's summons. We do not know when the Lord will call us. Do you want to appear before the Lord in good condition when you are called? Be always in a state of true repentance; be always as you wish to be at your death, as you wish to be summoned. Do you want to die in a blessed state? Remember the hour of your death and live piously. Wise and prudent people are vigilant and are always awaiting their master's summons. Christian! You should imitate "the sons of this world [who] are more shrewd in their generation than the sons of light" (Luke 16:8): be alert and await the call of your Lord. Be prudent and wise in this important matter, and you will be blessed. This is where the door to either a blessed or an unhappy eternity opens. From here you will go either to eternal life and consolation or to eternal death and torments. You see how terrifying this hour is. Blessed is he who is vigilant and awaiting this hour! You should be vigilant, my soul, and await this hour and them with joy you will be able to sing, "Lord, now You are letting Your servant depart in peace," and so on (Luke 2:29–32). "O Lord, tell me mine end, and the number of my days, what it is, that I may know what is wanting to me. Behold, Thou hast made my days as it were a span long, and my existence is as nothing before Thee; verily, every man living is altogether vanity. Therefore man walketh as a shadow, and disquieteth himself in vain; he heapeth up riches, and knoweth not for whom he gathereth them" (Ps 38:5–7). O Jesus, my Redeemer! Cleanse me before You take me from here.

It happens that a servant, neither caring for his master nor fearing him, thinks to himself, "My master will not summon me today or even longer. I shall go with my friends to have a good time and amuse myself." So, going out, he begins to drink heavily. Then a messenger runs up to him unexpectedly and calls him, saying, "Come, the master needs you." Then his merriment turns into woe, and his audacity, into fear and trembling. And he goes to his master trembling, thoughts rushing around in his head, thinking, what answer I can give to my master, without whose leave I absented myself, went my own way, and acted scandalously. Likewise the Christian who does not fear God and does not take care for his salvation thinks to himself: "I am still young and healthy, my death is not in sight, I shall not die soon. I will have a good time and amuse myself on earth, to enjoy the good things of this world. I will acquire fame, so that people will know me. Then I shall have a considerable income, I'll gather quite a bit and fill up my chests. Now people only work to accumulate; why should I be different? Having accumulated, I will buy up more villages and peasants. I have little land; I'll add some more. I'll take away from this widow and from that base fellow. There is no one to stand up for them and to hinder me. It is far to the King, and I shall bribe the judge, and everything will turn out fine. Then I will build myself a mansion and decorate it. I will buy myself an English carriage, and a team of fine horses. I will plant a beautiful garden with avenues and porticoes, I will dig nice ponds in it so that there will be somewhere to stroll, have a good time, and amuse ourselves with guests. I'll buy wine and will set a table, just as others do, and socialize with people. I'll go to visit them, and they'll come to visit me. I'll get together a good number of servants, dress them in proper livery, so there will be someone to serve me and the guests who come to me. I'll try to have vocal and instrumental music to better entertain me and my guests." The poor man, having fussed around in his thoughts, plans to do such things, and what he foolishly thinks of, he carries out in fact. Another thinks up other plans. We see this among the poor Christians of the present age. We see that all their cares are not of salvation and eternal life, to which they are called by God's Word and renewed by Holy Baptism, but of vanity. We see this and feel pity. But during such thoughts and undertakings, unexpectedly, like a speedy messenger, death silently comes to all and says, "Come, O man! The Lord Almighty is calling you." Here fear and trembling seizes the poor soul. His conscience denounces him and torments him. He thinks of God's Judgment. The soul is pressed from all sides; he does not know what to do. "Ah, the Lord is calling me, but I am deficient. A door to eternity, which I had never thought of before, has opened to me." O world, world! "Vanity of vanities, all is vanity!" (Eccl 1:2). "And so His spirit shall go forth, and he shall return again to his earth; in that day all his thoughts shall perish" (Ps 145:4). So dies one who promised himself a long life. He who wished to have a good time and amuse himself tastes the sorrow of death. He who wished to have a multitude of servants and peasants remains alone. He who thought to travel in a tandem carriage lies on his deathbed. He who thought of living in an opulent and beautiful house is being laid in his coffin. He who dreamed of expanding his land holdings is being buried in a six-foot hole. He who wished to entertain himself with music is being accompanied with tears and lamentations on the way of all the earth. This is how death comes unexpectedly, and the Lord calls us when we do not expect it. "O turn away mine eyes, O Lord, lest they behold vanity; give me life in Thy way" (Ps 118:37). Foolish Christian, whose heart has cleaved to vanity and who is neglecting your salvation! You see what happens to people; expect it for yourself. Death befalls them; it will befall you, too. The Lord and Judge calls them to Himself; He will call you, too. And He will call when, and where, and how you least expect it. Upon their death, they tremble before God's Judgment seat and are troubled, and you too will tremble and be troubled. So prepare ahead of time, so that that hour, fearsome for all, will not be so fearsome for you. You will be blessed when, having turned from vanity ahead of time, you will think of that hour when the door to eternity is opened to everyone.

# 40. Servants Awaiting Their Master

It happens that a master leaves his house for a certain reason. So Christ the Lord, having completed the great work of our salvation, departed this world and, having ascended into heaven, sat at the right hand of God the Father. The master, leaving his house, says to his servants, "Stay home, and each one do his work; I will soon return." So Christ the Lord, leaving this world, ordered us, his servants, saying, "I shall come again to you, and I shall come quickly. And behold, I am coming quickly, and My reward is with Me, to give to every one according to his work" (John 14:4; Rev 22:12). Be ready: "Let your waist be girded and your lamps burning; and you yourselves be like men who wait for their master, when he will return from the wedding, that when he comes and knocks they may open to him immediately" (Luke 12:35–36). Good and faithful servants do what their master has ordered and await his arrival. Likewise, good and faithful servants of Christ act in accordance with the word of Christ their Lord, wait for His coming, and prepare to meet Him. "For our citizenship is in heaven, from which we also eagerly wait for the Savior, the Lord Jesus Christ" (Phil 3:20). It happens that servants, not expecting the impending arrival of their master, say, "Our master won't come for a while." And they begin to carouse and behave outrageously. But then suddenly the cry is heard—the master is coming! Likewise, Christians who are evil-minded and negligent of their salvation, thinking in their hearts: "Our master is a long time in coming," will begin carousing and behaving wickedly. But then suddenly is heard a cry and the sound of a trumpet: "Our master is coming! Go out to meet Him." Blessed are those servants whose master, on coming, will find them keeping watch and going out to meet him. And so blessed are those Christians whom Christ the Lord, at His coming, will find keeping watch and ready to meet Him. Wretched are those Christians, whom Christ the Lord, on coming, will find unfaithful to Him and walking after their fancies. The master will hand over the careless servants for punishment. Likewise, Christians who do not do the will of their Lord Jesus Christ will be handed over for eternal punishment. "And cast the unprofitable servant into the outer darkness. There will be weeping and gnashing of teeth … Watch therefore, for you know neither the day nor the hour in which the Son of Man is coming" (Matt 25:30, 1). For as Christ the Lord has appointed an unknown end for us, so that we would always anticipate it; likewise He fixed an unknown day of His coming into the world, so that we would await Him every day. And as we do not know when the Lord will call us to Himself, let us be ready every day and hour to meet Him. Christian! You see that a person dies when he does not expect it and leaves for the other world. So think and ponder that the Lord too will come to us unexpectedly. Then the cry will be heard unexpectedly, "Behold, the bridegroom is coming; go out to meet him!" (Matt 25:6). The sound of the trumpet will be heard: "Rise up, ye dead! Go to your judgment!" "Then the sign of the Son of Man will appear in heaven, and then all the tribes of the earth will mourn, and they will see the Son of Man coming on the clouds of heaven with power and great glory. For as the lightning comes from the east and flashes to the west, so also will the coming of the Son of Man be" (Matt 24:30, 27). So, as you await your end and prepare for it, in order to have a blessed repose, look also for the coming of your Lord and prepare to meet Him in order to be vouchsafed at His coming to stand at His right hand and to hear with those who hear His sweet voice: "Come, you blessed of My Father, inherit the kingdom prepared for you from the foundation of the world" (Matt 25:34).

# 41. A Man Summoned to Court

We see that when a man is summoned to court, he thinks only of this; he exerts all his efforts and consults his friends so that he will not be shamed in court and convicted. Christian! You will be called not to a human court but to a Divine one. "For we must all appear before the judgment seat of Christ, that each one may receive the things done in the body, according to what he has done, whether good or bad" (2 Cor 5:10). The more so should you prepare and exert all your efforts so that you will not be shamed at the Judgment and be condemned. It often happens that a man avoids having to appear in a human court. No one can avoid that Judgment, since it will take place for certain and will be for everyone. This is truly so, as surely as there was a yesterday and there is a today. For finding out the truth at a human court, witnesses are required; these often gain an acquittal for a guilty man. At that Judgment, it will not be so. That Judge will not require witnesses, but He Himself knows everything. At a human trial, silver and gold often help a guilty man, as happens at malfeasant courts. It is not so at that Judgment, because That Judge does not demand gifts and does not accept them. In a human court, exalted and powerful persons and other allies often defend a guilty man. At that Judgment, they can do nothing; they themselves will go into hiding and will be like reptiles. In a human court, there is often a respect of persons. Often the rich is preferred to the destitute, the honored to the base, and the well-born to the low-born. At that Judgment it will be different because That Judge does not consider position, but conscience and deeds. Then everyone will stand side by side before Him: servants and masters, kings and their subjects, rich and poor. In a human court, guile often gains an acquittal for a guilty man. At that Judgment, it will fall silent and dumb. There will be no place for it there because the Judge, being Omniscient, knows everything. In a human court, a person is judged before a few people. At that Judgment, he will be judged before the whole world, before the angels and people. In a human court, only a few know the vices of the accused. At that Judgment, the evil deeds, words, and thoughts of accused sinners will be exposed to the whole world. In a human court, the accused feels shame before a few people. At that Judgment the poor sinner will be shamed and disgraced before the whole world. From a human court, only temporal death or some other kind of temporal punishment will result. By that Judgment, the condemned sinner will be consigned not to temporal but to eternal death. You see, Christian, some aspects of a human court and Christ's Judgment. You also see how a person prepares with all apprehension for the human court, which in comparison with that Judgment is nothing. People prepare with all diligence for this court, however, lest they be put to shame. O careless Christian, cleaving to the vanity of this world, not ceasing to boldly transgress God's law, considering sin as insignificant or, what is worse, nothing at all! Have mercy on your poor soul. Lift up your mental eyes to that fearsome universal spectacle, at which "for every idle word men may speak, they will give account of it in the day of judgment" (Matt 12:36). And prepare with all apprehension for that day, when each must go either into eternal torment or into eternal life. In this important matter, imitate even the sons of this age, who being summoned to a human court, prepare for it with all thoroughness, lest they be put to shame. You will stand before God's Judgment Seat, not man's, at which there will be no respect of persons. Think about this beforehand and prepare yourself for this great day.

It happens that people, having committed some crime and realizing their sin, may, before they are summoned to trial, come to the king or to some other authority and with humility confess their sin, fall down before the authority, ask forgiveness, and receive it. Christian! You know that you will be summoned to God's Judgment, and you will be tormented for all your sins in deed, word, and thought. So do what sensible sons of this age do. Turn away from your sins and come to Christ the Judge, the Heavenly King, against Whom you sinned; confess your sins to Him with humility; fall down before Him; and convict yourself before Him now; and you will not be condemned by Him later. Call to Him with the publican's voice: "God, be merciful to me a sinner! ... bear fruits worthy of repentance" (Luke 18:13, 3:8). Then all your sins and iniquities will be expiated and will not be remembered because He will judge not those without sin but those who have sinned and have not repented. That is why repentance was preached: so that those who have sinned would repent and receive mercy from Him. Repent and expiate by your sighs and tears your sins written in your conscience, and they will be erased in God's book and will not appear at that Judgment. This is a preparation for the Dread Judgment. There is none other besides that one. Always be in true repentance. And you will be prepared for that Judgment, at which you will appear without fail. And so, having started a new Christian life, expect mercy from Him. One who repents and is living a new Christian life will not be harmed by his former wicked life. One thing alone is required of us: that we mend our ways and change for the better. Always remember that day and firmly bear in mind that you, just like everybody else, will be summoned to that Judgment, God's Judgment, and not a human one, and you will be summoned unexpectedly when the Archangel's trumpet sounds. This thought will move you to true repentance and will maintain you in humility and contriteness of heart. Remembrance and reflection on that Judgment will prevent you from committing sin, taking vengeance on your neighbor, but will prompt you to diligent and fervent prayer. If you remember that Judgment, you will not seek amusing days in the world but will rather desire tears, weeping, and lamentation. That people amuse themselves, and please their flesh, and act lawlessly comes from forgetfulness and lack of reflection on that Judgment. Remember the Judgment, and you will repent truly, reform, and change for the better every day. And you will not be the same as you were before. As fire drives out every stench, so fear of that Judgment will drive out every rottenness and stench from the soul and will purify it hour by hour.

In the world, we see that for an unjust trial there is an appeal or report to the king or some other authority, and those who have judged are themselves summoned to court and the unjust judges are tried. Thus, the injustices, coercion, animosity, and offenses that are done to poor people, and unjust judgments by kings, princes, lords, pastors, and other authorities cry out to heaven, and their cries are heard by the Almighty Lord, the King of kings and Lord of lords, and beg a hearing by Him. Poor people, not being able to find anyone to hear their lament, stave off offenses and coercion, and wipe away tears, sigh and cry out to God in heaven, the Father of orphans and Judge of widows: "O God! You are our Creator and Lord, You are our Protector and Helper. We do not find satisfaction on earth for our poverty and tears. Hear us and have mercy on us, poor ones, and wipe away the tears of Your creations that are enduring evil. The powerful help the powerful, the noble help the noble, masters help masters, the rich help the rich, and judges help judges. We cannot find help anywhere, so we ask it of You!" "The poor man is abandoned unto Thee; Thou art the helper of the orphan" (Ps 9:35). The Lord sees the wickedness of the lawless authorities and judges them. Their outcry, like that against Sodom, goes up to the Lord, and He hears the sighs of His wretched people, and the Judge judges all the earth. From this, we see the terrible punishments sent from God's righteous Judgment seat upon states and cities. We see terrible wars and bloodshed. We see pestilences. We see tempters, and disobedient sons, and mutineers against the homeland, who assume the names of high-ranking personages, and inflict upheaval and damage upon the homeland. We see terrible fires, and famine, and other punishments. All of this is sent down by God, the King of Kings and Lord of Lords, for unjust judgments, offenses, and coercion inflicted on poor people, as the Righteous Judge Who judges all the world. But besides this, all judges and authorities will be summoned to the universal Judgment. Then those who have judged His people will themselves stand before God the Judge and will give answer. Kings will stand and will have their say. Princes and grandees will also have their say. Masters will stand and have their say. All authorities from highest to lowest will stand and have their say for their unjust judgments and unscrupulous and wicked treatment of the people entrusted to them. Then woe will it be to the iniquitous authorities who by injustice and cruelty have done harm to God's people! "God will make a careful search of your works and examine closely your plans, because as servants of His kingdom, you did not judge rightly; neither did you keep His law, nor did you walk according to the plan of God; He shall come upon you terribly and quickly, because severe judgment falls on those who govern. For the least is pardoned in mercy, but the powerful shall be strongly examined" (Wis 6:3–6). Authorities, masters, and judges! Your unjust acts cry to heaven and to God as if raising a denunciation against you. God hears their cry and will summon you to His Judgment. Repent, beloved, before He calls you! He sees all your undertakings and all your injustice, "but is longsuffering toward us, not willing that any should perish but that all should come to repentance" (2 Pet 3:9). And if you do not repent now, you will repent when He calls you to His Judgment, but it will be too late and to no avail. Ponder on Solomon's words just quoted, and you will learn how terrible God's Judgment will be for you. "Convert us, O God; show the light of Thy countenance, and we shall be saved" (Ps 79:4).

It happens that when criminals and scoundrels are brought to court, they are led there in the same shackles in which they had been bound. Likewise the poor sinners will be led to God's Judgment with their sins, with which, like chains, they are bound, and they appear with them before the Righteous Judge and the whole world. And whatever they did in a secret place, or thought evil in their hearts, will all become known before all the angels and people. Then fornication and adultery will appear with the fornicator and adulterer, every theft and embezzlement with the thief and embezzler, their flattery and lying with the flatterer, liar, and cheat, all their cunning plans and hypocritical endeavors with the sly person, the evil person or the hypocrite, and all their abusive and pernicious words with the slanderer, foul-mouthed person, and gossip. In like manner, the evil deeds of each will appear with every guilty person. With every person in authority will be neglect of subordinates and their other transgressions: with a pastor, neglect of his flock and his other sins; with a judge, unjust trials and his other transgressions; with a master, the offenses and harm that he has caused to his servants and peasants, and his other transgressions. In a word, all his deeds, words, and impious thoughts, like complainants and accusers, will appear with every sinner at that Dread Trial, unless he is delivered from them here, in this world, by true repentance, heartfelt contrition, and tears. Then it will be said of every sinner: "Behold the man and his works! Behold the man, who was called a Christian, but did not do Christian works, was called a servant of God, but served the devil. Behold the man and his works!" O poor sinner! Woe will it be to you there, if you do not deliver yourself from these cruel complainants and accusers here, in this world! So try, beloved, ahead of time, now, to be delivered from them, lest they go with you into the next world. Free your soul from them, lest they surround you then and disgrace you. Give them up, and they will give up on you. Break away and depart from them, and they will break away and depart from you, and so you will be free from them. And repent for the things you have done and throw yourself down before the merciful eyes of Jesus, so that He may cleanse you from them by His Blood that He shed for you. Then you will be truly pure and free! "If the Son makes you free, you shall be free indeed" (John 8:36). "I am an image of Thine ineffable glory, though I bear the wounds of sin; take compassion on Thy creature, O Master, and cleanse me by Thy loving-kindness; and grant me the desired fatherland, making me again a dweller of paradise."[3]

One who is summoned to court is judged by a jury, is accused by witnesses, and endures a rebuke from the judges: they say you did such and such, broke such and such a law and decree, and so on. Thus will a poor sinner, not cleansed here by repentance of his sins and summoned to that Judgment, be judged by God, be exposed, and see his sins laid out before him and hear the rebuke from the Righteous Judge: "For thou hast hated correction, and hast cast My words behind thee. If thou sawest a thief, thou didst run with him, and hast been a partaker with the adulterer. Thy mouth hath embroidered evil, and thy tongue hath woven lies. Sitting, thou didst slander thy brother, and hast laid temptation on thine own mother's son" (Ps 49:17–20). And again: "I was hungry and you gave Me no food; I was thirsty and you gave

Me no drink; I was a stranger and you did not take Me in, naked and you did not clothe Me, sick and in prison and you did not visit Me" (Matt 25:42–43). Then will the Word of God said to the sinner in Holy Scripture come to pass: "I will reprove thee, and set thy sins before thy face" (Ps 49:21). Shame and fear will seize the one standing in court and being exposed. Likewise, shame beyond measure, fear, trembling, and terror will seize sinners at that Judgment. They will be exposed by God Himself, Whom they did not want to honor; they will be exposed for the ingratitude that they displayed to Him; they will be exposed before the whole world. The wrongdoer exposed in court is excluded from the number of good citizens and is considered a malefactor, and not a son of the homeland. Likewise, Christians who are wrongdoers and do not repent are excluded from the ranks of good Christians at that Judgment and, as the goats will be separated from the sheep, they will be considered unfaithful, and not faithful, false, and not true Christians. In court, the wrongdoer is condemned to death or another punishment as determined by the law. Likewise at that Judgment sinners will be condemned to eternal punishment. "Depart from Me, you cursed, into the everlasting fire prepared for the devil and his angels" (Matt 25:41). The criminal condemned to lawful punishment is separated from his kinsmen and friends at home and goes with inconsolable weeping to the punishment meted out to him. Likewise sinners, condemned at that Judgment to eternal punishment, are separated from God Himself, from His holy angels and God's chosen ones, and are separated for endless ages and will go with inconsolable weeping, trembling, terror, and endless despair into eternal torment. "And these will go away into everlasting punishment" (Matt 25:46). Poor sinner! Repent and wash away your sins by heartfelt contrition and tears, lest you suffer all this there. Have mercy, O Lord, have mercy on your creation! "Have mercy on me, O God, according to Thy great goodness, and according to the multitude of Thy mercies do away mine offenses. Turn Thy face away from my sins, and put out all my misdeeds" (Ps 50:3, 11). "If Thy shouldst mark iniquities, O Lord; Lord, who shall stand" (Ps 129:3). Turn Your face away from my sins, O Master, turn Your face to Christ, my Lord, Jesus Christ, Your only-begotten Son, Who for me, an unworthy and poor sinner, suffered and died, and for my sins offered Himself as a sacrifice and as an odor of sweet fragrance to You, His Heavenly Father and my Creator. And by His grace and love for mankind pour out Thy mercy on me and blot out all my transgressions and sins by His Blood, which was poured out for my sake!

# 42. A Person Covered with Wounds

In the world, we see that people have many and various diseases, and sometimes a person may be all covered with wounds and sores. What wounds and sores are to a person, sins and transgressions are to a sinful soul. A body is scathed and covered with wounds; the soul of a sinful person is scathed and covered with sins. It happens that bodily sores and wounds stink and fester. Likewise, the sores and wounds of sin stink and fester on the soul. The Psalmist says concerning this, "My wounds stink, and are corrupt, because of my foolishness" (Ps 37:6). It happens that a person is covered head to foot in sores and wounds. Likewise, a sinful soul, which abides in sins and compounds its sins, is covered in sores and wounds. This is spoken of in the prophet: "From the feet all the way to the head, there is no soundness in them" (Isa 1:6). The more bodily wounds and sores fester, the more they emit a stench. And the more a sinful soul sins, the more it is scathed and covered in wounds, and its scabs of sin are irritated, and from this a worse stench results. People see bodily wounds and sores and smell their stench. God sees the wound and sores of the soul. The stench of bodily wounds and sores are distressing and intolerable to people. The stench of wounds and sores on the soul are distressing and intolerable to God. People are revolted by bodily wounds and their stench. God is revolted by wounds on the soul, festering and stinking. It is terrible, beloved Christian, to be a person covered in wounds, wounds purulent and stinking, but it is even worse for the soul to be covered in its sinful and stinking wounds. The body is mortal and corruptible but the soul is immortal and incorruptible. If it is not healed from its wounds now, it will stand before the Judge in those wounds at that Judgment and will remain like that forever. A person covered with wounds, a beloved creation of God, created in God's image, having come into such a vile state, is worthy of tender feeling and pity. Sin is at fault for this. "O Lord, righteousness belongs to You, but shame of face belongs to us" (Dan 9:7). Turn your eyes from this disgrace to the soul that is stung by sins, as by wounds, and you will see a horrid spectacle worthy of even more pity and tender emotion. Its wounds and sores are pride, envy, malice, impurity, greed, etc. The longer it abides in them, the more it is wounded. The more it is wounded, the more its wounds fester and stink. Poor sinner! Enough of being wounded, and the wounds of your soul stinking and festering so! It is now time to be healed, time to apply the bandages of repentance to your sores and wounds. You heal your sick body, but your soul languishes from wounds and sores, and you do not care about this! O poor sinners! Let us run with faith to Jesus Christ, the Physician of souls and bodies, and not daring to approach Him because of our festering and stinking wounds; let us stand if even from a distance and from the depth of our hearts raise up the voice of the ten lepers to Him: "Jesus, Master, have mercy on us!" (Luke 17:12–13). There are no terrible wounds and sores, which He would not wish to and could not heal with one word, because He is all-powerful, merciful, and a friend of man. As the Gospel recounts, He healed mortal and corruptible bodies—would He not wish to cure immortal souls, which He came to save? He will indeed cure them if we come to Him with faith and fervently ask Him for healing. He sees our wounds and sores and wishes to heal them; for this He came into the world. But He wishes us to acknowledge before Him our sores that we have not been able to heal, which only He alone can heal. Heal me, O Lord, for I have sinned against Thee! "Heal me, O Lord, and I shall be healed. Save me, and I shall be saved … You are God my Savior! (Jer 17:14). "Lord, I am not worthy that You should come under my roof. But only speak a word, and my servant (my soul) will be healed" (Matt 8:8). "I am an image of Thine ineffable glory, though I bear the wounds of sin; take compassion on Thy creature, O Master, and cleanse me by Thy loving-kindness; and grant me the desired fatherland, making me again a dweller of paradise."[4]

When we see a person covered in sores or with some other fearsome disease, we pity him and sympathize with him. When we see a person covered in sins should we pity him and feel sympathy for him even more. For we have a common nature and common afflictions and sinfulness. If we feel sympathy and compassion for bodily human affliction, all the more should we feel sympathy and compassion for the affliction of the soul of our neighbor. If our neighbor's terrible bodily disease moves us to mercy, even more should his soul's disease move us to mercy and compassion. The soul is more honorable and more precious than the body. Therefore, its affliction and sinfulness are more terrible and dangerous than that of the body. The body, mortal and corruptible, decays in the earth, although it will be sound. The soul is immortal and will forever remain unhealed if it is not healed now. It is important to show sympathy and compassion to one covered in wounds and sores of the soul and who is adding the sores of sin to these sores. Why, then, O man, seeing your brother sinning, do you condemn him and do not pity one who is in extreme danger? You take pity on a suffering body; this is good and praiseworthy. Why then do you not take pity on a suffering soul but even judge and condemn it? It is better in such a case to sigh over our brother to the Lord and say: "Lord, have mercy and deliver him from this sinfulness, and restrain me from such by Thy all-powerful right hand." But turn your eyes on yourself, too, and into your own conscience. You will see that you too are covered with similar wounds, and perhaps, in ones that are greater and fouler still. That you judge and condemn your neighbor very much wounds and stings your soul and makes it foul and stinking in God's eyes: judging is the prerogative of the Son of God (see John 5:22); you are boldly arrogating this prerogative, even while still being a sinner. Why do you, a sinner and wounded one, despise, disparage, and judge another sinner who is wounded? You are no better than he is. He, you, I, and others are all equal, "for all have sinned and fall short of the glory of God" (Rom 3:23). Our enemy Satan has so wounded us that without God's help, we will only fall and be injured. "Remember us, O Lord, according to the favor that Thou bearest unto Thy people; O visit us with Thy salvation, that we may see the goodness of Thy chosen, and be glad in the gladness of Thy nation, and glory with Thine inheritance. We have sinned with our fathers; we have done amiss, and dealt wickedly. O God, be merciful unto us, and bless us; shine the light of Thy countenance upon us, and have mercy upon us, that Thy way may be known upon earth, Thy salvation among all nations" (Ps 105:4–6, 66:2–3).

# 43. A Blind Man Restrained

It happens that when a blind man walks by himself, he comes to a ditch or some other hazardous place where a serious accident can happen. Another person, seeing this and wishing to warn him against this threat, cries after him, "Come back! Don't go there!" or, taking him by the arm, leads him away from that dangerous place. Beloved Christian! Your brother and your neighbor, one of God's creations with you, created in the image of God and in His likeness, is walking like a blind man into the ditch of perdition when he transgresses. The fornicator and the adulterer are walking into the ditch of perdition. The irascible, the rememberer of wrongs, and the murderer are walking into the ditch of perdition; the thief, the swindler, and the usurer are walking into the ditch of perdition; the foul-mouth, the blasphemer, and he who talks foolishly are walking into the ditch of perdition; the slanderer, the backbiter, and the name-caller are walking into the ditch of perdition. Every wrongdoer is walking into the ditch of eternal perdition. He is walking like a blind man and may fall and not get out of it! Cry after him, beloved, when you see him walking, cry, "Brother! Don't go there!—a ditch has been dug in front of you into which you may fall and never get out." Take hold of him, beloved, take hold, before he falls! He is your brother; he is your neighbor, of your own nature, a human being like you, endowed with a rational soul, and walking into the ditch of perdition. Have mercy on him and retrieve him, if you can. He himself does not know where he is going. His eyes have been obscured by the enemy's delusion. You pity the blind man walking into a visible ditch, where only a temporal misfortune may occur. Much more should we pity a blind man who is heading into the ditch of eternal perdition. This action, although it is incumbent on every Christian, as Christian love demands, is especially incumbent on pastors, bishops and priests, and parents, civil authorities, and masters. For every ruler, if he is a Christian and is placed over Christians, is their shepherd. And he must, as much as it is possible, restrain the people entrusted to him who are heading for perdition and return them onto the path of salvation with the staff given him from God. Thus it is written of David, the King of Israel: "He chose David also His servant, and took him away from the sheepfolds. From the freshening ewes He took them, that he might tend Jacob his servant, and Israel his inheritance. And he tended them in the innocence of his heart, and guided them by the skillfulness of his hands" (Ps 77:70–72). Beloved pastors! The Lord entrusted you with His flock. Tend it and guard it against spiritual wolves. Parents! The Lord gave you children. Raise them in the fear of God. Instruct and admonish the youth inclined to evil to return. Civil authorities! The Lord placed you over His people and gave you a sword. Use it to cut every evil away from your subordinates. Masters! You must not only shear Christ's sheep but tend them. But what if the pastor and rulers, like a blind man, walk into the ditch of perdition, and drag along the people entrusted to them? "If therefore the light that is in you is darkness, how great is that darkness!" (Matt 6:23). O Most Good and Merciful God! Turn away this evil from Israel. "Hear, O Thou Shepherd of Israel, … O remember not our old sins; but let Thy mercy overtake us, for we have come to great poverty. Help us, O God our Saviour, for the glory of Thy Name; O Lord, deliver us, and wash away our sins, for Thy Name's sake, lest the nations say, Where is now their God? … O Lord God of Hosts! convert us; show the light of Thy countenance, and we shall be saved" (Ps 79:2; 78:8–10; 79:4 LXX).

# 44. A Tall Tree in the Midst of Short Trees

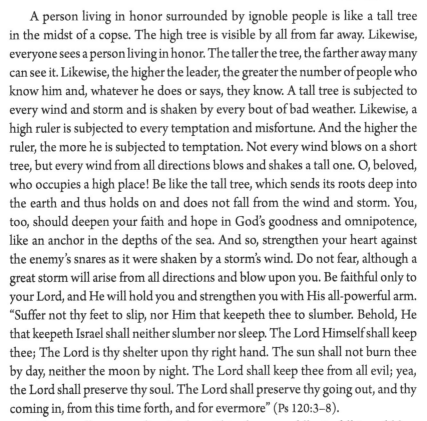

A person living in honor surrounded by ignoble people is like a tall tree in the midst of a copse. The high tree is visible by all from far away. Likewise, everyone sees a person living in honor. The taller the tree, the farther away many can see it. Likewise, the higher the leader, the greater the number of people who know him and, whatever he does or says, they know. A tall tree is subjected to every wind and storm and is shaken by every bout of bad weather. Likewise, a high ruler is subjected to every temptation and misfortune. And the higher the ruler, the more he is subjected to temptation. Not every wind blows on a short tree, but every wind from all directions blows and shakes a tall one. O, beloved, who occupies a high place! Be like the tall tree, which sends its roots deep into the earth and thus holds on and does not fall from the wind and storm. You, too, should deepen your faith and hope in God's goodness and omnipotence, like an anchor in the depths of the sea. And so, strengthen your heart against the enemy's snares as it were shaken by a storm's wind. Do not fear, although a great storm will arise from all directions and blow upon you. Be faithful only to your Lord, and He will hold you and strengthen you with His all-powerful arm. "Suffer not thy feet to slip, nor Him that keepeth thee to slumber. Behold, He that keepeth Israel shall neither slumber nor sleep. The Lord Himself shall keep thee; The Lord is thy shelter upon thy right hand. The sun shall not burn thee by day, neither the moon by night. The Lord shall keep thee from all evil; yea, the Lord shall preserve thy soul. The Lord shall preserve thy going out, and thy coming in, from this time forth, and for evermore" (Ps 120:3–8).

When a tall tree standing in the midst of a copse falls, its fall is audible a long way off, and it crushes many shorter trees standing near it. Likewise, when a pastor or other leader falls into serious sin, his fall will be heard from far away, and many will be scandalized. It is impossible, truly impossible, for the falls of a pastor or leader to be kept secret, no matter how hard they try to conceal them. Their fall will be heard afar off, like tall trees that have fallen. He did this or that. Who? A bishop or priest, governor or provincial leader, a prince or king, or some other ruler, or the householder at home. A father falls, and his children know about it. A master falls, and his servants know about it. A pastor falls, and his people know. A Judge falls, and everyone knows. A king falls, and everywhere this is heard of. Thus, David, the king of Israel fell, and all knew of it. Although he tried in every way to hide his fall, it spread everywhere so that the whole world learned of it. We see the same now. Authorities fall even now, and everyone learns of their fall. O, beloved, whom God placed in a high place! Avoid falls with all your strength, take heart, and be strong, lest you fall, and having fallen, you bring down others with you, as a tall tree does the short trees. "Therefore let him who thinks he stands take heed lest he fall" (1 Cor 10:12). And if you fall, do not tarry, but quickly get up and correct yourself. And then the fall will be recompensed by that rising and correction. David fell, but then he got up. And, as we see in his psalms, he made amends for his fall by repentance and warm tears. You should imitate this king of Israel, beloved. Stand aright and your fall will be covered. The Prophet Nathan was sent to him from God. And David himself, who fell and arose, and by his arising and correction teaches you how to get up and correct yourself, is sent to you. O you, Christ's sheep, who live in simplicity and humility! Do not let your soul grow faint, beloved, when you hear of the fall of a pastor or other kind of leader. He has the same kind of infirmity as other people but, as was said before, is subjected to greater and more numerous temptations than others. In visible warfare, the enemy tries to wound and bring down no one more than the commanders of the army. Likewise, the enemy of Christian souls, the devil, tries to cause to fall no one as much as pastors and other Christian leaders. All his efforts are directed toward injuring and infecting the pastor and Christian leader who may bring benefit to others. To injure, I say, and to infect, so that he could not bring benefit, but also so that he himself would go to perdition and bring others with him. So beloved Christian, shun judging the fall of a superior, although you know of it for sure. Shun much more exposing his fall to others and spreading temptation by gossip. May you not become like Ham, the son of Noah, who made known the shame of his father to others. It is better to conceal by your silence, as did Shem and Japheth, the sons of the same Noah, who, walking backward, covered the shame of their father. And know besides that many false rumors are spread about pastors and Christian authorities, and this is an action of the common enemy of all, the devil, for the spreading of temptation, and to cause every disorder and confusion in Christian society.

# 45. A Sensible Head

The pastor and leader in Christian society is what the head is to the body. When the body has a sensible head, the whole body is in good condition. Likewise, when Christian society has a sensible pastor and leader, that society is in good condition. Fortunate is the body that has a sensible head. Likewise, blessed is that Christian flock that has a sensible, good, and vigorous pastor. Blessed is that kingdom in which a sensible and good king reigns. Blessed is that city and country governed by a sensible and good ruler. Blessed are those servants overseen by a sensible master. Blessed are those children who have a sensible and good father. Blessed is every house that has a sensible and good householder. Everything, both happiness and unhappiness, in every society depends on the ruler, as the whole of the body depends on the head. Oh, beloved pastor and every authority figure! You are the light of the Christian society. All people look to you, at what you do and what you say, as everyone looks at a candle burning in the night. Be a light, so that those looking to you may be enlightened. Be like a mirror, looking into which people wipe away the blemishes on their faces. Be like the sensible head on a body. If you are sensible and good, all of Christian society subordinate to you will be blessed and you will be most blessed: "If ... the light that is in you is darkness, how great is that darkness" (Matt 6:23). And if the lamp goes out, then what will give light to those in darkness? And if the mirror becomes clouded, how will people see their blemishes? Beloved, be sensible and good, that you may gain blessedness both for yourself and for God's people. "Let your light so shine before men, that they may see your good works and glorify your Father in heaven" (Matt 5:16), Christ the Lord tells us. And inasmuch as all the blessedness of Christian society depends on sensible and good pastors and authority figures, you, the people named after Christ, should not cease praying to Christ, the common Master of all, so that He might teach and admonish pastors and other Christian authority figures, for this is your blessedness. "Therefore I exhort first of all that supplications, prayers, intercessions, and giving of thanks be made for all men, for kings and all who are in authority, that we may lead a quiet and peaceable life in all godliness and reverence" (1 Tim 2:1-2).

## 46. Desire

We see that people desire many things in the world, and what they yearn for, they seek. But let people desire and seek whatever they want. Christian! You should desire and seek your own, that is, whatever is proper and necessary. People desire to have happiness and prosperity in this world. You should desire and seek to have true piety in your heart. This is Christian desire! People desire to be freed from toil and be free. You should wish to be freed from sin and its toil. That is Christian desire! This is true freedom! "Whoever commits sin is a slave of sin ... if the Son makes you free, you shall be free indeed" (John 8:34, 36). People desire to master other people. You should desire to master yourself. This is Christian desire! This is a most glorious victory! People desire to be masters and to rule others. You should desire and endeavor to exercise dominion over your flesh and to rule it. This is Christian desire! This is true dominion! People desire to reign over people. You should desire and endeavor to reign over your passions and lusts. This is Christian desire! The true king is the one who is master of himself and his passions. "Those who are Christ's have crucified the flesh with its passions and desires" (Gal 5:24). There you have it, masters, sovereigns, and kings! Lord, help us! People desire to take vengeance on their enemies and return offense for offense. You, Christian, should desire and endeavor to yield to your enemies and to repay their offense with good works. This is Christian desire! This is the revenge of true Christians! "If your enemy is hungry, feed him; If he is thirsty, give him a drink; For in so doing you will heap coals of fire on his head. Do not be overcome by evil, but overcome evil with good" (Rom 12:20–21). People desire to have a healthy body. You should desire and endeavor for your soul to be healed and to be healthy. This is Christian desire! This is the health to be desired. People desire to speak and to converse with people. You should desire and endeavor to be silent more than you speak, so that you avoid sin. This is Christian desire! People desire to speak beautifully and fluently. You should desire to live beautifully and in a Christian manner. This is Christian desire! People desire to receive from people. You, Christian, should desire and endeavor to give to people, remembering the word of the Lord Jesus, for He Himself says, "'It is more blessed to give than to receive'" (Acts 20:35). People desire to live in a beautiful and luxurious house. You should desire and endeavor to live "in the house of God, which is the church of the living God and be fellow citizens with the saints and members of the household of God" (1 Tim 3:15; Eph 2:19). This is Christian desire! This is a splendid and palatial house. "Lord, who shall dwell in Thy tabernacle? Or who shall rest upon Thy holy hill? Even he that walketh blameless, and doeth the thing which is right, that speaketh the truth in his heart. He that hath used no deceit in his tongue, nor done evil to his neighbor, and hath not reproached his friend. He that setteth not by thee evil-doer, and maketh much of them that fear the Lord; He that sweareth unto his neighbor, and disappointed him not. He that hath not given his money upon usury, nor taken a bribe against the innocent; whoso doeth these things shall never fall" (Ps 14:1–5). "One thing have I desired of the Lord, which I will require; even that I may dwell in the house of the Lord all the days of my life" (Ps 26:4). "Lord, I have loved the beauty of Thy house, and the dwelling-place of Thy glory. O destroy not my soul with the ungodly, nor my life with the blood-thirsty; In whose hand is wickedness, and their right hand is full of bribes. But as for me, I have walked innocently; deliver me, O Lord, and have mercy upon me" (Ps 25:8–11). "I have preferred to be a doorkeeper in the house of my God, than to dwell in the tents of sinners" (Ps 83:11). People desire to wear beautiful and rich clothing. You should desire and endeavor to "put on tender mercies, kindness, humility, meekness, longsuffering" (Col 3:12) and so forth. This is Christian desire! This is the splendid Christian clothing! The Christian soul is adorned with these ornaments like a king's daughter. People desire to satiate their bellies. You should desire and endeavor to satiate your soul with the Word of God and with good and holy thoughts. This is Christian desire! This is the very sweet Christian food of the soul! People desire sweet and expensive wine. You should desire tears and spiritual lamentation, so that your heart may rejoice in God your Saviour. This is Christian desire! This is the sweet wine of the saints. Whoever wants to have true joy must beforehand weep much. People desire to have friendship with the exalted and famous of this world. You should desire and endeavor to have friendship with Christ and His saints. This is Christian desire! This is an excellent and most sweet alliance. "He who is joined to the Lord is one spirit with Him" (1 Cor 6:17). "'You are My friends if you do whatever I command you,' the Lord says" (John 15:14). Friendship is mutual love. Christ has loved you, and you should love Him, and there will be a friendship. "It is good for me to cleave unto God" (Ps 72:28). People desire to receive the king into their house. You should desire and endeavor to receive the King of Heaven, Jesus Christ, into the house of your heart. "If anyone loves Me, he will keep My word; and My Father will love him, and We will come to him and make Our home with him" (John 14:23). Oh, blessed is that heart in which dwells the Trihypostatic God! The Kingdom of God abides there, a paradise of sweetness and joy abides there. "Behold, I stand at the door and knock. If anyone hears My voice and opens the door, I will come in to him and dine with him, and he with Me" (Rev 3:20). Oh, Jesus, Pastor and Visitor of our souls! Do not pass by me, Your sinful servant, and let me hear Your voice, for it is sweet, and Your coming is salvific and peaceful. "My heart is ready, O God, my heart is ready" (Ps 107:2). People desire to have powerful persons as protectors and mentors. You should desire and endeavor to have God as your Mentor and Protector. This is Christian desire! This is a faithful Mentor and Protector! "O God, make speed to save me; O Lord make haste to help me. Thou art my helper; unto Thee will I sing, for Thou, O God, art my defender, and my merciful God" (Ps 69:2, 58:18). People desire to have riches in this world. You should desire and endeavor to grow rich in good deeds. These are the true Christian riches! People desire to have glory and praise in this world. You should desire and endeavor to avoid this, and you will have true glory. This is Christian desire! This is true glory and praise—to despise the glory and praise of the world. People desire to know much and to appear wise. But you should most of all desire and endeavor to get to know yourself. This is Christian wisdom! People desire to know what is happening somewhere or other. You should desire and endeavor to consider what is happening in your soul; what condition it is in; what thoughts, desires, and undertakings it gives birth to; which it aspires to—eternity or temporality? Where does it store its treasure—in heaven or on earth? Which is it joined to—God or the world? This is essential and vital knowledge! "For where your treasure is, there your heart will be also. The lamp of the body is the eye. If therefore your eye is good, your whole body will be full of light. But if your eye is bad, your whole body will be full of darkness. If therefore the light that is in you is darkness, how great is that darkness!" (Matt 6:21–23). People desire to please others. You should desire and endeavor to please the Lord your God. "For if I still pleased men, I would not be a bondservant of Christ" (Gal 1:10). "But this is also written: Let each of us please his neighbor for his good, leading to edification" (Rom 15:2). And when we thus please men, we please God, Who ordered us to do this. People desire to soothe the body. You should desire and endeavor to soothe and appease your conscience and your mind from evil and vain thoughts. This is Christian desire. This is God-pleasing rest and Christian tranquility. People desire bodily strength and power. You should desire strength and power for your soul. This is Christian desire. This is true strength—to be immovable in temptations, in troubles and misfortunes. "Thou, O Lord, of Thy favor hast given power to my goodness" (Ps 29:8). "The Lord shall give strength unto His people; the Lord shall bless His people with peace" (Ps 28:11). "The Lord is my strength, and my song, and is become my salvation" (Ps 117:14). "Therefore most gladly I will rather boast in my infirmities, that the power of Christ may rest upon me" (2 Cor 12:9). People desire to live long. You, Christian, should wish to die blessedly. "Lord, remember me when You come into Your kingdom" (Luke 23:42). "Be Thou also my guide, and my provider, for Thy Name's sake. Thou shalt draw me out of this net that they laid privily for me; for Thou art my protector, O Lord. Into Thy hands will I commend my spirit" (Ps 30:4–6). "My soul shall live, and shall praise Thee, and Thy judgments shall help me" (Ps 118:175). "Blessed be the Lord, Who hath not given us over for a prey unto their teeth. Our soul escaped even as a bird out of the snare of the fowler; the snare was broken, and we were delivered" (Ps 123:6–7). People desire to be in favor with the King, princes, and great lords. You, Christian, should desire and endeavor to be in favor with God, the Almighty, the Heavenly King. "O put not your trust in princes, in the sons of men, in whom there is no salvation" (Ps 145:3). "But ye shall die like men, and like one of the princes shall ye fall" (Ps 81:7). "O Lord, Thy mercy is for ever; despise not the works of Thy hands" (Ps 137:8). "Let Thy mercy, O Lord, be upon us, according as we have put our trust in Thee" (Ps 32:22). "It is better to trust in the Lord, than to put any confidence in man. It is better to trust in the Lord, than to put any confidence in princes" (Ps 117:8–9). People desire to see the King or a high-ranking personage. You, Christian, should above all else desire and endeavor to see God. This is the consummation of all desires! "For what have I in heaven, and what have I desired upon earth from Thee? My flesh and my heart have failed, O God of my heart, but Thou art my portion, O God, for ever" (Ps 72:25–26). "Like as the hart panteth after the water-brooks, so longeth my soul after Thee, O God. My soul hath thirsted for the mighty living God; when shall I come and appear before God's face" (Ps 41:2–3)? "The God of gods shall appear in Zion" (Ps 83:8). "For now we see in a mirror, dimly, but then face to face" (1 Cor 13:12). "We shall see Him as He is" (1 John 3:2). "Pursue peace with all people, and holiness, without which no one will see the Lord" (Heb 12:14). "Blessed are the pure in heart, For they shall see God" (Matt 5:8). This, beloved Christian, is the desire of the Christian soul! These are the sighing's and inner impulses of the Christian who cares about his salvation. What one fervently desires, he intently seeks and acquires. "Ask, and it will be given to you; seek, and you will find; knock, and it will be opened to you. For everyone who asks receives, and he who seeks finds, and to him who knocks it will be opened" (Matt 7:7–8). You should desire, my soul, and seek your own good, your health, your wealth, your rest and peace, etc. "Thou hast heard the desire of the poor, O Lord; Thine ear hearkeneth unto the disposition of their hearts" (Ps 9:38). "Lord, all my desire is before Thee, and my lamentation is not hid from Thee. My heart is troubled; my strength hath failed me, and the light of mine eyes, even that is gone from me, and so forth. Forsake me not, O Lord my God, be not far from me. Attend unto my help, O Lord of my salvation" (Ps 37:10–11, 22–23)!

## 47. Happiness

When they receive something that they desire, people are called happy. Likewise, a Christian is happy when he has that which he desires and seeks after. Happy are those people who are freed from slavery, or from prison, or from exile, or from captivity. The Christian is happy when he has been freed from the sins by which he had been bound as with chains and from slavery to the devil. Happiness for people is that they have a healthy body. Christian happiness is to have a healthy soul. Those soldiers are called happy who gain a victory over their enemies. Happy indeed is that Christian who is victorious over himself. Many consider it happiness that they have managed to take vengeance on their enemies. Happiness for the Christian is not vengeance: he does not repay evil for evil (see Rom 12:17). An even greater happiness is when he loves them and does good to them. Then he is a true son of the Heavenly Father, Who "makes His sun rise on the evil and on the good, and sends rain on the just and on the unjust" (Matt 5:44–45). Happiness for people is that they receive and gather much from others. Happy indeed is that Christian who from everything he has sets aside something for his neighbors. "Blessed are the merciful, For they shall obtain mercy" (Matt 5:7). "A good man showeth compassion and giveth, He will guide his words with discretion, For he shall never be moved" (Ps 111:5). Happiness for people is to be rich and famous in this world. For the Christian, happiness is to grow rich in good works and to despise the glory of this world. Happiness for people is to exercise dominion and reign over other people. The Christian is happy when he exercises dominion and reigns over himself, over his flesh, over his passions and lusts, and he commands them. There in truth is a master, king, and sovereign! Many people exercise dominion and reign over people but are themselves servants to sin and captives of their passions. Truly most glorious is the king and master who is in command of his own passions and lusts! Happiness for people is to lay a sumptuous table and to be sated at it. Happiness for the Christian is to hear the Word of God within one's heart and to gratify, comfort, and gladden one's soul with it. This is the sumptuous table, the most glorious and most sweet supper of the Christian soul. Happy is he who lives in the joy and gladness of this world. For the Christian, happiness is if he has sorrow in God and weeps for his sins. "Blessed are those who mourn, for they shall be comforted" (Matt 5:4). Happiness for people is when a person lives in a beautiful and palatial house. For the Christian, happiness is if he is truly within God's Church, if he is a true son of the Church, a companion of the saints, a member of the household of God, and a spiritual member of Christ. "Blessed are they that dwell in Thy house, for ever and ever will they praise Thee" (Ps 83:5). Happiness for people is to have powerful fellows as protectors and helpers. For the Christian, happiness is to have God as a Protector and Helper. "Blessed is the man whose help is from Thee. Blessed is he that hath the God of Jacob for his helper, whose hope is in the Lord his God, Who made heaven and earth, the sea and all that therein is, Who preserveth truth forever; Who rendereth judgment for the wronged, who giveth food unto the hungry" (Ps 83:6, 145:5–7). Happiness for people is to be strong in body and valiant in battle. For the Christian, happiness is if he is strong in soul, immovable and unvanquished in battle with the devil, and unbending in temptations, troubles, and misfortunes caused by him. This is Christian strength and nobility! This is a valiant soldier of Christ! Thou art my strength, O Lord, and Thou art my power, and so forth. With You, I can do everything. Without you, I can do nothing. "I can do all things through Christ who strengthens me" (Phil 4:13). Beloved Christian! Let people flourish in the happiness of this world. You will be happy enough when you have happiness within yourself. And this is the true, immovable, and inalienable happiness! Let people know much outside of themselves! You are happy enough when you know yourself and what is within you, even if you know nothing else. Let people show off their bodily health. You are happy enough when you have health of the soul, even if you are unwell in body. Let people abound in perishable wealth. You are happy enough when you bear piety and a treasury of virtues within you. Let people boast of their protectors and helpers: I, they say, have as my protector such and such a prince and lord; these men help me in my troubles and misfortunes. You are happy enough when God is your Helper and Protector. Let people show their freedom and nobility. You are happy enough when you have Christian nobility and a soul free from sins, even if you are in thrall to people or are imprisoned, or have been sent into exile, or are in captivity. Let people boast that they are in favor with the king, or lord, or prince. You will be very happy if you are honored to be in favor with God, the Heavenly King, even if none of the people hold you in favor. The favor of God alone will be more than the favor of the whole world for you. Let people live in beautiful palaces and mansions. You are happy enough when you live in the house of God, which is the Church of the Living God, and you are the companion of the saints and a member of the household of God, and a member of the family of Christ, even if you live in a hut or a cave, or have no place to lay your head. Let people be nourished and be satiated with a rich and sweet table. You are sufficiently happy when your soul is nourished and is satiated by God's voice, and is consoled by heavenly, holy, and spiritual thoughts, even if you eat only bread and water to ease your bodily infirmities. Let people boast of the power of their physical strength. You are sufficiently happy when your soul stands unmoving against the snares and temptations of the devil, even if you have no bodily strength. Let people dress in silken and beautiful clothing. You are sufficiently happy when your soul is adorned in the grace of Christ, faith, hope, love, and other spiritual ornaments, even if you are dressed in tatters. Let people boast that they are friends with the powerful and renowned of this world. You are happy and renowned enough when you have become friends with Christ, the Son of God, and have "fellowship ... with the Father and with His Son Jesus Christ" (1 John 1:3), even if you have no one as a friend, and so on. This is true happiness and real blessedness, which neither fire, nor water, nor prison, nor exile, nor captivity, not guile, nor human malice, nor death can take away. "If God is for us, who can be against us" (Rom 8:31)? A person carries this blessedness always and everywhere with him, for it is within him. "For indeed, the kingdom of God is within you" (Luke 17:21). "For the kingdom of God is not eating and drinking, but righteousness and peace and joy in the Holy Spirit" (Rom 14:17). The Christian departs for the next world with this blessedness and carries it with him from this world and brings it into his heavenly Homeland. He comes from blessedness into the most perfect, eternal blessedness, where he will be completely blessed in soul and body. Oh, truly the real Christian blessedness, truly a most precious happiness! What use is it to a person to be happy in the world, but not to have Christian happiness? What use is it to be healthy in the body, but to have an enfeebled soul? The sign of an enfeebled soul is depravity. What use is it to boast of nobility and bodily freedom, but to be a slave of sin and passions? "Whoever commits sin is a slave of sin" (John 8:34). "By whom a person is overcome, by him also he is brought into bondage" (2 Pet 2:19). What use is it to know much outside of yourself but not to know yourself? Poor person! Endeavor first to get to know yourself and then you will know much. What use is it to grow rich in corruptible matter but to be destitute in soul? That rich man is poor who grows rich in corruptible silver and gold but is destitute in virtue. What use is it to live in a luxurious and beautiful house but to be outside the house of God, the holy Church, like an outcast? What use is it to govern people to one who cannot rule himself? People! Learn first to govern yourself and then you will successfully rule other people. What use is it to adorn the corruptible body when the immortal soul is laid bare and covered with shabby, sinful rags? Foolish man! Leave alone the mortal body—dust, earth, and ashes, and adorn your immortal soul. And then you will have beauty—true and incorruptible—within yourself.

Christian! In this world, happiness is common both for the ungodly and for the pious but especially for the former. Who but the ungodly live mostly in worldly happiness? About them it is written, "For there is no fear in their death, and they are steadfast under the knout. They are not in the labor of other folk, neither are they plagued like other men" (Ps 72:4–5). But spiritual happiness is characteristic of true Christians alone. Have true piety within yourself, and then you will have true happiness, if only within yourself, but inalienable, and incomparably better than worldly happiness. "And as many as walk according to this rule, peace and mercy be upon them, and upon the Israel of God" (Gal 6:16). This offers consolation to people who are pious but unfortunate according to this world, that is, (1) the infirm. You, dear sufferers, should not lose heart. Although your body is wasting away, your holy souls are being cured and are receiving their health. "Even though our outward man is perishing, yet the inward man is being renewed day by day" (2 Cor 4:16). Here you are suffering with the pauper Lazarus, but you will inherit the bosom of Abraham with him (see Luke 16:22). (2) Servants and peasants under the command of masters. You, Christ's humble and meek sheep, should derive your consolation from the fact that, although you are called the servants of people, you are the free people of Christ. You work with your body for people, but your souls are free from slavery to sin. You do not have freedom and nobility as your masters do, but your souls are adorned with Christian freedom and nobility. Rejoice and be glad, for the inheritance of the sons of God awaits you. (3) The poor and wretched. You, servants of Christ living in scarcity and poverty, should not despair when you see others living in plenty. They shall leave behind whatever they have. "Be not thou afraid, though a man be made rich, or though the glory of his house be increased; for when he dieth, he shall carry nothing away, neither shall his pomp follow him" (Ps 48:17–18). You do not have corruptible gold, silver, or other matter, but within yourself, you bear an incorruptible treasure. Be happy with this. You do not live in palatial houses but are members of the household of God, of the family of Christ, and companions of the saints. Be happy with this. Wear rags on your body, but your holy souls are garbed in the clothing of salvation. You do not have the good things of this world, but good things are hidden up for you in heaven: "Eye has not seen, nor ear heard, Nor have entered into the heart of man The things which God has prepared for those who love Him" (1 Cor 2:9). Remember Christ's poverty: "For you know the grace of our Lord Jesus Christ, that though He was rich, yet for your sakes He became poor, that you through His poverty might become rich" (2 Cor 8:9). (4) Those mocked and ridiculed by the world. You who are trampled upon by the world like dirt receive in your heart a word of consolation. Let the world do to you as it wishes—you are Christ's. This is a great glory and praise—to be Christ's, Who is the Lord of glory! "In the Lord shall my soul be praised" (Ps 33:3). The world derides you, disparages you, and berates you, but your souls are precious for God. The world condemns you, but God vindicates you. The world curses you, but God blesses you. "They shall curse, yet Thou shalt bless" (Ps 108:28 LXX). The world spurns you as worthless, but God accepts you. "O God, be not silent of my praise, For the mouth of the ungodly, yea, the mouth of the deceitful is opened upon me, and they have spoken against me with a false tongue; They compassed me about also with words of hatred, and fought against me without a cause. Instead of the love that I had unto them, they would defame me, but I gave myself unto prayer. And they rewarded me evil for good, and hatred for my love" (Ps 108:1–4). Remember that Christ, our Head and the Lord of glory, was scorned, disparaged, derided, and berated by the evil world. "A servant is not greater than his master" (John 13:16). "If they have called the master of the house Beelzebub, how much more will they call those of his household" (Matt 10:25)? "Blessed are you when they revile and persecute you, and say all kinds of evil against you falsely for My sake. Rejoice and be exceedingly glad, for great is your reward in heaven" (Matt 5:11–12). (5) Those in prison. You, Christ's beloved sufferers, should endure your sufferings. Your body is imprisoned, but your spirit is free. Your hands and feet are bound, but your holy souls are released by Christ's grace. You do not see the sunlight, but the Divine light within enlightens you. Remember, O fellow-sufferers and partners of

Christ's martyrs and confessors, that Christ, our Lord, was bound because of our sins. After this prison, you will reign with Christ, with Whom you are suffering. "We suffer with Him, that we may also be glorified together ... The sufferings of this present time are not worthy to be compared with the glory which shall be revealed in us" (Rom 8:17–18). (6) Those in exile. You, exiles and wanderers, should remember Christ's saying: "And everyone who has left houses or brothers or sisters or father or mother or wife or children or lands, for My name's sake, shall receive a hundredfold, and inherit eternal life" (Matt 19:29). You are separated from your home, from your father and other beloved relatives and friends, but you are not separated from God and His holy house. They have abandoned you, but God has not. He is even in exile with you, and He is everything for you. Remember also that for pious souls living in this world, any place is exile. You live in this world as did the Jews during the Babylonian captivity. They sat down and wept remembering Zion, their Homeland (see Ps 136:1). So also every pious soul in this world, as by the waters of Babylon, sits and weeps, remembering his beloved heavenly Homeland and the Jerusalem on high. There is no true home and homeland in this world for the pious soul, but everywhere there is banishment and exile. Be patient, beloved, and wait until the Lord calls you out of this world, as from Babylon, into the Jerusalem on high. Then you will see your home and your homeland, but now a heavenly, eternal, blessed one. "Your heart will rejoice, and your joy no one will take from you" (John 16:22). "Turn our captivity, O Lord, as the streams in the south" (Ps 125:4). (7) All the pious who have ever suffered should lift up the eyes of their hearts to the mansions of the heavenly Father and consider those holy inhabitants. You will see no one there who has not gotten there by the path of sorrows. And you will hear from there a voice bearing witness to them: "These are the ones who come out of the great tribulation, and washed their robes and made them white in the blood of the Lamb. Therefore they are before the throne of God, and serve Him day and night in His temple. And He who sits on the throne will dwell among them. They shall neither hunger anymore nor thirst anymore; the sun shall not strike them, nor any heat; for the Lamb who is in the midst of the throne will shepherd them and lead them to living fountains of waters. And God will wipe away every tear from their eyes" (Rev 7:14–17). "But let none of you suffer as a murderer, a thief, an evildoer, or as a busybody in other people's matters. Yet if anyone suffers as a Christian, let him not be ashamed, but let him glorify God in this matter" (1 Pet 4:15–16).

# 48. A Burning Candle

Man! Your life is as a burning candle. The longer the candle burns, the shorter it becomes. So with you—the longer you live, the shorter the remainder of your life grows. The candle burns down and goes out. So also a person finishes his life and dies. When a candle goes out, it seems that it had not existed. Like this, when a person dies and is buried, it seems that he also did not exist. You see, Christian, what is a person and what is his life. Remember that so also your life will be extinguished, just as a candle you see going out. Prepare for your death beforehand, so that you may die a blessed death. "O Lord, tell me mine end, and the number of my days, what it is, that I may know what is wanting to me. Behold, Thou hast made my days as it were a span long, and my existence is as nothing before Thee; verily, every man living is altogether vanity. Therefore man walketh as a shadow, and disquieteth himself in vain; he heapeth up riches, and knoweth not for whom he gathereth them" (Ps 38:5–7).

# 49. A Sword Hanging over a Head

If anyone sat or stood in a certain place and over his head was hanging a sharp sword on a slender thread, everyone would have the opinion that he was in great danger, for in such a case certain death would be hanging over him. And everyone, seeing a person in such danger, would call him away from that place. The sword of Divine justice and anger hangs over every unrepentant sinner. It hangs over the fornicator and adulterer; it hangs over the thief and extortioner. It hangs over the slanderer and name-caller. It hangs over the ruler who seeks his own filthy lucre, and not the common good. It hangs over the pastor who does not care for the perishing rational sheep, who were redeemed by the blood of Christ. It hangs over bribe-taking judges who pass judgment influenced by bribes and partiality, and not according to the facts. It hangs over the master who torments his peasants like beasts or oppresses them with excessive quitrents or labor. It hangs over parents who do not teach their children the fear of God but, by their lawless life, tempt and corrupt them and spread out the path to perdition to those washed and saved by the laver of regeneration. Finally, it hangs over every wrongdoer who capriciously and fearlessly dares to break God's law. "The wrath of God is revealed from heaven against all ungodliness and unrighteousness of men" (Rom 1:18). It hangs, I say, and the moment it falls, nothing other than eternal death will follow for that poor sinner. God's wrath fell thus on the sodomites, and they perished. It fell on pharaoh, whose heart had been hardened, and he sank in the sea, like lead, with all his army. It fell on the impious Israelites in the deserts and destroyed them. "The heavy wrath of God came upon them, and slew the fattest of them" (Ps 77:31). Ah, poor sinner! A sharp sword hangs over you and threatens you with nothing other than death. And if you do not get out of the way, it will fall on you. Move, please move, lest it fall and strike you, and "will cut [you] in two and appoint [you] his portion with the hypocrites" (Matt 24:51). In His goodness, God is still showing His long suffering toward you, so correct yourself, while He is showing His long suffering! He has been patient up to this point, but whether He will be patient henceforward, I do not know. Get off, beloved, please quickly get off the path of the ungodly, over which the sword of God's anger is hanging, before it falls on them and you. "O man! Do you despise the riches of His goodness, forbearance, and longsuffering, not knowing that the goodness of God leads you to repentance" (Rom 2:4)? "Blessed is the man that hath not walked in the counsel of the ungodly, nor stood in the way of sinners, and hath not sat in the seat of the scornful" (Ps 1:1).

When a person evades the aforesaid danger, he walks freely and in safety. So too, the sinner, when he turns to God with his whole heart, leaves the path of the ungodly, and begins to live in true repentance, is now free from God's fitting anger. Now, instead of God's anger, he awaits God's mercy and hopes on it. God's Judgment and anger do not fall on repentant sinners, for God wishes and awaits from us that we turn to Him and repent. God's anger hung like this over the Ninevites, but when they turned and repented, God's anger did not fall on them, but instead of anger, they experienced the mercy of God. "And God saw their works, that they turned from their evil ways. And God had a change of heart about the evil which He said he would do to them, and did not do it" (John 3:10). "I will hear what the Lord God will say concerning me; for He shall speak peace unto his people, and to His saints, and to them that turn their hearts unto Him" (Ps 84:9). Every repentant heart will receive these words of peace. Oh, blessed indeed is that person who, leaving the path of the ungodly, finds himself in a state of true repentance. Of such a one "there is joy in the presence of the angels of God over one sinner who repents" (Luke 15:10). If, by the grace of God you make progress

toward this good cause, Christian, stand and persevere, beloved, in this to
the end and in the next world you will make your home with the angels, and
with them you will glorify the all-good God forever. Begin and end well, and
you will be blessed. The Lord tells you: "His salvation is nigh them that fear
Him" (Ps 84:10). "Be faithful until death, and I will give you the crown of
life" (Rev 2:10).

## 50. A Net

In this world, we see that fishermen throw their nets into the water and
spread them out in order to catch fish. In this way, the devil with his demons
has spread various nets for us, O Christian. He has spread them at home, he
has spread them on the way, he has spread them in cities and villages, he has
spread them in the desert, and he has spread them on the land and at sea. He
has hidden the nets in food, in drink, in sensuality. He has hidden the nets in
honor and in wealth. He has hidden the nets in conversations and in silence.
He has hidden the nets in vision and hearing—he has hidden them to catch us
for our perdition. He has as many machinations and ruses against us as he has
pernicious nets, and as many dangers, calamities, and misfortunes of ours as
he has ruses and machinations. Oh, who can recognize these hidden nets and
be delivered from them? There are many and varied nets, they are everywhere,
hidden and invisible, nets for our affliction and ruin! Who can see them and
avoid them, if You, O Lord, do not reveal them and by Your all-powerful right
hand save us from them? "Be sober, be vigilant; because your adversary the
devil walks about like a roaring lion, seeking whom he may devour" (1 Pet
5:8). "Whoso dwelleth in the help of the Most High shall abide in the shelter
of the God of heaven. He will say unto the Lord, Thou art my defender, and
my refuge, my God, and I will trust in Him. For He shall deliver thee from the
snare of the hunter" (Ps 90:1–3). "For unto Thee, Lord, O Lord, are mine eyes;
in Thee have I put my trust; O take not my soul away. Keep me from the snare
that they have laid for me, and from the traps of them that do wickedness"
(Ps 140:8–9). "In this way wherein I walked have they privily laid a snare for
me. I looked upon my right and saw: and there was no man that would know
me; I had no place to flee unto, and there was no one looking out for my soul.
I cried unto Thee, O Lord; I said, Thou art my hope; Thou art my portion
in the land of the living. Consider my petition, for I am brought very low;
O deliver me from my persecutors, for they have become too strong for me"

(Ps 141:4–7). "Keep me, O Lord, from the hands of the sinner; save me from the wicked men, who have purposed to trip up my steps. The proud have laid a snare for me, and spread a net abroad with cords for my feet. They set traps in my way. I said unto the Lord, Thou are my God; hear, O Lord, the voice of my supplication. Lord, O Lord, Thou strength of my salvation, Thou hast overshadowed my head in the day of battle. Give me not over to the sinner, O Lord, because of my desire; they have plotted against me; forsake me not, lest they be too proud" (Ps 139:4–9). "O deliver not the soul that confesseth Thee unto the wild beasts" (Ps 73:19), "that I may sing unto You the hymn of thanksgiving: Blessed be the Lord, Who hath not given us over for a prey unto their teeth. Our soul escaped even as a bird out of the snare of the fowler; the snare was broken, and we were delivered. Our help is in the Name of the Lord, Who hath made heaven and earth" (Ps 123:6–8).

A fish that does not escape the net of the fisherman is caught in it and becomes entangled. So whoever does not escape the devil's net gets entangled in it. The fornicator and the adulterer are entangled in his net, the slanderer and the back-biter are entangled in his net, and the drunkard is entangled in his net. The pastor who does not take care for his own salvation and that of Christ's flock is entangled in his net. The ruler who does not seek the common good, but his own filthy lucre, is entangled in his net. The judge who is corrupted by bribes and gifts is entangled in his net. The master who torments or burdens his peasants with excessive quitrents is entangled in his net. In a word, every sinner who does not repent and does not take care for his salvation is entangled in his net. All of them have "been taken captive by him to do his will" (2 Tim 2:26). The fisherman who has entangled a fish in his net takes it for himself. Likewise, the devil takes the sinner entangled in his pernicious net into perdition, his own state. Ah! He hauls and will draw him in, if he does not extricate himself from that net. Oh, poor sinner! Groan and cry from the depths of your heart to Jesus, the Liberator of our souls. Call out from this perdition, as Jonah from the belly of the whale, or as Manasseh from his bonds, to the all-powerful Jesus, so that He may send you His help and that fortified by it you will disentangle yourself from the net of perdition. Take care for this beforehand, beloved, before he draws you into perdition. Only make a good beginning and appeal to Him with all fervor. He, being Merciful and a Friend of Mankind, will stretch out to you His all-powerful hand and will disentangle you from this net of the enemy, and you will be free from it. Oh Jesus, Friend of Mankind! Have mercy on the creation of Your hands, for whose sake You came into the world and suffered, lest our enemy rejoice over our perdition. "If the Son makes you free, you shall be free indeed" (John 8:36). And when you receive this mercy from Him, then you will sing to Him with a joyful spirit, "Thou hast broken my bonds in sunder. I will offer unto Thee a sacrifice of thanksgiving" (Ps 115:7–8). And again, "I will thank Thee, O Lord my God, with all my heart, and I will praise Thy Name for evermore. For great is Thy mercy toward me, and Thou hast delivered my soul from the nethermost hell" (Ps 85:12–13). Having received such mercy from Him, henceforward be cautious and avoid the enemy's nets, calling on the Lord to help you. "Be my soul's helper, O God, for I pass through the midst of many snares; deliver me out of them, and save me, O Good One, for Thou art the Lover of Mankind."[5]

# 51. Drunkenness

There is drunkenness from wine and strong drink, and there is also drunkenness not caused by wine, as it is said, "those who are drunk without wine" (Isa 28:1). Drunkenness from wine happens when a person uses it beyond measure. Drunkenness not from wine is when a person is intoxicated by love of this world, vain thoughts, and lawless undertakings. One who is intoxicated with wine often does not know what he is saying or doing and has neither shame nor fear, and almost everything he does is worthy of laughter. Likewise, one who is intoxicated by love of this world and other lawless thoughts does not know what he is doing. He tries out one thing and then another, but all his initiative and work turn against him. He sees that everyone dies and no one takes anything with him. But he takes such care over the increase of his wealth, the expansion of his land, building of a house, and his other whims, over attainment of honor and earthly glory; he takes such care, I say, as if he alone in this world will live forever. "Fool! This night your soul will be required of you; then whose will those things be which you have provided" (Luke 12:20)? Such a person is indeed foolish and worthy of laughter, or even more so, pity! If someone were in a foreign country and were preparing to return soon from there to his homeland and his house but had amassed there many immovable things, would he not be worthy of laughter? Everyone, on seeing his work and initiative, would rightly tell him off: "You know, you will be leaving all of this here, so why are you stockpiling so much?" Similarly foolish and worthy of laughter is one who in this world stores up much but knows that he will have to leave it all behind in the world, as in a foreign country, and leave it soon. This is done by drunkenness, not from wine or strong drink, but of love for this world, which has so darkened his mind that the poor man himself does not know what he is doing. Drunkenness from wine and strong drink is bad, but this is even worse. He who is intoxicated by wine and strong drink will easily sober up, but he who is intoxicated by love of this world— only with great difficulty. The lust that lives in him and makes him foolish thinks up many reasons and does not allow him to sober up: *I need a lot for my wife, my children, my old age*, he thinks. And what use is honor and glory, which you desire not less than riches? What use is the rich finery of clothing, of houses, of tables, of servants, of horses, of carriages, of diamonds, or other forms of vanity? Oh, you who have become intoxicated not by wine or strong drink, but by the lust of the vain world! Open your eyes and look at those who were such as you. Where are their riches? Where their honor and glory? Where their whims and arrogance? Where their vain attire? Everything left them when they left the world, or rather, the world left them unexpectedly. The same happened with them as with those people who in their dreams have much and drink much, but, having woken, they see nothing in their hands and feel great thirst. Thus, those who have become intoxicated by the lust of the vain world, while they were living in the world, as in sleep, had much and drank much, but at death, and more so after death, saw themselves poor and felt very thirsty, and beg for a drop of water, but it is not given to them. They will hear the answer: "Son, remember that in your lifetime you received your good things" (Luke 16:25). And they will experience the useless repentance of the ungodly:

> What has arrogance profited us? And how has our wealth with its false pretention helped us? All those things have passed by like a shadow, and like news that escapes notice; Like a ship that passes through the waves of water, which after passing through, no trace can be found, nor the pathway of its keel in the waves; Or like a bird, when it flies through the air, no proof of its journey is found; and the light air, whipped by the beating of its pinions and divided by the force of its rushing motion, is travelled through by the movement of its wings, but after this no sign of its approach is found therein; or like an arrow, when it is shot at an object, the divided air immediately comes together, so that no one knows its pathway. Thus we also, after we are born, come to an end, yet have no sign of virtue to show, but have been entirely consumed in our vice. (Wis 5:8–13)

Take care lest you too come to this late and useless repentance. Wise and blessed is he who learns by the misfortunes of others to avoid it himself.

It often happens that one who is intoxicated with wine does much harm to people. Then his mind is darkened and he therefore does not have healthy reasoning, but only the impulsiveness from the wine is acting, and he is therefore like one possessed, who himself does not know what he is doing. In like manner, one who is intoxicated by the evil lust of the vain world causes much harm to people and much more than one who is drunk from wine. From whom do the poor and helpless endure violence and insults? From whom do widows and orphans weep and wash themselves with bloody tears, than from the powerful, besotted by the love of this world? Where are the most poor, wretched, half-naked, and those who suffer every shortage for subsistence and existence, than among the peasants who are governed by masters who love this world? What country has more extortion, thefts, violence, brigandage, murders, and other lawless acts than one in which the ruler is besotted by love of this world? The insatiable drunkenness of the vain world causes all this, and even more, evil. We see wicked drunkenness, which is spreading everywhere; we see too the intoxicated ones, gone mad in it; we see this and sigh. Is there anything that a drunkard has not thought up? What will he not contemplate to stifle the craving hiding in his heart? He would like to live in a luxurious and beautiful house, to set a sumptuous and plentiful table, to go out in rich and beautiful clothing, to have servants attending oneself, wife and children in proper attire, to go for rides with splendid horses and rich carriages, to have delightful ponds, gardens, porticoes, and to do other such things. But how to get it all? Where can you find the money for all that? A master needs to collect it from the peasants; he needs to impose higher quitrents on them! A judge needs to collect money from those coming to court, and instead of justice, to mete out injustice, not to concern himself about God's law or about God, not to regard the innocent and guilty, to acquit the unrighteous and to convict the upright! The lawless merchant must lie, cheat, flatter, and sell a bad item for a good one and a cheap one for an expensive one. Likewise, in the rest of the ranks and professions, drunkenness, not from wine, but from the world, causes much evil and harm. Oh man, who has become intoxicated not with wine but with the lust of this world! Reflect on this and see how much offense and harm you are causing people, indeed more than one drunk with wine! One who has been intoxicated with wine, upon sobering up, often regrets that in his unruly conduct he has offended someone or other. But the one besotted with the lust of the world does not regret that he has caused and is causing offense to people like himself. He has no regret inasmuch as he has a darkened mind like one who is drunk. Oh, evil and pernicious drunkenness! Wretched is he who is in captivity to it! Blessed is he who is not defiled by it! O Christian who is drunk not with wine but with the lust of the vain world! Abandon this soul-destroying drunkenness and sober up, lest you appear with it before that Dread Judge and your Lord! Sober up, please, and you yourself will see how your mind was darkened and how badly you have acted. And you will without fail regret and repent of your actions! "Thus says the Lord, the Holy One of Israel: 'When you return and groan, then you will be saved and know where you were'" (Isa 30:15). "The lamp of the body is the eye. If therefore your eye is good, your whole body will be full of light. But if your eye is bad, your whole body will be full of darkness. If therefore the light that is in you is darkness, how great is that darkness!" (Matt 6:22–23). "Do not love the world or the things in the world. If anyone loves the world, the love of the Father is not in him. For all that is in the world—the lust of the flesh, the lust of the eyes, and the pride of life–is not of the Father but is of the world. And the world is passing away, and the lust of it; but he who does the will of God abides forever" (1 John 2:15–17). "Set your mind on things above, not on things on the earth" (Col 3:2). "O turn away mine eyes, lest they behold vanity" (Ps 118:37).

As we see, those who become intoxicated with wine learn this iniquitous practice from each other. Lust, hiding in the human heart, is excited and aroused by our vision and hearing. It is very hard for a young man or any man to not learn drunkenness and thus not become corrupted if he associates with a drunkard. Likewise, people learn drunkenness not from wine but from the lust of the world from others. We see this iniquitous zeal everywhere. This evil is whirling about before the eyes of all. How many changes in the construction of buildings, in the design of clothing, in the preparation of repasts, in the appointments of carriages and horses, and other vanity, beauty, and splendor of this world we see. How many, I say, changes we see. But they are all for the worse. Godliness is always same. As it was from the beginning of the world, so it is now, and so it will always be. Truth is always true, always immutable: it was, and is, and shall be. Vanity and allurement are inconstant and are always changing. Look at the vanity! One person has built such and such a mansion, has begun to wear such and such clothing, has hung such and such a mirror in his house, has begun to ride in such and such a carriage, has so many hand-picked horses, has set such and such a table, has attending servants in such and such livery, and so on. Another sees this and imitates him. Everyone sees this and does the same as the first. And so luxury spreads everywhere and increases and from hour to hour intensifies. And with luxury increases every evil and devours human souls exactly as a fire that having started in one house burns down the whole city or village or like the plague that, having started in one person, infects and kills many nearby people. In our homeland, we see this pernicious plague, which has infected not the bodies but the souls of Christians. If we look at the luxury of people, the lower nobility and the merchants, who formerly went about and lived like simple people, have become princes and lords. They now do not want to live otherwise than in luxurious and beautiful houses. They want to sit only at a sumptuous table covered with assorted foods; they want to drink only select and expensive wine; they want to wear only silken and beautiful clothing, in fox, marten, and sable coats; and they want to ride only in English carriages. And the vanity, pride, and splendor of this world has so entered into Christians and increases from day to day that if our ancestors rose from the dead, they would not recognize their homeland. "But our ancestors did not know how to live in the world, they did not know how to make use of their property." Take stock of yourself, friend, to whom this saying applies more, to you or to your ancestors? Your ancestors lived in simplicity and humility and therefore lived in a Christian manner and sensibly. You live in pride and splendor, and you are therefore far away from the Christian life. Your ancestors had fewer luxuries but more piety. And there were fewer poor and needy people, since they took less from the people and gave more to the needy and poor. Luxury has increased among you, and so the poor and needy have increased, weeping and shedding bloody tears. You began to live in luxurious homes, so many are found who do not have a hut where they can lay their heads. You began to set a sumptuous table and to drink expensive wines, so many do not have their daily sustenance. You began to wear rich attire, so we see that many go about in rags or half naked. You took it into your heads and desired to ride splendid carriages and horses, while many weep and complain that they have nothing with which to plough their fields, and so on. You yourselves judge: are you more sensible or were your ancestors? Oh, Christians who are intoxicated not with wine, but with the lust of this world! Is this why Christ has called you into His holy faith? In this world, He offers us not luxury but crosses and sorrow: "Enter by the narrow gate ... If anyone desires to come after Me, let him deny himself, and take up his cross, and follow Me ... In the world you will have tribulation" (Matt 7:13; Matt 16:2; John 16:33). Here you have the usual answer: "It is not for everyone to go to monasteries and hermitages." O beloved! When these words were spoken, there were no monasteries yet. They are put forward not only for hermitage- and monastery-dwellers, but for all Christians, living in cities and villages, and people of every profession and rank, and both sexes, who want to belong to Christ and to be saved. "Those who are Christ's have crucified the flesh with its passions and desires" (Gal 5:24). Consequently, those who have not crucified the flesh with its passions and desires are not Christ's. You see that your answer is incorrect. But reign, reign here with the world, whenever you want! Enjoy yourselves and take comfort in your luxury! Go visit each other, feast, and arrange your banquets and dances! How you will rejoice and dance in that place! We read in the holy Gospel that "[t]here was a certain rich man who was clothed in purple and fine linen and fared sumptuously every day" (Luke 16:19). But we see in the same passage that after death everything changed horribly. After his luxurious living, he went into fiery torment, and after expensive wines, he begged for a drop of water—and it was not given to him. He heard the answer, "Son, remember that in your lifetime you received your good things" (Luke 16:25). Take care, beloved, lest after your life of luxury you come into that place. God is not a respecter of persons. God has given us the good things of this world and permitted us to make use of them, but for our necessities, not for luxury. He has ordered us to cleave with our hearts and our love to Him alone. "For what have I in heaven, and what have I desired upon earth from Thee" (Ps 72:25)? "Save me, Lord, for there is not one godly man left, for truth is minished from among the children of men" (Ps 11:2). O you, pious soul, who do not have this soul-destroying drunkenness and live in the world like Lot in Sodom! Stop, strengthen yourself, and be immovable. "Fret not thyself because of the wicked, neither be thou envious against them that do unlawfulness, for they shall soon wither like the grass, and quickly fall away even as the green herb" (Ps 36:1–2). You should be like Daniel in Babylon, who looked through open windows toward Jerusalem, his homeland, and bent his knees and prayed (see Dan 6:11). You should look by faith and the eye of the soul to the Jerusalem on high from this world, as from Babylon, and kneeling down, raise your eyes to the Lord. "Unto Thee have I lifted up mine eyes, O Thou that dwellest in heaven" (Ps 122:1).

While he is drinking, one drunk from wine does not feel how harmful drunkenness is. Likewise, one who is intoxicated with the lusts of this world does not know how harmful these lusts are as long as he remains in them. For as with one, so with the other, the mind is darkened. One who is intoxicated with wine, as he begins to sober up, learns how harmful drunkenness is. Likewise, one who is intoxicated with the lusts of this world, when he begins to come to his senses, learns how harmful the lusts of this world are. One sobering up from drunkenness feels in his body a considerable weakness. Likewise, one leaving behind the lusts of this world will experience a weakening of the soul. As drunkenness from wine weakens the body, so the lusts of this world weaken the soul. A person, upon sobering up from drunkenness, feels regret and is ashamed that he consumed wine immoderately, lost consciousness, and behaved scandalously, and thus harmed himself and made himself a cause of laughter for people. Likewise, the Christian, upon coming to his senses, feels regret and is ashamed, repents, and grieves that he pursued the lusts of this world and abandoned true wealth and weeps for all his bygone days as ones lost. Then he will learn in what vanity and deception he had lived. Thus, Solomon, coming to his senses and having learned of his vain actions, confessed, saying,

> I made my works great; I built myself houses and I planted vineyards for myself. I made myself gardens and parks, and planted all kinds of fruit-trees in them. I made pools of water for myself from which to water growing trees. I acquired male and female servants, and servants were born in my house; and I had abundant possessions of herds and flocks, more than all before me in Jerusalem. I also gathered silver and gold for myself and the abundant treasures of kings and countries. I provided male and female singers for myself, the delights of the sons of men, and male and female cupbearers. So I became great and advanced beyond all before me in Jerusalem; my wisdom established me. Whatever my eyes desired, I did not keep from them. I did not withhold my heart from any merriment. For my heart was made glad in all my labor, and this was my portion from all my labor. Then I looked on all the

works my hands had done, and on the labor in which I had toiled, and indeed all is vanity. (Eccl 2:4–11)

Likewise you, Christian, when you sober up from this pernicious drunkenness, you will indeed learn that everything you have done, thought, planned and undertook is vanity and delusion. And what seemed to you beautiful is ugly within; and what seemed to you good is evil within. And you will acknowledge that everything is vanity. For it always seems of deception that it is something, but as you examine it, you will see that within it is nothing, and it seems something sweet, but within it is bitter. Having gotten drunk with wine, usually you must drink a lot of water in order to more easily drive out with the water the heat that had increased from the wine. You, Christian, should take into consideration the last four things: think frequently of death, upon which you will leave behind all your whims; of the Dread Judgment of Christ, before which you will have to appear, as will everyone; of a blessed eternity, into which will go the lovers of God; and of an unfortunate and an agonizing eternity, which those who love this world and all sinners will not avoid. By such reflection, extinguish drunkenness as with water hiding in your heart. Indeed, I tell you, all the vanity of this world will leave your head when you frequently think about these points! You will desire weeping and tears more than happy days. You will be satisfied with a hunk of bread with cabbage soup and a cave and a hut instead of a luxurious and beautiful house, and you will consider all the beauty of this world as carrion. When people pursue vanity and go mad in the fancies of this world, like drunkards, they forget about eternity and its circumstances. This forgetfulness is caused by the enemy of human souls, Satan, so that people, not remembering eternity, will not remember and not take care for their eternal salvation, which Christ, the Son of God, effected by His suffering and death. Remember, beloved Christian, please, remember and think about eternity. And you will sober up, and will have a healthy intellect, and all the beauty and fancies of the world you will count as nothing. This is Christian wisdom! Your soul, for which Christ, the Son of God, suffered and died is more precious than the whole world. Be diligent and take care that it be saved. The image of God, in which we were created, is the most beautiful and magnificent beauty of the soul. Seek this beauty by true repentance and faith. If it is found here, it will abide forever. If it is not found here, it will never be found. "And the world is passing away, and the lust of it; but he who does the will of God abides forever" (1 John 2:17).

# 52. A Mirror

We see that a mirror depicts whatever it is turned toward. Likewise, the human soul depicts whatever it is turned toward and connected to with love. When a mirror is turned toward the sky, the same can be seen, and when it is turned toward the earth, that is seen. The same thing with the human soul: when it is turned toward heaven, a heavenly image is reflected in it, and when it is attached to what is earthly, an earthly and brutish image is reflected in it, and thereby it ruins its nobility and its heavenly beauty. Therefore the Holy Spirit admonishes us through the apostle, "Do not love the world or the things in the world. If anyone loves the world, the love of the Father is not in him. For all that is in the world–the lust of the flesh, the lust of the eyes, and the pride of life–is not of the Father but is of the world" (1 John 2:15–16). The soul will appear at the Judgment of Christ with whatever is now depicted in it, if it does not sincerely repent now. And so each person will have his denunciation within himself and see in himself what he contemplated in the world: the heavenly or the earthly? Christians are called by the Word of God and renewed by holy baptism for eternal life and heavenly blessings; these must be zealously sought out. But when they cleave to what is earthly, they anger God. We read that the Israelites, leaving Egypt led by the servant of God Moses, greatly aroused the anger of God when they turned back in their hearts to Egypt and wanted its food (see Num 11:1–11). Likewise, Christians, led out by holy baptism from the slavery of the devil and called from earth to heaven as to the Promised Land, kindle God's righteous anger against them when they turn back in their hearts to the world. And what happened with those called to the splendid supper, but refused to go, of whom it was said, "None of those men who were invited shall taste my supper" (Luke 14:24), "for many are called but few are chosen" (Matt 22:14). All Christians are called to the sumptuous supper of eternal life. But many refuse to go, if not by word, then by deed. They wish to reign here on earth, rather than to go into that Kingdom. And so "none of those shall taste my supper." The life of Christ teaches us how to abide and live in this world. Christ could have everything in this world, as the Lord of all, but did not desire that. He lived in great poverty and humility, sorrows and abuse, showing us an example. Whoever follows this Leader will taste that supper and will reign with Him there as a member with its head. "If anyone serves Me, let him follow Me; and where I am, there My servant will be also. If anyone serves Me, him My Father will honor" (John 12:26). "But you are those

who have continued with Me in My trials. And I bestow upon you a kingdom, just as My Father bestowed one upon Me, that you may eat and drink
at My table in My kingdom" (Luke 22:28–30). "And he who does not take his
cross and follow after Me is not worthy of Me" (Matt 10:38). "O Lord God of
Hosts, convert us; show the light of Thy countenance, and we shall be saved"
(Ps 125:4). "Turn our captivity, O Lord, as the streams in the south" (Ps 125:4).

# 53. One Emerging from Darkness, Prison, Captivity, and the Like

As one emerging from the darkness into light, so is one who has turned
from an iniquitous life to God. For he found himself in an iniquitous life, as
in darkness, and felt his way around by touch, just as those who walk in the
darkness, like blind men. One abandoning an impious and godless life and
living in true repentance is as one emerging from prison. He found himself
in a godless life as in a prison and was bound by sins and transgressions, like
shackles, and could not walk freely. One who has escaped and been freed from
a sinful and impure life and who works with a free spirit for the Lord is as one
who has been freed from captivity. This person was in captivity not to a human
tormentor, but to the devil, and he worked for him and did his evil will. One
who has come from an unrepentant life into repentance and is abiding in it
is as one who has crawled out of a ditch and is walking on a safe path, for he
too was in a ditch, not in body, but in soul. One who has ceased to sin and has
begun a new Christian life is as one who has been saved from a flood and come
onto dry land, for he was submerged in sins as in the depths of the waters, was
drowning, and had nothing ahead of him but eternal death. One who has lived
wickedly and having recognized his soul's ruination—as one who was walking toward a ditch and has seen it and turned back—has now turned to true
repentance (for he was walking into the pit of eternal perdition but has turned
away from it) happily emerges from the darkness into light, for he sees the light
of this world. Much happier is he who emerges from the darkness of sin, since
he is illuminated not by the light of this world but by divine light. "He who
follows Me shall not walk in darkness, but have the light of life" (John 8:12).
Therefore He says: "Awake, you who sleep, Arise from the dead, And Christ
will give you light" (Eph 5:14). Happy is he who has come out of prison and

been freed from his bonds. Much happier is he who has been freed from the prison of an unrepentant life and the bonds of sin. Happy is he who has been freed from physical captivity. But much happier is he who has been freed in soul from the captivity of the devil. Happy is he who has gotten out of a visible ditch. But much happier is he who has gotten out of the ditch of sin. Happy is he who has been saved from sinking in water. But much happier is he who has been saved from sinking in sin and the depths of iniquities. If there is such a person and he has been blessed with such happiness, I congratulate him with this and declare from God's Word, "There is joy in the presence of the angels of God over one sinner who repents" (Luke 15:10). But, O beloved, hold to what you have begun! Remember Lot's wife, and do not look back to Sodom and Gomorrah. "No one, having put his hand to the plow, and looking back, is fit for the kingdom of God" (Luke 9:62). "And also remember what is written: My son, if you draw near to serve the Lord, prepare your soul for temptation" (Sir 2:1). The devil with his snares, from whose bondage you have been freed, will come after you like pharaoh after Israel and will try to again subjugate you. You should stop, not be afraid, and not become despondent, calling on Jesus, the all-powerful Redeemer of our souls. And you will see His salvation and with a joyful spirit will sing to Him: "The Lord became my helper and the shield of my salvation; He is my God, and I will glorify Him" (Exod 15:2). When the same enemy throws you into the fiery furnace of temptation, pray with the three holy children. And there Jesus, the Son of God, will come to your aid, as He came to those holy children in the "form of an Angel," and will cool you, as He cooled them (Dan 3:49–50). Complete the undertaking that you have begun with the help of Christ. Happy are you that you have made such a beginning, but you will be perfectly happy when you finish happily. Many begin, but not many finish. "Many are called, but few are chosen" (Matt 22:14). Therefore, Jesus, the Author and Accomplisher of our salvation, says to you, "Be faithful until death, and I will give you the crown of life" (Rev 2:10). "Forsake me not, O Lord my God, be not far from me. Attend unto my help, O Lord of my salvation" (Ps 37:22–23). "Suffer not thy feet to slip, nor Him that keepeth thee to slumber. Behold, He that keepeth Israel shall neither slumber nor sleep. The Lord Himself shall keep thee; the Lord is thy shelter upon thy right hand; the sun shall not burn thee by day, neither the moon by night. The Lord shall keep thee from all evil; yea, the Lord shall preserve thy soul. The Lord shall preserve thy going out, and thy coming in, from this time forth, and forevermore" (Ps 120:3–8).

# 54. Shame

We see that subjects before their monarch, subordinates before their lord, servants before their master, children before their father are ashamed to do what is unseemly. They are ashamed, and even afraid. Christians! God is in every place and is everywhere present and looks upon us and upon our affairs. He sees whatever we do, think, and undertake and hears whatever we say. The Holy Scriptures bears witness to this in many places (see Ps 32:13–15; Ps 138:1–16; Sir 23:27–29; Jer 32:17, 19, 27; and others). The most wise Augustine speaks to God about this: "I acknowledge, O Lord, that whatever I do and whatever activity I occupy myself with, I do in Your sight. And You see everything that I do better than I, who am doing it. For whatever I always do, You also are always present, being the constant observer of all my thoughts, intentions, pleasures, and actions."[6] What Augustine acknowledges about himself, everyone should acknowledge about himself. We who acknowledge and confess God, and call upon Him and sing to Him in prayer, and hope for and expect mercy from Him, I say, must be ashamed to do what is unseemly and offensive to His majesty and harmful to us. We must be ashamed and even afraid, since "our God is a fire consuming [the ungodly]" (Heb 12:29). Listen! You are ashamed to act badly in front of a person. All the more should you be ashamed before God! You do not see Him and cannot see Him, but He sees you and looks upon your acts, undertaking, and thoughts and hears every word of yours. "He that planted the ear, shall He not hear? Or He that made the eye, shall He not see" (Ps 93:9 and others)? The king is insulted when his subject behaves outrageously before him; and the master, when his servant acts unbecomingly before him; and a father, when his children act dishonestly before him. We all see this. Christian! Think and remember that this is how God is insulted when people, and especially Christians, who know and confess His name, transgress before His most holy eyes. His righteousness is insulted by your unrighteousness, His truth by your lie, His holiness by your impurity, His goodness by your mean-spiritedness, His meekness and long-suffering by your anger and malice, and His love by your hatred. O, how grave it is to insult the Great, Good, and Man-loving God! For whom? For you and me, little worms, earth and dust, to insult our Creator, our Redeemer, Protector, Nourisher, in a word, our most high Benefactor, by whose benefactions we are surrounded, and so many of which we receive every day, that without them we cannot live for a minute. It is a grave thing to insult Him, and a terrible thing!

For the one who insults will experience His righteous judgment if he does not have a change of heart and repents. God is good, long-suffering and plenteous in mercy; He awaits the repentance of the sinner, and therefore He is patient. But if he does not repent, he will then experience His righteous anger. You feel shame and fear before your king, before your master, before your father, not only to indulge in lechery and to commit another wicked act but even to speak an idle word and laugh. But before God, the all-seeing and fearsome King, you are not ashamed and do not fear not only to engage in idle talk and to laugh, but to commit serious transgressions: to commit fornication or adultery; to swindle, rob, steal, lie, slander, condemn, backbite, curse; and to do other shameless things. O Christian! Cover your eyes, if you do such things. Be ashamed, if you confess the Omnipresent, True, Almighty, Righteous, God, who cares about you and about your salvation, and Who renders to all according to their works. Blind and poor is that Christian who before people like himself, even if they are high-ranking and honored, is ashamed to display bad behavior, but before God, the omnipresent and all-seeing, is neither ashamed nor afraid to transgress. Oh! If a person saw even a little bit of the fearsome glory of God, he would fall down like one dead and would consider how he acts badly and shamelessly, how he offends the One from Whom he has received his life and all his good things, and he would weep and sob inconsolably. It is written of the ungodly: "They have not set God before them" (Ps 53:5) and therefore are not ashamed to transgress before Him. Christian! You should imagine God before you, and believe and remember that no matter where you are, and whatever you are doing or saying, God is present with you. And always look at Him with the eye of your mind, as the prophet says of himself: "I foresaw the Lord always before me" (Ps 15:8). Thus, seeing Him and looking at Him, fall down before Him with humility, repent and feel sorry for your past sins, for your shameless deeds and words, and ask forgiveness, often repeating: "I have sinned, Lord, have mercy on me!" And in future, be ashamed and be afraid of behaving badly and violating His holy law, lest you experience His avenging hand and be shamed at the universal reckoning. "Look upon me, hear me, O Lord my God; lighten mine eyes, that I sleep not in death. Lest mine enemy say, I have prevailed against him" (Ps 12:4–5). "Open Thou mine eyes, that I may recognize the wondrous things of Thy Law. I am a pilgrim upon earth, O hide not Thy commandments from me. My soul hath been consumed with longing for Thy judgments at all times" (Ps 118:18–20). "O Lord, Thou hast examined me, and known me; Thou hast known my down-sitting, and mine up-rising. Thou hast understood my thoughts from afar off. Thou hast searched into my path and my lot, and all my ways hast thou foreseen" (Ps 138:1–3).

# 55. I Cannot Escape Anywhere from You

It happens that, for certain reasons, a person tells another person, "I cannot escape anywhere from you." We hear this expression among people, but if we think about it, it is incorrectly ascribed to any person, whoever he may be, for it is possible to escape and hide from not only a simple person, but even from kings, even though they have a long reach, as we can see. Therefore these words, "I cannot escape anywhere from you," are befitting to say only to God. We cannot escape anywhere from Him, wherever we run, and cannot hide anywhere, no matter where we take it into our heads to hide. He anticipates wherever we may want to run and is present wherever we may want to hide. Are you in your house? God is there. On the road? God does not abandon you. Have you come to your apartment? God is here. Are you staying in a city or village? God is present there. Are you running into the desert or to the end of the earth? God is there before you. Do you wish to hide in the earth or in the depths of the sea? He is with you even there. You think, "Can't I hide in the darkness and night from Him?" No, that is an unreliable refuge! We have day and night, light and darkness, but with God there is no darkness, no night—everything is light and day. "The eyes of God are incomparably brighter than the sun, and look upon all the paths of men, and observe even the secret places" (Sir 23:27–29). The Psalmist learned that there is nowhere to escape from God, nor is it possible to hide from Him, and cried to Him whither shall I go then from Thy Spirit? Or whither shall I flee from Thy presence? If I climb up into heaven, Thou art there; if I go down to hell, Thou art there also. If I take up my wings early, and dwell in the uttermost parts of the sea, even there also shall Thy hand lead me, and Thy right hand shall hold me. And I said, peradventure the darkness shall hide me, and the night is light in my pleasures. "For the darkness shall be no darkness with Thee, and the night shall be bright as the day, for as is the darkness thereof, even so is the light of it" (Ps 138:7–12). Once the Prophet Jonah tried to run from the face of the Lord.

"But he was detained by God's right hand and saw himself in the belly of the whale, and from there was brought out onto dry land by the same right hand of God" (John 1:3, 2:1–11). It is impossible either to escape or to hide from God. Oh, poor sinner! Where will you escape from Him Who is everywhere? And where will you hide from Him Who sees all? Do you know where to run? Run from His justice to His goodness and from His judgment to His mercy. "As His majesty is, so is His mercy" (Sir 2:18). And hide with faith in Christ's most holy wounds. "This is the refuge to which Christians run and where they hide in safety from the anger of God! O Jesus! So shall the children of men put their trust in the shelter of Thy wings" (Ps 35:8). As chicks under the wings of a bird, so do sinners find refuge under the shelter of Your goodness and love for mankind. "Lord, Thou hast been our refuge from generation to generation" (Ps 89:2). "Come to Me, all you who labor and are heavy laden, and I will give you rest" (Matt 11:28).

## 56. The Master Is Here

It happens that when the master is somewhere nearby, but his servants do not see him or do not know that he is near, a servant, knowing of his presence, warns the other servants lest they anger him by their noise or other form of rowdiness and be punished, saying to them quietly, "Quiet!" or, "Be silent–the master is here." Likewise, the servants of God, the prophets and apostles, inspired by God's Spirit, warn us, O Christians. And they say to us: Hear this: the master is here, "Who is everywhere present and fills all things." "Let your gentleness be known to all men. The Lord is at hand" (Phil 4:5). Christians! Look out—*The Lord is at hand*. Look out for sin in word, deed, and thought— *The Lord is at hand*, He, Who hates sin and is offended and angered by it and punishes those who sin. You, who have gathered in the Lord's church for prayer and glorification of God, hear this: The Lord, before Whom you stand pray-ing, *is at hand*, and is watching how you stand before Him, in what spirit and heart you pray, how you sing and glorify Him. When you bow your knees and head to Him, do you bow your heart as well? When you ask mercy from Him, do you yourself show mercy to your neighbors? When you ask forgiveness of sins, do you yourself forgive people their sins? When you stand before God in your body, do you stand before Him in your spirit and heart? Praying to Him with your tongue and saying, Lord, have mercy, do you pray with your mind and heart? You sing and glorify Him with your lips, but do you sing with your hearts as well? Heed this, beloved: The Lord is at hand, the Lord Himself, before Whom you stand, Who looks at you and hears how you pray and hymn Him. Look out, beloved, lest your prayer and glorification be counted as a sin against you. We stand before a human king—a man—with fear and humility if we are asking something of him, and we pay attention to him with all our mind. All the more should we do this when we stand before God and pray to Him. The Lord is nigh unto all them that call upon Him, to all such as call upon Him in truth. "He will fulfill the desire of them that fear Him, and He will hear their prayer and save them" (Ps 144:18–19). You who sit in a place of judgment, who judge and deliberate between innocent and guilty, between aggrieved and offender, hear this: The Lord is at hand. The Master is here, the Judge of judges, and "He Who judges the whole earth" righteously, the King of Kings and Lord of Lords. He Himself is invisibly present here; sees your concerns, endeavors, and thoughts; hears your words; and looks upon you as you judge His people, how and whom you acquit, whom and for what you indict. Take care, beloved! The Lord is at hand. God standeth in the gathering of the gods, for in the midst of the gods He shall judge. How long will ye judge unjustly and accept the persons of sinners? Judge for the fatherless and the poor; do right unto such as are humble and needy. "Rescue the needy and the poor; out of the hand of the sinner deliver him" (Ps 81:1–4). So then, beloved, act in your court as God has commanded you. And besides, your oath, which you gave before Him, obliges you to do this, and justice, to which you are called, demands this, lest God, exasperated by our falsehood pour out His righteous anger upon you. You, who in this world are called masters and have under you servants and peasants, hear this: The Lord is at hand; the Lord Himself is near and sees your affairs and watches how you behave with His people who are your subordinates. He is not like a human—He is not partial to persons; all are equal before Him: both masters and their servants. Be careful, beloved, lest you anger your Lord, Who Himself is present here. You, who are called parents, have children, hear this: The Lord is at hand. The Lord Himself is here, Who sees all your affairs and hears your words. How do you behave with your children? How do you teach and admonish them? Do you not teach them vanity instead of truth and carelessness instead of fear? And instead of admonishment and beneficial training, do you not give the poison of temptations to young hearts? Watch, beloved, behave carefully before God, who is watching you, and before your young children, who take note of what you do and what you say, and themselves learn to do and speak thus. You, who preach the Word of God, listen to this: The Lord is at hand. The Lord Himself is here and sees with what hands and tongue you touch His sacred treasure. Do you use that great gift of God for his glory and the benefit of your neighbor, or to your own praise? The Lord Himself is here, trying the very hearts and reins ... God said to the sinner: Why dost thou preach My statutes, and takest My covenant in thy mouth? For thou hast hated correction and hast cast My words behind thee. If thou sawest a thief, thou didst run with him, and hast been partaker with the adulterer. Thy mouth hath embroidered evil, and thy tongue hath woven lies. "Sitting, thou didst slander thy brother, and hast laid temptation on thine own mother's son" (Ps 7:10; 49:16–20). You who buy and sell, hear this: The Lord is at hand. The Lord Himself is here, Who sees your affairs and watches how you buy and how you sell. Do you not sell something rotten for sound, bad for good, and cheap for expensive? Do you not lie, do you not cheat your neighbors with your goods? And, what is even worse, do you not swear falsely in God's name for the sake of foul gain? Be ashamed and fear to lie before the eyes of God, and to call upon His fearsome name in a lie, and to cheat His people. You, who sit at a table and taste the gifts of God, hear this: The Lord is at hand. The Lord Himself is here and is watching you. How do you taste God's good things? With prayer and thanksgiving? You taste God's benefactions, but do you remember the benefactor? All good things are God's, and not ours. "The earth is the Lord's, and the fullness thereof" (Ps 23:1). You who, gathering together, converse, hear this: The Lord is at hand. The Lord Himself is here and is watching you and hears what you say and about whom. Take care that your conversation not be counted as sin against you. We speak carefully in a King's presence; the more carefully should we speak in God's presence, Who is here, and there, and everywhere. Watch how, and what, and of whom you speak. You who wish to defile your soul and body with impurity, hear this: The Lord is at hand. The Lord Himself is here, Who sees your lawless undertaking. Be ashamed and afraid to transgress before the eyes of God. You, who are angry with your neighbor and think of taking vengeance on him and hurting him, hear this: The Lord is at hand. The Lord Himself is here and sees your evil intention. Be ashamed and afraid of the Lord Who is present, and abandon your evil undertaking. You, who think to steal and swindle, hear this: The Lord is at hand. The Lord Himself is here and sees your intended act. Be ashamed and afraid before the eyes of God to commit this lawless deed. You, who either out of you own malice, or from evil habit, slander and pass judgment on your neighbor, hear this: The Lord is at hand and hears your slander, by which you sow temptations for people, and your judgment, by which you judge sinners like you.

Be ashamed and afraid of the Lord, before Whom you slander and judge His people, and restrain your tongue from this lawless deed. And why do you look at the speck in your brother's eye, but do not consider the plank in your own eye? Or how can you say to your brother, "Let me remove the speck from your eye"; and look, a plank is in your own eye? "Hypocrite! First remove the plank from your own eye, and then you will see clearly to remove the speck from your brother's eye" (Matt 7:3–5). Do not speak evil of one another, brethren. "He who speaks evil of a brother and judges his brother speaks evil of the law and judges the law" (Jas 4:11). Every Christian, hear: The Lord is at hand. Wherever you are, whatever you are doing, whatever you say and think, He is present with you, and sees every one of your actions, and hears every one of your words. Be ashamed, beloved, and afraid of sinning before your Lord, as you are ashamed and afraid of breaking the law before an earthly king and other authority. "Beloved, do not become like the ungodly, who have not set God before them" (Ps 53:5), "but be like that holy man who wrote of himself, I foresaw the Lord always before me" (Ps 15:8). You should always see your Lord before you always and everywhere. And whatever you are doing: either speaking, or thinking, or eating and drinking, or sitting at home, or going on your way, or selling or buying, or keeping silence, or conversing with someone, or praying, or singing praises to your Lord, may He always abide before the eyes of your mind, even if you do not see Him. Honor Him with your heart, lips, and deeds as you honor a king who is present. And if, being human, you commit an offense and sin before Him in something, do not tarry, but immediately fall down before Him with humility and beg forgiveness: I have sinned, O Lord, have mercy on me! And your sin will be forgiven, for He is merciful and a Lover of Mankind, and knows our weakness. Hear this, my soul, and be ashamed, and fear your Lord always and everywhere! Hear, O God-fearing and pious soul, who sincerely honors your Lord, hear this: The Lord is at hand— He Who tells you, "You are Mine. If you pass through the water, I am with you, and the rivers shall not overflow you. If you pass through fire, you shall not be burned up, nor shall the flame consume you" (Isa 43:1–2). O beloved! Suffer not thy feet to slip, nor Him that keepeth thee to slumber. Behold, He that keepeth Israel shall neither slumber nor sleep. The Lord Himself shall keep thee; the Lord is thy shelter upon thy right hand; the sun shall not burn thee by day, neither the moon by night. The Lord shall keep thee from all evil; yea, the Lord shall preserve thy soul. "The Lord shall preserve thy going out, and thy coming in, from this time forth, and forevermore" (Ps 120:3–8).

# 57. A King Who Enters a City or House

It happens that when a king wishes to enter some city or house, his servants and envoys tell other people living in the city or house, "Open the gates, the King is coming." And so the king enters and is received with honor by the citizens or the people of the household. Like this, Christ the Lord, the Heavenly King, coming to earth and having effected eternal salvation on earth, sent to all countries and cities of the whole earth His holy disciples and apostles to proclaim to them His coming and His saving entry. "Go into all the world and preach the gospel to every creature" (Mark 16:15). "These envoys of God and faithful servants of Christ went out and preached everywhere, the Lord working with them and confirming the word through the accompanying signs" (Mark 16:20). They said to the people living in each city and each country, "Open the gates and the Heavenly King, your King, still unknown to you, will enter to you. He wants to reign among you, and to lead you into His eternal kingdom: Open the gates, and He will come in to you. Lift up your gates, O ye princes, and be ye lift up, ye everlasting doors, and the King of glory shall come in" (Ps 23:7). And so the king of glory with His grace and eternal salvation came into the pagan cities and countries. The Jews, to whom He was sent, did not receive "Him as their true King, as it was written, He came to His own, and His own did not receive Him" (John 1:11). Therefore, the kingdom of God was taken away from them. Peoples, not knowing and not expecting Him, with joy and faith opened their cities to Him, received Him, worshipped Him, and took upon themselves His sweet yoke. Therefore, the kingdom of God was turned over to them, for where Christ, the Lord and King of Glory, is, there also is the Kingdom of God. Thanks be to God that the King of glory and peace, Jesus Christ, came into our country, into our homeland and cities, and with Him the Kingdom of God! But we see that He has departed again from many countries and cities for ingratitude and disdain for His holy Word, and with Him the Kingdom of God has been taken away from them too. Since we see that every injustice has multiplied in our homeland, love already has almost dried up, excessive luxury has increased, carnal and flippant life is observed almost everywhere, and so the Word of God is held in extreme contempt, and almost everyone pays attention to carnal and worldly fancies and not to God's lips; almost everyone pleases the flesh and the world rather than God and seeks temporary and earthly blessings rather than eternal ones; there is danger, Christians, extreme danger, that Christ the Lord with

His kingdom might leave our country and cities. For nothing else will result from this if people imagine that they know him, but do not honor Him, and instead of Him honor the Mammon of injustice, scorn His holy Gospel, flout His holy law, and seek the world and vanity, and not His kingdom. Such people, following the Jews, drive Christ away from themselves, and He thus is persuaded to depart from them, and He says to these people what He says to the Jews: "See! Your house is left to you desolate" (Matt 23:38). These words are frightening, very frightening! What is there without Christ, except undeniable perdition? Let us turn, Christians, to Christ with our whole hearts, and let us repent and weep before Him, lest he abandon us, lest the Kingdom of God be taken away from us, as it was taken away from the obdurate Jews. "Forsake me not, O Lord my God, be not far from me. Attend unto my help, O Lord of my salvation" (Ps 37:22–23).

# 58. Woe

Woe to that place in which there is no light. People wander around there, like the blind; the harmful is not distinguished from the beneficial there and often stumbling or falls happen. In a word, every kind of misfortune, disaster, and injury takes place. Woe especially to those souls, in which Christ, the true Light, is absent. There is nothing there, except the darkness, the shadow of death, tribulation, sinfulness, and perdition. "I am the light of the world. He who follows Me shall not walk in darkness, but have the light of life" (John 8:12). "Awake, you who sleep, Arise from the dead, And Christ will give you light" (Eph 5:14). Woe to that house in which there is not a prudent householder; every kind of disorder reigns there. Even more so, woe to the souls in which Christ, the Master of the House, does not have His abode! Every kind of real disorder and disarray reigns there; it is the habitation of all kinds of evil spirits. Woe to the ship that lacks a good helmsman, since it is close to sinking. Even more so, woe to the soul that sails the sea of this world and that lacks Christ, the Wise Guide, for it is close to sinking. "Now if anyone does not have the Spirit of Christ, he is not His" (Rom 8:9). Woe to those people who do not have bread and water, for they waste away and die from hunger and thirst. Even more so, woe to those souls that are deprived of the Bread of Life, Jesus Christ, for they are wasting away from hunger and may die. "I am the bread of life. The bread of God is He who comes down from heaven and gives life to the world" (John 6:33, 35). "But whoever drinks of the water that I shall give him will never thirst. But the water that I shall give him will become in him a fountain of water springing up into everlasting life" (John 4:14). The body is satisfied by bread and refreshed by water; without bread and water it languishes and dies. The True Food and Drink of the soul is Christ. With this Food and Drink, it revives and lives. Without this Food and Drink, it languishes and dies. If one does not have the Spirit of Christ, he does not have Christ either: If Christ lives in someone, the life of Christ manifests itself in that person, and His humility, love, patience, and meekness manifest themselves in him. Christ's dwelling in a person cannot be idle: it will unfailingly be manifested through such effects as Christ desires, as the shining sun is manifested through its rays, or like the stove heated by fire through its warmth, or as a good tree through its sweet fruits. If Christ, the Light of life, lives in someone, His light is also manifested in that person, and the darkness is driven out, and dark deeds are not manifested. If Christ, a purifying, illuminating fire, lives in someone, the warmth of love and mercy makes itself felt in him. "If Christ, the humble and meek Lamb of God" (John 1:29, 36) lives in someone, His humility, meekness, and patience are manifested in him. If Christ, the Tree of life and thought, lives in someone, His sweet fruits are manifested in him. You can tell a tree by its fruit. Whoever is joined with Christ, as the member with the head, or as the branch with the vine, bears fruit like He does. So Christ's dwelling in a person cannot be idle but is felt without fail through internal spiritual movements and is manifested through similar external actions. Let us turn, O Christian, with a whole heart to Christ, let us sigh and weep before Him, and let us repent with a contrite heart, and let us earnestly pray to Him. May he also come to us sinners and "dwell in [our] hearts through faith" (Eph 3:17) and take possession of us. And until that time, we shall not cease asking, and seeking, and knocking at the door of His mercy "until Christ is formed in [us]" (Gal 4:19).

## 59. A Good Tree

As a good tree, so is a good Christian who thinks spiritually. A good tree comes from a good seed. A good Christian is born of the heavenly and good seed, according to the Scriptures: "having been born again, not of corruptible seed but incorruptible, through the word of God which lives and abides forever" (1 Pet 1:23). A good tree is known by its good fruit. Likewise, a good Christian is known by his good works. A good tree bears good fruit from within. Likewise, a good Christian does good works from within, sincerely and from the heart. Good fruits reveal a good tree but do not make it good. Likewise, good works reveal a good Christian but do not make him good. "It is first necessary for the tree to be good, and then to bear good fruit, for a bad tree cannot bear good fruit" (Matt 7:17–18; Luke 6:43). Likewise, a Christian must first become good, and then do good works, for evil cannot do this. A good tree bears fruit for its owner and other people. Likewise, a good Christian does good works for the glory of God's name and the benefit of his neighbors. The good fruits of a good tree, although they hang from and are visible on the tree, are ascribed to not to the tree itself but to the good seed from which the tree grew. Likewise, good works, although a good Christian does them, should be attributed to the good and man-loving God, Who sowed the good seed in the human heart, and made it good, is helping him and strengthens him to do good. Without God, it is impossible either to be good, or to do good, according to God's Word: "Without Me you can do nothing" (John 15:50). The more a good tree is pruned by a worker, the more fruit it bears. "Likewise, the more a good Christian is punished and corrected by God, the Heavenly Vinedresser, the better he is and the more good deeds he does" (John 15:1–2). A good tree bestows its fruits on all indiscriminately, household members and strangers alike. Likewise, the good Christian does good to all, friends and enemies, people known and unknown, imitating the Heavenly Father, Who "makes His sun rise on the evil and on the good, and sends rain on the just and on the unjust" (Matt 5:45). His house is open to any wanderer, and every hungry person is nourished with his bread. He will not part with the naked without clothing him, if he has anything to clothe him with. He will not refuse anyone asking for help, if he can give it. He will shed tears and weep with one who is suffering and weeping. He first goes with consolation to the sorrowing, and tries, as much as he can, to heal a wounded heart. With one who rejoices, he rejoices for his well-being, as for his own. He seeks and begs mercy from God for everyone, as for himself. He would be overjoyed if he saw everyone saved. And if it were possible and he had the means, he would help all those in need. Seeing a brother sinning, he does not judge him but sympathizes in a spirit of charity. This and other things are the fruit of a good tree. Christian! Become good and then you will do good works. And to become good, you must (1) turn to God with your whole heart and be truly repentant. Without this, a person cannot be good. (2) Read God's Word and other Christian books with attention and intently reflect on them. "All Scripture is given by inspiration of God, and is profitable for doctrine, for reproof, for correction, for instruction in righteousness, that the man of God may be complete, thoroughly equipped for every good work" (2 Tim 3:16–17). (3) Try to perceive the corruption and sinfulness of your heart. From knowledge of yourself will follow humility and diligence in reforming yourself. For first the sick person must perceive his infirmity and then seek healing. The beginning of health is the perception of infirmity, and the beginning of reformation is a perception of one's misery and sinfulness. Who, seeing in himself a deadly poison, does not eagerly wish to be delivered from it? And who, seeing his ruination, will not try to be delivered from it? Knowledge of oneself is the beginning of salvation. Know yourself, O man, and sincerely acknowledge your poverty and sinfulness before God. And give yourself into the hands of Christ, as a sick man gives himself over to a physician, and then Christ will heal you. (4) Shun every sin and compel yourself to every good deed, even if the heart is unwilling. The Lord, seeing such effort and zeal for the good, will show mercy to one who exerts himself and day by day will change him for the better. The sick man, when he wishes to be healed, avoids everything that the doctor forbids him, even though his appetite draws him to it. Likewise, the Christian should avoid everything that Christ, the Heavenly Physician, forbids, even if the heart is unwilling. Otherwise, he cannot be healed. (5) Pray fervently and ask correction from Christ Himself, Who cleansed the lepers, gave sight to the blind, and cured the sick. He will heal our immortal souls as well, if we pray fervently and exert our own effort for this, according to His truthful promise: "Ask, and it will be given to you; seek, and you will find; knock, and it will be opened to you. For everyone who asks receives, and he who seeks finds, and to him who knocks it will be opened" (Matt 7:7–8). "Turn me back, and I shall return" ... "Heal me, O Lord, and I shall be healed" (Jer 38:18 LXX; 17:10 LXX). Without Him conversion and healing do not take place.

# 60. Slime or Mud on the Bottom of a Spring

We see that although in a spring there is clean water, on the bottom there is slime or mud. Likewise, in the depth of the human heart there is every impurity. Like stinking slime and stench, hidden there are pride and haughtiness, greed, anger, malice and envy, brutish impurity and every kind of abomination. In a spring, the impurity lying at its bottom can be seen when it is struck with a staff or some other implement; then from the slime or mud lying there all the water in the spring is disturbed and becomes turbid. Likewise the impurity of the passions and the brutish depravity, lying in the depths of the human heart, are manifested during temptation and enticement. Who would know that on the bottom of a spring there is slime or mud if it did not rise from there and reveal itself if you strike it? So from whence would we know that in the depths of the human heart is hiding such abomination and impurity, if it did not emerge from there and did not manifest itself by external deeds? We see how a person, it happens, is in a bad temper. He yells, curses, and engages in other types of rowdiness. This is anger, like poison, hidden in his heart and manifested in the event of temptation and grievance, working in him and impelling him to such rowdiness. We see how much a person gathers for his poor and mortal body, which is satisfied by a small piece of bread and some clothing. How much, I say, he gathers, although he knows that he will leave it all behind upon his death. This is greed and the cruel lust for wealth, lodged in the heart, working in him. We see that a person is conceited; how many ways he devises for people to know, praise, extol, and honor him. We see how he despises people like himself and considers them his footstool, how he judges and criticizes their affairs, although he is the same; how he everywhere tries to take first place and be in charge of others, and so on. This is pride, lodged in his heart, working in him. Sexual impurity, hiding within a person, manifests itself through such sordid, such loathsome, such foul and shameless deeds that it is ignominious to even speak of! Penetrate, O man, into the depths of your heart, examine and find out what a foul slime of passions lies in it. Whatever evil you see in your neighbor, the same is in your heart—that for which you judge and condemn your neighbor is also in you, although it is not manifested externally. God's eye sees not only outward action but also the depths of the heart. Many think of themselves that they are humble and meek, but upon temptation, something else comes to the surface. "Many call themselves sinful and greatly sinful (without doubt, *every* person is a *sinner*, according to the Scriptures" (1 John 1:8)—but do not tolerate hearing this from other people. Whoever truly and sincerely in his heart calls himself a sinner will calmly endure every abusive word and will not show a sign of anger, for he is humble. So, take note, O man, and examine and test what evil lies hidden in your heart, what pride, love of fame, self-love, anger, envy, greed, impurity, and other loathsomeness. How can good fruit come from a poisonous seed and how can a good deed come from an evil heart? How can evil create good? And how can someone be good when Christ's grace does not correct him? Christ corrects him who learns his sinfulness and poverty, and acknowledges it before Him, and asks help and amendment from Him. We read in the Gospel that He healed those who acknowledged their poverty before Him and asked Him for healing. Likewise, now He heals those souls who acknowledge their infirmity and ask Him for healing. Look into your heart frequently, O man, and you will come to know it. The beginning of correction depends on this. The more often you search within and scrutinize, the more you will recognize it. The more you come to know your heart, the more you will come to know the evil hiding in it. The more you come to know the evil in yourself, the more you will come to know your poverty and sinfulness. Recognition of poverty and sinfulness will convince you to humble yourself and seek help and deliverance from Christ, Who can do all and make good out of evil. "God ... gives grace to the humble" (Jas 4:6). "Make me a clean heart, O God, and renew a right spirit within me. Cast me not away from Thy presence, and take not Thy Holy Spirit from me. O give me the comfort of Thy salvation, and stablish me with Thy governing Spirit" (Ps 50:12–14).

# 61. A Person Who Has Fallen among Robbers and Been Injured by Them

A person falls into the hands of robbers who strip him and seriously injure him. We see such evil in the world. Thus, the entire human race, after its departure from God and transgression of His holy commandments, fell into the devil's hands, as into a robber's, and remained without holy and God-woven clothing, and was unspeakably covered with wounds, and lay ulcerated on the path of this world. So serious were his wounds that no one could heal them. God's Law was sent to him from heaven. But this only reproved him and showed him his wounds but did not heal them; it threatened him with death but did not help him. Prophets were sent, but even they could do nothing. The poor human race lay unhealed! It lay covered with wound and sores, exhausted, shamed, outraged by the robber, the devil. He lay "half dead" (Luke 10:30–32). Ah, the most beloved creation of God, man! Into what a condition, what tribulation, what dishonor you have come by the serpent's cunning! Where is your splendid beauty, with which your Creator adorned you? Where is your honor, with which He did homage to you? Where is the image of God and the likeness of God, in which you were created? Where is that blessedness for which you were created? The evil serpent envied our blessedness, and cunningly tripped us up, wounded us incurably, and deprived us of our blessedness. And we became acquainted with good and evil by the very experience. We were deprived of good and learned what it was. We fell into evil and learned what it was. We wanted Divine honor and were deprived of God's image. "But man, being in honor, understood it not; he shall be compared unto the brute beasts, and is become like unto them" (Ps 48:13). The ulcers and wounds with which our enemy incurably wounded us are pride, haughtiness, excessive self-love, unseemly desire, vainglory, ignorance of God and remissness toward Him, hatred, envy, anger, malice, impurity, and so on. What does a person not renewed by the grace of God plan and desire, if not just evil and vanity? As only a bad smell emanates from a stinking spring, so nothing except evil comes from a human heart not renewed by the power of God. This evil is all the more dangerous, in that it is hidden deep inside a person. And it is only recognized by those who examine their internal condition with all diligence and find themselves in various temptations. Our enemy has so seriously wounded and infected us, O man, that no power could cure us. This requires the power of God, which created us from nothing. The Creator Himself had to come to His creation, which was incurably wounded by the enemy and prostrate on the path of this world, whom neither the law nor the prophets could heal, and the Creator Himself had to cure him who could not be remedied by any other power. The Creator came and *took pity* on him. "He came in human form to a human covered with wounds and *half-dead* in order to more easily cure him and to bring him into his original blessedness, which was lost through the serpent's cunning" (see Luke 10:33–35). I hymn you, my God and Creator! I have heard Your report and was afraid. You came to me, seeking me who was lost! And I glorify Your great condescension toward me, O Greatly Merciful One! Learn, O man, the wounds of your soul, if you want to be cured of them, and with all fervor pray and sigh to Christ. May He heal you—He without Whom your healing cannot take place, since this is impossible for any created actor. Only God, Who creates everything from nothing, can create light from darkness and good from evil.

# 62. A Hospital or Infirmary

What a hospital is to a sick person, the holy Church is to Christians who are spiritually ill. Sick people enter a hospital through a door. The spiritually ill enter the holy Church by faith and holy baptism. Sick people enter the hospital in order to be cured from illness and recover their health. The spiritually ill enter the holy Church in order to be cured from diseases of the soul and be saved. In a hospital, there is a physician who visits the sick, examines them, and treats them. In the Church there is the holy Doctor, Christ, Who visits and heals Christians, the spiritually ill. In the hospital, the physician forbids patients everything that hinders the treatment he is giving them. Christ orders Christians in the holy Church to refrain from everything that hinders the healing of their souls and their attaining eternal salvation. In a hospital, patients who wish to be healed obey the physician and are healed. Likewise, Christians, if they wish to be healed and be saved, must listen to Christ the Physician and avoid everything that he forbids. In the hospital, those patients who do not obey the physician and do not abstain from what he forbids them are not healed and do not regain their health. Likewise, those Christians who do not obey Christ and who live by their fancies and not by the rule of His teaching will remain unhealed and will be deprived of salvation. In the hospital the patients declare their ailments to the physician: "I am sick with something." Likewise, Christians must declare their ailments to Christ, the Heavenly Physician, and ask healing of Him. "Those who are well have no need of a physician, but those who are sick" (Matt 9:12). In the hospital, it happens that not all patients are healed. There are incurable diseases, and a person cannot have everything that he wants. In the holy Church, it is otherwise. There is no illness of the soul that Christ does not wish to and cannot heal, if only the patient himself wishes this and earnestly desires, asks, and seeks it from Christ. Everything is possible for Him Whose word and gesture everything obeys, Whose wish and word is deed, by Whose command "the lepers are cleansed, the blind receive their sight, the deaf hear, the dumb speak, the paralytics and those lying on their beds stand up, and the dead are raised" (see Matt 11:5). Only become aware of, Christian, and acknowledge your infirmity, and with humility ask healing of This Physician, and wait without doubting, and you will surely receive it. Only beware of what hinders His saving treatment. In a hospital, the patients wishing to be healed give themselves over to the will of the physician, so that he can act as he wishes. Likewise Christians, if they truly want to be cured, must commit and entrust themselves to the most wise and faithful Physician, Jesus Christ, so that He would do with them as He wishes. He will give bitter or sweet medicine—all must be taken as he thinks best. For Jesus Christ is the wise, faithful, and man-loving Physician and very much wants to heal our souls, and so save them. For this He came into the world and suffered and died for us. He healed our corruptible and mortal bodies, as His Gospel preaches. Will he not heal immortal souls? Let us entrust ourselves to him—that He will heal us, as He wills. But we will try to abstain from everything that He forbids us and hinders His treatment. What use is medicine to a patient if he acts according to his own will and not according to the will of the physician? Reflect on this, O Christian, if you want to be cured and so be saved. All of us are sick and need a Doctor to heal us. But not everyone is aware of and acknowledges his illness. The beginning of healing is to be aware of your infirmity. Many are not healed since they are not aware of their infirmity. They are not aware because they do not try to be aware. And so, not being aware of and not acknowledging their infirmity, they do not seek healing. A person sees bodily infirmity and seeks healing. Oh, with what zeal he would seek healing of his soul, if only he saw its serious illness! But the problem is that like the soul itself, its infirmity is not visible and is only perceived by them who examine its condition with all diligence. Examine it, O man, and learn the multifarious infirmities of your soul, that you may look for its healing by Christ, the Heavenly Physician. The more you examine and learn of its infirmity, the greater eagerness and desire you will exert in seeking its healing. Unhealed bodily illness threatens temporal death. Unhealed illness of the soul threatens eternal death. Cease looking and seeking what is outside you and for the most part brings harm and not benefit. Examine and learn what is happening in your soul and how many and which illnesses torment it and lead it to death. You have entered into the sacred clinic of the holy Church to seek healing of your soul from Christ the Saviour and thus to be eternally saved, and not to seek honor, glory, and riches, not to put on banquets, not to go visiting or to receive guests, and not to chase after other types of vanity. People come to the infirmary to be healed, not to carry out their fancies. Poor Christian! Become aware of your error, and turn from vanity to Christ, and try to perceive the infirmity of your soul, and acknowledge it before Christ, that you may receive healing from Him. "Those who are well have no need of a physician, but those who are sick" (Matt 9:12). "I said, Lord, have mercy on me; heal my soul, for I have sinned against Thee. My wounds stink, and are corrupt, because of my foolishness" (Ps 40:5, 37:6).

"It happens that a sick person seeks healing from many physicians but does not find it, as we read in the Gospel about the woman who was suffering from a flow of blood" (Mark 5:25–26). Likewise, the poor Christian, seeing his terrible infirmity of the soul, seeks help first from one place, then from another, but does not find it. He reads many books with no small diligence but cannot find healing in them. Beloved Christian! No matter how hard you try, or where you turn, you will not receive healing anywhere or anyhow except from Christ. Without a doubt, it is helpful and necessary to read Christian books, and to reflect on them, and to study them. They enlighten the mind, give understanding, move to repentance, and prompt us to prayer. But all of them, as we see, point to Christ and refer us to Christ and guide us to seek healing and salvation from Him. He alone, being the Eternal Light, gives light to the blind and, being a Physician, heals the sick and, being Life, gives life to the dead and, being all-powerful, raises up the paralytics and makes the lame whole. That poor woman suffering from a flow of blood, when she could not obtain healing from any physicians, but rather grew worse, heard about Jesus, about whom news was spreading everywhere, that He was accessible to all, and that he healed all kinds of ailments not by herbs, but by His Word and His power. And she thought this: "I will go to that Great Wonderworker and Physician, and on account of the shame of my infirmity, I will not appear before His face, I will not declare my foul infirmity, but will come up from behind and touch His robe, and I shall be cured." And with such faith, "she came behind Him in the crowd and touched His garment. For she said, 'If only I may touch His clothes, I shall be made well.' Immediately the fountain of her blood was dried up, and she felt in her body that she was healed of the affliction" (Mark 5:27–29). You see, Christian, the faith of the poor woman! You see the power, effect, and fruit of her faith! This woman teaches us where and how to seek healing of the infirmities of our souls, that is, with Christ and by faith. She said to herself, "If only I may touch His clothes, I shall be made well." Here is the nature of faith! And she obtained what she hoped for. Where there is true faith, there is also hope. Let us take this woman as an example. We will draw near to Christ with faith and hope, and though silently we will fall down before His all-seeing eye. When we pray it shall be with faith and hope. When we approach His holy and life-giving Mysteries, we will draw near with faith and hope of healing and renewal, remembering and imitating that woman who suffered from a flow of blood. So our infirmity of soul will be healed, and the source of our ruinous passions that torment our souls will dry up. A sign that affliction of the soul has begun to be healed is when pernicious passions begin to calm down and abate, when pride, self-love, greed, hatred, envy, anger, rage, stinginess, love of fame, impurity, and other evils subside in a person, like a sign of a body that has begun to heal, when it begins to be freed from harmful humors. What harmful humors are to the body are what sinful passions are to the soul. Harmful humors torment and kill the body. Sinful passions torment the soul and lead it to eternal death. The body becomes healthy when it is healed from evil and harmful humors. Likewise, the soul becomes healthy when it is freed from evil and sinful passions. "Have mercy on me, O Lord, Son of David! My daughter (my soul) is severely demon-possessed ... Lord, help me!" (Matt 15:22, 25). A sin that lives in the soul and torments the soul is great demon. It does not give it peace. It inclines toward and darts first to one, then to another, then to a third impious and ruinous undertaking. "Lord, help me!" And she said, "Yes, Lord, yet even the little dogs eat the crumbs which fall from their masters' table." And may I, the unworthy, hear too: "Let it be to you as you desire," as the Canaanite woman heard (Matt 15:27–28).

# 63. Poison, Hidden in a Person

Bad people may give poison to a person. So the ancient serpent, our enemy the devil, has poured a sinful and deadly poison into our nature. A person, although he may be healthy, becomes seriously ill if he somehow accidentally takes poison. Likewise, our nature was pure, chaste, holy, and good. But when it was infected by the poison of that cunning and evil serpent, it fell into incurable disease and misfortune. The poison present in a person infects his whole body. Likewise, the deadly poison of the serpent infected all our powers of soul and body. It happens from this poison that "For from within, out of the heart of men, proceed evil thoughts, adulteries, fornications, murders, thefts, covetousness, wickedness, deceit, lewdness, an evil eye, blasphemy, pride, foolishness. All these evil things come from within and defile a man" (Mark 7:21–23). "From here proceed: adultery, fornication, uncleanness, lewdness, idolatry, sorcery, hatred, contentions, jealousies, outbursts of wrath, selfish ambitions, dissensions, heresies, envy, murders, drunkenness, revelries, and the like" (Gal 5:19–21). From these come pride, haughtiness, contempt for neighbors, condemnation, slander, revenge in deed and word, desire for and seeking one's own honor, glory and praise. From these come flattery, slyness, cunning, falsehood, and hypocrisy. From these come shameful acts and filthy language. From this come excessiveness in food and drink and solicitude for feasting. From this people so devise changes in clothing, in construction and decoration of houses, in arrangement of carriages and horses, and other vanity. All this and other similar things proceed from carnal thinking and the serpent's deadly poison, sown in the human heart. The poison, present within a person, torments them and with time causes an unbearable illness. So also this poison of the serpent, hidden in the soul, very much torments it and causes various illnesses.

See what pride does in a person! How it torments him! How many ways does he devise to acquire honor, glory, and praise in this world! Having acquired it, with what labor and care does he guard this, his treasure! How indignant he is when he is held in contempt by someone! How he suffers, is troubled, grumbles, and uses bad language when he is deprived of honor, so much so that many kill themselves!

It is impossible to say what greed does, what harm and illness it brings the poor human soul. We see with what indefatigable effort and constant labors these poor people seek riches. With what fear and dread they look after and guard what they have obtained! Having lost it, how they become sad, depressed; they grieve, lament, and torment themselves and, not enduring this unbearable illness, will often even consign themselves to death.

Everyone, especially those living a celibate life, knows what torment and what burning in the heart and in the person's whole body sexual desire creates. Like a raging fever, it creates burning and stirring in a person's whole body. It is impossible to depict how a poor soul is tormented by envy. The body itself grows pale and withers from envy.

Take a look, too, at anger, what signs of its torment it produces! Look what a person does in anger. How indignant he is and how he kicks up a fuss, curses and swears, torments himself and beats himself, strikes himself on the head and face and, as if in a fever, shakes all over. In a word, he becomes like one possessed. If the external appearance is so sordid, what is going on inside the poor soul! How the demon is tormenting it!

You see, O man, what terrible serpent's poison is hidden in the soul and how bitterly it torments it! Get to know with all diligence and examine this deadly poison hiding in your heart and soul. Its terrible and noxious action manifests itself. If it were not in your heart and in your soul, you would not have such terrible and bitter illnesses. For everything is known by its actions.

Thus, a serpent's poison, hidden in the human heart and soul, is known by its terrible and excruciating actions. He who knows this great and pernicious evil needs to seek healing from it, lest he die from it in soul and body forever. The poison, present in the body and unhealed, is death for a person. Likewise that most ruinous poison, if it is not healed by Christ's power, threatens nothing other than eternal death to the soul. When the body is ill, you seek a physician and try to heal it, although you know that this house will be destroyed and will be turned into dust and earth. Is it not necessary to care much more about the immortal and incorruptible soul, which exceeds the whole world, heaven and earth in preciousness and value, and to seek healing for it? The soul is, so dear, created in the image of God and redeemed by the priceless blood of the Son of God, and you do not care about it! You do not care because you do not see and do not know its cruel and deadly illness and the poison hidden in it. Oh, if it were possible for a person to see the cruel contagion of the soul! He truly would be terrified and would weep inconsolably and would sob about its misfortune and ruination, and having left everything behind him, would seek how to heal it and bring it to its former comeliness and beauty! Who, upon seeing his extreme misfortune, will not seek a way to be freed from it? We see that those sick in body, having sensed in themselves some kind of illness, seek healing. So, having learned of and experienced a serious and ruinous illness, will you not try to heal your soul? It is impossible not to. A recognized misfortune convinces a person to seek a method and help for deliverance from it. Recognize and examine, O man, the cruel infirmity of your soul and you will try to heal it. Without awareness of infirmity, its healing does not take place. We become aware, beloved, of the cruel infirmity hiding in our souls, and turn to Christ, the Physician of souls and bodies. We will seek healing from Him with all effort and zeal, often and from the depths of our heart raising up to Him the call of the ten lepers: "Jesus, Master, have mercy on us!" (Luke 17:13). But we will also take care of ourselves, avoiding every sin because He is offended by it. Who will anger a physician from whom he is seeking healing? Is it not better to try to please him? The cruel serpent has infected us with his cruel poison, and we will seek healing from Christ the Son of God. Only He can heal us from it, and He makes well those who sigh and pray with faith in Him. "The Israelites, bitten in the desert by serpents, looked at the copper serpent and so were healed" (Num 21:6–9). So should we too look with faith to Christ, the Son of God, Who was lifted up on the tree for our sins and Who by His Cross crushed the head of that serpent, that we may be healed from his deadly poison. "And as Moses lifted up the serpent in the wilderness, even so must the Son of Man be lifted up, that whoever believes in Him should not perish but have eternal life" (John 3:14–15).

# 64. Warfare

In the world, we see that when one nation rises up against another, the other state prepares to defend itself and take up arms against the aggressor and join battle with him. Likewise, inasmuch as our flesh with its passions and lusts rises up against us, Christians, we should not slumber but should defend ourselves and resist it. When one state resists another and one tries to overcome it, then a battle takes place between them. So, when a Christian resists the flesh with its passions and lusts and does not do what it wants, but even more so tries to subdue its spirit, then a battle takes place between the Christian and the flesh. And this is what the Apostle writes about: "For the flesh lusts against the Spirit, and the Spirit against the flesh; and these are contrary to one another" (Gal 5:17). In visible warfare, when one side does not wish to submit to the other, and so give itself up into slavery to it, it fights against it with all its power. Likewise, the Christian must stand up and fight against the flesh with all endeavor and diligence if he does not want to be conquered by it, be subjugated by it, be its captive and slave. In warfare, the soldiers who are fighting against their enemy receive directions from the commanders and help from each other. Likewise, a Christian fighting against the flesh must ask and expect instructions and help from Christ, the author and judge of struggles, and by His power subdue the uprising of his flesh. The flesh wishes to be haughty and arrogant, but the Christian must suppress it by Christ's humility. In this world, the flesh desires to become rich and to acquire much, but the Christian must cut off this desire by Christ's poverty. The flesh wishes to become angry at a person and take vengeance on him for an offense, but the Christian should tame its impulses by Christ's meekness and calm. In misfortune, the flesh is agitated, rushes about, wishes to grumble and not have patience, but the Christian must calm its unseemly impulse by Christ's power and patience. The flesh wishes to hate those who are at enmity with it and to be angry at them, but the Christian should overcome it with Christ's goodness and love. So also in other cases the Christian should stand up and fight against the flesh by the power and example of Christ and overcome it. In visible warfare, it happens that a defeated side again rises up and reorganizes and fights even more vigorously against the side that had defeated it. Likewise the Christian, after being defeated by the flesh, must stand up and, calling on the help of the all-powerful Jesus, be fortified by His power, and again stand up and fight against the flesh, and not permit it to master and exercise dominion over it. In visible warfare, the more one side is defeated, and the other side wins, the weaker the defeated side becomes, and the stronger and more powerful the winning side is. So also is it in the battle between the flesh and the Christian. The more the Christian overcomes the flesh, the more the flesh weakens, its passions and lusts are calmed and subside, and the Christian is filled with great power and is strengthened and improved. In visible warfare, the soldier stands and fights not against a single enemy but against all of them. Likewise, the Christian should stand and fight not just against only one passion but against all of them. What use is it for a soldier to stand and fight against one enemy and not to oppose the other and to be defeated and killed by them? A soldier, if he wants to preserve his life and be the victor, must oppose all the enemies coming against him. What use is it for a Christian to stand and fight against one particular passion but to be subdued by the others and fall into slavery? Many struggle against lust, which is praiseworthy and excellent but are overcome by anger and rage. Others are generous and merciful to their neighbors, but do harm to a person with their tongue, slandering him and passing judgment on him. Many restrain their bellies from overeating and drunkenness but do not want to fast even a little from remembering of wrongs. It is likewise in other things. As we arm ourselves and stand against one passion, so must we arm ourselves against others and fight with them.

"The Apostle says concerning this, Beloved, I beg you as sojourners and pilgrims, abstain from fleshly lusts, which war against the soul" (1 Pet 2:11). Christian! As you have armed yourself and fight against one particular passion, likewise arm yourself against the others and do not permit them to defeat you. As you fight against lust and do not allow it to master you, struggle and wage war against pride; fight with haughtiness; contend with vainglory; grapple with anger, rage, and remembering wrongs; battle with greed and miserliness; tussle with hatred and envy; and so on. As you restrain your belly from overeating and drunkenness, restrain your tongue from slander and condemnation, idle talk, foul language, and backbiting. As you keep your hands from murder, theft, stealing, and robbery, keep them too from fighting. As you fast from food and drink, abstain also from every evil. This is Christian fasting!

This is true abstinence! This struggle is difficult, but Christian duty requires it. Many conquer people, states, and cities but do not want to conquer themselves. This is Christian victory: to conquer oneself, that is, one's flesh. The more often a soldier takes part in battle and fights against enemies, the more skilled and braver he becomes. Likewise, the more a Christian fights against the flesh, its passions and lusts, and defeats them by Christ's grace, the more skilled in the Christian calling and better he becomes hour by hour. For the Lord, seeing his effort, endeavor, and struggle, pardons and corrects him; frees him from slavery to the passions; and makes him a good tree that bears good fruit. "For if you live according to the flesh you will die, but if by the Spirit you put to death the deeds of the body, you will live" (Rom 8:13). "Those who are Christ's have crucified the flesh with its passions and desires" (Gal 5:24). "There is therefore now no condemnation to those who are in Christ Jesus, who do not walk according to the flesh but according to the Spirit" (Rom 8:1). "Beholding the sea of life surging with the tempest of temptations, I run to Thy calm haven and cry unto Thee: Raise up my life from corruption, O Greatly-merciful One."[7]

# 65. Calling

In the world, we see that people are named by various callings. Some are judges, others soldiers, commanders, herders, and so on. Likewise, every Christian has been called to repentance by Christ the Lord, Who says, "I did not come to call the righteous, but sinners, to repentance" (Matt 9:13). "But since we are all sinners, for all have sinned and fall short of the glory of God" (Rom 3:23), we all are called to repentance. For the Christian calling, to which they are called by Christ, is true repentance; Christ has called them to this. For every person, his calling is his very first concern while he is in his calling. The first concern of judges is to try to find the truth and to rule according to the laws, as long as they are in this calling. Likewise, the first calling of Christians is to be in repentance, since Christ has called them to this. Look, Christian: what have you been called to? Not riches, not honor, not to seek glory in the world, not to host banquets, not to go visiting or to receive guests but, having turned away from all of this, to be in repentance and by this to receive eternal salvation in Jesus Christ, to which you were called. Salvation consists not only in breaking with external serious sins but also in a change of mind and heart and in renewal of one's internal condition. That is, one must turn away from all the vanity of the world, since it hinders everyone who desires to be saved; to examine each separate infirmity of the soul, that is, pride, anger, envy, impurity, greed, and so on; to feel regret and contrition that through the serpent's poison such an evil entered our soul, which was created pure and immaculate; and to pray with such regret and contrition to Christ, so that He would correct and heal us by His power. And when the heart or internal condition changes and reforms, then the external life and deeds will be good. The feet will not walk toward evil if the soul does not desire it. The hands will not do evil if the will does not desire it. The tongue will not speak evil if the heart does not desire it. The body will not commit fornication if the heart does not desire it. What is the use of not doing wrong on the outside but being evil on the inside? What is the use of not stealing but being covetous on the inside? What use is it not to kill with the hands but to breathe malice and murder within? The murderer, adulterer, and thief live in the heart. There is no use in a vessel that is clean on the outside but is filled with all kinds of stench and filth inside. So there is no use for a person who is good on the outside but evil on the inside; is humble and quiet externally but filled with pride, envy, and malice internally; he speaks affectionately and smoothly but has flattery and craftiness in his heart; he restrains his hands from theft and robbery but gives nothing of his own to anyone, and so on. Therefore, people who are good on the outside, but are evil on the inside, are likened to "whitewashed tombs which indeed appear beautiful outwardly, but inside are full of dead men's bones and all uncleanness" (Matt 23:27). Christian, our God tries our very hearts and reins (see Ps 7:10) and "the Lord sees into the heart" whereas "man looks at the outward appearance" (1 Kgs 16:7 LXX). He looks at what is inside, hidden in the heart, not what is outside; He judges a person by this. You are humble on the outside—that is good, but haven't you become haughty in your heart? You do not show anger on the outside and do not show a bad temper—that is good, but aren't you consumed inside you with malice against your neighbor? You do not kill your brother with your hands—you do well, but look—don't you hate him in your heart? "Whoever hates his brother is a murderer" (1 John 3:15). You do not get involved carnally with a woman—you do well, but you lust in your heart and are a fornicator. "Whoever looks at a woman to lust for her has already committed adultery with her in his heart" (Matt 5:28). You do not purloin someone else's property, but inside, in your heart, you wish to do this—you are truly a thief. You do not steal another's property, but out of your stinginess you do not give to a poor person—you are truly a thief. If you keep for yourself alone God's bounties, which were given to you not just for yourself but for others as well, then you are wronging people to the degree that you are able to give of the riches that you are keeping for yourself, and so on. The human heart is a vessel filled with filth and the stench of lusts. Beloved Christian! Let us try to clean this vessel within us, and our external acts will be pleasing to God. God has promised us a great thing—He promised that He Himself would live in our hearts: "I will dwell in them and walk among them. I will be their God, And they shall be My people" (2 Cor 6:16; Lev 26:12). There is not and cannot be a greater, more precious, more pleasant, and more beloved treasure than having God living within us. And there is no greater honor for a person than to be the temple of God. God lives in a pure soul as in His most welcoming temple. And He loves to dwell in a pure soul more than in temples built with hands, inasmuch as the image of God is in the soul. Let us too cleanse our hearts, O Christians! May the image of God, the splendid beauty of our souls, appear also in us, and so we shall be the temple of our God. "Therefore, having these promises, beloved, let us cleanse ourselves from all filthiness of the flesh and spirit, perfecting holiness in the fear of God" (2 Cor 7:11). "I will pour out my prayer unto the Lord, and to Him will I proclaim my grief; for with evils my soul is filled, and my life unto hades hath drawn nigh, and like Jonah I will pray: From corruption raise me up, O God."[8]

# 66. Your Father Has Been Waiting for You a Long Time. Do Not Tarry!

A person speaks like this to another person who has absented himself from his father and is procrastinating: "Your father has been waiting for you a long time. Why are you tarrying?" This is how the prophets, apostles, pastors, and teachers of the Church speak to and exhort every sinner who at holy baptism was joined to his Heavenly Father and was numbered with His holy people but later was separated from Him by an iniquitous and debauched life, and as it were went away into a far country: Your Heavenly Father has been waiting for you a long time. Why, poor sinner, are you tarrying in this iniquitous country and ruinous separation? You have lost the inheritance given to you. You are deprived of your daily sustenance. A pernicious hunger has befallen you. Having left your merciful and compassionate Father, you have fallen into slavery to an evil and harsh tormenter; you tend his dumb and unclean beasts, swine. And you do not have anything to fill your belly while doing such hard and loathsome work. You have gotten to the point where you desire and seek the pods with which the swine were fed, but no one gives you even such meager and vile food. You yourself see what misfortune, poverty, and wretchedness you are in. You have fallen from great wealth! Into what baseness you have come crashing down from such high honor! What great blessedness you have been deprived of and into what great misfortune you have fallen! All this happened to you because you willfully separated yourself from your good and compassionate Father, from His house, His holy family. Complete abundance flows out to everyone living in His house—you have been deprived of everything! Everyone there lives in complete prosperity by the grace of your Merciful Father—and you live in complete poverty! Everyone there is sufficiently sated with food and refreshed with drink, and you are dying from hunger! There is enough tasty food and pleasant drink for all His people, and you have come to such scarcity that you wish to fill your belly with pods that swine eat, but no one gives you even these! Everyone in that house finds repose under the protection of their Merciful Father, but here you are among unclean beasts, swine! Everyone there wears nice clothing, but you are covered with torn and stinking rags, like some pauper! Everyone there is consoled, but you lament. Everyone there rejoices, but you weep. Everyone there enjoys himself, but you grieve and are sad. Everyone there eats and drinks plentifully, but you are deprived of everything. Oh, into what a difficult affliction you have come, you, who was in honor, glory, wealth, plenty, peace, rest, and all blessedness, living with your compassionate and most merciful Father! The straying son often hears such words and admonitions, but he tarries in his calamitous separation. The compassionate Father waits and often checks to see when His straying son will come to Him. But His son has no such thought or feeling for returning to his Father. His Father wants to show mercy to him, but the son does not care about mercy. The Father wants to receive him again as his son and give him his inheritance, but the son does not want to come to his Father. His Father wants to make him a participant in His blessedness, but the son does not understand that. The Father with His family awaits him in His home, but the son tarries, as he lingered in iniquitous separation and in a pernicious country. He wishes more to be with the evil tormenter than with his good and compassionate Father. He wishes more to be covered with stinking and foul rags than to wear good clothing at his Father's. He wishes more to fill his belly with pods, the food of swine, than to enjoy the good things of his Father's house. He wishes to be in an impoverished condition than to be in blessedness. Oh, the goodness, oh, the compassion of his Father, Who does not despise, does not forget, does not reject the son who willfully broke away and angered Him by his evil disposition, but with great yearning waits for His straying son to return to Him! Oh, the blindness, the callousness of a son who prefers to stay in a foreign land, enduring extreme misfortunes, rather than to return to his Father and to live in His house in complete well-being. O poor son, come to your senses and leave this iniquitous and pernicious country! Remember the compassion of your Father, and recall His great munificence! You have angered Him, but He does not take away His mercy from you. You left Him, but He expects you to return to Him and wants to take you back. Remember what abundance of good things were in the house of your Father, "How many of my father's hired servants have bread enough and to spare, and I perish with hunger!" (Luke 15:17). Get up and return to your Father. You have squandered His wealth, but do not be afraid. He is compassionate, long-suffering, and greatly merciful. He will not remember your willfulness; He will not reprimand you for your behavior that was offensive to Him. He is generous and wealthy; he will make you rich again. Get up and go boldly to your Father and, falling down before His merciful eyes, acknowledge your guilt, and say to Him with contrition and sorrow of heart: "Father, I have sinned against heaven and before you, and I am no longer worthy to be called your son. Make me like one of your hired servants" (Luke 15:18–19). He awaits you with great longing and will receive you with joy. As soon as He sees you returning, even from afar, He will mercifully and lovingly look upon you and take pity on you; His merciful heart is troubled for your sake, and pardoning you, he will have mercy on you. "Ah! My beloved child, My lost child, is returning to me. My son, who has been separated from Me, is coming back to me: "'This my son was dead and is alive again; he was lost and is found' ... I will surely have mercy upon him" (Luke 15:24). Going out to meet him, "his father saw him and had compassion, and ran and fell on his neck and kissed him" (Luke 15:20). Indeed, you will still be afar off, and your Father will see you and take pity; and, running up, He will fall on your shoulder and kiss you, will lead you into His house and will give you the best clothing and dress you in it, will give you a ring for your finger and shoes for your feet, and will order His whole holy family to rejoice and be glad for you, saying, "This my son was dead and is alive again; he was lost and is found." And they will begin to make merry for you (see Luke 15:13–24). "There is joy in the presence of the angels of God over one sinner who repents" (Luke 15:10). The more sincerely you repent and reform, and change for the better, the sooner you will go and draw near to your Heavenly Father. For we come to Him not with our feet but with our hearts, not by alteration of place but by change of our will and morals. As by sins we separate ourselves and withdraw from Him, so by true repentance, reform, and change of our will and habits for the better we draw hear to Him. Turn, my soul to your Heavenly Father, and you will receive from Him rest and blessedness. Say as did the prodigal son: "Father, I have sinned against heaven and in your sight, and am no longer worthy to be called your son ... make me like one of your hired servants" (Luke 15:18–20).

# 67. And We Will Go There

It happens that when people go to some place, city, or some kind of business, others say to their family or neighbors, "Your people went someplace or to some kind of business." And they answer them like this: "And we too will go there." Christians! These words, "And we will go there," will befit us if we remember our departure from the world. Our brothers and ancestors left this world and went into the next, and we shall go there. They left behind the world, and we shall leave it behind. They left behind their pleasures, and we shall leave ours behind. They left behind their relatives and friends, and we shall leave ours behind. They left behind their houses and all their expensive attire, and we shall leave ours behind. They left their estates and their villages behind, and we shall leave ours behind. They left gold, silver and all their wealth behind, and we shall leave ours behind. They left their ranks, titles, names, and all their glory behind, and we shall leave ours. They left all their luxury behind, and we shall leave ours behind. In a word, they have left everything behind, and we shall leave everything behind. They took nothing with them, and we shall take nothing either. They left this world naked, and we shall leave it naked and leave it soon. Why are we toiling and accumulating? They went to the Righteous Judge to receive according to their works, and we shall go, too. Ah! We shall go to the Judge of all, to God, Who regards not persons, but the conscience and the works, with Whom kings and their subjects, masters and servants, renowned and low-born, rich and poor, princes and tillers of the soil, are all equal. Christians, our ancestors and brothers went to this Judge in the next world, and we shall go there, too. Highly honored kings! Your ancestors and brothers went there to receive their lot, and you will go there and will stand before the Judge with your subjects, and give an answer to Him—how you ruled His people that he entrusted to you. Lords, princes, and masters! Your brothers and forebears went there to receive their recompense, and you will go there and will stand next to your servants and peasants before the Judge, and will give an answer as to how you behaved toward them. Judges! Your forebears and brothers went there, to the Righteous Judge, to give an answer, and you will go there, and will be intensely interrogated by Him as to how you judged His people. Pastors (bishops and priests)! Your brothers and forebears went into the next world to receive according to their deeds and their labors—you too will go, beloved, and Christ, the Chief of pastors, will ask of you concerning the Christian souls that He obtained by His blood. Rich men! Your brothers went into the next world to give an answer as to how and for what they expended the wealth given them—you too will go and will give an answer for all your possessions. Christians! Everyone is going there, and no one returns from there—we shall go and we shall not return. Those who have departed for there are all in their places and are awaiting the general resurrection and last judgment; we too shall go and everyone shall be in his place. Let us repent, beloved, and correct ourselves and prepare ourselves beforehand for the hour of death. Let us depart from here with good hope, and we shall receive mercy from Christ the Lord, and so we shall be in the place of rest, where the righteous and His saints find repose. "Let Thy mercy, O Lord, be upon us, according as we have put our trust in Thee" (Ps 32:22).

# 68. *Spring*

Spring is the image and sign of the resurrection of the dead. What happens during this season will also happen in the resurrection of the dead, as we see in the Sacred Scriptures and as we believe. During spring, all of earthly creation is renewed. Likewise, during the resurrection everything will be renewed, according to God's faithful promise. "Behold, I make all things new," the Lord says (Rev 21:5). "There shall be a new heaven and a new earth," and so on (Isa 65:17). We, "according to His promise, look for new heavens and a new earth in which righteousness dwells" (2 Pet 3:13).

During spring, all creation, as we see, comes to life. Likewise, in the resurrection of the dead all human nature will come to life. During spring, every kind
of grass and verdure emerges from the depths of the earth and appears in its
own form. Likewise, on the last day, the dead will come out of their graves
and will each be in their own image. "For the hour is coming in which all who
are in the graves will hear His voice and come forth–those who have done
good, to the resurrection of life, and those who have done evil, to the resurrection of condemnation" (John 5:28–29). In the winter, trees and grass seem
dried up, but in the spring their vitality shows forth. Likewise, for those not
knowing of the resurrection of the dead, the deceased seem lost. But the holy
faith teaches us that their life will be made manifest on the last day. During
winter, both the dried-up and the thriving trees seem alike, but in spring, the
difference between them becomes apparent. Likewise, in the present age and
in death itself, the righteous and the ungodly have the same external appearance. But during the resurrection of the dead, the great difference between
them will be revealed. In springtime, the thriving trees and grass are covered
with leaves and various flowers. Likewise, in the resurrection of the dead,
the bodies of the pious and righteous will be transformed into a new, bright,
pleasant, and beautiful form, according to God's truthful promise. "For our
citizenship is in heaven, from which we also eagerly wait for the Saviour, the
Lord Jesus Christ, who will transform our lowly body that it may be conformed to His glorious body, according to the working by which He is able
even to subdue all things to Himself" (Phil 3:20–21). "Beloved, now we are
children of God, and it has not yet been revealed what we shall be, but we
know that when He is revealed, we shall be like Him, for we shall see Him
as He is" (1 John 3:2). "Then the righteous will shine forth as the sun in the
kingdom of their Father" (Matt 13:43). Dry trees and grass, both during the
winter and during the spring, have a constant and identical appearance, that
is, unpleasant and dark. Likewise, impious and irreligious people both now
and then will have an unpleasant, or rather, a very mean-spirited appearance.
Christian! You see in spring the image and sign of the resurrection of the
dead. And you see what kind of resurrection there will be of the righteous
and of sinners (then everyone will receive according to their works). Live
now as you want to arise then. You look for the resurrection of the dead, and
the life of the age to come—live not contrary to this but worthy of it. You
want to have fellowship with pious, righteous, and holy people then—live a
pious, holy, and righteous life now. What a person now has on the inside will

then be revealed on the outside. Is there piety? It will be revealed then. Is there dishonesty and hypocrisy? It will reveal itself then. Then the children of God and the children of the devil are manifest; then "the sheep [will be divided] from the goats" (1 John 3:10; Matt 25:32–33). "If we want, beloved, to attain the resurrection of the righteous, we must now resurrect spiritually with the risen Christ, that just as Christ was raised from the dead by the glory of the Father, even so we also should walk in newness of life" (Rom 6:4). "Awake, you who sleep, Arise from the dead, And Christ will give you light" (Eph 5:14). "Blessed and holy is he who has part in the first resurrection" (Rev 20:6).

## 69. Get Up!

It happens that someone rouses a lazy person and says to him, "Get up, it's time to go to work." So also God's saving grace rouses the Christian who is lazy and careless about his salvation: "Get up," and go about the work to which the Lord has called you. Every careless and unrepentant sinner is lying down and does not work out his own salvation with fear and trembling; does not labor in the Lord's vineyard (see Phil 2:12; Matt 20:1–16, 21:33). The fornicator and adulterer are lying down. The thief, extortioner, and robber are lying down. The malicious man and misanthrope are lying down. The slanderer, name-caller, vilifier, and he who disparages his neighbor and beats him with his tongue as with a weapon are lying down. The drunkard and the voluptuary are lying down. In a word, every unreformed and unrepentant sinner is lying down. God's grace comes to every such one, and strikes him, and says to him, "Get up! It's time to go about the Lord's business. It's time to repent; it is the moment to labor at the business of salvation. Get up! Time is going by and will not return. Your life is growing shorter. Death is coming unexpectedly. Satan, like a cunning thief, is stealing your salvation. Get up and wipe the sleep from your eyes." "Awake, you who sleep, Arise from the dead, And Christ will give you light" (Eph 5:14). Get up! God, like a compassionate and merciful Father, awaits you as a prodigal son. "When you return and groan, then you will be saved and know where you were" (Isa 30:15). Get up! Christ the Lord suffered and died for your sake. Christ's blood was poured out for your sake. Salvation was obtained for you not by gold or silver, not for any other price, but by the most precious blood of Christ. Do you want to lose such a dear treasure through negligence and cause yourself to fall into the eternal dominion of the devil, and into everlasting torment, from which Christ by His blood saved you? Remember that the death and blood of Christ will not help the unrepentant sinner, just as medicine will not help the sick person who does not care for himself. Get up! The Lord threatens punishment for the impious and iniquitous: may punishment not befall you as well. "Though they may attempt to bury themselves in Hades, from there My hand shall drag them out, and though they climb up to heaven, from there I shall bring them down. Though they hide themselves on top of Carmel, from there I shall search and take them. Though they hide from My sight at the bottom of the sea, from there I shall command the serpent, and it will bite them. And though they go into captivity before their enemies, from there I shall command the sword, and it will slay them. And I shall set my eyes on them for evil and not for good" (Amos 9:2–4). "Except ye be converted, He will whet His sword; He hath bent His bow and made it ready. He hath fitted it with the instruments of death; He hath forged His arrows in the fire" (Ps 7:13–14). "He shall pour out their blood as dust and their flesh as dung. Their silver and their gold shall not be able to deliver them in the day of the wrath of the Lord, but the whole land shall be consumed by the fire of His zeal" (Zeph 1:17–18). Poor man! Repent, and you will escape God's punishment. God's threats are not hollow: they will come true if sinners do not repent. Get up! Your life is growing shorter, and every day, a certain part of it is taken away, and death approaches and will come to you like an express messenger. And it is already closer to you today than it was yesterday and the day before. However it finds you, that is how it will send you into the next world. Take care, lest it find you unrepentant and careless. It comes unexpectedly, like a thief, and carries off people when, where, and how they least expect it. Take care, then, and expect it every day and hour. And, having gotten up, be sober and vigilant and be such as you wish to be in that hour. Do you remember where are those who lived in sins; in luxury; in voluptuousness; in the gaiety of the world; in honor, glory, and wealth? They have died. "Everything that pleased them has left them and they are now in their places and await Christ's universal Judgment. Get up! Christ the Lord will come to the Judgment and will call all to His Judgment that each one may receive the things done in the body, according to what he has done, whether good or bad" (2 Cor 5:10). You too will be called to that Judgment, and it will be rendered to you for every impious deed, word, and thought. All the people there will be divided into two parts; some will stand on the right side of the Judge, and others on His left. Some will hear from the Righteous Judge, "Come, you blessed of My Father, inherit the kingdom prepared for you from the foundation of the world"; others will hear, "Depart from Me, you cursed, into the everlasting fire prepared for the devil and his angels" (Matt 25:34, 41). Blessed are they who will hear, "Come," but cursed and poor, to whom will be said, "Depart from me." Get up, poor sinner, and work out your own salvation with fear and trembling (Phil 2:12), that you will be deemed worthy then to be among the blessed. Get up! Eternal torment awaits careless and unrepentant sinners! What should you expect if you do not wake up and do not repent with contrition of heart? Today God's mercy is promised and given to everyone who repents. Then all mercy will cease to be granted. But then the word will be heard spoken, "Son, remember that in your lifetime you received your good things" (Luke 16:25). You too will hear these words. You will suffer without end. You will always be dying but never die. You will be both living and dying. You will be on fire but never be burned up. You will taste the sorrow of eternal death. The fire that torments you will not go out; the worm eating you will not die, if you do not repent. Having gotten up, repent, and with weeping and tears turn to the Lord your God, that he would have mercy on you, lest you fall into endless misfortune. Get up! God promises eternal life, eternal joy, and eternal blessedness to the righteous, to saints, and to all sinners who repent with a contrite heart. They will be with God forever. They will see God face to face and will delight in this, like a sweet drink, forever. They will be endlessly consoled; they will rejoice and exult forever. They will, like kings and lords, reign without end. No sinner will enter into that eternal life if he does not wash himself and be purified by contrition of heart and warm tears, if faith has not "made [their robes] white in the blood of the Lamb" (Rev 7:14). "But outside are dogs and sorcerers and sexually immoral and murderers and idolaters, and whoever loves and practices a lie" (Rev 22:15). Get up and repent, and work for the cause of your salvation, lest you be deprived of that blessedness. Today if you will hear His voice, "Harden not your hearts, as in the provocation, and as the day of temptation in the wilderness; when your fathers tempted Me, proved Me, and saw my works. Forty years long was I grieved with that generation, and said, they do not always err in their hearts, for they have not known My ways; so I swore in My wrath, that they should not enter into My rest" (Ps 94:7–11). We then, as workers together with Him, also plead with you not to receive the grace of God in vain. For He says: "In an acceptable time I have heard you, And in the day of salvation I have helped you." Behold, now is the accepted time; behold, now is the day of salvation (2 Cor 6:1–2).

## 70. Livestock

The kind of ill temper that is seen in livestock and wild animals is also present in a person who is not reborn and not renewed by the grace of God. In livestock, we see self-love. We see how it wants to eat all the food, grabbing it and devouring it, and does not allow another animal near and chases it away. This also is seen in a human. He offends others but he will not tolerate an offense himself. He holds others in contempt but will not tolerate contempt himself. He slanders others, but he does not want to hear slander about himself. He steals others' property but does not want his property to be stolen. He himself does not help others in need, but he wants someone to help him when he is in need. He wants people to feed him if he is hungry, clothe him if he is naked, let him in their house if he is wandering, and so on but does not do this for others. He does not want any evil for himself but rather wishes every good thing for himself; to others he does evil and does nothing good. He wants to have everything but is not disturbed that his neighbor has nothing. In a word, he wants to enjoy complete well-being himself, and to avoid misfortune, but does not think of other people who are like himself. This is bestial and loathsome self-love. Pride can be seen in a beast. The same thing can be seen in a human. We see the poor person disparages others but exalts himself. As he despises others, he glorifies himself. As he accuses others, he excuses himself. As he condemns others, he justifies himself; as he backbites and abuses others, he praises himself. We see that everywhere he seeks the first place and wants to command others, rule over them, give orders, and to be deferred to by all. What meaning has thinking up beautiful and gold-threaded attire, palatial houses, rich carriages and expensive horses, splendid banquets, filled with all kinds of foods and drinks, and other vanity and magnificence—what, I say, does all this signify, if not pride hiding in the human heart that seeks glorification in everything? Pride wants to show itself everywhere and to everyone, and humility, beloved of God and people, wants to hide itself. You see, O man, human pride, but be aware that the more loathsome the vice is before God, the more hidden little recognized by anyone it is. But it is recognized only by those who examine themselves with all assiduousness and find themselves in various temptations. And why should earth, ashes, and the shadow of death be proud? We see anger and rage in an animal. The same thing is present in a human. We see how he is enraged, how he is indignant, how he grumbles, how he is in a bad temper, how he agonizes, all from anger! How he shakes like a leaf in the wind; how he swears; how he vilifies, curses, and often spews out horrible blasphemies; how he threatens one who has offended him; how he holds a grudge and seeks how to get revenge on him. This is the effect of hideous and pernicious anger, hidden in a person's heart! We see that animals fight. We see the same among humans. We see how many quarrels and blood shedding of all sorts happen between the wretched people. Cunning and slyness is observed among animals. The same pernicious evil is present in a human. We see how he pretends, how he puts in a show of being good, although he is evil inside. We see how he dissembles, is cunning, flatters, lies, cheats, and is hypocritical. Thievery is observed among livestock. The same is seen in a human. How many manifest, secret, and crafty methods of thievery a man thinks up, and will not even think of it, consequently few are free of it, especially merchants, artisans, petty officials, masters, landowners who have peasants, treasurers, the rich, the famous, and others who love the world, riches, glory, and honor. Gluttony is observed among livestock, the same as among people. Impurity is seen among livestock. We see the same among humans. We see that the wretched man, like a swine in mud, wallows in sensuality. Laziness is observed among livestock. We see it also in man. We see how he is negligent for himself and for his salvation. But what is worse than this and further increases human poverty and wretchedness is that of those evil dispositions that are found in various beasts, all are found in a single unreformed human. Some dumb animals are proud, but others are humble. Some are cunning and sly, but others are guileless. Some are sullen and irascible, but others are meek. Some are lazy, but others are vigorous. But every depravity of a beast is present in the wretched sinner; he is proud, irascible, greedy, lazy, cunning, sly, impure, and so on. Oh, what a lethal poison, and what a colossal and pernicious evil is hidden in the human heart! How miserable and wretched is man! The external appearance shows a person how he was created, but within is a true animal, even worse than an animal, since he has in himself the depravity of not one particular animal but those of all the animals. O miserable man! Into what condition have you come, having sinned against your Lord and Creator by listening to the advice of your cunning enemy? O highly respected divine creation, enriched with God's image and likeness, into what baseness and foulness you have fallen! Where is your primordial beauty and grandeur? Where are your holiness, purity, righteousness, and innocence? Where is your divine light, which enlightened your soul and reason? Where is your Godlike blessedness, which your Creator granted you in the beginning? All of this has left you! Your sin deprived you of all of this. It deprived you of blessedness and plunged you into all kinds of misfortune and wretchedness. It deprived you of the beloved light and plunged you into pernicious darkness. It deprived you of the image and likeness of God and bestowed beastliness. You were created in the image and likeness of God but became hideous and like an animal. "Man, being in honor, understood it not; he shall be compared unto the brute beasts, and is become like unto them" (Ps 48:13 LXX). He was free but became a captive; he was holy and pure but became defiled and loathsome. He was comely and bright but became ugly and dark. He was a temple of the Holy Spirit but became an abode of unclean spirits. O terrible fall! O most disastrous changes! Terrible was that time, day, and hour, in which man listened to the crafty counsel of the serpent and transgressed the commandment of his Creator! "O Lord, remember what happened to us; look upon us with favor and see our disgrace. The joy of our heart has ceased; our dance has turned into mourning. The crown fell from our head; woe to us because we sinned! Because of this, our heart has become painful; Because of this, our eyes have remained in darkness" (Lam 5:1, 15–17). Poor man, you, who were baptized in the name of the Holy Trinity and enrolled your name for Jesus Christ, the Son of God! Look what vileness is hidden in the human heart! What use is it to you that you confess God's name and often cry out, "Lord, Lord," but have an evil and bestial nature within you? How can someone who harbors such impurity enter God's kingdom if he has not turned with his whole heart to God and renewed himself with true repentance, heartfelt contrition, warm tears, and the grace of the Holy Spirit? "But outside are dogs and sorcerers and sexually immoral and murderers and idolaters, and whoever loves and practices a lie" (Rev 22:15). "But there shall by no means enter it anything that defiles" (Rev 21:27). Remember us, O Lord, according to the favor that thou bearest unto Thy people; O visit us with Thy salvation, that we may see the goodness of Thy chosen, and be glad in the gladness of "Thy nation, and glory with Thine inheritance. We have sinned with our father; we have done amiss, and dealt wickedly" (Ps 105:4–6).

# 71. *Turning*

When a servant turns away from his master and leaves him, he shows him his back, not his face, and what his master says, he does not hear—likewise a poor sinner, when he reorientates his love and obedience away from God and turns to evil deeds. As it were he turns his back on Him and leaves Him, does not pay attention to what God says in His holy Word, and does not care about it. Concerning this, the prophet passed on God's lament about the transgressors: "They have turned their backs to me and not their faces" (Jer 2:27). And the prophet said against the ungodly: "[They] have not set God before them" (Ps 53:5). This is a loathsome turning away and departure from God! Not only do people depart from God when they renounce His holy name and approach strange gods, but also when they do not wish to do His will and fearlessly transgress, as the Apostle wrote, "they profess to know God, but in works they deny Him, being abominable, disobedient, and disqualified for every good work" (Titus 1:16). Understand this, Christian, who confess the name of Christ but are not living a Christian life! Know for sure that there are many pagans hiding under the name of Christian, especially in the present terrible times, in which carnal lust, lust of the eyes, and worldly pride are more esteemed among Christians as a triple god than God, the Creator of heaven and earth, higher than any human reverence and glorification. When a servant turns toward his master and stands before Him, he faces him, and what the master tells him, he listens to and heeds. Likewise, the sinner, when he has a change of heart and turns to God from his sins, is already as it were standing facing Him, renders Him reverence as his God and Creator, heeds His holy commands, and tries to fulfill everything that is said in the sacred Scripture. Wherever he is, he sees God before himself with the eyes of his soul and with faith and avoids every sin in deed, word, and thought, so as not to anger Him. The prophet says about this, "I foresaw the Lord always before me" (Ps 15:8). This is real conversion, true awakening from the sleep of sin, genuine repentance, authentic resurrection of the soul! Blessed is the person who arises thus and abides in this until the end! Indeed such a one will arise on the last day, not to death but to life and eternal blessedness. "Blessed and holy is he who has part in the first resurrection. Over such the second death has no power" (Rev 20:6). Christian! Hasten to turn to the Lord your God, and without fail you will be saved by Christ's grace. "O Lord God of hosts, convert us; show the light of Thy countenance, and we shall be saved" (Ps 79:8). "O remember not our old sins, but let Thy mercy overtake us, for we are come to great poverty. Help us, O God our Saviour, for the glory of Thy Name; O Lord, deliver us, and wash away our sins, for Thy Name's sake" (Ps 78:8–9).

When a person turns and comes to another person, he turns his body and comes to him, although it often happens that he has a heart and spirit that are pointed in a different direction. A turning toward God is not like this. We do not turn and come to God with our body and legs. For how and where shall we turn to Him, Who is everywhere and is already where we wish to go before we arrive? Turning to God, Who is omnipresent, depends not on place, body, and feet but on heart and spirit. We turn to God when we come to know Him, conscious that He is our Highest Good and Blessedness and, having abandoned other created things, the world, its vanity, and all sins as things offensive to Him, we desire, love, and seek Him alone and revere Him above all created things and always remember Him and taking care lest we offend Him in any way. This is true turning to God! For turning to the world takes place when a person directs his heart to worldly things, that is, to honor, glory, riches, luxury, and every vanity, drawing nearer to worldly things and seeking them as his beloved treasure. So also turning to God takes place when a person, having left all of this, loves God alone, desires, comes near in his heart to Him and seeks him as the Highest Good. Whatever a person comes to recognize and acknowledge as his good and blessedness, that also does he love. And what he loves, that also does he desire. What he desires, that also he always thinks about. What he thinks about, that also he seeks with eagerness. Do you seek honor, glory, riches, luxury, and other vanity in this world? This means that you esteem this for your welfare and blessedness, and love and desire it, meaning that you have turned away in your heart from your God and Creator. You have turned to His creation, that you esteem this more than the One who made you. But when, having despised and abandoned all of this, you seek God alone, and Him only do you desire to acquire and possess, it means that you esteem Him more than all creation, and you find your delight in Him, and you place your uttermost welfare and blessedness in Him. So, in Christ's words, "Where [a man's] treasure is, there [his] heart will be also," his love, his thoughts, his desire will be there; it is what he thinks, cares, and talks about, and what he seeks (Matt 6:21). Whoever sees the honor, riches, and glory of this world and everything contained in it as his treasure has his heart with its desire and love there also. And whoever holds God alone as his treasure clings to Him alone. Oh, the eternal treasure! How precious, priceless, incomparable, more longed-for than the whole world, most beloved, and sweet You are for souls that love You! In you they find everything that those who love the world find in the world. They find it all but incomparably better. In You they find riches, honor, glory, rest, peace, consolation, joy, sweetness, and incomparably more blessedness than the whole world contains. God is such a dear and lofty good, for it is uncreated, everlasting, and eternal, from Whom, as from a spring, every good flows, whatever is and can be, but is despised and scorned by those who love this world. O poor Christian! You will seek this good someday but will not find it if you do not sincerely look for it now. Turn to Him now, and seek Him, and you will find Him, "Seek the Lord and be strengthened; seek his face always" (Ps 104:4). "I will hear what the Lord God will say concerning me; for He shall speak peace unto His people, and to His saints, and to them that turn their hearts unto Him. Surely His salvation is nigh them that fear Him, that glory may dwell in our land" (Ps 84:9–10). "For what have I in heaven, and what have I desired upon earth from Thee? My flesh and my heart have failed, O God of my heart, but Thou art my portion, O God, for ever. For lo, they that go far from Thee shall perish; Thou hast destroyed all them that are unfaithful against Thee. But it is good from me to cleave unto God" (Ps 72:25–28). "I will love Thee, O Lord, my strength. The Lord is my firm foundation, and my fortress, and my deliverer; my God is my helper, and I will trust in Him, my defender, the horn also of my salvation, and my protector" (Ps 17:2–3).

How and where should I seek God? The answer: (1) Do not desire and do not seek anything except God and His holy will, following the prophet, who desired nothing either in heaven or on earth except "[f]or what have I in heaven [accept Thee], and what have I desired upon earth from Thee [besides Thee]" (Ps 72:25 LXX [Ps 73:25])? And you will seek God. (2) He Who is everywhere is sought and found everywhere and in every place. Wherever you may either be or live, God is near you; seek Him there. Do you live in the city? God is there; seek him there. Do you live in a village? God is there; seek him there. Do you live in a monastery or in a hermitage? God is with you; God is found there, too; seek Him there, too. In a word, wherever you are, God is near you. Seek Him near you, as is proper, and you will find Him. "Behold, I stand at the door and knock. If anyone hears My voice and opens the door, I will come in to him and dine with him, and he with Me" (Rev 3:20). See, God Himself wishes to come to us and to grant us knowledge of Himself. He stands at the doors of everyone and wishes to be known to everyone, but few hear Him knocking at the door, since every person's hearing is muffled by sinful lusts and the love of the world (see Rev 3:20). And so, having knocked at the door and receiving no answer, He leaves with nothing from the person. Calm and quiet your heart and mind from carnal lusts and the noise of worldly desires. Turn away from all of this and heed Him alone. Then you will indeed realize that He stands near you and knocks at the door of your heart, and you will hear His most sweet voice, and you will open your doors to Him. Then He will enter your house and will dine with you, and you with Him. Then you will "taste and see that the Lord is good" (Ps 33:9). Then you too will cry out with love and joy, "The Lord God, compassionate, merciful, long-suffering, abounding in mercy and true" (Exod 34:6). Further, I will love Thee, O Lord, my strength, and so on. And further, for what have I in heaven, and what have I desired upon earth from Thee? and so on. Seek Him in all places Who is everywhere, and leaving everything, seek Him alone. Then without fail you will find Him.

# 72. Imitation

In the world, we see that subjects imitate their King, servants their master, children their father, pupils their teacher, and so on. What one does, another copies, then a third, until all act in the same way. One has built a certain kind of chamber, and another and a third build the same. One has begun to wear a certain type of clothing, and others follow after. So it is in other things. You see, Christian, what the sons of this age do and how they imitate each other. What should we do? Whom should we imitate? We, Christians, are from Christ; whom then should we imitate, if not Christ, after Whom we are named. He is our King, and we are His subjects. He is our Master, and we are His unworthy servants. He is our Father, from Whom we were born again; we are His unworthy children. He is our teacher, and we are His unworthy pupils. Whom should we imitate if not Him? Let the sons of this age imitate each other. We will place before ourselves Christ and His holy life and will imitate Him Who presents Himself to us as a model and object of imitation: "For I have given you an example, that you should do as I have done to you" (John 13:15). He was humble, meek, quiet, patient, merciful, charitable, so needy that He had no place to lay His head, as He testifies of Himself: "Foxes have holes and birds of the air have nests, but the Son of Man has nowhere to lay His head" (Matt 8:20). Let us picture these and His other excellent virtues before our minds' eyes and let us try as far as we can to imitate them. He was humble: let us be humble before God and people. He loved everyone so much that He laid down His life for everyone—let us too love each other, and Him first and foremost. He was meek to all those who abused Him—let us also be meek toward those who revile and reproach us. He was patient in all His sufferings—let us endure everything disagreeable that may happen to us. He disdained all the glory, honor, and riches of this world, being the Lord of all, for His is "the earth and the fullness thereof" (Ps 23:1)—let us too disdain them, and let us love eternal good things. We see that people emulate others for various reasons: some to please those whom they imitate, others for their own enjoyment and to please themselves, others for their own benefit. We Christians should emulate Christ, our Lord, for all these reasons. It is pleasing to Christ when we imitate Him, for He wants this from us not for His own sake, but for ours. It is pleasing and advantageous also to us. What is more agreeable, advantageous, and sweeter than to follow the humble Heavenly King, Who for our sake became impoverished, meek, long-suffering, plenteous in mercy, most good, compassionate, a gentle Lamb of God, innocent, and most pure? He is the light of the world. If we follow Him, we will not be in the darkness, but in the light. "I am the light of the world. He who follows Me shall not walk in darkness, but have the light of life" (John 8:12). "I am the way, the truth, and the life" (John 14:6). If we stay on this path, we shall surely not lose our way. If we follow this Truth, we shall not be enticed by the evil and seductive world. If we abide with this life, we shall not die but will be alive forever. You see, Christian, that it is not only beneficial but even necessary to follow Christ. We poor ones, like lost sheep in this world, do not know the way to our heavenly Homeland. Let us entrust ourselves to the leadership of our Saviour Jesus Christ, and let us follow Him, and He will lead us to His Heavenly Father, and into His kingdom, for He says, "No one comes to the Father except through Me" (John 14:6). Christian! If you are afraid of perishing eternally, and sincerely wish to be saved forever, believe in Christ, and humbly live on earth as He lived, and you will be saved, which I wish for myself and for you.

# 73. The Safe Path

In this world we see that people move from place to place, and there is one dangerous path, and another safe one. Christians! From our birth to our death, we are wayfarers, and we are trying to reach eternal life and the Kingdom of

God, to which we have been renewed by holy baptism and called by the Word of God. Let us choose the safe path to this blessedness. Which path is safe for us? To sincerely believe in Christ and to entrust our salvation to His sufferings and death. To put your hope only in Him as Redeemer and Saviour. To know no other means besides Him for attaining eternal salvation and to live humbly, meekly, and patiently on earth after His example. This is the safe path. O Lord, set me on this path! If in this world you seek honor, glory, riches, concupiscence, know that you have gotten off the safe path and are going by a dangerous path. If you do not believe this, study God's holy Word and other Christian books, and you will learn this truth. Christians in this world are called to bearing the cross and not to honor, glory, riches, or concupiscence. They have their honor, glory, riches, joy, and sweetness, but within themselves not on the outside—it is all spiritual and not carnal. Beloved, heed what the eternal Truth, Christ our Lord, says: "Enter by the narrow gate; for wide is the gate and broad is the way that leads to destruction, and there are many who go in by it. Because narrow is the gate and difficult is the way which leads to life, and there are few who find it" (Matt 7:13–14). You see what the safe path is. This path is low and humble but leads to our sublime Homeland, heaven. If you want to come into the Homeland, go by this path. "Guide me, O Lord in Thy way, and I will walk in Thy truth; O let my heart rejoice to fear Thy Name" (Ps 85:11).

# 74. A Mirror

We see that people have mirrors in their chambers for their needs. Christians! What the mirror is for the sons of this age; let the Gospel and the chaste life of Christ be for us. They look at the mirror from time to time and adjust their bodies and cleanse blemishes on their faces. Let us do likewise. Christ, the Son of God, gave us Himself and His holy life as a model, as we saw earlier: "For I have given you an example, that you should do as I have done to you" (John 13:15). Let us picture in the eyes of our soul this pure mirror and see in it whether our life is in conformity with the life of Christ. It is absolutely necessary that it be in conformity. As we were created in conformity with the old Adam, so we must be created in conformity with the New Adam, Jesus Christ, if we wish to enter eternal life. And as we became like that first man in depravity, so must we become like that second Man, the Lord from Heaven, Jesus Christ, in decency that we may be "a new creation" (2 Cor 5:17).

"As was the man of dust, so also are those who are made of dust; and as is the heavenly Man, so also are those who are heavenly. And as we have borne the image of the man of dust, we shall also bear the image of the heavenly Man" (1 Cor 15:48–49). Look more frequently at the spotless mirror of the immaculate life of Christ, and by repentance and contrition of heart wash away the vices that have adhered to your soul and, as much as you can, conform yourself to Him. Conform yourself to Christ, the Son of God, in humility, meekness, patience, love, and other virtues now, and you will be in conformity there. But do not conform yourself to contemporary Christians. The life of contemporary Christians is for the most part opposed to Christ, not in conformity with Him. Christ lived in humility, and contemporary Christians love to live in pride and splendor. Christ treated everyone sincerely and unassumingly, but contemporary Christians treat everyone slyly and craftily. Christ lived in great poverty and so did not have anywhere to lay His head, although He could have had everything because He is the Lord of all, but contemporary Christians only think and care about amassing great wealth, and if it were possible, they would have all the treasures of the world. Christ, worthy of every reverence and glorification, avoided honor and glory, but contemporary Christians exert all their strength and effort in order to be honored and glorified. Christ lived in love and mercy, bur contemporary Christians hate one another, slander each other, backbite each other, abuse each other, steal from each other, swindle each other, defraud each other, and weave intrigues and snares for each other. Christ took revenge on no one for an offense, although He could have routed all His enemies by a nod of His head, but contemporary Christians take revenge on each other both in word and deed. Christ was meek with his abusers: they reproached Him, and He did not reproach them in return. But contemporary Christians reproach each other and cut each other to pieces with their tongues as with sharp swords. Christ lived in great patience, but contemporary Christians, even if only some minor misfortune or trouble happens, grumble and vilify. Christ tried only to fulfill the will of His Heavenly Father, and complete the work of our salvation, and did realize and complete them. But among contemporary Christians everything is different—they do not care about the will of God but exert all their efforts to pleasing the world and fulfilling their whims. You see, Christian, what Christ did in this world, and you see what Christians do. You yourself should learn what kind of Christianity there is among present-day Christians! You yourself see that it is false. Do not conform to present-day Christians since all their schemes, undertakings, endeavors, and deeds are offensive to Christ. But just as you check the mirror to touch up your face, check the mirror of the immaculate life of Christ, and touch up your disposition, and cleanse your soul. "Let this mind be in you which was also in Christ Jesus" (Phil 2:5). "I beseech you therefore, brethren, by the mercies of God, that you present your bodies a living sacrifice, holy, acceptable to God, which is your reasonable service. And do not be conformed to this world, but be transformed by the renewing of your mind, that you may prove what is that good and acceptable and perfect will of God" (Rom 12:1–2).

# 75. Plague

What a plague is for the body, temptation is for the soul. The plague infects and kills the body. Temptation infects and kills the human soul. As we see, the plague starts first in one person, then the whole house, and from there the whole city or village, and further the whole country is infected and perishes. Likewise, temptation begins in one person and then passes on to many. Lust, hiding in the human heart, is roused by sight and hearing, as fire by the wind, and is inflamed to evil. We see this in the world whatever the eyes see and the ears hear strikes the human heart. One has begun to build himself a certain kind of house, to wear a particular kind of clothing, to ride in a specific kind of carriage and horses, to have precise kinds of draperies and decorations in his house, and so on. Another sees this, then a third, and others, and then all the rest. And everyone does the same. One landowner takes so much in fixed rent from his peasants, or requires they work so many days a week for him. Others see this and behave the same with their peasants. One judge is infected with bribery and has collected some thousands from this iniquitous practice. Another sees this, then a third, and others, and they contemplate such an iniquitous practice. He, they say, has collected so very much, and I shall do the same. And so this terrible evil spreads from one to another and then from him to others and then to everyone. We see how our poor homeland has been infected by this terrible plague! Nowhere is there a trial without the passing of money. They do not judge but only buy and sell. One has begun to arrange banquets and invite and receive guests. Others do the same, and already they do nothing but go to visit each other. Thus, temptation, like the plague, infects not bodies, but human souls, and takes from them not temporal but eternal life. We see that one city abounds in one iniquity, and another city in another.

This happens from nothing else but temptation. Oh, what a terrible evil is temptation. "It is for this reason that Christ the Lord so strong forbade giving temptation" (see Matt 18:6–9). Christian! Avoid temptation and avoid causing temptation like the plague. Sincerely love the law of God, and you will avoid stumbling blocks. "Great peace have they who love Thy Law, and nothing can trip them up" (Ps 118:165). Despise this world with its delusion, and love the one God and eternal life, and you will live unharmed in the world, as Lot in Sodom.

What a person infected by the plague is, so also is a slanderer. The one infected by the plague infects whoever associates with him and does not behave cautiously. The slanderer harms whoever hears his slander. From the infected person, the infectious plague passes to another, then to a third, then to a fourth, and so on to all the people, if they are not careful. And it happens that many thousands of people are infected from one infected person and perish. Likewise, one person hears slander from a slanderer and tells another, and he tells a third, the third tells a fourth, and thus everyone hears and they are harmed by the slander. And it happens that the whole country and the whole state hear it and are harmed. Some, hearing it, condemn the one about whom the slander is being spread: he did or is doing a bad thing, they say. And so they sin seriously, appropriating for themselves what belongs to Christ, the Righteous Judge, alone. He alone is the Judge of all. Others are roused to the same iniquitous action; they hear of it and they do it. The slanderer, the scatterer of evil is guilty of all this ruinous evil. And so you see, Christian, what a ruinous evil is slander, although contemporary Christians comfort themselves and enjoy themselves with nothing as much as slander. What is on the tongues of people when they gather together? The name of one and then another is fussed over. What else are their conversations about? First about one and then about another poor sinner. One will talk about one, a second about another, a third about a third, and so, as many sins and transgressions take place during the gathering as the words spoken. The cause of all this evil is the slanderer from whom the slander initiated. The slanderer harms the one whom he slanders, for with his tongue he wounds him as with a sword, and tears to pieces his reputation, as a dog tears clothing with its teeth: he, they say, does this and that. He also harms himself, for he sins seriously. He harms those who hear his slander, too, for he gives them occasion for slander and judgment and so leads them to the same iniquitous deed in which he finds himself, and as from one infected person many people are infected in body and perish; likewise from one slanderer, the source of the slander, many Christian souls are infected and perish. O unbridled tongue! How much evil you do to the world! As the wind spreads the fire throughout the whole city or village, so also an unbridled tongue spreads every kind of evil throughout the whole state and throughout the whole world. One slanderer learned of something—and now everyone knows; one spoke—and everyone speaks. Oh, it is a hundred times better to be tripped up by the feet than by the tongue. The tongue is a little member but does great evil (see Jas 3:5–6). It is guarded by a double fence, that is, by the teeth and the lips, but it very easily breaks loose and springs out. Christian! Beware of the slanderer, as you avoid a person infected with the plague, lest you be infected and yourself perish because of him. Slanderers usually investigate other people's business: he, they say, does such and such, and so, having investigated it, they spread the slander. They know each other and meet together and ask each other about one thing and another. And so, having found out, they spread the slander. Beware such people as you would lepers. Beware also of investigating people's sins yourself, lest you judge and slander your neighbor. Investigation and learning of another's sins is the beginning of judgment and slander. Turn your eyes away from your neighbor and turn them instead to yourself. Examine and learn your own sins and cleanse them by sincere repentance and faith. This is the Christian work to which you are called by Christ. Try by any means to hold your tongue, and you will avoid many sins.

# 76. Following Like Cattle

We see that where one beast goes, the others follow it, although there will be harm to them there. Many people recklessly do the same and act according to feelings, and not reason, and follow each other after the example of the cattle, not thinking whether this will be beneficial or harmful. We see this iniquitous and ruinous eagerness in the world. One person has begun to put on frequent banquets, to drink, to carouse, to get drunk, and to make others drunk, and the second does the same, and the third. One has begun to dress foppishly; others will follow him. One has amassed great wealth, and others take trouble to do the same. One shameless woman applies powder and coloring to her face, and others follow her, and they all act ruinously, as one. One wicked merchant asks prices higher than the goods are worth from a tradesman, and gives an oath on it, and calls on the holy and awesome name of God in this iniquitous matter. And others do the same as he does. Likewise, these poor people imitate each other in other things. They imitate, but it is to their harm and their perdition. This is a reckless pursuit. This is following like cattle! This is a plague with which Christian souls, redeemed by the most holy Blood of Christ, are being infected and are perishing! This is a soul-destroying fire, which, having begun in one person, burns up other houses of the soul. Alas, the calamity! Alas, the sorrow! Evil begins in one, and then everyone does likewise, and this comes into common practice and gains such a strong hold that to root it out becomes impossible, like a chronic disease. "People will laugh at me if I do not do as they do." The answer to this is: (1) Ungodliness always mocks piety and reviles it. Let some rich man sell his palatial house, all his belongings, and let him disperse his property, and distribute it to the poor, and let him love the poverty of Christ. You yourself will see what the evil world will do to him. "What a fool," they will say, "look what he did! He gave away what other people accumulate." Thus piety seems like obstreperousness to the sons of this age. (2) Christ, our Saviour, the Lord and King of glory, was mocked and sworn at by the lovers of the world. Let the world mock and swear at you too. You should keep on and do what is pleasing to Him, and not to the world. Conform yourself to Him as your author and not to this age. (3) Should we really do what the world does? Many kill, commit adultery and fornication, steal, swindle, and so on. And what should we do? Let it not be this! They are going to perdition, and should we go too? May God preserve us from that! (4) We have not only feeling/sense but also reason, and we may judge what is good and what is evil, what is beneficial and what is harmful. And so, when we see what people are doing, we should follow not our senses, after the example of the animals, but our reason. Those who follow their senses alone, rather than their reason, are not people but animals. (5) We are Christians. We have the holy Word of God. We see in it what is good and what is evil, what is beneficial and what is harmful. So God forbids what is evil and what is harmful to us and commands that which is good and beneficial to us. What are people doing? Let us hold this up to the Sacred Scripture, as to a clean mirror, and look into it. Are people doing what is compatible or incompatible with it? If they are doing what is compatible, that is good, and it is beneficial for us to do it. If incompatible, let us turn our eyes away from this and listen to what the Sacred Book teaches. (6) Let even the whole world do what is hateful to God and ruinous for itself; you, however, should do what is pleasing to God and edifying for yourself. The whole world will not intercede for you at the Judgment Seat of God. You will not say there: "But so and so did this." You will hear one thing from the Judge: "Why did you not do what I ordered you?" You should honor God alone more than everything in the world. Be in the world like Lot in Sodom, where everyone transgressed; he did not imitate them but did what was pleasing to the holy will of God. You should do the same; do not imitate what the evil world does. You see or hear what evil people do, be as if not seeing and not hearing. Always turn the eyes of your heart to eternity, and all worldly things will be as it were left behind you, and you will live in the world as if alone, knowing your Creator and His holy will. "If then you were raised with Christ, seek those things which are above, where Christ is, sitting at the right hand of God. Set your mind on things above, not on things on the earth" (Col 3:1–2).

# 77. A Lamp

What a lamp is in the house, living faith is in the human heart. A lamp is lit by a person. The lamp of faith is lit by the Holy Spirit through the Word of God that is heard, as it is written: "So then faith comes by hearing, and hearing by the word of God" (Rom 10:17). When a lamp burns and shines in a house, everything is clear in the house; those living in it see everything, those walking do not stumble, and everyone does his work because he is given light by the lamp. So, when the lamp of faith shines in the heart, the person sees everything spiritual clearly: he sees the invisible God as visible, and other things invisible as visible, and does deeds befitting the Christian calling. When there is no lamp in the house, it is dark in the house. So, when there is no lamp of faith in a person's heart, there is nothing other than darkness and every kind of error there. So a burning lamp in a house does not go out, we must add oil. Thus, the lamp of faith in our heart does go out, we must (1) read or listen to, and discuss the Word of God and other Christian books; (2) pray diligently to God; (3) commune of the holy and life-giving Mysteries of the Body and Blood of Christ; (4) do works of mercy. "Blessed are the merciful, for they shall obtain mercy" (Matt 5:7). The signs in Holy Scripture of a lamp of faith, burning in the human heart, are the following: (1) Such a person reads or listens to the Word of God and studies it diligently. (2) He calls on God with a warm heart, prays and thanks Him for all His benefactions. (3) He strives with all zeal to live worthy of the calling of a Christian and the Gospel. (4) He shows his faith in God by good works, as the Apostle demands: "Show me your faith without your works" (Jas 2:18). (5) He bewares of every sin, and fights against it, and does not allow it to control him. (6) He lives in this world as a wanderer and stranger and always raises the eyes of his heart to the heavenly Homeland and sighs, and for this reason, his heart does not cleave to worldly things but uses everything with fear and according to need. Nothing in the world gladdens such a person except God alone and the hope of eternal life. (7) A manifest sign of a lamp of faith that burns in the human heart is spiritual joy that is felt in the heart, a joy in the Holy Spirit, a joy in God, which is depicted in the psalms: "My heart and my flesh have rejoiced in the living God" (Ps 83:3), for where there is faith in God, there is love of God; where there is love for God, there is joy in God; for what we love, we also rejoice in. From this it is obvious what are the signs of faith that has died out in the human heart, namely: (1) An iniquitous life, contrary to the word of God. Faith has died out in the fornicator, the adulterer, and every unclean person. Faith has died out in the thief, violator, and the robber. Faith has died out in the malicious, the hate-filled, and the one breathing vengeance. Faith has been extinguished in the slanderer, the antagonizer, the reproacher, the maligner, and the foul-mouthed. Faith has been extinguished in the hypocrite, the deceitful, and the flatterer. In a word, faith has been extinguished in every lawbreaker who does not guard his conscience but acts against it, and instead of a lamp of faith, the darkness of ignorance of God is in them. For what communion has light with the darkness of a wicked life? The light is faith, and the darkness is a wicked life. What does faith have in common with the darkness of a wicked life? Such people, although they pray to God, do so hypocritically, for their hearts stand far from God. "These people draw near to Me with their mouth, And honor Me with their lips, But their heart is far from Me" (Matt 15:8, Isa 29:13), befit them. (2) Disdain for the Word of God and aversion to it. (3) Abandonment of prayer. (4) Withdrawal from reception of the Holy Mysteries of Christ. Without them, faith cannot exist and be preserved in the human heart. (5) A predilection for temporal things: riches, honor, glory, and luxury. Faith is a gift from heaven, and therefore it diverts the human heart from an earthly mind-set and induces to a heavenly mindset. Such a person sins against the word of the Apostle, "Set your mind on things above, not on things on the earth" (Col 3:2). Christians who have the lamp of faith burning in their hearts and who will have it until the end will go out to meet the Bridegroom Christ, who has come to judge the living and the dead, and will enter with Him into the heavenly bridal chamber, like the wise virgins, "Be faithful until death," having that lamp in yourself, "and I will give you the crown of life," the Lord Christ tells you (Rev 2:10). But those who will not have this lamp in their hearts will not be found worthy to meet Christ the King, and will not be admitted into that bridal chamber, but will remain outside of it and will hear from Christ the King: "I do not know you" (Matt 25:12). Christian, it is terrifying to hear these words from Christ to Christians: "I do not know you!" Let us turn with our whole hearts to God, and let our lamps be lit by His grace. "Awake, you who sleep, Arise from the dead, And Christ will give you light" (Eph 5:14). "Thou shalt light my lamp, O Lord my God; Thou shalt make my darkness to be light" (Ps 17:29).

# 78. A Blind Man and a Sighted Man Accompanying Him

It happens that there is a sighted person with a blind man, but the blind man does not know that he is there with him. Likewise, God, being omnipresent, is with every person, but the person who is not enlightened by faith, inasmuch as he does not see Him, does not know that his Lord and Judge abides with him invisibly. It often happens that the blind man, not seeing the person present with him, commits indecent and shameless acts, thinking to himself that no one sees him. Likewise the sinner, like the blind man not seeing other people near him, thinks and imagines that no one sees him, just as he does not see anyone, and so dares to commit wicked acts. But the poor man is greatly deceived, for God, Who is present with him, and before Whom he does and thinks everything, sees him and sees every deed and thought of his, and entering it into His book, and on the last day will expose him. God says to the sinner, "I will reprove thee, and set thy sins before thy face" (Ps 49:21). He would say "You thought that no one saw you when you did wicked deeds, but I saw you, I saw how you violated My law, and I will present your transgressions to you. You did them in secret, but I will expose you before the whole world, angels and people. Then you will learn, sinner, that I saw everything that you did, began, or contemplated in your heart. You escape notice from people, but you cannot escape notice anywhere from Me." Such a blind man is every fornicator, adulterer, defiler, and lover of impurity, every thief, extortioner, robber, and bribe-taking judge, every slanderer and distorter of his neighbor's reputation, whoever treats others flatteringly, slyly, cunningly, falsely, and hypocritically, and so on. All such are blind not in their bodily eyes, but in the eyes of their souls, and attempt to escape people's notice, but they cannot hide from God the all-seeing; they hide their wicked deeds from people, but God sees them better than the people of the entire world. "Take heed, ye thoughtless among the people, and ye fools, when will ye be wise? He that planted the ear, shall He not hear? Or He that made the eye, shall He not see" (Ps 93:8–9)? "The Lord looked down from heaven, and beheld all the children of men; From his prepared habitation, He considereth all them that dwell on the earth, Having made the hearts of every one of them, and understanding all their works" (Ps 32:13–15). "Your eyes are on the ways of the sons of men, to give everyone according to his way" (Jer 39:19 LXX). "Whither shall I go then from thy Spirit? Or whither shall I flee from Thy presence? If I climb up into heaven, thou art there; if I go down to hell, Thou art there also. If I take up my wings early, and dwell in the uttermost parts of the sea, Even there also shall Thy hand lead me, and Thy right hand shall hold me. And I said, Peradventure the darkness shall hide me, and the night is light in my pleasures. For the darkness shall be no darkness with Thee, and the night shall be as bright as the day, for as is the darkness thereof, even so is the light of it" (Ps 138:7–12). You see, O man, that although you seem to be alone, God the Judge is present with you. And although no humans see you, your deeds are seen by God, before Whom you should fear and feel shame more than before the whole world, more than all the angels and people, for before Him all creation is as nothing. Fear and repent. And in future avoid transgressing before the eyes of God, lest you yourself experience His avenging hand!

When a blind man, although he does not see the person near him, knows for sure that someone is there, he avoids doing anything indecent. Likewise, a Christian, enlightened by faith, although he does not see God present (for to see him is impossible), he does, however, see Him with the internal eye of faith and sees the invisible before him, as if it were visible. This is how the Psalmist, enlightened by faith and the Holy Spirit, spoke of himself: "I foresaw the Lord always before me" (Ps 15:8). Thus, it is written about the Prophet Moses: "For he endured as seeing Him who is invisible" (Heb 11:27). For this is a characteristic of faith that it presents the invisible God to the eyes of the soul as visible. The soul enlightened by such faith walks everywhere and in every place before God with fear and reverence, avoids everything that is hateful to Him, and behaves before Him like pupils before their teacher, servants before their master, children before their father, and subjects before their monarch. With such a soul, the man-loving God in all misfortunes, disasters, and temptations is a protector, helper, and defender. "You are Mine. If you pass through water, I am with you; and the rivers shall not overflow you. If you pass through fire, you shall not be burned up, nor shall the flame consume you. For I am the Lord your God, the Holy One of Israel, who saves you," says the Lord (Isa 43:1–3). Concerning this, the faithful soul takes courage and proclaims, "The Lord is my shepherd; therefore can I lack nothing. He maketh me to lie down in a green pasture; He leadeth me beside the still water. He hath converted my soul; He hath set me on the paths of righteousness, for His Name's sake. Yea, though I walk through the valley of the shadow of death, I will fear no evil, for thou art with me" (Ps 22:1–4). "The Lord is my light, and my Saviour; whom then shall I fear? The Lord is the defender of my life; of whom then shall I be afraid? When they that had enmity against me, even my enemies, and my foes, came nigh to eat up my flesh, they faltered and fell. Though a legion were laid against me, yet shall not my heart be afraid; and though there rise up war against me, yet will I put my trust in Him. One thing have I desired of the Lord, which I will require; even that I may dwell in the house of the Lord all the days of my life, to behold the fair beauty of the Lord, and to visit His holy temple" (Ps 26:1–3). Therefore, faithful soul, "Suffer not thy feet to slip, nor Him that keepeth thee to slumber. Behold, he that keepeth Israel shall neither slumber nor sleep. The Lord Himself shall keep thee; the Lord is thy shelter upon thy right hand. The sun shall not burn thee by day, neither the moon by night. The Lord shall keep thee from all evil; yea, the Lord shall preserve thy soul. The Lord shall preserve thy going out, and thy coming in, from this time forth, and for evermore" (Ps 120:3–8).

# 79. A Subject Who Violates the Law in the Presence of His King

If someone were to become so audacious that in the presence of his king he began to violate the law, tell me, please, O man, tell me whether this troublemaker has not greatly insulted and scorned his monarch and not moved him to righteous anger? Indeed the monarch would consider such a deed a great disgrace and would be justifiably angered at that wrongdoer. Christian! We all walk and live before God, the King of heaven and earth, omnipresent and all-seeing. And everything that we may do, think, and say, we do, think, and say before His holy eyes, although we do not see Him. His holy Word assures us of this. Every wrongdoer breaks His holy law in His presence. Every blasphemer vilifies His holy and fearsome Name in His presence. Every liar swears falsely by His holy and fearsome Name in His presence and calls falsely on His great Name in His presence. Every evildoer and murderer kills a person in His presence. Every fornicator, adulterer, and lover of impurity transgresses in His presence. Every thief, extortioner, and robber breaks the law "thou shalt not steal" in His presence. Every slanderer, name-caller, reproacher, foul-mouth, and blasphemer transgresses in His presence. Everyone who either contemplates or thinks craftiness and evil in his heart contemplates it in His presence, for God sees both out heart and our thoughts. What scorn and insult to our Creator may be greater than this? Oh, how many enemies of God there are in the world, not only those who do not know Him, but also those who think that they revere Him and boast of His holy faith! In truth, an enemy of God is not only he who spews forth explicit blasphemies against His holy name, but also he who without fear dares to sin. All such say in their hearts, "The Lord shall not see, neither shall the God of Jacob comprehend. Take heed, ye thoughtless among the people, and ye fools, when will you be wise? He that planted the ear, shall He not hear? Or He that made the eye, shall He not see" (Ps 93:7–9)? Oh, man, called by the name of Christian, but who acts as one with idolaters. You confess God, but in works are distant from Him. You honor the name of God, but by transgressing the law of God, you dishonor Him! Please be aware of what sort of person you are in God's sight, and where and to what end your depravity is leading you. Be aware, before the end overtakes you, and you receive according to your works. God has been and is long-suffering to you, expecting your repentance, but we do not know whether He will show patience into the future. The Lord is good and merciful but also just. Those who have been converted and have repented will experience his mercy, but unrepentant sinners will experience His justice and righteous judgment. Be converted and repent, so that you may not experience His righteous judgment, and what is more, that you will be found worthy of his mercy. "Have mercy upon me, O God, after Thy great goodness, and according to the multitude of Thy mercies do away mine offenses" (Ps 50:3).

# 80. A Servant Offended
## in the Presence of His Master

It happens that some coarse man offends a servant before his master. Likewise the sinner, when he inflicts some offense on a Christian, inflicts it in the presence of the Lord God, Who is omnipresent and all-seeing. Among these are: (1) adulterers, who lawlessly defile another's bed; (2) those who harm people's health in some way; (3) murderers, who beat and kill a person; (4) those who vilify and reproach their neighbors; (5) those who secretly or openly slander their neighbors; (6) thieves, extortioners, and robbers, who unjustly appropriate other people's good for themselves; (7) merchants who, when selling goods, cheat people and sell a shoddy imitation for the real thing, and a cheap one for an expensive one; (8) landowners who either brutally torment their peasants, or burden them with excessive quitrents, or prevail on them to work excessively for them; (9) judges who pass judgment based on bribes and not on justice. (10) those who do not give pay to hired help, or give it, but not in full; (11) hired help who took sufficient pay for their labors, but do not want to work for it, or who work, but slyly and hypocritically; (12) bosses/superiors who do not give the agreed salary to subordinates, or give it, but not in full; (13) anyone who behaves slyly, cunningly, and hypocritically with his neighbor and cheats him, and in any way offends him and belongs to this same number. All such offend His people in the presence of the Lord God. An offense done to a servant in the presence of his master bears upon the master as well and vexes him greatly. Likewise, an offense inflicted on Christians also bears on Christ the Lord Himself and vexes Him greatly. As Christ the Lord regards a good deed done to Christians as one done to Himself, as it is said, "And the King will answer and say to them, 'Assuredly, I say to you, inasmuch as you did it to one of the least of these My brethren, you did it to Me'" (Matt 25:40), so also the Lord regards an offense inflicted on Christians as one inflicted on Himself. A servant who suffers an offense in his master's presence looks to his master and consigns his offense to him. Likewise, the Christian, as one offended in the Lord's presence, should look to Him and convey his offense to Him, as one who judges righteously, for He says, "Vengeance is Mine, I will repay" (Rom 12:19). From this, it can be seen: (1) Whoever sins against a person sins also against God. Whoever offends a person offends God. Whoever vexes a person vexes also the Lord. For, in offending a person, he is breaking the commandment of God and offends a person, the servant of God, in the presence of his Lord. (2) You see how seriously such persons sin, Christian! It is vexing to you, very vexing, when someone offends your servant in your presence. But you dare to offend a Christian, a servant of Christ, before his Lord. Do you really think that the Lord of all does not see you, as you do not see Him? No! No! No one is doing evil and none of his evil deeds is concealed from His all-seeing eye. Whether you do evil on the road, or in the desert, at home or in the marketplace, alone or in public, secretly or openly, or in the depths of your heart you contemplate falsehood, He is present everywhere, He sees everything, whatever and wherever you do and contemplate it, and writes it down in His book, and on the last day, He will expose you in all this before the whole world, as it is said, "I will reprove thee, and set thy sins before thy face" (Ps 49:21). Do you reproach, backbite, vilify, and malign your neighbor? He is present here, hears your evil word, and sees the offense. Do you slander your brother? He is here and hears your slander. Do you beat up or kill your neighbor? He is not far from you and sees your evil deed. Do you steal another's property? You are stealing it before His holy eyes. Do you lie and deceive your neighbor? His eyes see your lie. In a word, everything that you do to your neighbor is all done before the Lord of all. And from this, you yourself can see how you vex His majesty, and how seriously you sin. Oh, better, truly better to die repeatedly than to vex Christ the Lord, Christ, Who so loved us worthless servants that he did not refuse to die for us. O man, who has in any way offended your neighbor! Take a look, please; take a look at what you are doing both to whom and before Whom. Take a look before it is too late! You call yourself a Christian, you sign yourself with the cross, you go to church, worship and pray to God, sing *Alleluia*, and what is most important of all, you approach the altar and commune the life-giving Mysteries of Christ, listen to the Word of God, and so on. All these, indeed, are signs of Christianity. But if you do not cease offending your neighbor and sinning, take care lest you become an enemy of Christ rather than a Christian. Examine yourself and think how you treat your neighbor, and repent, and correct yourself, while there is time for repentance. "Or do you despise the riches of His goodness, forbearance, and longsuffering, not knowing that the goodness of God leads you to repentance? But in accordance with your hardness and your impenitent heart you are treasuring up for yourself wrath in the day of wrath and revelation of the righteous judgment of God, who 'will render to each one according to his deeds': eternal life to those who by patient continuance in doing good seek for glory, honor, and immortality; but to those who are self-seeking and do not obey the truth, but obey unrighteousness–indignation and wrath, tribulation and anguish, on every soul of man who does evil, of the Jew first and also of the Greek" (Rom 2:4–9).

# 81. Royal Mercy Promised to Transgressors, and Announced, and Shown to Those Who Turn Themselves Around

It happens that a king, wishing to pardon and reform criminals and corrupt people who are both themselves perishing and are causing great harm to the homeland, diverts them from villainous deeds by promising mercy, and in leading them to a righteous life, promulgates an edict everywhere that if they, freely admitting their transgression, reform and in future live decently, then all their villainous deeds will be remitted and will not be remembered, and they themselves will live in peace and tranquility, like other sons of the homeland. And those who, having felt the king's mercy to them, act according to the promulgated decree are favored with mercy from the king. In this way, God, the Heavenly King, the King of Kings, and Lord of Lords, wishing to pardon sinners, declares repentance to them through His holy Word, so that they will leave their sins and turn to Him with true regret and contrition of heart and reform themselves. "Repent!" (Matt 3:2). And when they do this, the good and man-befriending God promises to remit and not remember all the sins that they have committed. "If a lawless man turns from all the lawless deeds he commits ... he will surely live and not die. None of the transgressions he commits will be remembered" (Jer 38:34 LXX [Jer 31:34]; Ezek 18:21–22). The Merciful God affirmed His promise even *by His oath*, so that poor sinners would not doubt His promise and would not fear to reform and to come to Him with repentance. "As I live, thus says the Lord: 'I do not will the death of the ungodly man. So the ungodly man should turn from his way and live'" (Ezek 33:11) (see Heb 6:13, 17–18). This great and unparalleled mercy of God, declared to the whole world, was heard by many sinners, many robbers, fornicators and adulterers, and other serious sinners, who embraced it with love and, leaving their loathsome deeds, hastened with repentance to their Merciful Creator, and received mercy from Him and, having been cleansed by repentance, became His friends and entered His eternal kingdom. Sinner! Why are you tarrying, hearing such a merciful utterance from the Heavenly Father? Repentant publicans and fornicators are delighted by the heavenly kingdom; why are you abiding in your sins and tarrying in them, as in a foreign country? God, like a Father who loves His children, awaits you! Well, come to yourself too, and hasten with repentance to your Heavenly Father. Indeed, I tell you, He will receive you with joy, and with merciful eyes will lovingly look upon you, and "will have compassion on you, and run and fall upon your neck and kiss you." Do not fear! He will not inflict any rebuke on you for your carelessness and separation but will order that you be dressed in the *best robe* and a ring be put on your hand, and sandals on your feet. Then there will be joy among God's angels for you. Then it will be said, "This my son was dead and is alive again, and was lost and is found" (see Luke 15:20, 22, 24). Quick, let us hasten, poor sinner, to the Heavenly Father, while He waits and the doors of His kingdom are open!

Wrongdoers who disdain the royal pardon declared and are hardened in their villainy do not wish to make a break with the evil and ruinous deeds, rightly turn the royal pardon into great anger, and already convicted by the court, will be punished according to the full extent of the law. They did not want to accept the royal pardon declared for their correction and benefit, so they will experience his justice and his righteously avenging hand. Then the royal anger will flare up against such insensible and ungrateful people. Likewise sinners, who now hear repentance being preached and God's mercy shown to sinners, but do not want to sincerely reform, to make a break with sin, and to repent, will instead of God's mercy experience His righteousness and avenging hand. "Upon sinners He shall rain down snares; fire and brimstone, and the stormy wind, shall be the portion of their cup" (Ps 10:6). "But the cowardly, unbelieving, abominable, murderers, sexually immoral, sorcerers, idolaters, and all liars shall have their part in the lake which burns with fire and brimstone, which is the second death" (Rev 21:8). Then they indeed will experience those fearsome threats, which they hear now in the holy Word of God. They do not want to experience God's manifest mercies, so they will experience His avenging righteousness. Now God calls and promises mercy, but then He will send down and pour out His righteous anger upon them. Now He says, "Repent," but then He will say, "Answer." Now He says, "Come unto Me," but then He will say, "Depart from Me." Where? "Into the everlasting fire prepared for the devil and his angels" (Matt 25:41). Now He hears those repenting and praying to Him, but then sinners will hear, "I do not know you, you did not get to know Me, and I do not recognize you, you did not listen to Me, and I do not hear you." "I called, but you did not obey, And spoke at length, but you paid no attention, But made my counsels invalid, And were not persuaded by my reproofs; Consequently, I will laugh at your annihilation, And will exult when ruin comes to you" (Prov 1:24–26). And again, "I called you, but you did not obey; I spoke, but you refused to listen. You did evil in my sight, and did not choose the things I willed." Therefore, thus says the Lord, "Behold, My servants shall eat, but you shall hunger. Behold, My servants shall drink, but you shall thirst. Behold, My servants shall be glad, but you shall be ashamed. Behold, My servants shall rejoice exceedingly in gladness, but you shall cry out because of the pain in your heart; and you shall wail from the crushing of your spirit" (Isa 65:12–14). Sinners! Let us fear the prohibitions of God, let us repent while repentance is being preached. Let us accept God's mercy, while it is still available. Let us turn to God, while He calls and waits. Let us pray to Him, while He listens to those who pray. "We are ambassadors for Christ, as though God were pleading through us: we implore you on Christ's behalf, be reconciled to God. For He made Him who knew no sin to be sin for us, that we might become the righteousness of God in Him. We then, as workers together with Him also plead with you not to receive the grace of God in vain. For He says: 'In an acceptable time I have heard you, And in the day of salvation I have helped you.' Behold, now is the accepted time; behold, now is the day of salvation" (2 Cor 5:20–21, 6:1–2). "Come to Me, all you who labor and are heavy laden, and I will give you rest. Take My yoke upon you and learn from Me, for I am gentle and lowly in heart, and you will find rest for your souls. For My yoke is easy and My burden is light" (Matt 11:28–30). "Or do you despise the riches of His goodness, forbearance, and longsuffering, not knowing that the goodness of God leads you to repentance? But in accordance with your hardness and your impenitent heart you are treasuring up for yourself wrath in the day of wrath and revelation of the righteous judgment of God, who 'will render to each one according to his deeds': eternal life to those who by patient continuance in doing good seek for glory, honor, and immortality; but to those who are self-seeking and do not obey the truth, but obey unrighteousness—indignation and wrath, tribulation and anguish, on every soul of man who does evil, of the Jew first and also of the Greek" (Rom 2:4–9).

# 82. Tares among the Wheat

It happens that tares grow among the wheat. The pious and the impious are like the wheat and tares. The tares grow among the wheat. Likewise the impious are present and circulate among the pious. The tares at first do not differ from the wheat, but later, when the wheat begins to ripen and bear fruit, it turns out that they are not wheat but tares. Likewise, the impious are not immediately recognized, but later, little by little their wickedness and depravity are manifested: "By their fruits you will know them," the Lord says (Matt 7:16). There is a great difference between the tares and the wheat. It is the same between the impious and the pious. Tares, as we see, are good for nothing, but wheat is useful for everything. Likewise, the impious are fit for nothing, but the pious are useful for everything. The tares, being worthless, are gathered during the harvest into sheaves and burned, but the wheat is gathered into the granary. Likewise the impious, being fruitless at the end of the age will be gathered, bound into sheaves and consigned to eternal fire. Fornicators and adulterers, defilers, and the depraved will make up their own sheaf. Thieves, extortioners, and robbers, who steal another's goods, will make up their own sheaf. Liars and the sly and cunning will make up. Slanderers, backbiters, and the foul-mouthed will make up their own sheaf. Hypocrites, who show themselves outwardly and holy, but inside are evil, will make up their own sheaf. These and other transgressors, being fruitless for their Lord, will be thrown into the eternal fire. But the pious, righteous, holy, and good, as ones bearing in patience the fruit of God's Word, some a hundred fold, some sixty-fold, and some thirty-fold, will be gathered into the heavenly kingdom, as wheat into the granary. "He who sows the good seed is the Son of Man. The field is the world, the good seeds are the sons of the kingdom, but the tares are the sons of the wicked one. The enemy who sowed them is the devil, the harvest is the end of the age, and the reapers are the angels. Therefore as the tares are gathered and burned in the fire, so it will be at the end of this age. The Son of Man will send out His angels, and they will gather out of His kingdom all things that offend, and those who practice lawlessness, and will cast them into the furnace of fire. There will be wailing and gnashing of teeth. Then the righteous will shine forth as the sun in the kingdom of their Father. He who has ears to hear, let him hear!" (Matt 13:37–43). Sinners, let us repent! Let us not burn in the eternal fire, like tares, and let us create worthy fruits of repentance. May we be by the grace of God the wheat that is gathered into the heavenly granary! "Convert us, O God; show the light of Thy countenance, and we shall be saved" (Ps 79:4).

## 83. Why Are You Here?

It happens that a person, upon seeing an acquaintance who has come to the village, or the city, or to some other kind of place, asks, "Why are you here?" This may be asked of a Christian who has come into the holy Church or Christianity for the sake of salvation but does not take care about it. We could ask of him, "Tell us, why are you here?" Why have you embraced Christianity but do not live a Christian life? Why have you entered Christ's vineyard but do not cultivate it? Why have you united yourself to the holy community but do not live a holy life. Why are you here? After all, you came here not to gather wealth, gold and silver, not to seek honor and glory, not to please the flesh and the world, not to serve sin and the passions, but to serve and please Christ the Lord and thus to gain salvation. "And [Christ] died for all, that those who live should live no longer for themselves, but for Him who died for them and rose again" (2 Cor 5:15). Remember what vows you gave to God, when you joined Christianity; how you renounced Satan and all his evil works; how you renounced the world and all its whims; how you promised to serve Christ, the Son of God, who died for you and rose again. Where are your vows now? Remember how the priest greeted you then with the great mercy of God: "Thou art washed, thou art justified, thou art sanctified in the name of our Lord Jesus Christ, and the Spirit of our God." Where are those vows that you gave to God and before God and His holy Church? Where is that righteousness and holiness that you received for free without any merits of yours, and by God's mercy alone? Show me them by your works. You received holiness—where is it? Why do you not live a holy life? You received righteousness. Where is your righteousness? Why do you not do works of righteousness? You were washed in the holy laver from the pollution of sin—so why are you defiling yourself again by sins? For what the proverb says happened also with you "A dog returns to his own vomit" and "a sow, having washed, to her wallowing in the mire" (2 Pet 2:22). As the farmer goes out into the field to cultivate the earth, the merchant arrives at his shop to conduct business; the pupil comes to school to learn; the judge enters the courtroom to judge, and seek justice; the soldier sallies forth out to battle to fight against enemies and to defend the homeland; so also the Christian embraces Christianity to live a holy life, to please Christ the Lord and with faith in Him, to seek eternal salvation from Him. As He who called you is holy, you also be holy in all your conduct, because it is written, "Be holy, for I am holy" (1 Pet 1:15–16). Why are you here, Christian, you who defile your body and soul by impurity. You, who breathe a spirit of malice and revenge against your brother. You, who stretch out your hand to steal another's goods. You, who cause the shedding of tears of widows, orphans, and other poor people. You, who slander your brother, and beat him with your tongue as with a sword. You, who lie, cheat, and lead astray your neighbor with your slyness, and so on? All this, as darkness from the light, are far removed from Christians. Why are you here? Why do you intermingle light with darkness? "For God did not call us to uncleanness, but in holiness" (1 Thess 4:7). Christian! Remember the vows you gave at holy baptism, which you gave not to man, but to God. It is fearsome to lie to God! God is not mocked. He will call you to account for your vows when He calls you to His Judgment. Then you will see Whom you lied to and before Whom you did not keep your vows. Remember this now, and repent, and do works worthy of your vows. May you not appear at that Judgment with a lie and share the fate of liars. "[They] shall have their part in the lake which burns with fire and brimstone, which is the second death" (Rev 21:8). "Awake, you who sleep, Arise from the dead, And Christ will give you light" (Eph 5:14).

# 84. A Lie

We see that various lies exist in the world. A merchant lies when he says goods of his are of such a value, when actually they are otherwise. A witness in court lies when he tells what he did not see and hear, or does not recount what he saw and heard, and calls black white, and bitter sweet. A servant lies when he tells his master what did not happen. A judge lies who promised and swore to act according to his conscience in court, to preserve and seek justice, but does not do this. A worker lies who having taken a suitable wage promised him who hired him to work earnestly but works lazily or does not work at all. A debtor lies who borrows money from a lender and promises to pay it back but does not do so. Anyone lies who hires others to work for him and promises to pay them a suitable wage for their labor but does not pay it. A soldier lies who swore to serve the Sovereign and society but does not do it. A pastor lies who promises and swears to tend the flock of Christ's sheep but does not tend it or negligently tends it and so on. Similarly, a Christian lies who promises in holy baptism to serve Christ the Lord but does not. Everyone does likewise who after holy baptism transgresses and cleaves to the vanity of this world. The fornicator, adulterer, and every defiler lies to Christ the Lord. The extortioner, thief, and robber lie. The blasphemer, the foul-mouthed person, and the one who talks foolishly lie. The backbiter, slanderer, and user of bad language lie. In a word, every transgressor lies. For an iniquitous and unchristian life is contrary to those vows that are made by Christians in baptism. Every Christian promises in baptism to live a holy, chaste, and pious life in Jesus Christ and to serve Him: without a holy and pious life, it is impossible to serve Christ. But when he lives not piously, but iniquitously, he does not serve Christ, does not keep his vows, and so lies to Him. And he will remain in sin for as long as he lives an unrepentant life. Christian! It is serious to lie to a person, a simple person, more serious to an official, and much more serious to the king. How incomparably more serious and terrible is it to lie to God! Remember to Whom you made your vows in baptism and, when you do not keep them, to Whom you have lied. You have lied to God, and not to a human. Repent before time runs out, and fulfill your vows, and may the Lord receive you into His mercy. "Have mercy upon me, O God, after Thy great goodness, and according to the multitude of Thy mercies do away mine offenses. Wash me thoroughly from my wickedness, and cleanse me from my sin. For I know my fault, and my sin is ever before me. Against Thee only have I sinned, and done evil before Thee" (Ps 50:3–6).

## 85. A Hen

We see that a hen gathers her little chicks under her wings and warms them. Likewise, Christ the Lord wants to gather sinners under the wings of His goodness and warm them, for He says to Jerusalem, "O Jerusalem, Jerusalem … How often I wanted to gather your children together, as a hen gathers her chicks under her wings, but you were not willing!" (Matt 23:37). Christ the Lord wishes, I say, to gather sinners. And how could He, Who created us in His own image and likeness, not wish this? And how could He, Who sympathizes and feels pity for our misfortune, not wish this? And how could He, Who sent the prophets to call us to Him, not wish this? And how could He, Who Himself came to us for our sake, lived on earth, labored, suffered, and died for us, not wish this? How could One Who so loved us not wish to gather us under His wings? O sinners! He wishes it, He wishes it, and, having stretched out the wings of His goodness, awaits us. "Come to Me, all you who labor and are heavy laden, and I will give you rest" (Matt 11:28). All the saints were gathered under His wings and are receiving rest under the shelter of His wings. Sinners! What are we waiting for? Why, having been scattered, do we roam and wander, like chicks that have been separated from their mother? Christ the Lord awaits us and, like a hen, wants to gather us under His wings. We even hear His voice calling: "Come to me." Well, let us run toward His voice, as chicks run to the voice of their mother, let us run to Him, and hiding under the shelter of His goodness, according to the admonition of the Psalmist: "Today, if you will hear His voice, Harden not your heart" (Ps 94:7–8). Let us run with repentance and regret. And may the saying not befit us that He spoke to the hard-hearted Jerusalem: "O Jerusalem, Jerusalem … How often I wanted to gather your children together, as a hen gathers her chicks under her wings, but you were not willing! … See! Your house is left to you desolate." "Your house is left to you desolate" are terrible words. Let us fear this and return to the Shepherd and Visitor of our souls. For nowhere will we find rest other than with Him. Without Him there is no rest; without Him there is no salvation, but unmitigated misfortune and perdition. Let us turn to Him while He waits, calls, and wishes to take us under the wings of His goodness. "The one who comes to Me I will by no means cast out" (John 6:37). "Come to Me, all you who labor and are heavy laden, and I will give you rest."

# 86. A Poultice

What a poultice is for a bodily sore or wound, so the Gospel is for a sinful soul, wounded by fear of God's judgment and sadness for sins. A bodily wound receives a slackening of pain and healing from the poultice. So the sinful soul, trembling before God's judgment, stricken with sorrow and grief before it, receives a slackening, a lively consolation and healing from the Gospel. This is what the Psalmist sang of concerning God's love for mankind: "Who healeth those that are broken in heart and bindeth up their wounds" (Ps 146:3). Do not fear, soul that is sinful but repents and sorrows for your sins! Only believe in the Gospel, and you will feel in your hearts its vitality. Judge for yourself: for whose sake did Christ, the Son of God, come into the world? For the sake of sinners. For whose sake did He live and labor on the earth? For the sake of sinners. For whose sake did He suffer, die, and rise again? For the sake of sinners, as the Apostle, to our consolation, says: "This is a faithful saying and worthy of all acceptance, that Christ Jesus came into the world to save sinners, of whom I am chief" (1 Tim 1:15). O, the immeasurable love for mankind of God! O, the great consolation for sinners! The Lord and God Himself came into the world to seek out and save those who were perishing. You are one of the sinners and are perishing, so He came to seek out and save you too. Only hold to the faith of the One who came to seek out and save sinners, and strengthen your hope in Him. Then he will without fail seek out and save you. And it is not said that Christ came for the sake of such and such sinners, but for the sake of each and every one, no matter how great and serious their sins may be. One thing only is required of them, that they give up their sins, repent, and have a contrite heart. And the spiritual poultice of the Gospel will be applied to their wounds, and they will feel in their hearts the joyfulness of God's mercy to them. For they are already beginning to offer a contrite spirit as a sacrifice to God on the altar of their heart. "The sacrifice unto God is a contrite spirit; a contrite and humble heart God shall not despise" (Ps 50:19). Sinful soul, crushed by fear and sadness! Picture within yourself how the compassionate father mentioned in the Gospel parable receives his younger son, who has returned from straying. How lovingly he looks upon him still from afar, how he meets him, how he falls upon his shoulder, how he embraces and kisses him! How he orders his servants to bring the best robe and clothe him, and to put a ring on his finger and sandals on his feet, and how orders his whole family to rejoice and be glad for him! "Ah, my son has returned to me! My son has come to me safe and unharmed!" "This my son was dead and is alive again; he was lost and is found" (Luke 15:20–25). Likewise, God, the Heavenly Father, lovingly receives the sinner who repents and comes to Him with a contrite heart, does not remember his sins and transgressions, and commands His whole heavenly family to rejoice for him. Thus, the Lord says, "There is joy in the presence of the angels of God over one sinner who repents" (Luke 15:10). And indeed, it is so. If for the sake of a sinner He did not spare His Son but gave Him over to death, how will He not receive the repentant sinner? "He who did not spare His own Son, but delivered Him up for us all, how shall He not with Him also freely give us all things" (Rom 8:32)? How will He not have mercy on us, who ask mercy of Him? How will He not receive us who turn to Him? How will He not remit us our sins? How will He not save us? "If God is for us, who can be against us" (Rom 8:31)? "The God of our salvation ... Our God is the God that saveth" (Ps 67:20–21). A father or a mother does not take pity on a sick child as much as the Merciful God takes pity on a sinner who sighs to Him in contrition and pain of heart. Then He is deeply moved over him, and then He will have mercy on him, pardoning him. For as great as His majesty is, such is His mercy! Glory be to His generosity! Glory to His goodness! Glory to His love for mankind! "Blessed be the Name of the Lord henceforth and forevermore! O praise the Lord all ye nations; praise Him, all ye peoples, for His merciful kindness is ever more and more towards us, and the truth of the Lord endureth forever. O come, [sinners], let us worship and fall down before Him, and weep before the Lord that made us. For He is our God, and we are the people of His pasture, and the sheep of His hand. For with the Lord there is mercy, and with Him is plenteous redemption, and He shall redeem Israel from all his iniquities" (Ps 116:1–2, 94:6–7, 129:6 [7–8 in Slavonic]). From this you see, Christian, on whom the Gospel bestows its consolation, to wit, not on fornicators, not on adulterers, not on thieves, not on extortioners, and not robbers, and not on other people living lawlessly. To these it is said, "Lament and mourn and weep! Let your laughter be turned to mourning and your joy to gloom" (Jas 4:9). When they do this, then they too will be consoled by the Gospel as by food after a fast. Then the Gospel will be affixed to their wounded heart like a poultice to a wound. For whom is the Gospel suitable? The answer: sinners, who have turned from their sins to God, who are sorry for the sins they have committed, who fear God's judgment, who are stricken with sorrow, who seek God's mercy, and who fall down to Him with humility. Therefore it is written, "Repent, and believe in the gospel" (Mark 1:15). Without repentance, the Gospel will bring no benefit. The Gospel brings us consolation. But what good is consolation to one who does not have a sorrowful and broken heart? And this is what Christ the Lord says of Himself: "He has anointed Me to preach the gospel to the poor; He has sent Me to heal the brokenhearted" (Luke 4:18). You see to whom Christ is preaching the good news. Repent and turn from sins to God and have a contrite heart. Then the holy Gospel will befit you, too, as a poultice does a bodily sore.

## 87. Where Are You Going? There Will Be Misfortune for You There

It happens that a person warns a person who is going toward a certain danger, saying, "Where are you going? There will be misfortune for you there." So the holy Christian books warn and restrain the careless sinner who is headed toward perdition, saying, "Poor sinner! Where are you going? There will be misfortune for you there." Where are you going? What misfortune can be greater than eternal perdition and eternal death? For as only true good is eternal good, so also the only true evil is eternal evil. Where are you going, poor sinner? To perdition! Fornicator, adulterer, and lover of impurity! Where are you going? To perdition! You malicious one, and you who breathes vengeance against your brother and who defile your hands with human blood! Where are you going? To perdition! Thief, extortioner, and robber! Where are you going? To perdition! Slanderer, name-caller, backbiter, and user of foul language! Where are you going? To perdition! Drunkard and every troublemaker! Where are you going? To perdition! Sly one, flatterer, and cheater! Where are you going? To perdition! Careless and scandalizing pastor! Where are you going? To perdition! To perdition, and you will drag many with you, many, for whom Christ poured out His blood. Judge, perjurer, and bribe taker! Where are you going? To perdition, and by your example, you are laying the path there for your minions. Ruler who serves your own whims and not society, and seeks your own gain and not the general benefit! Where are you going? To perdition! Landowner who torments or burdens your peasants! Where are you going? To perdition! Lying merchant, who sells a cheap item for an expensive one, a shoddy item for a good one, and a rotten one for a sound one! Where are you going? To perdition! Hired hand who accepts appropriate pay, and does not work, or pretends to work! Where are you going? To perdition! Money-grubber, who withholds the pay of a hired hand! Where are you going? To perdition! Sorcerer and one who calls on him for help! Where are you going? To perdition! Every unreformed sinner who does not repent! Where are you going? To perdition! The life of every person, while he lives in this world, is his path. As his life is, so is his path. And as he lives, so does he walk. And whatever kind of life he has, such a path does he walk. He walks either to eternal blessedness or to eternal perdition. He who lives piously in Christ Jesus walks by a pious path and walks to eternal life. He who lives iniquitously walks by the path of iniquity and walks to eternal perdition. Ah, he walks to perdition, he for whom Christ died; he walks and will be lost if he does not return! Poor sinner! Stand firm while you are still on the path; return before you are lost. When you are lost, you will not escape. You will, like a corpse, forever be in perdition and in eternal death. Turn back! Christ the Lord, Who suffered and died for you, calls you and summons you to repentance. "I did not come to call the righteous, but sinners, to repentance" (Matt 9:13). Turn and get on the path of repentance, the path leading to eternal life, that going by it, you will come to a blessed end and enter eternal life. "Do not be deceived. Neither fornicators, nor idolaters, nor adulterers, nor homosexuals, nor sodomites, nor thieves, nor covetous, nor drunkards, nor revilers, nor extortioners will inherit the kingdom of God" (1 Cor 6:9–10). "The cowardly, unbelieving, abominable, murderers, sexually immoral, sorcerers, idolaters, and all liars shall have their part in the lake which burns with fire and brimstone, which is the second death" (Rev 21:8). "Come to Me, all you who labor and are heavy laden, and I will give you rest" (Matt 11:28).

# 88. Why Have You Stopped?

It happens that when people who have gathered for some undertaking are working and toiling, that one of them, getting lazy, stops. Then another says to him, "Why have you stopped?" Likewise, you can say in encouragement to one who has begun but is slackening in the struggle of piety, "Other Christians are toiling in their undertaking, but why have you stopped?" Others are repenting and sighing with fervor for their sins—why have you stopped? Others are battling against sin, the devil, the world and passions—why have you stopped? Others are diligently cultivating the Lord's vineyard—why have you stopped? Others are serving the Lord with zeal—why have you stopped? Others are fervently praying, beseeching, and knocking on the door of God's mercy— why have you stopped? Others are sowing their spiritual seeds—why have you stopped? Others generously give alms—why have you stopped? Others do good to their neighbors—why have you stopped? Others, despising wealth, honor, glory, and every vanity of this world, look toward eternal blessedness and hasten toward it—why have you stopped? Others humble themselves before God and people—why have you stopped? Others serve their neighbors with love—why have you stopped? Others go and hasten to the honor of a higher calling—why are you watching, why have you stopped, and why are you not going? Others strive for eternal life—why have you stopped and are not striving? Others, denying themselves and taking up their cross; follow Christ, follow Him with patience, love, meekness, humility; and follow Him into eternal life. "How joyful are all they whose habitation is in thee!" (Ps 86:7); where there are joy, gladness, sweetness, honor, glory, and eternal blessedness; where they see God face to face; where sickness, sorrow, and sighing have ceased; where the sound of joy and gladness is heard, and the sound and clamor of those feasting and making merry is heard; where the hymn "Alleluia" is sung continuously and sweetly; where there is sweet and blessed friendship with the angels, that is, where those who follow Christ, like sheep after their shepherd, go: "My sheep hear My voice, and I know them, and they follow Me. And I give them eternal life, and they shall never perish; neither shall anyone snatch them out of My hand," says the Lord (John 10:27–28). Why have you stopped? Why are you not hastening there to a tranquil, peaceful, and sweet place? All the saints went there and entered, the patriarchs, prophets, apostles, holy hierarchs, martyrs, holy monastics and everyone who pleased God by faith from time immemorial; are settled there, rejoice and are glad; and await the general resurrection and the most perfect blessedness in accordance with God's true promise. Why have you stopped? Why are you not hastening there? They are awaiting with great eagerness for us to arrive there. The Heavenly Father, Who did not spare His Son for our sake, but handed Him over to death, awaits us. He awaits those whom He created in His image and likeness. He awaits that He may make us happy with eternal blessedness in His kingdom. Why have we stopped? Why are we slumbering? Why don't we go? Why do we not hasten there? What blessedness do we see in this world? What rest, peace, and good? What gladness and joy? "Vanity of vanities, all is vanity" (Eccl 1:2)! Troubles in cities, troubles in villages, troubles in deserts, troubles on land, troubles on sea! Troubles from open enemies, troubles from secret ones, troubles from the tongue, troubles from human hands, troubles from the flesh and passions that fight with the soul, troubles from the devil, who "walks about like a roaring lion, seeking whom he may devour" (1 Pet 5:8)! Troubles from false seducers and tempters, troubles from relatives and from false brethren, troubles from the entire world! "The whole world lies under the sway of the wicked one" (1 John 5:19). What in the world is not woeful? Wealth is linked with poverty, glory with disgrace, honor with dishonor, rest is

not without agitation, peace is not without agitation and revolt, love is hypocritical, friendship is not without suspicion, sweetness is diluted with grief. In
all quarters of the world are found fear, dread, suspicion, danger, and sorrow.
There is no truth; there is no faithfulness. Truth has diminished among the
sons of men. Indeed, "the whole world lies in evil." What good do we expect
from this world? "Vanity of vanities, all is vanity". They have talked of vanities
every one with his neighbor (Ps 11:3). Lying lips are in the heart, and in the
heart they spoke evil. Woe is me, that my life in a foreign land is prolonged.
O Jesus, sweetness of life, joy and consolation of those who love You! To You,
Who lives in heaven, I lift up my tearful eyes from this bitter vale of tears:
draw me after You. We will run to the habitation of all those who keep festi-
val. "Unto Thee have I lifted up mine eyes, O Thou that dwellest in heaven.
Behold, even as the eyes of servants are upon the hand of their masters, and
as the eyes of a maid are upon the hand of her mistress, even so are our eyes
upon the Lord our God, until He have pity upon us. Have mercy upon us, O
Lord, have mercy upon us, for we have had our fill of humiliation. Our soul
is fed up with the scornful reproof of the wealthy, and the disparaging of the
proud" (Ps 122:1–4).

# 89. Fasting

As we see, there is a fast both of the body and of the soul. The bodily
fast is when the belly abstains from food and drink. The fast of the soul is
when it refrains from evil thoughts, deed, and words. An excellent faster is
one who restrains himself from anger, rage, malice, and revenge. An excellent
faster is one who imposes abstinence on his tongue and restrains it from idle
talk, foul language, foolishness, slander, judgment, flattery, lying, and every
kind of malicious talk. An excellent faster is one who restrains his hands from
theft, extortion, robbery, and his heart from desiring others' property. In a
word, the good faster is one who withdraws from every evil. You see, Christian, the fast of the soul. The bodily fast is beneficial for us since it serves
for the mortification of our passions. But fasting of the soul is absolutely
essential because without it, bodily fasting is nothing. Many fast in the body
but do not in the soul. Many fast from food and drink but do not abstain
from evil thoughts, deeds, and words. What benefit do they get from this?
Many fast for a day or two or more but do not want to abstain from anger,

remembrance of wrongs, and revenge. Many abstain from wine, meat, and fish but with their tongues they bite people like themselves, and what benefit do they get from this? Some often do not touch food with their hands but reach them out to bribery, extortion, and robbery of another's goods. What benefit do they get from this? True and real fasting is abstinence from every evil. Christian, if you want fasting to be beneficial for you, then, while fasting bodily, do so also in the soul, and fast always. As you impose fasting on your belly, impose it on your evil thoughts and whims. May your mind fast from vain thoughts! May your memory fast from remembrance of wrongs! May your will fast from evil desires! May your eyes fast from evil sights: Turn away thine eyes, lest they behold vanity (see Ps 118:37). May your ears fast from foul songs and slanderous whisperings! May your tongue fast from slander, judgment, blasphemy, lies, flattery, foul language, and every idle and corrupt word! May your hands fast from fighting and from embezzling of another's property! May your feet fast from going about evil business! "Shun evil, and do good" (Ps 33:15; 1 Pet 3:11). This is the Christian fasting that God requires of us. Repent and, abstaining from every evil word, deed, and thought, and learn every virtue, and you will always be fasting in the sight of God. "'If you fast for condemnations and quarrels, and strike a humble man with your fists, why do you fast to Me as you do today, so your voice may be heard in crying? I did not choose this fast, and such a day for a man to humble his soul; nor if you should bow your neck like a ring and spread sackcloth and ashes under yourself, could you thus call such a fast acceptable? I did not choose such a fast," says the Lord;

> rather, loose every bond of wrongdoing; untie the knots of violent dealings; cancel the debts of the oppressed; and tear apart every unjust contract. Break your bread for the hungry, and bring the homeless poor into your house. If you see a naked man, clothe him, nor shall you disregard your offspring in your own household. Then your light shall break forth as the morning, and your healing shall spring forth quickly. Your righteousness shall go before you, and the glory of God shall cover you. Then you shall cry out, and God will hear you. While you are still speaking, He will say, "Behold, I am here." If you take away your fetter and the pointing of the finger, and the word of grumbling, and if you give bread to the hungry from your soul, and satisfy the humble soul, then your light shall rise up in the darkness, and your darkness shall be as midday. (Isa 58:4–10)

# 90. Renunciation of Christ

People only understand renunciation of Christ to be when a Christian renounces Him by the lips and with words. Indeed, this is renunciation of Christ; this is a serious and destructive deed since to renounce Christ is to renounce life and to plunge oneself into self-evident death. But there is another renunciation of Christ similar to it. It is affected by deeds and an iniquitous life. Of such a renunciation, the Apostle says, "They profess to know God, but in works they deny Him, being abominable, disobedient, and disqualified for every good work" (Titus 1:16). There is a renunciation of Christ by the tongue, and there is a renunciation of Christ by deed. Christian, do not comfort yourself that you are a Christian if you live not piously but iniquitously. Whoever disdains a command disdains and abandons the one who gave the command. He is an unfaithful servant who does not evince obedience to his master. What kind of servant of Christ is the Christian who does not obey Christ? The Lord says, "But why do you call Me 'Lord, Lord,' and do not do the things which I say" (Luke 6:46)? And again, he says, "He who is not with Me is against Me" (Matt 12:30). Every transgressing Christian is not with Christ but is against Christ, is an enemy of Christ, and has renounced Christ even though he calls Him, "Lord, Lord." Whether you commit fornication, Christian, or adultery, or in any other way defile your soul and body, you renounce Christ. If you reach out your hand for theft and robbery of someone else's goods, you renounce Christ. If you flatter and are sly and cheat your neighbor, you renounce Christ. If you slander, abuse and vilify your neighbor, you renounce Christ. In a word, in doing any wicked deed against conscience and with intent, you renounce Christ. And as often as you offer sacrifice to your passionate desires as to an idol, that often do you obey it. Repudiate the desire that is persuading you to do an evil deed, and obey Christ, and you will not be renouncing Him. It is easy to shun gold, silver, copper, and wooden idols, but it is very difficult to shun those that are within us, that is, in our hearts. "Those who are Christ's have crucified the flesh with its passions and desires" (Gal 5:24). Consequently, those who have not crucified the flesh with its passions and desires are not Christ's. But if they are not Christ's, then think: what are they in God's eyes? What are their prayers like? What are their sacrifices and offerings like? Oh, there are so many false Christians! So many idolaters hide under the name of Christian! The tree is known by its fruit, and the Christian, by his faith and good works. "Show me your faith without your work" (Jas 2:18), the Apostle requires of you, Christian. Reform, Christian, and repent, mortify your flesh with its passions and lusts. And may you be a true Christian and have a good hope in Christ Jesus.

# 91. A Servant Who Knows, and One Who Does Not Know, the Will of His Master

It happens in the world that some servants know the will of their master and do not do it, and others do not know it and do not do it. And for this they receive a punishment from their master. The one who knows the will of his master and does not do it is punished harshly, but the one not knowing and not doing it is punished less, as the Lord says, "That servant who knew his master's will, and did not prepare himself or do according to his will, shall be beaten with many stripes. But he who did not know, yet committed things deserving of stripes, shall be beaten with few" (Luke 12:47–48). Such are the pagans and the Christians in the sight of Christ the Lord. Pagans, not knowing Christ the Lord, do not know His will either, and do not do it, and will be punished in the age to come less than evil Christians. Christians know Christ, Who came into the world, and always hear the word of Christ being preached, and the will of Christ their Lord contained in it, but do not want to do it. For this reason in the age to come they will be tormented harshly and to a greater degree than pagans and idolaters. Woe will it be then to Christians who knew Christ, but did not do His will. Then they will hear from Christ, "I tell you I do not know you, where you are from. Depart from Me, all you workers of iniquity" (Luke 13:27). Of this it is said, "that it will be more tolerable in that Day for Sodom than for that city" (Luke 10:12); that is, it will be more tolerable for those who do not know God and do not hear the Word of God but act wickedly, than for wicked Christians, who hear the Word of God and confess God with their lips but renounce Him by their deeds. "Not everyone who says to Me, 'Lord, Lord,' shall enter the kingdom of heaven, but he who does the will of My Father in heaven" (Matt 7:21). Repent, Christian, and do the will of Christ, Who for your sake suffered and died, lest you be condemned more severely than the pagans on Judgment Day.

# 92. Take Stock of Yourself!

We often hear that people on various occasions say, "Take stock of yourself!" You, Christian, who confesses God and hears His holy Word and knows that sinners will receive eternal torment, and the righteous, eternal life—it is especially fitting to say to you, "Take stock of yourself!" You renounced Satan and all his evil deeds at baptism, but have you not reverted back to him by your evil and dissolute life? "Take stock of yourself!" You promised and made a vow then to serve Christ the Lord, who died for you, but do you not serve sin and the world instead? "Take stock of yourself!" "Whoever commits sin is a slave of sin" (John 8:34). "You cannot serve God and mammon" (Matt 6:24). You were washed then, you were sanctified, you were justified in the name of our Lord Jesus Christ, and the Spirit of our God, but have you not been defiled and are you not being defiled again by wicked deeds? "Take stock of yourself!" The proverb is suitable for such people: "A dog returns to his own vomit," and, "a sow, having washed, to her wallowing in the mire" (2 Pet 2:22). You were called by the Word of God and renewed by holy baptism to eternal life and heavenly good things, but do you not think of what is earthly? Do you not seek how in this world to be glorified, to become rich, to be honored? Do you not join your heart with the vanity of this world? Are you not walking by the path of the impious to destruction? Take stock of yourself! "For wide is the gate and broad is the way that leads to destruction, and there are many who go in by it. Because narrow is the gate and difficult is the way which leads to life, and there are few ho find it," says the Lord (Matt 7:13–14). God is in every place, He looks upon all of us, He hears every one of our words, He sees our deeds and thoughts, and He examines our hearts and reins, as His holy Word preaches and our holy faith teaches. How do you walk in the sight of the omnipresent and all-seeing God? How do you speak before Him Who hears your every word? How do you act and think before Him Who sees your every deed and thought and writes down everything in His book, and on the day of His Judgment will declare it to you? What thoughts about Him do you cherish in your heart—are they consistent with the Word of God and the holy faith? Take stock of yourself! You confess the fearsome and holy name of God, you call upon and sing to Him in prayer, but do you not defile those lips with which you confess and hymn God, and do you not defile them, I say, by foul language, slander, backbiting, foolish words, blasphemy, judgment, flattery, lying, and every rotten and idle word? Take stock of yourself! You lift up your hands to the Great and Holy God, but do you not cover them with shame by extortion, robbery, and every wrong? Do you not harbor hatred and malice against your neighbor? Do you not desire to wreak vengeance on him and harm him in some way? Look around you! You approach the holy and life-giving Mysteries of Christ. Oh, how great is that deed! How great is the goodness of God! How great is His esteem, too, for man! Man, earth and ashes, touches the divine Body and Blood! "Bless the Lord, O my soul" (Ps 102:1)! Beloved Christian! How do you approach this great and fearsome mystery? With what faith? With what fear? With what heart? With what lips? With what hands? Take stock of yourself! For this is a fire that burns the unworthy. "But let a man examine himself, and so let him eat of the bread and drink of the cup. For he who eats and drinks in an unworthy manner eats and drinks judgment to himself, not discerning the Lord's body" (1 Cor 11:28–29). God is your greatest benefactor, greater than whom there never was, is not, and cannot be. He created you out of nothing, just as everything else, and grants you every good thing. Without His goodness, we could not live for even a minute. The sun, moon, and stars that shine on you are His goodness. The air that maintains your life is His goodness. The Earth on which you live, which brings forth fruit for you and your livestock, is His goodness. The livestock that serve you are His goodness. The water that you and your animals drink, and the fish that live in it, are His goodness. The house in which you take your rest and that protects you from storms and bad weather is His goodness. The food and drink with which you strengthen and refresh your infirm body are His goodness. The fire and firewood on which your food is cooked and with which your house is heated are His goodness. The clothing with which you cover and warm you naked body is His goodness. All this and more He gives you with His invisible and almighty hand, He gives it from His special kindness and love for you. His nature is such that He cannot not do good. You see His love for you, but do you feel in yourself love for Him in return? Love is recompensed by nothing other than by love. You receive benefactions from Him, but do you remember the benefactor and do you thank Him? Take stock of yourself! Ingratitude toward a person from whom we receive some small favor and we do not thank him is serious. Incomparably more so is ingratitude to God, when we receive each and every good thing from Him but are ungrateful. Without love, there cannot be gratitude toward Him. And he who does not do the bidding of His holy will show ingratitude to Him. "His lofty and incomprehensible love for us is revealed by the coming to us by His good will of His only-begotten Son to seek us out and save us, the perishing" (Matt 18:11). Christ the Lord Himself tells us of this love, "For God so loved the world that He gave His only begotten Son, that whoever believes in Him should not perish but have everlasting life" (John 3:16). Poor sinner! For your sin, by which you have dishonored and angered the Righteous and Infinite God, you, like a corpse that has been reduced to dust, should have died the eternal death in hell and drunk without end the bitter cup of God's anger, and been counted as one with Satan and his angels, and suffered in the unquenchable fire. These are the fruits of sin, "For the wages of sin is death" (Rom 6:23). God, the Lover of Mankind, in His goodness and love for us, would not permit you to come to this. Glory to His goodness, glory to His love for mankind, glory to His generosity and mercy! He would not, I say, permit you to come to this. Whom? An apostate and His enemy. He had mercy on you, He took pity on you, He loved you, He sent His only-begotten Son to you to save you. He came to you, the Creator to His creation, the Lord to His unprofitable servant, the Holy and Great God to a sinner. The King of Heaven appeared on earth, and He who is inaccessible to the cherubim and seraphim became accessible to poor outcast people and sinners, became man in a body like you, lived on earth, and dwelt among sinners, as light in the midst of darkness, "and the darkness did not comprehend it" (John 1:5). He worked, was ill, wept, suffered, and died for you. You see, sinner, what God did for your sake. "Blessed is the Lord God of Israel, For He has visited and redeemed His people, And has raised up a horn of salvation for us In the house of His servant David" (Luke 1:68–69). What more can you expect of God, sinner, when He did not spare even His only-begotten Son for your sake? What love, what benefaction could be greater than this! Do you remember this great deed of God, of which there could not be a greater? Do you remember this deed, by which you were delivered from eternal death and hell, and in which your eternal life and all your eternal happiness consists? Do you remember this, and do you thank God, your benefactor and redeemer, from a pure heart? Take stock of yourself! Do you sincerely, and not hypocritically, honor the Lord, who has so honored you? Take stock of yourself! Do you observe His holy commandments, without which love for Him is impossible? Take stock of yourself! "He who has My commandments and keeps them, it is he who loves Me. He who does not love Me does not keep My words," says the Lord (John 14:21, 24). "And He died for all, that those who live should live no longer for themselves, but for Him who died for them and rose again" (2 Cor 5:15). God, Who created and loves every person, created and loves you as well, and from His love gives His good things to all, including you, and showed such merciful and marvelous man-loving providence in the work of salvation to all, so also to you. God, I say, Who so loved you and is your benefactor desires and commands that you love your neighbor, that is, every person, as you love yourself. Do you comply with the holy wish of the One who has loved you and is your benefactor? Do you do the bidding of His holy will? Do you render diligent obedience to Him? Do you love your neighbor who is loved by God? Do you not do to him what you do not want for yourself? Do you give him in his need the helping hand that you would want for yourself? Take stock of yourself! The time of our life is short, passes like flowing water, and once lost, does not return like a spoken word. How and in what do you spend it? Is it not in idleness? Is it not in vanity? Is it not in parties and banquets? Is it not in acquiring honor, glory, and riches? Take stock of yourself! God has given you time for repentance and not for concupiscence. Are you spending it as God wants? Take stock of yourself! A person can find everything in this world, but he cannot find lost time. Death comes for a person by an invisible road and snatches him away when and where and in what manner he least expects. Our death is both known and unknown to us: known, that we shall die; unknown, for we do not know when, where, and how we shall die. The longer we live, the fewer our days grow and the closer we are to the end of our life. Christian! Do you remember that terrible hour at which all the saints looked and wept, the hour in which everyone should go either into a blessed or a tormented eternity, and are you preparing for this with true repentance? Take stock of yourself! However that hour finds you is how you will stand before God's Judgment. Blessed is he who remembers that hour. "O Lord, tell me mine end, and the number of my days, what it is, that I may know what is wanting to me. Behold, Thou hast made my days as it were a span long, and my existence is as nothing before Thee; verily, every man living is altogether vanity. Therefore man walketh as a shadow, and disquieteth himself in vain; he heapeth up riches, and knoweth not for whom he gathereth them" (Ps 38:5–7). All of us must appear before Christ's Judgment seat. You too will appear before that judgment, God's Judgment, not man's. A just and strict examination of deeds, words, and thoughts will take place there. Everything whatsoever we have done in our whole lives will be exposed and will be revealed before the whole world, and each will be rebuked by his own conscience. Kings and their subjects, masters and their servants, parents and their children, pastors and their people, noble and low-born, rich and poor will stand side by side there, and each will answer for himself. The sins that the sinner has expiated here by repentance, contrition of heart, and tears will not even appear there. But whatever sins an unrepentant sinner may have committed in word deed, or thought, will all be exposed to the whole world. Then will be said of him, "There is the man and his works!" All the people gathered there will be divided into two parts: some will stand on the right side of the Righteous Judge, and the Lord, the King of Glory, will call them into His eternal kingdom; others will stand at the left side of this Judge, and he will send them into eternal fire, prepared for the devil and his angels. "And these will go away into everlasting punishment, but the righteous into eternal life" (Matt 25:46). Christian! Do you remember this terrible day, and do you have a burning lamp and oil in a vessel, and are you preparing to meet that Judge Who is coming? Take stock of yourself! You, too, look around, beloved pastor, how you tend Christ's flock? Christ the Lord entrusted you to tend His flock, not dumb sheep, but rational ones, Christian souls, redeemed by His holy blood. How do you tend them? Do you nourish them with the food of God's Word? Do you go before them as a model of good works? Do you show them the way of salvation? Do you protect them from the wolves of the soul, the demons? Take stock of yourself! Authority figure and ruler, how do you treat God's people entrusted to you? Do you care about them and look after the common weal, which your office and the force of your oath require of you? Do you not seek your own filthy lucre? Take stock of yourself! Judge, how do you judge, whom do you acquit and why, and whom do you prosecute? Take stock of yourself! Master, how do you treat servants and peasants, people like you? Take stock of yourself! Servant, how and with what kind of conscience do you serve your master? Take stock of yourself! Father, how are you raising your children? What are you teaching them? Are you not pouring the poison of temptations into their young hearts, instead of healthy teaching and instruction? Take stock of yourself! Child, how do you honor the father who begot you? Do you render your parent and breadwinner his due? Take stock of yourself! Husband, are you faithful to your wife, and wife, are you faithful to your husband? Take stock of yourself! Merchant, how do you trade and how do you sell? Take stock of yourself! Look around, please, every Christian—what and why do you now act, speak, and think? Everything that you do, say, and think now will be revealed before you at that shame-filled spectacle. Do not be careless about yourself, beloved. God wants to save you: may that be your desire, and you will be saved. Whoever wants something earnestly seeks it earnestly. Take stock of yourself! You, too, should look around, my soul; how you live; how you treat people; how you behave, speak and think; what you love and what you hate; how you relax; what comforts you and what delights you; what grieves you and what saddens you; and in what you place your hope. "Look upon me, hear me, O Lord my God; lighten mine eyes, that I sleep not in death. Lest mine enemy say, I have prevailed against him" (Ps 12:4–5). "See then that you walk circumspectly, not as fools but as wise, redeeming the time, because the days are evil. Therefore do not be unwise, but understand what the will of the Lord is" (Eph 5:15–17).

## 93. A Shield

We see in the world that people in a battle defend themselves from the enemy's arrows with a shield. Christian! Our life is nothing other than a battle and a contest against various enemies; a battle against the devil and his angels; a battle against the flesh with its passions and lusts; a battle against the evil and hostile world; a battle against false brethren; a battle against secret and open enemies—a continuous and terrible battle. What kind of shield do we have to protect us from the arrows of enemies on that terrible day? God's holy Word directs us to faith and the Lord's name, and the examples of all the saints show this, and all true Christians in the day of their sorrow resort to this shield and thus protect themselves from the enemy. "God is our refuge and strength, a very present helper in the troubles which greatly afflict us. Therefore will we not fear, when the earth be shaken, and the hills be cast into the midst of the sea" (Ps 45:2–3). "Our fathers hoped in Thee; they trusted, and Thou didst deliver them. They called upon Thee, and were saved; they put their trust in Thee, and were not confounded" (Ps 21:5–6). "Lord, Thou hast been our refuge from generation to generation" (Ps 89:2). This shield, like a mighty wall, protected our forefathers, Abraham, and Isaac, and Jacob, as was written of them: "He allowed no man to rule over them, and he reproved kings for their sakes" (1 Chr 16:21). Joseph, beautiful in soul and body, was kept safe under this shield, and the arrows of temptations and troubles shot at him did nothing. By this shield, Israel coming out of Egypt was kept safe; it was kept safe from its enemy and tormentor, the pursuing Pharoah, and from the enemies whom they met on the way and who rose up against it; under this shield it was kept safe from the multifarious enemies living in the Promised Land. "If the Lord Himself had not been on our side, may Israel now say, If the Lord Himself had not been on our side, when men rose up against us, then would they have swallowed us up alive; When their wrath was kindled upon us, then would the waters have drowned us" (Ps 123:1–3/4). The holy David, king of Israel, resisted all his enemies with it, as he says of himself: "All nations compassed me round about, but in the Name of the Lord have I driven them back. They kept me in on every side, but in the Name of the Lord have I driven them back. They came about me like bees on a honeycomb, and burned even as a fire among the thorns, and in the Name of the Lord have I driven them back" (Ps 117:10–12). The prophets, apostles, hierarchs, martyrs, holy monks, hermits, and all the saints who have pleased God from time immemorial were kept safe under it. They were kept safe in multifarious temptations, misfortunes, disasters, tortures, and sufferings. True Christians even now take shelter under this secure and invincible shield and, being protected from the enemy, make bold and sing the beautiful hymn: "God is our refuge and strength, a very present helper in the troubles which greatly afflict us … The Lord of hosts is with us; the God of Jacob is our protector" (Ps 45:2, 8). "If God is for us, who can be against us? He who did not spare His own Son, but delivered Him up for us all, how shall He not with Him also freely give us all things" (Rom 8:31–32)? Saint Paul, the God-loving soul, makes bold and triumphs over all of hell and the power of the enemy. Beloved Christian! Satan and all his evil spirits have an unbridled fury against man, and especially against the true Christian and, like wild animals in the night, encircle him invisibly and in many ways attack him, and try to destroy him, either themselves or through false Christians and other evil people, their servants. Who could be saved from their slanders and arrows, if the Lord did not protect them with the shield of his goodness, and the shelter of his grace-filled wings? In truth, he would perish in one minute. In truth, what the holy David sang of the old Israel and of its defense and protection, "If the Lord Himself had not been on our side, may Israel now say, If the Lord Himself had not been on our side, when men rose up against us, then would they have swallowed us up alive; When their wrath was kindled against us, then would the waters have drowned us," befits the new Israel, the Christians. Indeed our enemies would have swallowed us up alive, if God were not with us and were not preserving us. "Blessed be the Lord, Who hath not given us over for a prey unto their teeth" (Ps 123:6). From this we see how vain is hope on everything except God, and what an unsound support for any person, and a false shield for any creature. Therefore, leaving all else, let us flee to this safe and impregnable shield. "It is better to trust in the Lord, then to put any confidence in man. It is better to trust in the Lord, then to put any confidence in princes" (Ps 117:8–9). Let some protect themselves by cunning and contrived speech; others with gold, silver, and their other treasures; some by their office and their high titles; some by the mediation of princes and lords; some by other means that they wish. But everything with which they may protect themselves is a false and unsound shield. Their hopes will disappoint them. We defend ourselves with the Name of the Lord and will not be put to shame. Look, Christian, belong only to God, and the Name of the Lord will defend you from all the slanders of the enemy. "I will love Thee, O Lord, my strength. The Lord is my firm foundation, and my fortress, and my deliverer; my God is my helper, and I will trust in Him, my defender, the horn also of my salvation, and my protector. Giving praise, I will call upon the Lord, and so shall I be safe from mine enemies" (Ps 17:2–4). "Yea, though I walk through the valley of the shadow of death, I will fear no evil, for Thou art with me" (Ps 22:4). "Thou art my refuge from the afflictions that overwhelm me; my Joy, deliver me from them that circle me round about" (Ps 31:7). "Thou art my helper; unto Thee will I sing, for Thou, O God, art my defender, and my merciful God" (Ps 58:18). When a Christian dwells in the grace of God and in the help and protection of the Most High, then, even though all the evil people, all of society, the whole world, all the devils and hell stirred themselves and rose up against him, and all the misfortunes and disasters that happen in the world besieged him, they would in no wise succeed since God is more powerful than all of them, for He holds him in His almighty hand, protects him, and keeps him safe. Do not fear, pious and God-loving soul. "For He shall deliver thee from the snare of the hunter, and from every mutinous word. With His wings will He overshadow thee, and thou shalt be safe under his feathers; His truth shall compass thee round about like a shield. Thou shalt not be afraid for any terror by night, nor for the arrow that flieth by day; For the thing that walketh in darkness, for sickness, or the demon of noon-day. A thousand shall fall beside thee, and ten thousand at thy right hand, but unto thee it shall not come nigh" (Ps 90:3–7). The entirety of the psalm teaches this.

# 94. Peace

In the world, we see that when one kingdom with another, city with another city, village, with another village, neighbor with neighbor, wife with husband, and others living in one home have peace with one another, then everything goes well, and they fear no evil from each other, provided that it is true peace, and not a hypocritical one, which often occurs between people. So, when a Christian has peace with God, then he carries all blessedness within himself and drives away all calamity and misfortune. Then a person dwells in the mercy of Almighty God, Who covers His servants; he does not fear the wrath and judgment of God; he is not terrified of hell and Gehenna; he is not frightened of the devils and all the slanders of the enemy; he hopes without doubting for eternal life and the promised good things and every blessing of God. He fears only one thing—that he will sin before God and will anger Him and so be deprived of this very sweet peace. This peace may only be in a pure and innocent conscience—this is the most sublime gift of the Holy Spirit. The holy Apostle wishes Christians this peace in almost all of his epistles: "Grace to you and peace," and so on. Priests also wish us this peace at all public divine services, "Peace be unto all!" Christ the Lord, having risen from the dead, proclaimed this peace to the apostles: "Peace to you" (John 20:21). In Adam, we had lost this peace, peace with God, but regained it in Christ, our Lord. He became the Mediator between God and people, as the Church sings to Him: "Thou wast a Mediator between God and man, O Christ God" (Sunday Octoechos, Canon 5th Ode, Tone 2). By His suffering and death, He made satisfaction for our sins, took away our sins, introduced eternal righteousness, and propitiated God: He thus reconciled us with God and God with us, the angels with people, and people with the angels. He joined the heavenly with the earthly and the earthly with the heavenly. The Lord, our Defender and Helper, as One mighty in power, conquered and trampled down death, hell, and the whole demonic horde, and all of our enemies, and granted us the good hope of eternal life, so that we hope in accordance with His truthful promise to triumph over all our enemies in a blessed eternity. "O Death, where is your sting? O Hades, where is your victory" (1 Cor 15:55)? Let us depend on this Victor over death and hell and all our enemies! Let us boast in this Defender and Helper! Let us trust in this Protector in all of our calamities, misfortunes, temptations, and snares of the enemy inflicted upon us! He stands up for us, as our Defender and Helper. He is all-powerful. If He is for us, who can be against us? "Thou art my strength, O Lord, Thou also art my power, Thou art my God, Thou art my exceeding joy, Who without leaving the bosom of the Father, hast none the less visited our poverty" (Sunday Octoechos, Canticle 4, Tone 8),[9] and so forth. Thanksgiving be to God, who has given us the victory by our Lord Jesus Christ. Therefore, let us offer a sacrifice of praise and thanksgiving to Him alone, as the author and finisher of our world, the Father of the age to come, the pastor and overseer of our souls, the author of faith, the mediator of the New Testament/Covenant and Great Hierarch, the author and finisher of our salvation and of all our eternal blessedness, Jesus Christ, our Lord with the Father and His Holy Spirit. "Blessed be the Name of the Lord, from this time forth and forever more" (Ps 112:2). "Therefore, having been justified by faith, we have peace with God through our Lord Jesus Christ, through whom also we have access by faith into this grace in which we stand" (Rom 5:1–2). "And [Christ] came and preached peace to you who were afar off and to those who were near. For through Him we both have access by one Spirit to the Father" (Eph 2:17–18). "For the kingdom of God is not eating and drinking, but righteousness and peace and joy in the Holy Spirit. For he who serves Christ in these things is acceptable to God and approved by men" (Rom 14:17–18). "O Lord, our God, grant us peace, for You render everything to us. O Lord our God, possess us; O Lord, we know no other besides You; we name Your name" (Isa 26:12–13).

# 95. A Straight and a Crooked Tree

Righteous and unrighteous hearts are like straight and crooked trees. As straight and crooked trees are to each other, so are righteous and unrighteous hearts—the straight does not get on harmoniously with the crooked; likewise, between the righteous and unrighteous heart there is no similarity and harmony. But let us take a look at what sort are the righteous and unrighteous heart, and we shall see what the difference is between them and whether there can be harmony between them. The righteous heart is God-fearing, but the unrighteous has no fear of God. The righteous heart follows God and His holy will, but the unrighteous, its own evil will and whims. The righteous heart avoids every sin, but the unrighteous heart is not troubled about this. The righteous heart humbles itself and thinks humbly, but the unrighteous one becomes conceited and behaves haughtily. The righteous heart thinks of heaven and aspires to future good things, but the unrighteous heart thinks of what is earthly and allies itself with the vanity of this world. The righteous heart loves every person and does not withdraw its love even from those who hate it, but the unrighteous heart only loves those who love it and often hates even them. The righteous heart deals with its neighbors artlessly, unflatteringly, and unhypocritically. But the unrighteous heart deals craftily, slyly, and hypocritically with every person. What the righteous heart has on its tongue and declares in speech is what is within itself and what it is thinking. But the unrighteous heart speaks something else, thinks something else, has something else on the tongue, and has something else within itself. The righteous heart neither desires nor touches another's goods. But an unrighteous heart both desires and reaches out his hands for them. A righteous heart desires and tries to do good to all. But an unrighteous heart does not care about that. What the righteous heart does not want for itself it does not do to its neighbor. But the unrighteous heart does to its neighbor what it does not wish for itself: it judges its neighbor, slanders, backbites, blasphemes, and curses, although it does not at all wish this for itself. A righteous heart does not take revenge for an offense; it bears it and forgives. But an unrighteous heart does not want to endure any offense, although it itself offends everyone. The righteous heart, although it may stumble and fall, immediately gets back on its feet with repentance. But the unrighteous heart, having fallen once, stays down. The righteous heart thanks God for everything that it has received from Him, but the unrighteous heart forgets every one of God's benefactions. The righteous heart is patient in misfortune and distress, but the unrighteous one is indignant, grumbles, and often even blasphemes. The righteous heart honors God in truth, and spirit, and earnest obedience, but the unrighteous one with only the lips and outward appearance. Of such, the Lord says, "These people draw near to Me with their mouth, And honor Me with their lips, But their heart is far from Me" (Matt 15:8; Isa 29:13). The righteous heart ascribes every good thing that it does to God, as the Source of every good thing, but the unrighteous, to itself and its own endeavor. The righteous heart works to the glory of God and the benefit of its neighbor, but the unrighteous heart does everything for its own praise and vainglory, and so forth. You see the portrayal of a righteous and unrighteous heart. Think for yourself what similarity and harmony can be between them. What does light have in common with darkness, sweet with bitter, white with black, or straight with crooked? Do not seek, oh, do not seek peace and harmony between a bad-tempered wife and a good-natured husband, and a good-natured wife and a bad-tempered husband; between a bad-tempered mother-in-law and a good-natured daughter-in-law, and a bad-tempered daughter-in-law and a good-natured mother-in-law; between a bad-tempered brother and a good-natured brother, between a bad-tempered sister and a good-natured sister, between a bad-tempered neighbor and a good-natured neighbor, and between any bad-tempered and good-natured persons. No, there has not been, nor can there be peace and harmony between them. "Do you suppose that I came to give peace on earth? I tell you, not at all, but rather division. For from now on five in one house will be divided: three against two, and two against three. Father will be divided against son and son against father, mother against daughter and daughter against mother, mother-in-law against her daughter-in-law and daughter-in-law against her mother-in-law" (Luke 12:51–53). They will unfailingly be divided from each other when some follow Christ, the Light, and others follow the darkness; some think about the heavenly, and the others about the earthly. A straight tree is useful for any purpose; everything can be made from it, but a crooked tree is not good for anything. In like manner, a righteous heart is useful and necessary for every rank and calling and for general benefit, but an unrighteous heart is not useful for any calling and rank. Wherever it may be, it will follow its own will, and not God's, everywhere it will seek its own filthy lucre and not the common benefit. O man, turn to God, and correct yourself, and follow God's will, and you will be a straight tree, and your undertakings will be righteous. "And as many as walk according to this rule, peace and mercy be upon them, and upon the Israel of God" (Gal 6:16). But an unrighteous heart is deprived of all of this, and "the wrath of God abides on him" (John 3:36). "Make me a clean heart, O God, and renew a right spirit within me. Cast me not away from Thy presence, and take not Thy Holy Spirit from me. O give me the comfort of Thy salvation, and stablish me with Thy governing Spirit" (Ps 50:12–14). Pray, Christian, with all fervor that God Himself would correct and mend your heart by His grace. Without it, our heart cannot be righteous. When God's grace takes up its abode in your heart and lives there, you will day by day be renewed, changed, and reformed.

# 96. Water Flows from High Mountains to Low-Lying Areas

We see that water flows down from mountains to low-lying areas. In the same way, God's grace pours out from the Heavenly Father to humble hearts. But let us look at the characteristics of the humble heart and we will see this truth. (1) The humble heart sees in itself its sins, sinfulness, affliction, baseness, and nothingness, and from all this gets to know its unworthiness. Such a heart does not dare to lift up its eyes to heaven and to say much to God but beats its breast and, sighing, falls down before God and prays, "God, be merciful to me a sinner!," as did the publican (Luke 18:13). He judges himself unworthy to look upon God and to approach Him. Peter showed such humility when he said to Christ, "Depart from me, for I am a sinful man, O Lord!" (Luke 5:8). (2) The humble heart flees every dignity, honor, and fame. And if some kind of honor and dignity is thrust upon it, it assumes these with extreme unwillingness and for the sake of obedience, since it sees its ignorance and unworthiness. (3) The humble heart shows obedience to those above, does not despise those equal and lower than itself, but treats all as brethren, even if it is more respectable than them and has greater talents than them, for it looks not on talents but on its own baseness and understands that the talents are not its own but someone else's, and it is only their receptacle, and not their master, but baseness and nothingness is its own, as with all people, for every person is in himself poor and wretched. And that is why it treats inferiors as if it is one of them. (4) If it somehow offends someone through ignorance or carelessness, as this happens with everyone, it is not ashamed to fall down before him and ask forgiveness, even if the offended one were below him or its subordinate. What a fine sight it is when a higher-ranking person bows to an inferior and asks forgiveness! (5) A humble heart considers itself unworthy of any benefaction and worthy of every distress. Therefore, when it finds itself in misfortune, it does not grumble; it is not indignant but endures it magnanimously, considering itself deserving of it. (6) When anyone offends it by word or deed, it does not become angry at the one who offends and particularly does not exact revenge on him, for it considers itself deserving of this. (7) When it sees or hears someone sinning, it does not judge him, for it sees that it itself too is such a sinner. (8) Whatever good and benefaction it receives from God, it sees that it receives it for free, without any merit of its own and from His mercy alone, since it sees its unworthiness, that it is unworthy of everything that it receives. And for this reason it thanks God warmly for everything that it receives. (9) Whatever good it itself does, it ascribes it all to God, for it sees its feebleness and nothingness, that, like a dried-up tree, it cannot of itself bear any good fruit without God's help. (10) At a meeting, at lunch, and at supper, it sits "in the lowest place" (Luke 14:10). (11) It does not seek the best house, the finest clothing, the highest quality food, and so on but is satisfied with what it has. And it considers itself unworthy of what it has. And how can it desire and seek something better when it considers itself unworthy of what it already has? You see, Christian, some depictions of a humble heart. A stream of God's grace flows onto such a heart. God looks mercifully on such a heart. Give me, O Lord, to know myself, and to see my wretchedness, poverty, and nothingness, and I shall have a humble heart. "Look upon me, hear me, O Lord my God; lighten mine eyes, that I sleep not in death. Lest mine enemy say, I have prevailed against him" (Ps 12:4–5). Man is poor and wretched, but he is so much the poorer and more wretched, in that he does not see his poverty and wretchedness. He thinks that he is white, but he is black as a raven. He thinks that he sees and knows everything, but he is blind and knows nothing. He thinks that he is rich, but he is really poor and wretched. He thinks that he is honorable, but he is dishonorable and has become like an animal. He thinks that he is good, but in actual fact, he is evil. He thinks that he is healthy, but in actual fact, he is feeble. He thinks that he is happy, but he is poorer and more wretched than any creature. Sin has made him such. "Lord, what is man, that Thou hast had such respect unto him? Or the son of man, that Thou so regardest him" (Ps 143:3)? But the poorer the person, the greater and more amazing was God's grace to him. God Himself became man for man's sake. "Praise the Lord, O my soul" (Ps 145:1). The beginning of well-being is to become aware of your lack of well-being, as the beginning of health is to become aware of your infirmity. Christian! Become aware of your poverty and acknowledge it, and you will be well because you will be humble. "God resists the proud, But gives grace to the humble" ... "for everyone who exalts himself will be humbled, and he who humbles himself will be exalted" (1 Pet 5:5; Luke 18:14).

## 97. Water Flowing By

As water is flowing by, so is our life and everything that happens in life. We see that water in a river continuously flows and everything floating on the surface of the water, for example, wood, litter, and so on, passes by. Christian! This is how our life, and with life all well-being and ill-being, goes by. I did not exist before, and now I am here in the world, like other creatures. "Thy hands have made me and fashioned me," O Lord (Ps 118:73). I was a baby, and that passed. I was a boy, and that passed. I was a youth, and that left me. I was a mature and strong man, and that passed. Now my hair is turning gray, and I am growing weak from old age. But that too will pass, I am approaching the end, and I shall go on the path of the whole earth. I was born in order to die. I die in order that I may live. "Lord, remember me when You come into Your kingdom" (Luke 23:42)! What has happened with me will happen with every person. I was healthy and ill and again healthy and again ill, and this passed. I was in well-being and ill-being, time went by, and with time everything passed. I was in honor; that time passed, and honor departed from me. People honored me and kept bowing to me; that time passed, and I do not see it any more. I was cheerful, and I was sad; I rejoiced and I wept. And now the same thing happens with me: the days pass; sorrow and cheerfulness, joy and weeping pass with them. People complimented me and sang my praises; they reviled me and they vilified me. And some praised, then the same cursed me, and some reviled, and then complimented me—time passed; everything passed; praise and abuse, glory and infamy passed away. I hear the same even now: first they praise, and then they revile; first they glorify, and then they defame. I know that this too will pass: time will pass; the abuse and praise, glory, and infamy will pass. What has happened and is happening to me, the same will happen to every person living in this world. Such is the world, such is its constancy, and such is our life in the world. Man is poor from his mother's womb even to the grave: he is born with tears; he lives in the world as a ship sails in the sea, and first rises, then falls, first rises then falls, and dies with weeping. I lived in a palatial house, and I lived in a hut. Time passed, and such peace left me. I live now cooped up in a hut, and this will not last. I sat at an opulent table, and I sat at a meager one. Those days passed, and everything that was in them passed as well. This is happening even now, and this will pass. I tasted sweetness and grief; the taste receded, and the sweetness and grief receded from me. I heard sweet music. The time for listening passed, and my merriment ceased. I dressed in good clothing. That time passed; the attire departed from me. I rode in a carriage. That time passed, and the carriage is no more. Servants stood before me. That time passed and they departed from me. I had friends and acquaintances. Those days passed, and some of them turned into my enemies, and some into false brethren. What happens to me happens with everyone. Where is that time in which I was happy; in which I was healthy, cheerful, joyful, celebrated, praised, honored; in which I was comforted by a sumptuous table and music, and rode in a tandem carriage? Time has passed, and all my happiness and my consolation have passed with it. Where is that time when I was unhappy, ill, sad, mournful, reviled and vilified, reproached and sworn at, and so on? Those days have passed, and all that unhappiness of mine has passed as well. Everything will pass that happens at present, as everything passes with the fleeting time. What one person experiences happens with everyone. There is no person who from birth to death abides in unchanged well-being or ill-being. As under the sky there is fine weather, then overcast, then bad weather and storm, then clear and quiet prevail; likewise it falls to every person to be in well-being, then in ill-being, then in fear, then in sadness, then in joy. But as days and hours pass, so every happiness and unhappiness pass with them. You see, Christian, that like water flowing by and everything floating on it, so the time of our life and all our well-being and ill-being passes with time. And so all our life will pass by. As now our bygone days and everything that happened in them are happiness and unhappiness, so too the rest of our life, and everything that takes place in it will be. And as we see as in sleep our bygone days, and with them all our well-being and ill-being, likewise at the end of our lives we shall see the rest of the time as in sleep. And we will only remember then and dream that such and such happened with us. Such is our life in this world! Life in the age to come will not be like this, as the word of God and our faith assure us. Our life there will begin one day, but it will never end; it will be continuous and permanent. Our body will not have infirmities, decrepitude, old age, death and decay, but it will be a spiritual body, imperishable, immortal, healthy, strong, light, and flourishing. The body is sown in corruption, it is raised in incorruption. It is sown in dishonor, it is raised in glory. It is sown in weakness, it is raised in power. It is sown a natural body, it is raised a spiritual body ... For this corruptible must put on incorruption, and this mortal must put on immortality. So when this corruptible has put on incorruption, and this mortal has put on immortality, then shall be brought to pass the saying that is written: "Death is swallowed up in victory." "O Death, where is your sting? O Hades, where is your victory" (1 Cor 15:42–44, 53–55)? Glory, honor, rest, peace, consolation, joy, gladness, and all blessedness will also be there continuously. God's chosen ones will continuously see Him face to face, and continuously be consoled, will rejoice, and will be glad; they will continuously reign with Christ, as members with the head. "We suffer with Him, that we may also be glorified together" (Rom 8:17). Likewise, in an unfortunate eternity, death will be continuous. Having once died, the condemned will continuously die and desire death; they will continuously be tormented and suffer, and none will feel consolation, refreshment, or relief. This is the second death and eternal death. From this, it follows: (1) Inasmuch as our temporal life is inconstant, and all in it changes and passes by, we should not cleave to temporal and worldly things but seek eternal life and those good things with all possible zeal. "Set your mind on things above, not on things on the earth" (Col 3:2). (2) Do not become puffed up by the well-being of this world, that is, riches, glory, honor, praise, and other things—just as they come to us, so also they leave us, and we become as one of the unfortunate, needy, poor, and despised. (3) In ill-being, do not become despondent since this too will pass. And as after the night that is passed, the day dawns, and after a storm and bad weather, fine weather shines through, so also joy comes after grief and sorrow, and well-being comes after ill-being. (4) Gently endure slander, abuse, reproaches, and vilification of willful and wicked people and not to be distressed, for even all this will pass. For God is powerful, and He will turn their curse into a blessing for us, as it is said, "They shall curse, yet Thou shalt bless" (Ps 108:28). (5) Whoever will be equally steadfast in patience during well-being and ill-being will always abide in repose and peace and will have a pleasant, sweet life, similar and conforming to Christ's life and on earth will feel heavenly joy, and in this temporal life taste the sweetness of eternal life. "O Lord, help me! And let all them that put their trust in Thee be glad; they shall ever rejoice; and Thou shalt dwell in them and they that love Thy Name shall be joyful in Thee" (Ps 5:12).

# 98. Now You Are Freed from All Misfortunes

It happens that people in various situations say: "Now you are freed from all misfortunes." This is said to one who was in captivity but is leaving it. Although this saying is said to people living in this world, it is not quite suitable for them. It is impossible for a person who lives in this world to be freed from all misfortunes. He has been freed from one misfortune, but another happens to him. As seafarers always expect bad weather and storms, likewise one who lives in this world must always expect misfortunes and disasters. One misfortune has passed; now another unexpectedly comes along—the world is always like that. For this reason, this saying, "Now you are freed from all misfortunes," is suitable only for a faithful and pious person at the time of his death. He then indeed is freed from all misfortunes. Beloved Christian, who are completing this much-suffering life, you are now being freed from all misfortunes.

You were born in order to die—you are dying now in order to live. You were born to misfortunes and sorrows; now you are ending your life, and your misfortunes and sorrows are ending, too. You lived through diverse misfortunes and disasters—now you will no longer see them. You wept and were ill; now there will no longer be any of that. You endured illness of the soul and body; now you will no longer feel any of that. You endured tedium and grief; now it will no longer bother you. You endured every shortage and distress; now it is departing from you. Not without grief and labor have you fought against the flesh with its passions and lusts; now it will no longer bother you. You endured the attack of the devil and his evil spirits and did battle against them; now they will leave you. You endured insult and animosity from evil people; now they will no longer insult you and cause evil. You labored and did not have real rest; now you will have it. You feared everything deadly and injurious; now you will have no fear and be in safety. You required food, drink, and clothing for your feeble body; now you will not require them. You inadvertently saw the temptations of this world; now you will not see them. You inadvertently heard the impious and pernicious words of willful people; now you will not hear them. You endured the reproaches and abuse of your enemies; now you will not have any of this. You are being separated from your father and mother but are going to God, your Eternal Father. You are leaving both your friends and brethren, but the angels and assembly of saints will be your friends. You will not see this sun, but Christ the Lord, the Sun of Righteousness, will shine on you, Who both died for you and by His death enlivened you. You are leaving this world, but you are leaving all your misfortunes and disasters with the world and are entering the kingdom of God. You are ending temporal life but are beginning the eternal and blessed one. You are temporarily tasting the sorrow of death, but you will taste the sweetness of eternal life. You will not see day and night, but the day will always and continuously shine for you. Your body, as dust, will be consigned to the dust but will be awakened by the voice of the Son of God and will arise, and the corruptible will be invested with incorruption, and the mortal will be invested with immortality, and that of the soul will be invested by that of the spirit, and the feeble will rise up in strength, and the dishonored will rise in glory. "Thanks be to God, who gives us the victory through our Lord Jesus Christ" (1 Cor 15:57). "For blessed is the way on which thou shalt walk today, my soul: for a place of rest is been prepared for thee [Prokeimenon, Order for Burial of the Dead (Laymen)]." All the saints, patriarchs, prophets, apostles, hierarchs, martyrs, monastic saints, and everyone who has pleased God from the beginning have gone there and find repose there. You too are going there where all the saints find repose. You will behold, and your heart will rejoice, and "your joy no one will take from you" (John 16:22). You will behold the glory of God, and your heart will rejoice. You will behold Christ, the Son of God, Who suffered and died for you; you will behold in glory, and your heart will rejoice. You will behold the choirs of angels and archangels, and the chosen ones of God, and your heart will rejoice. You will behold the splendid Jerusalem on high, and its unspeakable beauty, and your heart will rejoice. You will behold the house of the Heavenly Father and His many habitations, and your heart will rejoice. You will behold there everything else, incomparably better and more splendid than you see here, and your heart will rejoice. You will behold good things, "Eye has not seen, nor ear heard, Nor have entered into the heart of man The things which God has prepared for those who love Him" (1 Cor 2:9). You will behold, and your heart will rejoice. You will see wondrous, excellent, and fearsome things, of which there is no number, and your heart will rejoice. Will you say: "I am unworthy of the Heavenly Kingdom?" The answer is: Really, no one is worthy of it. But Christ, our Lord, Who by the price of His priceless blood earned it for us, is worthy. Our worthiness depends on His worthiness. He, by His worthiness made even us, the unworthy, worthy, and by His grace, the good and man-loving Heavenly Father, in His unspeakable mercy, bestows it. He is the Father to you as to all the faithful and opens the doors of His kingdom and will grant the inheritance of eternal life. You will say, "I am a sinner?" The answer is: "Christ Jesus came into the world to save sinners, of whom I am chief" (1 Tim 1:15). This is our justification, "[He] became for us wisdom from God–and righteousness and sanctification and redemption" (1 Cor 1:30). "I have committed many sins?" The answer is: "But where sin abounded, grace abounded much more" (Rom 5:20). Many sins are cleansed by the multitude of God's compassions. Do you say, "I fear the judgment?" Christ answers: "Most assuredly, I say to you, he who hears My word and believes in Him who sent Me has everlasting life, and shall not come into judgment, but has passed from death into life" (John 5:24). Do you say, "I fear that I shall perish?" The Psalmist answers: "The God of our salvation ... Our God is the God that saveth" (Ps 67:20–21). Do you say, "I fear hell and eternal torment?" The answer is: Christ the Lord redeemed us from it by His death and His blood. And the Church sings, "From the belly of hades hath He delivered us" (Troparion of the Resurrection). Do you say, "How can I rejoice with the saints, who shone forth in so many virtues?" The answer is: Even the saints were saved by the grace of Christ. You should sing with the thief: "Lord, remember me when You come into Your kingdom" (Luke

23:42). The whole Church offers such a cry to Him. "Be of good courage and let your heart stand firm" (Ps 30:25). The Lord is your helper, the Lord is your protector, the Lord is your defender, the Lord is your redeemer, the Lord is your deliverer. The Lord is your Saviour; He, Who loved you and gave Himself over for you, and suffered and died for you, defeated all our enemies; He by His all-powerful hand preserves you. God's angels are your companions. "The Lord is my light, and my Saviour; whom then shall I fear? The Lord is the defender of my life; of whom then shall I be afraid" (Ps 26:1). "Turn again then into thy rest, O my soul, for the Lord hath prospered thee. For He hath delivered my soul from death, mine eyes from tears, and my feet from stumbling. I will be well-pleasing before the Lord in the land of the living" (Ps 114:7–8). "For we know that if our earthly house, this tent, is destroyed, we have a building from God, a house not made with hands, eternal in the heavens" (2 Cor 5:1).

# 99. A Small Sapling

We see that a small sapling inclines easily in any direction: it will grow in the direction toward which it inclines. Likewise a young boy: whatever he is taught, he becomes accustomed to, and whatever he is accustomed to, he will do for the rest of his time. If he learns goodness in his youth, he will be good all his life. If he learns evil, he will be evil for all his life. And from a small boy may develop either an angel or a devil. How he turns out depends on what kind of upbringing and instruction he will have. The whole remaining time of his life depends on his upbringing, as fruits depend on the seeds. Therefore God's Word admonishes parents: "But bring them up in the training and admonition of the Lord" (Eph 6:4). And in the Proverbs of Solomon, it is written, "He who spares the rod hates his son, But he who loves him instructs him with care" (Prov 13:26). Many teach their children worldly etiquette; some teach foreign languages, to speak French, German, Italian, and allot no small sums for this; others try to train them in trade and other skills; hardly anyone teaches children to live in a Christian manner. And without this, every learning is nothing and every wisdom is ignorance. What use is it to a Christian to speak Italian, French, or German, but to live godlessly? What good is to be skilled in trade and arts but not to have fear of God? Such artists and wise men can be worse than unskilled simpletons. The young heart, as one inclined to evil, strives for every evil if it is not restrained by the fear of God and the bridle of discipline. And even more so those who sharpen their minds by studies and arts, but do not correct the will, become skilled at everything bad, and themselves display examples of this. Therefore, Christian, let your first effort be to teach your children to live in a Christian manner. All your teaching and instruction are nothing without this. God will not call you to account for whether you taught your children worldly etiquette and foreign languages, but He will call you to account as to whether you taught them to live in a Christian manner, whether you instructed them in piety. Woe to young children who have evil fathers! What can they learn from them except evil? For how can an evil person teach goodness? Although it happens that an evil father punishes his children for willfulness, he teaches it by his example. Young people learn more from deeds than from words and punishments. From this it happens that if the fathers are bad, the children are worse, and the grandchildren are even worse. And so the poor person, having learned evil and become used to it, becomes sated with ungodliness, as with bread, and falls from evil to evil and from iniquity to iniquity, and plunges into perdition, as a rock dropped from the top of a mountain. And although it happens that some of them realize their misfortune and ruin, and shudder, and are horrified, and begin to repent, they return to their wickedness, drawn by habit as if by a rope. This evil proceeds from an evil upbringing. Woe to the young children but worse is the woe to fathers who not only do not teach their children goodness but by their bad example give cause for every evil! Such fathers kill not the body but Christian souls for which Christ died and deprive them not of temporal but eternal life. They will realize this terrible harm where everything will be revealed, and the deeds of each will be displayed before the eyes of all. Therefore, fathers in whom there is a spark of piety must try in every way to teach their children to live in a Christian manner, and to pour the milk of piety into their young hearts, "that you may grow thereby" (1 Pet 2:2). It is useful to teach sciences and arts, but it is necessary to teach how to live in a Christian manner, since every science and art without Christian life is nothing. Heed this, parents, lest you be murderers of those children whom you have brought into the world. A true father is not he who has begotten children, but he who has brought them up and taught them well. He who begot has only given life, but he who has brought them up and taught them well has helped them to live well. Pagans also live in the world, dwelling in darkness and idolatry, worse than the very animals. But only Christians live well. Therefore we are in debt to the fathers who have begotten us. But we are in even greater debt to fathers who have brought us up and instructed us in piety, for fathers who have begotten us, begat us to temporal life, but fathers who have brought us up and instructed us in piety beget us to eternal life. "Blessed is he who does good, and teaches good" (see Matt 5:19). Blessed is the parent who has begotten his children to temporal life and has given birth to them for eternal life. Wretched is the parent who begat his children to temporal life but has closed the doors to eternal life—has closed them either by neglecting a good upbringing or by his bad example. It is better for a person not to be born than to be born and to find himself in eternal perdition.

A small sapling, when it pulled out from the earth, is pulled out easily. Likewise, every evil passion, before it has taken root in the heart and become firmly established, is removed from a person without difficulty. A big tree is pulled out of the earth with hardship and great difficulty, since it has taken root deep within the earth. Likewise a firmly established passion that has taken root deep within the human heart is uprooted with great hardship and difficulty. Much difficulty and struggle is required for those in the habit of drunkenness to be freed from drunkenness; for those in the habit of fornication to be freed from fornication; for those in the habit of greed to be freed from greed; for those in the habit of thievery and stealing to be freed from stealing; for those in the habit of slander, judgment, and backbiting to restrain their tongues from this; for those in the habit of swearing not to swear; for those in the habit of lying not to lie; for those accustomed to grandeur, pride, and the vanity of this world drunkenness to be freed from this; and so forth. Many try to free themselves from the passion in which they dwell, and repent and weep, seeing their misfortune, and with time break themselves of it, but then return to it again. The passion, like a magnet, draws them to itself. Therefore, Christian, arm yourself against your flesh from the beginning, while you are still young; arm yourself against the flesh, which with the passions and lusts wages war with your soul and wishes to destroy it. Uproot the passions and lusts from your heart, while they are still young and have not grown, lest they, when they grow, destroy your soul. These are your foremost enemies and familiars and are ever with you wherever you may be, since they are within you. They surround your soul and continuously oppress it, and take away its nobility, and deprive it of its sweet freedom. They turn it away from God and

His holy love. They prevent it from doing His will, serving and pleasing Him, saying pure and God-pleasing prayer, contemplating heavenly things, hearing the word of God and bearing its fruit, to be nourished and comforted by heavenly, holy, and kind thoughts, to strive for and run toward eternal and blessed life; as real enemies they prohibit it. The soul is surrounded by these enemies, and confined in this darkness as in a dungeon, and is deprived of its sweet freedom and its nobility. "Bring my soul out of prison, that I may give thanks unto Thy Name; the righteous await me, until Thou shalt requite me" (Ps 141:8). "O Lord, remember what happened to us; Look upon us with favor and see our disgrace" (Lam 5:1). Destroy these hostile and iniquitous infants that your passionate flesh has begotten. Kill the enemies while they are still young, lest they kill you when they grow up and become stronger. Let them die, that your soul may live. Be a fighter and a kicker, and not a sluggard. Be a valiant warrior against these enemies, and not their prisoner; their sovereign and not their subject; their master, and not their servant. Stand up against them, and do not yield to them, lest they overcome you and take you captive, and will possess you, like a prisoner. Woe to that soul that these foes possess! Obey the Lord, and not them, that you may be the Lord's servant, and not theirs. It is impossible to work both for God and for the passions, and to please God and the passionate flesh; and to do the will of God, and the will of your flesh and its lusts, since one is contrary to the other. What God desires, the passionate flesh does not desire, and what God does not desire, the passionate flesh does desire. Renounce the passionate flesh, "crucify it with its passions and desires, that you may be a slave of God and man of God. And those who are Christ's have crucified the flesh with its passions and desires" (Gal 5:24). "My soul shall live, and shall praise Thee, and Thy judgments shall help me. I have gone astray like a sheep that is lost; O seek Thy servant, for I have not forgotten Thy commandments" (Ps 118:175–176). "O God, make speed to save me; O Lord make haste to help me. Let them be ashamed and confounded that seek after my soul" (Ps 69:2–3).

## *100. Repose*

As we see, there is bodily repose, and there is repose of the soul. The body finds repose when it rests after a journey or labors. Likewise, the soul finds repose when it rests in a pure and innocent conscience and is not disturbed by anything. This is the sweetest repose of the soul. The body finds sweet repose when it rests after labors; the soul is also in sweet repose when it has a pure and innocent conscience. The body has its unrest, and the soul also has its. The body is deprived of repose when it is involved in labors, and the soul is deprived of repose when it is disturbed by a bad conscience.

Repose of the soul is taken away:

(1) By every sin and transgression. A fornicator, an adulterer, and any lover of impurity cannot have repose of the soul. The malicious person, the vengeful person, and the murderer cannot have repose of the soul. The thief, extortioner, robber, and judge who takes bribes cannot have repose of the soul. The slanderer, the name-caller, and the backbiter cannot have repose of the soul. The liar and the cheat cannot have repose of the soul. In a word, every sinner who breaks the law of God cannot have repose of the soul, for, having violated God's law, he violates the repose of the conscience and vexes the conscience, which rebukes and torments the soul that has sinned. Whatever God's law says is also said by the conscience, and for whatever God's law rebukes a person, his conscience also rebukes him. If a person sins against God's law, he also sins against his conscience and vexes it. If something is done against the conscience, it is also done against God's law. Which is why it happens that when a person who is God-fearing and is trying to maintain a clean conscience sins in something, and commits an offense, immediately his conscience jabs him and troubles his soul and bothers it until it cleanses the sin by repentance, sighing, and contrition of heart, and so rest of the soul returns. And although even among people living an iniquitous life the conscience for a time is silent and as it were sleeps, when it wakes up and it sees its sins and transgressions, then it will rise up strongly against them and begin to haunt and torment them, and so trouble them that some give in to despair, and often even kill themselves, not enduring the pangs of conscience, as it happened with Judas, the betrayer of the Lord. "Then he threw down the pieces of silver in the temple and departed, and went and hanged himself" (Matt 27:5). Therefore, in order to have repose of the soul, people who transgress must turn from their sins to God, and cleanse their conscience, sullied by sin, by repentance, and calm its vexation. And thus rest and quiet of the soul will return to them. Without this, there is no way they can have repose, no matter how they console their conscience. And there is a danger that one might go from this temporal anxiety to eternal anxiety, in which the conscience of the soul that has sinned will always visualize its sins and will haunt and torment it by remembrance of them. This

is the fruit of sin. Sin is sweet for people, but its fruit is bitter: "For the wages of sin is death" (Rom 6:23).

(2) Satan tries to take repose of the soul away from pious people by all kinds of temptations and evil thoughts, when he tries to lead them into sin and so vex and trouble their conscience. O beloved! Beware of this evil whisperer, lest you lose repose of soul. Whenever you feel any evil thought that arises in your heart, know for sure that the enemy has approached your soul and is giving it his evil counsel, as the serpent did to Eve. A spirit is known by its odor. An evil spirit emits an evil odor. You sense an evil odor, know for sure that an evil spirit is there, letting forth its foul and stinking odor. Drive away this evil odor from yourself, and you will drive off the evil spirit. "Therefore submit to God. Resist the devil and he will flee from you" (Jas 4:7). Do not allow your soul to long listen to his whisperings, lest he entice you as the serpent did Eve. But immediately upon hearing his evil advice, turn away from him and turn to Almighty Jesus, your Defender and Saviour, and pray to Him, that He would help you in your struggle. This struggle is tiresome and difficult, but a most glorious victory will follow. We are struggling and will not yield to the enemy, but Jesus Christ, the Victor over death and hell, will help us and win the victory in us. To Him be thanksgiving and glory. "Bless the Lord, O my soul!" (Ps 102:1). "The Lord became my helper and the shield of my salvation; He is my God, and I will glorify Him" (Exod 15:2). As often as we oppose our enemy and ward of his evil counsels, we defeat and shame him. As often as we defeat him, we gladden the holy angels and glorify our God and Father, Who is in the heavens. If the evil enemy approaches you, and you hear his evil counsel, immediately take heart and stand like a warrior of Christ, and remember that God sees all, and is looking at you, and awaits your struggle, and wants to help you. And as often as you enter the struggle with your enemy and defeat him, Jesus, the Judge of the struggle, crowns you, and His holy angels rejoice for you. "There is joy in the presence of the angels of God over one sinner who repents" (Luke 15:10). For this struggle, the struggle against the devil and sin is necessary for true repentance. One who truly repents fights against every sin and its inventor, the devil. Therefore, be firm in your struggle, and do not yield to your enemy, lest he mock you, or even disgrace you. Christ the Lord from the Throne of His Glory looks on your struggle and prepares a crown of eternal glory for you. The holy angels also look upon you and rejoice on your struggle. Christ the Lord tells you, "Be faithful until death, and I will give you the crown of life" (Rev 2:10).

(3) The same evil adversary tries to take away rest of the heart when he disturbs a person who is pious and cares about his salvation with fear and terror of eternal death and hell, and with despair of God's mercy. Such thoughts are the fiery arrows of the evil one that he shoots at the faithful soul and thus troubles it greatly. Such anxiety tempts our faith and hope: whether a person stands strong in the faith and hope, and whether he unrelentingly expects the mercy of God, which He has promised to his faithful people. So the troubled and confused soul must, with God's help, be confirmed in faith and hope, looking to God's truthful promise, and firmly and steadfastly holding on to it, that He who has promised to save those who believe in Him will save them without fail; and "hope does not disappoint" (Rom 5:5). "I believe that I shall see the goodness of the Lord in the land of the living. Wait thou on the Lord; be of good courage, and let thine heart stand firm, and wait thou on the Lord" (Ps 26:13–14). The believer must both be patient and wait. "For He who promised is faithful" (Heb 10:23). "If God is for us, who can be against us? He who did not spare His own Son, but delivered Him up for us all, how shall He not with Him also freely give us all things" (Rom 8:31–32)?

(4) The same enemy troubles the pious soul through evil people. Hence, it happens that the pious soul undergoes every hatred, animosity, persecution, defamation, slander, and other afflictions. And these are the snares of the evil spirit. First he himself tempts and troubles the pious soul. But if he does not succeed in carrying out his evil desire and seducing it, he invents another method for its oppression; he dispatches to it evil people who do his evil will. Then a storm of persecutions, defamation, slander, and affliction will rise up against the person from here, there, and everywhere. The pious soul in such a disastrous situation must not be despondent and troubled but flee to the calm refuge of patience. Patience is the truly calm and safe refuge for the soul, which is tossed and distressed on the sea of this world. And the soul should remember God's comforting words, "In the world you will have tribulation" (John 16:33). "If they have called the master of the house Beelzebub, how much more will they call those of his household!" (Matt 10:25), "We must through many tribulations enter the kingdom of God" (Acts 14:22). A voice from heaven, testifying about the saved, was heard concerning this: "These are the ones who come out of the great tribulation" (Rev 7:14), and so on. "For whom the Lord loves He chastens, and scourges every son whom He receives" (Heb 12:6). "If you endure chastening, God deals with you as

with sons; for what son is there whom a father does not chasten" (Heb 12:7)? Thus, pious souls are becoming conformed to the only-begotten Son of God, Jesus Christ, Who was dishonored, cursed at, insulted, and suffered the death of the cross. Tell me, please, is it not comforting to a person to be in conformity with the Lord of glory and to follow after Him as after the Lamb of God? In conformity here in this world, in suffering, and in eternal life, in glory? "We suffer with Him, that we may also be glorified together" (Rom 8:17). There cannot indeed be a greater consolation for the Christ-loving soul. The soul will indeed rejoice and be glad in all suffering when it understands this. Consider, beloved, who you are and consider Christ to Whom you are conforming yourself. You are earth, and ashes, and even more, a sinner. Christ is the Lord of glory, the only-begotten Son of God, the Eternal King, and the eternal Son of the Father, the Great and Powerful God, your Creator Who loved you, your Redeemer, your Saviour, Who so loved you that He gave Himself for you, and suffered and died for your soul, and so delivered you from death and hell. He did this for your sake because He could not see you in perdition. "Praise the Lord, O my soul … Who has loved [you] and given Himself for [you]" (Ps 145:1; Eph 5:2). Christian! You, earth and dust, are becoming conformed to the Lord of Glory. Oh, it is indeed a great honor, a great glory, a great blessedness, a great praise, a great consolation, joy, and gladness, to be conformed to the only-begotten Son of God both here and in His eternal kingdom! O Jesus, joy and sweetness of the holy angels! ["Having run the course, I flee to Thee, O Lord" (Canticle VIII)][10] Draw me after you: We shall run …. "Thy garments smell of myrrh, frankincense, and cassia" (Ps 44:9). The spirit is vigorous, but the flesh is weak. The spirit wishes, but the flesh turns away. The spirit is delighted, but the flesh is a burden. The spirit runs, but the flesh holds back. So then, pull along the weak, O Mighty One, and as the strong giant the weak child, pull me. We shall run. How? On Your splendid and saving path by which you walked from birth until to death, for the sake of me, the poor one. "Thy goings were seen, O God" (Ps 67:25). Where? Into Your eternal and most glorious kingdom. Let us run there, that I will be conformed with you both here and there. Amen. "If anyone serves Me, let him follow Me; and where I am, there My servant will be also. If anyone serves Me, him My Father will honor" (John 12:26). "Be sober, be vigilant; because your adversary the devil walks about like a roaring lion, seeking whom he may devour. Resist him, steadfast in the faith" (1 Pet 5:8–9).

# 101. A Bridle

What a bridle is to a raging and rampaging horse, abstinence is to the passionate and lustful flesh. The horse is restrained by the bridle and obeys the desire of the rider. Likewise, the Christian must restrain the flesh that is filled with lust and subdue the spirit or the mind. Let us look at thoughts and fleshly desires, and the kind of battle they have with the spirit.

The flesh desires to be proud and conceited—the spirit does not desire this.

The flesh desires to disdain and despise others—the spirit does not desire this.

The flesh desires to slander, judge, and defame a person—the spirit does not desire this.

The flesh desires to live in the pride and splendor of the world—the spirit does not desire this.

The flesh desires to seek and have riches, glory, and honor in this world—the spirit does not desire this.

The flesh desires to have every amusement in this world—the spirit shuns them.

The flesh desires to arrange banquets, to feast and make merry—the spirit does not desire this.

The flesh desires to dress in beautiful, foppish clothing—the spirit does not desire this.

The flesh desires to become angry at a neighbor for an offense, to feel malice, to seek revenge, to repay evil for evil, scorn for scorn, to reproach him who reproaches, to vilify the vilifier, to offend the offender and to quarrel with him—the spirit shuns all this.

The flesh desires to commit fornication, adultery, and to wallow in impurity—the spirit shuns this.

The flesh desires to get drunk and carouse—the spirit does not desire this.

The flesh wants to lie, flatter, and cheat—the spirit does not desire this.

The flesh wants to live in idleness—the spirit does not desire this.

The flesh desires to engage in idle talk, to speak foolishly, and to blaspheme—the spirit does not desire this.

The flesh desires to extort others' property, to steal, to defraud, and in every way to appropriate for oneself—the spirit does not desire this, and so on.

This is the carnal will and mindset.

On the other hand, whatever the spirit desires is not desired by the flesh.

The spirit desires to follow the will of God and to do it—the flesh does not desire this.

The spirit desires to humble itself before God and people—the flesh does not desire this.

The spirit desires to render obedience to God and to keep His holy commandments—the flesh does not desire this.

The spirit desires to act lovingly, peacefully, sincerely, and simple-heartedly with its neighbors—the flesh does not desire this.

The spirit desires to live abstemiously and chastely—the flesh does not desire this.

The spirit desires to have mercy on its neighbor, and to provide for his needs, and to help him—the flesh does not desire this.

The spirit desires to endure offenses and to forgive people their trespasses—the flesh does not desire this.

The spirit desires to love enemies, to do good to those who hate it, to bless those who curse it, and to pray for those who cause temptation—the flesh shuns all this.

The spirit desires to keep silent, endure, and meekly remain firm in misfortunes, temptations, trials, and every suffering—the flesh does not desire this.

The spirit desires to place all its hope in God—the flesh does not desire this.

The spirit desires to do every righteous act—the flesh does not desire this.

The spirit desires to please God in everything—the flesh does not desire this, but desires to please itself, and so on.

This is the spiritual will and mindset.

You see what a battle and discord there is between the flesh and the spirit. The Apostle speaks of exactly this: "The flesh lusts against the Spirit, and the Spirit against the flesh; and these are contrary to one another" (Gal 5:17). You see fleshly thinking and spiritual thinking. You see what the flesh desires and what the spirit desires.

As a horse is restrained and by the bridle submits to the wish of the rider, so also we, Christians, must subdue the flesh to the spirit, and mortify fleshly thinking by the spirit, and do not what the passionate and lustful flesh desires, but what the spirit desires. "Be ye not like to horse and mule, which have no understanding" (Ps 31:9). "For those who live according to the flesh set their minds on the things of the flesh, but those who live according to the Spirit, the things of the Spirit. For to be carnally minded is death, but to be spiritually minded is life and peace. Because the carnal mind is enmity against God; for it is not subject to the law of God, nor indeed can be. So then, those who are in the flesh cannot please God. Therefore, brethren, we are debtors—not to the flesh, to live according to the flesh ... For if you live according to the flesh you will die; but if by the Spirit you put to death the deeds of the body, you will live ... Make no provision for the flesh, to fulfill its lusts" (Rom 8:5–8, 12–13; 13:14). "Walk in the Spirit, and you shall not fulfill the lust of the flesh. For the flesh lusts against the Spirit, and the Spirit against the flesh; and these are contrary to one another, so that you do not do the things that you wish. And those who are Christ's have crucified the flesh with its passions and desires" (Gal 5:16–17, 24).

## 102. Follow Me

It happens that in various circumstances one says to another, "Follow me." Christian! Similarly, Christ says to each of us, "Follow Me." Read the holy Gospel, and pay attention to it, and you will hear His most sweet voice: "Follow Me."

I am your Creator, and you are my creation: "Follow Me."

I am your Lord, and you are My servant: "Follow Me."

I am your King, and you are My subject: "Follow Me."

I am your God, Who was clothed in servile flesh for you. "Follow Me."

I came into the world for your sake: "Follow Me," Who came to you and for your sake.

I, the Invisible One, appeared in earth for your and everyone's sake: "Follow Me."

I, Who am inaccessible to the cherubim and seraphim, became available to sinners and to you: "Follow Me."

I, the King of Heaven, lived for a time on earth for your sake: "Follow Me."

I, the all-powerful and omnipotent, became weak for your sake: "Follow Me."

I, the rich One, became poor for your sake, that you may become rich by My poverty (2 Cor 8:9): "Follow Me."

I, the Lord of Glory, was sworn at and disgraced for your sake: "Follow Me."

I, the eternal and everlasting One, tasted of death, the death of the cross, for your sake: "Follow Me."

I, Who sits on the throne of glory, and am worshipped by the angels, and am praised, and glorified, was abused by sinners for your sake: "Follow Me."

I, Who alone has immortality and lives in inapproachable light, was counted among the dead and laid in a dark tomb for your sake: "Follow Me."

I am your Redeemer, your Deliverer, your Saviour, Who redeemed you from the devil, death, and hell not with silver and gold but by My blood: "Follow Me."

You see My love for you; you should show your love to Him who has loved you, and "follow Me" with love. Your love is of benefit to you, and not to Me, just as lack of love harms you, and not Me: "Follow Me." "Lord, what is man, that Thou hast had such respect unto him? Or the son of man, that Thou so regardest him? Man is like to vanity" (Ps 143:3–4). I hymn You, for "I have heard Your report and was afraid" (Hab 3:2) for You have come to me, seeking me, the lost one. Therefore, I glorify Your great condescension toward me, O greatly merciful One. "My heart is ready, O God, my heart is ready" (Ps 56:8). Help me, O Lord my God, and save me in accordance with Thy mercy.

What, Christian, do you want to renounce such a Lord and benefactor of yours, Who calls you after Himself, and not follow Him? It is terrible and shameless! It is terrible to rouse Him to righteous anger, and to fall under his righteous judgment, and so to perish. It is shameless since He is your greatest lover and benefactor. Tell me, please, if an earthly king called you to follow himself, would you not hurry after him, having abandoned everything with joy for the sake of modest and temporary honor and gain? The King of Kings and Lord of Lords, the Heavenly King calls you to Himself: "Follow Me," and calls not to temporary honor and glory and gain, but to an eternal life, kingdom, honor, and glory. "Follow me, follow me," and I will lead you into My eternal kingdom, to My eternal and heavenly Father: "No one comes to the Father except through Me" (John 14:6).

Fornicator, adulterer, and lover of impurity! Hear the Lord's voice: "Repent and follow Me."

Malicious avenger and murderer! Hear the Lord's voice: "Repent and follow Me."

Thief, extortioner, robber, and extortioner! Hear the Lord's voice: "Repent and follow Me."

Reproacher, reviler, slanderer, and every kind of backbiter! Hear the Lord's voice: "Repent and follow Me."

Liar, cheat, seducer, hypocrite! Hear the Lord's voice: "Repent and follow Me."

Every kind of sinner, living in unrepentance! Hear the Lord's voice: "Repent and follow Me."

Hear the Lord's voice calling you. Hear the voice of Him, Who so loved you and displayed such merciful, man-loving, and wonderful providence concerning you. Hear his voice: "Repent and follow Me."

Man, my beloved creation! I came down from heaven, that I may raise you up to heaven: "Follow Me."

I lived on earth, that I might make you an inhabitant of heaven: "Follow Me."

I did not have a place to lay My head, that I might lead you into the house of My Heavenly Father: "Follow Me."

I labored, that I might bring you into eternal repose: "Follow Me."

I became poor, that I would enrich you: "Follow Me."

I wept, was troubled, lamented, grieved, that I might give you true consolation, joy, and gladness: "Follow Me."

I was cursed, sworn at, and dishonored, that I might honor and glorify you, My dishonored creation: "Follow Me."

I was bound, that I would release you from the bonds of sin: "Follow Me."

I, the Judge of the living and the dead, was tried and condemned, that I might deliver you from eternal judgment: "Follow Me."

I was numbered among the iniquitous, that I might vindicate you: "Follow Me."

I tasted death, the death of the cross, that I might enliven you, my creation, killed by the snake's venom: "Follow Me."

I rose from the dead, that you also might rise in soul and body: "Follow Me."

I ascended into heaven that you also might ascend: "Follow Me."

I sat at the right hand of God the Father, that you also might be glorified: "Follow Me."

I was likened to you in everything, except sin, that you would be like Me: "Follow Me."

I assumed your image, that you might be conformed to My image: "Follow Me."

I came to you, that I might draw you to Myself, you, my beloved creation who had fallen away: "Follow Me."

You see, O man, what love I showed to you; you see, too, My providence for you. I demand nothing from you for this, only that you would be grateful to Me and followed Me, and thus would receive salvation with eternal glory. I wish from you, that it be your wish as well. "Follow Me," Who hungers and thirsts after your salvation, and I will grant you My salvation.

Love My poverty, and you will be truly rich.

Love My humility, and you will be truly glorified and great.

Love My meekness and patience, and you will be truly quiet, calm, and peaceful.

Give up the earth, and you will have heaven.

Give up the world, and you will have God within you.

Renounce yourself, and you will truly be master of yourself.

Give up the pleasure of the flesh and the world, and you will have true comfort.

Give up perishable riches, and you will have imperishable riches.

Give up earthly honor and glory, and you will have heavenly honor and glory.

"Follow Me," and you will have everything that your soul desires, but true and incomparably better than everything that you give up.

Listen and pay attention, sinful soul, to the voice of your redeemer Jesus, Who loves you, and follow him, that you may find your way. Hurry, hurry, beloved, while He calls and the doors are open. Heaven is open, and publicans, adulterers, and every kind of repentant sinner is entering it.

You should hurry there, too, poor sinner, that you, too, may receive the kingdom of heaven. The Apostles, martyrs, holy hierarchs, holy monastics, and all the saints of God have entered it and are settled now in the mansions of the Heavenly Father. Many are going and arriving there even now—but only those who follow their most sweet Jesus—and by His grace take up their abode in eternal repose.

My soul, you should also hear the Lord's voice and join this holy fellowship, and with them follow Jesus, the faithful leader. And may you hear in the hour of your departure his voice saying: "All who have gone on the sorrowful narrow path and have taken up the cross like a yoke and, having followed me in faith, come, enjoy the honors and heavenly crowns that I have prepared for you." "Christ also suffered for us, leaving us an example, that you should follow His steps: 'Who committed no sin, Nor was deceit found in His mouth';

who, when He was reviled, did not revile in return; when He suffered, He did not threaten, but committed Himself to Him who judges righteously" (1 Pet 2:21–23). "If anyone serves Me, let him follow Me; and where I am, there My servant will be also" (John 12:26). "And he who does not take his cross and follow after Me is not worthy of Me" (Matt 10:38). "I am the light of the world. He who follows Me shall not walk in darkness, but have the light of life," says the Lord (John 8:12).

It happens that one calls a person, saying: "Follow Me;" but another says to him, calling him to himself, "Follow Me." Thus, Christ the Lord says to every Christian, "Follow Me," as said earlier, but Satan, the enemy of the human race, whispers in the ear of man and calls him to himself, saying, "Follow Me." A person hears his evil whisperings as many times as he senses evil and impious thoughts rising up in his heart. This is all his loathsome whispering.

O man! Whom is it better for you to hear? Christ, your Lord, Who showed such wonderful providence for you, and desires to save you, and to lead you into his eternal kingdom, as you saw earlier; or the evil whisperer, the devil, who wants to draw you away from Christ your Saviour, and to cast you into eternal perdition?

Christ is Light; the devil is darkness.

Christ is Life; the devil is death.

Christ is Truth; the devil is a liar and the father of lies.

Christ has loved you; the devil is your enemy.

Christ is your benefactor; the devil does evil to you.

Christ is the true and highest Good; the devil is the uttermost evil.

Christ is your Saviour; the devil is your destroyer.

Christ wishes to save you forever and came into the world for your sake; the devil wishes to destroy you forever.

Christ desires to grant you eternal life; the devil desires to kill you forever.

Christ desires to lead you into His eternal kingdom; the devil desires to lead you into eternal torment.

Christ desires to enrich you forever; the devil desires to make you destitute forever.

Christ desires to glorify you forever; the devil desires to disgrace you.

Christ desires to eternally honor you; the devil desires to eternally disgrace you.

You see who is Christ and who is the devil, and why he whispers to you and calls you away from Christ, your Lord, after himself. He desires to be your eternal undoing, as he himself is in perdition. This is his cunning; this is his malicious intent against us. Renounce, beloved, renounce this evil whisperer, and spit on him, as you did in holy baptism, and, having turned away from this seducer, turn to Christ, your Lord, and follow Him in faith and truth, as you promised Him in baptism. He is your God, your Lord, Who had loved you, Your benefactor, your eternal life, your everlasting light, your true and eternal blessedness, without which we cannot be blessed either in this world or in the world to come. Join yourself to the Lord your God: "it is good for me to cleave unto God" (Ps 72:28).

But in spite of the devil being a destroyer, many obey him, and follow him in great multitudes.

Fornicators, adulterers, and all lovers of impurity follow him.

Those who remember wrongs, haters of people, murderers, and those who spill human blood follow him.

Those who oppose their parents, backbite them, and do not honor them follow him.

Thieves, extortioners, robbers, judges who take bribes, those who withhold the pay of hired hands, and those who by every injustice and flattery snatch away someone else's goods follow him.

Slanderers, the foul-mouthed, and everyone who cuts and wounds his neighbor with his tongue as with a sword follow him.

Drunkards and lovers of pleasure follow him.

Tricksters, the deceitful, tempters, and all who entice their neighbor, follow him.

All sorts of transgressors, who oppose God's word by his depraved life, follow him.

Finally, those who love this age, who think of the earthly and not of the heavenly, who love to live in the pride and the splendor of this world, follow him. In a word, everyone who does not care about God's Word and about God, who are joined in their hearts with the earthly, and who do not care about their eternal salvation, obtained by the blood of Christ—all such people are following after Satan. The Apostle's saying is befitting for all such people: "For some have already turned aside after Satan" (1 Tim 5:15). All such people are ashamed of the words of Christ and of Christ Himself and are appalled at Him, humble, abused, and disgraced, and withdraw from Him; they do, however, want to be glorified with Him. They have no desire to be with Him in this world and to follow after Him, but they do want to be participants in His kingdom, which is impossible. Whoever will be with him in this world will be with Him in the age to come.

O man, who bears the name of Christ, but who follows Satan! Remember what renunciations and vows you gave at baptism, how you renounced Satan and all his works and his pride, how you spat on him, how you departed from him, how you joined yourself to Christ, how you promised and swore in faith and truth to serve Him, to follow Him in humility and love, as a bride follows a bridegroom. Where are those renunciations now, where are your vows, where is your oath, where is your service to Christ, where is your following of Him? You lied to God, and not to man. You abandoned God, and not man; you abandoned the light, and loved the darkness; you abandoned life, and loved death.

Remember this, and turn to Christ, your Saviour. Flee from that seducer, as Israel did from Pharoah, and although he will chase after you, since he has lost his catch, take courage, and from the bottom of your heart sigh to the omnipotent Jesus, that He not remember your transgressions and that He will help you. He Who died for you will await you with joy, and with compassionate embraces, "like the prodigal son, will fall on your neck" (Luke 15:20). And when you are freed from the heavy bondage to that tormentor, then with joy you will sing the hymn of victory to your Helper: "The Lord became my helper and the shield of my salvation; He is my God, and I will glorify Him; my father's God, and I will exalt Him" (Exod 15:2). The angels in heaven will rejoice for you. "There is joy in the presence of the angels of God over one sinner who repents" (Luke 15:10).

# 103. Study

We see that people learn various arts and sciences. Some learn to sew clothing; others, to carry on trade; others, to build houses; others, to learn foreign languages; others, to beautifully and mellifluously speak and write; others, to philosophize or to excel in the natural sciences, and so on. Likewise, Christians should learn to live in a Christian manner. Without this, any art or science is nothing.

Christian! External science and art are common for pagans and Christians, since pagans, as we see, also study arts and sciences. But the knowledge and art of living piously and in a Christian manner is characteristic only of Christians. A Christian is known not by his speaking and writing beautifully, but by his living beautifully and God-pleasingly, not by external love of wisdom, but by instruction in evangelical and Christian philosophy. Many people speak and write beautifully, but live bestially. Many people philosophize superbly about natural things but do not even know the basics of Christianity. The truly wise man is he who is foolish for the world but wise for Christ. Truly lacking wisdom and foolish is he who, although he knows everything, does not know God and Christ, the Son of God. Learn, O Christian, the Christian evangelical philosophy and you will be truly wise, although the world will consider you foolish.

Christian teaching consists of the following:

(1) In knowing God. When you get to know God, you will become wiser, but within, not without. And the more you get to know Him, the wiser and more proficient you will be in the Christian calling.

When you truly learn that God is Omnipresent and Omniscient, and sees your every deed, thought, undertaking, and intention, and hears your every word, and your life and death are in His Almighty hand, this knowledge will without fail teach you to fear Him and tremble, and everywhere to behave carefully, speak carefully, work carefully, and think and act carefully.

When you learn that God is just and will render to each according to his deeds, this knowledge will move you to fervent repentance for past sins. And you will sigh and sing to Him from the bottom of your heart, "Enter not into judgment with Thy servant, for before Thee shall no man living be justified" (Ps 142:2). "If Thou shouldest mark iniquities, O Lord; Lord who shall stand" (Ps 129:3)?

When you learn that God is true, omnipresent, and immutable goodness and love, you will without fail love Him. Who, having come to know goodness, does not love goodness? And from such knowledge will unfailingly follow fervent obedience, submission, and submission to Him, and from obedience, painstaking fulfillment of His holy commandments.

(2) In restraint and mortification of the passions and lusts that war with the soul. But knowledge is needed even here. Come to know what is hidden in your heart. Check there often, and you will see that pride, haughtiness,

self-love, greed, anger, envy, love of fame, impurity, desire for revenge, and every sinful abomination lurks there. "For from within, out of the heart of men, proceed evil thoughts, adulteries, fornications, murders, thefts, covetousness, wickedness, deceit, lewdness, an evil eye, blasphemy, pride, foolishness" (Mark 7:21–22; Matt 15:18, 19). And if they come forth, it means that they are present there. And what is present in one person is in another, for we all are infected with this poison. All of this evil leads a person to nothing else than perdition.

Learn to get to know the pernicious evil hiding within you, and then you will learn to restrain and mortify that which leads you to perdition, and you will try to defeat and kill those enemies who always want to destroy you. It is absolutely essential to crucify the flesh with its passions and desires if you desire to live in a Christian manner and be Christ's. According to the apostle's teaching, only those are Christ's who "have crucified the flesh with its passions and desires" (Gal 5:24).

Learn to know yourself in order to know what a great misfortune is hidden within you, and you will endeavor to be delivered from it.

Learn to know the enemies that are within and not outside you, and having recognized them, destroy them, lest they destroy you forever. If they are dead, then your soul will be alive. But if they are alive and possess you, then your soul will be dead. Defeat and destroy them, so that your soul may live.

Beloved! Conquer yourself in this way, and you will possess yourself, and you will be truly noble, a master, king, and sovereign.

(3) In justice and love to your neighbor. Even here knowledge is needed. Learn that your neighbor is the same kind of person as you, and has everything, as you have, and does not want the same things as you. Like you, he wants every good thing and does not want any evil. Do not do to him what you do not want for yourself and do what you want for yourself. Christian justice and love for your neighbor consists in this. And this is what the Lord wants from us: "You shall love your neighbor as yourself" (Matt 19:19). Love does not do evil to a neighbor but wishes him every good. Love your neighbor, and you will not do to him what you do not wish for yourself, and you will wish to do everything that you want for yourself.

This is what must be taught to a Christian from infancy to the end of his life. This is the Christian science. This is the sublime art. He is a true lover of wisdom who studies this philosophy. Those beginning to study art and sciences acknowledge their ignorance and endeavor to learn what they do not know. In other words, the reason why they study is that they do not know.

Likewise, Christians, if they wish to study and learn the Christian philosophy, must acknowledge their ignorance and foolishness. Without this, instruction will be in vain and useless. The ignorant study, not the wise.

As we see, the longer and more carefully those who study the external sciences and arts study them, the more proficient they become. Also, the more diligently and carefully one studies the Christian philosophy and reforms himself in accordance with its rules, the more proficient a Christian he becomes. The more he gets to know God, the more he fears and loves Him. The more he examines himself, the more he humbles and reforms himself. The more he thinks about his neighbor, the more justly and lovingly he treats him and behaves with him. And thus he arrives at perfection, as far as this is possible to one living in the flesh.

(4) Any human effort and diligence is in vain without God's help. For the flesh always wishes to possess a man, and our reason is blind without God's enlightenment; the devil always and everywhere throws out snares beneath our feet and in every way tries to make us stumble, and the world with its temptations surrounds us and wants to enfeeble and corrupt us. Therefore, it is absolutely necessary to sigh and pray to the Lord often and with all fervor that He would direct us in our studies and help us to study successfully. He mercifully promised to grant us His grace. And if He promised, He will grant it to those who ask. "Ask, and it will be given to you; seek, and you will find; knock, and it will be opened to you. For everyone who asks receives, and he who seeks finds, and to him who knocks it will be opened" (Matt 7:7–8).

Christian, study the Christian science in order to be a true Christian and disciple of Christ. Christ the Lord will not ask us at His dread Judgment whether we were skilled in trade, oratory, astrology, geology, and other sciences. He asks whether we studied and did that which His holy Gospel teaches and what in holy baptism we promised and took an oath to Him to do. He will ask us only about these arts and sciences then.

"O God, make speed to save me; O Lord, make haste to help me (Ps 69:2). O look Thou upon me, and have mercy upon me, according to the judgment of them that love Thy Name. Direct my steps according to Thy word, and let not any wickedness have dominion over me" (Ps 118:132–133).

# 104. The Alphabet

What the alphabet is for those who are beginning to learn reading, humility is for Christians desiring to learn the Christian life. Those who are learning to read need first to learn the alphabet. Likewise Christians, if they want to successfully learn the virtuous life must first of all learn humility. The alphabet is the beginning and foundation of all book learning. Likewise, humility is the beginning and foundation of the Christian virtues. Without this, every spiritual building is disturbed and falls. There can be no true virtue without humility, and if it even does appear, it will again be brought to ruin. A person can neither begin nor do anything without God, as was said: "Without Me you can do nothing" (John 15:5). And according to the testimony of the apostle, "God resists the proud, but gives grace to the humble" (1 Pet 5:5). Learn, O Christian, this Christian alphabet, and you will successfully learn the Christian philosophy.

But in order to successfully learn humility, you must learn to get to know yourself and your poverty. Humility unfailingly results from knowing yourself and your poverty. Who, seeing his poverty, will not be humbled? Man is truly poor, but not everyone perceives his own poverty. Man is born into troubles and, as if having a premonition of them, cries, for every baby is born with crying. It lives and is brought up in troubles. The longer he lives, the more his troubles multiply. He dies with fear, and if he does not die in the Lord, even greater troubles await him. Man is poor on the outside but is poor even on the inside. Various infirmities and illnesses dispirit and torment him. The flesh with its passions and lusts rise up against him and wish to possess him and hand him over to eternal death. A person constantly feels this upheaval and anguish. And the more he resists it, the more it rises up against him. And this affliction and evil within him, this poison with which man is infected, does not destroy him temporarily, but forever. Externally, the devil is constantly laying his snares out for him and tries to entrap him for his perdition. The various temptations of the world, like thorns, tear at him and wish to destroy his soul. Every person lives in such tribulation. But he is that much poorer, if he does not see this.

For what is there for a person to become conceited and to boast about? Isn't it only poverty, corruption, and sins? What kind of praise is that? This is not praise, but abuse, not glory, but obscurity, not honor, but dishonor. What will you boast of, O man? Only that you have wealth, glory, honor, and the wisdom of this age? What kind of praise is there in this? Not external, but internal, well-being makes a person laudable and blessed. For any external well-being is nothing. It is not a tree that is beautiful on the outside and has many branches and leaves, but one that is good on the inside and bears good fruit that we call good. It happens that a person is rich on the outside, but poor and wretched on the inside; externally renowned and honorable, but internally inglorious and dishonorable; in appearance wise, and inside foolish; outwardly successful, but inside more cursed than all. And this is what happens, for the most part. People do honor to those who are conspicuous in this way, but in God's Word honor is due those for whom the Lord is their God. "Blessed are the people whose God is the Lord" (Ps 143:15).

And so, do not look at how a person is on the outside (for outwardly even the most impious of people are alike), but what he is like on the inside; not what he is like in front of people, but what he is like in the sight of God. It often and for the most part happens that a person is wise before people but foolish before God; renowned before people but inglorious before God; rich before people but very poor before God; great before people but nothing before God. And this blossoming of well-being, which appears and shines before people, soon wilts. When the storm of misfortunes comes, it, having withered up, falls, and death snatches it away from everyone. Life as a prince, or a lord, or a famous man, or a rich man, or a wise man exists only until the grave. Likewise all the treasures of this world only serve man until the grave. And then everything departs from him. Then everyone will know themselves as needy, miserable, poor, and wretched, as they were. Then princes, lords, and masters will become like their lowest servants. Then the rich will realize their neediness and will be poorer than paupers.

Be conceited and boast about these treasures, O man, if you wish. I tell you the truth that you are really poor, no matter how renowned you were in the world. Look at the dead in their coffins, and you will be convinced. Where princes, lords, and masters lie, and where their servants lie, it is impossible to tell. Where do the rich and poor, where the wise men and simpletons, where the noble and low-born, where the renowned and dishonorable lie, you indeed cannot tell! Everyone there is equal and has turned into earth, as if they were the earth. Looking at this decomposition, boast of the good fortune that you have, count your names and titles, be haughty with your riches and wisdom. You see here that everyone is equal. As all are born equal, so all die equal, except that one is saved and is going into eternal life, and another perishes and is consigned to eternal death. "Blessed are the dead who die in the Lord" (Rev 14:13). "Lord, remember me when You come into Your kingdom" (Luke 23:42).

Man was originally blessed but lost his blessedness. He was like God, created in the image and likeness of God, but "he shall be compared unto the brute beasts, and is become like unto them" (Ps 48:21). He was incorrupt but became subject to decay; he was immortal but became mortal; "for the wages of sin is death" (Rom 6:23). He was wise but became foolish. He was rich but became needy. He was beautiful but became ugly. He was holy and pure but became foul and impure. He was a temple and dwelling of the Holy Spirit but became the abode of unclean spirits. He was a master and owner but became a slave and captive. He was an inhabitant of the most sweet paradise, like the king of a fine palace, but was banished to this world, as into exile. Man was deprived of such blessedness and subjected to such troubles. All of us, his sons, were also subjected to them. "O Lord, righteousness belongs to you, but shame of face belongs to us" (Dan 9:7). "We have sinned with our fathers; we have done amiss, and dealt wickedly" (Ps 105:6). For what is a person in such misfortune to think and say but one thing: "Lord, have mercy on me ... for I have sinned against Thee" (Ps 40:5)?

As the beginning of health is the perception and acknowledgement of illness, so also the beginning of Christian blessedness is to perceive and acknowledge one's poverty and sinfulness. And this happens not from the perception and acknowledgement itself, but from the merciful and man-loving God's looking on such perception and acknowledgement and sending down His grace, as is written, "God ... gives grace to the humble" (1 Pet 5:5). God wishes one thing from us: that we perceive and acknowledge our poverty and humble ourselves before Him and walk and live in humility. And then He himself will lead us to our blessedness. The Apostle wrote of this: "Therefore humble yourselves under the mighty hand of God, that He may exalt you in due time, casting all your care upon Him, for He cares for you" (1 Pet 5:6–7). Our God is God the Almighty, who "made everything from nothing" (2 Macc 7:28). We see what excellent works He "created–heaven and earth, and all that therein is" (Ps 145:6). Thus, whoever perceives and acknowledges himself as nothing makes of this something, moreover, something good, that is, a wise, pious, virtuous, and holy person. God only makes that which is good since He Himself is good. But a person's greatest poverty and wretchedness consists in him thinking highly of himself, although, in actual fact, he is nothing. He thinks that he knows everything, but in reality he knows nothing. He thinks that he is intelligent, but in actual fact he is foolish and senseless. He thinks that he is blessed but is in reality needy and poor. He thinks that he is rich, but he is actually poor and wretched. He thinks that he is good, but he in reality is evil. He thinks that he is holy and righteous, but he is actually sinful and defiled. He thinks that he is something, but he is in reality nothing. What is Almighty God, Who made everything out of nothing, to do with such a person? He leaves him in his false blessedness and does His work on the one who abases himself, and He makes him blessed who perceives and acknowledges himself poor and wretched. Therefore the Lord says to the Heavenly Father, "You have hidden these things [the mysteries of the Gospel] from the wise and prudent and have revealed them to babes" (Matt 11:25). The scribes, Pharisees, and teachers of the law thought of themselves as wise and intelligent: "Are we blind also" (John 9:40)? Therefore, God's light and wisdom was hidden from them. The Apostles, like children, were simple and humble, but they were enlightened and made wise by God Himself.

Christian! Pride is profound blindness and foolishness. It prevents us from learning of and acknowledging our poverty and wretchedness. Humility is profound enlightenment and wisdom, which comes from perception of our poverty and wretchedness. The humble person will unfailingly achieve Christian blessedness because God, who loves the humble of heart, will not abandon him. "Blessed are the poor in spirit, For theirs is the kingdom of heaven" (Matt 5:3).

Christian, get to know yourself and your poverty, and you will be humble. And if you are humble, you will be blessed, as well.

Perceive and acknowledge your indigence before God, and you will be rich.

Perceive and acknowledge your blindness before God, and the eyes of your heart will be opened.

Perceive and acknowledge your foolishness before God, and you will be wise.

Perceive and acknowledge your sins before God, and you will be justified by Him.

Perceive and acknowledge your impurity before God, and you will be pure and holy.

Perceive and acknowledge your imperfection before God, and you will be set aright.

Perceive and acknowledge your infirmity before God, and you will become healthy.

Perceive and acknowledge your straying before God, and you will be searched for. "I have gone astray like a sheep that is lost; O seek Thy servant" (Ps 118:176).

Finally, perceive and acknowledge that you are poor and wretched, and you will be blessed. Everything in you will be put aright by God's grace, which will be with you, if you are humble.

There, Christian, is the alphabet of Christian teaching. Learn it, and you will successfully learn the Christian philosophy. "Everyone who exalts himself will be humbled, and he who humbles himself will be exalted" (Luke 18:14).

# 105. Teacher and Pupils

We see that those who study arts and sciences study with teachers. So Christians who are studying the Christian life must study with Christ since Christians are nothing other than pupils of Christ. "As we see, in the Acts of the Holy Apostles, in the beginning the Christians were called *disciples*, and only later were called *Christians*" (Acts 11:26). In teaching their pupils arts and sciences, teachers show them an example, and whatever they are teaching they themselves do and thus lead them to success in their studies. He is a good teacher who both teaches and shows an example for imitation in whatever he is teaching. Thus Christ the Lord, living on the earth, taught goodness and did good, and what He taught is what he did, and by His example, He taught us a holy and Christian life. Therefore the holy Evangelist Luke says, "The former account I made ... of all that Jesus began both to do and teach" (Acts 1:1).

Do you wish, Christian, to learn to live in a holy and Christian manner (and it is absolutely necessary, if you want to be Christ's, to be a true Christian, and not a false one)? If you do wish this, then put before you the holy Gospel and the immaculate life of Christ, and learn from them. As you scrutinize your face in the mirror, and, having seen smudges on it, you wipe and wash them off, lest you be ridiculed upon going out in public, so let the Gospel and the holy life of Christ written in it be a mirror for your soul. And seeing the smudges on your soul, wipe them away by repentance, regret, and tears, lest you appear at Christ's dread Judgment with your smudges, and you be ashamed before God, the righteous Judge, and His holy angels, and the people. It is absolutely necessary to have the sign of Christ and to appear there with it and to show that as we confessed the name of Christ here, so in actuality we were in the image of the life of Christ. We should be afraid lest we hear, "I never knew you" (Matt 7:23).

Everything that you see in yourself contrary to the Gospel and Christ's holy life is a vice. Correct everything that is not in keeping with it. Do not follow the will of your flesh, although it even comforts you, but follow Christ's will, which will lead you to your good and blessedness. Do you say that this is difficult and unpleasant?

The answer is:

(1) It is not difficult, but easy, to bear Christ's yoke, according to Christ's own testimony: "For My yoke is easy and My burden is light" (Matt 11:30).

Judge for yourself what is harder and what easier: to take revenge or to forgive, to be angry or not to be angry, to hate or to love, to live in pride or humility, to seek riches, honor and renown or to scorn them, and so on.

The conscience itself prevails on us to acknowledge that it is much easier to forgive than to avenge; to be meek than to be angry; to have patience than to be impatient; to love than to hate; not to care for earthly good things than to seek them; to think of the heavenly than of the earthly. To take revenge requires considerable effort; to forgive does not amount to any effort. To love is easy and sweet; to hate is difficult and unpleasant. Hatred binds and oppresses the heart, but love unbinds, expands, and relieves the heart and thus makes a person joyful and cheerful. Humility is not afraid to fall, since it lies on the ground and moves along the ground: where can one who moves along the ground fall? Pride lifts itself high and becomes haughty but is always in fear and trembling, lest it fall. And although it worries and guards with all its might against falling, it falls and shatters. The patient soul is always in repose and stillness, but the impatient one is in confusion, unrest, and upheaval. And the greater impatience it is in, the greater unrest and upheaval it experiences. Whereas the more a patient soul has patience, the greater repose and stillness it feels within itself. O, if only you could see the heart of the person who bears the yoke of the Gospel, the yoke of Christ! You would see in it a paradise of joy and sweetness, and the Kingdom of God in it, although from without it is worried in different ways and is surrounded by misfortunes and temptations, like a fragrant rose by thorns. There cannot not be consolation and true joy in that heart in which the Kingdom of God is felt.

My poor soul, sigh, pray, and try to bear Christ's good yoke, and you will live on earth in keeping with heavenly life. Grant me, O Lord, to bear your good yoke and light burden, and I shall always be calm, peaceful, joyful, and cheerful, and I shall eat the crumbs that fall from Your heavenly table, like the dogs from the table of their master. "Lord, help me!" (Matt 15:27). "Hear me, O Lord, for Thy mercy is gracious" (Ps 68:17).

(2) When you love Christ, you must also love His Gospel and His holy life. It is impossible for one who loves anyone's person not love his ways. If you love Christ, as you absolutely must love him, as the Lord who is good and loves you, your redeemer and Saviour, Who redeemed you not with gold and silver but with His blood from terrible misfortune and ruination; if you love Him, then love also His most holy and all-good ways. If you love His ways, then try to imitate and follow them, and take pains, as much as it is possible for a feeble human, to reflect them in your soul. And you will be compatible with Him both here in this life and in the glory of the future life. It is sweet for one who loves to be together with a beloved and to follow after him and bitter to be parted from him. As a magnet attracts iron, so do Christ's ways attract a Christ-loving soul. And as those who smell a sweet fragrance wish to smell it more and more, so those who come to know Christ and the saints and His most sweet ways try more and more to imitate them. "Thy garments smell of myrrh, frankincense, and cassia" (Ps 44:9), Word of God and Son of the Virgin, Jesus Christ.

Beloved Christian! The more we shall get to know Christ, the more we shall love Him. The more we shall love him, the more diligently we shall follow His most holy ways. It is impossible for one who smells a sweet fragrance not to wish and not to try more and more to smell it. Likewise, it is impossible for one who has felt Christ's love and humility in his heart not to follow Him and His holy ways. Get to know Christ, and you will love Christ and His holy lie, and you will follow His supremely good ways.

(3) You say that those who live by the rule of the Holy Gospel are hated by all; do you say that this is difficult?

The answer is:

They are indeed hated, as even Christ Himself predicted for our strengthening and consolation, "You will be hated by all for My name's sake" (Matt 10:22). And it is indeed difficult, and not a small cross, to be hated by all, but it is comforting that all of this is for Christ's sake, for whose sake we all must persevere with joy.

Hear the comforting teaching of Christ: "If the world hates you, you know that it hated Me before it hated you. If you were of the world, the world would love its own. Yet because you are not of the world, but I chose you out of the world, therefore the world hates you" (John 15:18–19). And again: "He who has My commandments and keeps them, it is he who loves Me. And he who loves Me will be loved by My Father, and I will love him and manifest Myself to him" (John 14:21). What can be more comforting for the Christian soul than these words? The world hates it, but God loves it. The world shuns it, but God selects and receives it. Tell me, please, tell me what is better: to be beloved of God or of the world? The whole world, compared to God, is nothing. The love of this world is bitter and leads to even more bitterness. It seems like a red apple on the outside that within is filled with rottenness and bitterness. God's love is sweet, comforting and engendering joy and leads to eternal joy and sweetness. It is better, incomparably better, to be beloved by God alone than by the whole world. I desire and choose this. Let the whole world hate me, if it wishes, and do to me as it wills, if only God alone would love and in His mercy protect me. "His love and mercy are greater for me than the love and mercy of the whole world." "Thy mercy is gracious" (Ps 68:17). "It is good for me to cleave unto God" (Ps 72:28). "I wish nothing either on earth, or in heaven, except You alone and Your love" (Ps 72:25–26). "I shall be alive and blessed with You even in the shadow of death" (Ps 22:4), but without "You even heaven is nothing" (Ps 72:25). "O look Thou upon me, and have mercy upon me, according to the judgment of them that love Thy Name" (Ps 118:132).

(4) You say that those who live according to the Gospel are held in contempt, and you are ashamed to be held in contempt?

The answer is:

It is true that pious souls are held in contempt in the world's opinion. But to warn us, Christ said of this, "Whoever is ashamed of Me and My words in this adulterous and sinful generation, of him the Son of Man also will be ashamed when He comes in the glory of His Father with the holy angels" (Mark 8:38). Then it will be shameful to hear from Christ, "I do not know you, where you are from" (Luke 13:27). You did not know Me, and I do not know you. You were ashamed of Me and of My humility, and I am now ashamed of you. It will be shameful then to hear these words, Christians, to hear them before the whole world, to hear them from Christ. It is shameful, but also terrifying, since they are followed by eternal perdition.

Pious souls are indeed held in contempt by the world but honored by God. "If anyone serves Me, him My Father will honor" (John 12:26). They are held in contempt by the world, but close to Christ, and "fellow citizens with the saints and members of the household of God" (Eph 2:19). They are held in contempt by the world, but friends of Christ the Lord and King of Glory. "You are My friends if you do whatever I command you" (John 15:14). They are held in contempt by the world, but they make up a living "body in Christ" (Rom 12:5) and have Him as their *Head*, "Who is higher than the heavens" (Eph 1:22; 5:30). They are held in contempt by the world, but are the "dwelling place and temple of the Holy Spirit" (Rom 8:19; 1 Cor 3:16; 6:19). They are held in contempt by the world, but are "sons of God" (Rom 8:14; Gal 3:26). They are held in contempt by the world, but they have fellowship with the Father and His Son, Jesus Christ. "Our fellowship is with the Father and with His Son Jesus Christ" (1 John 1:3). They are deprived of the fleeting glory and honor of this world but are vouchsafed God's "eternal glory" (2 Cor 4:17; Col 3:4).

Why, O man, would it be shameful for you to be held in contempt by the world, if you had dignity and glory from God? What is more dignified than this dignity, what is more noble than this nobility, what is more splendid than this splendor, what is more glorious than this glory, as for a person to be close to God, to be a friend of Christ, to be a temple and dwelling place of the Holy Spirit, to be a Son of the Most High God, to be a living member of the Body of Christ, to have fellowship with the Father and with His Son Jesus Christ? What can be more glorious and awesome than this? This surpasses by far all the glory of this world, which, and comparison with heavenly glory, is similar to carrion and dung.

O man! Do not look at how a person looks on the outside but look at what is inside; it is not important what he is like before the world, but what he is like before God. True Christians are held in contempt before the world, but within they have great glory and treasure. This treasure rarely and with great difficulty is found under crowns, under titles and names of this world, under purple robes and fine linen, within rich and beautiful walls, but mostly in tatters and in huts and caves; there it feels more at home. True Christians are like gold covered in soot, unknown and trampled on by people.

Glory to God's love for mankind, glory to His goodness, glory to His mercy and munificence, that He favored poor man with such honor and glory! Our Saviour and Lord earned all of this for us. What, Christian, do you wish to learn the philosophy of the Gospel and be Christ's disciple or do you wish to not be held in contempt by the world and not to learn it?

(5) You say that you wish to, but the struggle that the evangelical and Christian philosophy requires is hard: to crucify the flesh with its passions and lusts?

And indeed, this struggle is difficult but necessary and glorious. Even pupils study in the schools of this world with considerable effort. They study mainly for physical and temporal gain. We study for the benefit of the soul— eternal benefit, and not with people, but with Christ, the Lord of glory, it is most sweet and excellent. Also, soldiers fight in battles of this world with considerable effort. They fight for earthly and temporal honor, but we fight for what is heavenly and eternal and incomparably better. Merchants travel and wander through various countries and cities with considerable effort. They work for perishable treasure, but we for that which is imperishable and spiritual. Farmers cultivate and sow the land with considerable effort. They work in order to gather physical and temporal fruits. We work in order to have spiritual fruit. "But the fruit of the Spirit is love, joy, peace, longsuffering, kindness, goodness, faithfulness, gentleness, self-control" (Gal 5:22–23). For these most sweet fruits, Christians, we must study, work, and fight.

(6) Do you say that it is impossible to master yourself, which is required of a student of the philosophy of the Gospel?

And this is indeed so, but it is possible with Christ's help. As He commanded us to learn from Him, "Learn from Me, for I am gentle and lowly in heart" (Matt 11:29), so also He promised to grant us help, whenever we ask: "Ask, and it will be given to you; seek, and you will find; knock, and it will be opened to you. For everyone who asks receives, and he who seeks finds, and to him who knocks it will be opened" (Matt 7:7–8). You only need to try, take care, work, struggle, acknowledge your ignorance and infirmity before Him, and fervently pray to Him, and help will be given you. And so, what was impossible for you without His help will be possible with His help. "You can do all things through Christ who strengthens you" (Phil 4:13). His "strength is made perfect in our weakness," when we acknowledge our weakness (2 Cor 12:9). "Christ also suffered for us, leaving us an example, that you should follow His steps" (1 Pet 2:21).

"For I have given you an example, that you should do as I have done to you" (John 13:15). "If anyone serves Me, let him follow Me; and where I am, there My servant will be also" (John 12:26). "And he who does not take his cross and follow after Me is not worthy of Me" (Matt 10:38). "To him who overcomes I will give some of the hidden manna to eat. And I will give him a white stone, and on the stone a new name written which no one knows except him who receives it" (Rev 2:17). "Guide me, O Lord, in Thy way, and I will walk in Thy truth; O let my heart rejoice to fear Thy name" (Ps 85:11).

When boys and youths are given over by their parents for study of arts and sciences, they are fearful and terrified to start this and at first feel considerable sorrow. But when they become accustomed and experience some benefit from the instruction in arts and sciences, they feel not a little pleasure within themselves from the instruction, and the more they study and enlighten the intellect by study, the more they rejoice and are glad. Therefore it is said by many: "The root of education is bitter, but its fruits are sweet." Any art and science lead to this.

Likewise, it at first seems fearsome to those who approach the study of the philosophy of the Gospel and begin to study it, and they feel not a little sorrow: the spiritual Christian life is bitter for the flesh and Christ's yoke is heavy. But when they begin to study and they see spiritual benefit in their studies, then they rejoice, and they seek to do more and more. And the more they learn, the more delight they feel within themselves. So, to any carnal person, Christ is at first fearsome and bitter but later pleasant and sweet. Satan's yoke is at first pleasant and sweet, but later vile and bitter, as it is in reality. The yoke of Christ is at first fearsome and bitter, but later is pleasant and sweet. For one who has learned the Christian philosophy, to do good is joyful and sweet, but to one who has not studied it, it is difficult and tedious.

Imagine, Christian, two people, one having learned the Christian philosophy, and another who has not, and you will see a great difference between them. The former both thinks and speaks spiritually, and the latter carnally. With the former, both thoughts and speech are about God, the Word of God, and eternal life; with the latter, about the vanity of the world and luxury. The former thinks and cares about how to receive eternal life, the latter, how to amass wealth and find honor and glory in this world. It is all the same to the former where he lives: in rich and beautiful chambers or in a ramshackle hut; the latter would like to live only in a fine and beautiful house. For the former, it is all the same whether he sits at a rich or meager table; the latter always thinks of the best table. "The former dresses equally both in elegant and in humble clothing; the latter wants to wear only elegant dress and, as the rich man of the Gospel, to be clothed in purple and fine linen" (Luke 16:19). The former, whether he has the riches of this world or not, is not troubled about this and is satisfied with what he has. The latter is troubled about this and, if he does not get it, he grieves and complains. The latter, if he has wealth, spends it on the poor and homeless and other God-pleasing works; the latter, on luxury and his own whims. The former sympathizes with the poor person, as a suffering member of his own body. The latter thinks and says, "What do I care about his needs? After all, he's not related to me," and so on. The former, if he is reproached or otherwise offended, is silent or meekly answers the one who has given offense. The latter becomes incensed when offended and returns offense for offense, and harassment for harassment, and malice for malice, and tries to get revenge in another way, and so on.

You see, Christian, the portrayal of one who learns the Christian philosophy and one who does not, and you see how much they differ from each other. Join these pupils who study the evangelical and Christian philosophy and learn it with them from Christ, that you will indeed be a Christian and Christ's disciple. And although the beginning of this study seems fearsome and distressing, urge and force yourself, like a lazy donkey. Seeing this effort of yours, the Lord will help you, and day by day His holy yoke will seem lighter and sweeter.

# 106. I Am Greatly in Your Debt

You hear that people tell other people, "I am greatly in your debt." And such words show gratitude of heart. These people say this to those from whom they have received considerable good, benefactions, and help for free. Such words are correct and proceed from a grateful heart when they are said not hypocritically but from heartfelt sincerity. For people should be grateful to their benefactors.

Christians! It is especially proper to thank our God with humility and sincerity and to say to Him, "I am greatly in your debt, O Lord." And we should thank him every day, hour, and minute since we constantly receive good things from the Lord as a gift. "I will bless the Lord at all times, his praise is ever in my mouth" (Ps 33:2).

I did not exist, and then I came into being and live, like other people. "You, O Lord, granted me to exist and be counted among the works of Your hands, and to see the works of Your hands—heaven and earth and all that therein is" (Ps 145:6), and from contemplation of Your great and excellent works, to get to know You, the great and most glorious Creator, and to be satisfied and comforted by Your good things. "Thy hands have made me and fashioned me" (Ps 118:73). I am in great debt to you for this and have nothing with which to repay.

You created me not as a soulless creature, not a beast, not a bird, not a fish, not any other kind of dumb animal, which all have life but do not understand their blessedness; You created a person possessing reason. Therefore I can learn and understand that I have my beginning of existence and life from You; I am Your creation; You are my Creator. I am greatly in your debt for this and can in no way repay. Thus created by You, I cannot be and live without you and your good things. Your hand, O Lord, will support me and grant me Your good things (see Ps 103:28).

Without light, I cannot live and move: your luminaries, the sun, moon and stars give me light. I cannot live without fire: Your fire warms me and cooks my food. I cannot be either alive or healthy without air: Your air gives me life and maintains my life. I cannot exist without food: Your generous hand, O Lord, gives me food. I cannot be without water: Your kindness, O Lord, formed springs, rivers, and lakes for my sake, and using the water from them, I quench my thirst and wash myself. Stripped of my God-woven garment (The Great Penitential Canon of St. Andrew of Crete), I cannot exist without clothing: I even receive this from your generous hand. I cannot exist without a house: You also give me a house for the repose of my feeble and miserable body. I cannot be without livestock: Your creatures serve and work for me. Both other people—my brothers—and I receive these and innumerable other blessings from You. I am greatly in your debt for all of this. "What shall I render unto the Lord, for all that He hath rendered unto me" (Ps 115:3)?

What would happen to me, if You were to take away even one of these blessings from me? Would my eyes be of any use if Your light did not shine for me? I would certainly wander around like a blind man. "How could I live if You did not give me Your food? Without air, I cannot live for a moment. So every creation of Yours is very good" (Gen 1:25) and serves me, the poor one. But while receiving these blessings from You, I await future and better blessings in accordance with Your true promise; my spirit looks from those seen to the unseen, and from the present ones to future ones, and from the temporal to the eternal, and from the earthly to the heavenly. If You grant us such blessings in banishment and exile, what kind of blessings will you grant in the Homeland and Your house! And if You so generously open Your hand to those who know You and do not know You, who honor you and do not honor you, Your friends and enemies, what blessings will be vouchsafed in eternal life to those who love You? "Eye has not seen, nor ear heard, Nor have entered into the heart of man The things which God has prepared for those who love Him" (1 Cor 2:9). "Let Thy mercy, O Lord, be upon us, according as we have put our trust in Thee" (Ps 32:22).

I am blind, like others, without grace and your enlightenment: my sin has blinded me. Therefore, even in this regard, Your kindness has cared in Your love for mankind both for everyone and for me, the unworthy. For the enlightenment of all, You sent down to us Your holy Word through Your chosen servants. It shines for me like a candle for those sitting in darkness, and reveals the harm and benefit, evil and good, sin and virtue, lie and truth, what is unpleasing to You and pleasing, unbelief and faith, and so drives away my blindness and enlightens my mind. "Thy law is a lamp unto my feet, and a light unto my paths" (Ps 118:105). I am greatly in Your debt, O Lord, for all this, and I have nothing with which to repay.

From this, I recognize You, my God and Creator. I see that You have done and are doing excellent and wondrous works that neither the human hand nor any creature can do. And from Your Word, I know that You are always the same (see Heb 13:8), You marvelously and splendidly work miracles in the world that You created out of nothing (see 2 Macc 7:28), and from all of this, I know of Your almighty power. Both to create things from nothing and to change the things that were created are all in Your power. Is transforming rivers into blood, streaming water from a rock, changing fire into dew, giving sight to a man blind from birth, raising the dead, and performing other works similar to this, characteristic of anything other than Your all-powerful hand? "Reasoning upon this almighty power of Yours, I am convinced that I must tremble and humble myself before You" (Isa 66:2), "humble myself under Your mighty hand" (1 Pet 5:6). How can I not tremble and humble myself before the One Who has in His hands both me and all the ends of the earth? Both my death and my life are in His hands. Most gracious and merciful God! Spare me, a poor sinner.

I see in Your Word that Your almighty hand protects, keeps, and saves those who fear, love, and honor You; but it humbles, punishes, and chastises the self-willed, who do not fear and do not honor You; it rewards virtue and punishes sin. And from this I perceive Your righteousness, which will repay to all according to their works, and I fear your judgment, and thus I am moved to repentance for my past sins; I compel myself to cry out to You from the depths of my heart: "God, be merciful to me a sinner!" (Luke 18:13). "And enter not into judgment with Thy servant, for before Thee shall no man living be justified" (Ps 142:2). "If Thou shouldest mark iniquities, O Lord; Lord, who shall stand" (Ps 129:3)? This puts me on my guard against other sins, to which my weakness inclines me.

I see in your word that You call all who have turned away from you and the impious, and those who have turned back to you and with repentance come and seek and ask mercy from you, will receive in Your love for mankind, as a child-loving Father of straying sons, and will show them Your mercy, and will not remember their sins and transgression, and will add them to the number of those who love and honor You. From this, I learn of Your kindness and incomparable mercy toward poor sinners, and therefore do not myself despair of my sins, but I run with hope in You, the kind and merciful God, and ask mercy. "Have mercy upon me, O God, after Thy great goodness, and according to the multitude of Thy mercies do away mine offenses" (Ps 50:3).

All Your creations show Your kindness, and everywhere Your word is preached (see Ps 18:2); "even the cattle of the field also look up to You" (Joel 1:20), angels and people are astonished, repentant sinners kiss it and the righteous feel it, even insensate sinners are not deprived, as Your goodness is patient with them, "and leads to repentance" (Rom 2:4). Even I, a poor sinner, feel it and kiss Your goodness and with Your prophet I cry, "O taste, and see, that the Lord is good" (Ps 33:9). And as often as I feel Your goodness in my heart, my heart is roused and enkindled toward love for You.

Glory to Your goodness, glory to Your munificence, glory to Your mercy, glory to Your long-suffering, glory to Your love for mankind! "I will love Thee, O Lord, my strength. The Lord is my firm foundation, and my fortress, and my deliverer; my God is my helper, and I will trust in Him, my defender, the horn also of my salvation, and my protector" (Ps 17:2–3).

In Your Word, I see that everything that You reveal to us is exactly as it is; and whatever you predict comes true; and whatever You have promised and are promising, You always "fulfill, for The Lord is faithful in all His words" (Ps 144:13). And I see that Heaven and earth will pass away, but Your words will by "no means pass away" (Matt 24:35). And from this I perceive your truth, and I am confirmed in my faith, and I believe Your holy and merciful promise without doubting, and I am steadfast in my hope. Your mercy, O Lord, and Your truth enlivens me, supports me, keeps and strengthens me, and leads me to Your future and eternal blessings. I know that the house of my body will fall into ruin, and my body, as earth, will be consigned to the earth. But your mercy assures me that the same body in which my soul now lives will arise by Your power and Your almighty voice (see John 11:43) and will be transformed by Your grace into the best and most beautiful form. "It is sown in dishonor, it is raised in glory. It is sown in weakness, it is raised in power. It is sown a natural body, it is raised a spiritual body. For this corruptible must put on incorruption, and this mortal must put on immortality" (1 Cor 15:43–44, 53). And so, with Your holy Church, "I look for the resurrection of the dead, and the life of the age to come, Amen."[11]

I see in Your holy Word that You have neither a beginning nor an end. All things created by You may come to an end just as they began and may cease to exist just as they did not exist. That they exist depends on Your holy will and all-powerful strength. But You, as You abide without beginning, so will be without end and cannot not exist. "Before ever the mountains were formed, or the earth and the world were created, even from age to age Thou art" (Ps 89:3). "In the beginning, O Lord, hast Thou laid the foundation of the earth, and the heavens are the work of Thy hands. They shall perish, but Thou shalt endure; yea, they all shall wax old as doth a garment, and as a vesture shalt Thou change them, and they shall be changed. But Thou art the same, and Thy years shall not fail" (Ps 101:26–28). "And from this I see that You alone have immortality, dwelling in unapproachable light" (1 Tim 6:16); "You alone are everlasting, You alone have unchangeable life, and You are everlasting eternity and eternal everlastingness, eternal life, without Whom we may not live and be alive, with Whom is the fountain of life" (Ps 35:10).

To be with You is life; without You is manifest death.

To be with You is blessedness; to be without You is wretchedness.

To be with You is consolation, joy, and sweetness; to be without You is sorrow and grief.

Those who live with You truly live; those living without you have died while alive; they live in people's eyes, but before Your eyes, they are dead; they abide in death. He is dead who is withdrawn from life; just as he is in darkness who is withdrawn from the light. Contemplating on this, I tremble and am afraid to withdraw from You, my life. I seek and try to be with You, Your unworthy creation. O Lord, "cast me not away from Thy presence, and take not Thy Holy Spirit from me. O give me the comfort of Thy salvation and stablish me with Thy governing Spirit" (Ps 50:13–14). You are my Creator; You are my life; You are my strength, O Lord, You are my power, You are my God, You are my joy. "For what have I in heaven, and what have I desired on earth from Thee? My flesh and my heart have failed, O God of my heart, but Thou art my portion, O God, for ever. For lo, they that go far from Thee shall perish; Thou hast destroyed all them that are unfaithful against Thee. But it is good for me to cleave unto God, to put my trust in the Lord" (Ps 72:25–28).

My soul, heed diligently, very diligently, this saying: "Behold, those who withdraw themselves from Thee will perish." Beware withdrawing from life, lest you be in death. Beware withdrawing from the light, lest you dwell in darkness.

Sin cuts us off from God and separates us from Him. The angels sinned, and were cut off from God, and perished. Our first parents sinned in paradise and were cut off from God and died. People nowadays sin and are cut off from God and abide in death.

Beware, my soul, lest you suffer in the same way.

Draw near to life, that you may live in Him and with Him.

Adhere to the light, that you may have in yourself the light of life.

Draw near to blessedness, that you may be blessed.

Draw near to the good God, that you may be good.

Adhere to joy and sweetness, that you may abide in consolation, joy, and gladness. Die to sin and the vanity of this world, that you may live with God. "But it is good for me to cleave unto God!"

I see in Your holy Word that You have incomparable and incomprehensible holiness, at which Your chosen and holy angels are amazed and terrified, so that with trembling and terror they are compelled to cry out, "Holy, holy, holy, is the Lord of hosts!" (Isa 6:3). And I know that to be with You is life, to be without you is death. It is fearsome to be separated from you, but it is impossible for one covered with shame and defiled to be with You. And he who wishes to have fellowship with You, the *Light* of life, in Whom there is "no darkness at all," must be and walk in the light (1 John 1:5–7). This reflection teaches me to fear any sin and retreat from it, and to be in repentance and contrition for sins previously committed, and to pray to You with humility and repentance. "Turn Thy face from my sins, put out all my misdeeds" (Ps 50:11). O Lord, take away my iniquities from me, and I shall be Yours, and I shall be with you. "For it is good for me to cleave unto God."

I see in Your holy Word that You are everywhere and in every place, and there is no such place where You would not be present in essence, and wherever I go and stay, I move and abide before You; and whatever I do, say, think, undertake, I do, say, think, and undertake before You. You see and know all, and see and know much better than I myself know; and whatever I do, say, think, and undertake, you note down in your book, and will render according to my deeds, thoughts, words, and undertakings. Since You are everywhere, You see and know everything. That is why I can nowhere and in no way hide from you. "All my ways are before Thee, O Lord" (Ps 118:168). "Whither shall I go then from Thy Spirit? Or whither shall I flee from Thy presence? If I climb up into heaven, Thou art there; if I go down to hell, Thou art there also. If I take up my wings early, and dwell in the uttermost parts of the sea, Even there also shall Thy hand lead me, and Thy right hand shall hold me. And I said, Peradventure the darkness shall hide me, and the night is light in my pleasures. For the darkness shall be no darkness with Thee, and the night shall be as bright as the day" (Ps 138:7–12).

This precept and reflection teaches me to always fear You and tremble, to live with fear and apprehension and act, do, say, think, and undertake as children do before their father and servants do before their master, as subjects come before their king and address him, for everyone is in Your presence, and everything is revealed before Your all-seeing eye, and nothing is hidden. From this, I shall learn everywhere and in every place to bend my knees before You, and with humility call upon You, and seek mercy from You, and to put my hope in You, "Though I walk through the valley of the shadow of death, I will fear no evil, for Thou art with me" (Ps 22:4). "Thou art my helper; unto Thee will I sing, for Thou, O God, art my defender, and my merciful God" (Ps 58:18).

I see too in Your holy Word that You are an immaterial Spirit, Whom it is impossible either for the eye to see, or the ear to hear, or the hands to touch, or any sense to perceive, but You are only visible and knowable by the eye of faith and the mind. "God is Spirit" (John 4:24). From this, I learn to honor You not in matter, but in spirit (for the Spirit is honored in spirit), and *worship You in spirit and truth*. O Lord, teach me to honor You and worship You in spirit and truth.

I see too in Your holy Word that You disclose there a way of salvation for us, where it is not noticed, and You direct everything in good order and to a good end. "And from this, I perceive Your incomprehensible wisdom and am amazed by it. And I see that You, having made everything in wisdom" (Ps 103:24), also direct all things wisely. And from this, I learn to rely upon your wise and wondrous providence in everything, in well-being and in troubles. "Everything that is sent to me from You is sent for my benefit and for my blessedness, as from the source of every good gift" (Jas 1:17). If You exalt me, it is good for me. If You humble me, it is good for me. If you send me joy, it is good for me. If You sadden me, it is good for me. Glory to You, O God, for all things! For You do all things in order to make me blessed. "I will bless the Lord at all times," both sad and joyful (Ps 33:2).

So from Your holy Word I learn to know You, my Creator and God, and knowing, to honor, and from this, I receive great and ineffable benefit for my soul. What would I be if Your holy Word did not guide me? I should certainly walk and go astray, as one blind and as one walking in the dark, as all the nations that do not have this lamp of Yours, and not heeding it, walk and go astray, and do not know You, their Creator, and being provided with Your good gifts that You are giving them, do not know You, the benefactor, but honor creation instead of the Creator, and rendering to Your creatures the honor that they should render to You, the Creator and benefactor. Your holy Word turns me away from such soul-destroying error, and points to You, my Creator, and leads to You, and it teaches both to know You and to honor You alone as my God and Creator, and to worship and serve You alone, and to render fitting honor to You. I am greatly in Your debt for this heavenly gift of Yours, O Lord, and I cannot repay anyhow or with anything.

I thank You, lover of mankind, that You have lit this divine lamp of Yours and placed it both before everyone, and before me, a poor one. Looking at it, I am illumined and enlightened, and I understand and know You, my Creator and God, and I am put on the true path.

In Your Word, I see what is demanded by the Creator from His rational creation, by the Lord from His servant, by the most-high benefactor from the one for whom he performs the benefaction, by God from man, that is, such reverence, subjection, worship, obedience, and love that should not be rendered to any creature. And from this, I learn to so honor You as my faith and Your holy Word teaches. My conscience also prompts me to this and motivates me to such reverence.

In Your Word, I see who I am and who is my neighbor and that I am in debt to him, that is, as I love myself, so I should love him, as a man should love a man and a kindred nature, one beloved and honored by You; and to do nothing to him that I would want for myself, and to do everything for him that I would want for myself. I owe this to him; I learn this from Your holy Word.

In Your Word, I see that You, as Creator, care for all of your creation so that not even a little bird "falls to the ground apart from [Your] will" (Matt 10:29), and even more so for man, whom You created in your image and likeness. In this, I see that You showed a wondrous providence, incomprehensible to our minds, for pitiful man. Man in his creation was truly honored by You, his Creator, more than all Your creatures by Your extraordinary counsel, "Let Us make man" (Gen 1:26). He was created in Your image and in Your likeness; he was created holy, pure, chaste, and wise, and was created for eternal blessedness. But enticed by the seductive counsel of the evil serpent, he was deprived of all his honor and blessedness and, having turned away from You, perished.

Oh, the ruinous counsel! Oh, the cruel fall! Man fell, and he, who was created in the image of God and the likeness of God, and was created for eternal blessedness, perished. "Adam, where are you" (Gen 3:9)? Ah, My beloved creation, created by My hands, created in My image and in My likeness, *where are you?* You have fallen from such a height to such lowness, from such glory to such ignominy, from such blessedness to such wretchedness. The evil serpent enticed My honored creation; the thief kidnapped man, created by My hands, and took him off into captivity; a wild beast has devoured My beloved child (see Gen 37:33). "Man, being in honor, understood it not; he shall be compared unto the brute beasts, and is become like unto them" (Ps 48:13, 21).

Thus perished the first-created man, and we, his sons, have perished! But You, the good, merciful, and man-loving God, did not bear to see miserable man in ruination but had mercy on him. You would have given him Your law so that it would turn him and lead him to You. But it only showed him his feebleness but did not cure it; it rebuked him and inspired fear but did not console; showed his ruination but did not save, and could not save, since man, so badly wounded and infirm, could not fulfill it. You sent your chosen servants, the prophets, to fallen man; and they only rebuked man but did not help him, but they did give indications of Him Who was coming to save man, and announced Him, and thus granted a certain consolation to miserable man, "He is coming, He is coming" (Mal 3:1; Isa 62:11; Ps 117:26); He "will come quickly and not delay" (Isa 13:22 LXX; 14:1).

Finally, the time came, and by Your most holy good will You sent us Your only-begotten Son Himself, co-essential, and co-eternal, and co-unoriginate with You. And He was clothed in flesh of like nature with ours and was born of the most immaculate Virgin Mother and, although being God without begin-ning, was an infant and, although being the Heavenly King, lived on earth, and You bore witness to Him from heaven with Your most divine voice, "This is My beloved Son, in whom I am well pleased. Hear Him!" (Matt 17:5).

He was sent from You, our God and Creator, to us miserable ones to seek us out and to save us, Your perishing creation, as He consolingly preached of Your love for us, the unworthy, "For God so loved the world that He gave His only begotten Son, that whoever believes in Him should not perish but have everlasting life. For God did not send His Son into the world to condemn the world, but that the world through Him might be saved" (John 3:16–17). On coming to us, He announced to us Your most holy good will and sublime mercy; and by Your Holy Gospel, which He brought us from You, He com-forted and cheered our hearts, embittered by the poison of the serpent; He preached to us that You are remitting for us our sins, by which we have angered You, our Creator and God, and that You are calling us to Yourself through Him, and are opening the doors of your eternal kingdom to those who believe in him and are obedient to Him, as He Himself witnessed to this for our con-solation, "The Spirit of the Lord is upon Me, Because He has anointed Me To preach the gospel to the poor; He has sent Me to heal the brokenhearted, To proclaim liberty to the captives And recovery of sight to the blind, To set at liberty those who are oppressed; To proclaim the acceptable year of the Lord" (Luke 4:18–19).

Bringing us these all-pleasant tidings from You to us poor sinners, He lived, as a man, with people on earth, and taught us by His example to please You and to do your will, and showed us the way, and called us to Your eternal kingdom and suffered and died at the hands of those who had not accepted Him, and rose from the dead, and ascended into heaven, from whence He had come, and sat at the right hand of You, God and Father. So, having cleansed us who believed in Him from our sins by His suffering and death and blood, shed for our sake, He, as the good shepherd, draws Your lost sheep to you, His Heavenly Father.

For such man-loving, saving, wondrous, providence of Yours, incompre-hensible to our mind, I, a poor sinner, as well as all people, are deeply in Your debt. "What shall I render unto the Lord, for all that He hath rendered unto me" (Ps 115:3)? I confess You, Father, with Your only-begotten Son and Your Most Holy Spirit! I hymn Your love for mankind! I, an unworthy and poor sin-ner, glorify your goodness and mercy! "Blessed is the Lord God of Israel, for

He has visited and redeemed His people, and has raised up a horn of salvation for us In the house of His servant David" (Luke 1:68–69).

Where would I, a sinner and wrongdoer, be, if not in perdition and in eternal death, like a fallen corpse? Like the demons, I would be eternally eating the bitter fruits of my sins. "For the wages of sin is death" (Rom 6:23). Your goodness, Your mercy and love for mankind has kept me from this, but You so wondrously saved me. I am greatly in Your debt for this! "Bless the Lord, O my soul, and all that is within me bless His holy Name. Bless the Lord, O my soul, and forget not all His benefits," and so on (Ps 102:1–2).

I see in Your holy Word that the devil, that ancient evil serpent, who enticed my ancestors in Paradise, envying our blessedness to which You lead us by the grace of Your only-begotten Son, even now "walks about like a roaring lion, seeking whom he may devour" (1 Pet 5:8). Your kindness puts everyone who knows You, as well as me, the unworthy one, on our guard against this enemy of ours, and Your all-powerful hand keeps us safe. Oh, could I really be unharmed? Would not the enemy swallow me alive, if Your almighty hand did not protect me? I am greatly in your debt for this, too! "Blessed be the Lord, Who hath not given us over for a prey unto their teeth" (Ps 123:6). "But forsake me not, O Lord" (Ps 37:22), "even unto the end, but deliver us from the evil one!" (Matt 6:13). "Arise, O Lord my God, let thy hand be lifted up; forget not Thy poor before the end" (Ps 9:33). "O deliver not the soul that confesseth Thee unto the wild beasts; forget not the souls of the poor forever" (Ps 73:19).

"I see in Your holy Word that Your holy Angels, standing before the throne of Your glory and seeing Your most holy face, protect those who know and fear You, and by Your command keep them safe from the evil demons" (Ps 33:8), and are "sent forth to minister for those who will inherit salvation" (Heb 1:14). For You do not abandon those whom You redeemed by the precious blood of Your only-begotten Son but keep them safe through Your holy servants and lead them to eternal rest. Even I, Your unworthy and worthless servant, am accounted worthy of this Your grace by Your mercy. I am greatly in your debt for this, too, O Lord.

I know and confess with humility that I have sinned much against You, my Creator and God, and I am sorry for this, and I see some sins in my conscience, but others I do not see, and I do not see more than I do see: "Who can understand his fallings into sin" (Ps 18:13)? I sorrow and grieve that I, the lowest worm, have foolishly insulted You, the Lord, greatly by them—You, my good and man-loving God, my Creator, my redeemer, my sublime benefactor,

Whom the holy angels honor with fear and trembling, hymn, and worship. You saw me sinning as often as I have sinned against You, and You were patient with me in your goodness as often as You saw, and you pardoned me as often as You showed patience with me. And if You had dealt with me according to Your most holy righteousness, my soul would have long ago gone down to hell, but Your goodness and love for mankind and Your long-suffering restrained You, and kept me, a poor sinner, from my perdition. I am also greatly in your debt for Your great mercy to me, O Lord. "I will thank Thee, O Lord my God, with all my heart, and I will praise Thy Name for evermore. For great is Thy mercy toward me, and Thou hast delivered my soul from the nethermost hell" (Ps 85:12–13).

I see from these and other benefactions toward me that I do not even know of that You guard me by Your love for me and goodness, love for mankind, long-suffering and munificence. Your goodness, O Lord, can be seen in that I have not yet perished but still live. I see that You are leading me to eternal salvation, which You promised to those who know and honor You. Have mercy on me, a poor sinner, until the end, and by the grace of Your only-begotten Son, wash away all my iniquities, and save me unto eternal life. With all Your chosen ones, may I thank you there for all your benefactions and praise and hymn You with Your only-begotten Son and the Most Holy Spirit. "*Now* I see all this *in part*, but there I shall see face to face unto the endless ages, Amen" (1 Cor 13:12).

Christian, you see the following from these discussions:

(1) You and I are in debt to God; that is, both you and I are obliged to Him for everything: that we live, that we move—this is God's goodness, and whatever you do, however much it may please God, even if throughout your entire life you suffered for His name's sake, even this would be nothing—you would still remain a debtor to God, since we receive everything from Him and are in debt to Him for everything! We cannot repay Him in any way or with anything for just His creating us, and what will we repay for all His other innumerable and unrivaled benefactions? "What shall I render unto the Lord, for all that He hath rendered unto me" (Ps 115:3)? There is only one answer: nothing.

(2) We shall learn from this to thank Him with humility from a sincere heart, and to learn our imperfection and poverty in that we receive benefactions every day and hour from Him, as our benefactor, but we have nothing with which to repay our benefactor.

(3) We should thank Him for all good things, but most of all for His Word, the most sublime gift He sent to us, and for the salvific coming of His only-begotten Son to us, and for eternal life and blessedness promised to us on His behalf. God's ineffable and incomprehensible goodness to us was revealed in it.

(4) From this you see, Christian, that you are poor and miserable, that without God's blessings, you could not live even minutes. Poor and miserable is he who has no food, has no clothing, has no house, and so on. You do not own any of these or anything else, but you receive everything from God, who is rich in mercy. And if the Lord did not give you all of this, you would be most poor and wretched, more than all creatures. You see now that you are poor and miserable. Perceive and acknowledge your poverty and squalor, that the Lord, plenteous in mercy, may enrich you.

(5) You see from this that we cannot merit anything from God on our own but receive everything for free from His generous hand. He, good and plenteous in mercy, seeing our poverty and destitution, opens His treasury of blessings, and from it gives us everything for free. His nature is such that He cannot not do good.

(6) From knowledge of God will follow renewal, correction, piety, and a holy Christian life, as you saw earlier. To truly know God and to live impiously is impossible, since one is the opposite of the other. It is impossible not to correct and renew oneself for one who has come to know God, and the more he knows, the more he reforms and renews himself, and becomes better.

(7) From this, it follows that Christians who live wickedly do not know God, although they confess His holy name, pray to Him, go to Church, commune Christ's Mysteries, and so on. The Apostle wrote of this, "Now by this we know that we know Him, if we keep His commandments. He who says, 'I know Him,' and does not keep His commandments, is a liar, and the truth is not in him" (1 John 2:3–4). Such people all abide in death, as ones separated from life; they live in the body but are dead in the soul; they are alive in the eyes of the world but have died in God's eyes. For it is impossible for one defiled by sins to have fellowship with a holy God, and if someone is separated from Him, he is separated from life—he is dead, as is written: "They that go far from Thee shall perish" (Ps 72:27). These include fornicators, adulterers, all kinds of defilers, the malicious and vengeful, extortioners, thieves and robbers, slanderers and backbiters, debauchers, cheats, and hypocrites and others of their ilk. All such have withdrawn from God by their depravity and therefore abide in death.

(8) When a transgressor turns to God with His whole heart, and will abide in true repentance, he will come to life again. If, O sinner, you wish to live by the soul, and not only by the body, turn with your whole heart to God, to Life, Who gives life to all, and keep to Him in faith and truth, and you will live truly both now and in the age to come, and although you will die, you will come to life again and will enter the resurrection of eternal life. "O praise the Lord, all ye nations! Praise Him, all ye peoples, For His merciful kindness is ever more and more towards us, and the truth of the Lord endureth forever" (Ps 116:1–2). "Praise the Lord, O my soul; While I live will I praise the Lord; I will sing unto my God as long as I have being" (Ps 145:1–2).

# 107. The Memory of an Absent Benefactor

It happens that a person receives many benefactions from another person and, remembering this, always remembers the benefactor, and out of love and gratitude to him, even mentions him to his friends. A thankful heart always remembers a benefactor and his benefactions, but an ungrateful one forgets both the benefactions and the benefactor, as was written of the ungrateful Israelites, "And they forgat His good deeds, and the wonderful works that He had showed for them" (Ps 77:11). And insofar as the grateful person remembers his benefactor and his benefactions, he often boasts of him before his friends, shows them the benefactions of his benefactor, and speaks of him, saying that he had done such and such a good thing for him: he built a house for him, gave him clothing, delivered him from some misfortune, and so on. This shows that his heart is grateful to his benefactor.

Likewise, a Christian should always remember God and His innumerable benefactions and say within himself in his soul: my God created me and brought me from non-being into being and grants me such and such a good thing. By His command, the heavenly bodies that I see, the sun, moon, and stars, give me, the unworthy one, light, and day and night show me the way, and with their help I avoid mishap and every injury. Oh, how unfortunate I would be, and in no way would I differ from a blind man if they were hidden from me! By His command, the air that I inhale and exhale serves and maintains my life. I should disappear immediately if even for one minute I were deprived of it. The clouds, which, like water skins, contain water and are borne from place to place, and moisten the air and the land, serve me by His good will. What use to me would fertile land and the seed sown on it be, if the clouds did not water it from above? It would be barren land, and my animals and I would perish without food, as happens during drought and famine.

His almighty hand built for me this house, in which I live and rest and take refuge from bad weather and storms. How bitter would my life be for me if I did not have it! His goodness even takes care about this. His generous hand gives me the food that I eat and fortify my feeble body and by which I am comforted, and the water, by which I quench my thirst and refresh myself. How could I live if He had not opened His treasury and given me His blessings? His holy and all-powerful hand sends me this clothing, with which I cover and warm my naked and miserable body. How could I go around without clothes and be unscathed by the cold and frost? His love for mankind took care for this, too.

His fire warms my house, and cooks my food, and at nighttime gives me light. His all-powerful and generous hand has filled the lakes, rivers, and springs for me and my livestock and brought forth in them all different kinds of fish and animals for my needs. I see various kinds of grass and herbs in the fields and steppes. By His command, the earth reveals its treasures. He gives these to both me and my livestock; they serve as medicine for my feeble body and as food for my livestock. He planted various trees, and those serve my various needs. By His command, various birds, livestock, and beasts propagate, and from them, I get either food, or clothing, or other diverse benefits.

He brings forth the winds from His treasure houses, and those cool me and my livestock during hot weather, cleanse the air, push along the clouds, and make the sky clear. Day and night are caused by His all-powerful word; the sun rises and sets; it rises, and we have day; it sets, and night falls. The day serves me, and night serves me, too: in the day, I go forth to his work, and to labor, until the evening (see Ps 103:23); at night I give rest to my feeble body, thus gather new energy for taking up the labors of the next day, and so on.

He sent me His holy Word like a king sends a merciful letter to his servant; He sent it through His servants, men chosen and consecrated for this. His Word enlightens me, who am living in the darkness of ignorance, and, like a lamp, shines for me and shows me the correct way, and teaches me to differentiate darkness from light, evil from good, flattery from truth, injury from benefit, sin from virtue, superstition and unbelief from faith, fraudulent blessedness from truth, foolishness from wisdom, impiety from piety, and thus teaches me and makes me wiser. In it, I see who I am and Who He is Who so mercifully and with love for mankind takes care of me. In it, I see that I am a creation, and He is my Creator. From Him, I have the beginning of my existence and I shall have its end. But He has neither beginning nor end, and as He did not begin, so too He cannot end, and He alone is immortal.

In it, I see that like all the ends of the earth, I too am held in His almighty hands. I see in it that as He wisely cares for all creatures, He even more so cares for man and for me. In it, I see that heaven and earth and all that is in them are the works of His hands. The sun, the moon, and the stars that give light to me are the works of His hands. The air that gives me life; the clouds that sprinkle water on me; the earth, which bears fruit for me and on which I live; the waters that cool and serve me; fire, which warms me and cooks my food; the animals that work for me; the trees that serve my needs—all are the works of His hands; the food and drink with which I strengthen my feeble body; the clothing with which I cover and warm my naked body, and so on, are His blessings. He gives me all of this.

His holy Word teaches me how to live, what to do, and what to avoid, how and with what to please Him, and it shows me my feebleness, and reproves my sins, and threatens me with His judgment for them, and so leads me into fear and humility, and persuades me to repent, feel contrition for my sins, and with contrition of heart to run to Him, to seek His mercy and to pray, "God, be merciful to me a sinner!" (Luke 18:13).

But it also encourages, enlivens, and comforts me, trembling and having a contrite heart, and fearing His judgment, lest I be engulfed in sorrow and complete despair of receiving His mercy. For in His Word I see that He opens the door of His mercy to all poor sinners who turn to Him and repent of their sins, fall down with humility before Him, and ask for His mercy, and He accepts them. If He has mercy on all, then he has mercy on me, too, inasmuch as I am also one of them. If He is good for all, He is good for me; if He is a friend of man for all, He is such for me; if He is merciful for all, He is merciful for me; if He accepts all, He accepts me. If He saves all who believe in Him, He will do the same for me, since I too believe in Him.

But where, O beloved, where is He, Who is such a benefactor to you? Where is He who so loves you, Who shows such love to you? Where is that great Benefactor of yours, Who shows so many benefactions to you? Where did He go? Where does He live and dwell? Tell me, tell me, beloved! He is everywhere. And He is not far from me but is close to me, even though I do not see him, and I grieve about this and am sorry that I do not see the One who loves me, my Benefactor. "While we are at home in the body we are absent from the Lord. For we walk by faith, not by sight" (2 Cor 5:6–7).

I see His blessings, but I do not see the giver of blessings. I receive benefactions from His merciful hands, but I do not see the Benefactor. I see heaven and earth and all that is in them, everything that His hand created, but He Himself, Who did the creating, I do not see. His sun, moon, and stars shine upon me; His air, clouds, rivers, lakes, and springs serve me; His earth brings forth all kinds of trees, grasses, flowers, and fruits for me, but He Himself I do not see. By His invisible hand, He sends me every good thing, but the very One Who sends them I do not see. He opens His treasure house and gives me food, drink, and clothing, but the giver I do not see: "For I walk by faith, not by sight" (2 Cor 5:7). His all-powerful hand protects me from the snares of the enemy, but I do not see my protector. He is my refuge, my protector, my helper, my support in various temptations, misfortunes, tribulations, and griefs, but I do not see Him Himself. He guards me when I am awake in the day, and He guards me while I sleep at night, but I do not see my guardian. If I sit at home, He is with me. If I leave the house, He does not leave me. If I go on my way, He is with me. If I am in the city, in the village, in the desert, with people or alone, He does not depart from me, but I do not see Him: *For I walk by faith, not by sight.*

Whether I do, or say, or think something, I do, or say, or think everything in His sight, but I do not see Him, "For we walk by faith, not by sight" (2 Cor 5:7). Whether I stand in prayer in church or at home, I stand before Him, but I do not see Him, *for I walk by faith, not by sight.* He looks at me, and sees me, and sees how I sit, and how I stand, and He understands my thoughts, but I do not see Him, *for I walk by faith, not by sight.*

I bend my knees before Him, and I fall down and I worship, and I sigh and pray to Him and ask and seek His mercy for myself, but I do not see Him, *for I walk by faith, not by sight.*

I stretch out my hands to Him and raise my eyes, but I do not see Him, *for I walk by faith, not by sight.*

I thank Him as my Benefactor, I hymn Him, I praise Him, I bless and exalt Him, but I do not see Him, *for I walk by faith, not by sight.*

I also feel His holy hand, touching me, the unworthy one, but I do not see Him, *for I walk by faith, not by sight.*

He smites my heart with His holy fear, and therefore I am afraid and tremble before Him, but I do not see Him, *for I walk by faith, not by sight.*

He also touches my heart with holy love, and then my heart feels joy, gladness, and exultation, but I do not see Him, *for I walk by faith, not by sight.*

He punishes me and has mercy on me as a Father Who loves His children;
He grieves and comforts me, but I do not see Him, *for I walk by faith, not by
sight.*

I attend too His holy Word and hear in it that although the house of my
body will be dissolved, it will, however, rise, and it will be reconstituted and
will never be destroyed, but I do not see the One who says this, *for I walk by
faith, not by sight.*

"When shall I come and appear before God's face" (Ps 41:3 LXX)? When
shall I see Him, after Whom my soul longs (see Ps 83:2 LXX [84:2])? When
shall I see Him, upon Whom the angels dare not gaze, Whom the cherubim
and seraphim hymn with amazement and dread, "Holy, holy, holy, Lord God
Almighty" (Rev 4:8)? When will I see the One Who is eternal life; to look on
Him Who is the only consolation, joy, gladness, sweetness, and exultation;
to stand before Him—not in faith, but face to face (see 1 Cor 13:12) which
is ineffable glory, honor, and blessedness? To be with Him means to be in a
continuous sweet life of joy, gladness, and continuous exultation. When will I
come and see my Creator, my provider, my Benefactor, He Who loves me, my
redeemer, helper, and protector, my deliverer and Saviour, glory, honor, joy,
gladness, consolation, and my eternal blessedness?

"Like as the hart panteth after the waterbrooks, so longeth my soul after
Thee, O God. My soul hath thirsted for the mighty living God; when shall I
come and appear before God's face" (Ps 41:2–3)? "Lord, remember me when
You come into Your kingdom" (Luke 23:42).

# 108. He Did His Work and Left

We hear that in various instances one says of another, "He did his work
and left." This is said most often when one asks of another where such and
such a person is. Then the other answers, "He did his work and left."

Christians! We can and should say these words about Christ our Saviour
and even more so when the godless and impious, who do not know and do not
accept Him, ask us. Then we with daring should answer, "He did his work and

left." Although he abides with us invisibly and unremittingly and will until the end of the age, according to His truthful promise, "I am with you always, even to the end of the age." Amen (Matt 28:20).

"His work is the work of our salvation, which He wrought in the midst of the earth" (Ps 73:12) and left. He spoke of this work to His heavenly Father: "I have finished the work which You have given Me to do" (John 17:4). Christian! This work is a great one and incomprehensible to our mind—this work the prophets foresaw from afar and were amazed and awestruck by it, and preached with amazement and awe, and announced to the world, "Behold, the Lord is coming He our God that is before the ages He will come quickly and will not delay Behold, our God ... will come and save us" (Mal 3:1; Mic 5:2; Ps 54:20; Isa 14:1; Isa 62:11; Isa 35:4). "The apostles, who from the beginning were eye-witnesses and ministers of the word" (Luke 1:2), saw this work, preached it to the whole world, and enriched the whole universe with this witness like a priceless treasure. "That which was from the beginning, which we have heard, which we have seen with our eyes, which we have looked upon, and our hands have handled, concerning the Word of life—the life was manifested, and we have seen, and bear witness, and declare to you that eternal life which was with the Father and was manifested to us–that which we have seen and heard we declare to you, that you also may have fellowship with us" (1 John 1:1–3). This work of His, great and glorious, proclaims to us and presents to the eyes of our soul His holy Gospel, which He left to us through His chosen servants, the apostles for our enlightenment, faith, confirmation, and consolation. We see there His great work, which He Himself, by His own will, accomplished for the sake of our salvation and ascended to His Heavenly Father.

We see there His salvific coming to us, His labors and His struggles that He took up for the sake of our salvation, and His departure.

"Having predestined His incarnation before the foundation of the world" (Eph 1:4–5), our God, for the sake of our salvation, sent His angel to the most holy and most blessed Virgin Mary to announce to Her that He would form and take to Himself human flesh. And it was so. We see this work that is incomprehensible for us. The Son of God, born of the Father before the ages, was born on earth of a Virgin Mother without a Father. Angels hymned His holy Nativity: "Glory to God in the highest, And on earth peace, goodwill toward men!" (Luke 2:14). Shepherds saw the Child that had been born and worshiped and glorified Him. The Magi came from the East, taught by the miraculous star, and brought gifts to the newborn King, "and fell down and worshiped Him" (Matt 2:11). "With great joy, the holy elder Simeon met Him, when He was brought to the temple, and took the pre-eternal Child into his arms" (Luke 1:2; Matt 1 and 2).

"O blessed womb that bore the Lord of glory! O blessed arms that took and embraced the Lord Who bore all creation! O blessed eyes that saw in the flesh God as an infant! Kings, prophets, righteous men wished to see Him and did not see Him" (Luke 10:23–24). "It was never seen like this in Israel!" (Matt 9:33). For He who appeared was the God of Abraham, of Isaac, and of Jacob. It was He, Who appeared to Moses in the bush that burned and was not consumed, and spoke with him. It was He Who struck Egypt with boils and led His people out of that land. It was He Who divided the Red Sea and led Israel across it. It was He Who spoke with Moses on Mount Sinai and gave Him His law. It was He Who led Israel, His people, through the desert and fed them with manna, and defeated all their enemies before them. It was He Who led Israel, His people, into the Promised Land, into a land flowing with milk and honey, and drove all the nations before them, and gave them that land as an inheritance. It was He Who sent into the world His prophets. He Himself has now come to us—come in a form like ours. "God was manifested in the flesh" (1 Tim 3:16).

You see, Christian, God's condescension and the value of man. Fallen man was exalted in his restoration as much as he was honored by God in his creation:

(1) God Himself came to him to search him out and save him. He honored man by creation in His own image, but He Himself came to save him who had fallen and perished.

(2) God assumed and joined to Himself living flesh from the human race and became man. And thus, the Lord became like unto us and became our brother, as He Himself says, "I will declare Thy Name unto my brethren" (Ps 21:23). And to Mary Magdalene, He said, "Go to My brethren and say to them, 'I am ascending to My Father and your Father, and to My God and your God'" (John 20:17).

Oh, the incomprehensible condescension of God! Oh, the unspeakable dignity of man! "For indeed He does not give aid to angels, but He does give aid to the seed of Abraham" (Heb 2:16). "O hear this, all ye nations; take heed, all ye that dwell in the world; High and low, rich and poor, one with another" (Ps 48:2, 3).

Listen, God Himself came to us, He came in our form, He became like unto people and mercifully visited us. Come, let us meet Him, and worship Him, and render glory to God, Who came to us. "Blessed is the Lord God of Israel, For He has visited and redeemed His people, and has raised up a horn of salvation for us In the house of His servant David" (Luke 1:68–69). "Praise the Lord, O my soul; While I live will I praise the Lord; I will sing unto my God as long as I have being" (Ps 145:1–2). "I hymn You, Lord, I have heard Your report and was afraid" (Hab 3:2). He came to me, seeking me, the lost one. It is for just this reason that I glorify Your great condescension to me, O greatly merciful One!

We see in the holy Gospel that they sought the Son of God as a Child in order to kill Him and, evading the hands of evildoers, He fled into Egypt with His holy Mother and hid there for a certain time. We see that the iniquitous King Herod, wishing and seeking to kill the innocent Jesus, Who had come to save the world, directed himself in his anger to the killing of innocent children who were in Bethlehem and in all its districts (Matt 2:16) and killed, according to Church tradition, 14,000 children, intending thereby to kill the new-born infant, Jesus, King of the Jews, along with the other innocents. But the iniquitous murderer did not succeed in accomplishing this. The infants suffered from the murderer and were crowned as martyrs. And Jesus, saved by God's counsel, was carried away by His holy Mother into Egypt. And so, still as an infant, the Lord was a stranger in a foreign land and stayed there until his return to the land of Israel (see Matt 2:13–18).

Note, Christian:

(1) What love of power does? Herod, fearing loss of his royal dignity, hunted after the innocent, newly born Jesus, King of the Jews, and in so doing, killed so many thousands of innocent infants. Oh, what a great and terrible evil is love of power! The power-loving and iniquitous king did not fear spilling so much innocent blood. Why? In order not to be deprived of his dignity. Even now we see this evil in the world. Love of power does not fear raising its sword against monarchs and staining their purple robes with blood, and otherwise to kill God's anointed ones and to create serious disorders and confusion in society. The king has as many enemies as there are power-loving hearts surrounding him, although they flatter him.

(2) The Son of God, evading misfortune and death, gives us a model not to give oneself up voluntarily into misfortune but to avoid it. He could have secured Himself even where they sought Him to kill Him, but He fled into

Egypt, into a foreign country, teaching us, that we, if they persecute us *in one city*, should flee "to another" (Matt 10:23).

(3) Christ, the Son of God, as soon as He was born on the earth, began to endure persecution. From this, we see that He began from His very birth to bear the cross for the sake of our salvation. He, Who created the whole world and all that is in it, was born in a cave and lay in a manger. He, in Whose hands are the life and death of all, fled, pursued by the murderer. Human pride should be ashamed, wanting and seeking as it does to take its repose in rich and beautiful palaces, to live in the riches and glory of this world, and not to bear hearing a contrary word. It should be ashamed, I say, when it looks at the Heavenly King, who was born in a cave and rested in a manger and gave place to the anger of the iniquitous king and yielded to him.

Tell me, please, tell me, Christian, could not Christ the Heavenly King have had a glorious and magnificent place for His Nativity in the flesh and repose? How could He not? He is the Lord of all. Both heaven and earth and all that are therein are His. But He chose a cave, as a beautiful palace, and a manger, as a sumptuous couch, in order to teach us by His example not to seek riches and glory in this world, but to be strangers and pilgrims in a foreign land (Heb 11:13) and to seek a heavenly country (Heb 11:14–16) for which we were created.

Poor is that Christian who seeks much in this world and stores them up for future use. This is an undoubted sign that he only desires and seeks that which he sees, but he does not desire and does not seek what he does not see. Christ could have not only kept Himself safe from the iniquitous murderers but could have struck them with Divine power and His righteous judgment, but He did not desire this. "For the Son of Man did not come to destroy men's lives but to save them" (Luke 9:56). Because of this, He evaded and fled from His enemies and thus gave us an example to withdraw from anger and to yield to those who hate us and offend us. The King of Glory and the all-powerful Lord yielded. What shall we, humble, poor, and feeble, do? Shall we, who are worthy of every punishment, take revenge? And revenge is not our work, but God's. "Vengeance is Mine, I will repay," says the Lord (Rom 12:19).

From this, we see that the world, blinded by delusion, hates true Christians, just as it did not love the Christ of Truth. No sooner had Christ the Lord appeared on earth from heaven, than He began to endure persecution from the evil world: in the same way the world will persecute with hatred whoever begins to come to Christ and draw near to Him in faith and love and does not accept him as its own but ostracizes him. The pious soul seems an enemy and miscreant in the eyes of the impious, although he does and thinks no evil to them at all. But the one thing they do not like is that a righteous person avoids their follies and by his holy life reveals their malice like a lamp and exposes the darkness. And this is what the Lord speaks of: "you will be hated by all for My name's sake" (Matt 10:22). And the Apostle Paul wrote, "all who desire to live godly in Christ Jesus will suffer persecution" (2 Tim 3:12).

Pious soul, do not, however, be confused by this; do not be despondent; and do not fear. Without God's counsel, nothing will happen to us. God permits sorrows for the pious, but He permits them in such measure that they can bear, and permits for great benefit to them, and does not leave them, being His children, without consolation, which is for them like cooling during intense hot weather.

Indeed, "[m]any are the troubles of the righteous" (Ps 33:20). But the impious have many more, especially in view of their eternal torment in hell. Although they run wild here, there they will taste the fruits of their pride and impiety. But even here they live in every kind of agitation and upheaval: they defraud one another; they despoil one another; they complain against, vilify, and swear at each other, and fill the courts with contrived and truculent complaints. What can we expect in such cases and circumstances, except confusion and trouble? And if we look into their conscience, what else is going on there, but constant judgment, condemnation, upheaval, and torment? A bad conscience offends more than any sorrow and torments a person more than any torturer. The impious flourish externally in their prosperity, but within they are like worm-eaten flowers. On the other hand, the pious, although they may be troubled externally, are calm, peaceful, and quiet. They are comforted here and will be comforted most abundantly and eternally in the age to come.

(5) We see in the holy Gospel that it is written of those who sought the infant Jesus to kill him, "Those who sought the young Child's life are dead" (Matt 2:20). Thus the judgment of God overtakes all those who vex and persecute the pious. Pious souls, like sheep, are humble, meek, and defenseless, but God stands up for them and protects them and humbles the self-willed and impious. From this, we see that God's wondrous judgments will overtake them, and they will fall into a ditch where they do not expect, and they are preparing for themselves the pit that they are digging for the pious. Thus Absalom, the son of David, sought to kill his holy father and to seize the kingdom of Israel, but instead of this, he found his own ruin (see 2 Kgs 15:1–18).

Haman had prepared a gallows for the innocent Mordecai, but he himself was hanged on the same gallows (see Esth 3:1–7, 10). Pharaoh, the king of Egypt, was closely pursuing Israel and wanted to again vex it with his tyranny but learned the righteous judgment of God and drowned in the sea with his whole army (see Exod 14:5–30). A similar judgment of God is even now overtaking all those who are self-willed, who vex and persecute the pious.

We see in the holy Gospel that Jesus Christ, the Son of God, *grew in the flesh,* which He assumed from the most-pure Virgin Theotokos (Luke 1:80; actually 2:40) like other people and, attaining maturity, "was baptized" (Mark 1:9) in the waters of the Jordan, sanctifying the waters by His touch, and instituting the Mystery of our saving baptism and the mystical washing of our regeneration (Titus 3:5), by which we, the defiled ones, are washed, and we who are dead are given life, and we who have perished are saved, and we who are decrepit and decayed are renewed, and we who are separated from God return again to God and join ourselves to Him, are reconciled with Him, and become inheritors of His eternal kingdom.

We see in His holy Gospel that Jesus Christ, after His baptism, was led up by the Spirit into the wilderness (Matt 4:1), "was tempted by Satan" (Mark 1:13), and defeated the tempter. From this you see, Christian, that everyone who is born of water and the Spirit, that is every Christian, awaits temptation by the devil and, with it, constant struggle. If the artful spirit dared to tempt Christ, the Son of God, will he really leave Christians alone? Christ the Lord gave Himself to us as a model in all things. He was tempted by Satan; we must be tempted. He defeated the tempter by His power; we must defeat the enemy by His power. Christians were called not to operas and luxurious banquets but to warfare and spiritual struggle, and struggle not against flesh and blood, but against the devil and his evil spirits. "For we do not wrestle against flesh and blood, but against principalities, against powers, against the rulers of the darkness of this age, against spiritual hosts of wickedness in the heavenly places" (Eph 6:12).

This battle begins well if our eye is watchful (see Matt 6:22–24). A battle with humans is difficult, but it is much harder to fight with the malicious spirits. They see us and they take note of what we do and say, but we do not see them. They try to take from us not cities, not objectives, not perishable treasure, but eternal salvation, which Christ the Son of God obtained for us by His precious blood and death. They try to snatch this priceless treasure away from us and take pains toward this day and night. They tempt us when we are awake, they tempt us too as we sleep, they set snares by day, and they set snares at night.

Christians! We too need to be watchful if we wish to save ourselves and not be their captives. They find their weapons within us ourselves. They fight us with our own passions and lusts. Whoever wishes to fight successfully against these enemies has no time to seek riches, honor, and glory in this world. And if someone, having abandoned the heavenly, thinks about the earthly, he does not please God, but the world and his own fancies; this is a sure sign that he is their captive. Such a person is defeated and held captive. Every fornicator, adulterer, and lover of impurity is held captive; the thief, extortioner, and robber is held captive; the sorcerer and he who summons him, the liar, cheat, and tempter are held captive; the slanderer, the name-caller, and the back-biter are held captive; every transgressor, who fearlessly breaks God's law, is held captive. Ah! He is held captive, and his enemy will lead him away after him into eternal perdition, if he is not delivered from his tyranny and does not flee to Christ with repentance and remorse.

You are poor, Christian, who works for the world and sin. Take stock of yourself and learn the delusion of the soul-destroying enemy and your ruination. The whims of this world amuse you, but they hold your soul captive. These are the devil's snares, in which not the bodies but the souls of Christians are caught. Sin seems sweet to you, but its fruit is bitter: the captivity and death of the soul: "For the wages of sin is death" (Rom 6:23). You are careful lest some tyrant and barbarian, who takes captive only the body, and not the soul, might take you captive. So much the more should you take care lest you be taken captive by this tyrant, who takes both the soul and body captive. Therefore the Apostle exhorts us, "Be sober, be vigilant; because your adversary the devil walks about like a roaring lion, seeking whom he may devour. Resist him, steadfast in the faith" (1 Pet 5:8–9). And again, "Submit to God. Resist the devil and he will flee from you" (Jas 4:7). And again, "Be strong in the Lord and in the power of His might. Put on the whole armor of God, that you may be able to stand against the wiles of the devil" (Eph 6:10–11). The Apostles and messengers of our Saviour Jesus Christ arm us in this way against this enemy and his evil spirits. Beware, beloved Christian, of this enemy and his evil spirits. They move invisibly around us, and shoot first one, then another arrow at us, and spread their nets under our feet, and try to bring us down and take us captive. Beware and stand firm, but do not become despondent because God stands for us, "at *Whose* Name … they tremble" (Mark 16:17; Jas 2:19). You should just stand armed with faith, take care, be strong, make an effort, pray, and call upon the name of the Lord in time of need, and His help will come to you in time. "If God is for us, who can be against us" (Rom 8:31)? "Thou, O God, art my defender and Thy mercy shall go before me. Thou art my helper; unto Thee will I sing, for Thou, O God, art my defender, and my merciful God" (Ps 58:10–11 and 18).

We see in the holy Gospel that our Lord Jesus Christ, after the temptations from the evil spirit, "began to preach the Holy Gospel" (Matt 4:17), which He brought to earth from His Heavenly Father. And, having gathered twelve disciples, whom He called Apostles, He went with them from place to place and from city to city and preached the Gospel of the kingdom of God and sowed the salvific seed of God's Word in the soil of human hearts. And He taught all to know His Heavenly Father, and to please Him by faith and righteousness, and to do His holy will. He served as a model for all and so taught all a heavenly and holy life. He was a visible image of the deepest humility, of the warmest love for His Heavenly Father and all people, of compassionate mercy for the poor, of inscrutable meekness and long-suffering to detractors and enemies and of other most sweet and divine demeanors, which manifestly shows that He was not simply a man, but the Son of God and incarnate God, and appeared in human form, and Who walked the earth. All God's goodness and love for mankind that is depicted in all the Sacred Scripture, we see depicted in Him, as in the living image of the invisible God.

Do you desire, Christian, to see God's heart and His most blessed nature? Look at Christ, His only-begotten Son. Do you desire to see Christ's nature and His heart? Read His holy Gospel, pay attention to it, and it will show them to you. "This is our God; no other shall be compared to Him" (Bar 3:36). And, behold, He appeared on earth and lived with people. "Thy goings were seen, O God" (Ps 67:25). They saw "Thy going and Thy coming in" (Ps 120:8). They saw Your treatment of sinners, whom You had come to seek and to save. They saw that You, Who gives food to all flesh, ate and drank, as a man. They saw that You, Who are unapproachable for the cherubim and seraphim, were accessible to sinners. They saw Your human eyes, on which the ranks of angels dare not gaze. Your voice was heard, as the voice of the Son of God, as the only-begotten of the Father and our incarnate God. "Full of grace are Thy lips" (Ps 44:3). They saw Your most glorious works that you did on earth. They saw Your divine and beautiful virtues that You showed and left for us poor sinners.

Oh, blessed time, in which the Sun of righteousness dwelt on earth! "The people who sat in darkness have seen a great light, And upon those who sat in the region and shadow of death Light has dawned" (Matt 4:16). Blessed are the eyes that have seen God in human form! Blessed are the ears that have heard the voice of the Son of God and the Heavenly King, Who have appeared on earth! The prophets the righteous and the kings wished to see this and did not see it; they wanted to hear it but did not hear it.

Christians! Blessed are we that see His image, depicted in the Gospel, and hear His voice in that same Gospel, and confess and call upon His name, and mystically commune His most pure Body and life-giving Blood. We shall fervently imitate His beautiful virtues, which He left for us for this. May we follow God, Who for our sake appeared and walked the earth in human form. Let us love His humility, love, mercy, meekness, patience, and most sweet nature. "I am the light of the world. He who follows Me shall not walk in darkness, but have the light of life" (John 8:12). This is how He calls us to follow Him closely. If we follow Him closely and love His most good nature, we shall not walk in the darkness but shall be enlightened by His light. But if we do not follow Him, but follow our own whims, we shall without fail dwell in darkness. He abides in darkness who withdraws from the light, and he abides in death who separates himself from life. "For lo, they that go far from Thee shall perish; Thou hast destroyed all them that are unfaithful against Thee. But it is good for me to cleave unto God" (Ps 72:27–28).

We see in the holy Gospel that our Lord labored and troubled Himself for the sake of our salvation and, preaching the Gospel of the kingdom and so accomplishing the work of our salvation, went on foot from city to city and to various places. Oh, the great miracle! The all-powerful and Almighty labored and took trouble, and He that sits on the throne of His glory walked on the earth on foot. Poor sinner! The Lord so condescended for your sake. "Bless the Lord, O my soul" (Ps 102:1). Let us, Your worthless servants and sinners, hymn and worship Your ineffable love for mankind and condescension, O Lord. Our sin is overabundant in Your sight, but Your love for mankind and goodness toward us, who have sinned against you, have prevailed.

From this, we learn, Christian:

(1) To live not in idleness but in good endeavors. Many Christians, inasmuch as they have bread, do not want to set about any work but live in idleness and exercise themselves in useless and idle conversations or constantly take strolls and spend time in going on visits. Such idleness teaches them every

evil. Such lovers of idleness and parasites constantly sin against God, Who says, "In the sweat of your face you shall eat bread" (Gen 3:19). It is shameful for sinners to idle away their time when the Lord Himself labored for their sake.

(2) To live not in the opulence and pride of this world but in humility. Many Christians do not wish to ride except with a team of horses harnessed in tandem and in high, rich, gilded English carriages. This is their splendor and pride. Let they themselves see and reason how far they are from Christ, who went from place to place on foot. May human pride be ashamed and its exalted horn be lowered when the Heavenly King and Lord of glory lived in such humility on the earth.

Poor man! Look on His humility and, setting aside your pride, humble yourself, if you wish to follow Him into eternal life. "Narrow is the gate and difficult is the way which leads to life" (Matt 7:14). It is impossible to enter there with a tandem team and wide carriage. We must lay aside all this splendor and pride and follow Christ in humility. Not by luxury, but tribulations, and moreover, "many tribulations do we enter the kingdom of God" (Acts 14:22).

We see in the holy Gospel that Christ the Lord, while living on earth, had nowhere to lay His head, as He Himself testifies: "Foxes have holes and birds of the air have nests, but the Son of Man has nowhere to lay His head" (Matt 8:20).

From this you see, Christian:

(1) Christ's life on earth as one of great poverty. He Who created the earth and all that is therein did not have a place to lay His head. As the Lord of all, He could have had everything, but He did not have His own home, He did not have a place to lay His head. Thus He humbled Himself; thus He who is so rich in mercy was reduced to poverty for our sake. Wonderful is His humility, marvelous too is His poverty, as is He Himself, Who is over all the eternally blessed God (Rom 9:5).

(2) From this we too learn not to desire and not to seek in this world riches and palatial houses but to be content in whatever state we are, and with what God in His mercy gave us (Phil 4:11; 1 Tim 6:6–8). Many Christians of the present age so try to accumulate that they would be glad if all the treasure of this world were to fall into their hands. They are not satisfied with many thousands but keep accumulating more and more and multiply their treasures. They are not satisfied with the land that belongs to them but keep expanding

it more and more and name the land after themselves. They are not satisfied with the houses of their ancestors but only constantly devise, and enlarge, and heighten, and decorate magnificently new ones. This is opulence and pride, and the cause of all evil, covetousness. They themselves see that their life is contrary to Christ, Who was poor and did not have a place to lay His head.

Poor man! Why are you "worried and troubled about many things" (Luke 10:41)? Everything that you accumulate and however much you accumulate, you will leave in this world. Why do you expand your lands? Look to your future, and you will see that they are already digging a hole six feet deep. Why are you enlarging your house? For soon you will move into a six-foot grave, which is being prepared for you. Look at it and you will see that all your plans and undertakings are in vain. Remember that you are a wanderer and wayfarer on the earth: why should a wanderer and wayfarer store up so much and so uselessly burden himself? The Lord Jesus teaches you with His example. Look at Him and come to moderation. Christ does not lead us astray but teaches us the truth.

Look upon those who lived before us and accumulated much: they left everything here and departed for the next world with nothing. They dwell now in their places and await the general resurrection and God's judgment. Only they are there, and all their treasure remained here. Now they see that everything that they had here was not even theirs, and they know that they chased after nothing other than a shadow and the wind. The same will happen with you. And you will leave everything, and you will follow after them, and you will see that everything for which you now seek and which you accumulate is not yours. Blessed and wise is he who learns from another's misfortune to act prudently. Look at the dead, and your death, and your grave, which is already being prepared for you, and you do not know when death will put you into it, and abandon vanity, before it deserts you. Not much is needed for our nature: it is satisfied with food, and clothing, and a hut. But desire wants many things and seeks luxury. Even a whole kingdom is not enough for it. It can never be satisfied, as how a fever in a sick person cannot be relieved, however much he may drink. Get to know lust, and natural need, and act according to the requirement of nature and not according to the desire of lust.

Beloved Christian! Remember and take stock of yourself, that you are a Christian, and not an idolater. Christians look for the resurrection of the dead and the life of the age to come, and you should raise up your heart to there. He who wishes to be resurrected later into eternal life must be resurrected in the soul here. Many Christians say each day: "I look for the resurrection of the dead" (Symbol of Faith), but are so closely linked to the vanity of the world and live as if there will not even be a resurrection of the dead. And perhaps, they even imagine this and tell fables. But let them imagine as they wish and speak of what they wish. It will take place without fail, only not to their benefit but to their shame and eternal reproach. When this comes true for themselves they will learn that the Word of God, which preaches the resurrection of the dead, is true. "[They shall] come forth—those who have done good, to the resurrection of life, and those who have done evil, to the resurrection of condemnation" (John 5:29).

You should avoid such Epicureans as you would the plague and confess that the inheritance for Christian, riches, honor, glory, and all blessedness are not here, not in this world, but in "the life of the age to come" (Symbol of Faith), as their homeland and home are there. The Heavenly Father has prepared for them all good things, and "Eye has not seen, nor ear heard, Nor have entered into the heart of man The things which God has prepared for those who love Him" (1 Cor 2:9). True Christians seek to receive only those good things and do not care over the worldly ones; they are satisfied with what they have, according to the teaching of the Apostle, "For we brought nothing into this world, and it is certain we can carry nothing out. And having food and clothing, with these we shall be content" (1 Tim 6:7–8).

Follow the example of this holy fellowship and follow them, or better, Christ, who was poor in this world and did not have anywhere to lay His head, even though He has the whole world, both heaven and earth, and all that is in them, in His hands. Plant deep in our memory the exhortation of the Apostle: "Set your mind on things above, not on things on the earth" (Col 3:2). This was said to all Christians who wish to be true, and not false, Christians. But do not look on those who constantly accumulate wealth and fulfill their whims and show off their frivolities in the increase of wealth, and in the seeking of honor and glory, and in the enlarging and decoration of houses, in the arrangement of horses and carriages, and in the fabrication of new clothing, and in the presentation of various repasts that serve sensuality, and in other ways. Such people have moved far from Christ and from His holy Word. And it is obvious that they, like animals, only desire and seek that which they see, and what they do not see, they do not seek. A veil lies over their hearts, like a haze, which conceals eternal salvation from them. Therefore, they pursue the shadow rather than the truth.

We see in the holy Gospel that people of both sexes went in great numbers after Christ, God Who appeared on earth and went about in human form, either to hear His holy Word or wishing to be cured of their ailments. And when they did not have food in the desert, He fed them in a miraculous way so that "many thousands were filled by five loaves, and the remaining fragments were collected into twelve baskets" (Matt 14:14–21; 15:32–38). He who created heaven and earth and everything from nothing, having appeared in the form of a man, was here and multiplied the loaves. The good shepherd appeared on earth. "It was never seen like this in Israel!" (Matt 9:33). The lost sheep recognized their Shepherd and heard His voice calling them and ran to Him. His divine power drew them to Him. They left homes, and property, and occupations, and ran to the new and unprecedented preacher and wonderworker Who had appeared. "It was never seen like this in Israel! No man ever spoke like Jesus!" (Matt 9:33; John 7:46).

As He Himself was from heaven, so also His Word was heavenly; He had the words of eternal life (John 6:68). Christian, let us too follow Christ, not with our feet, but with our hearts and a change of our ways. And let us hear His Words within us; He will nourish us, who hunger in the desert of this world, not with perishable bread, but with that which is imperishable, sent from His heavenly table. This bread will strengthen and console not our body but our soul. We see in the holy Gospel that all the poor who would approach Him with supplication and faith received what they desired. Lepers came and were cleansed, the blind came and recovered their sight, the lame came and were healed. He also healed the paralytic, raised the dead, delivered the possessed from the tyranny of the demons, gave hearing to the deaf, loosed the tongues of the dumb, and performed other remarkable and supernatural miracles.

From this, we see the following:

(1) He is that Messiah and redeemer of the world, Who was to appear on the earth, Who was promised by God, and preached of by all the prophets, and Who was expected by all the faithful. He appeared on earth, and God's wondrous works were manifested. The people saw works that a human hand could not perform. The blind began to see and the lame to walk, the lepers to be cleansed, and the deaf to hear, the dead to rise and the poor to hear the preaching of the good news with consolations and joy. And these miracles pointed out like a finger that this was that glorious wonderworker Whom the prophets foretold to the world. He appeared then and performed miracles. Therefore, the peoples, having seen His extraordinary and fearsome works,

exclaimed with great amazement: "We have seen strange things today!" (Luke 5:26), "It was never seen like this in Israel!" (Matt 9:33).

Indeed, it was never seen like this in Israel because God had never appeared like this in Israel. Previously, God had appeared in Israel in various forms, but this time God appeared in human form. Previously, God had performed wonders through prophets and His chosen servants, but this time He Himself worked miracles by His Word. Previously, He had spoken through the prophets, but this time, He Himself spoke in person. Indeed, *it was never seen like this in Israel!*

(2) Christ the Lord healed all who came to Him in faith. Christian! Let us too go to the heavenly physician, Jesus, with faith. He is our true and faithful physician. Let us entrust ourselves to Him; let Him heal us, as He wills, since we too are poor and infirm, and no one but He can heal.

We are blind. The mind is blind in the knowledge of God and His holy will, in the knowledge of truth and falsehood, faith and superstition, virtues and vices, good and evil, benefit and harm, and so on. Let us too cry to Him from the depths of our hearts, as the blind men cried to Him: "Have mercy on us, O Lord, Son of David!" (Matt 20:30).

We are deaf. Sin made us deaf; we cannot hear God's most sweet words. Jesus, Son of God! Open the ears (Mark 7:35) of our souls, that we may hear Your words, the words of eternal life.

We are not lepers in body but in soul. Sin is a fearful leprosy and foul in God's eyes. Let us lift up our voice to Him along with the lepers: "Jesus, Master, have mercy on us!" (Luke 17:13).

"Our souls are severely demon-possessed" (Matt 15:22). Sin is similar to a powerful and evil demon. Pride is a savage demon, anger and wrath are savage demons, greed is a savage demon, envy is a savage demon, impurity is a savage demon, cruelty and unmercifulness is a savage demon, hatred is a savage demon, and so on. These demons torment not our bodies but our souls. Let us, like the woman of Canaan, importunately call to Jesus, "Have mercy on me, O Lord, Son of David!" (ibidem). And although He may tarry in granting what we ask, let us not cease knocking at the door of His mercy, saying, "Lord, help me!" (Matt 15:21–28).

As we see in the Gospel, all the poor who came to Him received mercy from Him, and we shall receive it, too. He healed those sick in body—the more so will He heal immortal souls. He had mercy on needs of the body, so much the more will He have mercy on needs of the soul. He does not have compassion on affliction of the body as much as affliction of our souls. The soul is much more precious to Him than the body. He Himself exhorts us to ask for this, "Ask, and it will be given to you; seek, and you will find; knock, and it will be opened to you" (Matt 7:7). "Come unto Him, and be enlightened, and your faces shall not be ashamed," His prophet exhorts us (Ps 33:6).

(3) Christ did not refuse any of the poor. Let us not refuse any of those who ask of us, according to His Word: "Give to him who asks you" (Matt 5:42). Let us not refuse to give what we can, and so let us follow Him in this. If someone asks us for bread, let us give him bread.

If he asks for drink, let us give him drink.

If he asks for clothing, let us give him clothing.

If he asks for money, let us give it.

If he asks for lodging and rest in our house, let us give it.

If he asks for help and protection, let us give it.

If he asks for advice and instruction, let us give it.

If he asks for consolation, let us give it

If he asks for deliverance, let us give it.

If he asks for a kindness, let us give it.

If he asks for anything else in accordance with God's will and out abilities, let us give it. Our Christ requires this of us, Christian!

He does not require of us that we work miracles—this is God's work, and not ours, and it is impossible for us, for it is above our powers. But He does require that we love one another, and have mercy on one another, and offer each other a helping hand. Both the bond of Christianity and His holy will desires this, and we shall get great benefit from this. "The one who has mercy on the poor lends to God, and He will repay him according to his gift" (Prov 19:17; see also Ps 40:2–4; Matt 10:42; 25:40). What can be more excellent than to give the Lord a loan, and what can be more beneficial than to give into the hands of Him Who has everything in His hands and Who will repay with great gain to him who gives? Oh, the goodness and love for mankind of God! Christians, we receive from Him all that we have or can have. But His holy Word says, "The one who has mercy on the poor lends to God." He thus encourages us to love and mercy, so that the poor, with whom He, as a Father Who loves His children, is compassionate, would receive their consolation in their sorrows, and those who have mercy on them and lend them a helping hand would not lose their reward. May God, being all-powerful, open His treasuries, and with His invisible hand give what is needed to the poor, and so fulfill their desires. But He presents them to our eyes, points to them, and commands us to have mercy on them, and He Himself promises for them to repay us, so that the poor whom He, being merciful, has pity on may not remain without satisfaction, and we would receive a hundred-fold reward from Him.

Beloved Christian, let us show mercy to our neighbors and grant everyone his request, that we may hear from Christ the Lord the sweet voice before the whole world: "Come, you blessed of My Father, inherit the kingdom prepared for you from the foundation of the world: for I was hungry and you gave Me food; I was thirsty and you gave Me drink; I was a stranger and you took Me in; I was naked and you clothed Me; I was sick and you visited Me; I was in prison and you came to Me" (Matt 25:34–36).

(4) Those Christians who do not have mercy and compassion on the poor and who do not extend to them a helping hand in need but waste their resources on frivolities and luxury are lacking a Christian heart and disposition and stand far from Christ. Such Christians begrudge for Christ's sake to clothe a naked man, or build a hut for someone who does not have a house, or give a little money to one who asks for a great need, and so on. But they do not skimp for frivolity and luxury, for dowries for daughters and inheritances for sons, and for earning honor, and so on, they do not begrudge, I say, many hundreds or thousands. Such is their faith! Such is their Christianity! They begrudge giving for the sake of Christ, but for the sake of frivolity and the vanity of the world, and for the sake of flesh and blood, they do not begrudge any outlay. Whoever loves something or someone spares nothing for that person or thing, and does everything for his, hers, or its sake, whatever is needed. This is an undoubted sign that these Christians love the world, flesh and blood, and not Christ, even though He died for them. Therefore, they will hear his fearsome voice before the whole world: "Depart from Me, you cursed, into the everlasting fire prepared for the devil and his angels: for I was hungry and you gave Me no food; I was thirsty and you gave Me no drink; I was a stranger and you did not take Me in, naked and you did not clothe Me, sick and in prison and you did not visit Me" (Matt 25:41–43).

(5) The worst and most corrupt nature is in those Christians who take and extort property from other Christians. Among these are lawless judges, who judge according to payment, and not according to justice, and make the poor shed tears. Among them are landowners who burden their peasants either by quit-rents or excessive chores, and take away from them what is necessary for their sustenance and upkeep. Among them are gentlemen in

positions of power who do not give their subordinates the salary appointed by the Sovereign or give them only a portion. Among them are those unscrupulous people, who loot after a fire and add even more grief to the grief-stricken owner. Among them are merchants who cheat their customers and instead of the proper price demand a higher price. Among them are hired help who, having taken sufficient pay for their labors, do not work for it or work lackadaisically. And among them are proprietors who hire people to work but do not pay them or pay only a portion. Finally, among them are thieves, extortioners, and robbers, who in some manner appropriate someone else's property for themselves or swindle it, and so on. All of them and their like have a corrupt nature and are far from Christ, and to tell the truth, are Christ's enemies and are against Him. "He who is not with Me is against Me, and he who does not gather with Me scatters abroad" (Matt 12:30). Such people are not with Christ, "For what fellowship has righteousness with lawlessness? And what communion has light with darkness" (2 Cor 6:14)? They are against Christ. This saying is terrible, Christian, but true. Their judgment will be terrible, too. If those who do not give are sent to fiery Gehenna, then what will happen to those who steal? Poor Christian! Repent, lest you burn like matter in fiery Gehenna, but never be consumed.

We see in the holy Gospel that Christ the Lord entered the houses of the people who invited Him and ate with them. Oh, blessed are those houses that the Heavenly King visited and, He "Who giveth food to all flesh" (Ps 135:25), ate food in them! People consider it good fortune to receive an earthly king in their house. What an indescribably greater good fortune is it to receive the Heavenly King in one's house! Those who received Christ then in their houses only thought of Him that He was a prophet, a famous teacher and wonderworker, but did not know that He is the Lord of prophets, although the light of His Divinity was demonstrated like the sun from its rays by various miracles and His wonderful works, and His omniscience, and His authority, and other things. Oh, if only they knew that the Guest Whom they received is the true God, walking in human form on the earth, they would have received Him with great fear and unspeakable joy. But this Divine and eternal light was hidden from them then.

Christians! That light shined for us by the grace of God. We now believe and know that Christ is our Lord and God, Who came into the world to save sinners. Let us repent and turn to Him. Let us open the houses of our hearts and with humility invite Him to come to us, that He will visit us also, humble and sinful. Although we do not see Him, He even now abides among His faithful and visits them in His love for mankind, according to His promise: "Lo, I am with you always, even to the end of the age" (Matt 28:20). He, as we see in the Gospel, did not have an aversion to anyone who called Him to himself. He will not disdain us either, as the Lover of mankind, if we cleanse our houses by repentance and invite Him with humility. But He is ready and glad to come to us, if only He sees a welcome place for Him in us, for He Himself speaks thus: "Behold, I stand at the door and knock. If anyone hears My voice and opens the door, I will come in to him and dine with him, and he with Me" (Rev 3:20).

The guest is great and glorious, gracious and gladdening, being God. He will not demand of us a festal table or food and drink. He Himself will lay a table for us, not the kind of table that people present but a table that strengthens, consoles, gladdens our souls and has the sweetness of eternal life. At this most sweet supper, we shall partly taste the sweetness of the heavenly table, which His holy angels taste. Let us cleanse the houses, our hearts, by true repentance and drive out the noise of the varied cares and frivolities of this world, that we may hear His most sweet voice at our doors, and let us open the doors to Him, and so, the glorious Guest will come to us.

O Lord, sweetest Jesus, Shepherd and Visitor of our souls! Do not pass by me, Your poor and wretched servant, but in your love for mankind visit my humble soul, visit that sinner for whose sake You shed your precious blood and endured the death of the Cross. "My heart is ready, O God, my heart is ready" (Ps 56:8).

We see in the holy Gospel that Jesus was available even to sinners. "All the tax collectors and the sinners drew near to Him to hear Him" (Luke 15:1). And He did not disdain to sit and eat bread with them. "As Jesus sat at the table in the house, ... many tax collectors and sinners came and sat down with Him and His disciples" (Matt 9:10).

We see from this, Christian, that:

(1) He Who is unapproachable to the cherubim and seraphim, and is worshipped and hymned by them with fear and reverence, and Who "dwell[s] in unapproachable light" (1 Tim 6:16), became available to public sinners. Oh, your goodness and love for mankind, Jesus our God! Glory to Your goodness, glory to your love for mankind, glory to Your munificence, glory to Your condescension! Here indeed it is timely to be amazed with the prophet and to exclaim, "Lord, what is man, that Thou hast had such respect unto him? Or the son of man, that Thou so regardest him" (Ps 143:3)?

Listen, sinners, and understand! The great and incomprehensible God, in His love for mankind, became accessible for us, so that *all the tax collectors and the sinners drew near to Him.* The sinners got to know their Saviour, the infirm got to know their Physician, the lost sheep got to know their good Shepherd, those sitting in darkness got to know their Light, those perishing got to know their Life, the poor got to know their Blessedness, and *drew near to Him.* His divine power, and the man-loving appearance of His holy face, and His heavenly and most sweet holy speech attracted them. In Christ was seen only humility, meekness, long-suffering, mercy, compassion, and love for mankind.

"Sinners, why are we slumbering, why are we tarrying, why do we not also coming to Christ? Why do we abide in darkness? Why are we not drawing near to that Light? Why do we remain unhealed and do not seek healing from the heavenly Physician? Well, then, let us draw near to Him with daring and faith, and [our] faces shall not be ashamed" (Ps 33:6).

(2) From this it can be seen in actual fact that "This is a faithful saying and worthy of all acceptance, that Christ Jesus came into the world to save sinners" (1 Tim 1:15), "The Son of Man has come to seek and to save that which was lost" (Luke 19:10). Jesus Christ came to save sinners, and He became accessible to sinners. But sinners also need to pay attention to what He says: "Repent," and also, "I did not come to call the righteous, but sinners, to repentance" (Matt 4:17; 9:13). Sinners must repent and correct themselves, and then Christ will save them.

(3) Consolation flows from this to sinners who are in a state of true repentance. If He came to save sinners, then this includes you, inasmuch as you are one of the sinners. If He came to seek out the perishing, then He will seek you out, inasmuch as you are one of the perishing.

(4) We see that true holiness does not abhor any sinners. A truly holy person hates sin, and not sinners; he abhors sins, and not sinners. The scribes and Pharisees, haughty in their sham holiness, abhorred sinners, and therefore they reproached the Apostles, "Why does your Teacher eat with tax collectors and sinners" (Matt 9:11)? But Christ, the Holiest of Holies and the Source of holiness, did not abhor any sinners. He is emulated by His holy servants, who are repelled by sin, but not by the sinners; they hate the sins, but have pity and compassion for the sinners. May haughty Pharisaical pride, which abhors sinners like oneself, be put to shame!

(5) This teaches pastors how to deal with sinners and to lead them in any way to repentance but not to participate in their sins. The pastor's concern is to seek the lost sheep. And good physicians are most often found where the

sick are. "Those who are well have no need of a physician, but those who are sick" (Matt 9:12).

(6) This teaches masters, princes, lords, those in authority, and others of the renowned of this world, and all Christians not to abhor, despise, or disparage any person, even the most vile. Christ, the King of kings and Lord of Lords, abhorred no one and despised no one. So much the more should people, however renowned in the world they may be, not abhor people like themselves.

We are all people; we all have an identical nature; all the high-born have the same soul and body as the low-born. And it often happens, and even for the most part, that those of a low station are more upright with God than one of exalted station, and a servant and peasant are better in the eyes of God than his master, prince, and lord. For human dignity and integrity are judged not by the glitter of gold and silver, not by name and title of this world, but by the integrity of the soul and the dignity of virtue. And God judges by what is inside, not by what is on the outside. One pious and God-fearing person is better and dearer to God than thousands of impious, although they lived and were revered in this world like gods. May all Christians look to Christ, their Lord, a living image of humility and condescension and may they follow Him in all things and not despise anyone.

(7) This denounces the demonic pride of those masters, princes, and lords who consider their servants and peasants as footstools, and even lower than their dogs, and those rich people who despise the poor and wretched. "How can he who is earth and ashes be arrogant" (Sir 10:9)? Why does a sinner despise a sinner? Why does a poor man abhor a poor man? All people are equal, although not have equal good fortune in this world. Princes, lords, masters, and renowned people! Look at the graves of your ancestors, and you yourselves will learn that truth, that all people, both renowned and those of low birth, are equal. A characteristic of the noble soul is to pity and sympathize with the poor and sinful man, not to despise and not to abhor him.

We see in the holy Gospel that Christ our Lord innocently endured many reproaches and much abuse while living on earth and endured them from His own people and endured them with all meekness.

You see here, Christian:

(1) God, sitting on His throne of glory and worshipped and revered, both appeared in the flesh for our sake and endured both abuse and reproach from the mouths of sinners. Our sins are at fault for this. For because of our sins

by which we vexed our God, the merciful Jesus, our deliverer, endured every abuse. Oh, the goodness and love for mankind! Let us be grateful to Him for His love for us.

(2) We see that the blinded world does not love righteousness and truth. Christ the Lord, the eternal truth, worked only righteousness and truth, worked everything for the creation of mankind, and taught only righteousness and truth. Therefore, He was hated and abused by the world, which was blinded by delusion. Ailing eyes do not like the light, and unrighteousness hates righteousness, and falsehood hates truth.

(3) From this, it follows that pastors and teachers of the truth and preachers of the heavenly word are subject to hatred, the abuse of evil people, inasmuch as they chastise their malice, delusion, and shady deeds with the light of heavenly teaching. "He who chastises evil men shall receive dishonor to himself" (Pr 9:7). The impious man is pierced by chastisement as by an iron pitchfork. This is testified to by the examples of the prophets, Apostles, and all the faithful hierarchs who lived in ancient times, who all endured persecution and abuse for the Word of God's truth. What can the preachers of truth nowadays expect from this world? If someone is a God-fearing Christian, I advise him not to believe the abuse leveled against pastors and teachers and what is more, to stop the mouths of the abusers. The cunning of the devil is hidden here. He teaches his minions to spread defamation against the preachers of truth, so that people would think badly of them and not believe their word, and thus would perish. This is what the evil spirit strives for, and so defamation and all kinds of slander are leveled at pastors by his counsel. Avoid this, Christians! If you hear someone defaming and leveling slander at a pastor, know for sure that using that person's lips like a tool, the evil spirit is spewing his stench.

(4) All true Christians are subject to such reproach and hatred. We see in ancient history that the pagans thought up and contrived terrible and diverse slanders against the Christians and called them all kinds of defamatory names. This, as we may see, was done through the action of the devil, so that the Christians would depart from the Christian faith, and that idolaters would be afraid to draw near it. But the evil counsel of the evil spirit was scattered by the power of God. The more slanders, reproaches, and persecutions he instigated against the Christians, the more the Christians grew in numbers.

Similar slanders and reproaches are even now being thought up against Christians, no longer by the idolaters, but by false Christian and lovers of this world and its delusions, its opulence, and its pride. Christians endure all sorts of slanders and reproaches from these false brothers; they clothe their insults first in one garb and then in another. And besides the usual, wicked reproaches, they contrive various defamations and mockeries. If they notice that a Christian withdraws from luxury and their shady deeds, then they say he is a "schismatic." If someone lives humbly and hates dandyism, then they say he is a "goody-goody." If he goes into seclusion for the sake of repentance and to avoid sin (for it is easier to repent in seclusion and to guard against sin than among people), then they say he is "sanctimonious." If because of sin, someone repents, is distressed, laments, and sighs, they say he is a "melancholic." If someone gives alms, they say he is "vainglorious" and a "hypocrite." If they learn that a Christian often prays to God, now they open their mouths and think up a nickname: "praying mantis." If a Christian, after the Gospel rule, does not take revenge on someone who offends him, now they descend on him and call him a "fool," saying he doesn't know how to stand up for himself. If, after the rule of the same Gospel, he disperses his property and gives to the poor, now they turn against him and reproach him: he's lost his mind, they say, he is squandering what his ancestors put together. These and other such insults and mockeries are spewed out by impious lips against the soul of the pious. For our consolation, Christ the Lord said concerning this, "If they have called the master of the house Beelzebub, how much more will they call those of his household" (Matt 10:25)! They hated Christ, the Master of the house, and they will also hate Christians, those of His household. They abused Christ and cursed at Christ, the Master of the house, and they will also abuse Christians, those of His house, and will curse at them. They banished Christ, the Master of the house, and they will banish Christians, those of His household. "A servant is not greater than his master" (John 15:20). This is the condition of Christians in the present age!

Christians are not of this world, as Christ Himself says of them: "They are not of the world, just as I am not of the world" (John 17:14). Therefore, the world banishes and vilifies them, as not one of its own. And this is also done by the cunning of the devil in order to lead astray the pious soul. This is an artful fabrication of the evil spirit. But "[s]uffer not thy feet to slip, nor Him that keepeth thee to slumber. Behold, He that keepeth Israel shall neither slumber nor sleep. The Lord Himself shall keep thee; the Lord is thy shelter upon they right hand; The sun shall not burn thee by day, neither the moon by night. The Lord shall keep thee from all evil; yea, the Lord shall preserve thy soul.

The Lord shall preserve thy going out, and thy coming in, from this time forth, and for evermore" (Ps 120:3–8).

(5) It is unseemly for Christians to abuse those who abuse and to reproach those who reproach, for this is contrary to the Christian faith. Therefore they must look at the living example of the meekness of their Lord, Jesus, "Who, when He was reviled, did not revile in return" (1 Pet 2:23), and, "as a lamb is silent before his shearers, so He opens not His mouth" (Isa 53:7). Evil is not overcome by evil, nor is abuse by abuse, but is only exacerbated and grows more savage. And the Christian victory consists not in vengeance, but in meekness and patience. Therefore, Christians, as Christ's sheep, must vanquish their abusers by humility and meekness and not repay them evil for evil and scorn for scorn. And they should not be angry with them, but rather pity them inasmuch as the devil is master of such abusers and detractors, and pray for them lest they remain his captive forever.

(6) In times of their distress, may Christians heed the consoling words of Christ: "If the world hates you, you know that it hated Me before it hated you. If you were of the world, the world would love its own. Yet because you are not of the world, but I chose you out of the world, therefore the world hates you. Remember the word that I said to you, 'A servant is not greater than his master.' If they persecuted Me, they will also persecute you" (John 15:18–20). Therefore fortify your hearts, beloved! Let the lovers of the world do what they want to you; you should be happy that you are Christ's. Let them abuse you—you are of Christ's house. It is a great glory and honor to be Christ's, although this treasure is hidden from the world. Let the world hate you: God loves you. Let the world curse you: God blesses you. "They shall curse, yet Thou shalt bless" (Ps 108:28). Be happy with this and be comforted. The evil world plans evil against you, but God turns this into good for you. The tyrant Pharaoh became hardened against Israel, but Israel left Egypt with silver and gold and with treasure. You should endure everything that the world does to you. And you will leave the world and appear to your heavenly Father with a spiritual treasure, a treasure not of this world.

(7) Revilers and detractors will receive their portion. They make noise like water in springtime, but they disappear like water flowing by; they rise up like smoke, but they disappear like smoke. That is their characteristic; that is their portion. The righteous God hears their affronts and reproaches with which they wound pious souls. He hears, and notes down in His book, and will display it before them, will present them before them, and will show them

those who have been outraged and mocked by them, but no longer in the form in which he had been mocked and outraged by them, but in the glory of His chosen ones and in the number of the sons of God: this is your schismatic, your goody-goody, your melancholic, your rogue and spendthrift!

Look at him and notice whether it is he whom you laughed at, whom you cursed, whom you abused, whom you swore at. Oh, what shame and fear will then grip revilers! What shame will cover their faces! "Then the righteous man will stand with confidence In the presence of those who afflict him; And those who reject his labors, When they see him, will be shaken with dreadful fear; And they shall be amazed at his unexpected salvation. They will speak among themselves with regret, And in anguish of spirit they will groan and say, 'This is the man whom we fools once held in derision And made a byword of disgrace. We considered his life to be madness And his death as without honor. How has he been numbered among the sons of God? And how is his portion among the saints?'" (Wis 5:1–5). Poor person! God wants you too to live in humility and repentance, and so to be saved, and not to swear at the humble and pious. So repent, and the anger of God will not fall upon you.

We see in the holy Gospel that Christ our Lord, while preaching the gospel of the kingdom of heaven in word, showed it in visible form, in deed, for support of our faith and for consolation: having taken three of His disciples Peter, James, and John, led them up on a high mountain and there showed them a certain portion of the glory of His kingdom (see Matt 17:1). Beloved Christian! Let us also now ascend in our minds that holy mountain on which stood the most pure feet of our Saviour God, and we shall see there a most glorious sight unprecedented from the beginning of the world. We shall see there that the face of our incarnate God, Who walked the earth just like other people, shines like the sun, and his clothes become as radiant as the light. We shall see that standing before Him are two most glorious prophets, Moses and Elias, talking with Him. We shall see that Peter with his companions were so gladdened by the vision of that glory that they did not want to come down from that mountain, but in joy of their souls exclaim to Christ, "Lord, it is good for us to be here." We shall hear there the voice of God from the cloud, bearing witness of His Son, "This is My beloved Son, in Whom I am well pleased. Hear Him!" (Matt 17:1–5).

Looking at this most glorious spectacle with our mind's eye, let us linger here and reflect a little while for our benefit, so that our hearts too may rejoice in seeing and contemplating this most glorious sight.

(1) On seeing the God-befitting glory of Christ our God on Tabor, we see too how He humbled Himself for our sake. The same Christ, Whom we see on the holy mountain, walked the earth, and suffered, and dwelt among people in the form of a man like us. That same glory of His was always with Him but hidden from the eyes of men. Who would even dare to approach Him if He dwelt on and walked the earth even in the glory that He only partly showed on the holy mountain? But He, having hidden His glory under the flesh, went about in humility, like one of the simple people, and so was accessible to all the poor and sinners. You see that He, "Who being the brightness of *the Father's* glory and the express image of His person" (Heb 1:3), and "dwelling in unapproachable light" (1 Tim 6:16), dwelt on and walked the earth in the humble form of a man. Glory to His humility and glory to His condescension!

(2) Two great prophets, Moses and Elias, stood before Him: Moses, the lawgiver and leader during the exodus of Israel from Egypt, and Elias, a zealot for the glory of the Lord of Hosts, taken up as to heaven on a fiery chariot. Both the Jews and all Israel considered them the most glorious prophets. They appeared and stood before Christ on the holy mountain. You see here that Christ is the Lord of the prophets, Who appeared on earth in human form, and He is the true Messiah, preached by the prophets. Glory to the Lord who appeared in the flesh and to God Who came to save sinners!

(3) Christ's flesh glorified on the holy mountain assures us and gives us hope that God's chosen will have glory like Christ's in eternal life, as Christ Himself declared: "Then the righteous will shine forth as the sun in the kingdom of their Father" (Matt 13:43). And the Apostle wrote that He "will transform our lowly body that it may be conformed to His glorious body" (Phil 3:21). And again, another Apostle says, "Beloved, now we are children of God; and it has not yet been revealed what we shall be, but we know that when He is revealed, we shall be like Him" (1 John 3:2). Christian! Be assured of this and look at this glory.

(4) The Apostle Peter, as well as those with him, was so overjoyed, even though he only saw a certain part of that glory. What joy will pour out into the hearts of God's chosen ones in the future life, when not a portion of the glory, but all of it will be revealed. How greatly will they be delighted and will rejoice forever, when they see God face to face and Christ's glory, and will see it without end or satiation. God's saints on earth feel a small fraction of this joy and sweetness and, like the smallest fragments falling from the heavenly table, savor and delight the throats of their souls.

(5) This glory and joy should be an encouragement for pious people to the good struggle and staying in it until the end, according to the words of Christ, "Be faithful until death, and I will give you the crown of life" (Rev 2:10). In this way, the hope of soldiers for victory and glory encourages them to struggle against enemies. In this way, the hope of farmers for fruits encourages them to cultivation and labors. In this way, the hope of merchants for wealth encourages them to travel and wander through unknown and dangerous places. In this way, the hope of pupils for knowledge encourages them to work at their studies. So also, the hope of the pious Christian for future glory and joy should encourage him to the necessary struggle for piety and pressing toward "the upward call" (Phil 3:14).

Christian! In your melancholy and need, raise up your mind to where Christ's face shone like the sun and his garments were white as light; and to where the righteous shine like the heavenly bodies, and they see God face to face, and people have an amiable friendship with the angels, and in joy of spirit incessantly sing "Alleluia!" (Rev 19:1–6). Raise up your mind to there, and you will be strengthened in your faith and struggle. Blessed are they that dwell in Thy house, for ever and ever will they praise Thee, O Lord" (Ps 83:5).

(6) Lift up your eyes to this glory and joy, you who think of earthly and not of heavenly things; you wish and seek how to become rich in this world, to become famous, and to be awarded honors; you love to live in opulent and beautiful houses, to be driven in a high carriage with a tandem team of horses, to be garbed in purple and fine linen, and so to reign in this world. Not by the broad, but *by the difficult way*, and not by the wide, but by "the narrow gate do they enter there" (Matt 7:13–14). Not by luxury, but by tribulations, and many tribulations, do they enter the kingdom of God, as the Apostle said, "We must through many tribulations enter the kingdom of God" (Acts 14:22). Saint John heard a voice from heaven, bearing witness to God's chosen ones, "These are the ones who come out of the great tribulation" (Rev 7:14). You see that they come there out of tribulation, not out of luxury. The luxury and merrymaking of this world lead not to the kingdom of God, but to hell, as the example of the rich man of the Gospel, who "was clothed in purple and fine linen and fared sumptuously every day" (Luke 16:19), bears witness.

Get your bearings to see where you are going and by what path. Beloved! You are Christians, you are called by the Word of God to eternal good things and not to temporal ones; all good things in eternal life have been prepared for us by our Heavenly Father. Let us seek them with eagerness, but let us make use of earthly good things as wanderers, with fear and caution, and based on our necessity, and not for luxury. Whoever desires what is great does not worry about what is small, and whoever seeks eternal blessedness does not worry about anything temporal. "For we brought nothing into this world, and it is certain we can carry nothing out. And having food and clothing, with these we shall be content" (1 Tim 6:7–8).

(7) Lift up your eyes to there, you, who defile your souls and bodies by fornication and adultery; you, who swindle, steal, and rob other people's property; you, who flatter and dissemble with your tongues; you, who slander your neighbor and wound him with abusive words as with arrows; and others who break God's law without fear. Lift up your eyes to there and get your bearings, of what glory you are being deprived because of your unrepentant life. "But there shall by no means enter it anything that defiles, or causes an abomination or a lie … But outside are dogs and sorcerers and sexually immoral and murderers and idolaters, and whoever loves and practices a lie" (Rev 21:27; 22:15).

(8) All Christians, let us too lift up our eyes and get our bearings there, how we are living in this world. We are called by God's Word and renewed by holy baptism for this great glory. Let us get our bearings whether we are living worthy of this calling. Not only the confession of the Christian, but also faith and a nature in conformity with faith, makes a true Christian. We confess Christ the Son of God, but do we obey Christ Whom we confess? We know and believe that God sent His Son to us to save us, but we hear that the same God tells us from His holy heaven about him: "Hear Him" (Matt 17:5). Are we listening to Him if we wish to be saved by His grace? Let us get our bearings!

We see how it was said above that the glory of the chosen ones of God will be in conformity with the glory of Christ. Therefore, if we wish to obtain this glory, we must here, in this life, be compatible with Him. If we wish to be with him there, we must not separate ourselves from Him, but dwell inseparably with Him here. If we wish to be like Him, we must also here in this life be like Him. If we wish to come into eternal life after Him and through Him, we must follow after Him by His path and imitate His humility, love, patience, and meekness. If we wish to be participants of His eternal kingdom, we must be participants also of His sufferings and patience. If we wish to be glorified with Him, we must also suffer with Him, and bear His vilification, according to the Scripture: "We suffer with Him, that we may also be glorified together" (Rom 8:17). If we wish "that you may eat and drink at My table in

My kingdom" (Luke 22:30), we must even here, in this world, taste the gall of affliction with Him. So, if we shall be compatible with Him here, we shall be compatible with Him there as well. We saw Christ's glory on Tabor with our souls' eyes, and with the Apostle Peter, we were gladdened somewhat. But if we wish to receive that glory, we shall follow Christ even to Golgotha: "Let us go forth to Him, outside the camp, bearing His reproach" (Heb 13:13).

Everyone wishes to reign with Christ, but not everyone wishes to endure tribulations with Christ. We see what is written about Christ: "Ought not the Christ to have suffered these things and to enter into His glory" (Luke 24:26)? But we see what was written about Christians: "We must through many tribulations enter the kingdom of God" (Acts 14:22). Christians are called not to the opera, not to dances, not to banquets, not to the amusements of this world, but to repentance, and sorrows, and crosses. Each person has to carry his cross and follow Christ, Who carried His cross, and so enter God's kingdom after Him and through Him. Christians will have glory, honor, riches, inheritance, blessedness, consolation, joy, gladness, and a splendid supper to delight them, but in the age to come, although even now they do not remain without consolation. And even their tears, which flow from a contrite spirit, act in place of refreshment and consolation. They grieve and rejoice, are sad and are consoled; they weep and are glad. For they have the Comforter present, Who, being compassionate and a lover of mankind, consoles them in their sorrows. "Therefore I urge you, imitate me [as I do Christ]", says the Apostle (1 Cor 4:16).

We see in the holy Gospel that Christ our Lord wishing to show us the most perfect image of humility washed the feet of His disciples and Apostles. Dear Christian!

Let us now ascend in our mind to the upper room in which the mystical supper took place, and we shall see there a most glorious miracle. This supper will show us how the Lord of Glory rises from the table, how He takes off His outer garment, how he takes a towel and girds Himself, how He pours water into a basin, how He bends His knees and begins to wash their feet, and bends over, and washes their feet, and dries them with the towel with which He was girded, and goes to all of them, from one to the next, and then to the third, and so on in succession, and bends down and takes the feet of each one in His holy hands and washes them with water, and wipes them dry with the towel, and God, Who had appeared in human form, completes this demeaning work of a servant (John 13:4–15).

We see here, Christian:

(1) The humility of Christ our Lord is as great and profound as He is great and lofty. His highness and majesty are incomprehensible, and so too is His humility. Nothing like this has ever been seen on the earth. Nowhere do we hear that a human king has washed the feet of his servants. Nothing like this was ever heard of. God, the Heavenly King, appeared in human form and did this on earth, to show everyone a model of humility.

"Oh hear this, all ye nations, take heed, all ye that dwell in the world" (Ps 48:2). The Heavenly King and Lord of glory washed the feet of His servants. Oh, glorious and wondrous spectacle! The Lord serves in the form of a servant. Marvelous and wonderful are all Your Works, Lord Jesus Christ, our God! Marvelous are heaven and earth and all that is in them; marvelous are Your works, which we see in Your holy Word, but the most marvelous work that You did for our sake, we see here! In those works, we see your omnipotence; in this, we are amazed at Your condescension. Incomprehensible is Your omnipotence; incomprehensible too is Your humility. Glory to Your love for mankind, glory to Your condescension, glory to Your humility, glory to Your goodness! You did this marvelous deed for our sake. O Lord, Who loves the humble and meek! Write Your work on my heart, so that I may always see and follow it.

(2) Highly esteemed kings, princes, lords, masters, and all the renowned of this world! Look into this speckless mirror of humility and having seen its opposite vice on our souls, wipe it away. The Son of God and Heavenly King washed the feet of His servants—you, earth-dwellers, should act like this with your earthly servants and subjects. Do not be afraid; you will not be lessened by this but exalted even more; you will not be disparaged but will rise even higher; you will not be dishonored but will be honored more highly; you will not shame yourself but will be even more greatly glorified. Everyone "who humbles himself will be exalted" (Luke 14:11). This seems a small and mean matter in the eyes of the world, but in the eyes of God, it is great and lofty. Whoever is truly humble is great with God, Who loves the humble. But even intelligent people will be amazed at such an effort of yours. This is why we all are amazed by the humility of Christ, Christians, that He, being so great, so humbled Himself. Truly everyone who knows the power of virtue will be amazed when they see you too in similar humility.

(3) Look at this living example of humility, pastors, and be given an example of your humility to your people. Let people look at you and see in you

Christ's humility, and they will learn that Jesus Christ, the Chief of Shepherds, has sent you to them as a pastor.

(4) All you Christians, watch and imitate your Lord. He was not ashamed to serve people, so you should not be ashamed to serve and wash the feet of each other. By this, you will show that you belong to Christ. Follow Christ's humility, and you will belong to Christ. A servant of Christ is not recognized by anything so much as by humility. Heed this too, my soul, and love Christ's humility above all.

(5) Society is similar to the makeup of the human body. The members of the human body do not despise one another, but serve one another, and so maintain the integrity of the whole body. The head by intellect, the eyes by sight, the ears by hearing, the nostrils by smelling, the legs by walking and running, the belly by digestion—they all serve the whole body and each other. It is the same in society: leaders serve their subordinates by guidance, instructions, and care for them, and the subordinates serve leaders by work, service for their needs, by food, attire, and so on, whatever they need. In this way, leaders and subordinates are bound to each other by mutual duty and mutual service, like members in the makeup of the human body.

The condition of subordinates without leaders is bad and unfavorable, but what can the superior do without the service of subordinates? In the human body, the head is considered more important than other members, but what can it do without the eyes, the ears, the hands, and the legs? Likewise, in society, the superior is seen as more important than others but what will he do without the service of his subordinates? Nothing. For the head, even the most intelligent, to control the body well, it needs eyes to see, ears to hear, lips and tongue to speak, hands to work, legs to walk, and so on. Likewise, the superior, even the most intelligent, in order that he might successfully earn his living in society, needs other people: some, like eyes; some, like ears; some, like lips; some, like hands; some, like legs; and so on. Then his administration will be successful. What is the head without the other members of the body? Nothing. And what is a superior without subordinates? Nothing. What is a commander without officers and soldiers? Like an ordinary soldier. What is a prince, lord, or master without servants and peasants? Also an ordinary person. The army protects the integrity of its homeland, but the homeland supplies it with weaponry, provisions, and other necessities and replaces the fallen with new soldiers. What can the army do when the homeland will not give it what is necessary? Cities exalt themselves over villages and hamlets, but what are cities without villages and hamlets? Nothing. Villages and hamlets provide cities with grain and other supplies. Cities would disappear if villages and hamlets did not give them their grain.

So those who are considered the most contemptible are valuable and needed. This is put forward not to make subordinates disdain their chiefs—heaven forbid! They should be rendered their proper honor, as the Scripture says, "Render therefore to all their due: taxes to whom taxes are due, customs to whom customs, fear to whom fear, honor to whom honor" (Rom 13:7). But those who consider themselves the most valuable should not despise inferiors and pride themselves in their titles and names. One thing is required of Christian leaders—that they themselves live with the fear of God and serve Christian society in view of their oath and following the guidance of the holy Scripture. Then they will be truly great, great both here and great in the kingdom of heaven. But if they live here according to their frivolities, and do not obey the One Who gave them authority, then great will be their eternal misfortune. Their suffering will be increased to the extent that they have inspired fear here. "For the least is pardoned in mercy, But the powerful shall be strongly examined" (Wis 6:6).

Beloved, who occupies a high position! Frequently consider Christ's humility, and this will not permit you to become conceited and to disdain your lower-ranking brothers, and to senselessly grow furious in this world, and so to fall into ruinous misfortune. Who knows whether you or the one whom you despise is better and more valuable in the eyes of God, Who looks in the heart and judges by what is inside, and not by appearances, and by faith and deeds in conformity with it, and not by names and titles?

(6) God can make both a rich man poor, and a poor man rich, and make a high-ranking man low-ranking, as is written: "He raiseth up the beggar out of the dust, and lifteth the cripple up out of the dump; That He may set him with the princes, even with the princes of His people" (Ps 112:7–8). Why does a person exalt himself because today is in his hand, but tomorrow may be in someone else's, and why despise that brother who today is lower-ranking, but who may in time become higher than him? We see enough of such examples in this world. Pride is always laid low, but humility is always exalted. "God resists the proud, but gives grace to the humble" (1 Pet 5:5). Look in the mirror of Christ's humility, and follow Him, and you will always be at your best.

(7) All of us, high-ranking or low-ranking, are one. We acknowledge, and confess, and call upon a single Creator. We have our origin from a single father,

Adam. We are redeemed by the blood and death of the One Christ, the Son of God. We have one baptism and one faith; we are called by the Word of God to one eternal blessedness; we approach the one mystery of the most holy Eucharist; we are all called Christians from the one Christ. Oh, if only all were Christians, no one would despise anyone else! When we are all one, like members of a body, then why should we disdain and despise each other? He who disdains will be disdained and he who despises will be despised.

(8) All people, from highest to lowest, are equal. The day of birth and of departure shows this. "There is one entrance into life for all," says Solomon, "and a common departure" (Wis 7:6). Everyone is born naked, brings nothing into the world, and takes nothing out of the world. No one is born a prince, a lord, a master, rich, renowned, but a simple human, poor, wretched, naked, and with weeping. In like manner, all are subject to all kinds of changes and troubles. We see this in the world. Those of high rank are humbled, and those of low rank are exalted; the renowned become despised, and the despised become renowned; the rich become poor, and the poor, rich. As in the sea, where the waves now rise and then fall, it happens likewise in the world: first people rise and then they fall. Death is equal for everyone. All people leave this world without anything. They leave all riches, honor, glory, names, and titles here. A small grave receives all equally. Each is buried equally in a six-foot hole and is covered with earth. Each is given over equally to corruption.

Where are riches, where is honor, where is glory, where are names and titles? Consider this, O man. I see where the prince is laid, where the lord is laid, where the master is laid, where the renowned is laid, where the rich is laid, and where are laid the servant and the pauper. I see that the earth lies here, and in it are only bare bones. And indeed I cannot recognize the master and his servant, the renowned and the low-born, the rich man and the poor man, because I see only earth. I hear that such a master is laid in such a place, but I do not see him—I only see earth. And how shall I call him by his name, if I see not him, but only earth? Consider this, and learn and acknowledge, that all are equal. You will be the same as those who you see here. Why should an equal disdain and despise his equal? What is there for earth and ashes to be proud of? Look at Christ's humility.

Christian, hear Christ, Who says: "You call me Teacher and Lord, and you say well, for so I am. If I then, your Lord and Teacher, have washed your feet, you also ought to wash one another's feet. For I have given you an example, that you should do as I have done to you. Most assuredly, I say to you, a servant is not greater than his master; nor is he who is sent greater than he who sent him. If you know these things, blessed are you if you do them" (John 13:13–17).

But let us look, Christian, at Christ's saving sufferings; let us look at the sufferings that Jesus Christ, our Lord, endured voluntarily for our sake. Let us look at the sufferings in which glory, consolation, joy, and our life consist. Let us look at His sufferings; let us concentrate all our attention on them, so that the crucified "Christ is formed" also in us (Gal 4:19). Let us look at His sufferings and let us join ourselves to them, that we may also be the partakers of His glory (see 1 Pet 4:13). We shall not be separated from Him neither here nor there. Both in sufferings and in glory, we shall be with Him, as the body with the head, and the bride with the groom, and the servants with the master.

We see in the holy Gospel that those whom He came to save, who were waiting for Him, to whom He showed great benefactions, those, I say, did not accept Him, as the holy evangelist witnesses with compassion to all the world: "He came to His own, and His own did not receive Him" (John 1:11). And not only did they not receive him, but they became embittered against Him and tried to kill Him, as we see in His holy Gospel. You see here, Christian:

(1) Christ's goodness and love for mankind are unconquerable by any malice. Christ our Lord knew what His ungrateful people would do with Him, but He still came to them, came to save them, came to seek those who were perishing, came to call and bear them to His Father. He lived with them, associated with them, taught them, showed them the path to eternal salvation, turned them to repentance, exhorted them, showed them by signs and wonders that He is That Messiah Who was promised to them by God, preached by the prophets, and awaited by them. "Go and tell John the things which you hear and see: The blind see and the lame walk; the lepers are cleansed and the deaf hear; the dead are raised up and the poor have the gospel preached to them" (Matt 11:4–5). That is, the time has come in which the preaching of the prophets is being fulfilled, and you may learn Who I am from My signs, and miracles, and works. The Jews saw all this but they did not receive Him, being an obstinate and corrupt generation. "He came to His own, and His own did not receive Him" (John 1:11).

(2) If some king came into his city, and the subjects, would not receive him and dishonored him and treated him spitefully, such a scorning would be great and intolerable for him. The King of Heaven and Lord came to His subjects, the Jews, and they did not accept Him, but even dishonored Him,

and were embittered against Him. But He acted meekly toward them, and was long-suffering with them, and exhorted them, and did good to them, and wished and sought eternal salvation for them. Oh, Your long-suffering, Jesus! Oh, Your goodness and love for mankind! Truly from this you may learn, O man, that He is the only-begotten Son of the heavenly Father, the radiance of His hypostasis, the image of the invisible God, Who "makes His sun rise on the evil and on the good, and sends rain on the just and on the unjust" (Matt 5:45).

The divine and most loving nature of the Father is seen in His Son. Who among men can endure such things? Human meekness and patience change quickly.

(3) From this, we see how envy and malice blind a person. The scribes and Pharisees knew from the prophecies that Christ must come when "[t]he scepter shall ... depart from Judah" (Gen 49:10). The scepter departed from Judah, and Jesus Christ came. They knew that He must be born a Jew in Bethlehem (see Mic 5:1). "That is where Jesus was born" (Matt 2:1). They knew of John the Baptist, that he was a "prophet" (Luke 1:76; John 1:23; Exod 40:3–5). John "bore witness to Jesus" (Luke 3:16; Matt 3:11; John 1:6–36). They knew that the Messiah expected by them would perform spectacular signs and wonders. Jesus performed unheard-of signs and wonders. Therefore, the people, seeing His sensational miracles, exclaimed, "It was never seen like this in Israel!" (Matt 9:33). Therefore, even Nicodemus said to Christ, "Rabbi, we know that You are a teacher come from God; for no one can do these signs that You do unless God is with him" (John 3:2). And they themselves took counsel concerning Jesus Christ and said among themselves, "What shall we do? For this Man works many signs" (John 1:47). But, blinded by envy and malice, they did not receive Him. This is how envy and malice blind one! Oh, the terrible evil, envy and malice! Christian! Beware of this evil, lest it blind your inner eyes, and the unending evil, eternal perdition, befall you.

(4) The scribes and Pharisees and other Jews did not receive Christ, but many received Him. Nations that had never even heard of Him received Him and worshipped Him. Glory to God that He shone His light upon us. Let us receive Him worthily, and love His holy appearance, and serve Him as our King and God, and abide in faith and His confession to the end. May He also confess us before His Heavenly Father, as He says, "Therefore whoever confesses Me before men, him I will also confess before My Father who is in heaven" (Matt 10:32). If we confess Him as the Son of God, our God and Lord

and King, then we will obey Him, and work for Him, as our King, Lord, and God, and we shall live by the rule of the holy Gospel. So, if we belong to Christ here, Christ will acknowledge us as His own before His Heavenly Father there.

Listen, Christian, to what the Apostle declares to be the marks of those who belong to Christ. "Those who are Christ's have crucified the flesh with its passions and desires" (Gal 5:24). These are the signs of Christ's people. "They are also called men of God, as we see in many places in Holy Scripture" (1 Tim 6:11; Heb 4:19; 1 Pet 2:10). Let us be Christ's not by confession alone, but also in deed and in truth, so that both here and at His Second Coming, Christ may acknowledge us as His own. "The solid foundation of God stands, having this seal: 'The Lord knows those who are His,' and, 'Let everyone who names the name of Christ depart from iniquity'" (2 Tim 2:19). "I know My sheep, and am known by My own," says the Lord. And again, "My sheep hear My voice, and I know them, and they follow Me. And I give them eternal life, and they shall never perish; neither shall anyone snatch them out of My hand" (John 10:14, 27–28).

We see in His holy Gospel that one of His disciples, named Judas Iscariot, sold Him to those who were planning to kill Him, and sold Him for thirty pieces of silver, and by a sly kiss betrayed Him into their hands. The cunning flatterer had discerned that the chief priests, scribes, and Pharisees planned to kill Jesus, but he had a greedy heart. He came to them, who craved innocent blood, and said to them, "'What are you willing to give me if I deliver Him to you?' And they counted out to him thirty pieces of silver" (Matt 26:15). And for such a small sum, the iniquitous one sold the priceless One! You saw, Jesus, the sly designs and intrigues that Your enemies devised against You. You saw the iniquitous haggling, purchase, and agreement. You saw that You, the price-less One, are sold for such a small price. You saw but endured the brutality of your iniquitous people. Glory to Your long-suffering, O merciful One! You were sold, O compassionate One, so cheap, in order to redeem me, sold into sin. I sing and hymn your love for mankind!

We see here, Christian:

(1) What a great evil is greed. The greedy soul does not blanch at doing anything, and dares everything, in order to acquire filthy lucre. The iniquitous Judas did not blanch at selling and betraying Jesus, his Lord and Teacher, Him Whom he saw performing spectacular and wondrous works. Greed blinded his eyes. The root and origin of his wicked deed was greed. What a ruinous evil is greed! Christian, shun greed, lest it plunge you into all sorts of evil.

(2) Iniquitous commanders who betray many thousands into the hands of enemies for silver and so cause intolerable harm to the homeland imitate Judas. Iniquitous judges who sell justice and truth for payment and make the innocent guilty and the guilty innocent imitate him. False witnesses who are suborned with money and give false testimony in court imitate him. Other wrongdoers who acquire filthy lucre to replace truth with a lie also imitate him.

(3) Those people who slander their pastors and vilify them using bad names imitate Judas; children, servants, pupils, and other people who slander and denigrate parents, masters, teachers, and mentors, and benefactors before others and also imitate him. All such people as it were are selling out their benefactors and follow Judas the traitor, who sold out his Lord and Teacher and betrayed Him into the hands of His enemies. Concerning such people, it is written: "He who repays evil for good, Evil will not be removed from his house" (Prov 17: 14 LXX). Christian, beware being an imitator of Judas, lest you inherit his fate.

(4) Judas, in betraying his Lord into the hands of the iniquitous, kissed Him and said to Him, "Greetings, Rabbi!" but in his heart, he thought evil against his Lord and betrayed Him with an insidious kiss. "Now His betrayer had given them a sign, saying, 'Whomever I kiss, He is the One; seize Him.'" "Immediately he went up to Jesus and said, 'Greetings, Rabbi!' and kissed Him" (Matt 26:48–49). Oh, the meekness of Jesus, Who endured the flattering kiss of His enemy! Oh, the foul lips of the traitor, who did not fear to approach and insidiously kiss the Holiest of the Holies and the source of holiness, the Lord!

Those Christians who insidiously, craftily, and slyly treat their neighbors follow and imitate the sly one who gave the kiss; they utter something with the tongue; they think something in their hearts; sweet honey is on their tongues, but in their hearts they have bitter bile; they bless with their tongues but curse with their hearts; With their lips, they say, "I wish you health," but in their hearts, they think of how they can ensnare the one whom they greet in words and do harm to him. All such people have the nature of the insidious traitor, Judas. Christian! Shun treating your neighbor insidiously, lest you become a son of perdition like Judas. "God tests the hearts and reins of all" (Ps 7:10) and sees how you behave and treat your neighbor and how you speak and think about him.

(5) We see how Satan leads a person first into one sin, then into another, and then into other sins. First he put greed into Judas's heart, then the

betrayal of His Lord, and he then brought him into complete despair. He does the same even now. First, he teaches a person to live in idleness and laziness, suggests to the one living in idleness all kinds of evil thoughts, and leads him to all kinds of evil and sin. First, he casts greed into the heart of a person, and from this leads him to embezzlement, thievery, robbery, violence, lies, brigandage, murder, and other serious transgressions. "The love of money is a root of all kinds of evil" (1 Tim 6:10). First, by seeking it, a person comes to haughtiness and arrogance, and then he disdains, despises, and condemns his neighbor. He does likewise in other sins. Christian! Shun even one sin, lest you fall into another and many other sins and reach the depth of evils.

(6) Judas the traitor, having fallen into despair, "hanged himself" (Matt 27:5). He learned the magnitude of sin but did not learn the magnitude of God's mercy. Nowadays many do likewise and follow after Judas. They learn the magnitude of their sins but do not learn the magnitude of God's compassions, and so despair of their salvation.

Christian! Despair is the serious and worst blow of the devil. Before the sin, it presents God as merciful, but after sin, as just. This is his slyness. You should do the opposite. Before the sin, imagine God's justice, lest you sin, but when you backslide and sin, think of the magnitude of God's mercy, lest you fall into the despair of Judas. As His greatness is, so is His mercy. No matter how many sins you have and how great they may be, God has even more mercy and compassion. Only repent and henceforward avoid sinning, lest you experience God's justice.

(7) We see how terrible and serious the torment of a guilty conscience is. Judas could not endure the torments of his guilty conscience and therefore hanged himself. A guilty conscience led him to this. Therefore, he preferred to die, rather than to endure the torment of his conscience. He preferred death to life. Christian! Avoid exacerbating your conscience, lest you suffer as did Judas. But guard your conscience just as you guard your life. There is no more vicious tormentor than a guilty conscience. Avoid wounding and disturbing it by your sins. Prefer to die rather than to sin against your conscience. Christian duty requires this of you.

If a guilty conscience so torments a person here that he would prefer to die than to live, then how will it torment the condemned ones in the age to come, when it imagines all the sins committed by them and the anger of God and eternal despair. From this, they will wish to die but will never die. And it is this that is "the second death and the eternal death!" (Rev 20:6–14).

We see in the holy Gospel that when, wishing to betray his Teacher into the hands of His enemies, Judas with His evil accomplices came to Christ, Who was then in the garden with His disciples, Jesus Christ, our Lord, Himself came forth and said to them, "Whom are you seeking?" and when they answered Him "Jesus of Nazareth," Jesus said to them, "I am He." And as soon as He told them "I am He," they took fright from this answer and His voice and fell on the ground. "Jesus therefore, knowing all things that would come upon Him, went forward and said to them, 'Whom are you seeking?' They answered Him, 'Jesus of Nazareth.' Jesus said to them, 'I am He.' And Judas, who betrayed Him, also stood with them. Now when He said to them, 'I am He,' they drew back and fell to the ground" (John 18:4–6).

Here we see, Christian:

(1) Jesus Christ our Lord knew the future and everything that would happen to Him. "Jesus therefore, knowing all things that would come upon Him ... To know the future is characteristic of God alone" (Isa 61:22–23; 42:9; 43:12). We see that Christ is our God Who came into the world to save us and Who suffered for us.

(2) The traitor Judas and his accomplices so took fright that they fell on the ground. From this they should have learned how great and mighty is He Who struck them with His voice like thunder. But they did not further hesitate to approach and lay their iniquitous hands on Jesus, and take and tie up the all-powerful One. Do you see how malice and every kind of sin blind a person?

(3) That Jesus Christ Himself came out to His enemies who had come to Him and said, "I am He," He Whom you seek. From this we see that He of His own will gave Himself over to suffering for us and endured all the sufferings that happened to Him. It was the Father's good will that His only-begotten Son should drain the cup of sufferings for our salvation; it was also His Beloved Son's good will, and He drained the cup given to Him from His Heavenly Father. "He ... became obedient to the point of death, even the death of the cross" (Phil 2:8); as He said, "Shall I not drink the cup which My Father has given Me" (John 18:11)?

Do you see, Christian, the fervent love of the only-begotten Son of God for us, and do you also see that of His Heavenly Father? God loved us, the unworthy, and His only-begotten Son also loved us. The Father gave up His Son to death and suffering for us, and He gave Himself and His Son for us.

Glory to God, Who so favored us! Glory to His Divine love for mankind, glory to His goodness, glory to His mercy and compassion! "Lord, what is man, that Thou hast had such respect unto him? Or the son of man, that Thou so regardest him" (Ps 143:3)?

(4) Jesus Christ our Lord could have evaded the hands of His iniquitous enemies, but He did not wish to since the time had now come for Him to suffer for us. Christians! Let us not flee and let us not avoid the cross of sufferings that the Heavenly Father will lay on us. Although we may avoid it, let us bear it without grumbling and let us follow Christ even to Golgotha, if His Heavenly Father wills it.

(5) Christ could have struck down all those who had come to seize Him, but He did not wish to, and He allowed them to take him and tie Him up. Let us too follow our Author, Jesus, in this. And although we may be able to take revenge on those who do evil to us and harm them, we will not, however, either take revenge on or harm them, but will endure all their evil-doing with meekness. So shall we follow Christ, our Author, as the body follows the head; so shall we be in conformity with Him, so "[shall] we suffer with Him, that we may also be glorified together" (Rom 8:17).

But let us see how and what Christ our Lord suffered for us. We see that, having been sold and betrayed by His betrayer, he was tied up, was led away bound to the iniquitous council, was abandoned by His disciples: "all the disciples forsook Him and fled" (Matt 26:56). He was judged by the iniquitous court, was mocked and sworn at, had His ears boxed and was slapped in the face, and was condemned to death. "They answered and said, 'He is deserving of death'" (Matt 26:66). He, Who has the death and life of each person in His hands, was led away to Pilate the governor and slandered before him as a profligate. He, Who taught the truth and preached the Kingdom of God to those who had drawn near, and pointed out the path to it, was led away from Pilate to the wicked Herod, and before him was also slandered, and mocked and sworn at by him, and returned again to Pilate. So the Lord of glory was led back and forth through the streets of Jerusalem with ridicule. His iniquitous people begged Pilate with great persistence for crucifixion: "Crucify Him!" (You heard, O Lord, these wicked words and bore them), and was sentenced to death on the Cross (Mark 15:13–15). He was crowned with thorns by the soldiers; He was saluted by them like a king with mocking, "Hail, King of the Jews" (Mark 15:18); the King of Heaven and Lord of Glory was spit on and stuck on the head with a reed.

"The Lamb of God" (John 1:29) was led to crucifixion and carried His cross and led out with Him were two malefactors; and a multitude of people followed, and saw Jesus, "led as a sheep to the slaughter" (Isa 53:7); and the Son of God was led out of the city to crucifixion and the death of the cross. "Thy goings were seen, O God, the processions of God my King" (Ps 67:25). Thus led to the place of the Skull, the place of death, and no longer having the appearance and beauty, "fairer than the sons of men" (Ps 44:3), He was nailed naked to the cross and wicked people pierced His hands and feet (see Ps 21:17), and for greater insult and dishonor, they hung the glory and praise of Israel between two robbers; and the Righteous One Who justifies us was considered among the lawless. So His enemies passing by blasphemed the insulted, and dishonored, and tormented, and suffering One, "wagging their heads and saying, 'You who destroy the temple and build it in three days, save Yourself! If You are the Son of God, come down from the cross'" (Matt 27:39–40). And so the transgressors added to the afflictions of His wounds. So the tormented and suffering Son of God in His thirst was given vinegar to drink instead of water, as He himself said: "They gave me also gall to eat, and when I was thirsty they gave me vinegar to drink" (Ps 68:22). Finally Jesus Christ our Lord finished all His sufferings with death, "even the death of the cross" (Phil 2:8).

Glory to You, O God, glory to You! From Your suffering sprang forth consolation; Your death is our life; Your grief gave birth to joy for us; Your dishonor and abuse obtained for us honor and eternal glory; Your humility exalted us, who were fallen and humbled; Your wounds healed us; Your bonds set us free who were bound with sins. "Thou hast broken my bonds in sunder. I will offer unto Thee a sacrifice of thanksgiving" (Ps 115:7–8). Being sold, You redeemed us who were sold to sin; judged and condemned, you saved us from eternal judgment; mocked and sworn at, You delivered us from the abuse and mocking of the devil.

We hymn Your love for mankind, we worship your sufferings, O Lover of Mankind, we embrace your mercy, we glorify Your goodness; we sinners, pardoned and redeemed by You, Your perishing people who were saved by you, thank You. Glory to You, Son of God, with your compassionate Father and Your Most-holy Spirit, Amen.

"What then shall we say to these things? If God is for us, who can be against us? He who did not spare His own Son, but delivered Him up for us all, how shall He not with Him also freely give us all things" (Rom 8:31–32)?

Christians! We see in the Gospel the sufferings of Christ our God. Let us pause here and with our mind's eyes look at Christ's sufferings, in which all our blessedness consists.

We see here:

(1) Christ our Lord suffered in both soul and body. In His soul, He had grief, sorrow, anguish, and horror that was unspeakable and incomprehensible to the mind.

"He began," says the Evangelist, "to be troubled and deeply distressed. Then He said to them" (the Apostles), "My soul is exceedingly sorrowful, even to death" (Mark 14:33–34). Then, on His most holy body, "His sweat became like great drops of blood falling down to the ground" (Luke 22:44). The dishonor, reproach, insult, mockery that the wicked Jews did to Him unspeakably wounded His most pure soul because this blasphemy related to His *whole person*, Which is God and Man, for Christ is perfect God and perfect Man. His most pure soul was extremely wounded, that in Him God was blasphemed and insulted. His most holy, most pure, immaculate body, united with the Word of God, was beaten, wounded, injured, tortured, had His ears boxed, spit on, bloodied, crowned with thorns, stripped, nailed to the Cross, and more. Look, Christian, at Christ's suffering and pain. And you want to live in the luxury and amusements of this world!

(2) Christ's pains and sufferings were intensified by His suffering from His own people, as it was written, "He came to His own, and His own did not receive Him" (John 1:11). He suffered from those to whom He bestowed very many and great benefactions—from such people did Christ our Lord suffer. Such was their ingratitude to the Lord, their benefactor. The ingratitude of *His* people was painful for Him. Moreover, He suffered in the famous and distinguished city of Jerusalem and in front of a multitude of people, who had gathered from all countries then for the feast of Passover; and, for greater defamation and insult, He, Who alone is holy and righteous, was hung between two malefactors and was considered among the lawless (Isa 53:13).

Look, Christian, at the dishonor and insult to Christ! You are called a Christian after Christ, but you insatiably desire and seek the glory and honor of this world. Reason for yourself what is within you and whether it is in conformity with Christ, and whether you are one of Christ's servants.

(3) As Christ our Lord came into the world for our sake to save us, so He also suffered for us. Our sins were the cause of His sufferings; He took our sins on Himself; He accepted and endured execution, a consequence of sins. "He

was wounded because of our lawlessness and became sick because of our sins" (Isa 53:5). Wondrous is the goodness, mercy, and providence of God toward us. We sinned, and Christ our Lord endured execution for us. The servants sinned, but the Master was punished. Glory to His love for mankind! We became haughty, but the Lord of Glory humbled Himself so profoundly for the sake of us who had become haughty. We snatched away God's glory with our progenitors, and He rendered Divine justice its due, as He said through the prophet, "I paid them for things I never took" (Ps 68:5). Through disobedience and our sins, all kinds of afflictions, misfortunes, and wretchedness entered into us. But through the sufferings of Christ, every blessedness that we may have and will have has been returned to us. Through sin, we fell; through Christ's sufferings we rose up. We died by sin, and, we came to life by Christ's sufferings and death. Christ died for us and by His death brought us back to life. David, King of Israel, once wished to die in place of his son Absalom (Oh, what ardent love!) and, sobbing for him, spoke thus: "My son Absalom, my son. My son Absalom—why your death instead of mine; I instead of you! Absalom my son, my son" (2 Kgs 19:1 LXX [18:33]). In this way, Christ, the Son of God and Son of David according to the flesh, in seeing us, dead and lost, wept for us, and wished to suffer and die for us, and actually did suffer and die, to bring us who had died back to life.

Glory to His ineffable love! He died, and we come to life. His death is our life. We were separated from God by sin, and we returned and drew near to God by Christ's sufferings. We were corrupted by sin, and we were restored by Christ's suffering. The devil made us captive by sin, and celebrated, and raged over us, like a cruel tyrant, by His sufferings and death, Christ our Lord defeated and put to shame that cruel tyrant, and snatched us from his hands by His power, and bound that proud enemy of ours, and gave him up to his faithful servants for trampling and mockery. "Behold, I give you the authority to trample on serpents and scorpions, and over all the power of the enemy" (Luke 10:19).

Sin was the reason that we, having departed from God, were so darkened in mind and lost our way, and dwelt in such delusion that, instead of the living God, we deified and revered idols and, instead of the Creator, creatures. Into such error man, although gifted with reason and created in the image and likeness of God, fell. Having fallen he worshipped irrational and soulless creatures, and revered them as his God, and asked and sought help from them. A great and terrible darkening of the mind it is to worship feeble creatures and deify them, and to seek help from them. This is how the devil, having taken us captive, was enticing us!

Christ our Lord by His coming and suffering abolished this delusion, and by the preaching of the holy Gospel and the power of His Cross and sufferings, we were vindicated, and we turned from the idols to the living God, and began to glorify the holy name of the Father, Son, and Holy Spirit, the One God in Three Hypostases. From the east to the west, the name of the Living God is glorified.

By sin, we fell to the curse and its consequent eternal condemnation. Christian! The curse is terrible: it leads a person to eternal torment. In His sufferings, Christ our Lord, Who is Blessed unto the ages, having become a curse for us, obtained God's blessing for us rather than a curse. "Christ has redeemed us from the curse of the law, having become a curse for us (for it is written, 'Cursed is everyone who hangs on a tree'), that the blessing of Abraham might come upon the Gentiles in Christ Jesus, that we might receive the promise of the Spirit through faith" (Gal 3:13–14). By sin, we greatly angered God and did not have any boldness or access to Him. By His sufferings, Christ our Lord propitiated God, and opened up access to Him for us, and granted us daring. He reconciled God with us and us with God, made His Father our Father, as he said, "I am ascending to My Father and your Father, and to My God and your God" (John 20:17). And He taught how to pray to Him like this: "Our Father, Who art in the heavens" and so on (Matt 6:9–13). Heaven and paradise were closed to us by sin, and hell and every eternal affliction were opened to us. Christ our Lord redeemed us from hell by His sufferings, opened the doors to the heavenly kingdom, and so on. The salvific and most sweet fruits of Christ's sufferings and all of His providence concerning us, and for our warm consolation, are beautifully depicted in the Gospel, the epistles of the Apostles, and the prophetic books.

They are suitable, however, only for the faithful and those in true repentance, but they are not of benefit to others, as will be set forth later.

(4) Christ our Lord endured all His sufferings voluntarily, as was discussed previously. The betrayer wished to sell and betray Him into the hands of the iniquitous; Christ did not resist him, and he betrayed Him. The transgressors wished to seize Him and tie Him up; He did not resist them, and they seized and bound Him. They wished to take Him to the iniquitous assembly; He did not resist, and they brought Him there. They wished to judge the Judge of all; He did not resist, and they judged Him. They wished to curse at, mock,

and spit at Him; He did not resist, and they cursed at, mocked, and spit at the Lord of Glory. They wished to torment and wound Him; He did not resist, and they tormented and wounded Him. They wished to lead Him to death as one condemned; He did not resist, and they led Him to death. They wished to nail Him to the cross, hanging Him between two malefactors; He did not resist, and they nailed Him and hanged Him there. They wished to do other evils to Him; He did not resist, and they did it. This is what He says of Himself through the prophet: "I am not disobedient, nor do I contradict Him. I gave My back to whips, and my cheeks to blows; and I turned not away my face from the shame of spitting" (Isa 50:5–6). And in the Gospel it says, "Therefore My Father loves Me, because I lay down My life that I may take it again. No one takes it from Me, but I lay it down of Myself. I have power to lay it down, and I have power to take it again. This command I have received from My Father" (John 10:17–18).

And who would be able to do anything to Him, if He did not permit it? If He is true God, as He really is, who could torment Him, Who holds the life and death of everyone in His hands? Indeed, He could have struck down all His enemies with a nod and in the twinkling of an eye, if He wished. But He permitted it to be so, that He would see us saved.

(5) You see from Christ's sufferings, Christian, what a great and terrible evil is sin. Sin offends and angers the God's incomprehensible and indescribable majesty. There is no greater evil than sin. Man sinned and thus angered God. But it was necessary for the Son of God to cleanse sin by His suffering and blood and to propitiate God, Who was angered by sin, and thus to reconcile man with God, and to deliver him from eternal punishment, the consequence of sin. For man, having sinned against God and angered Him, subjected himself to eternal punishment.

However many illnesses, calamities, misfortunes, and evils there are, sin is the cause of them all. A person may sin easily, but he may not easily cleanse his sin. He must cleanse it by bitter tears and the blood of the only-begotten Son of God. Otherwise, a person will experience its bitter fruit—eternal death. "For the wages of sin is death" (Rom 6:23).

Christian! Beware of nothing as much as sin, as an utterly ruinous evil, if you wish to be a true Christian and not perish eternally. It is better to choose to die, if necessary, than to sin.

(6) We see that three characteristics of God, justice, mercy, and wisdom, are shown and fulfilled in Christ's sufferings.

We see that God's justice does not leave sin unpunished. God's justice demanded that man, having sinned, be eternally punished for the sin. God's mercy wished to pardon the sinner. God's wisdom devised a way by which both His justice and His mercy were fulfilled and reconciled. Jesus Christ, the Son of God, fulfilled God's justice by His sufferings and death. But God's mercy promoted our salvation. So we see that through Christ's sufferings, the satisfaction of God's justice and mercy was achieved. Justice was satisfied, and we are being saved through God's mercy. Glory to the wise God, Who so favored us!

Christian! Kiss God's mercy, and repent of your sins, and seek eternal salvation with your whole heart. Seek it while God's mercy still applies, lest you experience the judgment of God's eternal justice.

(7) We see from Christ's sufferings what fervent and ardent love God has for the human race, that He did not spare His own Son for our sake. And we see that Christ, the Son of God, explained in His own words, "For God so loved the world that He gave His only begotten Son, that whoever believes in Him should not perish but have everlasting life" (John 3:16). As a child-loving father, seeing his children in captivity or in some other serious misfortune, out of love for them, has pity and compassion for them (for it is characteristic of love to have compassion), so the man-loving God, seeing us in captivity to the devil and in ruin, had compassion and took pity on us. Therefore, it was not so difficult for Him to send His Son into the world and to deliver Him to sufferings and death for us, to see us saved.

You see, O man, God's love for you. As many times as you see an image of Christ's sufferings, or as many times you hear of them, or as many times as you remember them, you should remember God's love and be amazed by it. Do not be careless, but try for both God's desire and intention for your salvation, and Christ's sufferings bear fruit in you, that is, eternal salvation. God loved you, and sent His Son for your sake, and deigned for Him to suffer for you—be worthy of His love and holy will, and strive for your salvation.

(8) God's love for us that has been revealed in all things but most of all in the sufferings of Christ, motivates us to love Him in return as a compassionate Father. God is the highest, eternal, and immutable good, and therefore in and of Himself is worthy of our love. For who does not love a great and immutable good? It, both of itself, and upon experiencing it, draws the heart of everyone to its love. But the deeds of His love and more so the sufferings of Christ, in which His incomprehensible love for us was revealed, urge us to love Him in

return. He loved us, loved the unworthy; let us love Him, Who is worthy of all love. He is our Creator, He is our Provider, He is our Redeemer, He loves us, He is our Father. "Lord, what is man, that thou hast had such respect unto him? Or the son of man, that Thou so regardest him" (Ps 143:3)?

We feel His holy love, which, although it is in everything, is most of all in His saving providence for us. Let us also love Him as the highest good and blessedness and out of love show Him obedience and keep His holy commandments, avoiding every sin, which He hates. If we do His will, we shall show our love for Him. Without this, there can be no love (John 14:15, 21). One who loves must unfailingly do the will of the beloved. Otherwise, the love will be false and hypocritical.

(9) The same love of God exhorts us to love our neighbor, that is, every person. "If God so loved us, we also ought to love one another" (1 John 4:11).

Will you wish, Christian, to hate him who God so loved?

Will you wish to do evil to one to whom God out of His love does good?

Will you wish to harm one for whose sake Christ, the Son of God, came into the world, suffered, died?

Will you wish to deceive, entice, slander, dishonor one whom Christ the Son of God so honored?

Will you wish to steal, to swindle, to take some belonging from one for whom Christ, the Son of God shed His blood?

Will you wish to show no mercy to one to whom Christ, the Son of God, showed mercy?

Will you wish to begrudge money, clothing, bread, water, shelter, and other things for one for whose sake Christ, the Son of God, did not even spare Himself?

If you love God, you must love the one whom God loves. You do not love God if you do not love man. The source of love for man is love for God. From love for God also arises love for neighbor. Love for God is linked to love for neighbor, and one cannot exist without the other. But love for God becomes known from love for neighbor. If you sincerely love your neighbor, as one beloved by God, it means that you also love God, Who loves him. If you do not love your neighbor, whom God loves, then without doubt you do not love God either (1 John 4:19–21).

Between the one who loves and the beloved there should be like-mindedness: whatever the latter thinks, the former must think also. God thinks good for man, and loves him, and wishes him every good thing, and does good for him. This is how man, if he loves God, should think kindly of man, and love him, and wish him every good thing, and do good to him. From this it follows that, if he unfeignedly loves him, he should extend a helping hand to him in every need. One who loves will in no way deny help to a beloved if he can at all provide it, as we see in action in the example of love between husband and wife, between parents and children, between brothers and sisters, and between sincere friends.

If, O man, you love Christ, Who has suffered for you, show this love toward your neighbor, for whom Christ suffered just as He did for you. Man is God's beloved creation. If you love God, then love the creation that He loves.

(10) From this it follows that there will be no excuse for those Christians who do not love their neighbors and show their lack of love by not wanting to help them in time of need, but to abandon them and leave them, and often shamelessly say of those in need: "What business is it of mine?" This includes all those rich people who expend their resources on luxury, on building pala-tial homes, on carriages and horses, on silken and rich clothing, rich repasts and wine, pleasure gardens and ponds, and for other of their whims, but do not wish to help the poor, for whom Christ suffered and shed His blood. They love all similar frivolities but not Christ. Therefore they will not have an excuse and will be shamed at Christ's Dread Judgment.

O man! Christ did not spare Himself for you, but you for His sake even begrudge money! Every Christian must be ready if need be not to renounce Christ and to die for Him. If you begrudge your money for the sake of Christ, will you wish and desire if need be to die for Christ? There is nothing dearer to a person than life. How will you give your life for Christ, if you begrudge money for His sake? You begrudge the small; will you not begrudge what is great? Who will believe you in this?

(11) Christ our Lord suffered and died for all people, however many there have been, are, and will be. Since God "desires all men to be saved and to come to the knowledge of the truth" (1 Tim 2:4), He sent His only-begotten Son into the world to save all. "For God so loved the world that He gave His only begot-ten Son, that whoever believes in Him should not perish but have everlasting life" (John 3:16). "This is a faithful saying and worthy of all acceptance, that Christ Jesus came into the world to save sinners, of whom I am chief" (1 Tim 1:15). "For all have sinned and fall short of the glory of God" (Rom 3:23). For all are sinners, and Christ Jesus came to save all. "The Son of Man has come to seek and to save that which was lost" (Luke 19:10). For all have perished, and

Christ came to seek and save all, and suffered for all. "[Christ] died for all," testifies Saint Paul (2 Cor 5:15). "For there is no partiality with God" (Rom 2:11). He wishes to save all, and for the sake of all He even sent His Son. Glory to His love for mankind! But only those people who receive Him with faith, who love His salvific appearing, who give sincere thanks to Him, and who obey His saving words receive mercy from Him and are saved. The others perish in their wickedness and impenitence. The grace of God saves the willing, but not the unwilling. Christ prepared salvation for all, but it is required of all that they desire salvation, and desire it sincerely and in truth. But whoever does not want it certainly perishes of his own accord.

O man! God sincerely wishes to save you, as you see from Christ's sufferings. May your desire be the same, and so you will be saved by His grace.

(12) From this follows consolation for every faithful, true Christian. If Christ suffered for all, then he suffered also for you. If he died for all, then he died also for you. If He reconciled all with His Heavenly Father, then He reconciled you as well. If He opened access to Him for all, then He opened it also to you. If He effected salvation and opened the Kingdom of God for all, then He did the same for you. Be of good cheer and peaceful and await eternal blessings without doubting. But only be faithful unto death, according to Christ's words, "Be faithful until death, and I will give you the crown of life" (Rev 2:10).

(13) A consolation for Christians in temptations, misfortunes, and tribulations. If Christ suffered so much for us, will He abandon us in our need? Will He abandon those for whom He suffered and died? He gave Himself up for us and did not refuse to die for us. Will He refuse to help us in our need? Never. His help will without fail come to us, for whose sake He effected such a great act of His love. He watches and awaits struggle and patience in our need, and invisibly grants us help, and is victorious in us, and prepares a crown for our victory.

Stand fast, Christian, have courage, and persevere in the need that befalls you, and pray, and call on Jesus, and await His help, and you will feel His supporting hand, of Him before Whom the devil and all hell tremble.

(14) Consolation for those who repent and are troubled in their conscience for their sins. It happens that the evil spirit whispers to those who repent: you, he says, have done so very much evil, what kind of salvation are you hoping for? Through this, the evil spirit intends and wishes to bring a person into despair and to make him an accomplice in his own ruination.

Christian! Avoid assenting to the evil counsel of the evil spirit. Our hope is Christ the Lord. If He suffered and died for you, how will He not accept and have mercy on one who turns himself around and repents? He desires this, and He exhorts us through His Word and through preachers, and expects all sinners to turn to Him and repent, and thus be saved. He Who gave Himself up, and suffered, and died for all wishes for and craves the salvation of all. This is a faithful saying and worthy of all acceptance. And even if your sins were great and terrible, and there were a great multitude of them, all of them would be expiated and wiped away by his grace. Your sins are great, but His mercy is infinite. You have a multitude of sins, but His munificence is endless. As a drop of water compared to the sea, so are all your sins compared to God's mercy and Christ's priceless merits. Christ will forgive you all your sins and will no longer mention them to you. Since, when you repent, His holy desire and the fruit of His sufferings becomes a reality, and your entire past life, sordid and foul, will not harm you, like darkness that has come out into the light. Darkness is an unrepentant life and error. Light is correction. You, having renounced your former life and having begun a new one, as it were coming out from darkness to the light and, having hated the darkness, loved the light, and therefore have become a new person.

Have courage and persevere, and expect eternal salvation, as all true Christians expect it. Only beware that you do not return to your former life, as a dog "returns to his own vomit and a sow, having washed, to her wallowing in the mire" (2 Pet 2:22). Watch out, beware of this! Satan tries with all his might to return you back to your former life. You should stand fast and persevere, and carry out to the end what you have begun. Not the beginning, but the end is boasted of. And whatever weakness you see within yourself, correct them by daily repentance and prayer, and so from day to day, you will be better. And in everything call upon the all-powerful helper, Jesus Christ, for without Him, we can do nothing. The enemy attacks you violently—you should stand firmly against him with Christ's help. And thus he will be shamed, but you will be saved.

(15) Although we should thank God for all of His benefactions that we have freely received and receive from Him, we should most of all thank Him because He sent His own Son to us, who were perishing, and deigned that He suffer for us and so save us. His wondrous and incomprehensible goodness and love for us is revealed in this. So wondrously are we saved! The Son of God, the King and Son of the Heavenly King, suffered and died for our

salvation. Who can condemn a person who is a true Christian? The Son of God suffered and died for him, and cleansed and sanctified him by His blood, and God vindicates him.

Remember, Christian, this great and incomprehensible deed and sincerely thank God for it. "Blessed is the Lord God of Israel, For He has visited and redeemed His people, And has raised up a horn of salvation for us in the house of His servant David" (Luke 1:68–69).

(16) Christ's sufferings and death teach us to die to sin and to live for God through righteousness. The Apostle wrote concerning this, "And [Christ] died for all, that those who live should live no longer for themselves, but for Him who died for them and rose again" (2 Cor 5:15).

Christian! If you wish to live for Christ God, then you must die to sin and to yourself. It is impossible to live both for sin and for Christ. Christ purchased you for Himself with His blood; you are His purchased servant. He is your Lord; you are His servant, purchased at the price of His blood. Judge for yourself for whom you should live—for yourself or for Him, your Lord; to live according to your own or according to His will.

You yourself know that a faithful servant does the bidding of his master and not of himself. Unfaithful is that servant who lives not according to the will of his master, but according to his own will and whims. Likewise the Christian is not a true Christian, but a false and unfaithful servant of Christ, if he lives not by Christ's will, but his own. Therefore, Christ the Lord says to such people, "But why do you call Me 'Lord, Lord,' and do not do the things which I say" (Luke 6:46)?

Die to your own will and to sin, that is, to your whims, and you will be Christ's servant, and you will live for Him and work for Him. The fruit of the crucifixion and death of Christ is in the expunging of our sins. "[Christ] Himself bore our sins in His own body on the tree, that we, having died to sins, might live for righteousness" (1 Pet 2:24).

But where is this fruit in you, if you are sinning and living in falsehood? This is a sign that you are still living in sin and have not been freed from sins. And then you do not have any benefit from Christ's sufferings and death, although it is the all-powerful cure. Repent and do away with your sinful whims, and then Christ's death will be of benefit to you. Christ was crucified for our sins, and we must crucify our flesh with its passions and lusts if we wish to belong to Christ. "Those who are Christ's have crucified the flesh with its passions and desires" (Gal 5:24). Here are the signs and marks of Christ's servants, namely that they *have crucified the flesh with its passions and desires.* Christ died for our sins, and we must renounce them and take leave of them, and die to them, that we may come to life through and with Christ.

So take stock of yourself, Christian, as to whose servant you are, for whom you live, for whom you work, to what end you are going, to what side you belong—to Christ or His enemy, the devil. He is the servant of the one whose will he does, whom he pleases, for whom he works.

(17) Christ our Lord was despised, disparaged, mocked, cursed, and stripped naked in his sufferings. From this, we learn, Christians, not to seek riches, honor, and glory in this world, but to despise all of them, and to make use of them for our needs, and not for luxury and concupiscence. It is shameful for a Christian to seek honor and glory in this world, when Christ his Lord was mocked and cursed for him. It is shameful for a Christian to desire and seek riches, when Christ his Lord did not even have rags during his sufferings. It is shameless for a Christian to wallow in luxury and pleasures, when Christ his Lord drank the bitter cup of suffering for him. Poor is that Christian who wishes to become rich, famous, to gain honor and to live in luxury and merrymaking. This is a sign that he has forgotten that Christ suffered and died for him, and it is obvious that he does not revere the suffering and death of the Son of God as a great thing. Take stock of yourself, Christian, in this important matter, and turn your mind to the Passion of Christ, and you will realize that you are doing what is contrary to the Christian faith.

(18) From Christ's sufferings and from His saving providence for man, we perceive and see how great is the dignity, honor, and nobility of man. God Himself—who surpasses all reason and wonder—God Himself took human form and came down to man who had departed from Him. Indeed, "[g]reat is the mystery of godliness: God was manifested in the flesh" (1 Tim 3:16), and moreover, suffered for man. That for which such a great and incomprehensible providence of God was accomplished must be great; that for which such a high price, the blood of the Son of God, was given must be precious. It is clear that man, for whose sake He came into the world Himself and suffered in His life-giving flesh, is dear to our God.

What a marvelous and most noble creation of God is man! He was created by God's special counsel: "Let Us make man" (Gen 1:26). "Man was made in the image and likeness of God" (v. 27). But when man fell and was lost, God showed a wondrous and incomprehensible providence for him. Besides giving him His law, He gave him His Word, as a candle, shining in a dark place, sent him prophets, commanded his angels to guard him; besides providing him with innumerable blessings, visible and invisible, He Himself with His heavenly host came to seek this lost silver piece (Luke 15:9), and to deliver and free man, held captive by the enemy, and to return his kingly nobility to him.

Ah, poor man, a beloved and highly esteemed, but fallen and lost creation! Look what an honor from God you were favored with, and how God so highly honored you! God Himself with His angels came to you to seek out and save you and suffered for you. Do you see your honor? As much as man was dishonored by the fall, so much was he honored by the incarnation of the Son of God and His saving providence. Sin cast him into the most ignoble condition, for "man, being in honor, understood it not; he shall be compared unto the brute beasts, and is become like unto them" (Ps 48:13), but was exalted above all creation by the coming of Christ the Son of God.

Oh, if only man so honored God as much as he is honored by God! Learn, O man, your baseness and poverty, which arise from sin, and humble yourself. Learn also your honor, created for you by Christ's coming and suffering, and thank Him sincerely and with all humility. "Lord, what is man, that thou hast had such respect unto him? Or the son of man, that thou so regardest him? Man is like to vanity" (Ps 143:3–4). Man had become base, but God's wondrous goodness highly honored and exalted him.

Man! You are dear to God; you should hold His providence for you in the highest esteem. God so honored you; and with your whole heart you should honor God, Who has honored you. God poured out wondrous goodness and love on you—you should embrace this goodness and love of His. God is truly honored when we repent of sins, which offend Him, and we avoid every sin, lest we offend Him, and do what is pleasing to His holy will. So repent, and avoid sin, and do what His holy will wishes, and you honor God, Who has honored you.

(19) From this it follows that we must honor every person. Christ, our Lord, honored man, so we too must honor Him. We render honor to a person honored by an earthly king; so much the more should we render honor to the one whom the Heavenly King has honored. How will you disparage, disdain, slander, swear at, backbite, or mock one whom God Himself has honored? Watch yourself, Christian, and avoid disdaining and disparaging a person whom the Heavenly King has honored so highly.

(20) From this, you see that those Christians who disdain, despise, swear at, and vilify people sin grievously. Insult and disrespect is shown for the King

himself when honor is not rendered to a person honored by him. In such a way, insult and disrespect is shown for the Heavenly King Himself, Jesus Christ, when we disdain and disparage a person honored by Him.

Watch yourself, Christian, and think about what you are doing when you disparage and vilify your brother. He who disparages will be disparaged, he who disdains will be disdained, and he who insults will be insulted.

(21) By His sufferings and death, Christ, our Lord, delivered us from eternal death and all the torments in hell and bestowed eternal life on us. From this, you see, Christian, what a great calamity is eternal torment and what a great blessing is eternal life. We sinners could in no way be delivered from that eternal evil and could in no way receive that eternal blessedness except by the sufferings and death of the only-begotten Son of God. Christ our Lord did not spare Himself for this. He redeemed us at the price of His own blood. Glory to His love for mankind, glory to His goodness and His mercy!

Great is the evil from which we are delivered at a great price. And great and costly is the good that is bought at a great and costly price. For an infinite and terrible evil, there must be eternal torment, from which we have been redeemed by the inestimable price of Christ's death. And there must also be that great and incomprehensible blessedness for which an inestimable price was paid. We were deprived of it by sin and were made subject to that calamity. Avoid sin, Christian, lest it cause you to fall into that disastrous eternal plight.

(22) From Christ's sufferings and all His salvific providence for us, we learn that our very first work and endeavor must be for our salvation. Everything else relating to this world and temporal life is the very last. God very much desires, as we see from Christ's sufferings and all His providence, that we be saved. Our desire must also be such. If the most good God yearns for our salvation, we too must do the same. As a hungry man desires bread and a thirsty man water, so also must we desire and seek salvation. The merciful God exerts every effort, as we see, to turn us to repentance and save us. Let all of our effort be for this. We need food, clothing, shelter, and so on, but salvation is so necessary that without it the whole world is nothing. A very great price, Christ's blood, was given for our salvation. May it also be for us precious, more valuable than the whole world, more valuable than heaven and earth, more valuable than all the treasure of this world, for without it everything is nothing. There is no benefit where there is no salvation of the soul. We seek the good things of this world, so much the more should we seek eternal good things. We care for health of the mortal body—so much more should we take

care that our immortal soul be restored to health. We maintain temporal life; so much more should we look after eternal life, for the sake of which we must leave everything, even temporal life itself, if needed. The primary task and endeavor of all true Christians was and is to desire and seek their salvation with all zeal, as something purchased at a high price.

Christian! May this be also your primary task and endeavor if you want to be a true Christian! Christ the Lord Himself, sacrificing Himself, acquired salvation for you so take care lest Satan snatch it from our hands. Every sin and predilection for the world closes the door for eternal salvation. So shun all of this.

(23) From Christ's sufferings we learn that Christians must suffer in this world, be mocked, cursed at, and disparaged, and endure other torments from those who love this world. The members must be with the suffering Head, and His servants must be with their suffering Lord.

Christians are from Christ—Christ's servants, members of Christ's body, spiritual. The world, beclouded by delusion, hated and persecuted Christ the Lord; it also hates and persecutes Christians as belonging to Christ, adhering to Christ, loving Christ, and following Him. "A servant is not greater than his master" (John 15:20). They did away with Christ the Lord, so what can His servants expect, except persecution? This was foretold by God Himself and written of in the Holy Scripture: "You will be hated by all for My name's sake" (Matt 10:22). "In the world you will have tribulation" (John 16:33). "If the world hates you, you know that it hated Me before it hated you. If you were of the world, the world would love its own. Yet because you are not of the world, but I chose you out of the world, therefore the world hates you" (John 15:18–19). "All who desire to live godly in Christ Jesus will suffer persecution" (2 Tim 3:12). "We must through many tribulations enter the kingdom of God" (Acts 14:22). And a heavenly voice bears witness concerning God's chosen ones: "These are the ones who come out of the great tribulation" (Rev 7:14). Tribulation has been foretold to Christians that they may be prepared to endure the tribulation. "My son, if you draw near to serve the Lord, prepare your soul for temptation" (Sir 2:1). It is no use for Christians to dream about the golden days and to await them. Tribulation is foretold, and we see this. But from whom would Christians endure tribulation? Persecution from pagan tyrants has ceased. Christians live among Christians. Indeed, open persecutors and tormentors have disappeared, and glory be to God! But the devil, the very first tormentor, as before constantly raises up persecution against the pious, as the Scripture says: "And the dragon was enraged with the woman, and he went to make war with the rest of her offspring, who keep the commandments of God and have the testimony of Jesus Christ" (Rev 12:17). This is the very first tormentor of the Christians!

Jesus Christ our Lord suffered from His own, as was written, "He came to His own, and His own did not receive Him" (John 1:11). "His prophets suffered from their fellow countrymen, as we see in the Scripture" (Matt 13:57; 23:37). Likewise, Christians suffer from their own Christians, but false ones. An evil neighbor hates and persecutes a good neighbor; an evil husband hates and persecutes a good wife and an evil wife does likewise to a good husband; a brother and sister hate and persecute a good brother and sister. "A man's enemies will be those of his own household" (Matt 10:36). These are the persecutors of Christians: false Christians! These include masters who either punish and torment their peasants beyond measure, or who reproach and curse at them with disgraceful and abusive language, or maintain worse than their dogs those for whom Christ suffered and died, or burden them with excessive chores and quit-rents, so they do not have sustenance and clothing because of their squalor; the master alone gobbles up all their goods. These tormentors of Christians, just more refined!

You see, Christian, from whom Christians suffer. So you yourself should expect sufferings and prepare to endure them, if you wish to live a pious life. An evil tongue is a great persecutor of Christians. As the body is wounded by the sword and mace, so the soul is wounded by abusive speech. But for consolation, Christ tells Christians, "Blessed are you when they revile and persecute you, and say all kinds of evil against you falsely for My sake. Rejoice and be exceedingly glad, for great is your reward in heaven" (Matt 5:11–12).

(24) From Christ's great patience, we learn to magnanimously endure every anguish that besets us. Christ did not resist His enemies; let us not resist them either. Christ did not take vengeance on His enemies; let us not take vengeance either. Christ meekly endured reproaches, mocking, and humiliation; let us meekly endure them as well. Christ died for us; let us die for Him, if it becomes necessary. "Christ also suffered for us, leaving us an example, that you should follow His steps" (1 Pet 2:21). Christ prayed for His crucifiers: "Father, forgive them" (Luke 23:34). Let us too pray for our enemies: "Lord, do not charge them with this sin" (Acts 7:60). In this way let us deny ourselves, in this way let us bear our cross, in this way we shall follow

Christ, in this way we shall be *a new creation* in Christ, in this way shall we be like unto Him. In this way "shall we suffer with Him, that we may also be glorified together" (Matt 16:24; 2 Cor 5:17; Rom 8:17). We shall be true Christians, shall be His true servants, shall be His living members. We shall be with Him here and there. We shall have in His coming a second sign and witness that we belonged to Him in this world, and so He shall then acknowledge us as His own.

(25) Christ's sufferings and all His saving merits, that He accomplished for us, have infinite importance, power, and dignity because of His Person, Who is perfect God and perfect Man. Because of this, for one who repents and sincerely believes in Christ, every and all kinds of sins whatever he may have committed, however numerous, serious, and terrible they may be, are remitted, and they are remitted only by grace. Because Christ's merits are higher and more powerful than all and every kind of our sins. What ruins a person is not seriousness nor the multitude of sins, but an unrepentant and hardened heart.

(26) By His sufferings for us, Christ our Lord forever put us in His debt, inasmuch as He, Who suffered for us, is God, One of the Holy Trinity, and we are sinners and worthless servants, for whom He suffered. He forever put us in His debt, insomuch as He delivered us from eternal death and torment not by silver or gold, but by His precious blood. He forever put us in His debt, inasmuch as He redeemed us for eternal life and opened the door to God's eternal kingdom. Eternal benefaction, done in such a wondrous fashion and achieved by an infinite person, requires eternal thanksgiving. Therefore, with all the Holy Church, eternal thanksgiving, praise, singing, and glorification let us offer with the Father and the Holy Spirit. Glory to God, who has so favored us!

(27) We learn from the sufferings of Christ that both our justification and eternal salvation consists in God's grace and Christ's merits alone, received in faith. This is witnessed in many places in the Holy Scriptures. But we must show this faith by works, in accordance with the Apostle's teaching: "Show me your faith without your works" (Jas 2:18). True repentance and faith are unfailingly followed by correction and renewal of the heart and exterior life. True repentance and faith renew and correct a person, turn him away from the vanity of the world, induce him to desire and search for eternal life, teach fear of God, and incessantly exhort to fight against sin and to do good and to please God.

Christian! Salvation is prepared for you by Christ. Shun losing it by your carelessness. Abide in true repentance and faith until the end, and by God's grace you will attain salvation, which I sincerely wish for you.

(28) Christ's sufferings not only will not be of benefit for Christians living without repentance and correction but will even be for denunciation and a worse condemnation. Christ, Who suffered and died for the sins of the world, will also judge the world for its sins (John 5:22; 2 Cor 5:10). The world saw Christ, living on earth as a man—then it will see Him as God.

The world saw Christ on earth in humility—then it will see him in Divine and terrible glory.

The world saw Christ on earth in meekness and long-suffering—then it will see His righteous anger against unrepentant sinners.

The world saw Christ's love and mercy toward sinners on earth—then it will see His justice.

The world saw Christ on earth remitting the sins of repentant sinners—then it will see Him rendering to all according to their deeds.

The world saw Christ on earth, being judged by the iniquitous—then it will see Him judging the iniquitous. The world heard the cry of the iniquitous against Christ: "Away with Him, away with Him! Crucify Him!"—then the world will hear the cry of unrepentant sinners to the mountains and stones, "Fall on us and hide us from the face of Him who sits on the throne and from the wrath of the Lamb! For the great day of His wrath has come, and who is able to stand" (Rev 6:16–17)?

The world saw Christ condemned to death by the iniquitous—then it will see Him condemning the iniquitous ones to eternal death: "Depart from Me, you cursed, into the everlasting fire prepared for the devil and his angels" (Matt 25:41).

The world saw Christ nailed to the cross and hanging between two malefactors—then it will see Him sitting on the throne of glory, and surrounded by the heavenly host, and shining with ineffable light; and it will be terrified and tremble all over in fear of that glory.

Pious souls, rejoice and be glad, since your deliverance is drawing near. As living consolation flows from Christ's sufferings to the pious and repentant, so greater denunciation and condemnation will flow to impious and unrepentant sinners.

We see in the holy Gospel that after Christ's resurrection from the dead, traces of Christ's wounds remained on His body (John 20:27). This was done by God's providence. At Christ's Second Coming, these wounds will be for the consolation and joy of the faithful and His saints and for denunciation and greater condemnation for the impious and unrepentant sinners because they were ungrateful to Him Who suffered for their salvation, and was nailed to the Cross, and died, and neglected salvation, which was acquired for them at such a high price.

It is written of the Jews who crucified Christ, "They shall look on Him whom they pierced" (John 19:37; Zech 12:10). Impious sinners also shall look, and they will see the wounds on His hands and feet and side, and fear, trembling, and horror will seize them. And so Christ's sufferings will be for their accusation and greater condemnation, that they did not want to make use of such grace of God and be saved. Among these are fornicators, adulterers, and all who live disgracefully; thieves, extortioners, robbers, bribe-taking judges; landowners who oppress their peasants; merchants who cheat in trade, and who sell a cheap item as if it were an expensive one, and a shoddy item as a good one; those who hold back the pay of hired help; slanderers, revilers; liars, tricksters, and sly persons; drunkards; those who resisted their parents and the authorities; those who cast spells and those who summon them, and other wrongdoers who do not repent and correct themselves. For all like them, Christ's sufferings, and the holy Gospel, and Christ Himself, Who suffered for all, will not only not yield any benefit but will be for greater condemnation and denunciation.

Repent, Christian, and begin a new life, contrary to your former iniquitous life, and Christ will be yours, with all His merits and eternal blessings.

(29) You see, Christian, what benefit results from recollection and reflection on Christ's sufferings. Faithful and diligent consideration of Christ's sufferings teaches us: to repent and feel sorry for our sins, which were the cause of the Passion and afflictions of Christ our Lord; to realize what a terrible and ruinous evil is sin; to avoid every sin, as a mortal and most pernicious evil; to despise the world with all its delusions and lusts, not to desire the honor, glory, riches, and merriment of this world; to think of the heavenly, and not of the earthly; to hold as precious the treasury of eternal salvation as something purchased for the immense price of Christ's blood; to realize what we have become through sin and what we have obtained through Christ's sufferings, what calamity we have fallen into through sin, and what great and incomprehensible blessedness has been returned to us through Christ's sufferings, and to earnestly thank God, Who had such mercy on us, for all of this; to learn

of God's anger because of sins, God's indefatigable judgment, God's unalterable justice, since it does not let sin go unpunished, God's incomprehensible wisdom, which devises a means of salvation where it is not apparent and where it is impossible for us, everything being possible for God; to come to know God's fervent love for the human race, and to love Him in return and, in accordance with His Word, to love and honor our neighbor, and to do good to him, and so on.

In this way, reflection on Christ's sufferings changes and renews a person and makes him different from what he formerly was. Christ's sufferings are like a salvific book, from which we learn every good thing, that is, repentance, faith, veneration of God, love for neighbor, humility, meekness, patience, disdain for the world and all its vanity, and we are spurred on to incessant desire and a diligent pursuit of the future life and its eternal blessings.

Christian, turn the eyes of your heart to Christ's sufferings, and remember them often, and reflect on them, and you will be renewed. Whoever loves and esteems something always has it on his mind and in his thoughts, and his mind and heart are absorbed in it. Through the sufferings of Christ, we were delivered from eternal perdition and received everlasting blessedness. And how can a Christian not remember this? It is sweet and beneficial to recollect the means and way by which we were delivered from the great calamity and received every kind of eternal good thing. Christ our Lord did this for us by His suffering. Remembrance of former affliction and reflection on present blessedness console, enliven, make joyful, and delight a person. We were lost but were saved by Christ's sufferings, and received eternal glory, life, joy, and good things. It is sweet and joyful to remember this.

Only beware, Christian, lest you fall under the former affliction. The doors of God's kingdom were opened by Christ's death. Repentant sinners and those who do works of repentance enter through them. You should avoid closing those doors to yourself by sins and an unrepentant life.

People have the practice of depicting battles, struggles of soldiers against enemies, and the victories gained over them. And looking at those pictures, they recall the victories gained over enemies, and so are comforted. The Holy Church adopted the excellent and soul-saving practice of painting images of the Passion of Christ and presenting them to the faithful for great benefit and consolation.

Christian! These pictures depict for you the struggle that the Son of God accomplished out for us. And He battled not with weapons, but by enduring the Cross and suffering; He battled against the devil and all our enemies. And He gained a most glorious and eternal victory over them and granted it to us in such a way that we hope by His grace to someday triumph and to exclaim, "O Death, where is your sting? O Hades, where is your victory" (1 Cor 15:55)?

"But thanks be to God, who gives us the victory through our Lord Jesus Christ" (1 Cor 15:57). It is comforting and joyful to remember this struggle of the Son of God and His victory gained over our enemies and to look upon it. He accomplished that struggle for us, and He gained the victory over our enemies for us, too. There is no way we ourselves could have defeated our enemies and be delivered from them. Christ, our Lord and protector, stood up for us, and was victorious, and trampled on them, and triumphed over them, and so snatched us away and delivered us from them. Glory to the conqueror of death and hell, Jesus! Let us joyfully sing to Him a song of victory: "He is greatly glorified!" (Exod 15:1).

The image of Christ's sufferings depicts for us this glorious and soul-saving victory. This image is like a book in which we read what is depicted. In the book, we read what was done and how. The image and picture presents all this not only to the eyes of the soul, but also to the bodily eyes, and depicts them poignantly, and so strikes the heart of the viewer. For it is impossible for a person who looks upon an image of Christ's sufferings not to be touched and to shudder, not to feel fear in the heart, or consolation, or contrition, or remorse for sins, especially if he looks with reflection and reverence. The painted image of Christ's sufferings will bestow such benefit!

If you desire, Christian, to have the constant memory of Christ's sufferings and to receive benefit from it for your soul, keep a depiction of Christ's sufferings in your home, and look at it often with reverence, and they will serve for you as a visual sermon and a replacement for your customary reading.

Throw out of your house fancy pictures, which tempt, arouse, and weaken your flesh, and keep an image that depicts the struggle and victory of Christ over our enemies, which will edify your soul. You will learn all good things from it. It will always remind you Who your Saviour and redeemer is, from what and by what and how He redeemed you; remind you of His love for you and your obligation to Him; remind you of your former affliction and your present and future blessedness, and what you formerly were and what you have now become.

This salvific picture will depict for you who you are and how you should live in the world. Upon looking at this picture, you will not want to enrich yourself, become famous, amuse yourself, and live in luxury in this world but you will consider yourself unworthy of all that you have. It will always exhort you not to take revenge, but to forgive a neighbor's offences, to do good not only to friends, but also to enemies, and to pray for all. In a word, what is written in the holy Gospel is all depicted in Christ's sufferings, and is presented for our imitation.

(30) You will revere Christ's entire saving providence, as well as His sufferings, and Christ Himself Who suffered, when you revere the work of your redemption as most precious, and hold it in constant memory, and sincerely thank Him for it, and you will live in true repentance and remorse for your sins, since they caused such affliction and suffering for Christ, you will shun every sin, and you will do everything that is pleasing to His holy will and, having come to hate the vanity of the world, you will rush to Him alone, as to our light and life, and will follow Him with humility, love, meekness, and patience. This is how Christ and His saving providence are truly revered. Many Christians honor Christ's sufferings and the Christ Who suffered with their lips, but turn away from Him in their hearts. Christ says of such people, "These people draw near to Me with their mouth, And honor Me with their lips, But their heart is far from Me" (Matt 15:8).

(31) From Christ's sufferings, we learn to approach the Heavenly Father with humility and faith, and in Christ's name to ask Him everything needed and helpful for salvation, that is, remission of sins, grace, renewal, and the excellent gifts of the Holy Spirit—"love, joy, peace, long-suffering, kindness, goodness, faithfulness, gentleness, self-control," and finally, eternal life and heavenly good things (Gal 5:22–23). If he sent His Son to us, and handed him over to suffering and death for us, how can He not grant everything that is pleasing to His will and beneficial to us? "He who did not spare His own Son, but delivered Him up for us all, how shall He not with Him also freely give us all things" (Rom 8:32)? Only let us ourselves not be careless. "Ask, and it will be given to you; seek, and you will find; knock, and it will be opened to you," Christ our Lord Himself encourages and reassures us (Matt 7:7). "Make me a clean heart, O God, and renew a right spirit within me. Cast me not away from Thy presence, and take not Thy Holy Spirit from me. O give me the comfort of Thy salvation, and stablish me with Thy governing Spirit" (Ps 50:12–14).

(32) We believe that in Christ are two natures, divinity and humanity united in a single person, but unmingled, and therefore Christ our Lord is perfect God and perfect man, Who suffered for us. But He suffered and

died according to his human nature, and not according to His divinity. For divinity is passionless. It cannot endure or suffer from illnesses and die; it is always constant in its all-perfect blessedness. Christ our God suffered in His soul and His body, as said earlier, but His divinity was impassionate in His sufferings. Avoid, Christian, ascribing illness and suffering to Christ's divinity.

Read and listen attentively to the church verses read on Wednesdays, Fridays, and Sundays, and you yourself will see this. Christ our Lord, being God, was worshipped and glorified by the angels on the throne of His glory with the Father and the Holy Spirit even when He walked the earth in human and humble form and when He suffered for us. "In the grave bodily, but in hades with Thy soul as God; in Paradise with the thief, and on the throne with the Father and the Spirit wast Thou Who fillest all things, Oh Christ the Inexpressible" (From the Hours of Holy Pascha).[12]

But let us look further: what did Christ our Lord do for us? Christ died for our sins, and on the third day rose from the dead, and being seen during forty days by His disciples and Apostles, and other of His faithful, and in various ways proved to them His rising, and "speaking of the things pertaining to the kingdom of God" (Acts 1:3). Thus He did His work, for which He came into the world, and before the eyes of His disciples, He ascended from the Mount of Olives into heaven, whence He came, and sat at the right hand of God the Father (see Acts 1:9 & 12). So, Christian, He did His work and left. "Sing unto God, O ye kingdoms of the earth, sing praises unto the Lord, Unto Him Who hath gone into the heaven of heavens in the east" (Ps 67:33–34). I sing to Thee: "Lord, I have heard Your report and was afraid" (Hab 3:2). He came to me, seeking me, the lost one. Therefore, I glorify Your great condescension to me, greatly merciful One.

Christian, let us pause a while here and consider Christ's salvific rising and ascension.

(1) Christ rose from the dead. Great consolation and joy flow to us from this. Christ rose and thus showed us that He has triumphed over all our enemies, the devil, sins, death and hell, as one strong in might, and gave us victory over them. Now we no longer fear sins, the devil, death, and hell. Christ is "our righteousness, sanctification, and redemption; he was delivered up because of our offenses, and was raised because of our justification" (1 Cor 1:30; Rom 4:25). "If God is for us, who can be against us" (Rom 8:31)? Christ's rising grants us this consolation and joy. Therefore, after His rising, He said to the

myrrh-bearing women, "Rejoice!" (Matt 28:9) and proclaimed to the Apostles, "Peace to you!" (John 20:26), as if to say, "Do not be afraid. I have cleansed your sins by My Blood; I have reconciled God with you and you with God; I have made My Father Your Father." "I am ascending to My Father and your Father, and to My God and your God" (John 20:17). He defeated and shamed the devil and snatched you from his power; he delivered you from death and hell, and opened the kingdom of God to you. Preach about this to all the corners of the world. "Go into all the world and preach the gospel to every creature" (Mark 16:15). All the faithful commune this joy and consolation. "O Christ, great and most holy Pascha, Christ! O Wisdom, Word, and Power of God: grant that we may more perfectly partake of Thee in the never-ending day of Thy kingdom."[13]

(2) Christ rose. We too need to rise with Christ, and to ascend with him into heaven. The rising is a double one: in body and in soul. The bodily rising will be on the last day, of which we read in the holy Symbol of Faith, "I look for the resurrection of the dead." Rising of the spirit consists of giving up sins. And to turn away from the vanity of the world, and to abide in true repentance and faith, to battle against every sin, to do the will of the Heavenly Father, to live uprightly for Him, and to follow Christ, the Son of God in humility, love, meekness, and patience. This is *the new creation* of which the Apostle speaks, "if anyone is in Christ, he is a new creation" (2 Cor 5:17), a new person, renewed by repentance and faith, a true Christian, a living member of the body of Christ and an heir to God's Kingdom.

The work of this new person is: to live humbly on earth, to avoid glory, honor, and every luxury, to think about the heavenly, and not the earthly, not to repay evil with evil, and scorning for scorning; to love his enemies, to bless those who curse him, to do good to those who hate him, and to pray for those who cause him temptation and for those who persecute him (Matt 5:44), and so on.

This is the work of the person who has risen from the death of the soul and living in a new life. So whoever will now rise up from the dead will rise into eternal life on the last day. "Blessed and holy is he who has part in the first resurrection. Over such the second death has no power" (Rev 20:6).

(3) Christ ascended into heaven, and what He Himself had said was fulfilled: "The Son of Man has come to seek and to save that which was lost" (Luke 19:10). He sought and saved man who had perished, and He ascended into heaven, and led him to His Heavenly Father, and ordered His heavenly

Powers to rejoice about this, saying, "Rejoice with me, for I have found the piece which I lost!" (Luke 15:9).

A shepherd, upon seeing a sheep has been separated from the flock, goes in search of it, and seeks it through the mountain and deserts, and, having found it, lays it on his shoulders, and with joy returns to his flock, and adds the sheep to it. Likewise the good Shepherd Jesus Christ our Lord, seeing man, who had been cut off from the assembly of angels, like a sheep from the flock, and wandering through the desert of this world, came down to search for him, and found him, and having laid him on his shoulders, carried him to His Heavenly Father, and numbered him among the assembly of angels, saying to them, "Rejoice with me, for I have found my sheep which was lost!" (Luke 15:6). Or as a man-loving and powerful king, upon seeing his people taken captive, goes out with his army and follows after his captive people and the enemy who had captured them, and having attacked him, snatches his people from his hands, and returns with joy to his homeland, and then there is joy in the entire homeland for the people who had been returned from captivity.

Likewise, the Heavenly King, Jesus Christ, the Lord mighty and powerful, the man-loving King, upon seeing man held captive by his enemy, the devil, went out with His heavenly army, and struck the foe who was holding him captive, and snatched captive man from his tormenting hands, and returned him to the heavenly Homeland; thus engendering joy for all the dwellers of heaven. Concerning this, the holy prophet sang to Him, foreseeing His restoration of us from captivity, "Thou art gone up on high, Thou hast led captivity captive" (Ps 67:19). Concerning this, may He receive glory from us, with the Father and the Holy Spirit, Amen!

(4) Christ ascended into heaven in the presence of His holy Apostles and showed all His faithful people the way there. Christ, the Head, ascended into heaven, and the holy members of His body, true Christians, will also ascend there. The way there was closed to mankind but was opened by Christ's death. *The veil of the temple was torn* at Christ's death, and the way and entrance into the heavenly kingdom was opened to the faithful (Matt 27:51; Heb 10:19).

Christians! The way into the Kingdom of Heaven has been shown to us and opened for us. And Christ our Lord has entered there and calls us to join Him there—us, for whom He suffered and died—so let us not be careless about our salvation. If we wish to ascend there and be with Christ, we must be with Him here in this world. "If anyone serves Me, let him follow Me; and where I am, there My servant will be also" (John 12:26).

Those living on the earth must separate themselves in mind and heart from this world, and relocate to heaven, and hide our treasure there, if we wish to enter there, in the words of the Apostle, "For our citizenship is in heaven, from which we also eagerly wait for the Savior, the Lord Jesus Christ" (Phil 3:20). "Ought not the Christ to have suffered these things and to enter into His glory" (Luke 24:26)? And we, Christians, "must through many tribulations enter the kingdom of God" (Acts 14:22). The Christian needs to live piously, humbly, lovingly, meekly, and patiently on earth if he wishes to enter the kingdom of heaven. This way is narrow and humble, but safe, and it leads into the kingdom of God.

(5) Neither the suffering and death of Christ, nor His Resurrection and Ascension will yield benefits to those Christians who live in carelessness and have not risen up in their souls from death. "Awake, you who sleep, Arise from the dead, And Christ will give you light" (Eph 5:14). We see, Christian, the first coming of Christ; we await the second. Let us try to be participants of the first, and then we shall meet His second coming with joy.

# 109. Citizens Awaiting Their King in Their City

We see that when citizens await the arrival of their king in their city, they prepare a worthy reception for him and often say among themselves, "The king is coming! The king is coming! At some time he will be here, night or day, morning or evening, and with what size retinue will he come?" This and like things do the townsmen speak among themselves as they await the king's arrival.

Christians! We are awaiting the coming to us of the Heavenly King, Jesus Christ. We see His first coming to us; we await the second too, and we shall see Him. We shall see that His first coming was in humility, poverty, meekness, and long-suffering; the second will be in terrible and Divine glory. In the first, He came quietly, and came down "like the rain upon a fleece of wool, even as the drops that water the earth" (Ps 71:6; Judg 6:36–40). In the second, He will shine "like lightening," which flashes in the east and appears in the west (Matt 24:27). He will come then not to suffer for us (that already took place), but to judge us and to render to all according to their deeds.

We see in the Holy Scripture what will happen then. We see that "the day of the Lord will come as a thief in the night, in which the heavens will pass away with a great noise, and the elements will melt with fervent heat; both the earth and the works that are in it will be burned up" (2 Pet 3:10). We see that then even "the sky will recede as a scroll when it is rolled up; and every mountain and island will move out of its place. And the kings of the earth, the great men, the rich men, the commanders, the mighty men, every slave and every free man, will hide themselves in the caves and in the rocks of the mountains, and will say to the mountains and rocks, 'Fall on us and hide us from the face of Him who sits on the throne and from the wrath of the Lamb! For the great day of His wrath has come, and who is able to stand?'" (Rev 6:14–17). We shall see that everyone who has died from the beginning of the world will rise from their graves then, and "come forth—those who have done good, to the resurrection of life, and those who have done evil, to the resurrection of condemnation" (John 5:28–29).

We see that from all corners of the earth "all the nations will be gathered before Him" (Matt 25:32) and will stand before the Heavenly King, the righteous Judge. We see that then all the people gathered together will be divided into two parts: some will stand on the right side of the Judge, and others, on the left. Then there will be a complete and final separation from one another. We see that then a wife will be forever separated from her husband; father and mother from their children; kings from their subjects; princes, lords, and masters from their servants; friends from their friends; and acquaintances from their acquaintances.

We also see that a wife will stand on the right side of the Judge, but a husband on the left, or a husband on the right, but his wife on the left; father and mother on the right, but their children on the left, or children on the right, but father and mother on the left; one brother on the right, but another on the left. We see that then the same will happen with leaders and their subordinates; we see that the king will stand on the right, but his subjects on the left, or subjects on the right, but the king on the left; princes, lords, and masters on the right, but their bondmen and servants on the left, or their bondmen and servants on the right, but princes, lords, and masters will stand on the left. We also see that pretended saints now revered by people stand on the left side, and supposed sinners and those despised by the world as impious will stand on the right. Saints and the righteous will be on the right side; the sinful and impious will stand on the left side.

Then the truth and untruth, the virtue and sin, the holiness and filth of each will be made known. For the examination then be according to conscience, and not by rank; by works, and not by personalities, by what is internal, and not by externals and outward appearances. For the Judge will be God, Who tries the hearts and reins and judges by the internal state of the heart, and not by the outward appearance of deeds. A person looks at the exterior of a man, but God looks at the human heart. For it often happens that a man is good in people's eyes, but evil before God; holy in people's eyes, but foul before God; virtuous in people's eyes, but depraved before God.

We see that those standing on the right side will shine like the heavenly bodies: "Then the righteous will shine forth as the sun" (Matt 13:43). Those standing on the left side will turn black and take up an appearance of vile ugliness, since the sins that are hidden in them now will come to the surface and will create a terrible ugliness. Then it will be revealed to the whole world whatever they did, not only openly, but also secretly, and what kind of thoughts and endeavors they had in their hearts. Then every ugliness of the soul adhering to it from sins will appear on the body of the sinner. Thus they will see their ugliness and the sinful loathsomeness in which they remained while living in this world. We hear that then the Righteous Judge will say to those who are on his right side, "Come, you blessed of My Father, inherit the kingdom prepared for you from the foundation of the world" (Matt 25:34). But to those who are on His left side, He will say, "Depart from Me, you cursed, into the everlasting fire prepared for the devil and his angels" (Matt 25:41). This is the lot of those standing on the right side and of those standing on the left side.

Christian, it will be sweet and joyful to hear, "Come," and terrible and sorrowful to hear: "Depart from Me." But without fail everyone will hear either one cry or the other. Christ's Dread Judgment will end with the blessing of some and the cursing of others. Everyone then, having heard the word said to them by the Judge, will go to their own, separate places, but not uniformly. Some will go with joy, and gladness, and triumph into eternal life. Others will go with weeping, sobbing, and despair into eternal torment. "And these will go away into everlasting punishment, but the righteous into eternal life" (Matt 25:46).

Christians! Such is the coming of our King, Jesus Christ, that we are awaiting—let us prepare ourselves to worthily meet Him. Let us talk often about that day. Let us say to one another: "The Heavenly King is coming! The Heavenly King is coming to us! He is coming to save the righteous and to torment sinners. When will He come? Night or day? Morning or evening? In what month, day, and hour?" His preachers constantly proclaim to us: "The Heavenly King is coming, the Heavenly King is coming, get ready to meet Him." O beloved messengers, tell us, when will He come to us? When will the sun of righteousness appear to us? When will His lightening flash and illumine the universe? When will His holy Throne be set up at the Trial and we all shall see Him? "He is coming soon," they answer us, "He is coming soon and will not tarry." "The coming of the Lord is at hand. Behold, the Judge is standing at the door!" (Jas 5:8–9). But you do not know the day and hour, in which He will come. "Watch therefore, for you do not know what hour your Lord is coming" (Matt 24:42). "He who testifies to these things says, 'Surely I am coming quickly.' Amen. Even so, come, Lord Jesus!" (Rev 22:20). To Him be glory unto the ages of ages, Amen.

# 110. One Will Be Taken and the Other Will Be Left

We see in the world that *one will be taken and the other will be left*. For example, one is taken for an honored office and the other is left; one is taken into the army and the other is left; one is taken for a feast and the other is left, and so on. Christian! So it will be at the Second Coming of Christ. "In that night there will be two men in one bed: the one will be taken and the other will be left. Two women will be grinding together: the one will be taken and the other left. Two men will be in the field: the one will be taken and the other left" (Luke 17:34–36). The pious one will be taken, and the impious one will be left. The pious husband will be taken, and the impious wife will be left and the pious wife will be taken and the impious husband will be left. The pious father will be taken, but the impious son and daughter will be left, and the pious son and daughter will be taken, and the impious father will be left. The pious brother and sister will be taken, and the other, impious brother and sister will be left. The pious neighbor will be taken, and the other, impious one will be left. The pious superior will be taken, but the impious subordinate will be left; and the pious subordinate will be taken, and the impious superior will be left. The pious prince, lord, and master will be taken, and their impious servant and servant will be left; and the pious servant and servant will be taken, and the impious prince, lord, and master will be left. The pious rich man will be taken, and the other, impious one will be left. The pious poor man will be taken, and the other, impious one will be left. The pious judge will be taken, and the other, impious one will be left. The pious master will be taken and the other, impious one will be left. The pious merchant will be taken, and the other, impious one will be left. The pious farmer will be taken, but the other, impious one will be left. The pious craftsman and artist will be taken, but the other, impious one will be left. The pious bondman and servant will be taken, but the impious one will be left. So one will be taken and the other will be left.

To where? To Christ, to the Kingdom of Heaven. "Wherever the body is, there the eagles will be gathered together" (Luke 17:37). Wherever the head is, there will the body be. Where Christ is, there will Christians be. "Where I am, there My servant will be also" (John 12:26). For it will be a selection and gathering by faith and truth, and not by office, calling, appearance, names, and titles. God is not a respecter of persons, but judges by what is inside, by faith and conscience. Gold and silver that bears a royal inscription or seal is taken to the treasury and is rejected if it does not have it. Christ's truth in a pious soul is like a royal seal that shows that this soul belongs to Christ. Such a soul will be taken into God's kingdom as one belonging to Christ. Then by God's command, angels will disperse throughout the world and will gather the pious, justified by faith and having the seal of Christ's truth, as coins with the depiction of the king into the treasury, into eternal life.

"And He will send His angels with a great sound of a trumpet, and they will gather together His elect from the four winds, from one end of heaven to the other" (Matt 24:31). Then this saying will be fulfilled: *one will be taken and the other will be left*. The pious one will be taken and the impious one will be left. "But as the days of Noah were, so also will the coming of the Son of Man be" (Matt 24:37). Before the flood they were eating, drinking, marrying, and suddenly came the flood, and destroyed them all. Thus it will be at the coming of the Son of God: people will be eating, drinking, arranging banquets, making merry, marrying, and unexpectedly, "the Day of the Lord" will arrive (Matt 24:37–39). Then will be heard the sound of the trumpet: "Come to the judgment!" Then will be heard the cry, "Behold, the bridegroom is coming; go out to meet him!" (Matt 25:6). Then will be fulfilled the saying of the Apostle, "When they say, 'Peace and safety!' then sudden destruction comes upon them" (1 Thess 5:3).

The day of the Lord "is near" (Rev 1:3). Unexpectedly "the sign of the Son of Man will appear in heaven, and then all the tribes of the earth will mourn, and they will see the Son of Man coming on the clouds of heaven with power and great glory. For as the lightning comes from the east and flashes to the west, so also will the coming of the Son of Man be" (Matt 24:30, 27). Christians! Let us repent and try to have a treasury of piety within ourselves, so that we too may not be left, but that "we … shall be … caught up together … in the clouds to meet the Lord in the air. And thus we shall always be with the Lord" (1 Thess 4:17).

# 111. An Oath

We see that when a person is either chosen for the army or is elevated to some respected post, or is appointed to some other service of the Sovereign, he pledges and swears to faithfully and justly serve the Sovereign and society, and to act conscientiously. This is the force of the oath. Likewise, all Christians, upon entering the holy Church, accepting the honor and dignity of the exalted name of Christian, and enlisting in the army of the Heavenly King, take an oath to remain in it until the end; they swear and promise, while renouncing Satan and all his evil deeds, to serve only Christ the Lord and Heavenly King with faith and truth for the entire time of their lives. We see this pledge, oath, and promise among Christians.

Every Christian should read the words that are pronounced before holy baptism. Each person being baptized proclaims three times: "I renounce Satan, and all his works, and all his angels, and all his service, and all his pride"; and spits on him. He also approaches Christ and says, "I unite myself unto Christ", and says this three times. Christian! What do this renunciation and vows signify, if not a pledge and oath, by which we promise, by renouncing Satan, and sins, and our lusts, and pride, and the vanity of this world, to follow Christ the Lord by faith, humility, love, meekness, and patience? This is the force of our vows made by us before holy baptism.

People who do not keep their pledges to the Sovereign and to society sin gravely. Such people prove to be unfaithful sons of society and more harmful for society than even external enemies, and are called a dishonorable name— traitors. They betray their Sovereign and society and become like an injured member of a body that itself decays and harms the entirety of the body. While considered members of society, they are decayed members that harm the entirety of society. An evil person cannot be a good leader, and if he is highly regarded, he will do much more harm to society than an obvious malefactor and external enemy. This is rather well known from history, and we see the same even now.

Among Christians who pledge an oath, and promise to serve Christ the Lord, but break their oath through sin are fornicators, adulterers, and all defilers, the malicious, the vengeful, murderers, thieves, extortioners, robbers, thugs, oppressors of widows and orphans, slanderers, the foul-mouthed, tricksters, tempters, liars, sly people, those who do not submit to their parents or the authorities, blasphemers, sorcerers and those summoning them, those who love the vanity of this world, those who live in pride and splendor, and others who live in opposition to God's Word. All such have violated the pledge of a Christian; have not kept their oaths and promises made during baptism; severed the salvific union with Christ and separated themselves with Him, and have returned to the service of Satan, whom they renounced and on whom they spit, and betrayed Christ their Lord and King, to Whom they swore an oath. The Lord says, "He who is not with Me is against Me" (Matt 12:30). All such are not with Christ, but against Him. "What fellowship has righteousness with lawlessness? And what communion has light with darkness? And what accord has Christ with Belial" (2 Cor 6:14–15)?

Violation of the promises given at baptism leads to this calamity and wretchedness. Those who have violated a pledge to the Sovereign and their society are removed from the number of good people and according to civil laws receive punishment as liars and violators of their pledge. Likewise Christians who have violated the pledge given to the Lord Jesus Christ, and have lied to Him and have turned to wickedness, are separated from good Christians like the goats from the sheep, and will be punished with eternal fire as traitors, more wicked than Muslims and pagans. "But the cowardly, unbelieving, abominable, murderers, sexually immoral, sorcerers, idolaters, and all liars shall have their part in the lake which burns with fire and brimstone, which is the second death" (Rev 21:8).

Christian! Remember that you gave this pledge, and take stock of yourself, please, in so important a matter, whether you are keeping it. If you are not keeping it, your baptism has no benefit for you. Christ the Lord, as a lover of mankind, calls and awaits all who have turned to Him and promises to show

His mercy to them. Turn, beloved to Him with repentance and tears, and He will receive you. And henceforth do not separate yourself from Him, but always be with Him. For He alone is our light and life, hope and consolation, joy, gladness, and blessedness in this age and the age to come. Apart from Him and without Him, there is only affliction, wretchedness, and grief both here and there. Turn to Him while there is still time. "Behold, now is the accepted time; behold, now is the day of salvation" (2 Cor 6:2). My soul, you should remember this, and remember that to be with Christ is eternal life; to be without Christ is eternal death. "For lo, they that go far from Thee shall perish," O Lord (Ps 72:27).

# 112. A Bathhouse

We see that people, when they go to a bathhouse, are washed from bodily dirt and taints and come out of the bathhouse clean and wearing a white shirt. Likewise, Christians, going into the bath of holy baptism, are washed from the dirt of sins, are purified and sanctified, and are clothed in the most bright and precious clothing of Christ's truth, as in royal purple, and are made sons of the Heavenly King and heirs of the heavenly kingdom, and emerge from it clean, holy, righteous, as the Apostle comfortingly tells them, "You were washed, you were sanctified, you were justified in the name of the Lord Jesus and by the Spirit of our God" (1 Cor 6:11). Therefore the Apostle calls holy baptism "the washing of regeneration" (Titus 3:5). Because in holy baptism we are born anew, and, having been perishing, we are saved and renewed, and we are cleansed and washed, and are made "a new creation in Christ" (2 Cor 5:17).

From this, we see, Christian, how great is God's love for mankind toward us. He favors man, defiled by sin and His enemy, with such grace, mercy, and honor! Blessed is God, Who has had such kindness! Glory to His kindness! Glory to His love for mankind! This grace and mercy were earned for us by the only-begotten Son of God, granted to us as a gift by the Heavenly Father, and perfected by the Holy Spirit. Glory to the Trihypostatic God!

Christians who treat the world and sin with love and transgress lose all of this holy and great Divine treasure. That is why "it has happened to them according to the true proverb: 'A dog returns to his own vomit,' and, 'a sow, having washed, to her wallowing in the mire'" (2 Pet 2:22). They are like those people who, having gone into the bathhouse and washed, willfully go into mud and get dirty. In the same way, having been washed by holy baptism and forgotten this great mercy that God has shown them, they willfully give themselves over to the filth of sin, and are defiled more and more by it. You yourself consider what benefit such people get from holy baptism. Indeed, none. Therefore, it happens that in their morals, such Christians are worse than pagans and idolaters, since many pagans, guided by natural law, have an aversion to such sins that corrupt Christians boldly dare to commit. Such falsehood, thievery, robbery, violence, trickery, flattery, slyness, insatiable greed, loathsome impurity as is seen in corrupt Christians are not evident among educated pagans. And many have gotten to the point where egregious sins, prohibited by God's law, are not considered sins.

This is serious blindness, a darkening and delusion of the mind, and results from human ingratitude. So man, having come into the depth of evil, pays it no mind. A Christian should, as one who has been renewed by God's grace, make progress for the better, and grow in Christ, and "come ... to a perfect man" (Eph 4:13). But he regresses and becomes worse than a pagan and an idolater. For such a person, baptism itself will serve as a denunciation on the day of Christ's judgment, if he does not repent, and does not correct himself, and washes away his filth by contrition of heart and tears.

From this, you see, Christian:

(1) How beneficial and necessary it is for Christians to recall holy baptism, the renunciations and vows that they gave, that is, whom and what they renounced then, what vows they gave to Jesus Christ, and what great mercy they were vouchsafed from God, in order that they remember all this, and live in the fear of God, and that they do not lose the heavenly gift given to them in baptism, but having lost it, they would seek it with repentance and contrition of heart, and correction of their life and morals. It is fitting to make this reminder especially to pastors.

(2) How beneficial and useful is the good and God-fearing upbringing of children, and reminding them of holy baptism and its circumstances, so that, when they remember and think about this, they may not be corrupted and be deprived of the gifts given in baptism. This is the responsibility of their parents. The parents gave them birth into temporal life, and should by the grace of God assist their birth into eternal life as well. But those parents who do not bring up their children with good character, but even more, lead them astray with bad example, give them birth into temporal life, but open the door to eternal death—it is better for them not to be born.

Beloved Christian! Like all Christians, you also have been vouchsafed to receive as a gift this supreme mercy and grace of God and the heavenly gifts in holy baptism; and you from God's servers heard then the sweetest greeting: *You were washed, you were sanctified, you were justified,* and so on. Remember this and take stock, whether you too have lost this great and heavenly treasure. If you do not live by the rule of God's Word, but live contrary to it, and follow the sinners described earlier, this is a clear sign that you have lost this spiritual treasure. This is why the already-mentioned proverb befits you: "A dog returns to his own vomit," and, "a sow, having washed, to her wallowing in the mire."

You are sorry and weep when you lose a physical and perishable treasure. How much more weeping and tears it will take to mourn over this lost heavenly treasure, and to wash with tears the defiled soul, and beg, seek, and knock at the door of God's mercy that it may return again to us! When it is lost, eternal salvation is also lost. It will unfailingly return if we return to God with repentance, and weeping, and tears. For "the Lord is merciful and gracious" (Ps 144:8). "He accepts those who repent and return to Him, as the compassionate father received the prodigal son" (Luke 15:20–24).

You, too, should take stock of yourself, my soul: what are you thinking, what are you contemplating, what do you love and what do you hate, what are you seeking and what are you avoiding, where do you live, where do you frequent, what do you aspire to, what desires, what movements do you feel within you? This heavenly treasure is hidden within the heart, but it reveals its existence through heavenly movements and desires. Like attracts like. "For where your treasure is, there your heart will be also" (Matt 6:21). "Remember Thy loving-kindnesses, O Lord, and Thy mercies, which are from everlasting. O remember not the sins of my youth, and of mine ignorance; according to Thy mercy think Thou upon me, O Lord, for Thy goodness' sake" (Ps 24:6–7). So, having turned away from sins to our Creator, may we always send up sighs to Him, and He will have mercy on us.

# 113. A Maiden Betrothed to a Man

In the world, we see that maidens are engaged to be married to men. So Christian souls are betrothed by faith to the heavenly bridegroom, Christ, in baptism, like pure maidens as brides, as the Apostle tells Christians, "For I am jealous for you with godly jealousy. For I have betrothed you to one husband, that I may present you as a chaste virgin to Christ" (2 Cor 11:2). This is a great mystery. This a great mystery and one passing understanding, and such unsurpassed honor and glory, and dignity, for the human soul to be betrothed to the Heavenly King and to the Son of God "fairer than the sons of men" (Ps 44:3). Who can comprehend and analyze such love for mankind of God's? Who can speak of the nobility, honor, glory, and dignity of the Christian soul, which is betrothed to the heavenly bridegroom? Pay attention to this, my soul. Remember, Christian, that your soul too is betrothed to this most glorious bridegroom.

A bride loves her bridegroom alone and tries to please him alone, as we see. In the same way, the Christian soul should love Christ, the Bridegroom, alone and please Him alone. A bride who directs her love to others who love her does not please her bridegroom, and he is repelled by her. In this way, Christ is repelled by a Christian soul that directs his love to sin and the world and tries to pleases them.

Oh, how gravely such a soul sins before Christ! How ungrateful and shamelessly it acts! How great is its calamity if it, having turned away from the most sweet and loving heavenly bridegroom, turns to the unclean and loathsome love of sin and the world! Christian! Take stock of yourself, please: have you not also turned away from Christ your Saviour to the world and sin? Do you not love something equally to, or what is worse, more than Him? You should love Him more than your father and mother, more than your wife and children, more than your brethren and friends, and more than yourself (Matt 10:37–39). He requires this of you, since He Himself so loved you that He gave Himself over as a sacrifice for you.

You see how beautiful the sky, the sun, the moon, and the stars and His other creations are. But He has not been so favorably disposed toward anything as toward your soul. You see how He honored you, with what honor and glory He has favored your soul. "Praise the Lord, O my soul" (Ps 145:1). "Hearken, O daughter, and see, and incline thine ear, and forget thy people, and thy father's house. And the King shall greatly desire thy beauty; for He is thy Lord, and thou shalt worship Him" (Ps 44:11–12).

Listen, my soul, listen to the voice of your heavenly bridegroom, and wish for His fine and most holy goodness. "For what have I in heaven, and what have I desired upon earth from Thee? My flesh and my heart have failed, O God of my heart, but Thou art my portion, O God, for ever. For lo, they that go far from Thee shall perish; Thou hast destroyed all them that are unfaithful against Thee. But it is good for me to cleave unto God, to put my trust in the Lord" (Ps 72:25–28). May your love for loathsome sin and the world and unseemly self-love be loathsome for you, my soul. Love only Jesus, who loves you; desire Him alone Who desires you; reach out and draw near to Him alone, Who seeks you. And be diligent with Him Who is diligent toward you, solicitous with Him Who looks after you, pure with the One Who is pure, holy with the One Who is holy, loving with the One Who is loving, meek with the One Who is meek, humble with the One who is humble, patient with the One Who is long-suffering, kind and merciful with the One Who is merciful. Guard against being separated from Him here, and you will dwell inseparably with Him in the age to come. "It is good for me to cleave unto God!"

# 114. A Ship

We see in the world that there are ships built for various needs that sail the seas and travel from place to place. The Holy Church is in the world what a ship is at sea. The Church is like a ship. A ship sails the sea; the Holy Church sojourns in the sea of this world. A ship is steered by its helmsman; the holy Church is steered by its Helmsman–Jesus Christ, our Lord. A ship, while it is sailing in the sea, is subjected to all kinds of storms, bad weather, and winds, and is tossed about by waves; the Holy Church, while it is in the world, is subjected to all kinds of storms of misfortunes, tribulations, and temptations, and is tossed about by the enticements of this world, like waves, and suffers from persecutions by the lovers of the world. But as consolation, the Helmsman, Jesus Christ, tells it concerning this, "And the gates of Hades shall not prevail against it" (Matt 16:18).

When sailing in the sea, a ship heads to its harbor to which it is sailing. The Holy Church, abiding in the sea of this world, heads to the calm harbor of eternal life; it will have rest there. Those on board the ship always think, and dream, and wish that they will safely reach their destination. Thus true Christians, who are in the Holy Church, always have in mind, and always aspire to and care about coming to the harbor of eternal rest. Because of this, they do not care about temporal and worldly treasures, for example, honor, glory, riches, and other things of this world, but are satisfied by what they have received from God's goodness. They say with the Apostle, "For we brought nothing into this world, and it is certain we can carry nothing out. And having food and clothing, with these we shall be content" (1 Tim 6:7–8).

When a big storm or bad weather is coming, sea captains have the practice of throwing an anchor into the depths of the sea, thus securing and saving their ship. Likewise, true Christians, when a big storm of temptations arises against them, throw the anchor of their hope into the depths of God's mercy and promise and His most holy oath (Heb 6:17–19). And they draw near to Jesus, as to their Helmsman, with supplication and tears, saying, "Lord, save us! We are perishing!" (Matt 9:25).

Noah's ark serves as a type or prefiguration of the Church. Various beasts, livestock, and birds were gathered in Noah's ark. Likewise, various peoples, like the wild beasts, were gathered in the Holy Church. "Behold, the Philistines also, and Tyre, with the Ethiopians, such were there. Mother Zion, shall a man say, and the man was born in her," sings the holy prophet about the Church (Ps 86:4–5). It is marvelous that in Noah's ark ferocious beasts were meek and harmonious with each other. This happened by God's command, and so they put aside their ferocity and savagery; otherwise they could not be accommodated in the ark. Likewise, those that have entered the Holy Church lay aside their former ways, like those of the beasts and the livestock, and become meek, harmonious, and peaceful with each other. For in baptism, all are renewed and adopt Christ's most holy character, and so are added to the Holy Church. Therefore it is written in the Acts of the Apostles about the first Christians, "the multitude of those who believed were of one heart and one soul" (Acts 4:32).

All the people, beasts, livestock, and birds outside of the ark then perished under the water. Likewise, all people outside of the Holy Church are perishing forever. Christian, think about whether you are within the Holy Church. The Church is *holy* (Eph 2:21; 5:26–27). Its sons must also be holy. Compare your character with the measure of God's Word and take note whether they are alike. The "new man" (Eph 4:24), or true Christian and son of the Church, is depicted there.

What use is there to be called a Christian, but not to be a Christian; to be numbered in the Church in people's eyes, but to be outside the Church, like an outcast, in God's eyes? All wrongdoers and those living in the pride and opulence of the world are living outside the Church, even though they boast of their confession of Christ's name. "What fellowship has righteousness with lawlessness? And what communion has light with darkness? And what accord has Christ with Belial" (2 Cor 6:14–15)?

Think about this, Christian, and repent, and correct yourself, and pray. May you be a true member of the Holy Church, and be saved from the coming wrath of God, as Noah was from the worldwide flood. You yourself can judge: how possible it is to be within the Church for one who flatters and is cunning and sly like a fox; for one who snatches away like a wolf; for one who rages and grows savage like a fierce lion; for one who is lustful as a stallion; for one who is as bad-tempered as a viper; for one who is as proud as a peacock; for one who stuffs himself and is as gluttonous as a pig; for one who so desires and seeks worldly things like the pagans, who have no hope of eternal life, as if he would live in this world forever, and as if he had not heard of the resurrection of the dead and eternal life. But what can one say if all these bestial dispositions are shown in one person? Such a person is even worse than a beast. Not the external appearance and form but the inner disposition of a man reveals the man. You will see for yourself, Christian, that it is impossible for a Christian who is careless and not cleansed by repentance to remain within God's Church. Such a one is in danger of perishing forever, as did all those outside Noah's ark, if he does not repent and correct himself. "Flesh and blood cannot inherit the kingdom of God" (1 Cor 15:50). "But outside are dogs and sorcerers and sexually immoral and murderers and idolaters, and whoever loves and practices a lie" (Rev 22:15).

Repent and correct yourself, and change yourself, and turn a bestial temperament into a Christian one, and so, having renewed yourself, you will be a true son of the Church, abiding in good hope of eternal life.

## 115. Whose Are You?

We hear that one person asks another, "To whom do you belong?" and the other replies, "I am the servant of such and such master, or the son of such and such father," and so on. But when a Christian is asked this, what should he answer? Certainly, every Christian should answer, "I am Christ's slave; for he confesses Christ as his Lord" (1 Cor 7:22; Rom 10:9; Col 3:24).

But take a look, Christian, into your conscience: do you work for Christ, do you please Christ, as a servant does his master? The holy martyrs—when their tormentors asked them, "To whom do you belong?"—answered audaciously, "We are Christians, we are servants of Christ." But they were so faithful to Christ their Lord that they did not spare their blood and life for His holy name. They so loved Him that not only honor, glory, and riches of this world, the weeping and tears of fathers and mothers, wives and children, but even horrible torture and "death shall [not] be able to separate us from the love of ... Christ" (Rom 8:38–39). These are the true servants of Christ; these are the true Christians, the sons of light, the sons of the Holy Church, Christ's meek sheep, the valiant warriors of Christ the King, the beloved members of the body of Christ, the children of the most high God and the heirs to His kingdom!

But how, Christian, you who confess Christ, but live contrary to Christ, I say, can you say, "I am Christ's servant"? Truly great is the dignity of being Christ's servant. This honor and dignity are incomparably greater and higher than to be the son of an illustrious prince or earthly King. "In the Lord shall my soul be praised" (Ps 33:3).

Many boast: I, they say, am the servant of such and such a high-ranking master, or the servant of that prince or lord, or the courtier of such and such a king. But Christians truly and fittingly boast of their Lord: we are servants of the Heavenly King, Jesus Christ. This is really true praise, truly high glory, honor and dignity—to be and be called Christ's servant. But how can one call himself a servant of Christ if he works for sin, the world, and himself, and not Christ? What benefit is there to be called Christ's servant, but not to be Christ's servant; to be a Christian on the outside and by confession, but within, in character to be a pagan or, what is worse, a beast? The holy Apostle declares to us the marks of Christ's servants, so that we may test ourselves and learn whether we are Christ's. "Those who are Christ's have crucified the flesh with its passions and desires" (Gal 5:24). These are the signs of Christ's people or servants!

Christian, crucify your flesh with its passions and desires and you will truly be Christ's servant, a Christian both in confession and deed. Otherwise, that Christian is falsely called this, not having a Christian character or not living in a Christian manner. So, be a Christian on the inside, and not only on the outside, and then you will be a true servant of Christ. "But why do you call Me 'Lord, Lord,' and do not do the things which I say" (Luke 6:46)? Do what the Lord wants and then call Him your Lord, and He will acknowledge you as His servant.

# 116. They Are in Concert

We often hear from people, "They are in concert." This saying is spoken of those people who have like-mindedness, harmony, and peace between themselves in something. Accordingly, a faithful servant is in concert with his master, the obedient son is in concert with his father, the faithful friend is in concert with his friend, the lecher is in concert with the loose woman, a robber is in concert with a robber, a thief is in concert with a thief, when they want to steal and carry off something, and so on. This is how it occurs in the spiritual regard, as well.

Every person is in concert either with Christ or with His enemy, the devil. He is in concert with whatever kind and whoever's spirit he has; he is in concert with whomever he has like-mindedness, harmony, and peace. Whoever truly and sincerely believes in Christ, the Son of God, and confesses and acknowledges Him alone as redeemer and Saviour and knows no other mediator for receiving eternal blessedness, and sincerely reaches out to Him, flees to Him with supplication in needs and circumstances, and acknowledges and has Him as a protector and helper; he loves Him alone and, following His Word, every person as well; he fights and battles against every sin and does not permit it to master him; he thinks about the heavenly and not the earthly; he thanks God for everything and does His holy will; he forgives his neighbor for offenses and does not take revenge on him; he sympathizes in his heart with those living in poverty and those suffering; he earnestly wishes for all to be saved; he has mercy not only on other people, but even on his enemies, and does good to them; and he uncomplainingly bears the cross sent to him from the Heavenly Father, and follows Christ, his Saviour, with humility and meekness—he is indeed in concert with Christ and has like-mindedness, harmony, and peace with Him. "He who is joined to the Lord is one spirit with Him" (1 Cor 6:17). "If anyone loves Me," says the Lord, "he will keep My word; and My Father will love him, and We will come to him and make Our home with him. You are My friends if you do whatever I command you" (John 14:23; 15:14). All such people who have been favored with this heavenly gift are in concert with Christ.

Oh, beloved like-mindedness! Oh, most sweet harmony! Oh, much longed-for peace! Oh, salvific union! Oh, heavenly friendship! Oh, much longed-for blessedness!—to be loved by Christ and to love Christ; to be united with Christ and to be of one spirit with Christ; to be beloved of God and be the temple and habitation of God; to be and be called a friend of the Heavenly King! "God is love, and he who abides in love abides in God, and God in him" (1 John 4:16).

Christian! It is a great thing to have like-mindedness, harmony, and peace with Christ and to be in concert with Him. What can be greater than this? What is more beneficial and more salvific? This surpasses by far every honor, glory, and riches, and beauty, and artistry, and wisdom, and knowledge of this world. For in this are true and heavenly wisdom, true and heavenly riches, honor, and glory. This means to be with Christ, that is, to draw near with our hearts to Him, to have like-mindedness, harmony, and peace with Him and to please Him. The holy Apostle requires this of us: "Let this mind be in you which was also in Christ Jesus" (Phil 2:5).

Christian! Let us be like this here with Christ, and we shall be with Him in the age to come. For in holy baptism, we were conjoined with Him and united with Him, and we promised to be with Him all our lives. "But it is good for me to cleave unto God!" (Ps 72:28).

But let us see what kind of Christians have severed this salvific and most sweet union and have fallen into their previous misfortune. The Lord says, "He who is not with Me is against Me" (Matt 12:30). This saying is terrifying, Christian, but true. The devil is the author and inventor of sin. Our progenitors in paradise, when they listened to his evil counsel, seriously sinned before God, and departed from Him, and became in concert with the devil, and so made themselves subject to eternal death and torment. Their descendants, all humans, were made subject to the same misfortune.

Through holy baptism, Christians by the grace of God break from the devil and are liberated, are cleansed from sins, are reconciled with God, and become a new creation in Christ (2 Cor 5:17) and God's people, and are *grafted* and joined *to Christ*, as branches to the true vine (John 15:5). Envying this great blessedness of Christians, the devil entices Christians, like our progenitors in paradise, through evil thoughts, and leads them to every kind of sin and the love of the vain world.

Christians who obey his pernicious counsel and comply with it, and turn aside after it, are in concert with him, although they do not understand this, for he darkens their mind and the eyes of their hearts and deafens the ears of their souls, lest they pay attention to the God's Word and see their misfortune and ruin.

The murderer, the person who is malicious and burning with revenge, is in concert with the devil, for the devil is the spirit of malice and a manslayer.

One who lives in pride and opulence is in concert with the devil, for the devil is a proud spirit.

Those who rely on themselves and their own strength are in concert with the devil, for the devil relies on himself and his own strength and cunning.

The fornicator, the adulterer, and those who love impurity are in concert with the devil, for the devil is an unclean spirit.

Everyone who gossips, eavesdrops, tells tales, and plays other dirty tricks and causes injury to a person is in concert with the devil, for the devil is a foe and a plotter.

A slanderer is in concert with the devil, for the devil is a slanderer and gets his name from this ("devil" is a Greek word and in our language means "slanderer").

A blasphemer, a reviler, and backbiter are in concert with the devil, for the devil is a blasphemer and reviler.

An envious and spiteful person is in concert with the devil, for the devil is a spirit of envy and hatred. The thief, robber, and extortioner are in concert with the devil, for the devil always steals for himself God's glory and the salvation of man.

The lover of power and lover of glory are in concert with the devil for the devil always seeks glory and worship from people.

The sorcerer and those that call upon him are in concert with the devil, for they devote themselves to him and ask help from him.

In a word, everyone who lives contrary to God's Word, and does the devil's will, and sins arbitrarily, is in concert with the devil. For whoever does someone's will and agrees with it is in concert with him. Even the Apostle's teaching agrees with this: "Whoever commits sin also commits lawlessness, and sin is lawlessness. And you know that He was manifested to take away our sins, and in Him there is no sin. Whoever abides in Him does not sin. Whoever sins has neither seen Him nor known Him. Little children, let no one deceive you. He who practices righteousness is righteous, just as He is righteous. He who sins is of the devil, for the devil has sinned from the beginning. For this purpose the Son of God was manifested, that He might destroy the works of the devil. Whoever has been born of God does not sin, for His seed remains in him; and he cannot sin, because he has been born of God. In this the children of God and the children of the devil are manifest" (1 John 3:4–10).

From this we see, Christian:

(1) Into what a poor condition man has come—a man created in the image and likeness of God has become in concert with the devil, the enemy

of God. He listened to his evil counsel and concurred with it, and broke with God, and became in concert with His enemy. We cannot mourn over this enough. "O Lord, righteousness belongs to You, but shame of face belongs to us" (Dan 9:7). O Lord, spare us!

(2) Every person dwells either with Christ or with the devil; he belongs either to one side or to the other. "He who is not with Me is against Me," says the Lord (Matt 12:30). Ponder on this, Christian, and keep your eye on which side you belong to.

(3) In God's eyes Christians who transgress through serious sin are worse than pagans. For, having renounced the devil in baptism, they have joined themselves to Christ and, having broken with Christ, have again turned aside after the devil. "The latter end is worse for them than the beginning. For it would have been better for them not to have known the way of righteousness, than having known it, to turn from the holy commandment delivered to them" (2 Pet 2:20–21).

(4) A demon does not turn against another demon, but they stand up for one another. But miserable man turns against men who are like him and related to him. A person should in every way help another person, and all people should stand up together and fight against the demons, and help one another and defend one another, but the opposite happens through the devil's trickery. Man turns against man and offends and persecutes him, which is a great error and terrible darkening of the mind.

(5) Those people who turn against people, and offend and persecute them, have the spirit of the devil in them and are possessed by the devil. Therefore we need to feel sorry for them, lest they become his eternal captives.

(6) Temptation and struggle follow true Christians from the devil, for they resist him and do not assent to his evil counsels; therefore, he turns on them and fights against them.

(7) The devil does through malicious people, his servants, what he himself cannot do to the true Christian. From this, we see the various machinations of malicious people against the pious soul.

(8) Hence, the pious must live carefully and be prudent, lest he be caught in the devil's snares and the evil designs of malicious people, his servants. On this point, the Apostle admonishes, "Be sober, be vigilant; because your adversary the devil walks about like a roaring lion, seeking whom he may devour" (1 Pet 5:8).

(9) Hence, persecution will follow the pious. The devil, when he cannot entice a pious soul into following after him, raises up persecution against it

through malicious people in order to lead it astray, separate it from Christ, and to win it over to his side. This is his slyness and his effort.

Beloved Christian! Stand up, take courage, and be strong, and endure everything, looking to the future glory and Christ's great patience. In this way, you will conquer every grief that comes your way.

(10) Christian, who has turned aside to follow Satan! Remember the vows that you gave at baptism, and repent, flee with remorse and contrition to Christ, who suffered and died for you and, being good and a lover of mankind, will receive you. He awaits you to return to Him. So return to Him while He is waiting. "Nor is there salvation" and blessedness outside of Him and without Him (Acts 4:12). Woe to the soul that is not with Christ. Eternal misfortune will befall it. *It is good for me to cleave unto God!* To be with Him is life; to be without Him is manifest death.

(11) Pious soul! When you stumble somehow and sin, do not linger in your sin, lest you turn to the opposing side, but immediately, having acknowledged your sin, repent and pray to the Lord: "Lord, have mercy on me ... for I have sinned against Thee" (Ps 40:5), and your sin will be remitted. But in future shun sin, like a serpent's sting: "The sting of death is sin" (1 Cor 15:56). Shun this sting, lest you die. To sin is human, but to live and wallow in sin is of the devil. Since the time the devil sinned, he lies continuously in sin and bitterness and will remain in this forever. Shun adding sin to sin, lest you be with the devil.

# 117. A King Summons His Subject to Him by an Edict

It happens that a king, wishing to summon his subject, sends him an edict and in this way calls him to himself. Likewise, the Heavenly King, Jesus Christ, calls every Christian to Himself in the age to come; He calls them through death. A person sees his approaching end or death—an edict from the Heavenly King now invisibly comes to him, summoning him. What is on the poor man's heart then? What fear, what trembling and terror, what tumult, agitation, what despair will shake him!

Ah, the Heavenly King is calling me, but I am not ready! His edict has come to me, ordering me to appear before Him, and I am deficient. I see my approaching end, but I had never even thought of it. My death, which I had never borne in mind, has come to me. The gates to eternity, which I had never thought of, are already opening to me. I fear the Judgment of God, Whom I have angered. My conscience rebukes and torments me, presenting me with my sins. The unhappy and agonizing eternity, into which unrepentant sinners are departing, shakes me with fear and terror. How come I never thought about this fearful hour? How come my mind was occupied with vanity? Why did I accumulate so much property? Why did I chase after the glory and honor of this world? Why did I commit such and such sins? Why did I not pay attention to God's Word, which warned me? What benefit is there now to me of the riches, honor, and fame I attained? What use now is worldly opulence and pride? What use is my house, palatial and decorated in various styles? What use are the carriages, horses, multitude of servants, lands and villages, assorted names and titles? What use are pleasure gardens, promenades, and ponds? What use are the friends whom I often entertained with banquets and various wines, and in turn amused myself with them?

This vanity and everything else from this world darkened and blinded my mind, and so I could not distinguish delusion and truth, evil and good, harm and benefit, sin and virtue, wretchedness and true happiness; this vanity took away my memory, the remembrance of death, to which I have now drawn near, and that is putting an end to all this sham consolation, together with the recollection of eternity, which I am now entering. I am now learning what constitutes delusion and what truth, what is true good and true evil. Now I see that God's Word is true and teaches the truth. Blessed are they who heed this! Wretched are they who do not heed it!

Oh, world, world! World filled with vanity and delusion, how you entice miserable man! I am now leaving your treasure; instead of riches and a beautiful house, I will be taking up my abode in a small coffin; instead of silk and fine linen, I shall be covered with black garb; instead of many lands and estates, I shall be buried in a six-foot hole in the earth; instead of riches, honor, and fame, I am inheriting lifelessness and decomposition; and instead of the luxury with which I comforted myself, I shall be food for worms.

Farewell, everyone! Farewell, wife and children; farewell, my friends and acquaintances; farewell, my servants and peasants; farewell, my estates and lands! I am now leaving you. Farewell, world! I am now leaving you too and I am leaving to you all that is yours. "Naked I came from my mother's womb, and naked" shall I leave on the path of all the earth (Job 1:21). Now I see that whatever I had was not mine; as I am now leaving everything I had, and as I came into the world with nothing, so I am leaving the world without anything. The Heavenly King is calling me now, and I am going to Him, but I tremble before His righteous and fearful judgment. He is not a respecter of persons; He judges according to our conscience and our deeds, and not with partiality. With Him kings and subjects, lords, princes, masters and their servants, rich and poor are equal.

Christian! Remember that an edict is coming from the Heavenly King to you, too, and you do not know when it will come and summon you, and what happens with others at their death will happen with you. Be judicious and wise, and prepare for that hour well ahead of time by repentance and contrition of heart; prepare for the hour in which the gates to heaven will open to everyone. That hour will be fearful, not only for sinners, but also for saints, who, always contemplating it, grieved and wept. From this hour, each will either be saved eternally or perish eternally. Remember death—and you will not desire to be amused yourself along with the world. Indeed, all the vanity and luxury of the world will seem loathsome to you. You will rather seek weeping and tears than merriment and pleasures.

# 118. I Will Come Tomorrow

We hear this saying from people: "I will come tomorrow." A person says this when someone summons him; then he, if he is either occupied with some task or having some other need and not having the possibility of leaving his home, answers the one calling him like this: "I will come tomorrow."

Christians! Christ is calling us to Himself, and he calls at all times and constantly: "Come to Me, all you who labor and are heavy laden, and I will give you rest" (Matt 11:28). This is how Christ the Lord calls to repentance and through repentance calls all sinners to Himself. But many Christians put off this repentance and as it were, rebuff Christ, and if not with their lips, at least with their hearts say, "I will come tomorrow." Such a thought and saying, "I will come tomorrow," everyone who from day to day puts off conversion and true repentance has in his heart. All such say in their hearts, "I will come tomorrow." The fornicator, the adulterer, and the lover of uncleanness say, "I will come tomorrow." The drunkard and the glutton say, "I will come tomorrow." He who lives in pride, opulence, and in the vanity of the world says, "I will come tomorrow." The money-grubber, the thief, and the extortioner say, "I will come tomorrow." Every sinner who lives in sin and does not correct himself says, "I will come tomorrow." And many put off their repentance until illness or until their death. Such people do not even think of it. Such people say constantly in their hearts: "There is no God" (Ps 13:1).

Oh, miserable sinner! Why do you promise yourself a tomorrow, which is not in your hands, but in God's? What if you do not live to see tomorrow? The call to repentance ends when, by royal edict, the Heavenly King calls you to account and judgment. What fear, trembling, horror, and despair will then trouble your soul! Death comes by an invisible road for everyone and snatches away a person when he does not expect it, and where he does not expect it, and how he does not expect it. What if it comes to you while you are having such thoughts and silently proclaims to you, "Come, O man, the Lord Almighty is calling you!" What will you say then: "I will come tomorrow"? No! Even if you do not wish to, you will go. But with what hope, I do not know.

Sinful soul! God promised us His grace and mercy, but He did not promise us a tomorrow. And the Holy Spirit says, "Today if you will hear His voice, harden not your hearts as in the provocation, and as in the day of temptation in the wilderness" (Ps 94:7–8; Heb 3:7–8; 4:7). Christ's preachers constantly preach repentance and proclaim to sinners, "Repent and come to Christ." But the sinful soul answers in his heart, "I will come tomorrow." Blind sinner! Consider and take stock of whom you rebuff thus in your heart with "I will come tomorrow." Your God and Lord, your Creator, King of kings and Lord of lords, is calling you; the generous and merciful Lord, long-suffering and plenteous in mercy is calling; he calls with love; Jesus your redeemer, Who suffered and died for your salvation, is calling. He calls lest you fall into eternal perdition and death; He calls into His eternal kingdom and blessedness. Being merciful, He pities you lest you perish. But you answer Him with the thought, and unrepentant disposition, and an uncorrected heart, "I will come tomorrow." It is shameless to rebuff an earthly king, or even a lower-ranking ruler, and say "I will come tomorrow." It is extremely serious and shameful to rebuff the Heavenly King and answer "I will come tomorrow." Serious and shameless, but also terrible, since there will be a time when sinners will want to come to him, but the doors will be closed. Then they will hear, "I do not know you"; you did not know Me, and I do not know you; you did not hear me, and I do not hear you (Luke 13:25–27; Matt 25:10–12). "Since I called, but you did not obey, And spoke at length, but you paid no attention, but made my counsels invalid, and were not persuaded by my reproofs; consequently, I will laugh at your annihilation, and will exult when ruin comes to you" (Prov 1: 25–27 LXX [24–26]). Therefore He says, *Today if you will hear His voice, harden not your hearts.*

Sinner, do not tarry to turn to the Lord, lest you experience God's judgment rather than God's mercy. Let us come to Christ not with our feet, but with our hearts, not by change of place, but by change of will and of morals for the better. Whoever changes within himself and, having left evil practices behind, cleanses himself by repentance, and shuns every sin, and obliges the will of God, That one is coming to Christ and no longer says, "I will come tomorrow," but with the Prophet says, "My heart is ready, O God, my heart is ready" (Ps 107:2). See, I am coming! "I will arise and go to my father, and will say to him, 'Father, I have sinned against heaven and before you, and I am no longer worthy to be called your son. Make me like one of your hired servants'" (Luke 15:18–19).

"Oh, how lovingly Jesus Christ looks on such a soul that returns and comes to Him! Ah, my son who was dead is returning to me alive!" (Luke 15:24). "Being merciful, I will have mercy on him and will generously endow him" (Jer 31:20). Rejoice, angels, for the lost drachma had been found. My son, who had departed from Me has returned healthy to me. Man, My beloved creation, created in My image and likeness, but lost, has returned to life.

Poor sinner, let us also arise and hurry to our compassionate Father. He awaits us and embraces with outstretched arms those who come. We shall find rest nowhere and in nothing other than with him. He alone reassures us: "Come to Me, all you who labor and are heavy laden, and I will give you rest" (Matt 11:28). Enough of tarrying in foreign parts; enough of working for an evil master; enough of feeding on sins, like rotten pods. *Arising,* we will go to our Father, and he will feed us with the meal, which is intended for His sons. *Father, I have sinned against heaven and before you, and I am no longer worthy to be called your son. Make me like one of your hired servants.*

# 119. A Gardener Cuts Down
## a Barren Tree

We see that a gardener, waiting long enough for fruit from an apple tree or some other kind of tree and seeing that it is not giving him the desired fruit, cuts down this tree as worthless and barren and throws it in the fire.

So God's judgment overtakes and cuts down the unrepentant sinner. God, being all-good and a lover of mankind, awaits repentance from the sinner and is long-suffering toward him. But when He sees that he lives in unrepentance, as he lived previously, then in His righteous judgment he cuts him down and throws him into the eternal fire.

In this way, God awaited repentance from the wicked people who lived before the flood. But when He saw that there was no repentance in them, He destroyed them with a terrible and universal inundation. Likewise, He awaited repentance from the inhabitants of Sodom and burned with fire from heaven those who were unrepentant and were abiding in their wickedness. Likewise, He awaited repentance from pharaoh, the king of Egypt, for not a little time. But when pharaoh scorned His long-suffering and remained in his obduracy, he experienced the avenging hand of God; he was sunk like a rock in the depths of the sea with all of his army. Likewise, He awaited the repentance and conversion from the Israelites, who had left Egypt, had seen the glorious wonders of God, but had transgressed. But when, not having changed in the least, they became confirmed in their wickedness, by God's judgment they perished in various ways in the desert. Thus, Absalom, David's son, who planned to kill his father and seize the kingdom of Israel, but having been hanged on a tree, perished between heaven and earth, experienced God's judgment.

Even now, the same judgment of God befalls those who transgress, and scorn God's long-suffering, and do not wish to repent and correct themselves. We hear of the wondrous and terrible judgments of God. Lechers and loose women are often stuck down in the most iniquitous activity; God's judgment often carries away extortioners, thieves, and robbers during the very crime. The Dread Judgment overtakes murderers, the malicious, the vindictive, slanderers, the foul-mouthed, liars, debauchers, cheats, and others who devise cunning snares for their neighbors and often fall into the pit that they dig for others. Thus, God's wondrous and terrible judgment befalls every wicked one. And although, by God's unfathomable judgments, not all transgressors are punished here, they are all cut down by death, as by a pole-axe, and thrown into the eternal fire, and thus receive their deserved lot. The holy Forerunner spoke of this: "And even now the ax is laid to the root of the trees. Therefore every tree which does not bear good fruit is cut down and thrown into the fire" (Matt 3:10).

O Christian who does not care about repentance! Fear God's judgment and repent, lest it suddenly befall you and send you into the fires of Gehenna! You yourself do not know where and how judgment will befall you, and where you expect good things and gain, you will get evil. The hardened Pharaoh chased after Israel and expected gain, but instead found ruin and a grave in the Red Sea. A similar fate awaits other transgressors as well. Look upon God's wondrous judgments and cease sinning, and repent that you sinned, so that the Lord will be merciful to you. God has tolerated you up to now, seeing your iniquitous deeds, and awaits your repentance. But whether he will endure this henceforward is not known. We must understand this and remember God's universal and Dread Judgment.

The Lord is long-suffering toward wicked and unrepentant sinners and expects from them repentance and correction, as He was long-suffering to the wicked before the Flood and awaited repentance from them. But when he sees that the sinners have no repentance, no conversion, no correction, and the world stubbornly stands in its wickedness, then unexpectedly, like lightning the Judge, Christ the Lord will appear, and the trumpets will sound, "Come to Christ's judgment!" and the Apostle's saying will be fulfilled: "For when they say, 'Peace and safety!' then sudden destruction comes upon them, as labor pains upon a pregnant woman. And they shall not escape" (1 Thess 5:3). Then all the unrepentant sinners, as before perished in the waters of the flood, will perish and be plunged into *the lake of fire* and will reap the fruits of their iniquity and wickedness. And the Apostle Peter wrote about this, "The Lord is not slack concerning His promise, as some count slackness, but is longsuffering toward us, not willing that any should perish but that all should come to repentance" (2 Pet 3:9).

Watch out, sinner! God expects repentance from you. Do not be negligent in relation to God's goodness and long-suffering and repent, lest either your death or Christ's judgment find you unrepentant and careless. Blessed and wise is he who lives heedfully, and seeing God's judgments on others, himself evades misfortune with foresight. "Have mercy upon me, O God, after Thy great goodness, and according to the multitude of Thy mercies do away mine offences" (Ps 50:3).

# 120. Snares Placed on the Path

We see that people secretly spread out snares in the places, which birds and wild animals frequent in order to catch them. Like this, Satan, Christians, spreads out his snares for us and tries to catch us in them. At holy baptism, by the grace of God, we entered onto the path of salvation, and by this path we try to come to our heavenly Homeland, for which we were created by our Creator and, having fallen, were redeemed, called by God's Word, and renewed in the laver of regeneration. On this our path, our enemy spreads out many snares in order to entangle us to our perdition. This is his pursuit and concern.

His pernicious snares are as follows:

(1) Many and varied heresies, schisms, and superstitions. Oh, how many Christian souls the cunning and crafty enemy has caught and is catching with these snares. The past centuries have born witness to this, and we see this nowadays with pity and lamentation. He endeavors to entangle a person in the snares of heresy, and schism, and superstition and through him to entice, ensnare, and cause harm to many others. Heresy is like the plague, which, having begun in one person, infects many. Heresy is an opinion and teaching contrary to God and His holy Word and arises from ignorance and misunderstanding of Sacred Scripture. This is why we, in order not to get tangled in the webs of the evil one, must steadfastly hold to God's holy Word. God's Word is the rule of our faith, as the holy Prophet says, "Thy law is a lamp unto my feet, and a light unto my paths" (Ps 118:105).

The God-bearing fathers and teachers of the Church interpreted and explained Holy Scripture. To understand it, it is also beneficial to read their books. And so, hold to God's Word, lest you become tangled in the snares of heresy, and schism, and superstition. And when you hear a word contrary to God's Word from a person, avoid that person like one infected with the plague. An inimical spirit is known by an evil odor. A person's word is a witness of a man's heart and the spirit living in him. God's Word warns us of these snares of the enemy. "Beloved, do not believe every spirit, but test the spirits, whether they are of God; because many false prophets have gone out into the world" (1 John 4:1). And again, "Beware of false prophets, who come to you in sheep's clothing, but inwardly they are ravenous wolves. You will know them by their fruits" (Matt 7:15–16).

(2) He spreads out snares of love of this world, its pride and vanity. He presents to the Christian soul the honor, fame, riches, and luxury of this world and whispers in its ear how good and pleasant it is to be honored, to have respect and admiration, to be renowned and praised, to live in opulence, in a palatial and beautiful house, to have many servants, to dress in silk and nice-looking clothing, to go for drives in a tandem carriage, to associate with distinguished and renowned people, to offer a rich table every day and

enjoy oneself, and to entertain guests who come, and so on. In whispering like this, the evil spirit plans that the miserable person would become tangled up in such vain thoughts and not think about his Christian duty and calling and would forget that he is redeemed and called, and renewed for eternal life.

Oh, how many Christians are entangled in these snares, especially in the present day! Christian, answer the evil spirit like this: "For we brought nothing into this world, and it is certain we can carry nothing out. And having food and clothing, with these we shall be content" (1 Tim 6:7–8). The Word of God warns us of these snares. "Do not love the world or the things in the world. If anyone loves the world, the love of the Father is not in him. For all that is in the world—the lust of the flesh, the lust of the eyes, and the pride of life—is not of the Father but is of the world. And the world is passing away, and the lust of it; but he who does the will of God abides forever" (1 John 2:15–17). And again: "Set your mind on things above, not on things on the earth (Col 3:2). You cannot serve God and mammon" (Matt 4:24). "O turn away mine eyes, lest they behold vanity; give me life in Thy way. O stablish Thy word in Thy servant unto fear of Thee" (Ps 118:37–38).

(3) The enemy sets his snares for us when he entices us to every sin, and tries to catch and entangle us in them as in a snare. Oh, how many people are caught in his pernicious snares and become entangled in them! Wicked people and murderers are caught in these snares. Adulterers, fornicators, and all lovers of impurity are caught by him. Thieves, extortioners, robbers, and bribe-takers are caught by him; drunkards and gluttons are caught by him, foul mouths and blasphemers are caught by him. Those who quarrel and hurt each other are caught by him. Those who resist their parents and the authorities are caught by him. Slanderers, defamers, and blasphemers are caught by him. Liars, tempters, and cheats are caught by him. Sorcerers and those who summon them are caught by him. Those who live in idleness, insidiously eating up someone else's bread for free, are caught by him, and others of those who transgress and commit falsehood are caught by him.

God's Word warns us of these snares: "Come, ye children, and hearken unto me; I will teach you the fear of the Lord. What man is he that lusteth to live, and would gladly see good days? Keep thy tongue from evil, and thy lips, that they speak no guile. Shun evil, and do good; seek peace and pursue it" (Ps 33:12–14). And again: "Let everyone who names the name of Christ depart from iniquity. For the wages of sin is death" (2 Tim 2:19; Rom 6:23, and in many other places). As a caution for us, it is also written in the Holy Scripture about the punishments for sins. For this they are shown to us, that we may fear doing what the transgressors did and were punished. Christian, shun every sin. The devil's snare is sin. Shun the snare, lest you step into it and get tangled up in the snare.

(4) The devil spreads out his snares for us when he insinuates evil thoughts into us: every kind of unbelief and doubt; all kinds of blasphemies on the name of God, despair, and so on. This and suchlike are felt by pious souls and those struggling against him. God's Word warns us against these snares: "Be sober, be vigilant; because your adversary the devil walks about like a roaring lion, seeking whom he may devour. Resist him, steadfast in the faith" (1 Pet 5:8–9).

Christian! Beware of these snares of the enemy. Whenever you feel such an evil thought, the enemy is spreading out his snare for you and wishes to entrap you. We can recognize the foul spirit from his stinking odor.

(5) We see that he, when he himself cannot entrap a person, sends evil people, his minions, to him, through whom, as his tools, he tries to entrap him. Hence we see many seducers, tricksters, and deceivers who pretend to be good and try to steal into the pious heart and enter into friendship with it, but who within are wolves in sheep's clothing and a secret tool of the devil. Through such servants of his, the devil tries to entrap the pious soul and to entangle it in his snares. Such wolves are more dangerous than the devil himself, but they will be known by their fruits, for no matter how much they dissemble and conceal themselves, they reveal the poison hiding within them. Beware of such people, Christian! Our Saviour told us, "You will know them by their fruits" (Matt 7:16).

(6) The devil spreads his snares for us when he incites persecution, malice, hatred, mockery, and ridicule from people. And precisely for this reason it happens that pious souls suffer much from those who love this world and hear slander borne on people's tongues and lips concerning such sins that they do not know of in themselves. This is a machination and ruse of the devil to lead the pious person, not being able to bear such slanders and hatred from people, from the right path.

So, by the cunning of the devil, the idolaters contrived false and serious slanders against the ancient Christians, so that they, leaving Christian piety, would be converted to their ungodliness. In the same way, the perfidious spirit even now acts through false Christians. Christian! Christ the Lord cautions us against these snares and steadies us on His path, saying, "Be faithful until death, and I will give you the crown of life" (Rev 2:10). And further, "He who endures to the end shall be saved" (Matt 24:13).

(7) Among his secret and very concealed snares are when He presents us with evil under the guise of good and vice under the guise of virtue, like poison hidden in honey. Thus, he teaches a husband to distance himself from his wife and a wife to distance herself from her husband under the pretext of abstinence, but the evil spirit schemes thereby to cause them to fall into the pit of adultery. There is much of this evil in the world. He insinuates into a person's heart to abstain from certain food (for it is impossible to abstain from all), but he thereby contrives that the person denigrates God's creation and falls into haughtiness, and despises and disparages others for what they eat. There is much of this evil too in the world. "For every creature of God is good, and nothing is to be refused if it is received with thanksgiving; for it is sanctified by the word of God and prayer" (1 Tim 4:4–5).

He teaches a person to leave home and visit others under the pretext of love but wishes thereby to take him away from prayer, beneficial contemplation, and work proper to his profession, and plunge him into idleness, idle talk, slandering and judgment, and other evils. And it happens that a person returns home not the same person who left it. There is nothing more beneficial than to keep to home and solitude.

He teaches a person to seek honor under the pretext of serving society: "You will," they say, "being in a place of honor, serve society," but he thereby plans to corrupt him, and plunge him into incalculable evil, and harm him through many temptations. It is good to serve society but bad to commit falsehood and "serve mammon" (Matt 6:24). Such servants soon reveal themselves. Indeed, many people would be saints if they were not in places of honor. Honor for the unwise is like a sword by which he kills both himself and others. One needs first to learn to govern oneself and then others.

The enemy insinuates into a person's heart to amass riches for the sake of giving alms: "You will thereby provide for the poor," they say, "and have not a little benefit from this," but he is planning by this to implant greed in his heart and to lead him to every kind of deceit. From this it happens that many give generously to others but yet take away from others. Many masters are generous to the needy and poverty-stricken but are miserly with their own peasants and reduce them to indigence and destitution. It is beneficial to give alms but ruinous to wrong others. What kind of alms is this: to take from one, and give to another! This is not alms but inhumanity. The foremost Christian mercy is not to do wrong to anyone.

The enemy also teaches a person to arrange dinners and feasts under the pretext of entertaining out of love and to invite one's friends and play host to them. But thereby he is scheming to lead the host and the others into drunkenness, excess, luxury, and squandering of possessions and other evils. Hence, we see how many of such entertainments—loving, but harmful for the soul—have multiplied. It is good to open the doors of your house and receive guests and entertain them— but be willing to receive everyone without discrimination, including wanderers with no food of their own—and moreover entertain decorously and without any excess.

Hospitality to wanderers is a Christian virtue. But it is bad to please your own whims, and get drunk, and waste your resources on whims, and commit other evils that take place at banquets and feasts. Many expend a considerable amount on banquets and feasts, but give nothing to the needy and poverty-stricken. Many invite the rich and famous to dinners, but they close the doors to the poor, who have no sustenance. The foe leads a person to this under the pretext of a loving hospitality.

The enemy spreads these and various other snares on the path that Christians are taking to eternal life.

(8) No person can escape by himself from these and other snares of the enemy. What are we, Christians, to do so that we do not fall into the snares of the enemy? By his example, the holy Prophet shows the means by which we escape from his snares, saying, "I lifted up mine eyes unto the hills; from whence will my help come? My help cometh even from the Lord, Who hath made heaven and earth. Suffer not thy feet to slip, nor Him that keepeth thee to slumber. Behold, He that keepeth Israel shall neither slumber nor sleep. The Lord Himself shall keep thee; the Lord is thy shelter upon thy right hand. The sun shall not burn thee by day, neither the moon by night. The Lord shall keep thee from all evil; yea, the Lord shall preserve thy soul. The Lord shall preserve thy going out, and thy coming in, from this time forth, and for evermore" (Ps 120:1–8). This is the means of salvation—God's help.

Without God's help, all of our effort and labor are useless and in vain (see John 15:5). We need habitual and fervent prayer for God to help us in this important matter. He Himself knows that we need His help, but He wants us to ask, seek, and knock at the door of His mercy (see Matt 7:7).

(9) When the Israelites left Egypt and crossed through the Red Sea, and went through the desert into the Promised Land, then, although the holy Moses was their leader and Joshua son of Nun was his successor, the Lord

Himself was invisibly present there, led them, and struck their enemies who were opposing them, and so led them into the Promised Land, as the Prophet sings to Him, "O God, we have heard with our ears, and our fathers have told us, the work which thou hast done in their days, in the days of old; How Thou hast driven out the heathen with Thy hand, and planted them in; how Thou didst afflict the people, and cast them out. For they gat not the land in possession through their own sword, neither was it their own arm that saved them; but Thy right hand, and Thine arm, and the light of thy countenance, because Thou hadst a favor unto them" (Ps 43:2–4).

Through holy baptism, we have been delivered from slavery to the devil, and we are going along the path of this life, as through the desert, to our heavenly Homeland, for which we were redeemed by Christ's blood. But the devil with his crafty snares and the world, with its temptations, and the flesh, with its passions and whims, resist us and raise up obstacles for us and block our way. Let us not, however, abandon our quest, but let us go farther and farther along our path. For the same Lord Jesus Christ is invisibly present with us too, according to His truthful promise: "And lo, I am with you always, even to the end of the age." Amen (Matt 28:20). And He leads us and will bring us to the heavenly Homeland, if we will only follow Him with love, humility, and meekness. "He who promised is faithful" (Heb 10:23). He gives what He has promised. "My sheep hear My voice, and I know them, and they follow Me. And I give them eternal life, and they shall never perish; neither shall anyone snatch them out of My hand," says the Lord (John 10:27–28).

Christians! Let us be only Christ's sheep and commend ourselves and all our life into Christ's all-powerful hands. Then we will surely be in the heavenly enclosure and in the pasture of eternal life. And although we shall endure many temptations, misfortunes, and tribulations in this world, we shall be in eternal rest. And the saying of the psalm will be fulfilled: "Thou hast proved us, O God, Thou hast tried us, like as silver is tried. Thou broughtest us into the snare, and laidest trouble upon our back. Thou sufferest men to ride over our heads; we went through fire and water, and Thou broughtest us out into refreshment" (Ps 65:10–12). Let us think also of what the Apostle wrote: "the sufferings of this present time are not worthy to be compared with the glory which shall be revealed in us" (Rom 8:18). A good hope of reward alleviates every labor, struggle, affliction, and sorrow.

# 121. A Great Thing

We see that people esteem many things as great. But for Christians only one thing is great: what is Divine and eternal. For they see and think that everything earthly and temporal will like a shadow pass by, and that is why for them all of this is as nothing. This is the right opinion; this is the insuperable truth. People esteem it as great to be begotten by a king and to be and be called the king's child. But for Christians it is great to be born of God and be called and to be a child of God. The holy Apostle is amazed at this and says in astonishment: "Behold what manner of love the Father has bestowed on us, that we should be called children of God! Therefore the world does not know us, because it did not know Him. Beloved, now we are children of God; and it has not yet been revealed what we shall be, but we know that when He is revealed, we shall be like Him, for we shall see Him as He is" (1 John 3:1–2). "But as many as received Him, to them He gave the right to become children of God, to those who believe in His name: who were born, not of blood, nor of the will of the flesh, nor of the will of man, but of God" (John 1:12–13). "For you are all sons of God through faith in Christ Jesus. For as many of you as were baptized into Christ have put on Christ" (Gal 3:26–27).

It is for this reason that the Lord says to his Apostles and his other faithful: "I am ascending to My Father and your Father, and to My God and your God" (John 20:17). It is for this reason that He commanded us to call His Father "Our Father," and to pray to Him like this, "Our Father in Heaven" (Matt 6:9). Christian! It is truly great to be, and be called, a child of God; this is a great honor and glory; it incomparably surpasses all and every glory of this world, but it is disdained by those who love this world. Christian! Seek this great thing, and you will be truly in honor and glory. Children are born like unto their parents. Christians need to be like unto God if they wish to be children of God. "Be holy, for I am holy" (1 Pet 1:16; Lev 11:44; 19:2). "Therefore be merciful, just as your Father also is merciful" (Luke 6:36). "Be imitators of God as dear children" (Eph 5:1).

People consider it a great thing if a low-ranking person converses with the king. But for a Christian, it is great to converse with God, the Heavenly and Eternal King. And truly how great is it for a human, who is *earth and ashes*, and moreover a sinner, to approach God, the King of Kings and Lord of Lords, who lives in an inapproachable world, to approach I say, and stand before Him, and hold conversation with Him! Even the Archangel Gabriel boasts of this: "I am

Gabriel, who stands in the presence of God" (Luke 1:19). Truly a Christian stands before God and converses with God when he truly and sincerely prays and hymns Him (see Ps 144:1–8; 37:10; 18:15).

It is the angels' task to stand before God and hymn Him. The angels stand before God and sing, "Holy, holy, holy is the Lord of hosts" (Isa 6:3). People imitate the angels when they sincerely pray to God and praise Him, as Christians sing in the Liturgy, *Let us who mystically represent the Cherubim, and chant the thrice-holy hymn unto the life-creating Trinity*, and so on. You see, Christian, how great it is to pray to God and praise Him, but very many Christians do not care about this great thing; many abandon it; many do it, but with extreme carelessness, for they pray and sing either with great haste, as fast as the tongue can manage, or without any understanding, and so to speak, they do not know to whom or about what they are praying, and whom and about what they are singing. The Word of God applies to such people: "These people draw near to Me with their mouth, And honor Me with their lips, But their heart is far from Me" (Matt 15:8). That is why the Prophet tells those singing to God, "O sing unto our God, sing ye; O sing unto our King, sing ye. For God is the King of all the earth, sing ye with understanding" (Ps 46:7–8).

Christian, do you want to stand before God always and converse with Him? Always be in your mind and heart with the most kind God, and worship Him with your heart and mind, and pray to Him and praise Him, and you will always stand before Him and converse with Him. This will be possible for you to do always and at every place, day and night, morning and evening, and whenever you want, among people and in solitude, when busy or idle, on the way or staying at home, walking, sitting, lying in bed, in a word, always and at all times, and everywhere, inasmuch as God is everywhere, and is always and everywhere ready to hear you (see Job 19:23; Ps 33:16). The doors to Him are always open. But whoever wants to stand before God in prayer with effect, and to converse with Him, and to praise Him, and so to do what is typical of the dignity of angels, must imitate the angels both in purity and virtues.

People consider it a great thing to see an earthly king; therefore, everyone rushes to where he is in order to see him. But for Christians it is great to see the Heavenly King, Jesus Christ, King of Kings, and Lord of Lords, the One Who is of one nature and co-eternal with God the Father. He is the only-begotten Son, the King and Son of the King, Who is in the bosom of the Father, Who deigned to become incarnate, and lived on earth with people, and suffered, and died for people, and arose from the dead, and ascended into heaven, and sits at the right hand of the Father in His glory. It is great for Christians to see this King, for to see Him is extreme blessedness and eternal life, and joy greater than every joy. To see Him is food for the angels and most sweet drink of the chosen ones of God.

"When shall I come and appear before God's face" (Ps 41:3)? When shall I come and see Him, Who for my sake, a poor sinner, came into the world and lived in poverty, and suffered, and died, and in this way redeemed me from the devil, death, and hell? When shall I come and see the one Who so loved me, my Benefactor, my Redeemer, my Saviour? "For what have I in heaven, and what have I desired upon earth from Thee? My flesh and my heart have failed, O God of my heart, but Thou art my portion, O God, for ever" (Ps 72:25–26). I want nothing and desire nothing either in heaven or on earth except You alone, Oh Lord, the Word of God and Son of the Virgin, Jesus Christ, my God, the God of gods.

Christians! We wish to see this King, and we will cleanse ourselves by repentance and will whiten our clothing in the blood of the Lamb, so as to enter His most glorious chamber. We will see this King of ours, and of His kingdom there will be no end.

People consider it a great thing to receive an earthly king in their house. But for Christians, it is great to receive in the house of their heart the Heavenly King, Jesus Christ. And truly this is great. It is impossible to express what glory, what honor, what joy and gladness there will be in that house, into which this Heavenly and most glorious Guest comes. Peace and heavenly joy are there, and the Kingdom of God is there. Since where Christ God is, there is also the Kingdom of God and His blessedness. "Behold, I stand at the door and knock. If anyone hears My voice and opens the door, I will come in to him and dine with him, and he with Me" (Rev 3:20).

Oh, Your goodness! Oh, Your love for mankind, O Lord! What benefit is there for You, Who sits on the Throne of Your glory and Who lives in unapproachable light, what benefit is there that You wish to enter the house of our humble souls? Is not the temple of Your glory sufficient for You? "Thy kingdom is an everlasting kingdom, and Thy dominion endureth throughout all ages" (Ps 144:13). But the Lord Who loves mankind says, *Behold, I stand at the door and knock,* and so on. For He, being Good and the Lover of mankind, desires and seeks our benefit, and not His own, our blessedness, and not His own. Our salvation and blessedness are His beloved profit. An earthly king, by invitation, enters the house of his subject and enjoys the good things prepared

ortort

by his host. The King of Heaven, Jesus Christ, is not like this: He Himself comes to the doors of our hearts, knocks at the door, and wishes to come in to us. And, entering, he does not require our food from us, but Himself brings His own food, the most sweet heavenly food, and does not make use of our good things but gives us His invisible heavenly good things. "Praise the Lord, O my soul" (Ps 145:1).

But man, in his human poverty and wretchedness, does not perceive that this is the great and most precious heavenly Guest. He comes and knocks at the door of each one, but the poor soul, deafened by the love of this world and by the din of various carnal whims, does not hear His most sweet voice, and Jesus, the Lover of mankind, having stood by the doors in vain, leaves having accomplished nothing.

O man! It is shameful not to admit an earthly king or some lower-ranking ruler who wishes to enter our house. It is even more shameful not to admit the Heavenly King. Woe betide the soul without Christ! It is like a house without an owner, like a city ravaged and laid waste by enemies; like a ship sailing the sea without a helmsman; like a sheep wandering in the desert without a shepherd; like a person who has gone astray and lost his way; like a sick man abandoned by his doctor and others. But the soul itself is guilty that it does not have Christ living within it. "If anyone loves Me, he will keep My word; and My Father will love him, and We will come to him and make Our home with him," says the Lord (John 14:23). Beloved Christians, let us love Christ and one another, and this Heavenly and most dear Guest shall come to us with His Father and the Holy Spirit and make His habitation with us. Then we shall be really blessed even though the whole world may hate us.

People consider it a great thing to conquer a large number of people and to take impregnable cities. But for Christians, it is great to conquer ourselves, that is, our whims, self-love, greed, impurity, envy, anger, love of fame, and other evils hiding within the heart, or, as the Apostle wrote, "to crucify the flesh with its passions and desires" (Gal 5:24). This is the glorious victory; this is the glorious victor and soldier of Christ! Many conquer many people, and the powerful take cities, but they cannot conquer themselves and become the captives of their passions. "A patient man is better than a strong man. And he who controls his temper is better than he who captures a city" (Prov 16:30[32]).

Christian, let us try to conquer ourselves, and we shall gain a glorious victory. "[T]he Spirit says to the churches[:] To him who overcomes I will give to eat from the tree of life, which is in the midst of the Paradise of God." And again, "To him who overcomes I will give some of the hidden manna to eat" (Rev 2:7, 17). Yours is the victory, O Lord, Yours is the glory, for You are the boast of our power. "Therefore most gladly I will rather boast in my infirmities, that the power of Christ may rest upon me" (2 Cor 12:9).

People consider it a great thing to have a healthy, strong, and handsome body. But for Christians it is great to have a healthy, strong, and comely soul. Bodily health is good, but what use is it to have a healthy body, and a sickly and weak soul? What use is it to a Christian person that his body sees well, but his soul is blind in the knowledge of God and His holy will and of oneself; his body hears well, but his spirit is deaf and does not hear the Word of God; his body is erect, but his soul is crooked and bent; the body is not lame, but the soul is lame; the body is strong, and moves, and walks, but the soul is weak and immobile for any good deed; the body does not shake in ague and it does not burn with fever, but the soul shakes is scorched with anger and rage; the body is not tormented by the violence of the demons, but the soul is possessed by passions and sins. Passion and sin are a cruel demon. What good is it if the body is clean, but the soul is leprous and stinks all over from the wounds of sin; the body is handsome and comely, but the soul is foul and ugly? The body is mortal, but the soul is immortal. Bodily health only serves us until death, but after death, it disintegrates into dust, being frail. See, O man, what bodily beauties and comeliness there are here! Truly you will not be able to tell whether the body was healthy or sickly. But the health of the soul is inseparable from the soul, departs into the next world with it, accompanies it, and appears with it before God, and is favorable in His holy eyes. God loves a healthy and holy soul. Infirmity and debilitation of the body threaten temporal death, but infirmity and debilitation of the soul threaten eternal death.

It rarely happens that a healthy soul lives in a healthy body, but for the most part, and almost always, in an infirm one (2 Cor 12:10). Health of body opens the doors of a person to many whims and sins, but infirmity of the body closes them. A truculent and unbroken stallion rages, and often rushes to its destruction, but is restrained by a bridle, struggles, and suffers, and is broken, and thus becomes gentle. Our flesh is restrained by disease and infirmity, as by a bridle, and submits itself to the spirit. Oh, what great mercy God shows to those to whom he sends sickness! He afflicts his body so that the soul would become healthy; He delivers the flesh to exhaustion "that his spirit may be saved in the day of the Lord Jesus" (1 Cor 5:5).

Everyone experiencing illnesses knows and acknowledges this truth, and especially those living a celibate life. The rich man of the Gospel was healthy, and clothed himself in purple and fine linen, enjoyed himself happily, but after his death he went into the fiery flame and after temporal merrymaking, into eternal torment. Lazarus was poor and covered with pus, and lay in front of his doors, but after his death was carried away by the angels into the bosom of Abraham (see Luke 16:19–25). So one after temporal suffering went to eternal rest, but the other after temporal merrymaking left for eternal torment. The same thing happens now: even now, many receive their good things in their lives but suffer there, and many suffer here but are comforted there.

What good is it to have a healthy body but a feeble and infirm soul? It is a great thing to have health of soul, of an immortal soul created in the image of God, even if the body were infirm and unsound. Actually, we all want to have a healthy body, but we do not know how to have one. It is better to decay and putrify in the body, when this is pleasing to God and beneficial and necessary to us, just as long as the soul has its health. The Word of God and the holy faith teach us that someday the body will be joined with the healthy soul, and it will be healthy, strong, beautiful, spiritual, incorruptible, immortal, and flourishing forever. "Even though our outward man is perishing, yet the inward man is being renewed day by day" (2 Cor 4:16; see also 1 Cor 15:42–44 and 53; Phil 3:11).

People consider it a great thing to have the riches of this world. But for Christians, it is great to have the riches of the soul within themselves, that is, a living faith, God's grace, and the fruits of the spirit: "love, joy, peace, longsuffering, kindness, goodness, faithfulness, gentleness, self-control" (Gal 5:22–23). Christians consider this treasure of the soul a great thing. The riches of the world only serve a person and upon death departs from him, and he leaves for the next world like one of the poor and needy. "Be not thou afraid, though a man be made rich, or though the glory of his house be increased; For when he dieth, he shall carry nothing away, neither shall his pomp follow him" (Ps 48:17–18).

Even here, a person bears the treasury of the soul within himself, leaves for the next world with it, appears with it before the Heavenly Father, and gives testimony of himself that he is a Christian in name and in his essence. But what will the rich man, who has much material wealth but has no wealth of the soul, leave for the next world with, and what witness will he show that he was a Christian in this world? That he had much? Both the Turks and the pagans

have much. Or that he confessed God's name? "Even the demons believe–
and tremble" (Jas 2:19). What good is it to have chests filled with material
things but an empty heart? That rich man is poor who has no treasure of the
soul within, even though he has every external thing. People do honor to
him because they see that he has much of everything, but in God's eyes, he is
wretched, for God sees nothing in him except poverty (Rev 3:17).

Christian! Let us try to have the treasury of the soul within us, and we shall
be truly rich. Let us acknowledge our poverty, that God Himself will enrich us
with His grace. "For you know the grace of our Lord Jesus Christ, that though
He was rich, yet for your sakes He became poor, that you through His poverty
might become rich" (2 Cor 8:9). Wondrous poverty that enriches us, and wondrous wealth that comes from poverty! This is Christ's work, for everything
is possible for Him Who, though He was rich, became poor for our sake. It
is written, "All things are possible to him who believes" (Mark 9:23; see Matt
17:20).

People consider it a great thing to be a free man, to be noble, not to serve
anyone, but rather to command and rule over others. But for Christians it is
great to free from sin, to have a noble soul, not to serve any kind of sin, but to
serve God alone with faith and righteousness. This is a fine freedom and this is
true nobility! Every outward nobility and freedom only serves a person until
the grave, and there leaves him, and he becomes like one of the low-born. Now
it is impossible to know where the servant lies and where his master, and it is
not apparent who was the servant and who was the master. And what if in a
noble body lived an ignoble soul, and the one whom people served was a slave
to sin, for "[w]hoever commits sin is a slave of sin" (John 8:34).

With what will such a person appear at the universal Judgment? With sin?
This is terrifying. It will be there not as it is here: there will be no respect of
persons there; noble and ignoble, masters and servants will stand side by side
before the judge. Freedom of the soul is not like this. It is both here with the
person and leaves this world with him, accompanies him, stops the mouths of
slanderers, appears before God, and intercedes for him. See how great spiritual
freedom and nobility are! And although Christians are not without sin, they
are not deprived of freedom and nobility, inasmuch as feeling and seeing their
infirmities within themselves; they continually sigh to the Heavenly Father,
and acknowledging their sins, in harmony they raise up their voice to Him:
"Father! Forgive us our debts." And they receive what they ask, and so are not
deprived of their freedom.

Christian, you see both external and internal human freedom, and the nobility of this world and Christian nobility. You yourself judge: what use is it to be free on the outside, but inside to be ignoble and a slave—in the body, to receive service from people, but in the soul, to serve sin. Noble souls stand up against every sin and fight against it, and do not allow it to possess them. It is better to serve a person than sin, and through sin, the devil. "If the Son makes you free, you shall be free indeed," says the Lord, our Liberator (John 8:36). This is a most glorious freedom, our true nobility, our dignity, our honor, our glory, our beauty, our goodness, and our eternal blessedness! "Turn our captivity, O Lord, as the streams in the south. They that sow in tears, shall reap in joy. They went on their way and wept, sowing their seed, but they shall return in joy, bearing their sheaves" (Ps 125:4–6). "Have mercy on me, O God, after Thy great goodness, and according to the multitude of Thy mercies do away mine offences" (Ps 50:3).

People consider this and others a great thing. But for Christians only what is invisible, spiritual, divine, and eternal is great. Whatever someone considers great is what he desires and seeks with eagerness. Faith alone is the guide to invisible, spiritual, and heavenly things. "Now faith is the substance of things hoped for, the evidence of things not seen" (Heb 11:1). It presents the invisible as visible and the future as the present. This is why the faithful soul that has a living faith sees all this and seeks it, taking little or no care for the present. But whoever does not have such faith considers great and wishes and seeks only what he sees.

Christians, let us try to have the lamp of faith in our heart, and it will show us everything invisible, spiritual, divine, and eternal; then we shall be Christians. The whole essence of Christian blessedness depends on a living faith.

# 122. Do Not Be Afraid, I Am with You

It happens that a mother, seeing her child grieving and weeping, comforts him and says to him: "Do not be afraid, I am with you." Likewise, the merciful and man-loving God, the Creator and Father of bounties and God of every consolation, says to the faithful soul, which is living in temptations and trials, grieving, and lamenting, and fearing: "Do not be afraid, I am with you." I am your Creator; I am your redeemer; I am your Saviour; I am your helper and protector; I, Who hold everything in My hands, Whom all obey, am with you. "But Zion said, 'The Lord forsook me, and the Lord forgot me.' Will a woman forget her child, so as not to have mercy on the offspring of her womb? But even if a woman should forget these things, nevertheless, I shall not forget you," says the Lord (Isa 49:14–15). "If you pass through water, I am with you; and the rivers shall not overflow you. If you pass through fire, you shall not be burned up, nor shall the flame consume you. For I am the Lord your God, the Holy One of Israel, who saves you" (Isa 43:2–3).

Thus God was with His faithful Noah and preserved him from the universal flood. Thus He was with His faithful Lot and preserved the righteous man from the punishment of Sodom. Thus He was with His servants Abraham, Isaac, and Jacob, and preserved them on the land of their sojourn as was written about them, "He suffered no man to do them wrong, and reproved even kings for their sakes, saying, 'Touch not Mine anointed, and do My prophets no harm'" (Ps 104:14–15). Thus He was with Joseph and preserved him in the temptations and sufferings that came upon him and glorified him. Thus he was with Israel in Egypt; that is why He said, "I have seen the affliction of My people in Egypt, and have heard their cry because of their taskmasters" (Exod 3:7). He was with the same Israel during its exodus from Egypt, and He divided the Red Sea for it, made a path in the midst of the waters for it, led it through the Red Sea, and saved it from Pharoah the tyrant; therefore it sang the hymn of thanksgiving to God its Saviour. He was with the same Israel in the desert and fed it with the miraculous manna, and defeated its enemies before its face and led it to the mountains of His holiness. He was with the same Israel, living in the Promised Land, and saved them as the Prophet sings, "If the Lord Himself had not been on our side, may Israel now say, If the Lord Himself had not been on our side, when men rose up against us, then they would have swallowed us up alive" (Ps 123:1–2).

He was with David, His anointed one, in his various temptations and persecutions, and preserved His servant from his enemies. He was also with Jonah in the depths of the sea, preserved him in the belly of the whale, and delivered him from the sea monster. He was with the three children in the Babylonian furnace, quenched the fire's heat for them, and taught them to sing the hymn of thanksgiving. He was with Daniel in the lions' den, stopped the mouths of the lions, and delivered him from it. He was with the Apostles, was with the martyrs, and preserved them in the midst of terrible tortures. He was with the desert-dwellers, those living in caves, in dens and clefts of the earth, and preserved them from the enemy's machinations. He was, and is, and will be until the end of the age with His faithful servants, according to His truthful promise: "And lo, I am with you always, even to the end of the age." Amen (Matt 28:20).

"O how divine, how loving, how sweet is Thy voice! For Thou hast truly promised to be with us unto the end of the age, O Christ; having this foundation of hope, we faithful rejoice" (Paschal Canon Ode IX).[14] Therefore, His faithful servants, feeling His presence and living consolation near them, dare exclaim and sing a hymn in joy of soul: "God is our refuge and strength, a very present helper in the troubles which greatly afflict us. Therefore we will not fear, when the earth be shaken, and the hills be cast into the midst of the sea. The Lord of Hosts is with us; the God of Jacob is our protector" (Ps 45:2–3, 12). And again, "Yea, though I walk through the valley of the shadow of death, I will fear no evil, for Thou art with me" (Ps 22:4). And again, "The Lord is my light, and my Saviour; whom then shall I fear? The Lord is the defender of my life; of whom then shall I be afraid" (Ps 26:1)?, and so on. Take care, Christian; belong only to Christ, and "do not abandon your God" (Ps 33:22; 28:11; 31:11). Believe in Him sincerely as God; do his bidding in faith and righteousness; put all your hope in Him, and call on Him from your heart. And He is near to you; He is with you, keeping you safe, and wherever you will be, in whatever sorrow and temptation you find yourself, He is with you and looks upon your struggle and with an invisible hand strengthens you and helps you; and even if all the evil people rise up against you and the demonic hordes surround you, it will all be unsuccessful. "The Lord Himself shall keep thee; the Lord is thy shelter upon thy right hand; The sun shall not burn thee by day, neither the moon by night. The Lord shall keep thee from all evil; yea, the Lord shall preserve thy soul. The Lord shall preserve thy going out, and thy coming in, from this time forth, and for evermore" (Ps 120:5–8). "Forsake me not, O Lord my God, be not far from me. Attend unto my help, O Lord of my salvation" (Ps 37:22–23). "O Lord of hosts, be with us, for beside Thee, we have no other helper in adversity; O Lord of hosts, have mercy on us."[15]

# 123. A Belch

As a belch from the stomach is, likewise a word and deed proceeding from the heart. A belch begins in the stomach and comes out of the mouth. Likewise, that which is inside the heart of a person, good or evil, appears on the outside through word or deed. When a prayer is in the heart, and in abundance, then it will unfailingly be manifested either by raising the eyes to heaven, or lifting up of the hands, or speech proper to heartfelt prayer. Heartfelt prayer will find words fitting for itself. Then a person will cry out, "O Lord, have mercy! O Lord, hear me! O Lord, pity me!" or something similar.

When God's mercy and benefactions and gratitude for them are felt in the heart, it also comes forth through the corresponding words. Then a person exclaims and with a joyful spirit and lips of joy cries out to God the benefactor: "Glory to Thee, O God!" or, "Blessed is God!" or, *Bless the Lord, O my soul*, or suchlike. When sorrow for sin is felt in the heart, it manifests itself by sighing or tears. Sighing and tears, proceeding from a contrite heart, are expressions of heartfelt prayer. Then a person prays and cries out to God not with his tongue and lips, but his heart: "Hear my prayer, O Lord ... hold not Thy peace at my tears" (Ps 38:13). When God's love is perceived in the heart and its sweetness is experienced, then a person will cry out to God, "I will love Thee, O Lord, my strength" (Ps 17:2), or, "The Lord is compassionate and merciful, long suffering, and of great kindness" (Ps 102:8), or something similar to this. For love belches forth its signs.

When humility is present in the heart and is perceived, then a person disparages himself and acknowledges himself unworthy of everything, and everywhere seeks the very last place. When love and mercy for neighbor is present in a person's heart, it manifests itself through joy in the well-being of his neighbor and sympathy and compassion in his distress. Such a soul will not deny help to his neighbor, and if he cannot help, he will sigh for him to God, the helper of all, and so on.

From this, you see, Christian, what true prayer, thanksgiving, and true Christian piety is, when it is present in the heart, and comes forth from the heart. And whatever is not in the heart is not in the being itself.

In the same way, the kind of evil present in a person's heart issues forth through word or deed and reveals itself like a belch from the stomach. Anger reveals itself through rage, shouting, abuse, cursing, banging of hands, tearing out of hair, etc. Malice or remembrance of wrongs reveals itself by vengeance through word or deed, by injury, disgracing, slandering, and murder. These are the fruits of anger and malice. Concupiscence reveals itself through filthy thoughts, filthy dreams, and manifests itself through lustful looks, indecent jokes, touching, passionate words and the foulest actions, and so on.

Greed reveals itself through all kinds of seeking for riches, through miserliness, and hoarding of wealth, through thievery, extortion, robbery, violence, defrauding other people of their property, and other evils. Lying, hypocrisy, trickery, cunning reveal themselves through speech, inconsistent with the conscience and thought, and other signs, contrary to what is in a person. Pride reveals itself through seeking the honor and fame of this world and the fitting out of palatial houses, beautiful clothing, expensive horses and carriages and other splendors of this world. Pride is highly intolerant of contempt and obscurity. It everywhere and in everything seeks how to show itself off and to be something big in people's eyes.

Haughtiness reveals itself by display of one's good works, by disdaining and disparaging others and judgment of them, and exaltation of oneself above others. Although it does not pronounce the words of the Pharisee aloud, in its heart it says, "I am not like other men" (Luke 18:11). Oh, if only such a person pronounced these words *I am not like other men* both with his heart and with his lips in the opposite sense, that is, "Everyone is better than I am," and would cry out to God, "God, be merciful to me a sinner!" (Luke 18:13), indeed he would be better than many and would be righteous not by his own but by God's righteousness, which justifies the sinner!

Many think and say that they have hope in God, but in every instance, as from a belch, it comes to light on whom they are placing their hope. Temptation shows on whom we place our hope: on God or on man, or on another creation—whoever in time of need appeals to someone seeking help puts his hope on that person. If you appeal to a person and you seek help from him in any misfortune, then you are putting your hope on a person and not on God. If you are seeking to be delivered from misfortune by wealth and gifts, you are putting your hopes in wealth and not on God. If you try to be delivered through the intellect, trickery, and your own cunning, you are putting your hope on yourself and not on God. If you wish to be delivered through your office and rank, you are putting your hope on your honor and office, and not on God, and so on.

But whoever truly trusts in God, having abandoned everything except God, appeals to God alone in all occurrences and entanglements and asks help, as we see in the Psalms. In every kind of need and entanglements, such a soul sincerely says with the prophet, "The Lord is my helper, and I will not fear what man shall do unto me. The Lord is my helper, and I shall look down upon my enemies" (Ps 117:6–7). "In the Lord have I put my trust; how say ye then to my soul, Flee as a bird unto the hills" (Ps 10:1). This is why the Lord says of it, "Because he hath set his hope upon Me, therefore will I deliver him" (Ps 90:14).

So then, fortuity and temptation belch and reveal what kind of hope is hidden in the heart of a person. Many imagine that they love God and their neighbor, but inasmuch as they have no love in their hearts, they are deceived in this. Their deeds show that they love their whims and themselves, and not God or their neighbor. Love is great, and there is nothing greater than love. "All gifts without love are nothing" (1 Cor 13:1–3). Love should be in the heart, and not in words, and be known from deeds, and not from words. A constant wish and desire for God's glory, and the fulfillment of His will, insomuch as it is possible for a person in this world, are signs of heartfelt love.

Many people think that they are meek and patient, but occurrences and temptations, like a belch from the stomach, reveal the opposite, and then they themselves will learn that there is no meekness or patience in them. Many people think that they pray often, through the whole day, for they do many prostrations and read many written prayers, but since they do this without understanding and inner attention, they either seldom or never pray. Everything external without the internal is nothing. Every good thing and piety must be first in the heart and issue from the heart or from within, as a belch issues from the stomach.

The holy Prophet says, "My heart hath poured forth a good Word" (Ps 44:2). You should do likewise, Christian. If you pray, let your heart pour forth your prayer.

If you give thanks and sing to God, let your heart pour forth your thanksgiving and song.

If you humble yourself, let your heart pour forth your humility.

If you have mercy on your neighbor, let your heart pour forth your mercy.

If you speak quietly and gently with your neighbor, let your heart pour forth your quiet and gentle speech.

If you embrace and kiss your neighbor, let your heart pour forth your embrace and kiss.

If you receive and regale your neighbor in your home, let your heart pour forth your reception and regaling.

If you bend the head and knee to the Lord your God, let your heart pour forth your bows and prostrations.

If you lift up your hands and eyes to the One Who lives in heaven, let your heart pour forth the lifting up of hands and eyes.

If you sing to God with the prophet, *I will love Thee, O Lord,* and so on, let your heart pour forth this word.

If you say to God, "In Thee, O Lord, have I put my trust; let me never be confounded" (Ps 30:2), and so on, let your heart pour forth this saying and your hope.

If you repent to your Lord and confess your sin, saying, "I have sinned, O Lord," and so on, let your heart pour forth your repentance and confession.

If you confess and acknowledge before God your poverty, wretchedness, destitution, squalor, and nothingness, let your heart pour forth your confession and acknowledgement.

Therefore, Christian, heed the following points:

(1) People study what they do not know, and they seek what they do not have. They do not know arts and sciences, and so they go to academies and schools, and they study there, learn, and become educated. We should do likewise in the Christian calling. If we do not know how to pray, we must learn how. Therefore, the Apostles prayed to the Lord: "Lord, teach us to pray" (Luke 11:1). The canons that speak of repentance, of the sufferings of Christ, of the Resurrection of Christ, and which are read on other feast days, and other prayers of the Church teach us superbly to pray and glorify God. They teach and induce us to true prayer and glorification, but only if they are read with reasoning and understanding; otherwise, there is no benefit. If we do not have love, humility, meekness, and patience, we must seek them and study. And so that which we seek, we will find, and what we do not know, we shall learn.

(2) We must coerce and urge ourselves both to prayer and to every spiritual good thing, that is, to love, humility, meekness, patience, and other Christian virtues, although the heart does not desire this and avoids it. Seeing such labor and endeavor of ours, the Lord will grant us desire, zeal, and true prayer, and other Christian good things; He, Who can grant it and has promised, will grant it (see Matt 7:11, 21–22; John 16:23).

(3) Knowledge of his poverty teaches a person to escape from poverty. Lack of bread teaches to seek bread so as not to die of starvation; lack of drink persuades one to seek drink in order not to die of thirst; lack of clothing impels us to seek clothing, so that we do not go about naked; illness urges us to seek a physician, and so on. So also in the Christian life. When we come to understand the squalor and poverty of our souls, we shall seek our blessedness. It is bad to be a Christian without prayer, without love, without humility, without meekness and the other Christian virtues. Misfortune results from this. It is necessary to seek them with diligence. So an experienced misfortune impels a person to seek his blessedness. Learn, O Christian, the corruption, poverty, wretchedness, destitution, and squalor of your heart, and this very knowledge will teach you prayer and the Christian virtues.

(4) An excellent school of prayer and piety is sorrow and suffering. The Israelites, being in Egypt and enduring insults from the guards of the tyrant Pharoah, prayed diligently and cried out to God, as the Lord Himself said

of them, "I have seen the affliction of My people in Egypt, and have heard their cry" (Exod 3:7). Anna, the mother of Samuel the prophet, enduring reproaches, anguish, and sorrow because of her barrenness, prayed with all her heart to God, and she was heard by God (see 1 Kg 1). And King David's psalms bear witness to how, in his sorrows and persecutions, he was inspired to heartfelt prayer. The Prophet Jonah, in the belly of the whale, as in Hades, cried out from the depths of his heart to the Lord, as he himself says: "I cried out in my affliction to the Lord my God" (John 2:3). Susanna in Babylon, unjustly slandered by the wicked elders, and condemned to death, in this anguish and sorrow groaned unto the Lord and was heard by the Lord (see the Book of Daniel [Pramble (Susanna) LXX] [13:42–44]).

In this way sorrow teaches heartfelt prayer. When do we pray more fervently, than during illness, misfortune, adversities, temptations, upon the invasion of aliens, during famine, pestilence, and other calamities that threaten us with death? Then prayer pours out and rises up from the depths of the heart. Also we shall learn the Christian virtues nowhere better than enduring a cross, sorrow, and suffering and temptation. The soldier who, staying in the Homeland, studies the service regulations a great deal is not as skilled as the one who has often been in battles against the enemy. Likewise, the Christian who passes through the fire and water of temptations, misfortunes, adversities, and sorrows and battles against the invisible enemies is skillful in the Christian calling, and for this, besides other reasons, God permits sorrow and suffering for His servants, that is, so that they learn true and heartfelt prayer, and appeal to Him, and seek help, and learn the Christian virtues. "Tribulation produces perseverance; and perseverance, character; and character, hope. Now hope does not disappoint" (Rom 5:3–5)—without salt, meat, and fish rot. Likewise, without sorrows, a Christian becomes spoiled. Salt drives out worms from meat and fish. Likewise, sorrow expels corruption and passions from the soul. Salt preserves the integrity of things. Likewise, sorrow maintains the integrity of the soul. Salt is unpalatable but is beneficial for the body; sorrow is unpleasant but beneficial for the soul. "Blessed is the man whom Thou chastenest, O Lord" (Ps 93:12). "For whom the Lord loves He chastens, And scourges every son whom He receives" (Heb 12:6).

(5) Pupils in schools follow the regulations and the example shown by the teachers, and so learn arts and sciences. Christians, the rule for us is the holy Gospel, and the life and character of our Saviour, Jesus Christ, are a living example. We must look at this sacred rule and living example of virtues and learn the Christian art, that is, a virtuous life. Everything that we see in us contrary to the Gospel and the life of Christ is a vice.

The Gospel and life of Christ are light. Everything that is contrary to this light in us is darkness. As we hold up a mirror before our face and, having seen smudges on our face in it, we wipe them off, so should we hold up our souls before the mirror of the Gospel and life of Christ, and everything contrary to it, like a smudge, cleanse by repentance and contrition of heart. "I am the light of the world. He who follows Me shall not walk in darkness, but have the light of life," says the Lord (John 8:12). Let us approach this wondrous light, and let us follow Him, lest we dwell in the darkness.

(6) We must stand and fight against every evil that may arise from the heart, and not permit it to carry over into action, and to suppress it in the heart itself, and to cut it off with the sword of God's Word. Against malice and remembrance of wrongs, we must remember Christ's words: "If you forgive, and it will be forgiven you; if you do not forgive, and it will not be forgiven you" (see Matt 6:14–15). Against greed, and pride, and the opulence of this world, we must remember the words of the Apostle: "For we brought nothing into this world, and it is certain we can carry nothing out. And having food and clothing, with these we shall be content" (1 Tim 6:7–8). And Christ says, "You cannot serve God and mammon" (Matt 6:24). We will cut off carnal desire because the conscience is tormented and tortured for this sin. A bridle for haughtiness is remembrance of past sins, and reflection about our poverty and wretchedness, and of how a person may become the most loathsome and vile sinner, if God takes away His hand from him, for we see rather many of such examples. "Do not be haughty, but fear" (Rom 11:20).

You must act this way with other sins and fight against them. You must everywhere and always picture the presence of God before you and His omniscience and His righteousness. God is invisibly present everywhere, and sees everything, and may strike down a sinner during the actual sin. Be afraid to sin not only in word and deed, but even in thought (for God sees even thoughts), lest God's judgment befall you.

So is it seemly for a Christian to commit those sins for which Christ the Lord drained the bitter cup of suffering? Every sin closes the door to eternal life: "The wages of sin is death" (Rom 6:23). Shun every sin, lest you perish. A Christian cannot exist without a clear conscience. It is better for a Christian to die than to sin and trouble and vex the conscience. This struggle against sin is necessary for all Christians who wish to be saved. *Kill*, Christian, the wicked *children*, while they are young, lest they grow up and *kill* you (Ps 136:9).

Kill lust, lest it be carried out in action.

Kill a slight anger, lest it be turned into rage and malice.

Kill lustful thoughts, lest they multiply and defile you.

Kill the desire for wealth, lest you become a slave to Mammon.

Kill a slight haughtiness, lest you exalt yourself, and, having become exalted, you be humbled.

Kill every evil, while it is still small, lest it grow up and ruin you.

This struggle is hard, really hard, but necessary. Fight, and the crown of life will be bestowed on you from Christ, the Awarder of Trophies.

(7) Every effort and struggle of ours, both for good and against evil, is impotent without God's help, insofar as we are very corrupt and infirm. This is why our Saviour told us: "Without Me you can do nothing" (John 15:5). Therefore we must ask of Him and seek every good thing, and strength, and power against sin. The holy books teach us so that we would know what to do and what to avoid. But Christ the Lord enlightens our mind and grants us power and strength to desire and do, as the vine supplies its sap to the branches. And so, we must draw near to Christ and to sigh to Him, and ask and expect power and strength in everything. "He who promised is faithful" (Heb 10:23) and wants to help those for whose sake He came into the world and suffered.

# 124. A Boat or Vessel on a River

As a boat is on a river, so a person is in life. We see that a boat floats down a river on its own, but it can in no way sail against the current or up the river. But if it needs to go up the river, it requires powerful oarsmen or a sail with a favorable wind to move it. So it is with a person. Being corrupted, he lives comfortably and easily according to the flesh, his whims and passions, and according to his evil will, like a vessel floats on its own down a river. "The mind of man is diligently involved with evil things from his youth" (Gen 8:21). "For out of the heart proceed evil thoughts, murders, adulteries, fornications, thefts, false witness, blasphemies" (Matt 15:19). Our passions and whims are born with us, and that is why it is easy and comfortable to follow them and do their will, as it is to sail in a vessel down a river. But to live contrary to our evil will, to overcome it and to submit to the will of God, and to stand and fight against our whims and passions, to crucify and mortify them, and so to live piously and in a Christian way, is just as awkward and impossible as it is to sail a vessel against the current of the river without oarsmen and sails.

From this, we see how many books have been written that try to hinder the inclination of the passions; how many preachers labor and ring out in sermons against the passionate flesh and inspire fear of God's judgment in a person and disturb and restrain him with fear of temporal and eternal punishment, and the person himself, hearing the sermon, is terrified and disturbed and often repents. But he is going downstream according to the will of the whims and the passions, as a vessel rushes along a river. We have such a corrupted nature, Christian: man fell into such baseness and wretchedness through sin; this most wondrous beauty—God's image—has come into such disgrace by the devil's cunning!

What should we do? To live according to the whims and passions is contrary to Christianity, the holy faith, and the Word of God: This is clear calamity and ruin. We cannot stand against the rush of the passions, and calm and vanquish them by ourselves. A supernatural power must unfailingly help us, and push us forward, like a vessel against the stream. It will constantly inspire and strengthen us, and rouse us against the rushing of passions, vanquish them, and prompt our heart to sighing and heartfelt prayer and other Christian virtues. God's grace, living in a person, does all of this. With it, a person can do everything, but without it, he can do nothing. God's grace pushes a person forward and exhorts at any time and helps him to stand against the passions and vanquish them, and live in a Christian manner, as oarsmen move a vessel against the flow of a river. We need God's grace at all times, every hour, and every minute. God's grace is the life of our souls; without God's grace, a soul cannot be alive. Therefore, we are commanded to pray, "Ask, seek, and knock" (Matt 7:7). Thus we shall learn, Christian, our corruption and poverty (we are going downward, not upward, under our own power), and having learned, we shall humble ourselves before the Lord, that He give us his grace. "God resists the proud, But gives grace to the humble" (1 Pet 5:5). You see our physical poverty; why then do you not perceive poverty of the soul? You seek corruptible wealth; why do you not seek the incorruptible wealth of the soul? You recognize physical infirmity and cure it; why do you not recognize the infirmity of the soul and cure it? You flee from misfortunes and temporal death; why do you not flee from misfortunes and death of the soul, which leads to eternal death? You seek to be a proficient philosopher, a proficient poet, an eloquent orator, a wise astrologer, a skilled land-surveyor, a good architect, an adroit merchant, or some other kind of craftsman: Why do you not seek to be a true and good Christian? This surpasses any art and knowledge of this age; without this, everything is nothing.

We need to care more than anything else about what abides with us forever. "Make me a clean heart, O God, and renew a right spirit within me. Cast me not away from Thy presence, and take not Thy Holy Spirit from me. O give me the comfort of Thy salvation, and stablish me with Thy governing Spirit" (Ps 50:12–14).

# 125. The Knowledge of Misfortune or Trouble Induces Us to Seek Deliverance

Man consists of two parts: soul and body. The body has its misfortune and ill-being, and the soul has its. The body is visible, and its misfortune is visible; the soul is invisible, and its misfortune is invisible. The body is corruptible and mortal, and its misfortune will end; the soul is incorruptible and immortal, and its misfortune has no end, but remains with it forever, unless it is freed from it. The soul, being rational, immortal, and created in the image of God, is much more precious than the body, and this is why its misfortune is much more dangerous and harmful than physical misfortune. Physical misfortune dies and ceases with the body of the dying person, but an immortal soul's misfortune never dies unless it is delivered from that misfortune here.

Therefore, pay attention, Christian, to the following:

(1) It is difficult for a person to be in bodily poverty, but it is far more difficult to be in poverty of the soul. It is difficult for a person to have an infirm and weak body, but it is far more difficult to have an infirm and weak soul. It is difficult for a person to serve some kind of evil tyrant with his body, but far more difficult to serve sin with the soul and the devil through sin. "Whoever commits sin is a slave of sin" (John 8:34).

It is difficult for a person to be bound with iron shackles, but much more difficult to be bound with the shackles of sin: iron shackles torment the body, but the shackles of sin torment the soul. It is difficult for a person to bear a king's anger, but it is much more difficult to bear God's anger. It is difficult for a person to be bodily held captive by some enemy, but it is far more difficult to be held captive in the soul by the devil. It is difficult for a person to be banished from his homeland and his home, from his relatives and friends, but it is much more difficult for the soul to be banished from the heavenly Homeland

and God's house, from God Himself and His holy chosen ones. It is difficult for a person to be in prison and see little light, and to endure bondage, grief, and insult, but it is much more difficult for the soul to be in the prison of hell and to endure this misfortune forever.

It is difficult for a person to die in the body, but much more difficult to die in the soul. The body dies, and its hardship will come to an end; the soul never dies, and its death and its hardship never end. As the soul is much more precious than the body, so its hardship is much worse and more dangerous than bodily hardship. Therefore, we must seek deliverance from hardship of the soul more than that of the body. Bodily hardship, whatever it may be, and however long it may be, will all end, but that of the soul will never end.

(2) The misfortune itself leads to knowledge of misfortune, and knowledge of misfortune induces a person to seek deliverance. People see bodily misfortune, and feel its affliction, and therefore avoid it, and in every way seek how to be delivered from it. They do not see misfortune of the soul, which is much worse than that of the body, and do not feel its affliction, and this is why few fervently desire and seek to be freed from it. The Word of God presents misfortune of the soul to the eyes of our soul, and leads us to knowledge of it, and presents to us the image of deliverance, Christ. The more people perceive misfortune of the soul, the more zealously they seek to learn how to be delivered from it. "If the Son makes you free, you shall be free indeed" (John 8:36).

Glory to God, the Lover of Mankind! Idolaters realized their delusion and error, and from this, their ruinous misfortune; they learned from God's Word and His Most glorious miracles and were converted to Christ, and He freed them from ruinous misfortune, and they received eternal blessedness of the soul. Many who lived in ancient times realized their misfortune and made caves, deserts, and clefts of the earth their abodes. The martyrs realized this and desired rather to endure severe torture and die than to renounce Christ, inasmuch as to renounce Christ is to renounce every blessedness of the soul and eternal life and to incur ruination of the soul and eternal death. Many robbers, murderers, lechers and loose women, and other serious sinners came to know their souls' misfortune, zealously sought deliverance, and found it. Many even now are coming to know it and as a result are terrified and seek deliverance; consequently, they no longer care about bodily misfortunes, as long as they are delivered from misfortune of the soul. The fear of misfortune of the soul surpasses and makes bodily misfortune ineffectual, like a loud noise blots out a small and quiet voice. This is how a misfortune that is known moves a person to search for deliverance.

Christian, you should come to know your soul's misfortune and hardship, and without fail you will care about nothing as how to be delivered from this misfortune. Indeed, fear and terror will seize you as you come to know the misfortune of your soul, and you will wish to weep and sob rather than to rejoice. Blessed, blessed indeed, is the person who perceives the misfortune of his soul in good time. Knowledge of misfortune is the beginning of blessedness, as knowledge of an illness is the beginning of health. Come to know yourself thus, and you will be blessed.

(3) Temporal bodily misfortunes like illnesses, infirmities, poverty, persecution, ridicule, abasement, abuse, slander, exile, captivity, prison, bonds, loss of wealth and honor, beatings, wounds, and death itself in no way harm our soul, but what is more, "All things work together for good to those who love God" (Rom 8:28). And *blessed*, as God's Word teaches, are they who endure all this for Christ's sake (see Matt 5:11; 10:22).

Bodily and temporary misfortunes not only do not take away blessedness from our souls but even multiply it. "Even though our outward man is perishing, yet the inward man is being renewed day by day. For our light affliction, which is but for a moment, is working for us a far more exceeding and eternal weight of glory, while we do not look at the things which are seen, but at the things which are not seen. For the things which are seen are temporary, but the things which are not seen are eternal" (2 Cor 4:16–18). And this is what else is written: "But when we are judged, we are chastened by the Lord, that we may not be condemned with the world" (1 Cor 11:32). And again: "For whom the Lord loves He chastens, And scourges every son whom He receives" (Heb 12:6).

Not only church history but also sacred history witnesses how many bodily and temporary misfortunes have motivated people to true repentance. We see this even now. It is for this that God, the Lover of Mankind, sends misfortunes to us—that we may be motivated to true repentance and live in the fear of God. Both misfortunes and trials attest to God's goodness and love for mankind. Even in misfortunes and in trials, we should give thanks to God, the Lover of Mankind, for everything proceeds from Him for our good end. He cares for us. The Prodigal Son, when he had squandered his father's possessions and had come into such squalor and poverty that he had begun to die from hunger, finally came to himself and said, "How many of my father's hired servants have bread enough and to spare, and I perish with hunger! I will arise and go to my father, and will say to him, 'Father, I have sinned against heaven and before you'" (Luke 15:17–18). So also misfortune motivates a sinner to return to his Heavenly Father and true repentance.

The sinner encumbered by misfortunes and trials reasons like this: "I do not have bodily and temporary good things. My poverty, squalor, and wretchedness exhort me to seek the wealth of the soul; I will seek it with Christ, Who, "though He was rich, yet for [my] sake He became poor" (2 Cor 8:9). My bodily infirmity teaches me to seek my soul's health with Christ: He is the physician of our souls and bodies. I endure dishonor and ridicule from people; I seek glory and praise with God. The Lord says, "I will honor those who honor me" (1 Kg 2:30). I will endure the anger of the king or of my master; I will seek mercy from God. "Whoso putteth his trust in the Lord, mercy embraceth him on every side" (Ps 31:10).

If in the body I serve such and such a person and do not have freedom and nobility, I will seek freedom and nobility of the soul. If all people despise and abandon me, I will flee to God and draw near to Him, and He will neither abandon nor despise His creation: He does not abandon or despise anyone. "Forsake me not, O Lord my God, be not far from me. Attend unto my help, O Lord of my salvation. Hear us, O God of our salvation, the hope of all the ends of the earth, and of them that be afar off at sea" (Ps 37:22–23; 64:6). If I am banished from my country and home and am separated from my relatives and friends, I will try more earnestly to seek the heavenly Homeland and to have eternal friendship with the angels and saints of God. This prison in which I am confined and these bonds with which I am bound induce me to be delivered by repentance from the prison of hell and from the bonds of sin and hell, and so on.

Glory to God, "who desires all men to be saved and to come to the knowledge of the truth" (1 Tim 2:4). He sends me sorrow but converts me by it and cuts off the path to perdition, and returns me to Himself. *I will arise and go to my father.* So bodily and temporal misfortunes not only do not harm souls but are very beneficial for them. These misfortunes lead us to repentance and to God Himself and in a way induce us to enter into the Kingdom of God. Glory to God, the Lover of Mankind, glory to His wondrous providence for us! Through our misfortunes and trials, He seeks our true blessedness. So He turns all of our misfortune and wretchedness into our blessedness.

But bodily and temporary well-being more often than not corrupt and ruin a person. We see this in the example of the rich man of the Gospel, who did not know how to master his wealth and temporal well-being and went down to perdition (see Luke 16:23). In like manner, nowadays many people do not know how to master their wealth and scatter it not in accordance with God's will, but in accordance with their own whims, and become corrupted. Many people do not know how to master the health of their body, and become corrupted, and aspire to every evil. Bodily and temporal well-being, although good, is, however, for the corrupted human heart as a sword for a madman, by which he kills himself.

The Prodigal Son, while his father's property was still in his hands, did not think of returning to his father. But when he had finally lost it and had begun to endure deprivation and hunger, then he thought to return to his father, as said earlier. This is why it is written as a caution to us, "If riches increase, set not your heart upon them" (Ps 61:11). As bodily and temporary misfortune can be the cause of repentance and the soul's correction, so bodily and temporary well-being can often be the cause of corruption, and misfortune, and the soul's ruination, and especially when a young person has well-being. For such a person, it is extremely difficult not to be corrupted in his well-being. And this is one of the reasons why God permits misfortunes and trials to His servants, that is, that they not be led astray and so not be deprived of eternal blessedness. For in well-being, a person, being feeble, is easily led astray and corrupted.

And so, temporal and bodily sorrow is a bitter medicine, but one that is beneficial for the soul.

(4) Misfortune of the soul is always harmful and ruinous; it is always a great and cruel evil, being contrary to God and His holy will. Misfortune of the soul is self-love, pride, haughtiness, love of fame, ambition, self-importance, arrogance, despising and disparaging one's neighbor, darkness and delusion of the mind, ignorance of God, and truth, and righteousness, unbelief and superstition, envy, malice and remembrance of wrongs, greed and desire for wealth, lust, hypocrisy and craftiness, slyness, and other evils. This is a great misfortune of our souls. This fatal poison is hidden in our hearts, consumes and kills our souls, and leads a poor person only to eternal death. Learn, Christian, the affliction of your soul, that you may zealously seek deliverance from it. A misfortune that is perceived impels us to seek a means to be delivered from it, and to desire its opposite, and to seek blessedness.

Jesus, lover of Mankind! "Thou art my refuge from the afflictions that overwhelm me; my Joy, deliver me from them that circle me round about" (Ps 31:7). Sinful and poor, but created in the image of God, my soul groans and cries to You, my redeemer.

(5) Every misfortune is perceived most of all from the very experience. An illness is most of all perceived by those who are ill. Only the one being tormented by a toothache knows how terribly it is troubling him. Understand the same concerning other bodily and temporary misfortunes. Likewise, a misfortune of the soul, concealed within the heart, is most of all known in temptation. And the more a person finds himself in temptation, the better he perceives his poverty and wretchedness. Temptation reveals everything that is concealed within the heart, as an emetic brings up what is contained in the stomach. And the more a person recognizes his soul's misfortune and wretchedness, the more he is humbled. Recognition of misfortune humbles a person. And the more he is humbled, the more grace he acquires from God. "God resists the proud, but gives grace to the humble" (1 Pet 5:5).

Many people imagine of themselves that they do not have haughtiness, pride, envy, anger, malice, etc. But the temptation found indicates that this evil is concealed in their hearts, and so they are deceiving themselves. Lust is concealed for a certain time and is not recognized, but given the opportunity, like a venomous snake, it shows its head from a hidden place and wishes to sting the soul with its fangs. The well-being of others troubles us and reveals the envy hiding in our hearts; then it emerges from the heart and develops when we see our neighbor in good fortune. Anger and malice are perceived in offense inflicted on a neighbor. Hardheartedness and lack of mercy are shown when a person disregards the misfortune and suffering of a neighbor. Greed especially reveals itself upon loss of wealth and property; love of fame, in disgrace and dishonor; ambition, in deprivation of honor and office. We see how a person is anxious and grieves and how much he complains, weeps, and sobs upon losing either wealth, or office and honor, or the glory of this world. Many people, not being able to endure affliction and sorrow hiding within their hearts, kill themselves. Oh, the blindness! Oh, the insensibility! Oh, the misery! To destroy oneself for the sake of what in itself is almost nothing, like a shadow.

Whoever loves something feels sorry when he losses it; and the more he loves it, the more he feels sorry for what is lost. Likewise other afflictions of the soul are mainly perceived in temptation. Temptation opens our heart and makes the secret of our heart manifest. For God plumbs the whole depth and abyss of our hearts and sees what is hidden in it. Therefore God permits temptation to us and by this shows us what is hidden in our heart. Let us come to know, Christians, our soul's misfortune and evil, that in this way we may zealously seek deliverance.

(6) No one may deliver us from this affliction of the soul, no one except Jesus Christ. He is our deliverer. He knows our poverty better than we ourselves do. For this, He came into the world, lived in the world, suffered, and died in order to deliver our souls from this affliction and evil and to return to us our first blessedness and nobility and freedom, that is, this splendid beauty, God's image. All our blessedness and glory consists in Him. Let us acknowledge our poverty, and having humbled ourselves, let us seek deliverance with Him. That poor woman suffering from a flow of blood, finding nowhere a cure for her affliction, came to Jesus with faith and, only having touched His holy garment, received healing (see Mark 5:25–29). This woman exhorts us also to come to Jesus and ask His help and deliverance for our souls. For He is both able, being almighty, and wishes to deliver us, being a Lover of Mankind, and He is invisibly with us. Let us also approach with faith and in spirit touch His holy garments, and from day to day we shall feel that our affliction is lessening and freedom of soul is returning. But it is always true that knowledge of misfortune impels us to seek deliverance from misfortune. Come to know your misfortune, and you will seek deliverance. In this all the efficacy consists—to come to know yourself and your soul's affliction.

# 126. A Pauper

We see in the world that there are many paupers. A pauper is one who has nothing: neither bread, nor clothing, nor a house, nor money, nor anything else necessary for life, but instead asks people for everything and receives it from them. Every person, from high to low, and from rich to poverty-stricken, and from masters to servants, finds himself in such destitution and is actually destitute, although he does not realize his destitution.

(1) No matter what every person has, it is not his own, but God's; he has nothing from himself but receives it from God (see 1 Cor 1:7). God, being good and generous, opens His treasury and gives everything to all, as destitute and wretched, with His generous hand. Gold, silver, and copper are God's

good things and serve us in our needs. The bread with which we are nourished and the drink with which we quench our thirst are refreshed and consoled; clothing, with which we cover and warm ourselves; a house, in which we rest and shelter from bad weather and storms; fire, by which we warm ourselves and on which we our food; the air, by which our life is maintained; light, by which we are illumined; livestock, wild animals, birds, and fish, which serve our needs; and everything else are God's good things (see Ps 23:1). All this He, being a Lover of Mankind, gives us, destitute, wretched, and poor ones from His goodness alone. Therefore, we ask Him for everything necessary for our life in the prayer: "Give us this day our daily bread" (Matt 9:11). Under *bread* is understood everything necessary for the maintenance of our life.

You see, O man, your destitution. God gives you everything as to a pauper and beggar. He gives you everything of His own, inasmuch you have nothing of your own. Otherwise you would not be able to live for the shortest time. God anticipates your squalor and destitution and opens His treasure houses, and gives you His good things from them for maintenance and preservation of your life. Both the hour of your birth and the hour of your departure show your destitution. Naked you came from your mother's womb, and you enter the world with nothing; naked will you return from the world, and you leave with nothing (see Job 1:21; 1 Tim 6:7). Everything that you may have from birth to death only serves you, and all this is God's property, and not yours. God gives all this to you as to a pauper and beggar, for without this you cannot live.

From this, learn:

(a) To realize your destitution and poverty, and so be humbled. You are poor and destitute, inasmuch as you have nothing of your own, but receive all things from God.

(b) To realize God's goodness, which gives everything to us paupers and beggars.

(c) To thank God, as Bestower of every good, for everything. We receive every good thing from Him, like paupers and beggars, and we receive them without any merits of ours. As it says in the liturgy, "It is meet and right"[16] to thank Him always and for everything. Glory to God the benefactor for all things!

(d) From this you see that all people, being paupers and beggars, are equal. The equal destitution of all makes everyone equal. Whether one has much or little, he has someone else's, and not his own.

(e) Therefore, no one should exalt himself over others, nor disdain anyone. We all have someone else's property, and not his own.

(f) From this it follows that we should help each other in need. We all have God's property, and we should expend it as God wills. Our house should serve for rest for our neighbors. Our bread should also feed our neighbors; our silver and gold should also satisfy the needs of our neighbors; our livestock should also serve other people, and so on.

We learn this and other things from realization of our destitution and God's goodness to us. And this is that bodily destitution that we all have.

(2) When a person looks within his heart, and considers his inner state, he will see destitution of the soul, worse than that of the body, for he has nothing in himself except poverty, wretchedness, sin, and darkness. He does not have true and living faith, true and heartfelt prayer, true and heartfelt thanksgiving, his own righteousness, love, purity, goodness, mercy, meekness, patience, rest, quiet, peace, and other good things of the soul. So destitute and wretched is man! But whoever has this treasure receives it from God but does not have it of himself. He should attribute this to God's grace and not to his own effort. Therefore, this whole treasury is called the fruit of the Holy Spirit in God's Word. "The fruit of the Spirit is love, joy, peace, longsuffering, kindness, goodness, faithfulness, gentleness, self-control" (Gal 5:22–23).

Let us realize, Christians, our destitution of the soul, and let us seek our treasure of the soul with Christ, who, "though He was rich, yet for your sakes He became poor, that you through His poverty might become rich" (2 Cor 8:9). If we do not have a heartfelt faith, let us seek it, that He would enrich us with faith. "Lord, I believe; help my unbelief!" (Mark 9:24). If we do not have heartfelt prayer, let us seek it with Him, that He will teach us to pray through His Holy Spirit. "Lord, teach us to pray" (Luke 11:1). If we do not know how to give thanks truly and sincerely, we will ask this too from Him, that He will teach us to give thanks and to sing. If we do not have the fear of God and love, and any other treasure of the soul, let us knock on the door of His mercy, that he will open His heavenly treasury. He Himself commanded us to pray about all of this and promised to grant all of this. "Ask, and it will be given to you; seek, and you will find; knock, and it will be opened to you. For everyone who asks receives, and he who seeks finds, and to him who knocks it will be opened" (Matt 7:7–8). "Bow down Thy ear, O Lord, and hear me, for I am poor and in misery" (Ps 85:1). "O look Thou upon me, and have mercy upon me, according to the judgment of them that love Thy name" (Ps 118:132), and so on. "Upon whom will I show respect, but to the humble and the peaceful and to him that trembles at My words," says the Lord (Isa 66:2). "He hath regarded the prayer of the humble, and hath not despised their petition. Let this be written for another generation" (Ps 101:18–19).

(3) Man is destitute because he does not have faithful and sincere friends. True friendship cannot be without mutual and heartfelt love, without like-mindedness and harmony. Love is rare among the sons of men. Craftiness, cunning, falsehood, and hypocrisy appear almost in everyone. "Truth is minished from among the children of men. They have talked of vanities every one with his neighbor; they do but flatter with their lips, and dissemble in their double heart" (Ps 11:2–3). One deceives, another lies, a third and fourth do the same, and so one must beware of and fear everyone. "The human heart is deceitful above all things, and desperately wicked; who can know it?" (Jer 17:9 NKJV)

Often it happens that we have friends, but then they soon become our enemies, and so we learn that they were false friends to us. A sincere friend is always a friend. In our good fortune, we have many friends; this is like a shadow when the sun shines, but when the sunshine of our good fortune is hidden and the day of our prosperity grows dark, then like a shadow, they depart from us and vanish.

From this it is apparent that their friendship too was false, True love is always united with the beloved, both in good fortune and in misfortune. Since true love makes two into one, and hence where there is one, the other is constantly also there, although not always in body, but always in heart. Our true friend is one who does not abandon us even in misfortune. So seek such a friend, especially in the present time, when people learn to deceive and entice, ridicule and slander one another.

Oh, poor Christians, how far you have moved away from those Christians who "were of one heart and one soul" (Acts 4:32). And from this you can yourselves see that your Christianity is false. The devil, the father of lies, teaches people to lie to each other, deceive and entice one another, so that all loyalty and love would dry up from human hearts. O Lord, have mercy on Your inheritance and preserve the remnants of Israel! Each speaks vanity to his neighbor; everyone learns a lie; everyone sharpens his tongue, sharpens it for slander, mocking, degradation, and abuse. "Save me, Lord, for there is not one godly man left" (Ps 11:2).

Christian, what friends can you rely on here? Here there is clear trouble for a person: trouble from neighbors, trouble from one's own people, trouble from friends, trouble from brethren, trouble from servants and slaves. There cannot be a greater friendship than between husband and wife, but even here, how much enmity we see and how many complaints, and slanders, and other evils we hear from them against each other! What kind of friendship is this, to be complaining against and slandering each other?

You see, Christian, that we do not have faithful and sincere friends, and therefore, we are destitute, and there is nowhere to find them. Let us turn to Christ, let us join ourselves with Him and draw near with our heart. Without a doubt, He loves even us unworthy ones, being the Lover of Mankind, so that He even laid down His life for us. Let us also love Him, as One Who loves us, and so there will be friendship between us, but a faithful true, sincere, unceasing, blessed, and eternal one, for mutual love creates friendship. Then, although even the whole world will be at odds with us, truly nothing will harm us. "You are My friends," (Oh, the goodness, oh, the love for mankind of Jesus, oh, the Christian honor and dignity!), "if you do whatever I command you," says the Lord (John 15:14). "Hearken, O Lord, unto my voice, with which I have cried, Have mercy on me, and hear me. My heart hath said unto Thee, I will seek the Lord; my face hath sought Thee; Thy face, O Lord, will I seek. O turn not Thou Thy face from me, nor turn away from Thy servant in displeasure; be Thou my helper; reject me not, neither forsake me, O God, my Saviour" (Ps 26:7–9). "But it is good for me to cleave unto God, to put my trust in the Lord" (Ps 72:28).

Poor and destitute people, living in all kinds of penury and shortage, knowing a certain rich and generous person, all run to him, and each asks him for help in their penury. One asks him for money for his need, another bread, another clothing, another something else, and they receive what they ask for.

Christians! We are all poor, destitute, and wretched, as already said. No one can help our destitution, especially that of the soul, besides Christ. We know that He is rich, being God, and generous, merciful, and a lover of mankind. He is both able and willing to give to us. "For [our] sakes He became poor, that [we] through His poverty might become rich" (2 Cor 8:9). He took our destitution upon Himself to give us the wealth of His goodness. He is a refuge and enricher for us, poor, destitute, and wretched ones. Our forefathers and fathers turned to Him in their poverty, destitution, squalor, and wretchedness, and received help for what they were lacking, and were enriched by His all-generous hand. Even now, everyone who knows Him runs to Him and receives whatever is needed.

Let us too join and unite ourselves to this pious fellowship, and run to Him with faith and hope, that we too may receive mercy from Him, and He may enrich us with His grace. He drives no one away from Himself. "The one who comes to Me," He says, "I will by no means cast out" (John 6:37). "Whoso putteth his trust in the Lord, mercy embraceth him on every side" (Ps 31:10). Most of all, He calls us, poor and wretched, to Himself: "Come to Me, all you who labor and are heavy laden, and I will give you rest" (Matt 11:28). He will give bodily and temporal blessings to everyone—to all who know Him and do not know Him. Everyone receives them from His generous hand. He gives to us, too, and we receive everything needed. Glory to His goodness!

Being destitute and wretched, however, we must ask Him for everything, that we may realize and acknowledge our poverty, and the treasury of His goodness, which is opened up to us poor ones, and so, we will give thanks to Him. He gives blessings of the soul only to those who know Him and believe in Him and with faith ask them of Him. We shall come to know His inexhaustible treasury and Him, our Redeemer, Saviour, and Enricher. The Heavenly Father sent Him to us in order to enrich us, poor and destitute ones. The entire treasury of our blessedness reposes in Him.

Let us run to Him with faith, and declare to Him our penury and destitution, that He would look down upon us and grant us our petition and in place of our destitution grant us the wealth of his goodness. But it is required of us without fail that each one realizes and acknowledges his destitution, for without this we shall receive nothing. For "God resists the proud, But gives grace to the humble" (1 Pet 5:5). There can be no humility without realization and acknowledgement of poverty and destitution.

O poor and wretched people! What do we have to be proud of and extol ourselves for? We are poor in body and poor in soul. Although we may have physical and temporal wealth, this belongs to someone else and not us. Everything is God's, for "[t]he earth is the Lord's, and the fullness thereof" (Ps 23:1). We do not have a treasure of the soul. And we are all the poorer that we do not realize this, our poverty. We are blind, and we do not realize our blindness; poor, and do not realize our poverty; needy, and do not realize out neediness; wretched, and do not recognize our wretchedness. The wealth of God's grace is ready for all and is opened to all, but man does not want to realize and acknowledge his poverty and humble himself and so to receive God's grace. *Grace is given to the humble.*

Oh, how cruelly has sin infected and blinded the poor human! Into what baseness has fallen the image of God! Man is poor and does not realize and does not acknowledge his poverty and therefore receives nothing. God wishes to enrich him, but he does not wish to acknowledge his destitution.

Christian! The whole crux of the matter lies in our realizing and acknowledging our poverty and indigence before God. The wealth of His grace is ready for us. Our fault is that we do not have the treasury of the soul. So let us take stock of ourselves, and realize our poverty, that the Lord may fill our scarcity and deficiency with His grace. "For everyone who exalts himself will be humbled, and he who humbles himself will be exalted" (Luke 18:14).

# 127. A Treasure

The sons of this age have their treasure, and Christians have their treasure. The sons of this age have this treasure: corruptible riches, gold, silver, copper, and other matter. Christians have the treasure of God's grace, and this treasure is heavenly, spiritual, abiding in their hearts, as the Apostle wrote: "But we have this treasure in earthen vessels, that the excellence of the power may be of God and not of us" (2 Cor 4:7).

People who have a corruptible treasure use it to supply all their needs and whatever they lack. If they do not have bread, they buy bread. If they do not have clothing, they obtain clothing, and so on. Likewise, God's grace, the heavenly treasure living in Christian hearts, supplies all their souls' needs and deficiencies. Man of himself is blind—God's grace enlightens his heart's eyes and shows him the vanity of this world, the shortness of temporal life, and the duration of eternity; it shows that everything that is in this world passes like a shadow and that a person from birth to death is a wanderer and wayfarer, headed for the heavenly Homeland. It admonishes him at all times to be wary of everything and to relate with fear to all that exists in this world, and use them for need and not for pleasing of the flesh, and to shun the temptations of this world. This is why such a soul seeks in this world neither riches, nor honor, nor fame, nor any other treasure of this world, as do the sons of this age. But he always looks and aspires to eternal blessedness, and desires and tries to attain it most diligently. And this is why he sighs always to his Creator that he may obtain that grace of His, and praise and hymn Him with all the elect forever.

Man is feeble and he is powerless to stand against the urge of the passions and sin and overcome them—God's grace strengthens him, helps him to stand firm in this important struggle, shows him the loathsomeness of the passions and sin, and exhorts him at all times to shun this evil. Therefore such a person strongly guards against every sin, avoids situations that lead to sin, and tries to keep his conscience pure. It is difficult for such a person to sin, and he feels it better to die than to sin, knowing that every sin insults God's majesty, and the conscience is enflamed and troubled, which is unbearable for the pious soul.

A person does not see many sins within himself: "Who can understand his fallings into sin" (Ps 18:13)? God's grace exposes such sins in him. Everything is a sin that is done against God's will. This is why sorrow, melancholy, and lamentation rise up in the heart, and sometimes even torment makes itself felt. Therefore, the heart grieves, and it pours forth its signs, warm tears, weeps, and sobs, as if it had lost something great. And the very tears take the place of refreshment and consolation for such a heart. In this way, God's grace distresses the human heart, cures, saddens, comforts, overpowers, enlivens, and arranges everything for our benefit. The same grace of God shows a person not only his own wretchedness and poverty but also that of the entire human race. Therefore sympathy arises in a person's heart for other people too, for all people are of one nature and all have only infirmity and wretchedness. Therefore the pious soul laments and weeps not only for its own poverty but also for that of others.

Of himself, a person does not know and does not have true repentance and sorrow for sins: God's grace forms in him true repentance and sorrow. True repentance and sorrow is to regret and feel sorry for sins not on account of our perdition, but because by sin, we insult and anger the all-good God, Who is the compassionate Father and eternal goodness and love.

Man, realizing his baseness and God's incomprehensible majesty and His tremendous love for him and for everyone, is much grieved and wounded in his heart that he, "earth and ashes" (Sir 10:9; 13:31), and loved by God, has insulted and angered the One Who loved him. His angels, archangels, and all the heavenly powers honor, hymn, and worship Him with fear and love, but he, base, *earth and ashes*, has not honored nor obeyed Him. From this, a person feels a tremendous sadness in his heart and is wounded by this as by an arrow. And this is "godly sorrow," which "produces repentance leading to salvation" (2 Cor 7:10). God's grace produces this sorrow. He who has such sorrow will lament and grieve, even if there were no Gehenna.

Man does not have a true and heartfelt love for God in and of himself—God's grace arouses love in his heart, showing him that God is an uncreated, beginningless, endless, unalterable, everlasting, most loving Being and supremely high Good, from Whom all blessings and benefactions flow as from an ever-flowing spring and was created just as all creatures and people and, having fallen, was redeemed by Him for eternal blessedness. So God's grace, in enlightening the heart of man, kindles in it the fire of God's love.

Feeling such love in his heart, a person pours out words of love: "I will love Thee, O Lord, my strength" (Ps 17:2). And again: "For what have I in heaven, and what have I desired upon earth from Thee? My flesh and my heart have failed, O God of my heart, but Thou art my portion, O God for ever" (Ps 72:25–26). One who truly loves God desires nothing either on earth or in heaven except God alone. Such a soul cries with the Prophet, "Like as the hart panteth after the waterbrooks, so longeth my soul after Thee, O God. My soul hath thirsteth for the mighty living God" (Ps 41:2–3). For such a one, to be with God even in hell is paradise, but to be without God even in heaven is torment. Therefore, such a person tries to please God in everything and, seeing in himself many infirmities and shortcomings, grieves and is sad. And loving God, he loves his neighbor as well because God loves him and orders him to love.

If a person does not have true humility within himself, God's grace shows him his destitution, squalor, poverty, wretchedness, baseness, and nothingness. And so, by coming to know himself, a person is humbled and does not rely on himself in anything; he entrusts himself only to the omnipotence, wisdom, goodness, and mercy of God.

Man does not have righteousness in himself, with which he might appear before God's Judgment seat and be justified, but he sees in himself a sinner, for whom it is in no way possible to hold his ground at God's Judgment seat—God's grace comforts him and exhorts him for the sake of righteousness to sigh to God, and to seek justification in Christ, Who died and rose from the dead. Such a person cries out to God with the Publican, "God, be merciful to me a sinner!" (Luke 18:13). *O God, turn Thy face away from my sins, and turn to the face of Your Christ, my redeemer, Jesus, Who for the sake of me, a sinner, suffered and died. In you, O Jesus, my Holy One, I am justified.*

Man does not have in himself true and heartfelt prayer—God's grace teaches him what to pray for and arouses in him true and heartfelt prayer. And as the smoke of a fragrant powder placed on a burning coal rises, so prayer aroused by the grace of God rises up and ascends to God. Then a person briefly but earnestly prays and cries out: "O Lord, have mercy! O Lord, be generous! O Lord, hear and save!" Such words are heartfelt words and are pronounced by the lips. The lips say these words out of the fullness of the heart. Such a prayer, although short, passes through the heavens and enters the ears of the Lord Almighty.

Man does not know how to thank God truly and sincerely—God's grace teaches him this, showing him God's innumerable benefactions that have been and are being granted, of which he, base, wretched, squalid, poor, and unworthy of anything, has been favored from the goodness of God gratis and without any of his own merits. What is the sinner worthy of, besides punishment? But in spite of his being a sinner and disparaging Him, the all-good God who loves mankind grants him His innumerable blessings.

Realizing this goodness and love for mankind of God, and his own baseness and unworthiness, man thanks God, his most high benefactor, sincerely, bends his heart's knees, and falls down before Him, and even not with the lips, but with the heart cries out to Him: "Who am I, Lord, that You grant me such blessings of Yours? I am a sinner, I am a creation, who has sinned before you and grieved You, and who sins each day before You, but You do not leave me as such, but favor me with Your blessedness and mercy." "Lord, what is man, that Thou hast had such respect unto him? Or the son of man, that Thou so regardest him? Man is like to vanity; his days as a shadow pass away" (Ps 143:3–4), and so on. "Bless the Lord, O my soul, and all that is within me bless His holy Name. Bless the Lord, O my soul, and forget not all his benefits" (Ps 102:1–2). For in a thankful heart the good things given by its benefactor are always before the eyes of the soul and, looking at them and at its own unworthiness, it earnestly gives thanks to its benefactor.

The sign of an ungrateful heart is forgetfulness of benefactions, as was written of the ungrateful Israelites: "And they forgat His good deeds, and the wonderful works that He had showed for them" (Ps 77:11). God's grace turns a person away from this evil and at all times reminds him of God's benefactions, and that he must keep them in mind and earnestly give thanks to God the benefactor and acknowledge his own unworthiness.

If a person does not have the fear of God in him, God's grace teaches him the fear of the Lord, displaying God's majesty, omnipotence, omnipresence, and omniscience before his heart's eyes and so exhorts him to live circumspectly and with fear, to shun every sin in words, deeds, and thoughts, for this angers God and deprives the person who sins of God's mercy; and so teaches him always and everywhere to behave before the omnipresent and all-seeing God, as children behave before their father, and servants before their master, and subjects before their king, and dare not do anything improper. Therefore, such a God-fearing soul always and everywhere, secretly and openly, in the presence of people and in their absence, outside and inside, acts circumspectly and shuns every evil. It is surrounded by and maintained by the fear of God and is immovable toward any evil. And if any demonic temptation and evil thought attacks it, it is terrified of this and cries out to God, "O Lord, help me!" and so stands up and fights against evil. So the fear of God is the root of all blessings. "The fear of the Lord is the beginning of wisdom" (Ps 110:10).

Who is wise? He who always and everywhere acts circumspectly and has the invisible God before himself as if He were visible. "See then that you walk circumspectly, not as fools but as wise" (Eph 5:15). The beginning of this wisdom is the fear of the Lord. God's grace teaches the fear of the Lord within a person (see Ps 33:12). The same grace of God teaches a person to rejoice in God, his Saviour, and produces true, spiritual, heavenly joy in his heart, and a certain jubilation, and enjoyment, and rest, and peace in his conscience, and this is all a foretaste of eternal life and as it were a crumb from the heavenly table falling into the human heart.

The same grace of God changes a person and makes him loving, merciful, compassionate, meek, so that he becomes merciful even to his enemies, pities them and sympathizes with them, and is patient with them. God's grace sometimes so enflames the human heart with love that it would like to clasp everyone without exception in the embraces of his love and see everyone saved. This and other things are the action of God's grace living in a person's soul. This is the treasure of Christians that is within, and not outside, them, and that they carry with them always and everywhere. So they are poor and rich: poor in themselves but rich in the mercy of God. And although they have this heavenly treasure within themselves, they realize and acknowledge themselves to be poor and wretched, and always desire and ask it from their Creator, continually hunger and thirst for righteousness. God's grace, which dwells in them, also humbles them.

Christians, let us realize our poverty and the riches of God's grace and humble ourselves before our Lord, that He may grant us His grace. "God resists the proud, but gives grace to the humble" (1 Pet 5:5). It is easy for a heart that is humble and delivered from the love of the world and the whims of the flesh to take in God's grace, as it is easy for an empty vessel to receive water or some other matter. Water always flows downward from the mountains, and God's grace comes down from the heavenly high places into a free, humbled, and low heart. "Make me a clean heart, O God, and renew a right spirit within me. Cast me not away from Thy presence, and take not Thy Holy Spirit from me. O give me the comfort of Thy salvation, and stablish me with Thy governing Spirit" (Ps 50:12–14).

## 128. Witnesses

We see that in the world there are many witnesses who testify about things that take place in the world. People testify in court concerning the innocent and the guilty; a house and building testify about their architect and builder; a book testifies of its author and his intellect; cooked food testifies about the cook; a letter testifies about its writer; a person's tracks testify about the person who passed through a place; the tracks of livestock, about the livestock; the tracks of a bird, about the bird; and so on. In this way, the whole world witnesses about God, its Creator, and silently says to us rational creatures about Him: "He created me."

A great and wondrous building indicates a great and wondrous creator. The great and incomprehensible expanse of the heavens testifies: "He created me." "The heavens declare the glory of God" (Ps 18:2). The heavens are great and vast, but the Creator is incomparably greater, for Whom "Heaven is My throne, and earth is the footstool of my feet" (Isa 66:1).

The sun, moon, and stars testify: "He created us; we have light that He gave us, and we serve you, O people, with this. But our Creator, He Who gave us such light, is a Light incomparably better, more beautiful, more superb, and more wondrous" (see 1 John 1:5). He "wraps Himself with light as it were with a garment" (Ps 103:2). We enlighten your bodily eyes, but He enlightens the eyes of your soul. We show you the way, bodily good and evil, benefit and harm, but He by His holy word shows you the way to eternal life, the soul's good and evil, benefit and harm. The air testifies: "He created me. I enliven your bodies, but He enlivens your souls. I am the life of your bodies, but He is the life of your souls. Without me, animals cannot live; without Him, your souls cannot be alive. I enliven your mortal bodies, but with Him, you seek life for your souls. O God, *Thou shalt quicken us, and we shall call upon Thy Name*" (Ps 79:19).

The alternation of day and night testifies and silently cries to us about God: He arranged it like this. "Day unto day uttereth speech, and night unto night showeth knowledge. There is neither speech nor language, in which their voices are not heard" (Ps 18:3–4). In the east and the west, in the north and south, they testify silently. Night serves for our rest, and day for work. "Man shall go forth to his work, and to his labor, until the evening" (Ps 103:23).

Springs, river, lakes, and seas, and those that dwell in them testify: "He created us. We serve your needs; but He ordered us to serve you, so you will come to know your Creator and serve Him. We serve you, and you, the rational creation, serve your Creator and thank Him."

The earth testifies: He created me, and gave me to you for your habitation. "All the whole heavens are the Lord's, but the earth hath He given to the children of men" (Ps 113:24). You have your origin from me, but you will return again into my bosom, from which you were taken (see Gen 3:19). Realize that you are wanderers and strangers in this world. And so, seek your Homeland and Home, in which you will live permanently and find rest. "We ... look for new heavens and a new earth in which righteousness dwells" (2 Pet 3:13).

The fruits of the earth testify: "'He created us.' We, O people, have nourishing and healing power; He gave us such power for your sakes. We nourish and heal your bodies but seek food and healing for your souls with Him: He is the food and healing of your souls. Eating us, you "taste, and see, that the Lord is good" (Ps 33:9), Who gave you such good things for sustenance, consolation, and healing. We are a good creation of His, but our Creator is incomparably better. We are a good for your bodies, but He is the good for your souls. Love Him, give thanks to Him, seek Him, draw near to Him. "Taste, and see, that the Lord is good" (Ps 33:9 LXX).

The various trees testify: "He created us. We serve you, O people, with our fruits, and by giving you shade during hot weather; we serve too for the construction of your houses, and for heating of your rooms, and for the cooking of your food, and in other various needs. We serve you—you should serve our Creator and give thanks to Him."

The various wild animals, livestock, and birds testify: "He created us. He commanded us to serve you, O people! We serve you, giving you food, giving skins for clothing, working for you; we serve you and your needs: He so commanded us. You should serve the Lord, our Creator, and give thanks to and praise Him, for the Lord is good, Who created us for service to you."

The clouds, moving hither and thither and carrying the water like waterskins, and bedewing the air, earth, and fruits of the earth, and refreshing us, testify: "He created us." Marvelous is the creation, and marvelous is its arrangement: it has its place in the delicate element of the air; it contains such a great burden of water, but it does not fall down, and not suddenly but little by little pours it onto the earth, and having watered one area, moves to another, and pours out its treasure and waters the thirsty earth. The all-powerful and most wise Creator, Who "brings forth the clouds from the ends of the world" (Ps 134:7), arranged it thus.

"Look at us, O people," they silently cry out to us, "look at us and learn the might and wisdom of our Creator. He arranged and ordered us to be like this. We are carrying out His all-powerful word; we move from place to place and carry around water, as His servants, and humidify the air, and refresh you, water you fields, and yield your fruits. We serve you—you should serve your Creator, who ordered us to serve you, and give thanks to Him and praise Him, for the Lord is good. 'He did not leave Himself without witness, in that He did good, gave us rain from heaven and fruitful seasons, filling our hearts with food and gladness'" (Acts 14:17).

The lightning and thunder testify: "He created us." "He made lightnings into rain" (Ps 134:7). People, you are frightened of thunder and of lightning but you should fear Him Who created you. They are terrifying for you, but He is "feared exceedingly" (Sir 1:6–7 LXX). And so, fear Him, fear the One Who "is able to destroy both soul and body in fiery hell" (Matt 10:28); fear Him indeed, and repent, lest you perish.

The winds testify: "He created us." He "bringeth the winds out of His treasuries" (Ps 134:7). "We," they cry, "drive rain clouds to you, we purify the air and make it healthful, we drive away haze, and take away any mugginess and harm from the air, and make it beneficial and healthy for you, we help your fruits of the earth to grow, to develop, mature, and ripen; this is how we serve you. We serve you; you should serve the Lord, our Creator, and give thanks to Him, for the Lord is good."

The winter and summer, spring and fall testify: "He created us." All creation, too, testifies, "He created us." That created from nothing testifies of the almighty power of its Creator. The wisely created testifies of the wisdom of its Creator. "In wisdom hast Thou made them all" (Ps 103:24). Creation is good, and very good, and witnesses to the incomprehensible kindness and goodness of its Creator.

The human conscience testifies about God, our Creator. This faithful witness never is silent but always cries out to man: "There is a God, there is His righteous judgment. There is a God, Who rewards virtue and punishes sin"; therefore, it rebukes, troubles, and torments a person for sin but consoles and gladdens him for virtue.

The Word of God, contained in the Holy Bible, testifies to God. "The Law of the Lord is pure, converting the soul; the testimony of the Lord is sure, giving wisdom unto the simple. The statutes of the Lord are right, gladdening the heart; the commandment of the Lord is bright, giving light unto the eyes. The fear of the Lord is clean, enduring for ever and ever; the judgments of the Lord are true, and righteous altogether. More to be desired are they than gold and much precious stone; sweeter also than honey, and the honey-comb" (Ps 18:8–11). "Thy testimonies are very sure" (Ps 92:6).

The most glorious and wondrous works of God, which the whole world sees and gazes at in amazement, testify about God. Who brought on the worldwide flood, and saved the righteous Noah with his household and with a number of animals in the ark in the midst of the waters? God. Who tamed the various wild animals that were in the ark? God. Who burned Sodom and Gomorrah and their neighboring cities and led the righteous Lot out of them? God. Who led Israel out of Egyptian bondage? God. Who divided the Red Sea and led Israel through it? God. Who drowned the tyrant Pharoah with his whole army in the sea? God. Who led Israel through the terrible desert? God. Who fed such a multitude of people in the desert for forty years? God. God "giveth food to all flesh" (Ps 135:25).

Who struck down before their face the great king Sihon, king of the Amorites, and Og, king of Bashan? God. Who led Israel into the Promised Land? God. Who drove nations from this country and destroyed them, and settled Israel in it? God. Who saved Israel from the surrounding peoples who were living in that land? God. What was Israel against all the nations surrounding it? Israel can be likened to one person against thousands of people, or as two people against twenty thousand, or as a handful of water against the sea. But

Israel was kept safe; the nations of many thousands surrounding it could not destroy it. Who saved it, if not the all-powerful God, Whom it called upon and revered? The Psalmist sings of this: "If the Lord Himself had not been on our side, may Israel now say, If the Lord Himself had not been on our side, when men rose up against us, then would they have swallowed us up alive; When their wrath was kindled upon us, then would the waters have drowned us" (Ps 123:1–4). And although Israel sometimes found itself in slavery to other nations, this was sent to them by God as a punishment for their sins and iniquities; for God hates sins and iniquities even among His own people who know and honor Him and sends them punishment for them.

In the new age of grace, the deeds, performed by Christ, the Son of God, and described in the holy Gospel, show a marked and firm testimony about God and, as we point to the sun with a finger, they point to God and bring us to knowledge of Him. The Gospel is filled with such glorious and supernatural deeds. To change water into wine, to make a paralytic well by a word, to give sight to a man born blind, to the cleanse a leper, to drive out a demon from a man, to raise a dead man, and other such acts are impossible to do by any power found on earth. There must be present here an almighty power that can do everything, and from nothing can make something, from evil, good; from infirm, healthy; from darkness, light; from dead, alive; from non-existing, existing; and from non-being to bring into being, such a power, I say, whose wish everything obeys and which does everything that it wishes, for which there is nothing impossible. Such a power is our God, Who alone does everything that He wishes. And so that no one may doubt these glorious and wondrous works of God, even the very circumstances are described: where, in what country, in what city, or village; on the way or in the desert; when, morning or evening; on whom and who was there; and what happened after this; what was said; what was done; and so on. All of these details banish all doubt from a person and persuade us to see the truth in what the holy Gospel recounts. Christ the Lord changed water into wine. Where was this miracle? In Cana of Galilee. Under what circumstances? During a wedding. Who was there? The most-holy Mother of Jesus and His disciples. Why was the water changed into wine? Because there was not enough wine. Who reported this to Christ the Lord, Who Knows everything? His most-holy Mother said, "They have no wine." What did Christ the Lord answer her? "Woman, what does your concern have to do with Me?" What then did the Mother of Jesus say to the servants? "Whatever He [Jesus] says to you, do it." In what were the water changed into wine? In waterpots, filled to the brim. How did the wine changed from water seem to the master of the feast? Excellent. Therefore, having called the bridegroom, he said to him, "Every man at the beginning sets out the good wine, and when the guests have well drunk, then the inferior. You have kept the good wine until now!" (John 2:1–11).

The circumstances around other of God's wondrous works are described, showing the Gospel's truth clearer than the sun, so everyone who has common sense is sure to believe it. Therefore, those who do not believe the most holy truth of the Gospel and especially those were born in a Christian family and through baptism entered Christianity will not have an answer: their own conscience will convict them.

The conversion of nations to the Christian faith strongly testifies and resounds continuously to the whole world. This work is truly great and wonderful, and continuously in all corners of the world, in the east and in the west, in the north and in the south, and cries silently to all: "There is a God Who can do everything. There is a God Who creates light from darkness. There is a God Who takes care of all of creation, and especially for rational creation, that is, man. There is a God Who wishes that all people be saved and come to a knowledge of the truth. There is a God Who sent His Christ into the world to convert those who have gone astray, to seek and to save that which was lost" (Matt 18:11; Luke 19:10) and lead to Himself people, created in His own image, who have withdrawn from Him. This great and wondrous work, like a finger, points to God, the all-powerful, the all-good, the lover of man, the merciful, the long-suffering, and the most wise; this is the continuous silent sermon in all the ends of the earth about Christ, the Saviour of the world.

A marvelous work! The pagans, enticed by cunning, dreams, and diabolical apparitions; confirmed in idolatrous impiety; maintaining this from their ancestors, having become stagnant and worn out in this, and knowing what is conformable with carnal sophistication and acceptable to it, abandoned it and considered it a deception and falsehood. There must be here a supernatural Light, which enlightened the eyes of their souls and revealed the darkness and deception. To Whom were the pagans converted from their deception? To Christ, about Whom they never heard, Whom the Jews had expected, but rejected and Who suffered at their hands, was crucified, and hung between two thieves, and died, and rose on the third day, and ascended into heaven. And they acknowledged Him as the true God, and they placed and established all hope of eternal blessedness in Him alone; they recognized no other intermediary for eternal blessedness besides Him, worshipped Him as their true God, and glorified Him.

The power of the crucified Christ drew them to Him, Who died for all. Those who had become stagnant and worn out in polytheism acknowledged the One True God. They acknowledged God, One in essence, but Triune in Persons; they came to believe in the heavenly and supernatural mysteries, in the resurrection of the dead, in the heavenly and invisible blessings, and so on: they abandoned an iniquitous life, spent in pleasing of the flesh, vanity, and the opulence of this world and came to love the humble and virtuous life of Christ, and each taking up his cross, followed Christ, their Saviour. A supernatural light shined in their hearts and drew them after Christ.

Through whom were the innumerable peoples, who had been like wild animals, converted to the Christian faith? Through the twelve Apostles. What were they converted by? Not by the sword, but by the word. Who were they? Ignorant and very simple men. This is incomprehensible to the human mind! And nothing other than the power of Christ crucified did all of this. No matter how many obstacles the devil placed before the growing Christian faith and whatever tortures he devised through his votaries for preachers of the Word and the rest of the faithful, nothing worked for him: all his evil counsel crumbled by the power of the crucified Christ, our God.

The more they tortured and killed the Christians, the greater their number multiplied. Very many of them hurried to be tortured for Christ, as to a delectable feast, and entered through the fire and water to eternal rest (see Ps 65:12). This is something worthy of amazement! People saw the most horrible tortures that awaited Christians then, but daringly converted to the Christian faith, and hazarded all the tortures. They did not see the eternal blessings but strove for them as for visible ones and encouraged each other to that struggle and to those eternal blessings.

This was not a human work but a work of God. The power of God was acting. God, Whom they had come to know and were glorifying, granted them His light, strength, and power, according to what was written: "The Lord shall give strength unto His people" (Ps 28:11). And thus they prevailed over and defeated all the slanders of the enemy and the most horrible tortures. About this, Christ, our Saviour, said before His Passion, "And I, if I am lifted up from the earth, will draw all peoples to Myself" (John 12:32). And again: "Other sheep I have which are not of this fold; them also I must bring, and they will hear My voice; and there will be one flock and one shepherd" (John 10:16). He drew to Himself all His lost sheep, and all the ends of the earth worship Him with the Father and the Holy Spirit. "Blessed is the Lord God of Israel, For He has visited and redeemed His people, And has raised up a horn of salvation for us In the house of His servant David" (Luke 1:68–69).

You see, Christian, how many witnesses for God there are, and they continuously exhort us to believe in, honor, and glorify our Creator. Let us too honor Him with faith, fear, love, submission, and obedience. Let us come to know Him as Creator, God, Lord, provider, and our most high benefactor and our only blessedness and highest good, and He will know and acknowledge us as His people. And this is what eternal life consists of. "This is eternal life, that they may know You, the only true God, and Jesus Christ Whom You have sent," the Lord says (John 17:3).

# 129. Whom Should I Love, If Not Him?

We hear how one person says of another: "Whom should I love, if not him?" This is how one answers who is asked about someone, "You love him, right?" Then he who loves answers, "Whom should I love, if not him?"

Christian! It is fitting for us to wholeheartedly say this about our God: "Whom should I love, if not him?" God is without beginning, infinite, incomprehensible, eternal, immutable, the highest and dearest good, from whom, as from a spring, all blessings, visible and invisible, in heaven and on earth, proceed. "Whom should we love, if not Him?"

Everyone loves the good, and the greater the good, the more he loves it. And although people love evil, they love it not as evil but under the appearance of good. "No one is good but One, that is, God" (Matt 19:17). Whom should we love, if not Him alone?" As fire is always hot and always gives out warmth, as light is always light and gives light, as honey is always sweet and gives pleasure, so God is always and continuously good and always does good. And as fire cannot not give warmth, so God cannot not do good. It is His nature to do good. From Him alone is every good, whatever there is and can be. Consolation, joy, gladness, and blessedness emanate from Him. There cannot be true blessedness, consolation, joy, and gladness without Him. God does good for us even when He punishes us. For he punishes us in order to correct us; He beats us in order to show mercy to us; He crushes us in order to heal us. He does everything in order to gratify us.

Whom should we love, if not Him? God is our Creator. From Him, we have our origin and existence. Our soul, body and our entire constitution are from Him. We are the work of His hands. We did not exist, but now we do exist and are alive. His almighty power brought us from nonexistence to existence. "Thy hands have made me and fashioned me" (Ps 118:73). He made us not an insensible and dumb creation but a rational one: He honored us with reason. And moreover, He created us in His image and likeness.

Oh, what a beloved and highly honored creation is man! He bears God's image, as a seal and banner of the Heavenly King. Our all-good Creator so highly honored us, O people! It was said not of angels, nor of any other creation, but of man: "Let us make man in Our image, according to Our likeness" (Gen 1:26). Whom should we love, if not Him? God is our most high benefactor and has shown us as many benefactions as we take breaths, since we cannot even live a minute without His blessings. We are surrounded and enclosed in God's love and His blessings. From Him, we receive food; from Him, drink; from Him, clothing; from Him, shelter. His light illumines us and shows us the way, good and evil, benefit and harm. His fire warms us and cooks our food. Our life is maintained by His air. Livestock serves us by His command.

What would our life be like, if God took even some of His blessings away from us? What would be the use of our eyes, if God took His light away from us? We would wander about like blind men. Would the earth give us its fruit, if God did not send His rain down upon it? "For the Lord shall show loving-kindness, and our land shall give her increase" (Ps 84:13). Without air, a person cannot live even a minute. These and other innumerable visible blessings are God's benefactions, which He grants us only from love for us. Whom should we love, if not Him? Who does not love His blessings? Only the foolish and ungrateful.

The devil with his demons constantly wars against us and invisibly lays siege to us, and "walks about like a roaring lion, seeking whom he may devour" (1 Pet 5:8). Who among us could be saved from this devastating enemy, if the almighty right hand of God did not preserve us? God defends and saves us from him—God, Who has all the corners of the earth in His hands, and His holy angels "are encamped round about us" (Ps 33:8; Gen 32:1; Heb 1:14). And although our enemy tempts us and we endure against our will his onslaught and tyranny, this happens with God's permission for our benefit, as those who have been tempted will learn. And God allows him only as much as we can bear and is beneficial for us (see 1 Cor 10:13). This is a most high benefaction of God, but inasmuch as it is invisible, few recognize it. We receive so many of God's benefactions in every day and hour that we do not see and often do not know. And who may recognize and number them? As a river flows continuously and a spring continuously pours forth water, so God's benefactions continuously pour down on us.

God our benefactor loves us so! "The God of our salvation ... Our God is the God that saveth" (Ps 67:20–21). And so, whom should we love, if not Him, such a benefactor, Who loves us so?

Although even the entire world testifies of God, and everything in the world leads to knowledge of Him, and silently entreats us as to what kind of reverence rational creation should render to its Creator, our mind, however, obscured by the darkness of sin, is blind in the perception of God, and truth, and God's most holy will. Therefore, our all-good and man-loving Creator gave us His holy Word through His chosen servants. It shines for us like a lamp and reveals God and His divine attributes, and His holy will and His heavenly secrets, and shows us what is good and what is evil, what is truth and delusion, what is virtue and vice, that we owe to the Lord our God and to each other, and thus He leads us to our perfection and blessedness.

"All Scripture is given by inspiration of God, and is profitable for doctrine, for reproof, for correction, for instruction in righteousness, that the man of God may be complete, thoroughly equipped for every good work" (2 Tim 3:16–17). Those who hold this God-inspired lamp and heeding it walk in the light. Those who shun it dwell in darkness and wander about like blind men. For he who avoids the light will unfailingly be in the darkness. God's Word teaches us to love God with all of our hearts and our neighbor as ourselves (Luke 10:27). Whom should we love, if not Him, Who so takes care of and looks after us?

"For God so loved the world that He gave His only begotten Son, that whoever believes in Him should not perish but have everlasting life" (John 3:16). We were perishing, O people! God, our Merciful Creator, so loved us— us, unworthy of love—and showed such wondrous providence for us that He sent His only-begotten Son to us to seek us and save us.

Glory to His love for mankind! This love of His for us urges us to love Him. Whom should we love, if not Him? God is our Father. He talks with us as with His children in His holy Word; and in our hearts we feel His most sweet converse; and we pray and cry out to Him: *Our Father, Who art in the heavens,* and so on.

He cares for us, looks after us, nurtures us, and prepares an eternal legacy for us. Whom should we love, if not Him, our Father? What kind of child does not love his father, except perhaps a foolish and ungrateful one? God displays his great love and mercy even in that He punishes us: "For whom the Lord loves He chastens, And scourges every son whom He receives." "But when we are judged, we are chastened by the Lord, that we may not be condemned with the world" (Heb 12:6; 1 Cor 11:32).

"Does the Lord love," they say, "those whom He hands over to such sufferings?" Indeed, He does love them! What father does not punish his children? And if he punishes them, does it mean he does not love them? In no wise. He punishes them because he loves them; he punishes them but is preparing an inheritance for them. Likewise, God punishes us but is preparing an inheritance of eternal life and His kingdom. The prophets were punished, the Apostles were punished, the martyrs were punished, and all the saints were punished, but they were beloved children of God, and now have their abode in the house of their Heavenly Father, and will sing His praises throughout the ages of ages. Who would not wish to be there with them, with those who were so punished here? God punishes us for our benefit, "that we may be partakers of His holiness" (Heb 12:10). "Blessed is the man whom Thou chastenest, O Lord" (Ps 93:12; Job 5:17).

And so, the Lord shows us great love when He punishes us. Whom should we love, if not Him, and how can we not give thanks to Him for his Fatherly chastisement? O man, if you saw the glory of those who received punishment from the hands of the Lord, without doubt, you would embrace every one of God's punishments and wish for more suffering rather than well-being. True is God's Word: *whom the Lord loves He chastens.* When does a person become more corrupted and perishes as when he lives in well-being? The all-good God, in punishing us, does not allow this for us.

Glory to His wondrous providence for us! Whom should we love, if not Him, and how can we not give thanks to Him for this salvific providence of His for us. But it is written, "Do not love the world or the things in the world. If anyone loves the world, the love of the Father is not in him. For all that is in the world—the lust of the flesh, the lust of the eyes, and the pride of life—is not of the Father but is of the world" (1 John 2:15–16). And again, "He who has My commandments and keeps them, it is he who loves Me." And further, "He who does not love Me does not keep My words" (John 14:21–24). And again, "Friendship with the world is enmity with God; Whoever therefore wants to be a friend of the world makes himself an enemy of God" (Jas 4:4).

Christian! Contemplate these words of God and take stock of yourself, lest, instead of being one who loves God, you be among His enemies. A person who without fear breaks the commandments of God and is joined in his heart with the world, even if he confesses the name of the God, is certainly among their number. Of such, it is written, "They profess to know God, but in works they deny Him, being abominable, disobedient, and disqualified for every good work" (Titus 1:16).

Oh, how many of God's enemies are there even among those who think that they honor Him, who go to church and pray to Him and receive the life-giving Mysteries of Christ, and so on. "The enemies of the Lord have lied to Him" (Ps 80:16). This was written about the law-breaking Jews, but this saying also befits Christians who were washed by holy baptism, sanctified, justified, and promised to serve the Lord God in faith and righteousness but turn aside after their whims. Such people are fornicators and adulterers, defilers, thieves, violent men, blasphemers, liars, perjurers, and other wrongdoers, and everyone who lives in the opulence and pride of this world. My soul, do not enter into their counsel. "Doth not my soul wait still upon God? For of Him cometh my salvation. Yea, He is my God, and my Saviour, He is my defender" (Ps 61:2).

O God, eternal love and goodness! Vouchsafe me to love You, You, Who created me, Who redeemed me, the fallen one; converted the lost; and enlightened me by Your holy Word; You, who nourish me, clothe me, my Defender, Who keeps me safe from the calumnies of the enemy, and Who pours out other countless blessings on me; vouchsafe me to love You, my highest good and blessedness, and from love to glorify You, to thank You, to please You, to do Your holy will, to worship You in Spirit and truth, to hymn and praise You, the One Whom the angels in heaven continuously hymn and praise. And with the Prophet, I hymn You with all my heart in a joyful spirit: "I will love Thee, O Lord my strength. The Lord is my firm foundation, and my fortress, and my deliverer; my God is my helper, and I will trust in Him, my defender, the horn also of my salvation, and my protector" (Ps 17:2–3).

# 130. A Full and an Empty Vessel

As a vessel is, so is the human heart. The heart is like a vessel. A full vessel, filled with water or something else, accommodates nothing more. On the other hand, an empty vessel is suitable for holding everything. Therefore, people empty out a vessel when they want to pour or place something else into it. This is how the human heart is. When it is empty and does not have in itself worldly and carnal whims, it is suitable for receiving God's love, but when it is filled with love of this world, carnal desires, and sinful predilections, then God's love cannot fit into it. How can a heart filled with greed, love of fame, sensuality, anger, remembrance of wrongs, envy, pride, and other iniquitous predilections accommodate God's love? "For what fellowship has righteousness with lawlessness" (2 Cor 6:14)?

God's love is God's greatest gift and is accommodated wherever the heart has been freed from evil predilections and sinful habits by true repentance, contrition, and remorse, and is cleansed and prepared to receive this heavenly gift. Christians, if we wish for God's love to take up its abode in our heart, let us free it from love of this world and its whims and sinful habits, and let us turn our hearts to God, the only true Good leading to eternal blessings. Then God's sweet love will take up its abode in our hearts and then we shall taste and see, "that the Lord is good" (Ps 33:9).

Both the bitterness and sweetness of a thing are learned from tasting it. Only those who taste it find out how sweet honey is; only those who love God and feel in their hearts His sweet love find out how sweet God and His holy love is. "He who has an ear, let him hear what the Spirit says to the churches. To him who overcomes I will give some of the hidden manna to eat" (Rev 2:17).

# 131. Whoever Loves Something  Seeks after It

We see that if people love something, they seek after it diligently, and the more they love it, the more zealously they seek it. Whoever loves wealth seeks wealth; whoever loves honor and glory seeks that honor and glory. And whoever seeks something uses a suitable means and method to find what is desired and avoids every obstacle. Thus, merchants, wishing to amass wealth, wander through foreign lands and avoid and flee any obstacles standing in the way of their desire. Likewise, whoever truly loves God, the highest Good, seeks Him with all zeal and assiduousness, uses all means and methods for this, and flees every obstacle, which blocks his desire. The obstacles that impede our quest for eternal good things are sinful habit and the love of the vain world. Therefore, if we want to love God and seek Him, we must turn away from sin and repent, and abandon the world with its delusion and vanity, and in this way desire and seek the one God.

Christian! If you wish to love God, hate sin, which is offensive to God and hateful to Him. To love sin and God at the same time is in no way possible. If you wish to seek God, do not seek in this world either honor, or glory, or riches, or anything else pleasing to the flesh. He who seeks God must give up all of that; he must free the heart from all of that, so that there might be room in it for God, the Eternal Good, with His holy love. The holy David desired nothing either in heaven, or on earth, but God alone; for this reason he sang the sweet hymn: "For what have I in heaven, and what have I desired upon earth from Thee? My flesh and my heart have failed, O God of my heart, but Thou art my portion, O God, for ever" (Ps 72:25–26). So God's prophet teaches us by his example to desire and seek nothing but God alone if we wish to seek and find Him.

True heartfelt humility and fervent prayer are the method and means to find God. When God sees this in a person, He comes to him with His sweetest love and makes his heart His temple. "If anyone loves Me, he will keep My word; and My Father will love him, and We will come to him and make Our home with him," says the Lord (John 14:23). "For Thou, Lord, has never forsaken them that seek Thee" (Ps 9:11). "The rich have lacked, and suffered hunger, but they that seek the Lord shall want no manner of thing that is good" (Ps 33:11). "Let the heart of them be glad that seek the Lord. Seek the Lord and be strengthened; seek His face always" (Ps 104:3–4).

If someone asked: where should I seek God? In the desert, or in a monastery, or in Jerusalem, or in some other place? The answer would be: Seek Him where you are and where you live. God is present in every place, and there is no place where God is not present; He is everywhere present and fills all things, although His presence is invisible and incomprehensible to us. The Psalmist sings thus: "Whither shall I go then from Thy Spirit? Or whither shall I flee from Thy presence? If I climb up into heaven, Thou art there; if I go down to hell, Thou art there also. If I take up my wings early, and dwell in the uttermost parts of the sea, Even there also shall Thy hand lead me, and Thy right hand shall hold me" (Ps 138:7–10). For you can seek the Omnipresent everywhere. Only pay heed to yourself everywhere, and do not follow those of whom it is written: "which have not set God before them" (Ps 53:5), but follow the Psalmist, who says of himself, "I foresaw the Lord ever before me" (Ps 15:8). And avoiding every evil and leaving behind the world with its delusion and vanity look to the one God and place on Him the culmination of all your desires and call upon Him with a contrite and humble heart. Then you will learn and feel within yourself that He is close, and you will sing to Him with the Prophet, "Thou art nigh at hand, O Lord, and all Thy ways are truth" (Ps 118:151). "The Lord is nigh unto all them that call upon Him ... in truth" (Ps 144:18). And further, "The Lord is nigh unto them that are of a contrite heart" (Ps 33:19).

There is, however, no place so suitable to find God as in solitude and calm. Among people, there is vanity and temptations that pose hindrances to the God-loving soul. In solitude, there is quiet and peace, where eyes do not see and ears do not hear anything that could disturb a God-loving soul. Therefore, one holy father, when others asked him, "Why do you flee from us?," wisely answered, "I cannot be with God and people at the same time." Therefore he who seeks God must cherish solitude, and when he must go out in public, he must everywhere pay attention to himself, and before the eyes of his soul imagine God everywhere present, so as not to sin in anything before Him and not to offend Him. "See then that you walk circumspectly, not as fools but as wise" (Eph 5:15).

# 132. A Perceived Good Is Sought For

We see that people, when they perceive a good, seek after it. So if they perceive that wealth is a good is for them, they seek it; if they perceive that bread is a good for them, they seek it; they perceive that clothing is a good for them, they seek it; they perceive that a house is good for them, they seek it; if they learn that light is a good thing, they seek it; if they learn that skill, artistry, reason, and wisdom are good things for them, they seek after them, and so on. And the greater the good they perceive, the more zealously they seek after it. But an unperceived good is never sought: for how can we seek after that which we do not know? Therefore we must first perceive good and then seek after it.

So they seek after God, the supreme, innate, and eternal perceived Good; the more a person comes to perceive Him, the more zealously and diligently he seeks Him, and desires and seeks nothing either on earth, or in heaven, other than Him, singing in his heart with the Prophet, "For what have I in heaven, and what have I desired upon earth from Thee" (Ps 72:25–26), and so on. But, having left everything behind, he rushes to Him, yearning in spirit. "Like as the hart panteth after the waterbrooks, so longeth my soul after thee, O God. My soul hath thirsted for the mighty living God; when shall I come and appear before God's face" (Ps 41:2–3)?

Christian! If we wish to seek after God—and we absolutely must—we must first of all get to know Him and then seek Him; and the better we shall perceive Him, the more zealously we shall seek Him. A great and precious good is sought with great effort and zeal. Silver is sought with great eagerness by those who love it; gold, with even more eagerness; and a precious stone, with eagerness that vastly exceeds these. God is a good incomparably better and vastly superior to all creations, for He is the Creator of all. All creations are good and very good but incomparably better and more superior is He by Whom creations were made good. The air is bright, but the sun, from which the air gets its light, is much brighter. Water mixed with honey is sweet, but the actual honey that sweetens the water is sweeter. Likewise, God has incomparably better light than the sun, to which He gave light, and has incomparably better goodness and sweetness than all the creations that He made good.

God implanted love and mercy in human hearts, but He Himself has incomparably greater love and mercy. As His majesty, so also His love and mercy. And not only does He have love and mercy, but He is Love and Mercy itself; He is not only good, but He is Goodness itself; He is not only sweet, but He is Sweetness itself; He is not only wise, but He is Wisdom itself; He is not only beautiful, but He is Beauty itself, which is more beautiful than all beauties, and so on. But it is written, "O taste, and see, that the Lord is good" (Ps 33:9). Honey is recognized from its taste and a fragrant flower from its smell; so God's kindness and goodness is recognized from taste and sensation.

There are two books from which God is perceived:

(1) The book of nature, that is, the world, heaven, and earth with their fullness. Whoever looks at heaven and earth and God's other creations and diligently contemplates this cannot but come to a realization of the Creator and God. Therefore, from contemplating this, even the very pagans came to a perception of God and came to a knowledge of the greatness of God, Who created such a great world. "The heavens declare the glory of God," the Prophet

sings (Ps 18:2). For He Who created such a great and vast thing from nothing must be great. He Who created everything in wisdom must be wise: "In wisdom hast Thou made them all" (Ps 103:24).

He Who created everything good must be good. He Who gave light to the sun, moon, and stars is in and of Himself an incomparably better Light: "God is light and in Him is no darkness at all" (1 John 1:5; Ps 103:2). He Who made all things good is in and of Himself incomparably better. He Who gave reason to man has Himself incomparably better reason. He Who gave ears and eyes to animals has Himself incomparably better sight and hearing: "He that planted the ear, shall He not hear? Or He that made the eye, shall He not see" (Ps 93:9)? He Who gave nutritional value to grain has Himself what is incomparably better: "Man shall not live by bread alone, but by every word that proceeds from the mouth of God" (Matt 4:4). He can nourish us much better without bread and food than bread can nourish us. He Who gave healing properties to herbs has better properties, for He heals everyone with His word.

Water cools and enlivens us who thirst, but He cools and enlivens us incomparably better. "Jesus answered and said to her, 'Whoever drinks of this water will thirst again, but whoever drinks of the water that I shall give him will never thirst. But the water that I shall give him will become in him a fountain of water springing up into everlasting life'" (John 13–14). His fire warms us, but He Himself warms us much better. He warmed the heart of Cleopas and his companion when He accompanied them and spoke with them on the way; therefore they themselves acknowledged: "Did not our heart burn within us while He talked with us on the road, and while He opened the Scriptures to us" (Luke 24:32)? Honey delights us, but He Himself delights us incomparably more when we feel the goodness and love of His sweetness in our heart, and so on. God's creation is good, indeed, very good, but the Creator Himself is incomparably better (Gen 1:31; 1 Tim 4:4). As the mind of the author becomes known by his book, and the wisdom of the architect by his building, and the fire by its heat, so the Creator becomes known by His creation.

(2) The best and most perfect method by which to come to know God is Sacred Scripture. This book represents to us and depicts God with His divine properties. In it we are shown that the same God Who created the whole world has also done and does glorious works.

But truly we cannot perceive God without God. A person in his heart must feel that God is good, almighty, righteous, true, omnipresent, and so on, and *taste, and see, that the Lord is good*; then God is perceived somewhat. Therefore the Lord says, "And no one knows the Son except the Father. Nor does anyone know the Father except the Son, and the one to whom the Son wills to reveal Him" (Matt 11:27). And the holy Prophet prays, "Open Thou mine eyes, that I may recognize the wondrous things of Thy Law" (Ps 118:18).

For our eyes to see created things, they need natural light. For our reason to come to perceive and see God, it needs supernatural light to shine on it. God is hidden and "dwell[s] in unapproachable light" (1 Tim 6:17) but uncovers and reveals Himself to those who love Him, and are humble, and simple like children, but conceals Himself from the wise and disputers of this age. Therefore, the Lord says, "You have hidden these things from the wise and prudent and have revealed them to babes" (Matt 11:25).

Christian! Let us perceive God, and leaving everything, we shall without fail seek Him alone with love and diligence, and let us desire and seek nothing either on earth or in heaven besides Him. He alone will be our blessedness, both here and in the age to come.

# 133. Everything Finds Repose in Its Own Place

We see that all things find rest in places congenial for them. Fire rises, and there finds repose; air finds repose in the air; an earthly thing goes to the earth, and everybody finds repose on the earth; fish seek water and find repose there; water flows into the sea and finds repose there; in a word, everything finds repose in a substance congenial to it. And even if it is hindered, it seeks its place and repose. Fire, even if it is deflected, reaches upward; any weight, even if it is thrown upward, turns and fall to the earth, as to its place of repose. In this way, the human soul finds its rest in God alone and can find rest for itself nowhere, but in God alone.

God alone is repose for the soul. The soul is an immaterial spirit having the image and likeness of God: where can it have repose other than in its Creator, as its archetype? There is nowhere so favorable for God Himself to live, as in the human soul, as His image and likeness. Likewise, the human soul cannot be satisfied by anything as much as by its Creator and cannot seek repose anywhere as in the most kind Divinity. For what can soothe and satisfy the soul, being a spiritual being, conformable to and like God? Is it food? Clothing?

Expensive attire, house, riches, the beauty of this world, high honor, pleasure, and every seeming enjoyment? No! The soul cannot be soothed and satisfied by any of this. All this is corruptible, but the soul is incorruptible. This is temporal, but the soul is eternal. This is visible, but the soul is invisible. The soul has no similarity with all this: how can it be soothed and satisfied by what is dissimilar and unrelated? The spirit can in no way be satisfied by the body, or the immortal by the mortal, or the incorruptible by the corruptible, or the immaterial by the material, the invisible by the visible. There is something else by which the soul is soothed and satisfied.

The light of the sun, moon, and stars is a good but a physical good—it gives light to the body.

The air is a good, but a physical good—it gives life to the body.

Bread and every food is a good, but a physical good—it strengthens the body.

Drink is a good, but a physical good—it consoles the body.

Water is a good, but a physical good—it washes and refreshes the body.

A house is a good, but a physical good—it provides rest for the body.

Fire is a good, but a physical good—it warms the body.

Clothing is a good, but a physical good—it clothes the body.

The fruit of trees and grasses is a good, but a physical good—the body eats it.

Honey is a good, but a physical good—it delights the body, and so on.

All of these and others like them cannot satisfy the soul. Something else satisfies and gives repose to the soul.

There is a life by which the soul is enlivened; there is a light by which the soul is enlightened; there is bread and food by which the soul is strengthened; there is drink, by which it is refreshed; there is a house in which it finds repose; there is sweetness, by which it is delighted; there is attire, by which it is clothed, and so on. Only God is light, life, food, drink, strengthening, refreshment, consolation, enjoyment, joy, repose, peace, wealth, honor, glory, and all blessedness for the soul, as His image and likeness. The soul cannot live, find repose, and be blessed without God and apart from God. "God is love, and he who abides in love abides in God, and God in him" (1 John 4:16).

How many people devise methods to soothe and satisfy their soul but cannot devise anything in the world by which it would be soothed and satisfied. How much wealth they amass; how much high honor they try to achieve; how much great glory they try to acquire; how many types of food, drinks, confections, beautiful houses and buildings, clothing, and other whims they contrive but cannot calm and satisfy their souls, and with every passing day they increasingly desire and devise novelties and changes in everything. They cannot calm and satisfy their souls: what is the reason for this? Because they seek that which does not soothe and does not satisfy the soul, and do not seek that in which alone the soul finds its repose and satisfaction.

No creations can calm and satisfy the soul, the image, and likeness of God. They lead it to God, but it only finds calm in God. The holy David knew this well. Therefore, although he was the king of Israel, and had riches, honor, and great fame, all this he regarded as nothing but rushed in his soul to the *living Spring*, God. "Like as the hart panteth after the waterbrooks, so longeth my soul after thee, O God. My soul hath thirsted for the mighty living God" (Ps 41:2–3). And in another place, he sings, "When Thy glory is revealed, I shall be satisfied" (Ps 16:15); that is, my soul cannot be satisfied and contented by anything but You alone, O God! I shall be satisfied and contented, when the glory of Your most Holy Face shines upon me.

Christian! This holy prophet teaches us by his example to seek repose and pleasure for our souls in nothing but God alone. Why should we seek repose and pleasure where it cannot be found? A spirit finds rest in spirit and not in matter. The soul, having in itself the image and likeness of God, surpasses the entire world in dignity and preciousness, for heaven and earth with their fullness are not worth one human soul. The human soul is below God, but higher than all creation. A portrait of an earthly king is precious since the king's image and likeness are depicted in it; so too is the human soul precious and excellent, since the image and likeness of the Heavenly King is depicted in it. Why enslave it to the basest creation? Every creation is unworthy of it, for every creation is lower than the soul. Therefore, Christ, our Saviour, caring for the repose and blessedness of our souls, and seeing us, who are inclined to the basest condition and are practiced in earthly and vain things, and so toiling and troubling ourselves without any benefit, and deploring and pitying our misfortune, calls us to Himself and promises souls repose with Himself: "Come to Me, all you who labor and are heavy laden, and I will give you rest" (Matt 11:28–29).

O poor, lost people! Why do you labor and seek repose where you cannot find repose? Abandon your vain and useless plans and efforts, and come unto Me, and you "will find rest for your souls" (Matt 11:29).

Nowhere can you find rest except with Me. "Hearken, O Lord, unto my voice, with which I have cried, Have mercy upon me, and hear me. My heart hath said unto Thee, I will seek the Lord; my face hath sought Thee; Thy face,

O Lord, will I seek. O turn not Thou Thy face from me. When Thy glory is revealed, I shall be satisfied" (Ps 26:7–9; 16:15).

# 134. A Migrant

We see in the world that people migrate from place to place, from hamlet to another hamlet, and from village to another village, and from one city to another and move to live there, and transport all their personal property there, and are called migrants. This is how true Christians, who have a living faith like a lamp in their hearts and thoughts, migrate from this world to the next one; they are born into the world but are migrating into the heavenly Homeland. Saint Paul, Christ's chosen vessel, speaks of this with all the faithful, "For our citizenship is in heaven, from which we also eagerly wait for the Savior, the Lord Jesus Christ" (Phil 3:20).

We live on earth in the body, but our souls are turned to heaven. That is where Christ the Lord, our Head, went; that is where we, His members, hasten, aspire to, and long for. Our Forerunner, Jesus Christ the Lord, went there, and we too cast our eyes there and follow. He draws us there as His own. Our homeland is there; our home is there; our inheritance is there; our property, wealth, honor, fame, consolation, joy, and all blessedness are there. This is why such people seek nothing in this world except what is necessary, and nothing in this world that gladdens the sons of this world can gladden them. Such people do not lay up "treasures on earth, where moth and rust destroy and where thieves break in and steal; but lay up for yourselves treasures in heaven, where neither moth nor rust destroys and where thieves do not break in and steal" (Matt 6:19–20). They do not have it in their hearts to build palatial and beautiful houses; to add on to and increase their lands, estates, and peasants; to attain high honor; to acquire fame and praise in this world; and so on, for which the sons of this world are troubled about and care for. For "where their treasure is, there their heart will be also" (Matt 6:21).

Their treasure is in heaven, and that is where their heart is directed. But they are satisfied with the worldly and temporal things that they have, thinking and saying with the Apostle, "For we brought nothing into this world, and it is certain we can carry nothing out. And having food and clothing, with these we shall be content" (1 Tim 6:7–8). These are the signs and marks of the true Christian and the faithful servant of Christ. Such a one, although he may have wealth, although he may have honor and fame in this world, is, however, comforted by none of this, but his heart is always in heaven, where his true treasure is. For such a one, it is all the same to live anywhere in the world, for life in this world is exile and banishment. Anywhere, no matter where he is located, he raises up his tear-filled eyes to his beloved Homeland, heaven, and longs for it, "desiring to be clothed with our habitation which is from heaven" (2 Cor 5:2). And with the holy Prophet, he sings with all his heart, "How amiable are Thy dwellings, O Lord of hosts! My soul desireth and longeth for the courts of the Lord" (Ps 83:2–3), and so on.

Christian! Let us too migrate in our hearts to our heavenly Homeland, and let us not desire or seek anything in the world except what is necessary. Everything is prepared there by our heavenly Father. Why do we seek what is not ours? Let us seek that heavenly treasure that is truly ours and will be with us forever. Let us leave everything worldly in the world, and we shall depart the world naked, as we entered the world naked. "For here we have no continuing city, but we seek the one to come" (Heb 13:14).

# 135. Servants Sent by the Master to Invite Guests to Dinner

We see in the world that rich and famous people put on a feast in their houses and send their servants to invite various guests to that feast. In the same way, the Heavenly King, God, rich in mercy, has created the great and sweet supper of eternal life and sends His chosen servants to invite to that supper all people indiscriminately, rich and poor, famous and obscure, male and female, old and young, in a word, all people of every rank. "Come, for all things are now ready" (Luke 14:17). First, He sent the prophets and invited through them; then He sent the Apostles and invited through them: "Come, for all things are now ready." Now he sends bishops and priests and orders them also to invite everyone, for bishops and priests stand in the place of those chosen men and take on their duty. Therefore, being God's messengers, they must call energetically and exhort and entreat everyone, "Come, for all things are now ready."

O beloved (bishop and priest), messenger and servant of the Heavenly King: work to carry out your Lord's command; labor energetically. Go and invite to the supper of your Lord, and do not cease to call everyone; knock on the doors of the houses of their hearts that, when they hear, they will rush to this glorious supper and will recline with Abraham, Isaac, and Jacob in the kingdom of God. Invite them, beloved, invite them, while the doors are open; invite them, but go yourselves; and go in front of them and show them the way into that most excellent house of the Heavenly King.

Tell them in a loud voice, "Come, for all things are now ready." And do not just stand there but hasten to what you are calling the others: do not be a pillar standing in the path, which shows the way to the city, but itself does not move from its place, but be the leader, who both shows the way to others and himself leads the way. Your call will be effective when you yourself go where you are calling others; otherwise you will not achieve very much. People will follow your example more than your word. The words of your call will be powerful when the example of your life is consistent with your words. But when people hear your call, but see that you yourself are not moving, they will hardly believe your words, and so you will call them with your words, but you will hold them back by your example.

O beloved! Beware of this, lest these words of Christ be applicable to you: "He who does not gather with Me scatters abroad" (Matt 12:30). The prophets called, the Apostles called, their holy successors, pastors, and church teachers who lived in ancient times called but pressed with the most thirsting spirit for the prize of the upward call (see Phil 3:14), and nothing could hinder their call and striving. They regarded as nothing not only riches, honor, fame, and every comfort of this world, but also held in contempt bonds, prisons, exile, beatings, wounds, tortures, distresses, and every kind of death, and by these "tribulations enter[ed] the kingdom of God" (Acts 14:22).

Therefore, the people called by them, seeing such a striving of their leaders for a higher dignity, hurried after them with all zeal. Their example, consistent with the words of their call, encouraged and won over to it the ones invited. It was like this in old times.

Now people rush with merry and fleet feet to riches, honor, comforts, banquets, operas, and other amusements and merrymaking; they rush, inasmuch as they see what they are rushing to. But they do not see the supper that the Heavenly King, the Lord by His grace, has prepared for all, for it is seen with the eye of faith and not with physical eyes. People do not see it and therefore do not rush there. The temptations of this world, multiplied day by day, darken the eyes of the human soul and so extinguish the lamps of faith. From this it happens that people, like cattle, rush to what they see but do not seek what they do not see. This is the nature of beasts. Oh, if only people saw even a small part of that supper: having thrown away the treasure of this world, they would rush there with all zeal and haste! "Then the righteous will shine forth as the sun in the kingdom of their Father" (Matt 13:43).

It is said to pastors, *You are the light of the world.* When the light grows dark, how will people be enlightened? It is said to pastors, *You are the salt of the earth.* When the salt loses its flavor how will the people season themselves? Oh beloved pastor! You are the light of the world! Shine not only by your words but also by your life. You are the salt of the earth! Beware of losing your savor, lest others watching you also lose their savor. "Let your light so shine before men, that they may see your good works and glorify your Father in heaven" (Matt 5:13, 14, 16). Beloved, you have entered the apostolic calling and office; imitate the Apostles in teaching and life, so that you may take part with them at that supper and may draw many after you.

# 136. A Guard

We see that in the world various guards are posted: some guard the city, others guard a house, some are posted to guard something else, and they guard the place to which they are assigned. Like this, bishops and priests are chosen and appointed to guard the souls of Christians, entrusted to their supervision. The word of God spoken to the holy Prophet Ezekiel applies to them: "Son of man, I made you a watchman for the house of Israel" (Ezek 33:7). Watchmen who are assigned to guard houses, cities, and so on guard them from evil people. Against whom must bishops and priests guard the souls of Christians? The holy Apostle indicates the answer, saying: "Be sober, be vigilant; because your adversary the devil walks about like a roaring lion, seeking whom he may devour" (1 Pet 5:8).

Oh, how fierce is the enemy from which Christians must be guarded! Oh, how skillful and alert watchmen who are guarding Christians from this enemy must be! He desires and seeks not our houses, nor to take our cities, but to take our souls captive; not to take our property, gold, silver, and other material away from us but is trying to snatch away eternal salvation, acquired by Christ's blood and death. And he is cunning and sly as he is as evil. He has been learning this, his evil skill, from the beginning of the world; he knows how to make his approach, how to deceive, how to entice a person, how to sneak up on him, and so on. He steals and snatches away our salvation through unbelief, heresy, schisms, and every kind of sin. Bishops and priests are appointed to guard the souls of Christians from such a fierce and cunning enemy.

Do not doze, O beloved, but be sober and awake and guard the souls entrusted to you; warn and declare to the people the enemy's evil and ruinous approach. Be alert and continually speak the Word of God to the people. Exhort and entreat them to live by its rule and to correct their life, to plant faith into their hearts and to inculcate the fear of God. Caution them to refrain from sin and encourage them to virtue. Remind them of what God wants and requires of us; remind them of Christ, the Saviour of the world, of His life on earth, His sufferings, death, and resurrection, and for whose sake such a great and wondrous deed was accomplished, and that we are in debt to Him for this great love that He showed to us. Teach them what faith and unbelief, virtue and sin, falsehood and truth consist of, and so on.

This is the duty of the bishop and priest, watchmen of Christian souls. Watch over and protect the house of Israel, the Church, entrusted to you, which is the house of God. Watch over the Church, but first protect and watch over yourself and watch with all apprehension. For our enemy seeks to bring down no one more than a pastor. In war, the visible enemy takes more care how to take down the guard that is protecting the army; in like manner, the enemy of Christians, the devil, takes care for nothing more than to snatch away and take captive pastors, the watchmen over Christian souls. Take care, beloved; look after people and look after yourself. He invisibly walks around us, seeking how to swallow us up. He sees us, but we do not see him. But an evil spirit is recognized from its evil smell and stench.

And so, when you are taking care of and putting others on their guard, first take care of yourself and caution yourself. How will you caution and look after others when you do not look after yourself? How will you turn others away from sin when you yourself do not turn away from sin? How will you encourage others to virtue when you yourself are not prone to virtue? You will hear in your conscience the accusing word, "Physician heal yourself" (Luke 4:23). Read the First and Second Epistles of the Apostle Paul to Timothy and his Epistle to Titus and contemplate diligently, and you will see there how you should guard both yourself and the Christian souls entrusted to you. Be a faithful watchman, beloved, vigilant and indefatigable, of yourself and Christian souls, purchased not with silver and gold, but with Christ's blood. You have an answer to give for all them to the Righteous Judge, Who shed His most pure blood for them. Contemplate this; bear this in mind, pay attention to yourself and to all your flock; look after yourself and look after them.

Prayer is a powerful weapon against the invisible enemy. Therefore, you yourself should pray and you should teach your people to pray. Mutual prayer is like a strong wall against the enemy, that is, when a pastor prays for his people earnestly and with love, and the people cry out from the heart to God for the pastor. Need and misfortune urge to pray for oneself, but love urges to pray for one's neighbor. In a visible war, all the soldiers look after and protect the commander from the enemy, for their safety lies in his safety; likewise in the invisible war, all Christians should protect their leader, the pastor, against the enemy by prayer; for their safety depends on his safety.

When a pastor is good and wise, the sheep are in a good state. When such mutual love manifests itself, God Himself guards both the pastor and the flock, and without Him every effort is impotent, as is written: "Except the Lord build the house, they labor in vain that build it; except the Lord keep the city, the watchman waketh but in vain" (Ps 126:1). The holy prophet shows by his example whence comes help and safekeeping and says, "I lifted up mine eyes unto the hills; from whence will my help come? My help cometh even from the Lord, Who hath made heaven and earth," and so on, to the end of Psalm 120.

We see that when the watchman of a house raises the alarm about an evil coming upon the house, that is, of either oncoming malicious people or a fire that has begun, the residents of the house rise up and with all effort try to protect and save the house. So, when a pastor proclaims to the people God's coming wrath for sins and the consequent temporal and eternal punishment, and turns them to true repentance, the people must not scorn this but must have a change of heart, be converted, and repent for sins, and thus please God, and save their souls by His grace. The Apostle requires this: "Obey those who rule over you, and be submissive, for they watch out for your souls, as those who must give account. Let them do so with joy and not with grief, for that would be unprofitable for you" (Heb 13:17).

O Christian! The watchman announces a temporal evil to you, and you are on your guard. Even more should you be on your guard when eternal evil is announced to you. You guard your corruptible estate from the thief and the evil person; even more should you guard the incorruptible treasure of eternal salvation from the evil spirit. You guard your home from fire, even more should you guard your soul and body, lest they burn in the fire. The pastor, your watchman, proclaims all this to you and makes it clear to you. Learn about your approaching misfortune, and guard yourself, lest you fall into a misfortune from which you cannot get out. The fire there does not go out, and the worm does not die. Any and every temporal misfortune is nothing compared to the eternal one.

When the watchman of the house announces an evil coming upon the house to the people living there, and the residents ignore this and do not attempt to defend and save the house, and so the house is plundered and is ruined, they themselves are guilty of their misfortune, and the watchman is not to blame. So, when a pastor tries in every way to turn people to repentance, to exhort and entreat them about this, but they ignore this, do not have a change of heart, and do not repent, then they themselves are guilty in their own ruin, and the pastor will now not be held to account. And this is what God says to the Prophet Ezekiel: "But if you warn the ungodly man to turn from his way, and he does not turn from his way, he will die in his ungodliness; but you have delivered your own soul" (Ezek 33:9). How many times Christ the Lord Himself exhorted and tried to turn obdurate Jerusalem to repentance, but He finally said with pity and sorrow of His heart, "O Jerusalem, Jerusalem, the one who kills the prophets and stones those who are sent to her! How often I wanted to gather your children together, as a hen gathers her chicks under her wings, but you were not willing! See! Your house is left to you desolate" (Matt 23:38). This terrible saying applies to unrepentant Christians, who constantly hear God's Word and preaching of repentance, but do not turn around but abide in their impiety, and not only do not repent of their sins but even add sins to sins, and iniquities to iniquities, and so regress in their impiety and sink into the depth of evil; and as a blind man approaches a ditch into which he should fall, so they, having been darkened by the delusion of din and the vanity of this world, rush toward eternal perdition and should fall into it if he does not turn to God with a true heart and do not wash away their impiety with contrition of heart and warm tears.

Christian! This saying of Christ is fearsome: "Your house is left to you desolate." Be careful, lest it apply to you. A pastor should never cease, but should always resound with the word, while pitying and sympathizing in his heart with perishing Christians and not despairing of anyone while he still lives.

It happens that the watchman of a house, dozing off, will fall asleep or will absent himself from the place where he was posted, and at that time evil people will set upon the house, or a fire will start, and so there will be no one to warn those of the house about the oncoming evil. Then the master of the house will be angry with that watchman, interrogate him, and deliver him over to harsh punishment, inasmuch as because of his neglect, evil came upon the house. This is what happens with the pastor who dozes and does not guard Christian souls, who does not warn them of approaching evil.

The Church of God is "the house of God" (1 Tim 3:15). The master of this house is Christ the Lord; those of His house are the Christians; the bishop and priest are the watchmen of that house. If he dozes or sleeps and is careless about the house, and the adversary, the devil, who never sleeps, but is vigilant for the perdition of man and seeks someone to swallow up, comes upon that house and, seeing the dozing watchman, takes captive the souls of those of the house, then the master of the house, Christ, will justly be angered at the pastor, the watchman of His house, and will judge him for being negligent and unfaithful, "And will cut him in two and appoint him his portion with the hypocrites. There shall be weeping and gnashing of teeth" (Matt 24:51; see Ezek 33:8).

The pastor, the watchman of the Lord's house, dozes when he is silent and does not preach the Word of God, does not bring people to repentance, does not reprove people for their sins, does not teach the holy Christian life, does not protect them from the snares of the devil, does not show the path to eternal life, and does not inspire fear of God's coming anger for sins; in a word, he dozes when he takes no care to save for eternal life the people entrusted to him, for this is the essence of his calling and office. A pastor, the watchman of the Lord's house, sleeps and that deeply when he not only neglects his own salvation but is lawless. Then not only is he not watching over the Lord's house but is destroying it, and by his temptations he is dragging Christian souls after himself to perdition. This word of Christ applies to such a pastor: "He who is not with Me is against Me, and he who does not gather with Me scatters abroad" (Matt 12:30). There is no greater joy for the devil, the enemy of Christian souls, as when a pastor, the watchman of the Lord's house, is found in such a condition; then he does what he wants with the Christians. Woe unto people who have such a pastor! But even more woe be to that pastor, who tends only himself, and not the people entrusted to him! "If therefore the light that is in you is darkness, how great is that darkness!" (Matt 6:23). If the lamp goes out, with what will the people of the house be illumined? If the shepherd be snatched away by the wolf, who will guard the sheep? If the pastor, the "salt of the earth, loses its flavor" (Matt 5:13), then what tumult there will be among the people! If the guide goes astray from the path and gets lost, how lost will be the travelers!

O beloved pastor! You have been appointed as the watchman to guard not the material house, but the immaterial one, not walls of stone and wood, and other material, but the souls of Christians. Guard them and guard yourself. They are the beloved acquisition of Christ, the Son of God, the Lover of Souls. He acquired them for Himself not with gold and silver but by His precious blood. And He entrusted them to you to guard and tend: "Tend My sheep" (John 21:15–17). And you, upon entering on this office and calling, took them into your safeguarding. So keep them, guard them, and tend them. He will seek His acquisition back from your hands. It is terrible to ruin one Christian soul; it is much more terrible to ruin many souls. Think about this, beloved, and save them and save yourself. May the Shepherd and Author, Jesus Christ the Lord, help you, may He grant you wisdom, may He give you prudence, may He keep you and your people safe. Hear the word that the Apostle said to you and other pastors: "Therefore take heed to yourselves and to all the flock, among which the Holy Spirit has made you overseers, to shepherd the church of God which He purchased with His own blood" (Acts 20:28).

# 137. Do Not Touch It; You Cannot Lift It

We hear that one person says to another, "Do not touch it; you cannot lift it." This is said to someone who wants to take into his hands a stone or some other heavy object that exceeds his strength, and lift and carry it; then someone will rightly say to him, "Do not touch it; you cannot lift it."

Christian! Honor for a Christian is a heavy weight; and the greater and higher the honor, the greater its weight. And so, if you go to take on honor, consider your strength, and whether you can carry this weight. If you cannot lift and carry it, do not touch it, lest it overburden you, and you fall and lie under this heavy load, rather than carrying it. Whoever wants to look at many things must have many eyes. Whoever wants to rule others must first learn to rule himself; whoever wants to correct others must first learn to correct himself; whoever wants to teach others must first teach himself; whoever wants to enlighten others must first be a light; whoever wants to season others must be the salt; be the image and an untarnished mirror, in which many will look; be a father, who provides for his children in a fatherly way; be an unslumbering and vigilant watchman, who guards not a city and walls and material property, but the souls of Christians, for whom Christ the Lord shed His blood; be a skillful guide who leads not to a material city, but to eternal life. Whoever must bear the infirmities of many must be strong.

The higher the tree, the more often it shakes to and fro from any storm and bad weather. Such a wind blows little on a small tree and one standing in a low-lying spot, but a tall one and one standing on a mountain is subject to every wind and is shaken to and fro. It needs to have its roots deeply established in the earth, lest it be torn out by the assailing storm, and fall, and crash. Living in solitude and lowness, the Christian needs to bear his cross and follow Christ, for "many are the troubles" (Ps 33:20) that Christians have, but one living in honor must bear a larger and very heavy cross. And the higher the honor of a Christian, the heavier its burden. The devil, our adversary, rises up and fights against every Christian, but especially against a Christian authority figure. He exerts all his effort in order to cast down and take captive a Christian authority figure.

An enemy in a war of this world shoots at no one so much as the commanders and leaders; likewise, the enemy of Christians, the devil, takes up arms against no one as much as at those Christians who are in charge of other Christians and wish to save themselves and others. His favorite catch is a Christian in a leadership position, whom he has brought down and taken captive. And his captive is every one who lives contrary to the Word of God, seeks his own and not his subordinates' benefit, scandalizes, and does not guide or correct people. Then he easily takes other Christian souls captive, just as a visible enemy, having captured the superior officer, creates confusion among his subordinate troops and thus captures them easily as well. He has his own minions, false Christians, who have been planted and grow as tares among the wheat. Through them, he commits many slanders, machinations, and ruses against the Christian in authority.

All the past ages witness to this evil; we take note of this and see it even now. These slanderers are more dangerous for the Christian in authority than the devil himself, inasmuch as they are wolves, but ones hidden in sheep's clothing; they speak and, like Judas, greet affectionately, but in their hearts, they contemplate betrayal. A leader who wishes to save both himself and his subordinates must be sober-minded and prudent. These souls contrive much about the leader and sow these fabrications among the subordinates, and it happens that rumors fly from people's tongues concerning what had never even entered the leader's mind. And this way, the confusion, disorder, suspicion, and doubt about the superior becomes great among the subordinates. All this evil and evil talk strike at the soul of the leader. He needs to be strong, if he wishes to raise and carry this weight, and he unfailingly must.

Many Christians are troubled about nothing so much as how to attain honor and the highest honor. But they themselves do not know what they are troubled about. For the foolish and careless Christian, honor is as a sword is to a madman, who uses it to destroy both himself and others. All Christians take an oath and swear before God the Almighty and knower of hearts when they receive an honor, but many, upon walking out of the church, both forget and violate their promise under oath. It is obvious that the oath was only on the lips and tongue of such people, but in their heart godlessness was hidden. Society groans and suffers much from such oath-takers. It would be better for them not to be born, or if they had been born, to cultivate the land and feed themselves this way, than to attain honor and cause the tears of many innocent people to be shed.

Woe to such a leader! God, the Father of orphans and Judge of widows, will exact from him every teardrop of His offended people. "Take heed, ye thoughtless among the people, and ye fools, when will ye be wise? He that planted the ear, shall He not hear? Or He that made the eye, shall he not see? He that chasteneth the heathen, shall He not rebuke, He that teacheth man knowledge" (Ps 93:8–10)?

And so, watch yourself, Christian, and do not touch what you cannot lift. And although this is said to everyone who receives honor, it applies more so to the one who enters the calling and office of pastor and wishes to be a priest or bishop. Do not touch what you cannot lift; and do not seek and do not take up a burden, which is heavy beyond your strength, lest it overburden you and plunge you into the abyss. And when you are called to an honor, consider whether you can bear that burden. And when God's will intends honor for you, although you may even flee the honor, you will receive it. We see many examples of this in Church history. And indeed it is so! For God's determination has consequences.

# 138. Everyone Avoids a Perceived Evil

We see that all people, having recognized evil, avoid it. So, knowing that a serpent injures and kills with its venom, they avoid it; knowing that the teeth of animals deal injury and death, they flee the animals; knowing that fire burns and singes, and kills, that deep water drowns and kills, they beware water and fire; knowing that a scoundrel and robber strips and murders, they shun such pernicious people. In the same way, people avoid any other known evils.

Christian! Let us recognize our evil, which indeed is evil and ruinous for us. Let us recognize that sin is our bitter and cruel evil, and let us avoid it as a known evil. For who, having recognized evil and ruin, does not avoid it? It is impossible, truly impossible for one who recognizes evil not to hate evil and not to avoid it. That people love sin and do not avoid it is because they do not know this evil and its bitter fruits. It is impossible for one who recognizes sin as evil not to avoid it. Why do you run away from a serpent? Because it kills with its sting. *The sting of death is sin,* by which a man is killed (1 Cor 15:56). How, when you recognize this deadly sting, will you not avoid it?

Sin is recognized from the law of God and its bitter fruits.

(1) Sin is a great evil. For sin is an offense and breaking of the eternal and immutable law of God. "Sin is lawlessness" (1 John 3:40). What God commanded and made into law is violated through sin, becomes filthiness to the God Who commanded and made it into law, and proves to be disobedience.

(2) Sin is a great evil. Because the Great and Infinite God is offended by every sin, and He is angered Who created us from nothing, created us in His image and likeness; Who takes care of us, looks after us, is a benefactor for us, feeds us, clothes us, keeps us safe and calms us; He who so loved us, that He sent His only-begotten Son into the world for us and prepared for us an inheritance of eternal life and a kingdom, and grants us other countless blessings. By sin, we offend and anger our most high benefactor Who has so loved us.

Oh, what a cruel evil is sin! By it, we offend and anger our Creator and Father. Truly, it is better to die than to sin even slightly! The Holy and Righteous God is angered by sin. His angels hymn, glorify, honor, and worship Him with fear and reverence; but poor man, "earth and ashes" (Sir 10:9; 13:31), dares to offend and anger Him by sin.

Oh, how we, poor people have been sold to sin! "How will gold lose its brightness and fine silver become tarnished" (Lam 4:1)? How obscured has the splendid beauty of our souls become! Where is our beloved beauty—the image of God? "O Lord, remember what happened to us; Look upon us with favor and see our disgrace. The joy of our heart has ceased; Our dance has turned into mourning. The crown fell from our head; Woe to us, because we sinned!" (Lam 5:1, 15–17). "For what I will to do, that I do not practice; but what I hate, that I do. For the good that I will to do, I do not do; but the evil I will not to do, that I practice. O wretched man that I am! Who will deliver me from this body of death" (Rom 7:15, 19, 24)? "O Lord, righteousness belongs to You, but shame of face belongs to us" (Dan 9:7).

(3) Sin is a great evil, inasmuch as it brings great torment to a person's conscience. The conscience is wounded and exacerbated by sin and disturbs, rebukes, torments, and tortures the sinner. The sinner runs even though there is no one chasing him: his conscience is pursuing him more vigorously than any pursuer. When people are talking among themselves, he thinks that they are talking and conferring about him; he hears talk about a sin of which he is guilty, and he thinks that it is being spoken about him, although the talk applies to everyone in general.

This bad conscience, which judges and rebukes his sin, acts in him as a domestic judge and accuser and alarms and torments him. The sinner always and everywhere carries this internal and domestic evil with him until he cleanses the sin he committed by true repentance and contrition of heart. But with those who sin and do not feel torment of the conscience (which, it seems, is impossible), the conscience is sleeping for the time being. But when it wakes up and begins to denounce them and to present to them the sins that they committed, then they will learn how cruel its torment is, and how bitter is the fruit of sin. This torment is so cruel that the poor sinner goes to any evil than to endure that torment, and many, not being able to endure this, kill themselves, as did Judas, Christ's betrayer (see Matt 27:5).

We see this evil even now. In such a torment of conscience a person learns by experience to perceive sin and its bitter fruit. If the conscience so torments and burns a person for sin here in this world, how will it be in the age to come, where all his sins, committed from his youth to his death, known and unknown, are revealed clearly in his conscience and they will appear to him to rebuke, torment, and torture him?

Reflect on this, poor sinner, and recognize your sin. Sin seems sweet to you, but bitter is its fruit, which you will eat continuously, if you do not turn to God and cleanse yourself by true repentance.

(4) We see that various punishments have been sent and are sent by God for sin. For the righteous God hates sin and punishes the sinner for it. For sin, angels were cast down from heaven and became demons and were condemned to eternal torment. For sin, the first parents were expelled from paradise and sent into the world as into exile. For sin, the universal flood was brought on. For sin, Sodom and Gomorrah with the surrounding cities were burned with fire from heaven. For sin, Pharaoh, the pursuer of Israel, was drowned in the Red Sea with his whole army. For sin, the Israelites, having come out of Egypt, suffered diverse punishments in the desert and the Promised Land, as we see in the holy books of the Old Testament. For sin, there are even now various punishments, bloody battles, plagues, civil strife, fires, famine and earthquake, diverse diseases, and other misfortunes without number.

The cause of all misfortunes in the world, whatever they may be, is sin. The world sins, and for sin suffers in disasters and tribulation. In this way God's justice punishes sin, which is offensive to Him. Sin does not occur without punishment. If you sin, O man, await your punishment, either internally or externally, or both simultaneously. For this is the fruit of sin. It gives birth to nothing except punishment.

(5) For sin, entry into eternal life is barred. "But there shall by no means enter it anything that defiles" (Rev 21:27). Every sin defiles the one who commits it. "But outside are dogs and sorcerers and sexually immoral and murderers and idolaters, and whoever loves and practices a lie" (Rev 22:15; 1 Cor 6:8–9; Gal 5:19–21).

(6) A person is consigned to eternal fire and torment for sin, and he will be tormented with the devil and his angels without end. "'Their worm does not die, and the fire is not quenched'" (Mark 9:44, 46, 48). "But the cowardly, unbelieving, abominable, murderers, sexually immoral, sorcerers, idolaters, and all liars shall have their part in the lake which burns with fire and brimstone, which is the second death" (Rev 21:8).

You see, Christian, the bitter fruits of sin. And bitter is the sin that bears bitter fruits. As the fruits, so is the seed, for the seed yields fruit like itself. The fruits of sin are evil and bitter: sin is the evil and bitter seed; and there is no greater evil than sin. Pride and haughtiness are an evil and bitter seed. Disobedience and recalcitrance toward God and the authorities sent from him are an evil and bitter seed. Disrespect to parents and defiance of them and showing ingratitude to them are an evil and bitter seed. Malice and remembrance of wrongs, revenge and murder are an evil and bitter seed. Fornication, adultery, and every impurity are an evil and bitter seed. Theft, extortion, robbery, coercion, and every injustice are an evil and bitter seed. Contempt, disdain, and ridicule of a neighbor are an evil and bitter seed. Slander and condemnation of a neighbor are an evil and bitter seed. Mockery and defamation of a neighbor are an evil and bitter seed. Lying, flattery, craftiness and guile, and every wrongdoing are an evil and bitter seed.

Christian, recognize this evil and bitterness, and you will shun this evil. Shun the serpent, shun the teeth of the beast, shun the fire, shun the malefactor and robber, shun every evil that harms your body and takes away your temporal life. Sin harms you more than the serpent, more than the teeth of a beast, more than any malefactor and robber, more than any other evil; and takes away not temporal life, but eternal life; destroys not the body, but the soul; and causes not temporal, but eternal death.

What can be more terrible than this evil? This evil harms us even more than the demon itself. For the sin of the demon made the demon, who before the sin had been an angel of light. Why should you not shun such a great and terrible evil? Do you really wish to yield willingly to an obvious misfortune, as do those people who kill themselves with poison, stab themselves with a sword, hang themselves, throw themselves into a fire and are burned up, jump into deep water and drown, or plunge themselves into some other obvious evil? These people are rightly called irrational and mad because they kill themselves. Is not that person more mad and irrational, who knowing that sin is a terrible and deadly evil, willfully touches it and gives himself over to it?

Christian! You do not see this evil with your eyes, but you feel its bitter fruits in your conscience. And the whole world feels when it is being punished for sin by misfortunes and tribulations. Everyone calls him wise and blessed who is on guard against every evil, and avoids it; far more wise and blessed is he who shuns every sin. The first saves his body and temporal life, but the second, his soul and eternal life. This is Christian wisdom. This is understanding, enlightened by divine light to live carefully in the world, to avoid every sin, to deal with everything with fear, to avoid the vanity of the world, to think of what is heavenly, to always and everywhere have God before the eyes of our soul, and to honor Him with faith and holy obedience! "See then that you walk circumspectly, not as fools but as wise" (Eph 5:15).

It happens that parents warn their children, and other people warn others against harmful things and circumstances, and say, "Beware of such and such." But when the children or other people, not taking to heart this helpful advice, touch the thing they had been warned against, they are injured, and so learn the harm of what they were warned against. So small children touch a burning coal, and are burned, and learn that fire burns; people touch a poisonous plant, and are injured, and learn its harm.

Christian! In this way God, the Lover of Mankind, pitying and caring for us, warns us in His holy Word against every sin. "Come, ye children, and hearken unto me; I will teach you the fear of the Lord. What man is he that lusteth to live, and would gladly see good days? Keep thy tongue from evil, and thy lips, that they speak no guile. Shun evil, and do good" (Ps 33:12–15), and so on. But when we do not obey Him, which is our blindness and folly, and touch pernicious sin, as small children do fire, we are injured from this, and are burned as by fire, and then we learn what a cruel and pernicious evil sin is. This is how God warned our first parents away from sin in paradise: "But from the tree of the knowledge of good and evil you may not eat; for in whatever day you eat from it, you shall die by death" (Gen 2:17).

Our first parents did not believe God's holy command; did not obey God, their Creator, Who commanded it; touched the forbidden fruit; and so sinned grievously and then learned how cruel and ruinous it is to break God's commandment. They learned what a bitter seed sin is when they tasted its bitter fruit—death: "For the wages of sin is death" (Rom 6:23).

The same thing happens nowadays with Christians. God warns everyone against sin through His holy law: You shall not murder, you shall not steal, you shall not commit adultery, and so on (see Exod 20:2–17). It warns through punishments that sinners endured for sin, punishments described in His holy Word, and as it were says through them to everyone: "Sons of men, shun sin!"

You see that those who sinned suffered for the sin; you too will suffer if you sin. Blessed and wise is he who, seeing the affliction of others, is very careful and knows to avoid misfortune. But when Christians sin in spite of this, then they learn from the bitter consequences of sin—punishments—what a great and bitter evil sin is. A tortured conscience and every kind of oncoming punishment show the power and bitterness of sin. Then everyone will find out what sin is. True and salvific is the Word of God, which warns us against sin. God warns sinners against eternal punishment and torment. For this is written about eternal punishment, written about eternal fire, the worm that does not die, the gnashing of teeth, the inner darkness, and other evils. By means of this, the Lord seems to be saying, "Poor sinners! All of this evil awaits sinners in the age to come. Repent, lest you fall into this evil. "Thus says the Lord: 'I do not will the death of the ungodly man. So the ungodly man should turn from his way and live'" (Ezek 33:11). But if sinners do not believe this, and do not turn from their sins and repent, then they will learn from experience in the age to come what a great evil is sin when they taste its bitter fruits throughout all eternity. Those who have departed this world and not repented will now learn; lechers, thieves, extortioners, and other wrongdoers who have not cleansed their sins by repentance and been cast down into hell, in order to receive according to their deeds, will learn. The transgressors now living on earth will learn this, if they do not turn and repent; they will learn from experience that *the wages of sin is death*; when they will taste the bitterness of death without end, they will wish to die and will not die.

Christian! The Word of God is true and not false. "Heaven and earth will pass away, but [God's] words will by no means pass away" (Matt 24:35; Mark 13:31; Luke 21:33). What it proclaims is true. The righteous will receive eternal life, and sinners will receive eternal torment: "These will go away into everlasting punishment, but the righteous into eternal life" (Matt 25:46). Repent, that you may receive eternal life through Christ's grace. Shun sin, lest you die forever. *For the wages of sin is death.*

# 139. Little Children

We see that little children are unable to understand. When their games and playthings are taken away from them, they weep and sob, but when malefactors descend and plunder the house and property, they laugh and do not care about it. Many Christians are like such children. When someone takes something temporal away from them, they weep and sob and often give themselves up to death, but they do not care that eternal blessedness is being taken away from them by sin. If they are deprived of either riches, or honor, or temporal fame, they complain and are sad; they weep and sob, but they do not care that the malefactor of human souls, the devil, is by guile depriving them of eternal life, riches, honor, and fame, and of all eternal blessedness. Among these are lechers, adulterers, and all lovers of impurity, thieves, extortioners, robbers, sorcerers, and those who summon them, blasphemers, slanderers, revilers, sly tricksters, liars, and so on, who abide in sin.

It is obvious that all such people are neglecting the eternal treasure of salvation, taken from them by the devil's guile. It seems that they neglect what they do not see, but they care about what they do see and are sorry for what is lost, so they do not see eternal life and are not sorry about its loss. And so these people themselves see that they have faith only on their lips but in their hearts are hidden unbelief and godlessness, for it is impossible, truly impossible, for one who has the lamp of faith burning in his heart not to strive for eternal blessings with all zeal, and likewise not to abide in true repentance, and not to avoid every sin. For faith renews a person, deters him from sins and vanity, guides him to promised future blessings, and presents them to him as visible.

Oh, if only a person saw even a tiny bit of eternal life. Discarding all the vanity of this world, he would rush toward it with great yearning. But since he does not see it, and does not believe God's Word, which in various ways depicts the blessedness of that life, he does not seek it and does not regret his losing it but only seeks that which the senses represent to him and, being deprived of this, regrets its loss. This is the action of small and senseless children, or even of animal life, for animals seek after what they see, and what they do not see, they do not desire. "Man, being in honor, understood it not; he shall be compared unto the brute beasts, and is become like unto them" (Ps 48:21).

The Christian and pious soul, which has the lamp of faith burning in its heart, does not act like this. It hastens toward eternal life with all yearning and fears very much to be deprived of it, and this is why it turns away from every sin and the vanity of the world, as from manifest obstacles to this, and thinks of temporal good things in accordance with the words of the Apostle: "For we brought nothing into this world, and it is certain we can carry nothing out. And having food and clothing, with these we shall be content" (1 Tim 6:7–8). But when it is deprived of temporal blessings, it is not distressed like the sons of this age are but says with the righteous Job, "The Lord gave, and the Lord has taken away. As it seemed good to the Lord, so also it came to pass. Blessed be the name of the Lord" (Job 1:21).

Christian! It is great foolishness and manifest ruin to be sorry and weep about what like a shadow passes by, what we now have, and soon we shall not have (or the end of our life puts an end to it all), but not to feel sorry for what, having been once found, abides forever. God's Word is true: what it says will without fail come to pass. It splendidly and variously depicts and shows us eternal life and points the way to attaining it, that is, true repentance and living faith.

And so, keenly and truly believe the Word of God and, without a doubt, having changed and reformed, you will see the future life with the eye of faith, and while still living on earth, you will taste little grains of its sweetness. Then you, along with the Psalmist, will say with your heart, "How amiable are Thy dwellings, O Lord of hosts! My soul desireth and longeth for the courts of the Lord; my heart and my flesh have rejoiced in the living God" (Ps 83:2–3). Then (I am telling you the truth) the whole world with all its vanity, pride, and beauty will become loathsome to you. "Brethren, do not be children in understanding; however, in malice be babes, but in understanding be mature" (1 Cor 14:20). "I want you to be wise in what is good, and simple concerning evil" (Rom 16:19).

# 140. Those Who Eat and Drink at Table, and Others Who Are Hungry, but Not Allowed There for Their Own Fault

It happens that in a certain home, some eat and drink at table and are comforted, but the master of the house does not permit others to that table for a certain fault of theirs, and so grief and sorrow will envelop them, for they wish to eat and they are prevented from doing this. They see others eating and drinking, and being comforted, but they themselves hunger and thirst and so are consumed with sadness. The same thing will happen to sinners. Unbearable grief and sorrow will seize them, and they will feel sorry, but too late and to no avail, when they see the righteous in comfort, honor, glory, and eternal blessedness, eating and drinking at the table of the Lord and themselves deprived of all that blessedness and being in great torment. And this is what the Lord says to the Jews: "There will be weeping and gnashing of teeth, when you see Abraham and Isaac and Jacob and all the prophets in the kingdom of God, and yourselves thrust out" (Luke 13:28), and so on. And He says through the Prophet: "Behold, My servants shall eat, but you shall hunger. Behold, My servants shall drink, but you shall thirst. Behold, My servants shall be glad, but you shall be ashamed. Behold, My servants shall rejoice exceedingly in gladness, but you shall cry out because of the pain in your heart; and you shall wail from the crushing of your spirit" (Isa 65:14 [actually 13–14]).

So the rich man of the Gospel saw the wretched Lazarus comforted in the bosom of Abraham, while he himself was suffering in the burning flame; he saw him and exclaimed, "'Father Abraham, have mercy on me,'" and so on, but heard in answer, "'Son, remember that in your lifetime you received your good things, and likewise Lazarus evil things; but now he is comforted and you are tormented. And besides all this, between us and you there is a great gulf fixed, so that those who want to pass from here to you cannot, nor can those from there pass to us'" (Luke 16:24–26).

Other unrepentant sinners, who now are comforted by God's good things, but forget God and despise the wretched Lazaruses, will hear the same answer. Grief and unbearable sorrow will seize masters, princes, and lords who have disdained their servants, and treated them like a footstool and like cattle, but will see them in glory, but themselves in disgrace; it will seize the rich when they see the poor and wretched, whom they had despised, in the kingdom of God, and themselves outside of it; it will seize all revilers when they see in unspeakable glory those whom they vilified, backbit, swore at, dishonored, and looked upon as if they were dung, and themselves in dishonor and reproach. And this is what is written in the book of the Wisdom of Solomon:

> Then the righteous man will stand with confidence in the presence of those who afflict him; and those who reject his labors, when they see him, will be shaken with dreadful fear; and they shall be amazed at his unexpected salvation. They will speak among themselves with regret, and in anguish of spirit they will groan and say, "This is the man whom we fools once held in derision and made a byword of disgrace. We considered his life to be madness and his death as without honor. How has he been numbered among the sons of God? And how is his portion among the saints? Therefore we went astray from the way of truth, for

the light of righteousness did not shine on us, and the sun did not rise upon us. We were satisfied with the paths of lawlessness, and we traveled through impassable deserts; but the way of the Lord we have not known. (Wis 5:1–7)

Christian! We see that most sweet table in the Sacred Scripture, depicted in various ways for our encouragement and consolation. We see people eating and drinking at that table; we see those hungering and thirsting for that table, but not admitted by God's righteous judgment, and driven away from it. Those who have served the Lord with faith and truth and have pleased Him recline there; the holy patriarchs, prophets, apostles, hierarchs, martyrs, hermits, and holy monks recline there; and all the saints and righteous ones recline there. But sinners look upon that table from afar; they want to come to it but are not allowed; they wish to eat and drink, but it is not granted them; they repent and regret, but it is too late. And grief and anguish, sorrow and sighing will grasp them, but it will be too late and to no avail.

Christian! We, glory to God, are still living in this world, our hope has not yet perished, the doors to that table are still open, and the Merciful Lord is inviting everyone to it. And so, let us not neglect ourselves, lest we too be excluded from that most sweet table. Let us repent, and let us please our Lord Jesus Christ in faith and righteousness, that He may make us participants of that table. And since many sorrows meet those going to that consolation, we will not turn back, oppressed by them, but we will endure them. "But he who endures to the end shall be saved." "We must through many tribulations enter the kingdom of God" (Matt 24:13; Acts 14:22). And the voice from heaven witnesses of those reclining at that table: "These are the ones who come out of the great tribulation," and so on (Rev 7:14).

The hope of future good things encourages us to struggle and strengthens us in the struggle. The hope of acquiring wealth motivates and strengthens a merchant to wander through foreign lands; the hope of acquiring fruits motivates and strengthens the farmer to labor and sweat; the hope of acquiring understanding motivates and strengthens pupils to study in schools and to endure every want; the hope of victory motivates and strengthens the soldier to fight bravely against the enemy. Likewise, may the hope of future blessedness especially motivate and strengthen us in the struggle to the end. For a good end brings our blessedness to fulfillment, as was spoken: "Be faithful until death, and I will give you the crown of life," says the Lord (Rev 2:10).

# 141. Those Who Enter the King's Bridal Chamber

We see that people who wish to enter the king's bridal chamber dress in bright and clean clothes and enter like this, but they are not admitted there in rags and shoddy clothing. So too only those souls enter the bridal chamber of the Heavenly King who have bright and clean clothing, wedding garments, and clean linen; but those in the rags of sin are not admitted there. "But there shall by no means enter it anything that defiles" (Rev 21:27). In holy baptism, Christians by the grace of God shed the rags of sin and are clothed in clean clothing and wedding garments, and so are made worthy to enter that heavenly chamber, as written, "But you were washed, but you were sanctified, but you were justified in the name of the Lord Jesus and by the Spirit of our God" (1 Cor 6:11). They freely enter the house of the Heavenly King and are participants of all that blessedness. If one keeps this God-given garment, blessed is he, and truly blessed! "Blessed is he who watches, and keeps his garments, lest he walk naked and they see his shame" (Rev 16:15).

But many Christians—Oh, the poverty and wretchedness of man!—have lost that God-woven garment and have clothed themselves in the rags of sin. Such are fornicators, adulterers, and all who live uncleanly. Such are the greedy, thieves, extortioners, robbers, and all who steal what belongs to others. Such are slanderers, revilers, and liars and all who live lawlessly. All such wear the rags of sins and do not have wedding attire. And so, man, think: how can a person enter the heavenly bridal chamber in such vile clothing? People are not admitted into the palace of an earthly king in tattered clothing: will they be allowed into the palace of the Heavenly King in rags? No! Those who want to enter that beautiful bridal chamber must put off such vile clothing and put on clean linen. That radiant house shines with divine glory: those who enter it and who dwell in it must be clean and bright, as well. Otherwise, what accord does darkness have with light? "Lord, who shall dwell in Thy tabernacle, or who shall rest upon Thy holy hill? Even he that walketh blameless, and doeth the thing which is right, that speaketh the truth in his heart. He that hath used no deceit in his tongue, nor done evil to his neighbor, and hath not reproached his friend. He that setteth not by the evil-doer, and maketh much of them that fear the Lord; he that sweareth unto his neighbor, and disappointed him not. He that hath not given his money upon usury, nor taken a bribe against the innocent; whoso doeth these things shall never fall" (Ps 14:1–5). These are the marks of a soul wearing wedding garb and entering the bridal chamber of the Heavenly King.

Christian! Let us take stock whether we too have lost that salvific attire, and whether instead of it we are wearing the rags of sin, which bars the way into the heavenly chamber. If we see this, let us try through repentance and faith to put off the rags of sin and cleanse and whiten the robes of our souls in the blood of the Lamb, so that we with those who enter that splendid chamber may enter and appear before the Face of God and live in that chamber and praise God's goodness unto the ages of ages.

That God-woven and salvific robe is freely given to every Christian at baptism, but those who have lost it must seek it with great labor, repentance, regret, groaning, contrition of heart, weeping, and tears. "Blessed are they that dwell in Thy house, for ever and ever will they praise Thee" (Ps 83:5). And it is written: "Ask, and it will be given to you; seek, and you will find; knock, and it will be opened to you" (Matt 7:7). "I see Thy bridal chamber adorned, O my Saviour, and I have no wedding garment that I may enter there. Make the robe of my soul to shine, O Giver of Light, and save me."[17]

# 142. Light and Darkness

There is a physical and visible light, and there is an invisible light of the soul. There is also a physical and visible darkness, and there is an invisible darkness of the soul. The body is illumined by the physical light, but the soul is illumined by the light of the soul; so too the body grows dark and dimmed by physical and visible darkness, but the soul by the invisible darkness of the soul. God and the knowledge of God is the light of the soul, but ignorance of God is the darkness of the soul.

Faith is the light of the soul, but unbelief and superstition are the darkness of the soul; fear of God is the light of the soul, but lack of this fear is darkness of the soul. Every virtue is the light of the soul, but every sin is darkness of the soul. Humility, belittling, and disparagement of oneself are the light of the soul, but pride, haughtiness, and self-exaltation are darkness of the soul. Love for God and neighbor is the light of the soul, but immoderate self-love is the darkness of the soul. Hope and trust in God is the light of the soul, but hope in man and other creations is darkness of the soul. True and unfeigned prayer, singing, and praising of God's name are the light of the soul, but negligence of these is darkness of the soul. Good-naturedness and non-remembrance of wrongs are light of the soul, but malice and remembrance of wrongs are the darkness of the soul. Fasting and moderation are the light of the soul, but over-eating and drunkenness are the darkness of the soul.

Love of purity and its preservation are the light of the soul, but licentiousness, adultery, and every impurity are the darkness of the soul. Mercy, benevolence, and compassion for our neighbor are the light of the soul, but mercilessness and hardheartedness are the darkness of the soul. Generous distribution of alms from a pure heart is the light of the soul, but miserliness is the darkness of the soul. Disdain for the vanity and opulence of this world are the light of the soul, but love for it is the darkness of the soul. Remembrance of death, of Christ's Judgment, and of a blessed or unfortunate eternity is the light of the soul, but forgetfulness of them is the darkness of the soul. In a word, true repentance and fruits consistent with it—good works—are the light of the soul, but lack of repentance and the evil fruits connected with it—dark deeds—are the darkness of the soul.

Christian, you see light and darkness: flee darkness, lest you dwell in darkness, and be cast into eternal and outer darkness; love the light, so that you will dwell in the light and pass to the eternal light. He who lives in sin walks in darkness and does not know where he is going, for the darkness has benighted his eyes. He who knows God and is truly repentant flees dark deeds and bears the fruits of repentance walks in the light. "I am the light of the world. He who follows Me shall not walk in darkness, but have the light of life" (John 8:12).

We follow Christ not with our feet but with our heart, will, and morals. He follows the Lord who imitates Him through faith, humility, love, meekness, patience, and the other virtues and walks in the light, for he follows the light. He who lives according to his own will and does not reform his morals after the example of the Lord's life does not follow the Lord but walks in darkness, for he shuns the light. For he who shuns the light must be in darkness. For it is written:

> "And this is the condemnation, that the light has come into the world, and men loved darkness rather than light, because their deeds were evil. For everyone practicing evil hates the light and does not come to the light, lest his deeds should be exposed. But he who does the truth comes to the light, that his deeds may be clearly seen, that they have been done in God." (John 3:19–21)

Everyone who does good neither flees the light nor seeks the darkness, for he does not fear exposure because his deeds are righteous. But whoever does evil flees the light and seeks darkness, for dark deeds are performed in the darkness. The lecher, thief, extortioner, and every wrongdoer seek the darkness and a hidden place.

O poor man! No matter where you hide, in the darkness, or under the earth, or in the desert, or inside a building, you cannot hide anywhere from God and your own witness and accuser, the conscience. God is everywhere, and He sees your every deed. And your conscience is everywhere and exposes your every deed. It is not silent about any of your transgressions but says boldly, "You are doing evil; God's Dread Judgment awaits you! All your evil deeds will be exposed at it. Then God, the Righteous Judge, will render to you according to your deeds."

Christian! Let us hate evil and love the light, that we may be "sons of light" (John 12:36). Let us turn from deeds that are done in the dark; let us do deeds conformable to the day, that we may be illumined. "The night is far spent, the day is at hand. Therefore let us cast off the works of darkness, and let us put on the armor of light. Let us walk properly, as in the day, not in revelry and drunkenness, not in lewdness and lust, not in strife and envy. But put on the Lord Jesus Christ, and make no provision for the flesh, to fulfill its lusts" (Rom 13:12–14).

Christ, the True Light! Enlighten the eyes of our hearts, that we may see You, the inextinguishable light, and direct our feet to follow You, that we may have "the light of life" (John 8:12).

# 143. I Am Ashamed to Look at You

We hear that one says this to another: "I am ashamed to look at you." This is said by one who has received not a few benefactions from a certain person but has insulted him much and so has proved to be ungrateful to his benefactor, but then, feeling regret, he is contrite before him and declares his guilt to him, and confesses his sin, and is ashamed, and with remorse says to him: "I am ashamed to look at you."

In this way, the Christian soul that has sinned much before the Lord, but has later come to its senses and repented, fittingly says sorrowfully to God, its Creator: "I am ashamed to raise my eyes to You. I am Your creation and the work of Your hands. 'Thy hands have made me and fashioned me' (Ps 118:73). But I did not understand this, sinning and transgressing before You. You created me not as an insensible and dumb creature, but a man with senses and reason and, what is most important, You honored me with Your image. *I am the image of your ineffable glory.* But I did not understand that great gift of Yours, I did not obey you, I sinned and transgressed before you, and so insulted you, my great Creator and benefactor. Therefore shame covers my face; I am ashamed even to raise my eyes to You. 'O Lord, righteousness belongs to You, but shame of face belongs to us' (Dan 9:7)."

"You, as a God Who loves mankind and desires not the death of a sinner, washed, sanctified, and justified in the bath of regeneration me, who was defiled by sin, conceived in iniquities and born in sins (see Ps 50:7). But I did not understand this, Your great and incomprehensible gift, and again, alas, defiled myself with many sins, so grievously sinned before You and insulted You, as '[a] dog returns to his own vomit,' and, 'a sow, having washed, to her wallowing in the mire' (2 Pet 2:22). See the shame on my face! Woe is me, for I have sinned against You! My heart languishes from this. 'Because of this, our eyes have remained in darkness' (Lam 5:17)."

"I am ashamed to lift up my eyes to You. I am ashamed to look upon Your most holy Face. You called me to eternal life, opened to me the doors of Your kingdom and, in Your love for mankind, promised it as an inheritance. But I did not understand this; turned to the vanity of this world; sought its riches, honor, and glory; senselessly disregarded that eternal treasure that You promised me; and so seriously insulted You. I am ashamed to look at you. The shame of my face covers me."

"You feed me, clothe me, and with your generous hand give me every good thing that I have. But I did not understand your most abundant beneficence; I insulted you, my benefactor, and was ungrateful to You, my benefactor. Behold the shame of my face! I am ashamed to look at you. And now, I acknowledge and confess my ingratitude and sins before You; and I know and acknowledge that I am truly unworthy of heaven and earth, and a piece of bread, and the slightest other good, and of temporal life itself, but am worthy only of punishment. I deserve this because of my sins and my ingratitude."

"But, O Merciful and Man-loving Lord! May both your majesty and your mercy be upon me, a sinner! You did not destroy me, a sinner; do not destroy me now that I repent. You endured one who transgressed and awaited his conversion; have mercy and accept one who is turning to you. You had mercy on bandits, murderers, lechers, extortioners, robbers, and other grievous sinners who repented: have mercy on me too, who am like them. Knower of Hearts, You see the sorrow, grief, and regret of my heart, and the shame of my face, for I have sinned against You, my Creator and God. 'Have mercy upon me, O God, after Thy great goodness, and according to the multitude of Thy mercies do away mine offenses' (Ps 50:3 and on to the end of the Psalm). I do not want to sin against You again in any way, but will try to behave as Your word teaches and to correct myself according to its principles. Lord, help me, and stretch out Your holy hand to me, and strengthen me, for I am infirm. 'Thy mercy shall follow me all the days of my life' (Ps 22:6)."

Christian! Think well and learn who you are and against Whom you are sinning and Whom you are insulting whenever you sin. You, earth and ashes and a tiny worm, insult God's incomprehensible majesty by your sin, the Great God, Whom angels and all the powers of heaven hymn with fear and reverence and continuously glorify, and Whose desire and slightest gesture all creation obeys and fulfills His will. You alone do not obey Him and do not honor Him, but insult Him by sin. He is your Creator, Redeemer, and Benefactor, greater than Whom there is and cannot be, but you do not honor Him, for you sin against Him and so insult Him.

Think: is it not great madness and blindness not to honor and to insult the One from Whom we have our being and receive every good thing that we have? What subject dares to not honor and to insult his king? Only a madman, and to his manifest destruction. What son does not honor his father? Only an insensible one. What servant does not fear his master? Only one that has lost his mind. What person wishes to insult his benefactor? Only one who is worse than a brute or wild beast, for both brutes and wild beasts know their benefactors and remember their benefactions.

You render all this aforementioned recklessness to your Lord God when you sin. And this is what the Lord says: "A son honors his father, and a servant his master. If then, I am the Father, where is My honor? And if I am a Master, where is the reverence due to me" (Mal 1:6)? It is serious, truly serious, for a person to insult his benefactor, a servant his master, a son and daughter their father, a subordinate his superior; it is much worse for a subject to insult his king. How incomparably more serious it is to insult God, the King of kings, and Lord of lords, and the Father of our fathers, and the

Benefactor of our benefactors. God is insulted by sin, for due obedience is not rendered to Him.

Oh, what a cruel evil is sin! Sin is sweet to a person, but its fruits are very bitter. And do not think, O man, that you, when you sin against a person, do not sin against God. No, that opinion is wrong. For whoever sins against a person also sins against God, and whoever insults a person insults God. How? God commanded us not to offend and not to insult a person, but rather to love him and help him. If we do not do what He commanded, we do not render him obedience and we act contrary to His holy will and so madly insult Him. You see, O man, that sin against a person is impossible without sin against God, and an insult of a person does not happen without insulting God. If you hate a person whom God loves and commanded you to love, you also hate God Himself. If you offend a person, which God has forbidden, you are offending God Himself. Do you see where your sin against a person, your insult and your offense given him, arises to? To God Himself.

And from this it follows that if you wish to repent and be reconciled with God, it is necessary for you first to be reconciled with your neighbor whom you offended and insulted. And this is what the Lord says: "If you bring your gift to the altar, and there remember that your brother has something against you, leave your gift there before the altar, and go your way. First be reconciled to your brother, and then come and offer your gift" (Matt 5:24). And what increases the seriousness and vileness of the sin and shows a man's blindness and madness, every sin, just as every deed, is committed before God and His all-seeing eye, for God is everywhere and sees everything. Who would dare to behave badly before an earthly king, or even before a lower authority? The blind sinner dares to do this before God and His all-seeing eye. If a person reflects on all this and the aforesaid, he will without fail come to true repentance, contrition, and sadness of heart and will feel sorry and grieve in his heart that he sinned and insulted and angered God; and, not daring to lift up his eyes to God, his shame will acknowledge: "I am ashamed to raise my eyes to You, O Lord." And now henceforward he would wish rather to die than to sin.

Realize, Christian, Whom you are sinning against and Whom you are insulting by sin, and, I speak the truth, you will sincerely repent and guard against every sin. And so, enlightenment and knowledge of God, of oneself, and of sin is the beginning of repentance and salvation. "For thus says the Lord, the Holy One of Israel: 'When you return and groan, then you will be saved and know where you were'" (Isa 30:15).

# 144. Internecine Strife

We see and hear that in the world there is internecine strife. It happens when the inhabitants of one country or city rise up against one another. Christians engage in internecine strife like this when some rise up against others and offend them. Christians have a close alliance among themselves; they are connected by a greater alliance than the inhabitants of one country or city. They have one faith; they confess one God, the Father and the Son and the Holy Spirit, and they call upon Him, pray to Him, and hymn Him; they hear one Word of God; they are baptized with one baptism; they enter one church to pray; they commune the same Holy Mysteries; they are called to one eternal life; they are called Christians from the one Christ, and so on. You see, Christian, how you are connected to each other? More, indeed, than fellow citizens and brothers in the flesh. But when some rise up against others, then they are causing internecine strife.

These include the following:

(1) Thieves, extortioners, robbers, and others like them, who in any way steal property from Christians, that is, either money or clothing, or bread, a house, land, livestock, fishing ground, a grove, or something else.

(2) Merchants who cheat Christians during sale of goods and ask more for goods than they are worth.

(3) Masters who burden their peasants with either quit-rents or heavy work, or inhumanely torment them, or call them abusive names.

(4) Judges corrupted by bribery who, without a bribe, do not want to give satisfaction to Christians who are aggrieved and enduring evil.

(5) Lying slanderers and revilers who in any way abuse and vilify Christians.

(6) Tricksters, sly people, cheaters, who anyhow and in any way deceive Christians, and set traps for them.

(7) Finally, all who in any way cause offense and animosity to Christians. All these and the Christians described earlier rise up against Christians and incite strife against them. It is written about the first Christians: "Now the multitude of those who believed were of one heart and one soul" (Acts 4:32). And Christ the Lord demands this of Christians: "A new commandment I give to you, that you love one another; as I have loved you, that you also love one another. By this all will know that you are My disciples, if you have love for one another" (John 13:34–35). This is how it was

once, Christian. No, you can no longer search for that now. For the love of many has dried up; iniquity has multiplied; sin grows stronger day by day; offenses and animosity are increasing more and more. Against whom? Against Christians. From whom? From Christians! Brethren have arisen against brethren, "and 'a man's enemies will be those of his own household'" (Matt 10:36).

Complaining and weeping are heard everywhere; the very air makes a noise filled with mournful voices. A widow complains and weeps there: that powerful man, she says, took from me land, or a grove, or something else. The poor and wretched man groans: where can I live, he says, some violent man drove me from my land and destroyed my house. Elsewhere, a peasant sobs: I work so many days a week for my master; when can I work for my home and my family? Another is troubled similarly: my master or mistress alone eats up all my labor; how am I to feed my family and myself?

All complain almost in harmony: in such a place, they say, and in another, we do not find satisfaction for our grievances. Where should we go and where should we seek satisfaction? They do not pass judgment without money changing hands. Some are sad and complain: "A certain merchant cheated me for such and such goods." And another tells him: "Where won't you find that? In what city? Wherever you go and whatever you want to buy, everywhere you must beware of cheating, for everywhere they ask for prices higher than the goods are worth, and they all assert this by calling on the name of God, and everyone is already accustomed to this," and so on. See the Christians of the present age!

Oh, how far such Christians have departed from the first ones, among whom there was *one heart and one soul!* And from this it is obvious that their Christianity is false. Formerly Christians helped one another, but now they persecute and exasperate each other; and from this it is obvious that the Lord's coming has drawn near, and the day of the Lord "will come as a thief in the night" (2 Pet 3:10), unexpectedly.

O poor, blinded Christians! Who taught you to live like this? What prophet, what apostle and teacher? Do not all of them teach us to live in the fear of God, to love one another, to help one another, and to have harmony and peace among us? Take stock of yourself, and you will see that your deeds are from the devil. He, being the spirit of enmity and malice, hates love, harmony, and peace, and this is why he tries in every way to root out love and sow enmity, and so he teaches Christians to cause offenses and rancor.

God-fearing soul! Endure everything that false Christians and hypocrites do to you. "But he who endures to the end shall be save. Be faithful until death," the Lord tells you, "and I will give you the crown of life" (Matt 24:13; Rev 2:10).

The inhabitants of one homeland, as members of a single society, should help and protect each other and take up arms with one accord against external enemies. But if they do not do this, they give themselves over to everyone for mockery and to their enemies for defeat, and their homeland to ruin. For nothing ruins a homeland like internecine and internal strife. So, when Christians rise up against Christians and cause them harm, they give themselves over to the mockery of the devil and his minions, the idolaters. The devil, the enemy of Christians, rejoices in such Christians. All Christians should with one accord stand up and fight bravely against this enemy and help each other, and encourage each other against him, and so wage war with him alone, as the Lord requires (see Eph 6:10–18; 1 Pet 5:9). But when Christians rise up against Christians, then they are taking up arms not against the devil, but with the devil against Christians, and are helping him, and so are doing what is pleasing to him. This is indeed so, although such poor Christians do not perceive this. For whoever does someone's will pleases and serves him.

Oh, into what a sorry state Christianity has come: people wound and torment each other! In former times Christians looked after and protected each other from the idolators; now Christians rise up against Christians and guard against each other, inasmuch as one cannot believe anyone. For each flatters and deceives, acts crookedly and dissembles: on the tongue is honey, but in the heart he carries the bile of grief; he greets with his lips, but he is at enmity in his heart; he comforts and says pleasant things to one's face, but having moved away, he vilifies and abuses. Each seeks this and in his heart learns how to take possession of what is someone else's.

Oh, the terrible times! Oh, how the cunning of the devil is enabled, how sin has intensified, how love has vanished! What can a Christian God-fearing soul expect besides animosity and persecution? The Israelites, when they thought of leaving Egypt, endured very serious animosity from the tyrant pharaoh. So when holy and pious souls are growing scarce in this world, the devil very cruelly takes up arms against them and rankles them sometimes himself, other times through his minions; and the nearer the end of the world, the greater and more cruel will be the suffering for the pious. The devil most of all rises up against those who stand up and fight bravely against him, but he ignores those who submit to his will. He does his utmost to embitter this "little flock" (Luke 12:32). Leaving Egypt, the Israelites, even though pharaoh was rankling them, left with silver and gold, as was written, "He brought them forth also with silver and gold" (Ps 104:37); so Christians, although they suffer much from the devil and his minions in the end, leave the world with the priceless treasure of eternal blessedness.

Endure and strengthen your heart, pious soul! Everything worldly will remain in the world: you will depart here with an eternal and heavenly treasure. "Therefore be patient, brethren, until the coming of the Lord. See how the farmer waits for the precious fruit of the earth, waiting patiently for it until it receives the early and latter rain. You also be patient. Establish your hearts, for the coming of the Lord is at hand. Do not grumble against one another, brethren, lest you be condemned. Behold, the Judge is standing at the door!" (Jas 5:7–9).

# 145. A Bee That Wounds with Its Sting

They say that a bee, when it stings someone, itself dies. A Christian suffers just like this when he in some way offends and embitters his neighbor. He cannot offend his neighbor without a greater and more serious injury to himself. And the greater offense he gives his neighbor, the more he injures himself; and the more he wounds another, the more he wounds himself. Since, in offending his neighbor, he involves God Himself by his offense, for he is breaking God's commandment, which forbids offending anyone but commands to love everyone and to do good to everyone: "You shall love your neighbor as yourself" (Lev 19:18; Matt 22:39). Such a one injures himself more than the other person. Why? Because he injures the other in the body, but himself in the soul; he wounds and poisons the other's body, but his own soul. For as the soul is better and more valuable than the body, any injury, harm, and animosity to it are greater than that to the body. For a person's soul is wounded and rankled by every sin that he commits. He sins against his neighbor and incurs a wound in his soul. He wounds himself by his sin as by a bee's sting.

Satan, being a spirit hostile to man, always seeks and tries to lead a person to sin. Do you sin, O man? You give yourself over to harm by the devil. Do you oppress a person? The devil is oppressing you. Do you steal valuable from a person? The devil has stolen the valuables of your soul. Do you entice and deceive a person? The devil has enticed and deceived you. Do you slander a person? Then you have already given yourself over to the slander of the devil. Do you abuse and curse at a person? You have now given yourself over to the abuse of the devil. Do you beat and injure a person? The devil is now beating and injuring your soul. Do you laugh at a person? The devil is now laughing at you. Do you despise and disdain a person? The devil is despising and disdaining you, and so on.

Thus, every person sins and punishes himself! His very sin is his punishment. He offends another, and he is himself offended; he wounds and is himself wounded; he rankles, and he suffers evil; he beats and is beaten; he kills and is killed; he deprives and is deprived; he slanders and is slandered; he condemns and is condemned; he defames and is defamed; he swears at and is sworn at; he entices and is enticed; he cheats and is cheated; he despises and is despised; he mocks and is mocked.

In a word, whenever he does evil to his neighbor, he does a greater evil to himself; for he does evil to the body of his neighbor and for a time, but he does evil to his own soul and forever. So the measure that the sinner fills for his neighbor, he fills for himself and to spare. Therefore the Holy Spirit says, "Come, ye children, and hearken unto me; I will teach you the fear of the Lord. What man is he that lusteth to live, and would gladly see good days? Keep thy tongue from evil, and thy lips, that they speak no guile. Shun evil, and do good; seek peace, and pursue it. The eyes of the Lord are over the righteous, and His ears are open unto their prayers. But the countenance of the Lord is against them that do evil, to root out the remembrance of them from the earth" (Ps 33:12–17).

# 146. A Wounded Man Is Wounded Again

It happens that a torturer, having inflicted many wounds upon a man, beats him again and adds wounds to wounds and so causes him the cruelest sufferings. The world sees such cruelty. This is also done by those who bear

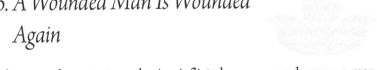

the name of Christians, who cause any kind of offense for poor people and so add misfortune to their misfortune.

These are those:

(1) Who craftily afflict one who is sad, or is in sickness, or is suffering from something else and vex him. This is what the stiff-necked and hard-hearted Jews did, who abused and reviled Christ, the Son of God, Who had already been outraged, wounded, tortured and was suffering on the Cross: "And those who passed by blasphemed Him, wagging their heads and saying, 'You who destroy the temple and build it in three days, save Yourself! If You are the Son of God, come down from the cross'" (Matt 27:39–41), and so on. And so they "added to the pain of my wounds" (Ps 68:27). Oh, the savage inhumanity! Oh, Your long-suffering, O Jesus!

(2) Judges who do not give satisfaction to a person suffering evil, and accuse and convict him who is innocent, as if he were guilty, and so add suffering to suffering.

(3) Masters who take from their poor and wretched peasants their last possessions, or burden them with excessive work, and so leave them without subsistence.

(4) Powerful people, who do not have the fear of God, who take away from widows, orphans, and other poor people land or anything else from which they gain their subsistence.

(5) People without a conscience who seeing a fire, carry off and steal anything from the person whose house is burning.

(6) Greedy rich men and other people who lend to the poor but charge interest from them, and the higher the interest they charge, the poorer they make them.

(7) People who withhold pay from hired hands.

(8) Masters and supervisors who without due cause do not give their subordinates the salaries appointed by the Sovereign.

(9) This includes also those shameless ravishers who for the sake of their foul lust take away other men's wives and so on.

The world sees these and other evils. All these people act like that torturer who again hurts one who has already been hurt and again torments one who has already been tormented. The cruel inhumanity! Such iniquities are seen among Christians. Such people have lost the last spark not only of Christianity but even of humanity. Such iniquities, like the sins of Sodom and Gomorrah, cry out to heaven. In whatever city and country this evil is committed, the people are seeking perdition for themselves.

Christian! What kind of mercy do you expect for yourself from God, the Father of orphans and the Judge of widows, you, who do any of the aforesaid evil to a poor person? And what do you expect for yourself in the age to come when you cause such torment for a person like you? Do you really wish to be with those inhuman people who once baked Christians like meat, burned them in fire, drowned them in water, gave them over to the teeth of wild animals, and subjected them to other inhuman tortures? You will, if you do not repent and wash away your iniquities with tears. For if *for every idle word men may speak, they will give account of it in the day of judgment,* as Christ said (Matt 12:36), even more will they be tortured for iniquities and such evil deeds. It will be more pleasant than for the Sodomites and idolaters than for such Christians, who always hear the Word of God rebuking them and teaching them, but not only do not want to correct themselves, but even sink into worse things.

Christian, realize your ruin and repent, while there is still time; repent, if you do not want to burn eternally in fiery Gehenna, as iron in the fire, but never be consumed. "Their worm shall not die, and their fire shall not be extinguished" (Isa 66:24; Mark 9:44).

# 147. A Mirror Shows the Smudges on a Face

What smudges are to the face, so sins are to the soul. What a mirror is for the face and smudges, a word of rebuke is for the soul and sins. A mirror shows us what there is on the face: when there are smudges on the face, it shows the smudges; when there are none on the face, it does not show any. Likewise the word of reproof, like the mirror, reveals the sins on the soul. Whatever sins there are in the soul, it shows and rebukes them; whatever sins the souls does not have, the word does not rebuke them. When a person, having seen smudges on his face, wipes them off, the mirror no longer shows them; so when the soul, giving up sins, cleanses them by repentance and faith, the word of rebuke no longer concerns it. And the conscience does to the human soul what the word of rebuke does. For the conscience is consistent with the law and the word of rebuke. The testimony of this internal witness is true: what it sees in the soul, it bears witness to and rebukes; what it does not see, it does not rebuke. Thus, God appointed two witnesses and accusers for the human soul: externally, His law; and within the soul, the conscience. Both of these witnesses truly and consistently testify to and rebuke us. They will be the witnesses for everyone at the Second Coming of Christ as well. They will bear witness there to whatever we have done now. If we have sinned here, they will denounce our sins there. If we have repented and wiped away our sins here, they will not denounce them there. If we have done good deeds here, they will witness to them there and praise us.

We see this now. When we do good, they praise us. The law praises us for the good, and the conscience praises us also; the law praises mercy, and the conscience does, too; the law honors the meek and patient, and the conscience honors them, too; God's word consoles one innocently enduring abuse, defamation, or exile, or bonds, or any other evil; his conscience consoles him, too. For as the sin itself is a punishment for a person, so virtue itself is a recompense and reward for him.

From this it follows:

(1) How necessary is the preaching of the Law of God, that from it people may know their sins, as from a mirror they know the smudges on their faces, and so, having learned of them, they would wipe them off by repentance and faith and in future would guard against them. This matter concerns mainly pastors.

(2) You should never be angry with anyone for a word of rebuke. You are not angry at a mirror for showing the smudges on your face: then why be angry at a preacher because he shows you your sins by his sermon? The mirror shows you what there is on your face: in the same way, a word of rebuke reproves you for what is in your soul.

(3) If someone is angered because of a word of rebuke, it is obvious that within himself he has those sins that the word in general rebukes. For this means that his conscience is also rebuking him for what he heard in the word. O man, when you become angry at a preacher for a word of rebuke, become angry as well at your conscience, which is rebuking you. But no matter how much you rage, it will not cease rebuking you and will always tell you what it sees in you. It is better to get angry at yourself, that you sinned and wounded your conscience. Repent and stop doing what wounds your conscience, and your conscience will no longer wound you, and the word of rebuke will not concern you. Then, by God's grace, rest, peace, and joy will take up its abode in your soul.

(4) As a mirror is used in order that smudges on the face may be seen and so be wiped off, so the word of rebuke should not be given for any other reason than that people recognize their sin and repent, and so correct themselves.

# 148. How Could I Forget Him!

We hear that one says such a thing about another: "How could I forget him!" This is said when one says to the other: "Often you mention him"—that is, such and such a person. Then he who mentions him answers, "How could I forget him! I have received many benefactions from him."

Christian, you and I most of all must sincerely say concerning our God: "How could I forget him!" We have been created and redeemed by our God and have received and always receive so many benefactions from Him that we not only cannot express them in speech but cannot even understand them with our minds, for they are measureless and innumerable, known and unknown; in a word, we are enclosed in God's benefactions and without them we could not live a minute. And so how could we forget Him, such a benefactor of ours! So let us not forget Him, O Christian!

God said to Old Israel through His Prophet: "I formed you to be my servant; therefore, you, O Israel, do not forget me" (Isa 44:21). The same God speaks like this to the Christian, "I formed you to be my servant; therefore, you," O Christian, "do not forget me." When the Christian is created, and when he is baptized in the name of the Father, and of the Son, and of the Holy Spirit, God makes the Christian a servant of God; formerly, he was a servant of the devil, but in holy baptism, he was made a servant of God. Remember, Christian, that you are a servant of God; the Lord created you His servant; and you, Christian, must not forget Him. The Christian is marked with the name of Christ as with a royal seal; he takes the name of Christian from Christ.

About the ancient Israelites we hear that when they worshiped the idol, "they forgat the God Who had saved them" (Ps 105:21), and so on.

So Christians forget the God Who saves them when after baptism they turn to iniquities and, having become servants of God, willfully become the servants of sin. "Whoever commits sin is a slave of sin" (John 8:34). Every wrongdoer and transgressor forgets God, his benefactor, for he forgets His holy commandments. The fornicator and adulterer forget; the thief, extortioner, and robber forget; the slanderer, the reviler, and every backbiter forget; the seducer, cheat, and liar forget; everyone who fearlessly breaks God's commandment forgets.

Christian, when you say about God, "How could I forget God?" do not forget His holy commandments but have them always before you, as God's commandments and always fulfill them. When you do this, you will surely not forget God Himself. Otherwise, although you may remember the name of God every minute, while neglecting God's commandments, you are forgetting God, your benefactor, and so are showing yourself ungrateful to Him, for your memory of Him is only on the lips and tongue, and not in the heart, where there is only forgetfulness.

For a man truly grateful to his benefactor remembers him not only on his lips but also in his heart and remembers his benefactions; likewise, the Christian carries God's name not only on his lips but should also have His memory in his heart, and love Him, and thank Him. For the memory, and gratitude, and love are inseparable. Whoever loves his benefactor always remembers him; whoever remembers him is motivated to gratitude for his benefactions, for it is impossible to not thank a benefactor, and not to sincerely remember his benefactions. For the very benefaction stimulates gratitude. Even livestock remember a benefaction, love the benefactor, and serve him.

Christian, if you do not forget God with your lips, do not forget Him with your heart; without this your memory is nothing. If you pray to God: "Remember me, O Lord, in Your Kingdom" (see Luke 23:42), then remember Him here, in this world just as it was said earlier. If you say to God, "Do not forget me," He says to you, "And you, Christian, do not forget me and my commandments."

A person is roused to remembrance of his benefactor upon seeing his benefaction, that is, either the house that he has built for him or the clothing in which he has dressed him, or anything else. "My benefactor has given me this clothing, he says, I received this bread that I am eating from him; in his mercy, he built for me this house in which I live," and so on. So all His benefactions should rouse a Christian to a loving remembrance of God, the Benefactor.

Christian! Each and every good thing that you have is God's good thing and benefaction. All of these prompt us to the remembrance of God. Whatever you see, contemplate and say to yourself: "This house in which I live and rest, this food that I eat, and this drink by which I am refreshed and comforted, this clothing by which I cover and warm myself, this livestock that serves me, this fire that warms me and cooks food for me, these luminaries (sun, moon, and stars), that give light to me and all creatures, and so on, are God's good things and benefaction." You always receive benefaction from God, and always use and are comforted by God's good things so that you cannot be without them for even a minute. You should always and at all times remember God, and thank Him for everything: *"I will bless the Lord at all times, His praise is ever in my mouth"* (Ps 33:2). The time, day, hour, and minute in which we do not bless the Lord are for naught, for the Lord's benefactions flow continuously like rivers and are generously poured out on us. "The Lord is merciful and gracious, longsuffering and of great kindness. The Lord is good unto all, and his mercies are upon all His works. Let all Thy works praise Thee, O Lord, and let Thy saints bless Thee" (Ps 144:8–10).

The holy icons especially bring to our mind God and His benefactions. The icon of the Annunciation shows us how the mankind-loving Lord, wishing to be born in the flesh of the Virgin, and to come into the world, and to appear to the world, and so effect our salvation, sent the Archangel Gabriel to announce this love for mankind to the most blessed Virgin and through her to the whole world. The icon of the salvific Nativity of Christ brings to our mind how the Beginningless God had a beginning, and the Invisible became visible, and the Immaterial became flesh, and the Intangible became tangible, and the Ancient of Days became an infant, and the Omnipotent became weak, and He who holds in His hand all the ends of the earth was carried in a mother's arms, and He Who gives food to all flesh was fed by his mother's milk, and He Who clothes the world as with a robe was wrapped in swaddling clothes. O the miracle—God became an infant! O man, our Lord did this for your sake and mine. Bless the Lord, all sons of men! Bless the Lord, O my soul! Remember this, Christian, and do not forget the Lord.

An icon of Christ's passion depicts for us how He cleansed our sins, and satisfied God's righteousness for us, and propitiated God, His Heavenly Father, and reconciled Him with us and us with Him, and redeemed us from death and hell, and opened the doors of God's kingdom, which were closed by our sins, and so effected salvation and eternal blessedness for us. The icon of Christ's passion depicts for us this and other sublime benefactions of God. Remember this, Christian, and do not forget Jesus Christ, the Son of God, who suffered for you.

Also, we are led to memory of God and his very great benefactions toward us by all of the Sacred Scriptures, being the Word of God, all the wondrous works of God described in them and His benefactions that have been shown to the human race, and all God's feast days, established by the holy Church; they inspire us to thanksgiving and glorification of God's Name, as we hear in church verses and hymns that are sung on holydays. Pay attention to yourself, Christian, and do not forget God, your benefactor.

Know for sure that those Christians forget God who live without the fear of God, and do not pay attention to His holy commandments, and sin and transgress against Him. They all walk in the darkness of ignorance of God; they do not know God, although they confess Him, and so they forget Him. They are satisfied with God's good things, but they forget God the benefactor. The Prophet says to such people: "Consider this,—that is, that God will display your sins before your face—ye that forget God, lest he pluck you away, and there be none to deliver" (Ps 49:22). Beware, Christian, of forgetting God and His holy commandments, lest you be forgotten by God forever. "My soul shall live, and shall praise Thee, and Thy judgments shall help me. I have gone astray like a sheep that is lost; O seek Thy servant, for I have not forgotten Thy commandments" (Ps 118:175–176). "Lord, remember me when You come into Your kingdom" (Luke 23:42).

# 149. We Shall Be Safe There

We hear that people say this: "We shall be safe there." Those who have been away from their homeland and their house, and wishing to return there, and so, consoling themselves, say, "We shall be safe there," that is, in their homeland and their house. The same is said also of any another place, where people hope to live in safety.

But it is not quite spoken truly of any place in this world. Why? There is no completely safe place in this world, as we shall see later. No matter where a person lives, while he is living in this world, he is not living without danger. From his mother's womb until the grave, a person has constant warfare. Therefore, it is proper and correct to say this to us about eternal life, Christian: there it will be truly safe for us. There we shall fear nothing; there we shall live without any fear and shall live in a tranquil and peaceful city; there we shall have perfect peace and rest, and that is why eternal life in the Sacred Scripture is called *rest* (Matt 11:29; Heb 4:11).

Living here, we fear wars and invasions of aliens and enemies; this will not happen there; for only the Kingdom of God, filled with peace, righteousness, and joy, will be there. Here we fear fires, famine, plague; none of that will happen there. Here we fear evil people who now openly, now secretly, set snares for us; that will not happen there, for they will not have a place there. Here we fear thieves and extortioners, who now openly, now surreptitiously, now by flattery take away our property from us; that will not happen there, inasmuch as they will all be banished from there. Here we fear the unbridled human tongue, for the slanderer is no small persecutor of ours; that will not happen there, for that place is inaccessible for such people. Here we fear false brethren, and "a man's enemies are all the people of his own household" (Mic 7:6; Matt 10:36); that will not happen there, for like-mindedness and loving brethren will be there.

Here even friendship is not without danger; there will be true and loving friendship, one without reproach, there, for all will have one heart, mind, will, desire, and perfect love for each other. Here we fear heretics and corrupters of the holy faith; that will not exist there, for they will be excluded from there and confined to their own places. Here we fear the flesh and the temptations of the world; these will not exist there. Here we fear sin; this will not exist there, for there will be perfect righteousness and love. Here we fear sickness and sorrow; these will not exist there, for there will be no sickness, sorrow, and sighing. Here we fear the devil and the evil demons; this will not happen there, for they will be confined to their place. Here we fear death and hell, which will not happen there; there we will eternally triumph over death and hell. "'O Death, where is your sting? O Hades, where is your victory?' The sting of death is sin, and the strength of sin is the law. But thanks be to God, who gives us the victory through our Lord Jesus Christ" (1 Cor 15:55–57).

You see, Christian, danger and safety. For one living in this world, it is always and everywhere dangerous to live; there is no danger in the future life. We may and should correctly and comfortingly say of it, "We shall be safe there." There we shall fear neither wars, nor enemies, nor famine, nor fire, nor plague, nor sly people, nor sicknesses, nor slanderers, nor revilers, nor thieves and extortioners, nor the devil and his evil spirits, nor temptations, nor death and hell, in a word, no ill-being. For every kind of ill-being is banished from there, and every kind of perfect well-being—perfect and eternal—will be there. And from this you see:

(1) How poor is our life in this world. Misfortunes and tribulations surround us and, like thorns, prick us. One misfortune passes, and immediately another comes forth, and after that one, a third, then a fourth, and so on. And so nothing else happens in this world except misfortunes; and like a ship tossed about by the winds and waves on the sea, so we in this life are tossed about by misfortunes and tribulations. Where and what kind of safety can we seek in this world? Will you withdraw to the desert and avoid all people and perfidy? A greater attack by the devil and even more of his snares will befall you there.

(2) From this it follows how carefully we must act while living in this world. "See then that you walk circumspectly, not as fools but as wise," the Apostle says (Eph 5:15). As a bird, sitting, looks everywhere, wary of the marksman and hunter, so the Christian should beware of everything in this world.

(3) Our efforts are feeble without God's help, especially during the attack of invisible enemies. Therefore, we must continually sigh and pray to God that He preserve us by His all-powerful hand. Christian! Read the holy psalms, and you will see how the holy David defended himself from his enemies by prayer and praise of God's name, as by a strong wall. "Giving praise, I will call upon the Lord, and so shall I be safe from mine enemies" (Ps 17:4). You should do likewise, that you be saved from the slanders of the enemy. "O how hast Thou multiplied Thy mercy, O God; so shall the children of men put their trust in the shelter of Thy wings" (Ps 35:8).

(4) If our life is so dangerous and miserable in this world, Christian, why should we wish a long life in this world? To live in this world is nothing other than to live always in poverty. Therefore, the holy Prophet laments and sighs about this, saying, "Woe is me, for my wandering hath been prolonged" (Ps 119:5). The day of a blessed death is better than of birth. We are born to misfortune, but a blessed death puts an end to all misfortunes. Wish for not a long life, as the sons of this age do, but wish for a blessed end.

(5) If safety, peace, rest, joy, gladness, and true, and perfect, and eternal blessedness are in eternal life, let us hurry there, Christian; let us hurry, despising all the vanity of this world. We shall have safety there. "Blessed is the man whom Thou hast chosen and taken unto Thyself; he shall dwell in Thy courts. We shall be satisfied with the pleasures of Thy house; Thy temple is holy.

Wonderful in truth; hear us, O God of our salvation, the hope of all the ends of the earth, and of them that be afar off at sea" (Ps 64:5–6). "How amiable are Thy dwellings, O Lord of Hosts! My soul desireth and longeth for the courts of the Lord" (and so on, to the end of Psalm 83).

# 150. A Painting Is Spoiled

If a picture by some artist were painted well, but some other, unskilled artist found and reworked the picture according to his own desire, everyone would laugh over this foolish undertaking, and the painter who had originally painted the picture would be not a little offended and chagrined. Those shameless women who daub their faces and decorate them with ceruse and coloring do something similar. Our God and Creator, as a wise painter, both gives the whole composition of the body and soul to each person and gives the rendering of the face to each one. But when people smear and decorate their own faces, they are redoing and spoiling the work of His holy hands, and as they are causing offense and chagrin to God Himself, their Creator, so also they are giving themselves over to reasonable people for mockery, or better, pity, and young hearts to temptation.

This is where the daubing and adornment of women's faces lead! God's work, supposedly not well created—which is terrible to think and say—is refashioned by such shameless ones. In young hearts, they inflame the flesh, already inflamed by passionate desire. This is done by those who confess Christ, the Son of God, Who was crucified and died for our sins!

Oh, the deception, oh, the cunning of the devil! Oh, how mighty the perfidy of the evil spirit! Such adornment of faces is a great weapon of the devil. There is nothing that he entices human hearts with more than with this net of his; there is nothing with which he fights Christians more than with this weapon of his. The flesh burns even without arson, and especially in a young man, but here the shameless ones also pour oil on the fire! Woe to them who add fire to fire! These shameless ones should be ashamed to come out in public!

Tell me, tell me, please, why do you go out among people wearing such a mask? To show yourself off? You really are showing yourself off, and you are showing what is hidden in your heart. And people see, but some are revolted by you, as by a freak; others turn their eyes upon you, and they conceive an affliction and give birth to lawlessness (see Ps 8:15). Such people do evil and do serious harm both to themselves and to neighbors when they go like this to dinners and other gatherings, but they do far greater harm to themselves, when with such ugliness they enter even into the holy churches, where the Word of God is preached, and God's holy name is glorified, and common prayer is offered to God by the faithful, and the holy and fearsome Mysteries are performed, and God Himself is especially present, they dare, I say, to enter the holy temples. If someone were to ask such a one, "Why have you come here into this holy and sacred place," if she answered, "To pray to God," one should say to her in chastisement, "Do you come for prayer with these beautifications? We approach God in prayer, we stand before God, we speak and ask mercy from Him: are such colorings and such attire needed here? Your speech, your attire, and your adornment show otherwise. You came to pray to God, but your adornment signifies otherwise. The proper adornment for prayer is sighing, tears, weeping, bending of knees, breast-beating, and not adornment of the body and face. If you sigh and weep, your attire will expose you, and will show your hypocrisy. You come in such attire to show off yourself, and not to pray."

Take stock of yourself why and into what place you are coming with such adornment, lest you come out with a very serious sin. "How awesome is this place! This is none other than the house of God" (Gen 28:17). Beware of having a heart that is filled with uncleanness in a holy and fearsome place and of scandalizing others in addition, and making God's temple a place of disgrace, lest you experience God's judgment on yourself. If you take stock of yourself, then you will later repent and regret that you adorned yourself with such colorings, and that you went out like this not only to the holy temples, but also to other places. I sincerely wish this for you.

"Do not let [women's] adornment be merely outward—arranging the hair, wearing gold, or putting on fine apparel—rather let it be the hidden person of the heart, with the incorruptible beauty of a gentle and quiet spirit, which is very precious in the sight of God. For in this manner, in former times, the holy women who trusted in God also adorned themselves, being submissive to their own husbands, as Sarah obeyed Abraham, calling him lord" (1 Pet 3:3–6), and so on. "In like manner also, that the women adorn themselves in modest apparel, with propriety and moderation, not with braided hair or gold or pearls or costly clothing, but, which is proper for women professing godliness, with good works" (1 Tim 2:9–10).

# 151. I Am Not Your Brother

We hear that one person says to another: "I am not your brother." It is amazing that a person says to another without shame: "I am not your brother." Examine, O man, in what kind of spirit you pronounce such words, "I am not your brother," and you yourself will see that the spirit of pride emits its evil smell in them. If you are not his brother, then whose are you? He is a human, but what should we call you? An angel or a demon? Tell me, please, tell me. For you yourself say to the person, "I am not your brother." I, you say, am tall, but he is short; I am rich, but he is poor; I am noble, but he is low-born; I am a master, but he is a servant; I am worthy, but he is unworthy; I am a good person, but he is evil, and so on. Look, O man, at Christ, the Son of God: who is higher than He, who is more noble than He, who is richer than He, who is more worthy than He, who is more glorious than He, who is better than He, who is wiser than He? No one can be compared with Him in any way, for He is the Eternal God, King of Kings and Lord of Lords, Who lives in unapproachable light. And while He is so great and glorious, He is not ashamed to call people *his brothers,* saying "I will declare Your name to My brethren," and again, "go to My brethren and say to them, 'I am ascending to My Father and your Father, and to My God and your God'" (Heb 2:13; Ps 21:23; John 20:17). And who are you, who says to a person, "I am not your brother," that you do not want to call someone who is like yourself your brother? Are you tall? But you are the same kind of person as a short one. Are you noble? But you are the same kind of person as one low-born. Are you a ruler? But you are the same kind of person as those subordinate to you. Are you a master? But you are the same kind of person as your servant. Are you rich? But you are the same kind of person as a poor one, and so on. But when you call yourself a good person, and another a bad one, it is unknown who is better: you or he whom you call evil. He is not good, who calls himself good, but he who does good and whom God, the Righteous Judge, praises. Take a look in the graves of the dead, and you will see that you are a brother to every person. *Ye*—princes, lords, the famous, noble, masters, the rich and all those who are exalted and revered like gods in the world—"shall die like men" (Ps 81:7).

And so, take stock of yourselves, beloved, and see that you are a man just like the others; see what your day of birth and of death show you; and putting aside pride, love Christ's humility. Then you will call every person, ever the basest, you brother. "Everyone who exalts himself will be humbled, and he who humbles himself will be exalted" (Luke 18:14).

# 152. The Path

Our life is as the path from village to village and from city to city, Christian! For our life is the path by which we constantly walk. Whether we sleep or are awake, we are always walking this path. We enter on that path when we are born; we finish it when we die. For one person, this road is very long—for another, very short—but its end is not known to anyone, for we do not know when we will finish it. This is how the Lord Who takes care of us has appointed, so that we would always await its end and prepare ourselves for it.

We see that one visible actual path is ample and wide, and another, strait and narrow. Likewise, one path of life is ample and wide, and another, strait and narrow. But we shall see which path of life is ample and which strait, and from this we shall learn to what end each leads.

On the wide road, there is unbelief; on the narrow road, a living faith.

On the wide road, there is flack of fear; on the narrow road, fear of God.

On the wide road, there are willfulness and disobedience; on the narrow path, submissiveness and obedience.

On the wide road, there is excessive self-love; on the narrow road, love of God and brotherly love.

On the wide road, there is love for the vanity of this world; on the narrow road, aversion to it.

On the wide road, there is seeking for honor, glory, and the riches of this world; on the narrow road, disdain for all of this.

On the wide road, there are luxury and sensuality; on the narrow road, moderation, fasting, and temperance.

On the wide road, there are pride and splendor; on the narrow road, humble-mindedness.

On the wide road, there is every sin and lawlessness; on the narrow road, every virtue.

On the wide road, there are licentiousness, adultery, and every impurity; on the narrow road, chastity and purity.

On the wide road, there are drunkenness and every wickedness springing from it; on the narrow road, sobriety and decency.

On the wide road, there are stealing, extortion, robbery, coercion, and every wrong; on the narrow road, withdrawal from all of this and doing righteousness.

On the wide road, there are anger, wrath, remembrance of wrongs, and vengeance in word and deed; on the narrow road, disdain for revenge, and meekness and patience.

On the wide road, there are hardheartedness, truculence, and savagery; on the narrow road, mercy and compassion.

On the wide road, there are slander, contempt, judgment, and reproach; on the narrow road, abstention from all these and prudent silence.

On the wide road, there are lying, craftiness, cunning, and hypocrisy; on the narrow road, simple-heartedness and speech consonant with sincere thought.

In a word, on the wide road, there are words, deeds, and thoughts contrary to God's will; on the narrow road, true repentance and its fruits, good works.

There, you see, Christian, the wide and narrow road of our lives. The wide road is opposed to God and therefore not pleasing to Him; the narrow road is in agreement with His holy will and therefore it is well pleasing to Him. The wide road leads a person to perdition, but the narrow road leads to life. Satan calls and attracts everyone onto the wide road, but Christ the Lord, who suffered and died for us, calls all from it and summons them to the narrow road.

Consider, O man, whom to obey: Christ or Satan, and by which road to go: the wide one or the narrow one, to perdition or to life. Christ the Lord wants to lead you into eternal life, being one who loves you and is your redeemer, but Satan, being your true adversary, wants to bring you into eternal perdition with himself. Hear the words of your Saviour, worthy of memory, and bury them in your heart, study them, and pay attention to them and yourself: "Enter by the narrow gate; for wide is the gate and broad is the way that leads to destruction, and there are many who go in by it. Because narrow is the gate and difficult is the way which leads to life, and there are few who find it" (Matt 7:13–14). His holy Apostle also instructs: "We must through many tribulations enter the kingdom of God" (Acts 14:22). "Guide me, O Lord, in Thy way, and I will walk in Thy truth; O let my heart rejoice to fear Thy Name" (Ps 85:11). The entire 118th Psalm instructs us how we should pray that the Lord Himself would guide us in His way, and keep us on it, and lead us along it.

# 153. The Belly

We see that the belly is insatiable. It requires food and cannot live without it. Today it is full, but tomorrow, and the next day and the next, it again requires food. So also with luxury. Luxury is like the belly, which devours everything, for luxury is capricious and can never be satisfied with anything.

But let us look at what luxury does, and from this we shall learn how harmful and pernicious it is.

(1) We see that luxury has designs on everything new and desires to re-fashion everything. It needs to change everything according to its own sophistic thinking. My house, he thinks, is not good, I need to rebuild it or build another. I do not like these clothes; I need to alter them or have new ones sewn. This food has become loathsome to me; I need to order the cook to cook such and such, and season it with this or that. I cannot drink ordinary vodka and ordinary wine; I must buy brandy and the best wine. It is unbecoming for my servants to serve me in such and such clothing; I must dress them better. It is shameful for me to go about in such and such a carriage and horses; I must obtain a better carriage and better horses. It is boring for me not to have music; I must try to have music in my house. Hunting with dogs provides no small gaiety; I shall try to have it, too. Card games drive away sad thoughts and boredom; what stops me from consoling myself with them, too? Pleasant ponds, gardens, and porticos provide no small gaiety; I will build both them and other things. Thus plans and reflects one who knows that Christ the Lord suffered for him and was crucified, and during His life had "nowhere to lay His head" (Matt 8:20), and for whom the narrow way to eternal life was shown by the same Lord.

Oh, poor Christian, who so aggrandize yourself! Take stock of yourself and you will see where your luxury will lead you. When will you, thinking such thoughts, be able to think about God, about Christ, crucified for your sins? When will you be able to think about your soul or of death? When will you be able to think about Christ's Judgment, before which you will stand and give an answer for everything? Or of a blessed or unfortunate eternity? What will you give to the poor and destitute, who beg in Christ's name, when you spend everything on luxury? I, you say, give to the poor. The answer to this: you give, but a kopeck or a half-kopeck apiece, and just to make a show of yourself, and not to make up for their shortage. But "everyone to whom much is given, from him much will be required" (Luke 12:48). In this way luxury turns away a person both from edifying thoughts and from giving alms and corrupts him.

(2) People learn to live luxuriously from each other, as we see. One has done so and so after his whims, he has built such and such chambers, has sewn such and such clothing, and so on. Another does the same thing, and then others do it. And so people follow each other, just like irrational cattle, who go wherever one of them goes, and do not consider whether what they are imitating others in is beneficial to them. They follow their feelings, but they do not consult with sound reason and the faithful counselor, God's Word, and so go astray. O man, do not do what people do, but what is consistent with sound reason and Sacred Scripture. You will indeed not go astray, if you hold on to this holy lamp and follow it.

(3) Luxury requires that a person live expansively. And for this, considerable sums are required. What does the lover of luxury intend? Where can he get it? There is none at hand. The lover of luxury must employ every kind of foul means. The lord must collect money from his subordinates; the landowner must impose excessive quit-rents on his peasants or force them to work for him more days a week; the merchant must sell a cheap thing for an expensive one, lie, and cheat customers; another, withhold a hired hand's pay; another, not give the salaries appointed by the Sovereign to his subordinates; another must turn to robbery, extortion, and every fraud. Luxury is the cause of this and every evil. From this, we see that many live in complete squalor and deficiency, many do not have houses, daily sustenance, and clothing. All of this results from luxury. Luxury teaches to offend and strip people bare. Some need much, and consequently others are left with nothing. Some deprive; others are deprived. Some are satiated; others hunger and thirst. Some are appareled in purple and fine linen; others go about half naked. Some expand and decorate their houses, and others do not even have a hut. Some go for drives in carriages and tandems; others have nothing with which to plow the earth and do other work, and so on. Such is the righteousness and love among present-day Christians, among those who always say: *I look for the resurrection of the dead, and the life of the age to come.*[18] Such ones look for the resurrection of the dead, and the life of the age to come, but live and behave as if there is no resurrection and eternal life.

(4) What is done in secret by lovers of luxury is shameful even to speak of. Where there is no fear of God, what can one expect, but all sorts of evil? The flesh runs wild with every person, but especially with the lover of luxury,

who has removed the bonds of moderation from it. But no matter how such people hide with their dark deeds, they hide from the all-seeing eye of God. He clearly sees both their thoughts and undertakings and their deeds, done in the darkness, and will proclaim them on the day of His Dread Judgment, as He says, "I will reprove thee, and set thy sins before thy face. Therefore consider this, ye that forget God, lest He pluck you away, and there be none to deliver" (Ps 49:21–22).

(5) Satan, the enemy of human souls, presents thoughts of whims and luxury, and entangles him in them: how good and pleasant it is to enjoy oneself, to do this and that, to comfort oneself this way or that, to go visiting and to receive guests, and so on. This is how the adversary plans that a person would consider this world as his homeland and a paradise of merrymaking, and forget about future blessedness, and so would perish; that he would also aspire to every unrighteousness and offense to poor people, which luxury teaches, and thus becoming entangled in all types of evil, would easily perish. Such is his cunning and design. Luxury is a powerful and effective rod with which he catches the souls of Christians and draws them after him into eternal perdition.

(6) We read in history that many cities and states perished from luxury, for luxury devours each and every good, like the belly or like an abyss, and makes even the most powerful people powerless and weak, and makes them unfit for struggle. The surrounding enemies experience joy when luxury increases in an opposing state. Woe to that country and state in which luxury increases! For along with luxury, every evil increases there, for which God's righteous anger hangs over it. From this, they have nothing else to expect, but ruin.

(7) You see, Christian, what luxury is and what it does. Shun luxury, lest you become corrupted and perish. "Others," they say, "do such and such, why shouldn't I do it?" What are you seeing, O man: "Others do such and such?" Others, acting lawlessly, are going to perdition. And you have to follow them? If you do what they do, then you will follow them to perdition. After all, you are a Christian; the lamp of God's Word enlightens you, and shows you what is good and what is evil, what is benefit and what is harm, what is virtue and what is vice, and to what end the narrow path leads, and to what the broad way leads. If you wish to be saved, you need to do not what people do, but what God's Word teaches.

In Sodom everyone broke the law, but the righteous Lot did not look at them, but lived in a holy and God-pleasing way. In the world, you should be like Lot in Sodom. Although everyone will be wallowing in luxury and iniquitous deeds, do not look at them, but do as God's Word teaches, and live as it is fitting for a true Christian. When you reflect upon a blessed or agonizing eternity, this reflection will disperse your thoughts about the whims and luxury as the breeze does the mist, and you will require nothing except what is necessary. Whims and luxury need many things; nature is satisfied by a little. "I beseech you therefore, brethren, by the mercies of God, that you present your bodies a living sacrifice, holy, acceptable to God, which is your reasonable service. And do not be conformed to this world, but be transformed by the renewing of your mind, that you may prove what is that good and acceptable and perfect will of God" (Rom 12:1–2).

# 154. A Man Falls into a Pit
## That He Himself Has Dug

It happens that a man digs a pit for a certain need of his but himself accidentally falls into that pit. Likewise, the evil that they have prepared for their neighbors often befalls deceitful people and malefactors. Often they themselves drink the poison that they prepare for their neighbors and die. Often they stab and kill themselves with the sword that they raise against their neighbor. Often they fall into a great defamation, when they plan to slander and denigrate their neighbors. Often they are deprived of their own land and other property when they desire and try to take possession of someone else's.

We see much of this in the world. This is how God's just and wondrous judgment befalls wrongdoers. This is how God's judgment befell the tyrant pharaoh, who pursued Israel, which had been freed from his slavery, and wanted to subjugate, enslave, and embitter it again, but instead found his own destruction, and where he expected gain, he saw his death, and was buried with his whole army in the water of the sea, as in a grave (see Ex 14:28). Absalom, the son of David, wanted to seize the kingdom of Israel, and plotted and sought to kill his holy and innocent father, but instead of this he was hanged on a tree and perished between heaven and earth, and so fell into the ditch that he had dug for his righteous father (see 2 Kg 18:9, 14). Haman experienced a similar judgment on himself, for he was hanged by the king's command on the same gallows that he had prepared for the innocent Mordecai (see Esth 7:9,

10). Thus God's judgment overtakes the proud and willful, and they unexpectedly fall into a ditch that they have dug for others. Such fates befall the lawless even now.

Hear, perfidious people and malefactors! People fall into the pit that they have dug out for their neighbors, they themselves drink the poison that they have prepared for others, and they suffer from that evil into which they wish to plunge others. Fear greatly and shun doing evil to your neighbors, lest you yourself first fall into that evil. "Behold, he hath travailed with unrighteousness, he hath conceived sorrow, and brought forth iniquity. He hath graven a pit, and digged it up, and is fallen himself into the hole he made, For his travail shall come upon his own head, and his unrighteousness shall fall on his own pate" (Ps 7:15–17).

# 155. Being Pleasing

We see that people try to be pleasing to other people. Subjects try to please their kings, subordinates try to please their superiors, servants their masters, children their parents, and others try to please other people. Likewise, Christian, we must try to please God.

He requires this of us:

(1) Our faith and confession. For faith must not be empty and vain, but fruitful, accompanied by love and good works, as the Apostle requires of us: "Show me your faith without your works" (Jas 2:18).

(2) Our promise that we gave to God at holy baptism requires this of us. For then, after having broken away from Satan, we promised to serve Him and do His bidding.

(3) Our very conscience requires this. For we are persuaded to do God's bidding by our very conscience and to honor Him with the highest reverence, which is impossible without doing His bidding.

(4) The essential need and matter of our salvation requires this of us. For it is necessary to continuously please Him of Whom we ask temporal and eternal salvation and from Whom we desire to receive every good thing of soul and body. For who does not try to please one of whom he asks and seeks mercy and every good thing? His natural reason itself convinces him of this. And so, Christians, do we too, wish to receive mercy from God? Then we must please Him. People try to please their kings. God is our king, and an eternal

King, the King of Kings, and a King Who is fearsome throughout all the earth. And so, we must try to please Him, as our Eternal God. People try to please the authorities and their superiors. God is our Supreme Ruler and Author, Whose power and command is eternal. And so, we must try to please Him, as our Eternal Ruler and Author.

People try to please their masters. God is our most high Lord, the Lord of Lords. And so, it is necessary to try to please Him as our most high Lord. People try to please their benefactors. God is our most high benefactor, from Whom we have received and are receiving innumerable benefactions, and there is no and cannot be a greater benefactor than He, for we are His creation, and all that we have is from Him. And so it is necessary to please Him as our most high benefactor.

People try to please their fathers. God is our Father; He begot us by His Holy Word and by the bath of spiritual baptism. And so it is necessary to please Him as our Merciful Father. We must try to be pleasing to Him Whose bidding all the holy angels do with fear, love, and joy; to Him Whom all creation serves and does His bidding; to Him before Whom all tremble; to Him Whom it is fearsome to resist or to displease; Him, Who is able to destroy both soul and body in hell (Matt 10:28); Him, Who has in His hand the life and death of all; Him, finally, from whom "we look for resurrection and life of the age to come." And we must try to please Him sincerely, wholeheartedly, and unhypocritically; that is, this action must proceed from faith and heart-felt hope. For He, as the Knower of Hearts, tests the depth of our heart and sees how we try to please Him: sincerely or hypocritically. Whom should we try to please, Christian, if not our God?

But let us see who pleases God and who does not, and how we must try to please Him.

(1) He who pleases God does His holy will. He who does not please God does not do His holy will. He who pleases God lives and acts humbly. He who does not please God has a high opinion of himself and is proud, and lives in pride and opulence. "God resists the proud, But gives grace to the humble" (1 Pet 5:5). He who pleases God places all his hope in Him, hope both of temporal and eternal salvation. He who does not please God places his hope on himself, on his honor, on princes and high-ranking people and other creations. He who pleases God calls on Him and prays to Him from a pure heart and asks help and protection in his needs and afflictions. He who does not please God abandons prayer and in his need resorts to feeble creation, and says either to

a person or to gold and silver: "You are my hope," which is proper and fitting to say to God alone.

He who pleases God sincerely thanks Him for all good things, praises Him, and sings, "I will praise the Name of my God with a song; and I will magnify Him with praise. And this shall please the Lord, better than a bullock that hath horns and hooves" (Ps 68:31–32). He who does not please God abandons this duty, and so is ungrateful to God. He who pleases God remembers His holy name with respect and reverence. He who does not please God does not render proper honor to His name, but, without any need, without fear or respect, and in all circumstances engages in unseemly swearing and mention of the fearsome and holy name of God, as has somehow entered into custom: "By God! I swear to God! With God is my witness!" and so on. He transgresses who takes the fearful name of God in jest or in a lie.

He who pleases God gives proper respect to his parents, authorities, and others in a place of honor. He who does not please God does not give them proper respect. He who pleases God maintains not only his own life, but that of his neighbor; he who does not please God neglects this. He who pleases God lives in honorable and chaste wedlock or, if unmarried, lives a pure and chaste life. He who does not please God does not preserve purity, but either commits adultery, as do those in the married state, or commits fornication, as do those living outside of legal marriage. "Marriage is honorable among all, and the bed undefiled; but fornicators and adulterers God will judge" (Heb 13:4).

He who pleases God shuns larceny, theft, and every fraud. He who does not please God reaches out his hand for these wicked deeds. He who pleases God restrains his tongue from slander, judgment, backbiting, idle talking, and all unsuitable and foul language. He who does not please God has an unbridled tongue. He who pleases God acts toward his neighbor and treats him sincerely, simple-heartedly, and unhypocritically. He who does not please God behaves falsely, flatteringly, craftily, or cunningly. He who pleases God does not desire anything of another's against the will of the owner. He who does not please God wishes to steal or take another's possessions.

In a word, he who pleases God amends himself and lives according to the rule of His holy Word; he who does not please God neglects this. "Nevertheless the solid foundation of God stands, having this seal: 'The Lord knows those who are His,' and, "Let everyone who names the name of Christ depart from iniquity" (2 Tim 2:19).

(2) We should please God, Christian, more than our kings, more than our authorities, more than our masters, more than our parents, and more than anyone to whom we are subordinate. For we must fear, and love, and honor Him more than any creation on heaven or on earth. For He is our most supreme Lord and is the King of kings and Lord of lords. Therefore, subjects should obey and please their kings, and subordinates their authorities, and servants their masters, and children their parents for the Lord's sake, as the Apostle says, "Therefore submit yourselves to every ordinance of man for the Lord's sake, whether to the king as supreme, or to governors, as to those who are sent by him" (1 Pet 2:13–14), and so forth.

(3) If, as it happens, the authorities direct or command something that is contrary to God's will, we must not obey them in this, even if they threaten us with death. Human authorities should be honored by us, but incomparably more honored should be God, Whom even the authorities themselves should obey with fear. The holy apostles, whom the iniquitous Jews forbade to teach and speak in the Christ's name, teach us this by their example; they did not obey them, and with boldness taught and spoke God's Word, and answered to those who forbade them, "We ought to obey God rather than men" (Acts 5:29).

(4) If we desire to please God, then we should not despise our neighbor and turn away from him but should have mercy on him and provide for him in his needs. "Let each of us please his neighbor for his good, leading to edification" (Rom 15:2).

If our neighbor asks us for advice, let us give advice when we can.

If he asks us for food, let us give food.

If he asks for clothing, let us clothe him.

If he asks shelter in our house, let us give him shelter.

If he asks a favor of us, let us do him the favor.

If he asks consolation in grief and sorrow, let us console him as we are able, and so on. For the will of God wishes this and Christian love requires it. "But do not forget to do good and to share, for with such sacrifices God is well pleased" (Heb 13:16).

(5) From this it follows that, if we want to please God, we must both love our enemies and do good to them, for God's will desires this (Matt 5:44). If we wish to do God's will, and so to please God, we must not deprive our enemies of our love and help them in their needs. This more than anything else reveals a Christian and a God-pleasing person. If you want to please an earthly king

and so receive mercy from him, then do not refuse to serve even your enemy when the king wishes this and commands you. You should especially do this for the Heavenly King, for Whose sake you should please the earthly king, and love your enemies, and serve them in their needs. For true Christian love consists in this, that is, to master oneself and render good for evil. "Therefore 'If your enemy is hungry, feed him; If he is thirsty, give him a drink; For in so doing you will heap coals of fire on his head.' Do not be overcome by evil, but overcome evil with good" (Rom 12:20–21).

(6) For all this to be pleasing to God, we must fulfill it all, that is, to avoid evil and do good, and not for vainglory and human praise, but for the glory of His holy name. Christ the Lord taught us this: "Let your light so shine before men, that they may see your good works and glorify your Father in heaven" (Matt 5:16). Otherwise, how can what is not done for God be pleasing to Him? From this, it follows that not every visible good work is truly good, but that which is done decently, that is, for the sake of the good, which is the glory of God's name.

Christian! God created the world for our sake, and does everything for our sake, and sent His Son into the world for our sake; handed Him over to death for our sake; thus redeemed us from sins, the devil, death, and hell; and has prepared an eternal kingdom: what more can God now do for our sake? Let us do everything for His sake, and let us love Him, honor Him, serve Him, and keep His commandments for His sake alone, and so we shall please Him from a pure heart.

(7) Temptation from the devil, as well as from evil people, follows after God-pleasing deeds and a holy intention. This happens through God's toleration for a person's testing: whether he is doing what he began for God's sake and whether he will continue steadfastly in the work he began. Therefore, everything that happens offensive to him must be accepted and be endured, as sent from the Lord's hand, and he should not slacken in what has been begun but carry on with it. "Wait thou on the Lord; be of good courage, and let thine heart stand firm, and wait thou on the Lord," the Prophet exhorts (Ps 26:14).

(8) We cannot please God without God Himself, Christian, for our blindness, and weakness, and corruption is great. Therefore we must pray to God with zeal and sigh to Him that He would set us on the path pleasing to Him, and would keep us on it, and lead us along it. We are taught this by the example of the holy David, who throughout the entire Psalm 118 prayed to God with

all zeal and desired a holy and God-pleasing life. Let us follow him in this. "Teach me to do Thy will, for Thou art my God" (Ps 142:10).

O Lord, grant me to desire, undertake, think, do, and speak what is pleasing to Your holy will. Do not permit me, O Lord, either to desire, or undertake, or think, or do, or speak what is not pleasing to Your will. "Guide me, O Lord, in Thy way, and I will walk in Thy truth; O let my heart rejoice to fear Thy Name" (Ps 85:11).

When subjects go before their king, subordinates before their superior, servants before their master, children before their father, and address them, they do so with all fear and apprehension, lest they make a false step in anything, and so offend and anger them, and therefore they avoid any improper words and actions, and this is how they please them.

Christian! Let us imitate such people who thus try to be pleasing to people, and let us behave thus before God and our Eternal King, and our Father, Who is in heaven, and let us avoid everything that is offensive and disagreeable to Him and so be pleasing to Him. For wherever and whenever we may be, we are in God's presence, and whatever we do, say, think, and undertake, we do, say, conceive, and undertake everything before Him. For God is present in every place, sees every deed of ours, and hears every word of ours.

Therefore, if we are at home, we are in his presence.

If we do any deed, we do it in his presence.

If we say anything, we say it in his presence.

If we conceive and start anything, we conceive and start it in his presence.

If we are with people and talking with them, we are talking in his presence.

If we eat or drink, we eat and drink in his presence.

If we buy or sell, we buy or sell in his presence.

If we love something, or hate it, if we desire something or are repelled by it, all this happens in his presence.

If we are lying in bed and resting, we are resting in his presence.

If we are walking in the way, He is with us, and we walk in his presence.

If we are in the desert or in solitude, or in a city or a village, in a hidden or open place, He is present with us, and we are in his presence.

In a word, wherever and whenever we may be, He is with us and we are in His presence, and whatever we do, think and say, everything is clear and open for Him (see Jer 23:24; Job 34:21; Sir 23:27–29; Heb 4:13). Let us behave before Him as subjects behave before their king and all subordinates before their authority figures, and so let us render fitting honor to Him, as our God, our King, our Master, and our Father, and in this way being pleasing to Him. Let us not become like those Christians who behave decorously before people and show themselves to be pious, but who in secret places transgress and do such things that are shameful even to speak of. Such Christians are hypocrites, impious, and godless. They are ashamed before people but not before God; they are afraid of people but not of God. God's prophet wrote of such people, "which have not set God before them" (Ps 53:5).

Oh man, where can you hide with your dark deeds from Him Who is everywhere present and sees all things? You avoid people, but God precedes you, and you cannot escape anywhere from Him (see Amos 9:2–4). You hide from people's eyes, but there is nowhere and no way you can hide from God's all-seeing eye. You take care that people not hear your foul and rotten words, but God hears them. You hide in the secret place of your heart flattery, cunning, slyness, and falsehood, and you take care that people do not learn of this evil of yours, but God, "Who [tries] the very hearts and reins," sees all of this clearly (Ps 7:10; 1 Chr 28:9).

But you say, "I do not see God." That is true, and it is impossible for anyone to see Him. "No one has seen God at any time" (John 1:18). God is a spirit, not subject to any of the senses, and therefore it is impossible to see him, but He is perceived only by faith and the intellect. The holy faith and God's Word teach us that God is everywhere, and sees everything of ours; and every deed, word, and thought are open to Him, as this is depicted especially in Psalm 138: *O Lord, Thou hast examined me,* and so on. If you believe the Word of God, then believe that God is in every place, and you walk and act before Him, although you do not see him, and He sees every one of your deeds, and you cannot hide anywhere and in any way from Him. The Word of God teaches all of this. If you do not believe the Word of God, why do you call yourself a Christian? "See then that you walk circumspectly, not as fools but as wise" (Eph 5:15).

We note also that when people wish to please their kings, authorities, and fathers, they do what they do, and so, in imitating their ways, please them.

Christian! Let us also imitate God our Heavenly King and Father; let us follow after His divine ways; and let us do what He does and so be pleasing to Him. He loves everyone, which is apparent from all His creations, and from His holy Word, and from the incarnation of His only-begotten Son. Let us also endeavor to love Him with our whole heart, Him, Who has loved us, and to love each other. "[L]ove is the fulfillment of the law" (Rom 13:10). He is Holy; let us too be holy, perfecting holiness in the fear of God. He is righteous; let us too be righteous, rendering to Him every honor and glory, and to our neighbors what is due them. He is gracious and merciful and feels pity for our affliction; let us also be merciful, as our Heavenly Father is merciful. He does good to all, good and evil, "He makes His sun rise on the evil and on the good, and sends rain on the just and on the unjust" (Matt 5:45), that we too may do good to all, to our kinsmen and non-kinsmen, to our friends and our enemies, to acquaintances and strangers.

He is long-suffering toward all and desires everyone to repent; let us be long-suffering, and let us not render evil for evil, and scorning for scorning. He is true and faithful in His words; let us be true and simple-hearted. He hates every sin and transgression; let us too hate sin and transgression, and turn away from them. He desires all men to be saved and to come to the knowledge of the truth (1 Tim 2:4); may we desire the same. He remits the sins of all who repent; let us sinners also remit sinners their sins; let us forgive, and He will forgive us our sins. He hears all who pray and fulfills their petitions; let us not turn away our ears from those who ask of us, and let us fulfill their petitions.

Thus let us become like Him; thus let us imitate Him; thus let us follow after His most holy ways; thus we shall be children of light; and ardent and true members of Christ, the Son of God, thus we shall show that we do not unjustly call Him Father: *Our Father, Who art in the heavens*, and so on. And this is how we shall be pleasing to Him. For His holy will, and His holy Word, and our promise given at baptism, and our Christian duty demand this. "Be imitators of God as dear children" (Eph 5:1).

We see that when subjects wish to please their kings, subordinates their superiors, servants their masters, and children their fathers, then they see and do what is desired by them, and not themselves, and so please them. Christians! Let us do likewise. Let us do not what we desire, but what God desires, and so please Him. God's Word shows us what is pleasing to God and what is not. May this sacred lamp shine for us in all our deeds, words, and endeavors, for this it is given to us by our Merciful Heavenly Father. "Thy Law is a lamp unto my feet, and a light unto my paths" (Ps 118:105).

It is pleasing to us to live in idleness and sloth, but for God it is not; let us do what is pleasing to God, and shake off the sleep of sloth and idleness, and let us dwell in useful and blessed labors. "In the sweat of your face you shall eat bread" (Gen 3:19). It is pleasing for us to live in the pride and splendor of this world, but that is not pleasing to God. What is pleasing to Him is our humbleness of mind. Let us love God-pleasing humility, and "let us live in humility" (1 Pet 5:5–6). It is pleasing to us to go by the broad path, the path of whims, luxury, and merrymaking, but to God that is not pleasing; let us avoid the broad and wide path, and let us enter by the narrow way, for it is pleasing to Him: "Enter by the narrow gate; for wide is the gate and broad is the way that leads to destruction, and there are many who go in by it. Because narrow is the gate and difficult is the way which leads to life, and there are few who find it" (Matt 7:13–14).

It is pleasing to us to become angry, and to render offense for offense, and evil for evil, and scorning for scorning, but that is not pleasing to God; let us do what is pleasing to God and forgive those who offend us, forgive from our hearts. "Beloved, do not avenge yourselves, but rather give place to wrath; for it is written, 'Vengeance is Mine, I will repay,' says the Lord" (Rom 12:19). It is not pleasing to us to love our enemies, to bless those who curse us, and to do good to those who hate us, but this is pleasing to God; let us do what is pleasing to God, and let us try to love not only our friends but also our enemies, and do good to those that hate us, and so on. "Love your enemies, bless those who curse you, do good to those who hate you, and pray for those who spitefully use you and persecute you" (Matt 5:44).

It is pleasing to us to indulge in lust, but this is offensive to God, and what is pleasing to Him is our chastity and holiness; let us do what is pleasing to God and "live in chastity and holiness" (Titus 2:12). It is pleasing to us to speak idly, slander, judge, and to speak other unsuitable and foul words with our tongue, but it is unpleasing to God; let us restrain our tongue and love prudent silence, and may whatever word that we may say be seasoned with the salt of reason and for the edification of our neighbor; for this is pleasing in God's eyes (see Eph 4:29).

Likewise in other things let us act and do not what is pleasing to our will and flesh, but what God's will desires, and so we shall please God. Let us descend with fear and zeal from that throne on which we sit, and let us relinquish it to our God, and honor Him, and worship Him, and always and in all words, deeds, and endeavors say to Him with humility and fear: "Father, Thy will be done, and not mine! Thy desire be done and not mine! I too wish what You wish; I do not wish what You do not wish. O Lord, help me, Amen."

# 156. A Swindler

We hear that those people who in some way, that is, either openly, or underhandedly, or by flattery steal what belongs to others are called by the dishonorable name of swindlers or thieves. This lawless activity is contrary to God's commandment: *do not steal*. Likewise, even more so those people who in some way steal and appropriate the glory, praise, and so on, due to God alone are swindlers and thieves. Among these are the following:

(1) Those who preach the Word of God for the sake of praise and glory. For God's Word is given to us for our salvation and the glory of God's name; it is for its sake that it should be preached. But when people preach it for the sake of their own praise and glory, then they steal the glory that is due to God alone. As a result, it happens that such preachers yield little benefit to people, although people even praise them, for they do not preach for the purpose for which the Word of God was given. This is why it is ineffectual in the hearts of listeners.

(2) Those rich men who spend their wealth on the building of palatial houses, on splendid clothing, on superb horses and carriages, on sumptuous meals, on expensive attire for servants, and other forms of opulence and vanity in order to have praise and glory from the world. Our wealth and our property are God's possessions and are given to us because of our poverty and need, and not for our praise and glory; they are given so that we ourselves would use them in moderation and would help our neighbors for the sake of the honor and glory of God's name. But if we do not do this, seeking instead to use it for our own praise and glory, then we are stealing the glory due to God alone. For everything belongs to God. "The earth is the Lord's, and the fullness thereof" (Ps 23:61). May each and every thing that belongs to God be for the glory of God and not ours. It will be enough for us to use what belongs to God and to thank God and glorify His holy name and not to seek our own praise and glory from it.

(3) Those people who give alms and do other good works in order to show themselves off; also those who build churches and adorn them, or found poorhouses so that people may celebrate and praise them. All such people are seeking their own, and not God's glory, and that is why they are stealing what is due to God.

(4) Those who show off either their mind and wisdom or eloquence so that people would glorify and praise them also belong to these. All such people, and those mentioned earlier, and others who do some kind of good but want to be glorified because of it are stealing God's glory. God is the beginning and source of every good; therefore glory and praise are due to Him alone for every good. Being poor and destitute and receiving good things from God for free, without any merits of his own, it is enough for a person that he makes use of God's good things for free, but he must ascribe and render glory and thanksgiving to God alone, his benefactor.

But when he seeks glory and praise for himself for God's good thing, he is stealing what is God's, and he departs from God in his heart, and what is terrible even to say, deifies himself, and in the place where he should have God, he places himself, and that honor that he should render to God, he draws to himself, which is a most loathsome Creator. Take care, O man, and think about where love of glory and pride are leading you!

(5) Whatever a person does and hides in his heart in the present age will be revealed at Christ's Judgment, and the whole world will learn of it; and everything whatsoever a person does, he as it were gives a loan to God, and it will be repaid then. If he glorifies God here, while living in the world, he will be glorified by God there. If he disdains and despises God, he will be disdained and despised there. Therefore the Lord says: "I will honor those who honor Me, and the one who despises Me shall be dishonored" (1 Kg 2:30).

(6) Bear in mind, therefore, Christian, what you are doing and for whom you are doing it: are you doing God's bidding or your own, are you seeking God's honor or your own in your action? When you do the bidding of your own will, and not God's, then you prefer your will to God's, which is grievous and terrible. When in your action, you seek your own, and not God's honor, you are abandoning God, and honoring and deifying yourself as a god, as you yourself can see, which is also terrible and wicked. God, Who tries hearts and reins, sees your heart too, and sees to what end you are doing things. So beware that instead of one who honors God, you may be an enemy of God. Self-love,

self-will, and love of fame lead a person into such ruin, although he, like a blind man, does not even see it. For self-love and love of fame blind a man.

And so, take stock of yourself, beloved, and throw the foul idol of pride out of your heart, and step down from that throne on which you sit and do homage to yourself, and yield place there to the Lord of Hosts, Whom angels worship with fear and all creation serves, and render to Him His glory, His praise, and His honor, and worship Him "in spirit and truth" (John 4:23), and honor Him as your God and Creator. To Him alone is due all glory, honor, and worship. "Glorify God in your body and in your spirit, which are God's" (1 Cor 6:20). "Fear God and give glory to Him" (Rev 14:7). "Do all to the glory of God" (1 Cor 10:31).

# 157. One Event Brings a Similar One to Mind

We see that one event reminds a person of a similar one: when he sees or hears something, something similar comes to mind. For example, when an educated man sees a pupil walking to school, he remembers how he himself walked to school; a farmer, upon seeing another farmer tilling the soil, remembers his own farming, and so on.

Christian! You too should be reminded by an event of a similar one that relates to the edification of your soul. You see how humbly, meekly, and prudently children come and behave before their father, or servants their master, or subordinates their superiors: remember that we come, live, and behave, think, speak, and work before the omnipresent God, Who looks upon all things. If persons appear before other persons with fear and decorum, and take care lest they anger them and incur punishment, even more should we appear before, live, and behave before our God with fear and reverence, and do nothing that is contrary to His holy will. For everywhere we are, we are in the presence of God, Who is Omnipresent. For God is everywhere, and in every place, as is witnessed in Psalm 138 and other places of the Holy Scripture, although we do not see Him at all (for it is impossible to see Him), and we do not understand how he is in every place.

Guard against sinning before God, lest you experience His avenging hand upon yourself. You are ashamed before a man, so much the more should you be ashamed before God. You try to please a man, so much the more should you try to please God. You fear man, so much the more should you fear God, before Whom all creation fears and trembles. "For our God is a consuming fire"—consuming the impious (Heb 12:29; Deut 4:24).

So take care, lest you be struck down in your wickedness. Render to Him everywhere and in every place, day and night, in an open or hidden place, in solitude or in gatherings of people, at home or on the road, and in every action render Him the fitting honor, glory, and obedience. This is required of you by your conscience, and the Word of God, and the Christian faith. If God is in every place, as is indeed the case, and sees all our actions and thoughts and hears our words, it follows that:

(1) It is impossible to hide or conceal ourselves from Him anywhere or in any place, inasmuch as wherever we may go and wherever we may think of hiding, He is there before us. O man! You flee from people, but from God you cannot flee anywhere. He precedes you everywhere. You hide from human eyes, but you cannot hide from God's: He sees you everywhere. You take care that people not hear your foul speech, but you cannot guard against God's ears: He is everywhere and hears every word of yours. You are ashamed to do evil before people, but God alone sees your evil better than the whole world: so be ashamed and fear to do any evil before Him anywhere. Everything you do now, while living in the world, secretly or openly, He will show you at that universal Judgment, and will set them before you, as He says, "I will reprove thee, and set thy sins before thy face" (Ps 49:21).

(2) From this, you see, Christian, how grievously those Christians vex God who transgress and do not fear to violate the law of God in His sight. If some wicked man dared to jump, dance, scream, and carry out other outrages in the presence of a royal personage, would this not be a great dishonor, scorning, and insult to the royal personage? You yourself see that such a ruffian shows the king great disrespect. Those people who act wickedly before the omnipresent and all-seeing God, and so behave outrageously before Him, commit a similar or an even incomparably greater outrage and show disrespect and scorning toward God. Among these are fornicators, adulterers, and every defiler; those who swear at each other, reproach each other, quarrel with each other, and fight with each other; slanderers and backbiters, who wound their neighbors with their tongues as with a sword; sly people and tricksters, tempters, cheaters, and hypocrites, who deal flatteringly and cunningly with their neighbors; sorcerers and those who summon them; those who sing filthy

and indecent songs, and those who raise up cries and howling; those who feast in a scandalous and reprehensible way; dancing ruffians and hussies; those who engage in fist-fights and those who watch them; thieves, swindlers, robbers, thugs, and all who steal someone else's property surreptitiously, or by flattery, or openly; merchants who cheat in dealings and ask a price higher than the item is worth, and especially those wrongdoers who do not fear to call on the name of God in a lie, and—O Your long-suffering, Lord!—affirm their lie with it as if it were the truth. Among these are judges and bureaucrats, who do their business according to their passion and for recompense, and not according to justice and the force of their oath; those who falsely swear by God's name; all users of foul language and blasphemers; in a word, everyone who is not ashamed and afraid to break the law. For every iniquity is done before God, whether it is done surreptitiously or openly.

(3) From this you see how grievously such Christians sin before God. They often hear the Word of God; they also hear that God is everywhere and in every place, but do not pay attention to this and disregard it, and do not correct themselves.

(4) You see again how great is God's goodness and long-suffering. People transgress before Him and dishonor and vex Him, but He does not punish them immediately but is patient and awaits their repentance. What meek king, seeing an outrage committed before him, will endure it? Soon human meekness turns into fury. Our God is not like that: He sees wrongdoing committed by a person before His Face; he sees, and is patient, not wishing the wrongdoers to perish, but he wants "that all should come to repentance" (2 Pet 3:9). You see God's grace; you also see His long-suffering.

(5) But hear, poor sinner, what the Apostle says to you: "Or do you despise the riches of His goodness, forbearance, and longsuffering, not knowing that the goodness of God leads you to repentance? But in accordance with your hardness and your impenitent heart you are treasuring up for yourself wrath in the day of wrath and revelation of the righteous judgment of God, who 'will render to each one according to his deeds'" (Rom 2:2–6).

Do you see a subject standing before a king, or a servant standing before his master, and talking with him and asking mercy of him? You see how he stands before him: he stands with humility and reverence, bows his head and bends his knees, looks at him with emotion, and asks with attention for what he wants to receive. Remember here that this is how true Christians stand before God in prayer: they stand with humility, reverence, and attention; bow their heads and bend their knees before him; look upon Him with faith; prostrate themselves before Him; declare their needs and what they are asking for; ask mercy and help from Him; confess their sins to Him;, and ask for absolution.

From this you see the following:

(1) True prayer consists not in outward words and speech alone; true prayer is "in spirit and truth" (John 4:23). When we pray to God, we must stand before Him not only in the body, but in the spirit as well, and say the prayer not only with the lips, but with both the mind and the heart, and bow not only our head and knees, but also our heart before Him, and lift up our mind's eyes to Him with humility. Every prayer must come from the heart, and whatever the tongue says, the mind and heart must be saying. Therefore, we should not learn anything as much as true prayer. God looks into the heart (1 Kg 16:7), and not at our words, and heeds the heart's sighing and not the lips' speaking. "Lord, teach us to pray" (Luke 11:1).

(2) Such prayer—that is, that done in spirit and truth—can be done in every place.

For you can freely stand before God and worship and pray in the spirit everywhere and in every place, at home or away from home; in a public or hidden place; among people or alone; walking, sitting, and lying; and on the road and at the market; and always and in every place. For the spirit is always free and may approach God everywhere and always, and speak with Him, and worship Him. And access is free to God always and at all times, as He is omnipresent, looks upon all of us, and cares for all of us, and He is ready to hear everyone everywhere and always. We cannot always approach a person with our petition, but to God, the doors are always open. And even if all the people scattered over the face of the entire earth approached and prayed to Him in spirit and truth, He would hear them all. "Hear us, O God of our salvation, the hope of all the ends of the earth, and of them that be afar off at sea" (Ps 64:6).

(3) Prayer should be with humility and reverence. Christian! Remember who you are and before Whom you stand in your prayer. Earth and ashes (Sir 10:9; 13:31), and moreover, a sinner, you stand before the holy, great, and incomprehensible God! Remember with Whom you speak in prayer, to Whom you say, *Lord, have mercy! Grant it, O Lord! To Thee, O Lord!* and so on. We speak humbly and reverently with a human king, or master, or some other authority; incomparably more humility and reverence are needed when we stand before God and speak with Him, for God incomparably surpasses every person, and His majesty is incomprehensible.

(4) What a great thing and honor for man it is to stand before God and speak with Him! It is excellent to speak with a human king: even more so is it with God, the Heavenly King, Who is the King of Kings and Lord of Lords. There is no greater honor for a person than to speak with God. Glory to You, O Lord, that You favored us, poor sinners, with this honor. Blessed be the name of the Lord forever!

(5) Prayers, canons, and church verses, read speedily and without reflection and attention, are nothing else than just noise, as you yourself see, Christian, and further, they vex God, rather than propitiate Him, when read like that. Such people, although they often think that they are praying, are never praying. It is better in God's sight to say from the heart and with humility and reverence two or three words than to read many prayers and canons speedily and without reflection. God heeds what is inside, and not outside, and hears cries from the heart and not the lips. Moses said nothing with his lips, but prayed to God only with his heart, when he led Israel to the Red Sea, but God said to him, "Why do you cry to Me" (Exod 14:15)? Also Hannah, the mother of Samuel, said nothing with her lips but only sighed and cried to the Lord with her heart alone; her prayer, though, was heard, and she received the hoped-for fruit of her prayer (1 Kg 1:13 and 20). Thus, God hears our heart, and not our lips.

Christian, learn to pray to God in spirit and truth, and so to worship Him, and call upon Him, and honor Him. God is in every place and is always ready to hear us; you can always and everywhere pray to Him and worship Him in spirit and truth.

(6) From this, you see that prayer can be said silently, without audible words, but done by the mind and heart, and be efficacious. But external prayer consisting only of words is not true prayer, but only a voice without understanding. This happens when a person reads a prayer but is thinking about something else. Therefore we must unfailingly pay heed to the words of the prayer being read, and to fasten our mind and reasoning to it, and to think that we are standing in prayer before God and are speaking to Him, and we are praying, and asking mercy of Him, and this is how to learn true prayer.

For prayer, inasmuch as it is a great good and the source of all blessings, requires much labor and training. And the devil tries to hinder nothing as much as our prayer, knowing that through it we receive all blessings from God. Therefore we must with all diligence take care that our prayer proceeds from the heart and that the mind and reasoning be bound to the words of the prayer being read.

Christian, when beginning to pray, remember that you want to come before God, stand in prayer, speak to Him, and ask mercy of Him just as a servant stands before his master, or a subject before the king, and bows to Him and asks mercy from him. Believe and think that God is near you and before you, and thus true, heart-felt, and reverent prayer will be enkindled. Then you will fall down before Him with humility, and pay homage, and sigh, and pray, and say: "O Lord! Have mercy! O Lord, have compassion! O Lord, hear me!" Then both your heart and your mind will be in harmony with the words of your prayer. "The Lord is nigh unto all them that call upon Him, to all such as call upon Him in truth" (Ps 144:18).

If you hear pleasant singing either in church or in another place, remember then that the angels in heaven hymn our Creator and God in such a way (see Isa 6:3). Imitate the holy angels and hymn your Creator and God while on earth, that some day you will be vouchsafed to hymn Him with them in heaven. Join yourself with those holy singers, and link your hymn with their hymn. Ensure that your singing may be pleasing to God, follow the heavenly orders in their purity and life and, singing with your lips, sing also with your heart. Music is sweet when the voices are good and in harmony with each other. Likewise, a hymn is pleasing to God when the singer lives a holy life and has good morals, and with oral singing harmonizes that of the heart, and the heart sings with the lips.

It is the angels' task to hymn God. For the angels do nothing other in heaven than continuously hymn God. And we, when we hymn God, imitate the angels and do their work. You yourself can see how very glorious this is. It is most glorious to live on earth, and follow the inhabitants of heaven, and to combine your own singing and voice with their most sweet singing and voice, and to hymn the Holy and Life-giving Trinity. But so that our singing be in harmony with their singing, let us also follow their holy life, and we will abide in love, harmony, and peace among ourselves, as they abide; then our singing too will be in harmony with their singing. Otherwise, the singing will not be beautiful on the lips of a sinner. "I will praise the Name of my God with a song; and I will magnify Him with praise. And this shall please the Lord, better than a bullock that hath horns and hoofs" (Ps 68:31–32).

If you see a sumptuous table, and people eating and drinking at it, or you yourself eat and drink with them, remember the table and the supper of the

Kingdom of God; remember that the pious, holy, and righteous sit at the Lord's table in His Kingdom, as was said: "Many will come from east and west, and sit down with Abraham, Isaac, and Jacob in the kingdom of heaven" (Matt 8:11). And the Lord also says, "Behold, my servants shall eat ... Behold, my servants shall drink, ... Behold, my servants shall be glad, ... Behold, my servants shall rejoice exceedingly in gladness" (Isa 65:13–14). But remember what is written: "For many are called, but few are chosen" (Luke 14:24; actually Matt 22:24); and again, "We must through many tribulations enter the kingdom of God" (Acts 14:22).

Live like this in the world in order not to be deprived of that joy and gladness. Serve the Lord with faith and righteousness and endure uncomplainingly every sorrow that befalls you, that you may be deemed worthy to eat, drink, and rejoice in the kingdom of God. Endure temporary sorrow, that you may receive the joy of eternal life. Taste the grief of the cross, and then you will taste sweetness in God's kingdom. "Lord, remember me when You come into Your kingdom" (Luke 23:48; actually 42).

When you look at the sun and are amazed at its beauty, remember what is written: "Then the righteous will shine forth as the sun in the kingdom of their Father" (Matt 13:43). You see how great the glory of God's chosen will be. "Beloved," says the Apostle, "now we are children of God; and it has not yet been revealed what we shall be, but we know that when He is revealed, we shall be like Him, for we shall see Him as He is" (1 John 3:2). For He "will transform our lowly body that it may be conformed to His glorious body" (Phil 3:21).

Christian! If we wish to be conformed to and like Christ in glory there, then we must be like Him and conformed to Him in life and patience here as well. Therefore the Apostle says, "And everyone who has this hope in Him purifies himself, just as He is pure" (1 John 3:3). Everyone wants to be glorified and exalted with Christ, but there are few who want to follow Christ and to bear the cross and to endure humiliation, disparagement, mocking, and grief with Christ. But He says, "And he who does not take his cross and follow after Me is not worthy of Me" (Matt 10:38).

And so, for one who wants to be with Christ in His kingdom and glory, it is necessary here too, in this world, to be with Him and to follow Him in humility and patience, and so to carry one's cross.

When you are in a bath and you feel a hotness and burning sensation of your body, or you have a fever or ague, or some other kind of serious illness, call to mind eternal torment, and how those condemned to the fire of Gehenna will suffer both in body and soul forever. "Their worm does not die, and the fire is not quenched" (Mark 9:44). "There will be weeping and gnashing of teeth" (Matt 25:30). Remember this misfortune, that you may not fall into it. Descend now with your mind into hell, that you may not go down there later in soul and body. The remembrance of Gehenna will prevent your falling into Gehenna. Every sin leads to this calamity: shun every sin, lest it plunge you into that calamity. People repent there, but too late; people sigh there, but too late; people weep there, but too late.

Christian! Glory to God, you have not yet perished; you are still living on the earth; you have not yet gone to this place of torment; you may still by the grace of God be saved and escape this evil and calamity. Repent now while repentance is still of use; sigh and weep, lest you come to that sighing and weeping later; pray and knock at the doors of God's mercy, that they may be opened to you that are opened to all those who truly repent. "Have mercy upon me, O God, after Thy great goodness, and according to the multitude of Thy mercies do away mine offenses" (Ps 50:3). "But the cowardly, unbelieving, abominable, murderers, sexually immoral, sorcerers, idolaters, and all liars shall have their part in the lake which burns with fire and brimstone, which is the second death" (Rev 21:8).

You see that small types of livestock give way to large ones, small beasts to large ones, small birds to large ones. Remember that in the same way physically small people yield to others and give way before anger, they do not reproach those who reproach them, they do not backbite backbiters, they concede to those who challenge them, and they do not resist those who hit them. Here true humility and meekness are acting in them. From this, you see what are humility and meekness.

But humility and meekness are recognized still more when equal gives place to equal, and although he can resist one who challenges him, he does not wish this and gives way to him. Even more humility and meekness are shown when the larger gives way to the smaller and does not resist him in word or deed. Oh, what a pleasant sight, when a high-ranking man gives way to a low-ranking and base one! Such a person is high ranking on the outside, but within himself is low; great on the outside, but unpretentious in his heart; rich on the outside, but poor and needy within. This high lowness is despised by the world, but exalted by the God. "Everyone who humbles himself will be exalted" (Luke 18:14).

Thus the holy David gave way to his adversaries, and although he could render them evil for evil, he did not wish to. The entire Holy Gospel preaches the humility and meekness of our Saviour: He gave way to all His enemies and detractors with all meekness. He was as humble and meek as He was great. This is why He commands us to learn humility and meekness from Him: "Learn from Me, for I am gentle and lowly in heart" (Matt 11:29).

This is not how mad pride is. It everywhere wants to show itself, does not want to give way to anyone, but resists either in word or deed. From this arise quarrels, mutual vituperation, backbiting, and fights. One says to another: "You are a scoundrel, or a wastrel," or something else. Pride answers: "So are you." This is what livestock and wild animals, and birds do when they see themselves equal to others: they do not give way to them but resist them; this is why they fight with each other until one overpowers the other. Proud and foolish people follow after these foolish animals, and do not wish to give way to one another, but like the animals quarrel and fight and injure each other either in word or in deed.

And so, you see, O man, what unregenerate man is, one who has not been renewed through God's grace. The pride and anger found in livestock and wild animals are also present in him. But it is written: "God resists the proud, but gives grace to the humble" (1 Pet 5:5). To Him be praise, honor, and glory unto the ages of ages. May it be! May it be! Amen.

*On the original, it is signed thus:*

*1779, 19th day of November*
*Tikhon (unworthy) Bishop*

# Notes

All references to source material in the original text were to the classic Russian language editions. The author followed a Russian cultural practice where one is not necessarily expected to provide all background detail and source material. Unless otherwise indicated, the quotations and their citations have been translated from the original text.

### 28. A Dinner or Supper

1    *The Evlogataria in the Funeral Service for the Laity* (Jordanville, New York: Holy Trinity Monastery, 2002).

### 37. Weeping

2    *The Great Canon: The Work of St. Andrew of Crete* (Jordanville, New York: Holy Trinity Publications, 2016), p. 11.

### 41. A Man Summoned to Court

3    *The Order of the Moleben and the Panikhida* (Jordanville, New York: Holy Trinity Publications, 2021), p. 70.

### 42. A Person Covered with Wounds

4    *The Order of the Moleben and the Panikhida* (Jordanville, New York: Holy Trinity Publications 2021), p. 70.

### 50. A Net

5    *The Prayer Book* (Jordanville, New York: Holy Trinity Publications, 2005), p. 58.

### 54. Shame

6    Soliloquia 14:14 [Augustine].

### 64. Warfare

7    *The Unabbreviated Horologion or Book of the Hours* (Jordanville, New York: Holy Trinity Monastery, 1997) p. 342.

### 65. Calling

8    *The Unabbreviated Horologion or Book of the Hours* (Jordanville, New York: Holy Trinity Monastery, 1997) p. 337.

## 94. Peace

9    *The Octoechos Saturday and Sunday Offices: Tones 1-8* (Orthodox Monastery of the Veil of Our Lady: Bussy-en-Othe, France, 1979) p. 215.

## 100. Repose

10    *A Psalter for Prayer*, trans. David James (Jordanville, New York: Holy Trinity Publications, 2019) p. 343.

## 106. I Am Greatly in Your Debt

11    This is a line from the Nicene Creed: *The Divine Liturgy of Our Father among the Saints John Chrysostom: Slavonic-English Parallel Text*, 5th edition (Jordanville, New York: Holy Trinity Publications, 2022) p. 165.

## 108. He Did His Work and Left

12    *Prayer Book* (Jordanville, New York: Holy Trinity Monastery, 2005) p. 208.

13    John Erikson, Paul Lazor, eds. *The Paschal Service* (Yonkers, New York: SVS Press, 1977) p. 38.

## 122. Do Not Be Afraid, I am with You

14    *Prayer Book* (Jordanville, New York: Holy Trinity Monastery, 2005) p. 199.

15    The Unabbreviated Horologion or Book of the Hours (Jordanville, New York: Holy Trinity Monastery, 1997) p. 227.

## 126. A Pauper

16    *The Divine Liturgy of Our Father Among the Saints John Chrysostom: Slavonic-English Parallel Text*, 5th edition (Jordanville, New York: Holy Trinity Publications, 2022) p. 167.

## 141. Those Who Enter the King's Bridal Chamber

17    This is an exapostilarion from the Bridegroom Matins service of Holy Week. Kallistos Ware and Mother Mary, *The Lenten Triodion* (London: Faber & Faber, 1977) p. 514.

## 153. The Belly

18    This is a line from the Nicene Creed: *The Divine Liturgy of Our Father among the Saints John Chrysostom: Slavonic-English Parallel Text*, 5th edition (Jordanville, New York: Holy Trinity Publications, 2022) p. 165.

# Scripture Index

23:1, pp. 82, 147, 183, 404, 408
23:7, p. 149
23:8, p. 19
23:61, p. 494
24:6–7, p. 356
25:8–11, p. 118
26:1, pp. 234, 388
26:1–3, p. 194
26:4, p. 118
26:13–14, p. 240
26:14, pp. 6, 8, 22, 489
26:7–9, p. 407
26:7–9; 16:15, p. 434
28:11, pp. 119, 420
29:8, p. 119
30:2, p. 391
30:4–6, p. 120
30:25, p. 234
31:7, pp. 222, 402
31:9, p. 244
31:10, pp. 400, 408
32:13–15, pp. 3, 14, 142, 193
32:22, pp. 23, 71, 120, 171, 267
33:11, p. 427
33:12, p. 413
33:12–14, p. 374
33:12–15, p. 449
33:12–17, pp. 92, 466
33:14, p. 90
33:15, pp. 90, 212
33:16, p. 380
33:19, p. 428
33:2, pp. 265, 272, 432
33:20, pp. 287, 443
33:22; 28:11; 31:11, p. 388
33:3, pp. 123, 361
33:6, pp. 7, 297, 301
33:8, pp. 275, 422
33:9 LXX, p. 415
33:9, pp. 9, 182, 268, 426, 429

34:1–3, p. 94
34:3, p. 72
35:8, pp. 145, 475
35:9–10, p. 68
35:10, p. 269
35:10–11, p. 71
36:1–2, p. 136
36:31, p. 79
37:10–11, 22–23, p. 121
37:22, p. 275
37:22–23, pp. 5, 141, 150, 388
37:22–23; 64:6, p. 400
37:6, p. 110
38:5–7, pp. 100, 127, 218
38:13, pp. 60, 389
38:13–14, p. 95
40:2–4, p. 297
40:5, pp. 92, 256, 366
40:5, 37:6, p. 158
41:2, p. 66
41:2–3, pp. 120, 282, 411, 429, 433
41:3 LXX, p. 282
41:3, p. 381
43:2–4, p. 378
43:27, p. 55
44:2, p. 391
44:3, pp. 290, 322, 357
44:9, pp. 241, 260
44:10, 14, p. 67
44:11–12, pp. 49, 357
44:16, p. 50
45:2, p. 11
45:2–3, p. 220
45:2–3, 12, p. 388
45:2, 8, p. 221
46:7–8, p. 380
47:9–10, p. 69
48:2, p. 311
48:2, 3, p. 284

## HOLY TRINITY PUBLICATIONS
### JORDANVILLE, NEW YORK

PSJP PRINTSHOP OF
SAINT JOB OF POCHAEV

HTSP HOLY TRINITY
SEMINARY PRESS

# The Collected Works of St Ignatius (Brianchaninov)

VOLUME I

## The Field
### Cultivating Salvation

The field is a place of cultivation and of battle. The author instructs his readers in the cultivation of the field of their hearts, with the aim of producing a harvest of virtues both pleasing to God and of benefit to all humankind. The Field draws deeply on the teachings of the ascetic fathers of the Church, from the desert dwellers of Scetis in Egypt to St Ignatius's Russian contemporaries, the Optina Elders.

ISBN: 9780884653769

VOLUME II

## The Refuge
### Anchoring the Soul in God

Prayer is a refuge of God's great mercy to the human race. A refuge is a place of inner stillness and peace where the heart is fully opened to the embrace of God's love. This text is an exposition of the concrete actions one needs to take to live with and in God. It weaves together meditations on Scripture (from the Psalms in particular) and amplifies these with the wisdom of early Christian saints.

ISBN: 9780884654292

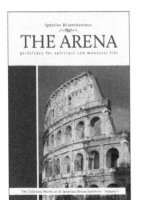

VOLUME V

## The Arena
### Guidelines for Spiritual and Monastic Life

This is one of the most important and accessible texts of Orthodox Christian teaching on the spiritual life, and not unlike the better known Philokalia. The author describes this work as his legacy "of soul saving instruction." In an age alienated from spiritual culture and rooted in materialism, his words pose an invitation to all who say to themselves "There must be more to life than this."

ISBN: 9780884652878